W9-BWI-815

The Writings and Speeches of Edmund Burke

General Editor: Paul Langford

VOLUME III

Party, Parliament, and
the American War

1774–1780

EDITED BY

W. M. ELOFSON

WITH

JOHN A. WOODS

TEXTUAL EDITOR FOR THE WRITINGS

WILLIAM B. TODD

CLARENDON PRESS · OXFORD
1996

Oxford University Press, Walton Street, Oxford OX2 6DP

Oxford New York
Athens Auckland Bangkok Bombay
Calcutta Cape Town Dar es Salaam Delhi
Florence Hong Kong Istanbul Karachi
Kuala Lumpur Madras Madrid Melbourne
Mexico City Nairobi Paris Singapore
Taipei Tokyo Toronto
and associated companies in
Berlin Ibadan

Oxford is a trade mark of Oxford University Press

Published in the United States
by Oxford University Press Inc., New York

© Oxford University Press 1996

All rights reserved. No part of this publication may be reproduced,
stored in a retrieval system, or transmitted, in any form or by any means,
without the prior permission in writing of Oxford University Press.
Within the UK, exceptions are allowed in respect of any fair dealing for the
purpose of research or private study, or criticism or review, as permitted
under the Copyright, Designs and Patents Act, 1988, or in the case of
reprographic reproduction in accordance with the terms of the licences
issued by the Copyright Licensing Agency. Enquiries concerning
reproduction outside these terms and in other countries should be
sent to the Rights Department, Oxford University Press,
at the address above

British Library Cataloguing in Publication Data
Data available

Library of Congress Cataloging in Publication Data
Data applied for

ISBN 0-19-822414-1

1 3 5 7 9 10 8 6 4 2

Typeset by Best-set Typesetter Ltd., Hong Kong

Printed in Great Britain
on acid-free paper by
Biddles Ltd., Guildford and King's Lynn

This edition is dedicated to the memory of

THOMAS W. COPELAND

(1907–79)

to whom it owes its conception and in large
measure the form which it takes. But for
his death his contribution would have been
still greater.

PREFACE

The need for a new edition of the writings and speeches of Edmund Burke has long been felt. Many editions have appeared in the course of the last hundred and fifty years, but all derive essentially from the first, which was commenced in Burke's own lifetime and finally completed in 1827. The work of the editors, French Laurence and Walker King, has many virtues, but, not surprisingly, it has proved less than adequate to the requirements of twentieth-century scholars. That it is now possible actually to undertake its replacement is owing to developments which have taken place only in recent years. The opening of the Earl Fitzwilliam's archive in 1948 has made available the great bulk of Burke's surviving papers. Closely related and equally important has been the publication of the definitive edition of Burke's correspondence. That work, which was begun in 1958, and has proceeded throughout under the direction of the late Professor Thomas W. Copeland, has now been brought to a triumphant conclusion with the production of the final (index) volume in 1978. Without this extensive and preliminary labour there could have been no question of re-editing the writings and speeches.

This edition makes no claim to be comprehensive. So far as the published writings are concerned, it is intended to present all the pieces known to have come from Burke's hand, together with a selection of those in which he can be shown to have collaborated and of those which he intended to print without actually doing so. Thanks to the scholarly labours of Professor William B. Todd, the identification and reproduction of the major works is a relatively straightforward matter, while the existence among the Fitzwilliam MSS. of a substantial number of drafts, fragments, and assorted papers makes it possible to attribute to Burke a small body of additional writings. The speeches, however, raise many more problems. Some of Burke's parliamentary speeches were published with his consent in his own lifetime and for the purposes of this edition have been treated essentially as if they were writings. For the vast majority, however, the only record is a mention or very brief account in a newspaper, or in a number of cases notes, drafts, or outlines, amongst Burke's papers at Sheffield or

Northampton. To reproduce a version of every known Burke speech would swell the edition to an enormous size, and much of what was reproduced would be of doubtful value, either because of the imperfections of newspaper reporting or because of the fragmentary and incoherent nature of the MS. However, this edition will endeavour to provide full texts for as many of Burke's speeches as is realistic considering all the difficulties and dangers. Such speeches are likely to be of intrinsic importance in themselves or to be in some way characteristic of Burke, as well as being based on a surviving record in which reasonable confidence can be placed. The editors will also provide the reader with as full a list as possible of the occasions and subjects on which Burke spoke on the theme or period covered by their volume, together with an indication of the most helpful source for those seeking a text.

This volume is the second of three particularly devoted to Burke's career in domestic politics. In it will be found five major pieces, his two speeches in 1775 on conciliation with America, his *Letter to the Sheriffs of Bristol* published in 1777, his speech on economical reform, and his well-known election address to his constituents at Bristol in 1780. There are also some ninety additional speeches, many of them published for the first time. Most of them relate directly to the evolution of Burke's political and constitutional ideals and/or to his philosophy of Empire and his approach to the American Revolution.

No study of this kind can be carried out without incurring a great many debts of gratitude. I should like to thank Olive, Countess Fitzwilliam's Wentworth Settlement Trustees for the use of the MS. collection at Sheffield and Northampton, and the staff at the City Library, Sheffield and Northamptonshire Record Office for their help and advice.

Along with the major manuscript collections the *Burke Correspondence* has been invaluable in the production of this volume. The time and energy which the editors painstakingly brought to bear on that work have made this one substantially less difficult than otherwise it would have been. Further, I should like to acknowledge the assistance which in the course of research I received from the staffs of the following institutions: the British Library; the Guildhall Library; the Public Record Office; the Bodleian Library; Nottingham University Library; the Huntington Library; New York City Library. I also cannot sufficiently stress the extent of my obligation to the Social Sciences and

Humanities Research Council of Canada for its generosity in providing crucial financial support for this volume. And I wish to record my gratitude to the History Department at the University of Calgary for providing typing and secretarial assistance and to Louis A. Knafla and other scholars in the department for their patience in helping to solve a great number of specific historical puzzles. Similarly, I am indebted to Dr. J. Vanderspoel and others in the Classics Department at the University of Calgary who have been a particular source of detailed assistance in identifying an almost overwhelming array of Latin, Greek, and other references and quotations in Burke's speeches and writings.

Finally, I must record my debt to the experience and learning of John Woods, who sadly died while this volume was in course of preparation and to Paul Langford, the General Editor, and Peter Marshall, the Associate Editor, who read the text in draft and made numerous suggestions for improvement. The value of their expertise and particularly their knowledge of parliamentary affairs and source materials cannot be overstated.

W.M.E.

University of Calgary
1991

CONTENTS

Contents

Contents

Contents

Contents

Contents

Contents

LIST OF SHORT TITLES

The following manuscript collections are cited in this volume by short title:

Add. MSS.
> Additional Manuscripts, British Library, London.

Eg. MSS.
> Egerton Manuscripts, British Library, London.

MSS. at Northampton
> Fitzwilliam MSS. on deposit at Northamptonshire Record Office, Northampton; part of the Fitzwilliam Burke collection, owned by the Earl Fitzwilliam and originally at Milton, Northamptonshire.

O'Hara MSS.
> National Library of Ireland, Dublin.

Portland MSS.
> Nottingham University Library.

P.R.O.
> Public Record Office, Chancery Lane and Kew, London.

MSS. at Sheffield
> Wentworth Woodhouse Muniments on deposit at Sheffield City Libraries, Sheffield; the larger part of the Fitzwilliam Burke collection, as well as papers of Burke's patrons Rockingham and Fitzwilliam, originally at Wentworth Woodhouse, Yorkshire.

The following printed works are cited in this volume by short title:

Brooke, *Chatham Administration*
> J. Brooke, *The Chatham Administration, 1766–1768*, London, 1956.

Chatham Correspondence
> *Correspondence of William Pitt, Earl of Chatham*, ed. W. S. Taylor and J. H. Pringle, 4 vols., London, 1838–40.

Commons Journals
    Journals of the House of Commons.
Corr. (1844)
    Edmund Burke, *Correspondence between 1744 and 1797*, ed.
    Charles William, Earl Fitzwilliam, and Richard Bourke, 4 vols.,
    London, 1844.
Commons Sessional Papers
    House of Commons Sessional Papers of the Eighteenth Century, ed.
    S. Lambert, 145 vols., Wilmington, 1975.
Corr.
    The Correspondence of Edmund Burke, ed. T. W. Copeland and
    Others, 10 vols., Cambridge, 1958–78.
Langford, *Rockingham Administration*
    P. Langford, *The First Rockingham Administration, 1765–1766*,
    London, 1973.
Lords Journals
    Journals of the House of Lords.
Namier and Brooke
    The History of Parliament: The House of Commons, 1754–90, ed. Sir
    L. Namier and J. Brooke, 3 vols., London, 1964.
Parl. Hist.
    *The Parliamentary History of England from the Norman Conquest
    in 1066 to the year 1803*, ed. W. Cobbett, 36 vols., London,
    1806–20.
Parl. Reg.
    *The Parliamentary Register; or History of the Proceedings and Debates
    in the House of Commons . . .* , ed. J. Almon, 18 vols., London,
    1774–80.
Rockingham Memoirs
    George Thomas Keppel, Earl of Albemarle, *Memoirs of the
    Marquis of Rockingham*, 2 vols., London, 1852.
Simmons and Thomas
    *Proceedings and Debates of the British Parliaments Respecting
    North America 1754–83*, eds. R. C. Simmons and P. D. G.
    Thomas, 6 vols., New York, 1982–7.
Todd
    W. B. Todd, *A Bibliography of Edmund Burke*, London, 1964.
    References in parentheses indicate item numbers of editions
    described in this bibliography.

Walpole, *Last Journals*
> Horace Walpole, *The Last Journals of Horace Walpole during the Reign of George III 1771–1783*, ed. A. Francis Stewart, 2 vols., London, 1910.

Walpole, *Memoirs*
> Horace Walpole, *Memoirs of the Reign of King George the Third*, ed. G. F. Russell Barker, 4 vols., London, 1894.

Works
> The collected series of Burke's works, published in many editions, of which the following are cited specifically:

Works (1792–1827)
> *The Works of the Right Honourable Edmund Burke, Collected in Three Volumes*, London, 1792. Further volumes were added to this, the first, quarto edition, in 1802, 1812, 1813, 1821, and 1827. This edition, along with the octavo issues of 1801 and 1803, has been collated throughout for textual purposes.

Works (Bohn)
> *The Works of the Right Honourable Edmund Burke*, 8 vols. (Bohn's British Classics), London, 1854–89. This edition is cited where it is necessary to direct scholars to a readily accessible version of an item not yet produced by the *Writings and Speeches*.

Wyvill Papers
> Christopher Wyvill, *Political Papers*, 6 vols., York, 1794–1802.

INTRODUCTION

By 1774 Edmund Burke had already gained widespread recognition for his skills as a writer, orator, and parliamentarian. Between 1774 and 1780, however, he was to see his reputation enhanced substantially. There were a number of reasons for this. One of the most important was the death in February 1775 of William Dowdeswell.[1] For a decade the latter had been a force of considerable weight and authority amongst the Rockingham Whigs. He had been the party's leader and most frequent speaker in the House of Commons and, as the Duke of Portland[2] once noted, its 'great luminary in all private consultations'.[3] When Dowdeswell was suddenly gone a void was created which, at least until Charles James Fox[4] asserted his dominance over the party in the early 1780s, threw heavier responsibilities on Burke's shoulders. Burke did not become the Rockinghams' leader in the House of Commons in these years. That mantle fell to Lord John Cavendish,[5] who merited it because of his bloodlines and landed wealth. However, he did of necessity become by far the most active advocate for the connection both in Parliament and outside. Cavendish was highly respected, an eloquent speaker, and by all accounts a thoroughly sensible politician,[6] but on a day-to-day level he lacked the industry and interest to be a regular man of business. Since all the rest of the country aristocrats and landed gentlemen in the central core of the Rockingham connection also suffered from that political short-coming, it was left increasingly to Burke to perform the functions which Dowdeswell alone or which he and Dowdeswell together had performed in the past.

The change in Burke's stature is demonstrated in the first place simply by the frequency with which he participated in the debates in the lower House. During the previous Parliament he had, to his credit, spoken on over two hundred occasions.[7] Between 1774 and 1780,

---

[1] (1721–75), M.P. 1747–54, 1761–75.
[2] William Henry Cavendish Bentinck, 3rd Duke of Portland (1738–1809).
[3] MS. at Sheffield, R1.1413: Portland to Rockingham, 21 November 1772.
[4] (1709–1806), M.P. 1768–1806.   [5] (1732–96), M.P. 1768–84.
[6] See e.g. Walpole, *Memoirs*, ii. 17.   [7] See vol. ii, p. 3.

however, he voiced his views almost four hundred[1] times and far more often than any other member of his own party. Indeed, in the first two or so years of this Parliament, he spoke more frequently than anyone but Lord North,[2] and, thereafter, more frequently than anyone but North and Fox. Moreover, he demonstrated ability second to none in two basic types of debates. The one occurred in the more or less spontaneous skirmishes between the Government and Opposition during discussion periods. Burke's wit and quickness of mind had always enabled him to perform admirably in these and by the mid-1770s his skills had been well tuned by time and practice. His chief adversary and only equal was North himself. Over the years their sardonic exchanges produced some entertaining moments. Such was the case, for instance, on 3 November 1775, when Burke in responding to points of law raised by the Solicitor-General, Alexander Wedderburn,[3] pointed out that the House had been subjected to a lot of legal double-talk. He declared that

the learned gentleman ... had ransacked history, statutes and journals, and had taken a very large journey, through which he did not wish to follow him, but he was always glad to meet him at his return home. Let us, said he, strip off all this learned foliage from his argument; let us unswathe this Egyptian corpse, and strip it of its salt, gum and mummy, and see what sort of a dry skeleton is underneath—nothing but a single point of law! The gentleman asserts that nothing but a Bill can declare the consent of parliament, not an address, not a resolution of the House, yet he thinks a resolution of the House would in this case be better than a Bill of Indemnity, so that we find a Bill is nothing, an address is nothing, a resolution is nothing, nay I fear our liberty is nothing, and that, ere long our rights, freedom, and spirit, nay the House itself will vanish, in a previous question.

This immediately brought North to his feet to inquire

whence the proofs and authorities of a point of law could be better drawn than from history, statutes and journals; he did not think it was from wit, or flowers of eloquence, that they should be deduced. He admired the honourable gentleman's method of proving a resolution to be, nothing; an address, nothing; a Bill, nothing; and by the same mode of reasoning he was inclined, he said, to conclude, that a long witty speech was—nothing.[4]

---

[1] See below, Appendix A.
[2] Frederick North, styled Lord North (1732–92), later (1790) 2nd Earl of Guilford, M.P. 1754–90.
[3] (1733–1805), later (1780), 1st Baron Loughborough and (1801) 1st Earl of Rosslyn, M.P. 1761–80.
[4] *Parl. Hist.* xviii. 835–6.

Burke met his match in North but not his superior and he appears to have thrived on the rivalry. In the discussions he and North both liked to wait for the other to speak first in order to have the last word. It looked most impressive that Burke scored his share of points and even 'caused a good deal of laughter' in the House at the ministry's expense[1] because he seemed to face rather unfair odds. North was usually supported in the discussions by Wedderburn, and a number of others including Charles Jenkinson,[2] Welbore Ellis,[3] and Richard Rigby.[4] Much of the time, however, Burke received only minimal backing from his own friends. Cavendish could intervene on his behalf with effect but he tended not to do so with a great deal of regularity. After the Americans declared independence Fox consistently spoke on the Opposition side and he moved increasingly towards the Rockingham camp. In the late 1770s he and Burke often baited the ministry together. However, at this stage in their relationship they seldom displayed the tactical co-operation and the team-work that North was able to draw on, or, indeed, that Burke had been accustomed to in earlier years with Dowdeswell.[5]

While Burke excelled in the spur of the moment encounters in the Commons, it was of course the major speeches which he had time to prepare in advance that really secured his reputation. Between 1774 and 1780 these tended on the whole to bring him more acclaim than the ones he had given in the past because of the standards they set for strength and clarity of argument and for the general wealth of ideas and information.[6] This was in part a reflection of the fact that Burke's overall party responsibilities changed in a qualitative as well as a quantitative sense. While Dowdeswell had been alive and making most of the crucial policy decisions for the Rockinghams, Burke's primary duties had been to keep his aristocratic leaders informed on political events in London and Westminster and, at every opportunity, to work on the party's public image. He had filled much of his time acting as a go-between or constructing speeches and producing works such as the

---

[1] Ibid. 768.
[2] (1729–1805), later (1786) 1st Baron Hawkesbury and (1796) 1st Earl of Liverpool, M.P. 1761–86, Secretary at War 1778–82.
[3] (1713–1802), later (1784) 1st Baron Mendip, M.P. 1741–94, Treasurer of the Navy 1777–82.
[4] (1722–88), M.P. 1745–88, Paymaster-General 1768–82.
[5] See vol. ii, pp. 5–8.
[6] See, for instance, opinions of his first conciliation speech (below, pp. 103–4).

Short Account of a Late Short Administration, Observations on a Late State of the Nation, and *Thoughts on the Cause of the Present Discontents*,[1] with the specific objective of glorifying the policies and character of the Rockingham Whigs. In the 1774–80 period, however, Burke devoted much less time to such matters. Amongst his writings only his *Letter to the Sheriffs of Bristol*[2] was undertaken directly for the purpose of political propaganda (and it much more to defend Burke to his own electors than to laud the party). From late 1774, when Dowdeswell became ill and unable to fulfil his duties, Burke was forced for the first time to play a leading role in establishing positions for the entire party with respect to many of the issues which emerged. By the end of the 1770s, the Marquess of Rockingham[3] himself had learnt regularly to entrust him with some of the most delicate political decisions. For example, in 1779, the Marquess called on him to supply their friends in Yorkshire with a set of instructions on the difficult question of how to deal with Christopher Wyvill[4] and the association movement.[5] Furthermore, in the same year, when the party leaders were approached to consider taking part in a new ministry, Rockingham asked him to outline a plan for the negotiations and a coherent set of conditions for assuming office.[6] Significantly, the last time the party had been involved in such negotiations, it had been Dowdeswell who had performed that function.[7]

It was in keeping with his role as a decision-maker in this period that Burke also developed some immensely significant measures for the party to propagate in the House of Commons. The most important of these, his two proposals for conciliation with America in 1775[8] and his civil establishment legislation in 1780,[9] he designed virtually alone and after only limited consultation with the other leading members of the party. Previously, the initiative in matters of that magnitude would almost certainly have been taken by Dowdeswell.[10] Just as Burke effectively assumed more influence in the development of party policies in these years, he also naturally took over the function, which

---

[1] See vol. ii, pp. 54–7, 102–219, 241–323.
[2] See below, pp. 476–8.
[3] Charles Watson Wentworth, 2nd Marquess of Rockingham (1730–82).
[4] (1740–1822).   [5] See below, pp. 288–330.   [6] See below, pp. 448–54.
[7] 'Thoughts on the present state of publick affairs and the propriety of accepting or declining administration, Written the 23d & 24 of July 1767', MS. at Sheffield, R1.842; Brooke, *Chatham Administration*, pp. 213–17.
[8] See below, pp. 102–68.   [9] See below, pp. 481–551.   [10] See vol. ii, pp. 8–9.

Dowdeswell had also previously performed, of actually presenting them to the House of Commons, and it is this which is reflected in the substance of his speeches. Now Burke was required to elucidate and elaborate a host of Bills and proposals rather than just extolling their virtues as he had in the past.[1] In part for that reason a number of the speeches transcribed in this volume more clearly spell out a logical thought process or a philosophy, than many he had delivered previously, they enlist a wider base of supportive evidence, and they have a more authoritative and a somewhat less sycophantic ring to them.[2] Perhaps nothing demonstrates this better than the contrast between the speech Burke had given on American taxation in 1774,[3] on the one hand, and his two speeches on conciliation with America in 1775, on the other. The former had been little more than a very eloquent rationalization of the Rockinghams' past policies and a full frontal attack on the North regime. The latter were extremely well-researched investigations into Anglo-American history and colonial society which provided a whole range of specific proposals and principles for the re-establishment of harmony within the empire.

If Burke's position in the Rockingham connection was raised by Dowdeswell's passing, it was also augmented by the fact that some great national and international issues emerged in these years to challenge his intellect and to provide him ample opportunities to display his abundant talents. The first of these was of course the American war itself. The dispute between the mother country and her colonies had been brewing for a decade or more by 1774. However, after the actual commencement of military operations in 1775 the background of real urgency was created which inspired Burke and others to search deeply for new answers to solve an old problem. Over the years, this required Burke to reassess and refine systematically his own ideas and to define more clearly all his leading premises. As will be seen, it also enabled him not only in the conciliation proposals but in numerous other speeches and writings as well, to articulate as never before a cogent philosophy of empire for himself and the Rockingham Whigs.

The other great issue which stimulated Burke's energies between

---

[1] See vol. ii, pp. 5–6.
[2] Note in particular the discussion which follows in this introduction relative to the conciliation with America proposals and the Civil Establishment Bills.
[3] See vol. ii, pp. 406–63.

1774 and 1780 was the question of constitutional amendment. During this Parliament he and the Rockinghams led their connection along the path of economical reform. In the historical development of the Whig party this was extremely important. It represented the first crucial step for the party which would lead it to parliamentary reform under Charles James Fox, and eventually to the ideals culminating in the first Great Reform Act under Lord John Russell and Earl Grey.[1] As will be argued here the Rockinghams were very moderate men. Their programme was the least radical of all those offered by any Opposition group in the late 1770s and early 1780s, and it was dictated by circumstance rather than zeal. The party was forced to address the question of reform because of the state of disrepute into which the North Government had fallen as a result of the American tragedy. To the Rockinghams, economical reform was largely a method of uniting all North's enemies and all the groups promoting constitutional amendment under their own leadership and of drawing support away from extreme measures. When designing his civil establishment legislation, therefore, Burke had to follow a very delicate course. He had in the first place to outline a string of measures which were moderate enough for the propertied classes and his own party to accept; and he had to offer a platform which was substantial enough to compete with men like Christopher Wyvill and his associates who were calling for changes both in Parliament and the system of representation.[2] This proved a difficult challenge and it forced him to think long and hard about sensible means to achieve economy in government and to re-establish the independence of the House of Commons. Burke's Civil Establishment Bills were the product of enormous effort and tireless research. Amongst his papers at Sheffield are dozens of documents which he used in estimating the numbers, costs, and origins of offices and officials and, as precisely as possible, the efficiencies and deficiencies of the entire system.[3] To read his speeches is to appreciate not only the logical development of his arguments but his familiarity with the internal operations of all the various departments in the

[1] Lord John Russell (1792–1839), later (1861) 1st Earl Russell, M.P. 1813–61; Charles Grey (1764–1845), later (1807) 2nd Earl Grey, M.P. 1786–1807. For further disussion see W. M. Elofson, 'The Rockingham Whigs in Transition: The East India Company Issue, 1772–3', *English Historical Review*, civ (1989), 947–74.
[2] W. M. Elofson, 'The Rockingham Whigs and the Country Tradition', *Parliamentary History*, viii (1989), 90–115.
[3] In particular, see MSS. at Sheffield, R1.18.1 to R1.18.41.

government and household and his knowledge and application of history. Clearly, only he amongst the Rockingham leaders could have measured up to the task of preparing this programme in the late 1770s and early 1780s.

Burke's activity in response to the major issues, and to many others as well after Dowdeswell's death, not only affected his standing within the Rockingham fold but it also brought him considerable public recognition. This came in part as a product of the fact that by this period British society in general was becoming increasingly well informed with respect to political and parliamentary affairs. The much publicized conflict between the House of Commons and the London printers in 1771 had for all practical purposes established the right of the unrelentingly competitive London newspapers to publish the debates.[1] Until 1777 attempts were frequently made to control the practice by both Houses, in particular through the closing of their respective chambers,[2] and therefore, reports had sometimes to be obtained through agreements between the press and individual members of Parliament who provided accounts of their own or others' speeches. Burke had always been keenly aware of the importance of out-of-doors opinion, and he was conscious of his standing in the eyes of the propertied classes. Therefore he learned to co-operate with the press himself when he felt that the public for whatever reason was likely to be denied access to accurate or sympathetic accounts of his performances. He learned methodically to prepare some of his speeches specifically for the printed medium,[3] and from time to time he made sure that legible handwritten versions were circulated to publishers like John Almon.[4] Consequently, any of his speeches that did not reach the press through the regular reporting network were normally made

[1] For an account of the history of parliamentary reporting in this period, see P. D. G. Thomas, 'The Beginning of Parliamentary Reporting in Newspapers, 1768–74', *English Historical Review*, lxxiv (1959), 623–36; and 'John Wilkes and the Freedom of the Press (1771)', *Bulletin of the Institute of Historical Research*, xxxiii (1960), 86–98.

[2] For instance, see below, p. 184. From 1777 the gallery of the House was closed much less frequently; see P. D. G. Thomas, *The House of Commons in the Eighteenth-Century*, Oxford, 1971, pp. 144–7, 336–7; A. Aspinall, 'The Reporting and Publishing of the House of Commons Debates', in *Essays Presented to Sir Lewis Namier*, eds. R. Pares and A.J.P. Taylor, London, 1956, pp. 227–57.

[3] For instance, his speech on the loss of Boston on 6 May 1776 was prepared for the press after the debate (below, p. 229), and that on Conway's motion on 22 May 1776 was prepared for the press before it was delivered (below, p. 232).

[4] For instance, his speech on the use of Indians on 6 February 1778 appears to have been given to Almon (1737–1805) by Burke or someone close to him. The draft is at Sheffield and transcribed below (p. 362).

available for public consumption one way or the other and, over the years, almost every significant statement he made in the course of virtually every day in the House of Commons could be expected to reach a wide audience. For a man with Burke's attributes this was an ideal situation. He was a master of parliamentary debate and during the years of the American Revolution his ability publicly to demonstrate his skills helped him to achieve almost universal commendation. Admittedly, those who viewed his performances sometimes criticized his rather notoriously fiery temper and his inclination to become sidetracked on secondary issues and they pointed to other minor failings. He is, wrote one, 'excursive, impetuous by frequently dwelling upon trifles, and pedantic'. His 'wit sometimes degenerates into buffoonery and ill-nature, and his oratory into bombast and mere fiction.' His 'voice is not of the best . . . and in the warmth of debate often becomes so hoarse as to render his accounts dissonant, and nearly unintelligible.'[1] Typically, however, Burke's contemporaries loudly applauded his eloquence, his 'copious, rich language', the clarity of his arguments, and, above all, his 'great information' and 'unbounded, comprehensive knowledge'. What becomes clear in the pieces in this volume is that before expressing his views on all but the most minor issues Burke did his homework. As a result he was able to convey to his audience the opinions of accepted authorities, and the historical and other evidence to support what he had to say. He is

so great a master of his own language, so well skilled in the characteristic marks of other authors, and blessed with so fruitful, various and pliant a genius, that he can assume at will the style and manner of any other writer [the above observer also reported]. Mr. Burke's knowledge is as uncommon, as it is universal; but, were it not, such are the powers of his understanding and memory, that he can make himself master of what subject and in what time he pleases—for which reason he always comes full furnished with matter into Parliament.[2]

Assessments such as these set Burke apart from almost all his contemporaries.[3] Late eighteenth-century pundits could incline to be eulogistic in describing political figures they liked but no British statesman in this period, in or out of Government, received more glowing tributes. In 1776, *London Magazine* declared that his

---

[1] *Universal Magazine*, lviii (1775), 349.   [2] Ibid.
[3] For a recent analysis of Burke's presentation, see C. Reid, *Edmund Burke and the Practice of Political Writing*, Dublin, 1985.

sources of knowledge are inexhaustible . . . and his materials drawn forth with great judgment. His memory is faithful, and his mind teems with the most luxuriant imagery, clothed in the most elegant language . . . This . . . at once renders him the fairest adversary, and stamps his speeches with a certain air of credit, veracity, and authority, seldom due to any of his contemporaries, in either house of parliament. His knowledge of parliamentary business is so vast and multifarious, that there is no subject that comes under discussion, whether politics, finance, commerce, manufactures, internal policie, &c. with all their divisions and subdivisions, which he does not treat in so masterly and technical a manner as to induce such as hear him to imagine he had dedicated a considerable portion of his life to the investigation of that particular subject.[1]

Interestingly, in this stage of Burke's career (and in contrast to much of that which was to follow), he was generously praised for the performances which roused in him a considerable amount of genuine emotion. Thus, for instance, he was highly commended after the first speech on conciliation with America in which he appealed on humanitarian grounds for American rights and liberties and laid out for the first time a list of proposals to save the empire.[2] He also received much praise for his speech in 1778 decrying the ministry's barbarity in employing vicious savages to fight what the Rockinghams considered a civil war against their fellow-countrymen in America,[3] and for the speeches in 1780 in which respectively, he declared the Whig party's historic conversion to a moderate reform programme,[4] and he defended the traditional constitution against John Sawbridge's[5] motion for shortening the duration of Parliaments.[6] The fact that Burke was able to comport himself in a dignified and sensible manner in such issues would seem to demonstrate that he had not yet begun significantly to experience the nervous disorder which would plague him in the later years of his life. It was in part that disorder which was later to make it difficult for him to react without extreme rancour to controversies such as the misdeeds of the East India Company's servants or to the revolution in France. In this volume statements quoted in the headnotes to many of the individual pieces help to demonstrate the regularity with which Burke's contemporaries acknowledged his talents while he was still able consistently to maintain a balanced perspective.

Burke's equanimity in the 1770s seems particularly note-worthy

---

[1] 6 April 1776.   [2] See below, p. 104.
[3] See below, p. 355.   [4] See below, p. 481.
[5] (c.1732–95), M.P. 1768–95.   [6] See *Corr.* iv. 237, n. 1.

when it is considered that notwithstanding his growing celebrity, the years of the American war were in many respects no less emotionally trying for him than those which were to follow. The sources of tension were many. In the first place his relationship with the city of Bristol was very difficult from the beginning. Burke began his term as representative for the city with enthusiasm and to all appearances with very high expectations[1] and over the years he dutifully fulfilled most of his responsibilities to his electors. He regularly represented the views and interests of his constituents to government and administrative officials in London and Westminster,[2] and, when called upon, he upheld the concerns of the Bristol commercial community in Parliament. In February 1775 he presented and actively supported a petition from his friend Richard Champion[3] to extend a patent for the manufacture of hard-paste porcelain.[4] A few months later, he spoke for the overseas traders, and earned a supportive petition from the merchants for his efforts, when he brought forth his Bill with respect to shipwrecks.[5] And, in 1777, he defended the African Company in the Commons (though he indirectly criticized the slave trade).[6] Yet for all his efforts Burke often found himself at odds with many of his constituents. Indeed, in his first major speech at Bristol he managed to stir considerable criticism by insisting that, unlike his co-representative Henry Cruger,[7] he could never consider himself dependent on the guidance of his electors in making the day-to-day decisions that affected them.[8] From that moment on the personal animosity between him and Cruger divided the Whig camp in the city and Burke found himself out of step with influential interests on almost every important issue from the American war to slavery to the trade and commerce of Ireland.[9] In the end, of course, the erosion of his support in the city led directly to his decision not to contest a second election in 1780.

Scarcely less discomfiting for Burke, at least in the earliest period of

---

[1] See below, p. 57.

[2] P. T. Underdown, 'Edmund Burke, the Commissary of his Bristol Constituents, 1774–80', *English Historical Review*, lxxiii (1958), 252–69.

[3] (1743–91).

[4] *Corr.* iii. 131.

[5] See below, p. 225 and n.

[6] See below, pp. 340, 341.

[7] (1739–1827), M.P. 1774–80, 1784–90.

[8] For Burke's relationship with Cruger, see P. T. Underdown, 'Henry Cruger and Edmund Burke', *William and Mary Quarterly*, xv (1958), 14–34; and see below, p. 622.

[9] For a thorough discussion of Burke's problems in Bristol, see below, pp. 620–3.

the American conflict, was his position as colonial agent for New York.[1] As a consequence of that position (and his own earnest desire for peace) he found himself required on a number of occasions to mediate between the mother country and the colonists. This brought him very little in the way of recompense because the two adversaries would not compromise their individual points of view for the sake of accommodation. From the American side, following the Boston Tea Party in 1773, Burke was faced not only with a demonstrated proclivity for violence but also an assault, which he himself could not condone, on the supremacy of Parliament. It made things particularly awkward for him, moreover, that this assault normally contained an implicit or even a direct attack on the Rockinghams' own Declaratory Act, which had laid down the maxim in 1766 that the King in Parliament 'had, hath and of right ought to have, full power and authority to make laws and statutes of sufficient force and validity to bind the colonies and people of America . . . in all cases whatsoever'.[2] One of the moments when Burke's discomfort became really intense occurred in 1775 when the New York Assembly called on him to present a petition to the House of Commons which expressed uncharitable opinions of the powers of the imperial Parliament while attacking his party's measure in direct terms. The disquiet he felt is demonstrated in the speech he gave in the House of Commons introducing the measure on 15 May[3] and in a letter which he wrote to the Assembly of New York shortly later explaining the stand he had taken. The fact that a portion of the letter reads like a study in diplomatic ambiguity is a reflection of Burke's inability at that stage unequivocally to take sides.

I shewed that although your opinion concerning the universality of the Legislative power of Great Britain might not meet with the Approbation of the house [he reported], yet as that opinion, however erronious, was expressed in Terms proper and decent; as it was accompanied with the most precise and full acknowledgment of our Legislative Authority in many, if not the most essential particulars, it could form no objection to the admission of the Paper.[4]

---

[1] Burke's last report to the New York Assembly as colonial agent was made on 7 June 1775, just before the battle of Bunker's Hill (*Corr.* iii. 164–7).

[2] 6 Geo. III, c. 12; for the passing of the Declaratory Act, see Langford, *Rockingham Administration*, pp. 149–98.

[3] See below, p. 172.

[4] *Corr.* iii. 164–5.

Early in the dispute the intractability of the Americans was a constant source of anxiety for Burke, but as the conflict developed into actual war it was unquestionably the attitude of his own countrymen which he found the most distasteful. In 1775 and 1776 he considered it astonishing that the North regime supported by very large majorities in the House of Commons should heighten the sense of injustice in the colonies through a series of blatantly coercive measures. On 9 March 1776, after a Bill was introduced to restrain the trade of New Jersey, Pennsylvania, Maryland, Virginia, and South Carolina, he told a friend that:

I have been a strenuous advocate for the superiority of this Country—but I confess I grow less Zealous when I see the use which is made of it. I love firm Government; but I hate the Tyranny which comes to the aid of a weak one ... We talk of starving hundreds of thousands of people with far greater ease and mirth than the regulations of a Turnpike—by far I assure you.[1]

Later he told the New York Assembly that:

There are certainly some Members in both houses, who earnestly desire, that measures of another complexion and tendency might be adopted. But these Men ... are not apparently much more numerous, or much more considerable in this Parliament than in the last. It is true, that the Numbers, which have divided in the Minority against some of the strong measures, are some what higher than those which divided on similar Questions in the last Parliament. But the Majority also is, greater. The Numbers against the Proceedings never exceeded in this Session one hundred and Six, where as those for enforcing them, have been raised to near three hundred. Such is the State of Parliament.[2]

For the most part, Burke was able in public to maintain his composure with respect to the American issue, but in private he unquestionably also felt profoundly his inability to ameliorate the dispute. At times he could become despondent enough to experience short but rather intense bouts of depression. 'Mr Burke takes it so to heart', Richard Champion once noted, 'that he is much fallen away and is far from well.'[3]

If the American war made Burke's life difficult, his sense of frustration was heightened prior to the mother country's pivotal defeat at

---

[1] Ibid. 132.
[2] Ibid. 135.
[3] Ibid. 137 n. 5. For other evidence of Burke's feelings of dejection over the American war, see the headnote to his *Letter to the Sheriffs of Bristol* (below, p. 289).

Saratoga in late 1777, by his own party's chronic inability to be aggressive in national politics for any prolonged intervals. The Marquess of Rockingham and his closest friends were country aristocrats and gentlemen rather than professional politicians. They always found sustained parliamentary or public action disagreeable, but while the vast majority in the House of Commons still supported North's strong stance, they were even more lethargic than at other periods in their career. Burke had been forced to play the role of a *'flapper'*,[1] as he himself put it, almost from the beginning of his association with the party, however, in these years he had to do so very often indeed.

We have been seduced, by various false representations, and Groundless promises, into a War [he warned the Marquess as the actual fighting began]. There is no sort of prospect or possibility of its coming to any good end by the pursuit of a continued train of Hostility. The only deliberation is, whether honest men will make one last Effort to give peace to their Country.[2]

Despite his efforts, however, Burke often found himself alone in London carrying the party banner with little or no support from the rest of the party leadership. On 10 May 1775, for instance, when he was asked by Lord Dartmouth[3] to arrange for a Memorial from the Assembly of New York to be presented to the Lords he was unable to find even one trusted friend to enable him to comply. 'He is much afraid', he replied to Dartmouth's request, 'that he may not be able to find a Peer, whom he can prevail upon to deliver the New York Memorial . . . as His particular friends in that house are not in Town.'[4] These fears were justified and, in the end, the Duke of Manchester[5] who was an ally but more closely associated with the Chathamites, had to be recruited.[6]

It was during the stage when the political situation associated with the American conflict seemed the most futile to Burke, that he poured out his feelings regarding the inaction of his own party in a long and well-known letter to Charles James Fox. That letter, written in the autumn of 1777, is worth quoting at length here, as it helps to demonstrate not only Burke's sense of dejection but also his pervasive

---

[1] *Corr.* iii. 389.
[2] Ibid. 183.
[3] William Legge, 2nd Earl of Dartmouth (1731–1801).
[4] *Corr.* iii. 155.
[5] George Montagu, 4th Duke of Manchester (1737–88).
[6] He presented it on 18 May 1775 (*Lords Journals*, xxxiv. 461).

ability to rationalize and to eulogize even those characteristics of the Marquess and others which he found the most disheartening.

You are sensible, that I do not differ from you in many things; and most certainly I do not dissent from the main of your doctrine concerning the Heresy of depending upon contingencies. You must recollect how uniform my sentiments have been on that Subject. I have ever wishd a settled plan of our own, founded in the very essence of the American Business, wholly unconnected with the Events of the war, and framed in such a manner as to keep up our Credit and maintain our System at home, in spite of any thing which may happen abroad. I am now convinced by a long and somewhat vexatious experience that such a plan is absolutely impracticable. I think with you, that some faults in the constitution of those whom we most love and trust are among the causes of this impracticability. They are faults too, that one can hardly wish them perfectly cured of, as I am afraid they are intimately connected with honest disinterested intentions, plentiful fortunes, assured rank, and quiet homes. A great deal of activity and enterprize can scarcely ever be expected from such men, unless some horrible calamity is just over their heads; or unless they suffer some gross personal insults from power, the resentment of which may be as unquiet and stimulating a principle in their minds, as ambition is in those of a different complexion. To say the truth, I cannot greatly blame them. We live at a time, when men are not repaid in fame, for what they sacrifice in Interest or repose. On the whole, when I consider of what discordant, and particularly of what fleeting materials the opposition has been all along composed, and at the same time review what Lord Rockingham has done, with that and with his own shatterd constitution, for these last twelve years, I confess I am rather surprized that he has done so much and perseverd so long, than that he has felt now and then some cold fits, and that he grows somewhat languid and desponding at last. I know that he and those who are most prevalent with him, though they are not thought so much devoted to popularity as others, do very much look to the people; and more than I think is wise in them, who do so little to guide and direct the public opinion. Without this, they act indeed; but they act as it were from compulsion, and because it is impossible in their situation to avoid taking some part. All this it is impossible to change, and to no purpose to complain of.[1]

It was only months after Burke wrote this letter that in fact the political situation for the Rockingham party began substantially to improve. In early 1778 the prospect of defeat in the American war became clearer in Britain,[2] and North's support in the House of Commons began to crumble. Under these circumstances the Rockingham leaders appear to have become a little more attentive and for the first time Burke was able to develop new offensives, including his economical

---

[1] *Corr.* iii. 381.   [2] See below, pp. 346, 367.

reform programme, with the hope of victory. Outright victory for the Opposition did not occur by the end of the Parliament in June 1780, but as was demonstrated by the success of two motions relating to the Civil Establishment Bill,[1] and of John Dunning's[2] historic motion declaring that the 'influence of the Crown has increased, is increasing and ought to be diminished',[3] the future suddenly looked much brighter. However, whatever satisfaction this brought Burke it was offset by new difficulties. The situation at Bristol gave him cause for concern, but the major source of anxiety appears to have been his inability to keep North's enemies united under the Rockinghams' leadership. He and the Marquess had dreamt for years of forming 'one grand constitutional party' with as many of their allies as possible. When 'bad men combine' they had argued as early as 1770, 'the good must associate; else they will fall, one by one, an unpitied sacrifice in a contemptible struggle'.[4] Now, however, just at the moment when a union of Opposition forces buoyed by the potential for victory in the Commons seemed within their grasp, they were unable to satisfy many of their allies with the moderate path of economical reform.[5] The malcontents included a number of London radicals and the Wyvill group from Rockingham's own county of Yorkshire, but what really disturbed Burke was that some important individuals with whom he had long been closely associated in Parliament were themselves unwilling to be restrained by his programme. In late September 1780 he was so discouraged by this, and his recent failure at Bristol, that he actually contemplated retirement from active politics. In a letter to one of his constituents he made it clear that his greatest regret was the fact that two old friends, the Duke of Richmond[6] and Sir George Savile,[7] had adopted frighteningly radical propositions. Some

of our *capital* Men entertain thoughts so very different from mine [he wrote], that if I come into Parliament, I must either fly in the face of the clearest lights of my own understanding, and the firmest conviction of my own con-

---

[1] See *Parl. Hist.* xxi. 150, 278.
[2] (1731–83), later (1782) 1st Baron Ashburton, M.P. 1768–82.
[3] See below, p. 588.
[4] Vol. ii, p. 315. For a discussion of this point, see Elofson, 'The Rockingham Whigs and the Country Tradition', 100–1.
[5] See below, pp. 588–9.
[6] Charles Lennox, 3rd Duke of Richmond (1735–1806).
[7] 8th Baronet (1726–84), M.P. 1759–83.

science, or I must oppose those for whom I have the highest value. The D. of Richmond has *voluntarily proposed* to open the Election of England to all those, without exception, who have [the] qualification of being 18 years old; and has swept away at one stroke all the privileges of Freeholders, Cities, and Burroughs throughout the Kingdom, and sends every Member of Parliament, every year, to the Judgment and discretion of such Electors. Sir Geo: Saville has *consented* to *adopt*, the Scheme of more *frequent Elections* as a remedy for disorders, which in my opinion, have a great part of their Root in *Elections themselves*; and while the Duke of Richmond proposes to annihilate the Freeholders, Sir Geo: Saville consents to a plan for a vast encrease of their *power* by choice of an hundred new Knights of the Shire. Which of these am I to adhere to? or shall I put myself into the graceful situation of opposing both? . . . In this situation with regard to those whom I esteem the most, how shall I act with those for whom I have no Esteem at all? Such there are, not only in the Ministry, but in the opposition.[1]

Burke and the Rockingham Whigs accomplished something of enduring significance during the years of opposition to North but for the most part their achievements were not the tangible kind in which they could regularly take immense pride. Perhaps their greatest success was in avoiding the dissolution of their own party. Except for a few people like Richmond, who had often complained that he was not consulted regularly enough by the inner circle of the party,[2] and Savile, who had often displayed considerable independence, the Rockinghams largely kept their following together during this extended period in the political wilderness. This was in part because most of the members of the party shared their leaders' lethargic attitude towards politics, and their relative indifference to the attractions of place and power, but it must have given Burke and the rest of the central core some satisfaction. After all they had been attempting since the 1760s, particularly in Burke's writings, to paint themselves to the world as a party of principles and their ability to remain by far the largest group in Opposition during the years when the battle against the North regime was the most hopeless, could only lend credence to that picture. The other central achievement for the party, though few of them would have recognized it as such, was in redefining the Whigs as an opposition connection and as a proponent of reform. For the most part of course they would continue to be both until long after Burke left them and until the party emerged from political obscurity in the 1830s. Accomplishments such as these were important but they also were not con-

---

[1] *Corr.* iv. 296–7.   [2] See, for instance, *Corr.* ii. 371.

crete, positive gains which might have enabled Burke to overcome all his frustrations. The latter he felt far more deeply and the fact that he was able to face them without succumbing to the melodramatic displays of the 1780s and 1790s, seems to demonstrate an emotional stability which eventually time and perhaps traumatic personal experiences such as the passing of Lord Rockingham in 1782, would damage.[1]

One of the major factors which helped Burke to maintain an even perspective in the 1770s was his constant pre-occupation with responsibilities in his own party. He was a man who needed an outlet for a huge reserve of intellectual energy and, in the period between Dowdeswell and Fox, he always had that outlet simply because he was required to take such a leading role in preparing and propagating virtually every stand his party made. At the beginning of each parliamentary session it was necessary for him to spearhead the attack on the Address to the King in the House of Commons often because he was the only Rockingham in town early enough to assume the responsibility.[2] Then, after each session started, he would find it necessary to become engrossed in an array of matters such as denouncing the Government over the land tax,[3] presenting and supporting petitions against the war,[4] dealing with special items on behalf of his constituents and producing parliamentary speeches and addresses on everything from the Government's coercive measures,[5] to the renovation of Somerset House,[6] to the regulation of butchers' meat,[7] capital punishment,[8] and the slave trade.[9] All of this did not prevent Burke from sinking occasionally into depression, but it does appear that it gave him a feeling of self-worth which may have helped him to view contentious matters in a reasonable light.

Burke's improved sense of his own importance in the 1770s can be detected in a new assertiveness in his relationship with Rockingham,

---

[1] Burke's major emotional outburst in the House of Commons in these years was that in 1780 during which he threatened a motion of impeachment against North and his colleagues (below, pp. 445–7). This appears, however, merely to have been the product of the fiery temper which his contemporaries had recognized years earlier; see below, p. 90.

[2] See, for instance, the work he did in preparing for the speech on the debate prior to the 1774–5 session (MSS. at Sheffield, Bk 27.231, 232; 6.34).

[3] See below, pp. 74–8. [4] See below, pp. 78–82.

[5] See below, pp. 82–4. [6] See below, pp. 169–71.

[7] See below, pp. 224–5. [8] See below, pp. 338–9.

[9] See below, pp. 340–1.

the Duke of Portland, Lord John Cavendish, and the small clique that made up the central core of the party. This is not to imply that Burke lost his profound admiration for his colleagues. However, one develops the impression that he grew a little less patient with their plodding, country approach to political events and less willing to await their lead. Earlier in his career Burke had been capable of following his own rather than the party line.[1] However, between 1774 and 1780, he demonstrated independence more frequently than before and on a greater and more important variety of concerns. For instance, in 1780 alone, he established his own approach to the Gordon riots and their aftermath, he refused to follow Sir George Savile's lead relative to Catholic schools,[2] and he spoke out in the Commons against John Sawbridge's motion for shorter Parliaments, though Rockingham, Cavendish, and others had agreed to support it.[3] Throughout the 1774–80 Parliament Burke also addressed most of what one might call the secondary issues with little or no consultation with the other members of his party. When his contemporaries viewed the energy he applied to such a wide range of activities, some of them wondered why he did not lose patience altogether with the Rockingham Whigs during the years of rather fruitless opposition. They searched for the reason for his continued attachment and loyalty to a group of men who under normal circumstances so completely lacked his enthusiasm in the political arena. The answer some of them believed lay simply in his character, consistency, and high moral standards. 'The sincerity of his friendship to Lord Rockingham and his party, and the frequent temptations to desert them, which he has certainly withstood,' they estimated, 'are strong evidence of the goodness and honesty of a heart which the industry and malevolence of Ministers and their adherents, have but too successfully called in question.'[4] Such statements were not altogether off the mark for it is clear that Burke shared with the other leading members of the party an unusually strong concern for principle. The Marquess of Rockingham and his aristocratic friends were often rather ineffective politicians because they cared relatively little about power and thus were able to put principles before political

---

[1] See vol. ii, pp. 5–12.
[2] See below, pp. 607–11.
[3] See below, pp. 588–602.
[4] *London Evening Post*, 7 May 1779.

expediency.[1] Evidence suggests that Burke himself may well have found the prospect of office attractive. He, unlike most of his associates, was constantly concerned about national politics and even between sessions of Parliament he kept his finger on the pulse of activity in London and Westminster. Moreover, his notoriously difficult financial position must have made office and a regular salary look attractive. However, his behaviour in this period makes it seem indisputable that he also cared too much about principles to be a successful politician. In Parliament he promoted Irish trade relief,[2] attacked slavery,[3] supported Catholic relief and the relief of insolvent debtors,[4] and he publicly and stead-fastly refused to accept a relationship of constant subservience to his electors, knowing full well that he was risking the wrath of many of his constituents at Bristol.[5] In all of these issues he felt that he was morally bound to take certain stands no matter what his constituents wanted and ultimately this may well have cost him his seat.[6]

It is apparent that nothing drew Burke to the Rockinghams more than their loyalty to principle. When he had first joined the fold he had recognized that their sense of public duty and their consistency, along with their politically unprofessional approach, presented real problems for the party in the competition for offices. Yet he had announced as early as 1767 that precisely because of their high ideals, he was pre-pared to endure a long period with them in the political wilderness. They are, he had told Charles O'Hara,[7]

by a good deal the strongest, of any, seperated from Government, and their connection the closest. They certainly stand fairest in point of Character; but that fairness which they have kept, and are determined still to keep, goes against their practicability; which is a quality ... indispensible ... [in the pursuit of power] ... [The] person now at the head of them, neither would, nor I am sure could, take a lead upon such Terms as the ... [present government] holds it ... [Their] turn never can be next, whilst any party, of not more strength, and more practicability, may be found; and it may very easily. I look therefore upon our Cause, viewed on the side of power, to be, for some years at least, quite desperate.[8]

Thereafter, even in the moments of his life when he became most frustrated as a result of the Rockinghams' other failings, Burke man-

---

[1] See Elofson, 'The Rockingham Whigs and the Country Tradition', 90–115.
[2] See below, pp. 435–7, 621.   [3] See below, pp. 340–1.
[4] See below, pp. 376–9.   [5] See below, pp. 340, 626.
[6] See below, pp. 630–57.   [7] (*c*.1715–76).   [8] *Corr.* i. 290.

aged to lift himself above despair by constructing euphonious declarations about their pristine public motives, their moral superiority, and disinterestedness.[1]

The other noteworthy quality besides a principled general approach to public affairs, which Burke shared with the Rockinghams in the years of opposition to North, was a consistent conservatism. In the strictly constitutional sphere this was grounded in the first place on a distinctly religious respect for all the institutions and conventions of government which had withstood the test of time.

I . . . believe from my soul [Burke himself once confessed] that Government is of divine *institution* and *sacred* authority, and no *arbitrary device of men*, to be modified at their *pleasure* or conducted by their *fancies*, or *feelings*, and [I] am persuaded that every one of us shall be called to a solemn and tremendous account for the part we take in it.[2]

During the course of the American war Burke expressed this view on behalf of the party on numerous occasions. He lectured the public at large, the members of the House of Commons, and even the King[3] himself on the importance of traditional values and the need to recognize the difference between 'the sacred name of Government' and the self-serving 'power of every miserable faction'.[4] Respect for tradition was reinforced in the minds of all the Rockingham leaders by a particularly strong sense of commitment to the system of government which had been established at the Glorious Revolution and during the so-called Whig supremacy.[5] The Marquess of Rockingham and his friends considered themselves the direct successors of court Whigs like Robert Walpole and Henry Pelham or Lords Somers and Sunderland.[6] They believed that men such as these had been responsible for the revolution and for the settlement which followed it and had established the immense prestige and influence of the Whig oligarchy upon that system. Therefore, their inclination was to worship the system itself and to 'avow and maintain in all its parts the same . . . government administered by their predecessors'.[7] 'I have supposed that

[1] See also *Corr.* vii. 52–3.
[2] See below, p. 208.
[3] See below, p. 261.
[4] See below p. 240.
[5] See Elofson, 'The Rockingham Whigs and the Country Tradition'.
[6] Sir Robert Walpole, First Earl of Orford (1676–1745), M.P. 1701–42; Henry Pelham (1695–54), M.P. 1717–54; John Somers, 1st Baron Somers (1651–1716); Charles Spencer, 3rd Earl of Sunderland (1674–1722).
[7] *London Magazine*, May 1777, 19.

the Constitution of this Country as settled at the Revolution was deemed the work and the Result of the Wisdom and Experience of Ages', Rockingham told a friend in 1780, 'I acknowledge these Prejudices, & I rather believe that they have taken some Root in general in the minds of the People of England.'[1] That line of reasoning Burke endorsed wholeheartedly. Like the Marquess, he constantly reflected back to a time when Whig pre-eminence and the British constitution had gone hand in hand. 'The most ardent lover of his country cannot wish for Great Britain an happier fate than to continue as she was . . . left' by George II, he wrote in 1770,[2] and some five years later he told the House of Commons of his

profound reverence for the wisdom of our ancestors, who have left us the inheritance of so happy a constitution, and so flourishing an empire, and what is a thousand times more valuable, the treasury of the maxims and principles which formed the one, and obtained the other.[3]

In this, Burke espoused a point of view which sounds rather Lockean. In his Address to the King in 1777 he made it clear that he saw the Glorious Revolution as a struggle against a ruler who had lost the right to govern because he had failed to provide for the liberties of his subjects. Fortunately, this had resulted in a reaffirmation of the first principles of government and, therefore, a new beginning for a chastened and better system worthy of the admiration and loyalty of posterity. He wrote:

It was not to passive principles in our Ancestors, that we owe the honor of appearing before a Sovereign, who cannot feel that he is a Prince, without knowing that we ought to be free. The revolution is a departure from the ancient course of the descent of this Monarchy. The People at that time reenter'd into their original rights; and it was not because a positive Law authorized what was then done, but because the freedom and safety of the Subject, the origin and cause of all Laws, required a proceeding paramount and superior to them. At that ever memorable and instructive period, the Letter of the Law was superseded in favour of the substance of Liberty. To the free choice therefore of the People, without either King or Parliament, we owe that happy establishment out of which both King and Parliament were regenerated. From that great principle of Liberty have originated the Statutes confirming and ratifying the establishment from which your Majesty derives your right to rule over us.[4]

[1] MS. at Sheffield, R1.1897: to John *Carr.* 22 May 1780.
[2] See vol. ii, p. 267.
[3] See below, p. 139.
[4] See below, pp. 273–4.

21

The deep respect for the British constitution which drew Burke and his friends together was thus a product of their commitment to Whig principles and to a Whig interpretation of history. It was all the more powerful in influencing their judgement because it was also a reflection of their basic view of society. This view most of the leading Rockinghams had inherited at birth as a result of the social prestige of their families. The Marquess and, with the exception of Burke himself, the other members of the central core of the party were a wealthy, landed, aristocratic clique. They considered themselves men of 'natural and fixed influence' and they clung together through common attributes such as 'vast property; obligations of favours given and received' and 'ties of blood, of alliance, of friendship'.[1] In their own counties these men wielded much influence. They were the landlords whose estates the lesser gentry and the yeomanry clamoured to rent. They were the heads of society who commonly decided who should be Justices of the Peace and who should sit in the House of Commons. As such, it was only to be expected that they should be comfortable with a traditional hierarchical view of society. They could see little reason to deny the natural evolution over the course of history which had placed unlimited prestige and almost all effective power in the hands of landed wealth, and which seemed to dictate that a few men in Britain were born to lead and the vast majority of the rest to follow.

This essentially élitist attitude is most clearly exhibited in the Rockingham's response to the ideals of more radical and democratic voices. In the 1770s noted reformers in Britain including John Wilkes,[2] William Beckford,[3] John Sawbridge, John Cartwright,[4] and Richard Price,[5] began to insist that the people should have a much stronger voice in government than the existing system allowed them and a more direct control over their representatives. To that end they began advocating measures such as shorter Parliaments, changes in the system of representation, and the extension of the franchise to more people.[6] The Rockinghams felt little sympathy for such objectives.

---

[1] See vol. ii, p 264.　　[2] (1725–97), M.P. 1757–64, 1768–9, 1774–90.
[3] (1709–70), M.P. 1747–70.　　[4] (1740–1824).　　[5] (1723–91).
[6] See E. Royle and J. Walvin, *English Radicals and Reformers, 1760–1848*, Brighton, 1982, pp. 13–31; J. Brewer, 'English Radicalism in the Age of George III', in *Three British Revolutions: 1641, 1688, 1776*, ed. J. G. A. Pocock, Princeton, NJ, 1980, pp. 323–67; and *Party Ideology and Popular Politics at the Accession of George III*, Cambridge, 1976, pp. 240–64; H. T. Dickinson, *Liberty and Property, Political Ideology in Eighteenth-Century Britain*, London, 1977, pp. 195–231; Lucy Sutherland, 'The City of London and Opposition to Government, 1768–74', *Politics and Finance in the Eighteenth Century*, ed. A. Newman, London, 1984, pp. 115–47; I. R. Christie, *Wilkes, Wyvill and Reform*, London 1962; S. Maccoby, *English Radicalism 1762–1785*, London, 1955.

They thought the will of the people (by which of course they meant only the propertied classes) should carry a great deal of weight with parliamentary and government leaders, but they did not consider the governing classes and M.P.s responsible to the people in any direct sense for their actions. They saw the representative in Parliament as a natural leader—a member of the governing classes—who ruled over his constituents by using his superior intelligence to provide for their liberties and welfare as he himself saw fit. In 1780 it was this philosophy which induced Rockingham, when he heard that Christopher Wyvill and his supporters were considering tests to select candidates at elections, to tell a friend that:

I don't like the Idea—of tests and especially on vague & inexplicit propositions. They being elected a Representative, if it implies a Trust—is most
highly Honourable, but if it is to lock up your reasoning Faculties of deliberating and judging, and is to tie you up beforehand—and preclude you from
acting according to your Conscience at the Moment—I think it would be a
disgraceful Bondage and what many men of the nicest Sense of Honour—can
not submit to.[1]

This was also the view which had prompted Lord John Cavendish a decade earlier, during the petitioning movement associated with John Wilkes and the Middlesex election, to declare that he had no doubt

the Gentlemen of the county will be ready to do anything; but we have been a
great many years teaching them to acquiesce & to be contented with what
their members do for them; if we encourage them, to take everything into
consideration they may choose to interpose much oftener than I am likely to
think convenient.[2]

The Rockinghams' attachment to a traditional view of society was, one supposes, strengthened by their identification with court Whigs who in the past appeared to have ruled the country basically as a birthright. Awareness of the important role their ancestors had played in British government gave the Marquess and his friends a sense of their own destiny. It confirmed in their minds that the clique which they themselves composed was one of select groups of natural leaders whose responsibility it was to 'guide and direct the public opinion'.[3] It may be that it was in part because this attitude meshed so well with the Whig view of history that Burke, himself, found it attractive even though he did not share his friends' aristocratic roots. Whatever the

[1] MS. at Sheffield, R1.1881: to Pemberton Milnes, 28 February 1780.
[2] MS. at Sheffield, R1.1219: to Rockingham [July 1769].   [3] *Corr.* iii. 381.

case, it is clear that Burke did embrace the élitist approach just as thoroughly as he did all the other Whig premisses. He believed that the traditional aristocracy represented the 'great Oaks that shade a Country and perpetuate your benefits from Generation to Generation',[1] and he unquestionably agreed that some men were born to lead and the rest to follow. His admiration for the highest orders of society was accompanied by a strong conviction that the lower orders lacked the capacity to grapple with complex affairs of state. Therefore, the idea of the governing classes accepting a position of strict subservience to their constituents, he found not only repugnant but an indication of intellectual and moral weakness. This, for instance, is largely why he detested election campaigns and the constant bowing to the whims of the people which they seemed to necessitate. As

to leaving to the Crowd, to choose for me, what principles I ought to hold, or what Course I ought to pursue for their benefit . . . [he told Portland during the 1780 campaign] I had much rather, innocently and obscurely, mix with them, with the utter ruin of all my hopes, (which hopes are my all) than to betray them by learning lessons from them. They are naturally proud, tyrannical, and ignorant; bad scholars and worse Masters.[2]

Burke's views on this subject were so strong that during his years as representative for Bristol, he felt obliged to proclaim them publicly on occasions when from a political standpoint he would have been well advised to withhold them. In his celebrated first major address to his electors he managed to stimulate some unneeded controversy when he insisted that:

it ought to be the happiness and glory of a Representative, to live in the strictest union, the closest correspondence, and the most unreserved communication with his constituents. Their wishes ought to have great weight with him . . . But, his unbiassed opinion, his mature judgement, his enlightened conscience, he ought not to sacrifice to you; to any man, or to any sett of men living. These he does not derive from your pleasure; no, nor from the Law and the Constitution. They are a trust from Providence, for the abuse of which he is deeply answerable. Your Representative owes you, not his industry only, but his judgement; and he betrays, instead of serving you, if he sacrifices it to your opinion.[3]

Burke was almost certainly aware of the reception this statement received amongst some of his electors at Bristol[4] but over the years

---

[1] Ibid. ii. 377.   [2] Ibid. iv. 274.   [3] See below, pp. 68–9.
[4] G. E. Weare, *Edmund Burke's Connection with Bristol, from 1774 till 1780; with a Prefatory Memoir of Burke*, Bristol, 1894, pp. 93–4.

which followed he was unable to restrain himself from reiterating it several times.[1] In 1780, for instance, when speaking of his attempts to attain certain objectives for interests outside the House of Commons, he went out of his way to explain that he had done so, not simply because his constituents wanted him to, but because reason convinced him that it was the right course of action.

> We are under infinite obligations to our constituents, who have raised us to so distinguished a trust, and have imparted such a degree of sanctity to common characters. We ought to walk before them with purity, plainness, and integrity of heart; with filial love, and not with slavish fear, which is always a low and tricking thing. For my own part, in what I have meditated upon that subject, I cannot indeed take upon me to say I have the honour *to follow* the sense of the people. The truth is, *I met it on the way*, while I was pursuing their interest according to my own ideas.[2]

For the most part, this type of reasoning worked to cement Burke's relationship with the rest of the leading members of the Rockingham connection in a defensive alliance against radical and threatening ideas. On rare occasions, however, it could work the other way. Ironically, this was because Burke tended to be even more defensive with respect to the entire range of constitutional conventions than the Marquess and others who had inherited wealth, social position, and Whig traditions directly from their ancestors. Amongst other things, his refusal to back Rockingham and Cavendish when they agreed, however reluctantly, to accept triennial Parliaments in 1780,[3] would seem to indicate the most powerful commitment in the party to the system which the Whig oligarchy had established in the past. When he claimed during the debate on that Bill that the last Triennial Act[4] had been the instrument of a Tory ministry, he appears to have been delivering a message not just to the general membership of the House of Commons but to some of his closest friends. He felt compelled to declare that the 'Septennial Parliament saved your constitution',[5] and he reminded his colleagues that they had never seen 'a more flourishing period for the union of National Prosperity dignity and Liberty than the 60 of the years[6] you have passed under that constitution of Parliament'. It would also appear to be a testimony to the depth of Burke's respect for the Whig system that he was more reluctant than most of his friends to

---

[1] Ibid.   [2] See below, p. 493.   [3] See below, p. 589.
[4] 6 and 7 Will. and Mary, c. 7.
[5] See below, p. 599.
[6] He meant, of course, until the fall of the Whigs at the beginning of George III's reign.

embrace the most basic general principle which eventually prompted the party to take the historic step of adopting a moderate reform programme. That principle was resistance to what by 1780 he singled out as 'the perennial spring of all prodigality and of all disorder'[1]—the undue influence of the Crown.

In 1780 Burke made the curtailment of the influence of the Crown (and economy) the basis of his party's 'economical reform' campaign which attempted to reduce Crown and ministerial patronage through a reformation of the King's household and public accounts, and the abolition of some fifty places of which a number were tenable with a seat in the House of Commons.[2] Long before Burke had set his mind to the development of his programme the struggle against the undue influence of the Crown had become practically an obsession with Rockingham and other leading figures in the party in their determination to find a great leading principle with which to attack the North regime. As early as 1771 the Marquess had determined that 'for the first time since the Revolution, the power and influence of the Crown is held out, as the main and chief and only support of Government,'[3] and many of his letters written after that are literally packed with statements such as: the 'Immense & dangerous Influence of the Crown';[4] his 'Majestys Advisers' fear 'the Influence of the Crown getting out of their Hands';[5] or the 'Causes of the increase of the power and influence of the Crown (which I take to be the grand disorder of the State) are by no means latent, but are easily traced to have arisen from various new Circumstances.'[6] Other leading members of the party regularly made similar assertions during these years,[7] but Burke himself displayed very little concern about the problem either in his private correspondence or in the House of Commons until the American war was almost over. His best opportunity to make a stand prior to designing his own economical reform programme came in 1777 when Parliament was asked to pay the arrears on the civil list. While that issue was being debated Opposition spokesmen generally

[1] See below, p. 483.
[2] See below, p. 482.
[3] *Corr.* ii. 194.
[4] MS. at Sheffield, R1.1876: to a representative of the Gentlemen of York, 30 December 1779.
[5] Portland MSS. PwF 9, 140: to Portland, 1 September 1780.
[6] MS. at Sheffield, R1.1897: to John Carr, 20 May 1780.
[7] MS. at Sheffield, R1.1898: to Sir Robert Clayton, 26 May 1780.

seized the moment to charge that the arrears were evidence that corruption was rife and the influence of the Crown out of control. The Marquess himself, in an uncharacteristically long and enthusiastic performance, urged against payment of the arrears because 'a further increase of the present overgrown influence of the Crown, would . . . enable the Ministers to carry on the delusive system which has been fatally adopted and which . . . must tend to the ruin . . . of this once great empire.'[1] Even on that occasion, however, Burke, while supporting the Opposition, intervened in the debate only briefly and, while he alluded to the subservience of the House of Commons and corruption, he had little of substance to say about the threat which the influence of the Crown presented to the nation.[2] He does not in fact appear to have become seriously concerned until he was called upon actually to design his Civil Establishment Bills. When he announced that his measure was forthcoming he apologized for having taken so long to make a stand claiming that he had

> been clear on the nature of this disease, and on the specific remedy for a long time. I however kept back my thoughts, partly for reasons of personal want of importance, partly from my own disposition. . . . I am besides cautious of experiment . . . and I have been reproached for it. But times alter natures.[3]

The reason for Burke's reticence seems to have been his defensiveness. It appears to have occurred to him that to concede that the influence of the Crown had subverted government was not only to admit the imperfections in the system he loved so much but, through such admission, to help to open the floodgates for reform propositions which aimed at significantly altering it. The charge that the weight of Crown patronage threatened the independence of the House of Commons had of course been a favourite of the enemies of Walpole and others during the Whig supremacy. The Whigs had established a policy of rejecting those charges, and it was difficult for a man of Burke's loyalties to take part in changing the trend. In his Address to the Colonists in January 1777 he told the Americans that 'Arguments may be used to weaken your confidence in that publick security; because from some unpleasant appearances, there is a suspicion, that Parliament itself is somewhat fallen from its independent spirit.' Feeling unable to bring himself to confirm those suspicions, he simply

---

[1] *London Evening Post*, 17 April 1777.
[2] See below, pp. 330–6.   [3] See below, p. 473.

added that how 'far this supposition may be founded in fact we are unwilling to determine'.[1] When finally he did endorse the principle of opposition to the undue influence of the Crown, Burke was careful, presumably in order to avoid giving credence to former attacks on the constitution, to argue that this had become a major threat only in recent years. 'Formerly', he pointed out, 'the operation of the influence of the Crown only touched the higher orders of the State. It has now insinuated itself into every creek and cranny in the kingdom.'[2]

Burke's conversion to a moderate reform stance thus was a slow and halting process because of his profound respect for the traditions of the Rockinghams' Whig predecessors. By the 1770s he appears to have become in fact more Whiggish than the Whigs themselves. One can only guess at the reasons for this. It may be that as a latecomer to the fold he felt less secure in his own Whiggery than the Marquess and others and needed to be doubly loyal and defensive in order to feel worthy of the title. There is no question that since he had adopted the Whigs he had learnt to see them as his family. His apologia for his years of devotion to them had inspired his compelling justification of party in the *Thoughts on the Cause of the Present Discontents*[3] as early as 1770, and while he grew somewhat less patient with the Rockinghams and less subservient as the years passed, he did not lose his admiration for them and his desire to be a Whig. It should be recognized that even his eventual conversion to the ideals of economical reform did not to any significant degree entail a weakening of his determination to defend and preserve the constitution. Indeed, quite the opposite was the case. Burke, it is apparent, rationalized his programme in his own mind as a means far more to protect the constitution than in any sense significantly to change it. In order to explain this statement properly it is necessary to examine his constitutional and political philosophy in more detail and to weigh a little more closely the forces which governed his approach to reform in the late 1770s and early 1780s.

Burke's desire to protect and preserve traditions of government and society naturally made him apprehensive about programmes aimed at change. It did not, however, force him to reject them altogether. Burke believed that flexibility and concession were necessary to preserve existing conventions. He was disdainful of the people but, possibly with

---

[1] See below, p. 284.   [2] See below, p. 471.
[3] See vol. ii, pp. 241–323.

the lessons of 1688 in his mind, he respected and even feared their collective power.[1] Throughout his career he operated with a firm conviction that it was necessary constantly to teach them to love and worship the status quo. The only way to do that he believed was to demonstrate through enlightened policies, that the existing system was able always to represent their will, secure their liberties, and work for their happiness. To him preservation could be achieved not through authoritarian policies, harsh laws or force, but through accommodation, compromise, and benevolence. This theme he enunciated many times. 'We have been too early instructed, and too long habituated to believe, that the only firm seat of all authority is in the minds, affections, and Interests of the People,' he argued in 1777. We must never 'change our opinion, on the Theoretick reasonings of speculative men, or for the convenience of a mere temporary arrangement of State.'[2] The key, he kept saying, was for the system to win the loyalty of the British people by demonstrating that it shared their values and aspirations. If loyalty appears only when it is based upon affection, affection is achieved only when government actions are in accord with what the people perceive to be for their benefit.

But, although there are some amongst us who think our constitution wants many improvements, to make it a complete system of liberty, perhaps none who are of that opinion, would think it right to aim at such improvement, by disturbing his country, and risquing every thing that is dear to him. In every arduous enterprize, we consider what we are to lose, as well as what we are to gain; and the more and better stake of liberty every people possess, the less they will hazard in a vain attempt to make it more. These are *the cords of man*. Man acts from adequate motives relative to his interest.[3]

Because Burke felt so protective towards the status quo he could advocate concern for civil liberties, proprietary rights, and the will of the people but he could not give in to calls for measures which might significantly alter the existing constitution or what he considered the traditional values of society. Indeed, what eventually encouraged him to design a moderate reform programme was not a desire to change, but to preserve. By 1779 he believed that the public was so disillusioned with the North regime that Britons might well take it upon themselves

---

[1] For Burke's view of 1688, see G. Watson, 'Burke's Conservative Revolution' and R. Kirk, 'A Revolution not Made but Prevented' in *Edmund Burke, Appraisals and Applications*, ed. D. E. Ritchie, New Brunswick, 1990, pp. 75–88, 89–102.
[2] See below, pp. 262–3.   [3] See below, p. 157.

to destroy the constitution altogether. During the war, hardships had ensued as a result of economic dislocation and rising taxes.[1] Moreover, after the defeat of British forces at Saratoga in late 1777[2] and the interference in the conflict of both France[3] and Spain,[4] almost everyone saw defeat and a substantial loss of international prestige as inevitable.[5] Discontent was widespread and it seemed to give weight to charges that the system was significantly flawed. How else, people appeared to be asking, could the country have sunk to so desperate a state? Many evinced signs of being swayed by 'Hazardous Experiments on the Constitution of the Country',[6] which roused real fears in the hearts of Burke, the Marquess, and many of their friends. In Yorkshire the Reverend Christopher Wyvill and his supporters began by late 1779 to push not just for shorter Parliaments and tests but also for the addition of more county seats to the House of Commons. What made the situation particularly threatening to Rockingham, moreover, was that they were appealing to those who wanted to strike a blow directly at aristocratic influence by entering 'into an Association to elect such Candidates only . . . as will engage to promote [our aims] . . . as something of this kind is plainly the Interest of independent men'.[7] It was also frightening that in the City of London some well-known radicals began vigorously espousing very democratic sounding principles which not only advocated direct controls by the people but also hinted strongly at a substantial extension of the franchise. The

meanest mechanic, the poorest peasant and day-laborer, [some of them were arguing] has important rights respecting his personal liberty, that of his wife and children, his property however inconsiderable, his wages, his earnings . . . Some share therefore in the power of making those laws, which deeply interest them, and to which they are expected to pay obedience, should be reserved even to this inferior, but most useful set of men in the community.[8]

When he turned his energies to his Civil Establishment legislation Burke did so with a sense of mission. He feared that all the conventions of government and society which he loved so much were under siege and he felt compelled to defend them. However, he could not

---

[1] See below, p. 396.   [2] See below, p. 346.   [3] See below, p. 367.
[4] See below, pp. 445–7.   [5] See below, pp. 393–7.
[6] MS. at Sheffield, R1.1897: Rockingham to John Carr, 22 May 1780.
[7] MS. at Sheffield, R1.1868: Wyvill to Pemberton Milnes, 5 December 1779.
[8] See the speech of John Wilkes when introducing his reform Bill in the House of Commons on 31 March 1776 (*Parl. Hist.* xviii. 1295–6).

stand against the tide of public opinion. He had a relatively low estimation of the people, but his conviction that governments to survive must be popular and thus must be seen to have the welfare and the will of the people at heart, led him to believe that a general but moderate programme must be developed. 'If any ask me what a free Government is,' he once said, 'I answer, that, for any practical purpose, it is what the people think so; and that they, and not I, are the natural, lawful, and competent judges of this matter.'[1] In other words, the government must be the kind of government the people think they want, and if the people believe that the system is not free enough, then it must be changed sufficiently to alter their opinion. Burke first applied this thesis to the question of reform when attempting to ease tensions in America. By late 1776 he had come to the conclusion that the colonists, whom he considered as Englishmen overseas, were more or less unanimous in their desire for change to make Parliament less subservient to the ministry. Therefore he reasoned that he should attempt to regain their loyalty not by standing against their will but by convincing them that the existing system had the capacity to conform to their wishes. In his 'Address to the Colonists' he made every effort to persuade the Americans that the British Parliament, if retained in its present form, could eventually cast out its evil ministers and make whatever adjustments were necessary to enable the system better to serve them.

we are well assured, from experience, that even if all were true, that is contended for, and in the extent too, in which it is argued, yet as long as the solid and well disposed forms of the Constitution remain, there ever is within Parliament itself a power of renovating its principles, and effecting a self-reformation, which no other plan of Government has ever contained. This Constitution has therefore admitted innumerable improvements, either for the correction of the original scheme, or for removing corruptions, or for bringing its principles better to suit those changes, which have successively happened in the circumstances of the nation, or in the manners of the people.

We feel, that the growth of the Colonies is such a change of circumstances; and that our present dispute is an exigency as pressing, as any which ever demanded a revision of our Government. Public troubles have often called upon this Country to look into its Constitution. It has ever been bettered by such a revision. If our happy and luxuriant encrease of dominion, and our diffused population, has outgrown the limits of a Constitution made for a contracted object, we ought to bless God, who has furnished us with this

---

[1] See below, p. 317.

noble occasion for displaying our skill and beneficence in enlarging the scale
of rational happiness, and of making the politick generosity of this Kingdom
as extensive, as its fortune. If we set about this great work on both sides, with
the same conciliatory turn of mind, we may now, as in former times, owe even
to our mutual mistakes, contentions and animosities, the lasting concord,
freedom, happiness, and glory of this Empire.[1]

By 1779 Burke had become certain that the desire for a freer system
had spread from America to the mother country. He believed that the
call for reform in Britain was so strong that unless the governing
classes could demonstrate that the constitution was flexible enough to
accept moderate change, the purveyors of radical and really threatening
ideas might some day have their way. 'Little more time remains for us',
he told the Duke of Portland in January 1780. 'It will not be borne by
the people, who are hungering & thirsting after substantial reformation, that we should balk their appetite'.[2] At that point he saw it as
the responsibility of the governing classes to protect the status quo
through mild alterations. That reasoning he explained most succinctly
when introducing his Civil Establishment legislation on 11 February
1780. Accept this temperate package, he told the members of the
House of Commons, or risk the wrath of the people and the consequent reduction of our cherished constitution to ashes.

Early reformations are amicable arrangements with a friend in power: Late
reformations are terms imposed upon a conquered enemy; early reformations
are made in cool blood; late reformations are made under a state of inflammation. In that state of things the people behold in government nothing that is
respectable. They see the abuse, and they will see nothing else—They fall
into the temper of a furious populace provoked at the disorder of a house of ill
fame; they never attempt to correct or regulate; they go to work by the
shortest way—They abate the nuisance, they pull down the house.[3]

Through his economical reform programme Burke was attempting
to use conciliatory means (in the sense that he was yielding or at least
giving concessions to the popular will) to reinforce the traditional
values which he and the Rockinghams believed in. In retrospect, one
might add, this was a thoroughly intelligent approach given the political
climate of the time. Even in that stage, some two years before the
Rockinghams would themselves assume ministerial office, the Civil

[1] See below, pp. 284–5.
[2] *Corr.* iv. 197: Burke to Portland, 16 January 1780.
[3] See below, p. 492.

Establishment legislation had a reasonable chance of success precisely because it was both moderate enough to alienate as few of the members of Parliament as possible and yet significant enough to seem attractive to those who were insisting that some measure of reform was necessary. The programme was moderate in principle. It would have reduced government patronage but, in theory at least only to levels which were thought to have been acceptable for strong and efficient government in the past. In planning the elimination of administrative offices Burke concentrated on the lower levels in the household and ministry.

We have ... several offices which perform real service—We have also places that provide large rewards for no service at all. We have stations which are made for the public decorum; made for preserving the grace and majesty of a great people.—We have likewise expensive formalities, which tend rather to the disgrace than the ornament of the state and the court ... To fall with the same severity on objects so perfectly dissimilar, is the very reverse of a reformation.[1]

He planned to discard the entire Board of Trade and the third secretaryship of state but these he could describe as ineffective and sinecurist[2] and, because the former was a product of the very distant and the latter of the very recent past,[3] he could satisfy himself and his own friends that they were no part of the Whig constitution. The other major offices of state would have emerged unscathed. They would have continued to operate with seats in the House of Commons and largely the same bureaucracies as they had enjoyed under the Rockinghams' Whig predecessors. While Burke was criticized for not going far enough, it would have been unrealistic to expect independent opinion in the House of Commons to accept anything more extensive. As it stood, the Commons did agree to consider the plan and accepted portions of it including the abolition of the Board of Trade.[4] If the scheme was realistic in its objectives, moreover, it was also substantial enough directly to address the two problems which most reform-minded people could agree upon in the dying days of the American Revolution. First, it aimed directly at cutting the cost of government. Burke estimated a saving of some £200,000 annually would ensue. Secondly, and even more importantly it could claim to be

---

[1] See below, p. 494.   [2] See below, p. 534.
[3] See below, pp. 533, 536.   [4] *Parl. Hist.* xxi. 278.

providing for a real reduction of the undue influence of the Crown. As is demonstrated by the success of Dunning's famous motion in 1780 and by volumes of political literature of the 1770s, the principle of opposition to the undue influence of the Crown had gained almost universal acceptance outside government.[1] Many so-called independent country gentlemen supported it and Opposition groups from Burke's own aristocratic friends to the London radicals had claimed to be deeply concerned about it.

If Burke's first brief flirtation with reform is seen as an attempt through conciliatory means to bolster traditional values and conventions, it in a sense acquits him of charges of inconsistency which historians have made against him for passing a less far-reaching scheme once he and the Rockingham party attained office in 1782. It should be remembered that Burke had never been a committed reformer. He was first, foremost, and always a defender. He loved the traditions of government and society which he felt had been in place at the beginning of George III's reign and the desire to protect them pervaded his political career. He offered his programme in 1780 because he felt the need to demonstrate that the institutions of government in Britain were essentially sound. He was attempting to show the world how flexible, just, and reliable the system really was so that the people could worship it as he, himself, did. By the time he designed his legislation in 1782, Burke almost certainly no longer felt quite the same sense of urgency in the pursuit of that objective. His standard for judging how free a system must be (and therefore how much modification it might require) had always been the opinion of the people. By 1782 he had reason to believe that the people would shortly become less alienated and therefore less likely to want radical measures of change. The American war appeared to be about to end, economic conditions were improving and peacetime levels of taxation could be expected to be the norm. Everyone of substance from the country gentlemen in the House of Commons to the propertied classes in the City of London could be expected to be more content. Moreover, and probably in Burke's eyes more importantly, the reins of power appeared to be firmly in the hands of men who could be trusted to do a much better job. The Whigs had once again asserted their influence and taken their natural position at the head of British government. This, Burke earnestly

---

[1] See below, pp. 438 and n., 588.

believed, would bring general satisfaction to the kingdom as wise, stable, and enlightened policies were revived. He once estimated that his 'Majesty's condescension in committing the direction of his affairs into the hands of the known friends of his family, and of the liberties of all his People',[1] could win back the loyalty even of the Americans. With the Rockinghams at the helm there was no danger that the patronage of the Crown would be abused the way it had been in the past. Burke was still committed to reducing influence in 1782 but he could see every hope that once the people saw it properly exercised they would learn to fear it less. Burke was unquestionably biased in placing so much faith in the Rockingham Whigs, but he had not in any respect given up his commitment to the traditions of his beloved colleagues' forefathers. Indeed, he almost certainly felt that they were now safer than they had ever been.

An acceptable term to describe Burke's political and constitutional philosophy would perhaps be conservation through change,[2] or preservation through concession, as long as it is recognized that in both cases the first word reflects his ultimate objective—to protect the status quo—and the last mainly his means to that end. In the 1774–80 period one can see this basic approach in Burke's response not only to the question of constitutional reform but to most of the controversies he addressed. Not all of these were major issues. It is a testimony to the strength of Burke's faith in concession as a method to preserve traditional institutions, conventions, and values that he found it appropriate in dealing with some of the most trivial matters. One of these appeared in April 1775 when the Commons was asked to vote £100,000 to convert Somerset House into a new public administrative centre and repository. In that affair some of the members of the House, no doubt in part concerned at the mounting costs of the American war, were anxious to appropriate as little capital as possible. However, Burke himself argued not for economy but for larger expenditure so that Somerset House could be made into a truly magnificent structure. His reasons were the same as those which governed his thinking relative to the question of constitutional reform. He wanted the House of Commons to be generous or, as he put it, 'liberal' (in this case with the public money) in order that the constitution could be

---

[1] See below, p. 285.
[2] In later years Burke would actually use these words himself; see vol. viii, p. 72.

strengthened in the hearts and affections of all Britons. Public buildings, he reasoned, indicate to the people the kinds of institutions they
house. It followed therefore that the great and glorious institutions,
which he believed existed in the British system of government, should
be contained in magnificent structures. Use this building, he told the
House, to display to the world the virtues of our constitution and it will
encourage the people to feel an everlasting loyalty to it.

There are few opportunities of doing any thing of this sort; this is one of
them, and I would wish the new edifice may be rendered an ornament to this
great, wealthy, and luxurious metropolis. When the public money is spent on
public works, the public spend it on themselves; they enjoy those works when
elegant and magnificent; they pride themselves on the glory of their country
possessing such. I never walk thro' Westminster Abbey but I think it mine; it
is every man's; and when such works are erected, they do honour to the age.
If we were upon an œconomical system only, and the old offices were to serve,
I should admit œconomy but if we are to go to a great expense, in the name of
national liberality, let it be compleat.[1]

Our government, he was saying, is tolerant, caring, and humane and
this fact ought to be displayed. When his views on Somerset House
were challenged, he clarified his position by pointing out that it was the
conciliatory nature of the constitution in particular, as demonstrated by
its deep respect for liberty, to which facilities such as fine buildings
would bring widespread public recognition.

Our freedom, Sir, ought to dictate the magnificence of our public works—
common wealths have ever shewn their glory and their liberality by these
splendid expenses. Reflect on the edifices of the common wealths of antiquity
more magnificent than those of emperors, as the buildings of the Republic of
Holland exceed the efforts of Kings. The Stadthouse of Amsterdam is a
greater and better work than Versailles; but, Sir, this country has been
niggardly throughout the present age—we have done nothing. Let this age
come in for a share of that fame which attends the exertion of these laudable
and useful expences. Who is it will say that Westminster Abbey and St Paul's
are not an honour and glory to this country?

The desire to teach the people to love their constitution, all of their
traditions, and, indeed, their entire society was on Burke's mind in
virtually all his public activities. He supported the theatre[2] and he
urged Parliament to make money available whenever possible for pro-

---

[1] See below, p. 170.
[2] See below, pp. 170–1.

jects such as the British Museum,[1] so that the 'liberal polite and arts' would flourish. He took a stand against what he considered inhumane practices such as the employment of Negro slaves and Indians in the American war,[2] and he worked for the amelioration of harsh legal measures such as the pillory[3] and capital punishment[4] in England, in part because he cared deeply about civilized standards and felt compassion for the downtrodden,[5] but also because he wanted Britain to be the most enlightened nation on earth. Then, he reasoned, she would be recognized as the best of all possible worlds and her people would see themselves as the most fortunate. This, in turn, would encourage them to protect and defend what they had rather than discard it for something new and untried.

In essence the philosophy which Burke employed so consistently in the years of the American Revolution he would modify only slightly after the outbreak of the French Revolution. The only thing which really differentiates his approach in the two periods is that in the earlier one he could still hold out hope that long-standing conventions would best be protected through concession. In the later period he seems to have come to the conclusion that both in France and England the opportunity for concession had, for the time being, been lost. The French he feared in 1789 had become so enraged at their government and society that they had delivered themselves into 'the worst of all Slavery'—'the despotism of their own blind and brutal passions'.[6] The 'prevalent part' of the people had 'murdered, robbed and rebelled.' They had 'put over their country an insolent tyranny, made up of cruel and inexorable masters ... hitherto not known to the world.' They had employed 'the practices of incendiaries, assassins, housebreakers, robbers, spreaders of false news, forgers of false orders from authority, and other delinquencies' and had acted 'more in the manner of thieves who have got possession of an house, than of conquerors who have subdued a nation.'[7] The following passage from the *Reflections on the Revolution in France* seems to demonstrate, however, that even in what

---

[1] See below, p. 336.
[2] See below, pp. 354–67.
[3] See below, pp. 583–6.
[4] See below, pp. 338–9.
[5] This is to be compared with his attitude in later years towards the unfortunate in India (see vol. v, pp. 104–6, 460–78).
[6] *Corr.* vi. 41–2.
[7] Vol. viii, pp. 332–3.

arguably was the most defensive period of his life, Burke continued to believe that when employed at the appropriate moment a conciliatory approach (or in this case the ability to give into demands for change) could be valuable when used as a means to bolster rather than effectively to alter tradition.

I think our happy situation [is] owing to our constitution; but owing to the whole of it, and not to any part singly; owing in a great measure to what we have left standing in our several reviews and reformations, as well as to what we have altered or superadded. Our people will find employment enough for a truly patriotic, free, and independent spirit, in guarding what they possess, from violation. I would not exclude alteration neither; but even when I changed, it should be to preserve. I should be led to my remedy by a great grievance. In what I did, I should follow the example of our ancestors. I would make the reparation as nearly as possible in the style of the building. A politic caution, a guarded circumspection, a moral rather than a complexional timidity were among the ruling principles of our forefathers in their most decided conduct.[1]

Evidently, Burke continued until the end of his life to be an advocate of conservation through change in so far as the British constitution was concerned. After the French Revolution he found it appropriate to stress his love of conventional institutions over his concern for liberty or flexibility, but he would never altogether lose sight of the need for compromise.

In Burke's career much of the significance of the years 1774 to 1780 is that they were a stage when he could express his belief in concession and his concern for tradition in more detail than he had in the past and with more freedom than he would be able to in much of the future. It should be noted as well that in these years he did so in response to two extremely important issues which, like lesser matters such as the 'polite and liberal arts', did not strictly and directly pertain to the question of constitutional reform. One of these concerned religion.

Before this period Burke had demonstrated both his willingness to advance the cause of greater religious liberty and his determination to preserve the pre-eminence of the Church of England and the traditional alliance between church and state. He had spoken out for religious liberty in particular when Dissenting clergy had applied to Parliament in 1772 for relief from subscription to the Articles which

[1] Vol. viii, p. 292.

they were required to subscribe by the Toleration Act. At that time he had supported the petitioners wholeheartedly and with one of the most logical and enlightened appeals for toleration made by any member of the House of Commons.

The opposer of the question is willing to grant them a toleration to a certain extent; that is, as far as their tenets correspond with those of the Church of England. But surely, Sir, this is not sound logick; for the very principle of toleration is that you will tolerate not those who agree with you in opinion, but those whose religious notions are totally different. For what merit, I beseech you, is there in tolerating your own doctrines? None at all. Christian charity consists in allowing others a latitude of opinion, in putting a restraint upon your own mind, and in not suffering the zeal of the Lords' House absolutely to eat you up.[1]

Burke's thought process with respect to religion, however, was exactly the same as with respect to the question of constitutional reform. He believed that conciliatory policies were necessary principally as a bulwark of convention. His concern in promoting religious freedom was at least as much to secure the position of the Church of England as to promote toleration for toleration's sake. Burke passionately supported the principle of establishment, even against his friends. In 1772 when a second petition was presented to the House of Commons for ending compulsory subscription to the Thirty-nine Articles because, as most people recognized, the Articles were 'outdated, contradictory and absurd',[2] he found that his sentiments were 'in opposition to the opinions of nearly all my own party'.[3] In the Commons he closed ranks with some High Church Tories like Sir Roger Newdigate,[4] to defeat the petition and he supported the Articles of faith because they were essential to the very existence of an established church. However outdated they might be, he insisted, subscription to them was the only basis upon which the institution could be identified, distinguished, and raised above all the rest.[5]

The degree of Burke's concern for the principle of establishment indicates a traditional position at a time when, at the other extreme, Dissenters and their spokesmen were upholding the principle that the 'Scriptures are the only rule to the Church of Christ, and [that]

---

[1] See vol. ii, pp. 369–70.   [2] *Parl. Hist.* xvii. 255.
[3] *Corr.* ii. 299.   [4] 5th Baronet (1719–1806), M.P. 1742–7, 1751–80.
[5] See vol. ii, pp. 359–64.

adhering to the Scriptures in opposition to human invention and corruption is the first Principle of Protestantism.'[1] One of the reasons that he so strongly supported establishment is that he saw it as a pillar of the status quo in both church and state. Like many others, Burke believed that the union between the ecclesiastical and the secular authority was ultimately necessary for the maintenance of both. Englishmen consider this

as the foundation of their whole constitution, [he would argue in the later years of his life] with which, and with every part of which, it holds an indissoluble union. Church and state are ideas inseparable in their minds, and scarcely is one ever mentioned without mentioning the other.[2]

Burke felt secure in the knowledge that when properly controlled the Anglican establishment could use its pre-eminent position to work hand in hand with the civil authority to proselytize the ideals amongst the people which would insure their love for church, country, and constitution. In defending subscription to the Thirty-nine Articles therefore he was defending tradition in the most general sense. He could accept that the Articles might be updated in the future but he insisted that in one form or another they were absolutely essential and he warned of the upheavals which might follow the abandonment of 'some criterion of faith more brief, more precise and definite than the scripture for the regulation of the priesthood'.[3] Forms 'of subscription', he said, 'are necessary for the sake of order and decorum, and public peace.'[4]

True to the conciliatory side of his philosophy, Burke considered enlightened and tolerant religious policies even more important to the preservation of the mother church than articles of faith or any laws and regulations. In his scale of values the Church of England could get the people to love it and to accept its ideals only if it could win their respect. This he anticipated it could accomplish not by preaching hate and intolerance, or by calling on the civil authority to establish or sustain harsh legal sanctions, but by acting itself as a shining example of magnanimity, understanding, benevolence, and freedom. It was for that reason that Burke gave his undivided support to Savile's Bill for the relief of Catholics in 1778[5] and that he supported the application

---

[1] *Parl. Hist.* xvii. 290.   [2] See vol. viii. 149.   [3] See vol. ii. 362.
[4] Ibid. 363.   [5] See below, pp. 376–9.

for relief of Scottish Catholics in 1779.[1] It was also largely the reason that in 1780 he was so outspoken in denouncing all the hypocrisy displayed by Lord George Gordon[2] and the Protestant Association and then opposed his friend Sir George Savile's Bill to restrict Catholic schools. Burke's belief in concession also helps to explain his determination to further the cause of moderate punishment of the anti-Catholic rioters in the wake of the Gordon fiasco.[3] In the resolutions he sent to Lord North after the riots he was emphatic that the Church of England should demonstrate that it was far too enlightened and too secure to succumb either to coercion or the obvious bigotry all around it. The

Truth and Evidence of the Christian Protestant Religion, the eminent Piety and Learning of sundry of its Professors, the Protection of the State, the Succession establish'd in his Majesty's Royal Family, the liberal Endowment of Churches, Universities, Schools, and Colleges, and the entire and exclusive possession of all offices and emoluments in Church, State, Law, Revenue, Army, and Navy, do, under the divine Providence, furnish a perfect Security to the said Protestant Religion, without any persecution of other his Majesty's Subjects.

Moreover,

all endeavours to disquiet the minds of the People, upon the said Prudent and Equitable Relaxation, as if any degree of Toleration were inconsistent with the safety, or irreconcileable to the Principles of the Protestant Religion, have a manifest tendency to disturb the public peace, to break the Union necessary at this time, to bring Dishonour on the national Character, to discredit the Protestant Religion, and to furnish occasion for the Renewal of the Persecution of our Protestant Brethren in other Countries.[4]

It may have been important to Burke that in the eighteenth century, and looking as far back as the Exclusion Crisis of the previous century, the protection of the status quo through conciliation could be seen as a Whig approach. In secular matters it reconciled a respect for the institutions of Crown, Lords, and Commons with a genuine concern for the liberties of the propertied classes. In religious affairs it sought to protect the pre-eminence of the Anglican Church and yet provide for toleration of various dissenting denominations. By 1780 it also

---

[1] See below, pp. 425–30.
[2] (1753–93), M.P. 1774–80.
[3] See below, pp. 602–3.
[4] See below, p. 104.

meant extending toleration to Catholics, Jews, and as Burke himself once argued, even to 'Pagans'.[1] One feels quite certain that Burke himself considered this a Whig approach and that this strengthened his resolve. An interesting feature of such an approach is that it often entailed working in two seemingly diametrically opposed directions at the same time. Obviously, if it is accepted that the more one supports liberty the stronger one's love for traditional values, then it follows that the deeper one's concern for traditional values the harder one must work in the cause of liberty. No one worked harder than Burke to defend and bolster the mother church and the principle of establishment and no one devoted to the Church of England, was more sincere and more energetic than him in promoting the rights of minority groups.

The other major issue in which Burke's actions could be properly described in something of this fashion is the American conflict. Few worked harder than him to defend and bolster the authority of the imperial Parliament and few devoted to the mother country were more sincere and more energetic in promoting the rights and interests of the colonial minority. Indeed, the determination to strengthen tradition with a policy of concession and appeasement governed virtually every position Burke took. In early 1774 he had resisted North's coercive measures—notably the Boston Port Act and the Massachusetts Bay Act—which brought the conflict to the point of war.[2] In the new Parliament, when the vast majority continued to demand strong measures, he stood for moderation and leniency and, after some hesitation for fear of encouraging American resistance and perhaps of alienating his electors,[3] he came down strongly and decisively on the side of American rights and liberties.[4] As the conflict deepened he kept arguing for greater and greater concessions and in every case his objective was, not to alter the traditional relationship between the mother country and her colonies, but to preserve as much of it as possible.

Burke may have been a champion of American liberty but constitutionally he was no champion of American equality. He saw it as his own duty to do everything possible to maintain the supremacy of the

---

[1] See below, p. 376.
[2] 14 Geo. III, c. 10, and 14 Geo. III, c. 45; see vol. ii, pp. 404–6, 463–5.
[3] See below, pp. 57–60, 72–4.
[4] See below, p. 97.

imperial Parliament over all the colonial possessions in the empire. In 1774 he argued in his widely publicized Speech on American Taxation that:

The Parliament of Great Britain sits at the head of her extensive empire in two capacities ... I think her nobler capacity, is what I call her *imperial character*; in which, as from the throne of heaven, she superintends all the several inferior legislatures, and guides, and controls them all without annihilating any. As all these provincial legislatures are only co-ordinate to each other, they ought all to be subordinate to her; else they can neither preserve mutual peace, nor hope for mutual justice, nor effectually afford mutual assistance. It is necessary to coerce the negligent, to restrain the violent, and to aid the weak and deficient, by the over-ruling plenitude of her power.[1]

As in domestic matters, however, Burke was driven by the conviction that central authority must be established through affection. He felt obliged constantly to promote lenient policies which would demonstrate that the mother country was anxious consistently to provide for the welfare and defend the liberties of the Americans. In his first speech on conciliation with America in early 1775, he told the House of Commons that:

my trust is in ... [America's] interest in the British constitution. My hold of the Colonies is in the close affection which grows from common names, from kindred blood, from similar privileges, and equal protection. These are ties, which, though light as air, are as strong as links of iron. Let the Colonies always keep the idea of their civil rights associated with your Government;— they will cling and grapple to you; and no force under heaven will be of power to tear them from their allegiance. But let it be once understood, that your Government may be one thing, and their Privileges another; that these two things may exist without any mutual relation; the cement is gone; the cohesion is loosened; and every thing hastens to decay and dissolution. As long as you have the wisdom to keep the sovereign authority of this country as the sanctuary of liberty, the sacred temple consecrated to our common faith, wherever the chosen race and sons of England worship freedom, they will turn their faces towards you. The more they multiply, the more friends you will have; the more ardently they love liberty, the more perfect will be their obedience. Slavery they can have any where. It is a weed that grows in every soil. They may have it from Spain, they may have it from Prussia. But until you become lost to all feeling of your true interest and your natural dignity, freedom they can have from none but you. This is the commodity of price, of which you have the monopoly.[2]

---

[1] See vol. ii, pp. 459–60.
[2] See below, pp. 164–5.

43

This kind of reasoning attracted Burke to the *laissez-faire* approach when he turned his attention to commercial matters. Economic freedom was like any other form to him and it seemed reasonable to argue that by providing for it in the colonies the mother country would see her own authority enhanced. If people like David Hume and Adam Smith[1] were right, this would bring increased prosperity to the entire empire. Therefore, instead of insisting on obedience to restrictive laws and regulations, the imperial Parliament should work to facilitate commercial development throughout the empire. This like enlightened policies in other areas would bring general contentment and help to establish the authority of the mother country on the only foundation which in the long term would endure. If you destroy the colonies with war, he told the House of Commons when that still appeared possible, you will lose a trader who has made you wealthy; but bolster American trade, enliven it, allow the colonies the liberty to pursue their commercial ambitions, and the whole empire will reap the rewards.

This is the true act of navigation, which binds to you the commerce of the Colonies, and through them secures to you the wealth of the world. Deny them this participation of freedom, and you break that sole bond, which originally made, and must still preserve, the unity of the empire. Do not entertain so weak an imagination, as that your registers and your bonds, your affidavits and your sufferances, your cockets and your clearances, are what form the great securities of your commerce. Do not dream that your letters of office, and your instructions, and your suspending clauses, are the things that hold together the great contexture of this mysterious whole. These things do not make your government. Dead instruments, passive tools as they are, it is the spirit of English communion that gives all their life and efficacy to them. It is the spirit of the English constitution, which, infused through the mighty mass, pervades, feeds, unites, invigorates, vivifies, every part of the empire, even down to the minutest member.[2]

The same position Burke advanced not just with respect to America but with regard virtually to all Britain's colonial and national possessions. Several years later he spoke for the opening up of the trade and commerce of Ireland by insisting that the policy of defending regulations rather than developing freer economies would ultimately threaten the supremacy of Parliament and the authority of the mother country.

[1] Hume (1711–76) and Smith (1723–90) were both on friendly terms with Burke; see *Corr.* i. 129 n. 1, iii. 152–3, v. 9–10, vi. 81 n. 1.

[2] See below, p. 165.

It had been pronounced dangerous for us to consider the laws relating to Ireland [he said]. And what was the reason given . . . Why, truly, that we ought to do nothing, because if we did grant her one thing, she might ask another. Such horrid reasoning was too gross to dwell upon! It was such narrow and illiberal policy as this that had lost us America for ever, and would in all probability prove the destruction one day or another of the British empire.[1]

A central premiss which governed Burke's approach to the American conflict was that nothing worthwhile could be achieved by force or intransigence on the side of the mother country. As is evident from his first speech on conciliation with America, he was not amongst those who believed that Britain and the empire would be better off without the laws of trade and navigation.[2] He merely considered them of secondary importance in comparison to 'the spirit of English communion'. However, had the Americans strenuously agitated against those laws with respect specifically to their own commerce and industry, it seems almost certain that he would have felt compelled eventually to back them. At any one time, he said over and over again, we must give in and give up, however reluctantly, all the laws and regulations which the colonists cannot or will not live with in order to preserve what is left. By 22 March 1775 he felt that in order to win back the Americans Parliament had no alternative but to relinquish all the coercive legislation and all Acts passed for the purposes of creating a revenue. By 16 November 1775 he believed that animosities had deepened to the point where Britain must promise never again to tax for revenue purposes and must offer to the colonists any revenues incidentally arising from taxes imposed for the regulation of trade. At that point he also thought Parliament should recognize the American Congress. By 6 April 1778 he was prepared to go on to the difficult expedient of discarding his own party's Declaratory Act and, finally, on 10 April 1778, he acknowledged the need for the acceptance of American independence. As the dispute continued, each of these steps was to Burke simply the minimum concession necessary to win back the love of Britain's American subjects and through that to re-establish whatever could be salvaged of the authority of Parliament. The following words written in the spring of 1777 outline the central logic behind the evolution of his policy of appeasement in defence of the traditional relationship between Britain and America. They

---

[1] *Parl. Hist.* xx. 137–8.   [2] See below, pp. 137–8.

also suggest that from early in the dispute Burke recognized that an approach such as his might well lead to total capitulation by the mother country on points both of law and principle.

It will be asked, if such was then my opinion of the mode of pacification, how I came to be the very person who moved, not only for a repeal of all the late coercive statutes, but for mutilating, by a positive law, the entireness of the legislative power of Parliament, and cutting off from it the whole right of taxation? I answer, because a different state of things requires a different conduct. When the dispute had gone to the last extremities (which no man laboured more to prevent than I did) the concessions which had satisfied in the beginning, could satisfy no longer; the violation of tacit faith required explicit security. The same cause, which has introduced all formal compacts and covenants among men, made it necessary: I mean, habits of soreness, jealousy, and distrust. I parted with it, as with a limb: but as with a limb to save the body; and I would have parted with more, if more had been necessary. Anything rather than a fruitless, hopeless, unnatural civil war. This mode of yielding would, it is said, give way to independency, without a war. I am persuaded from the nature of things, and from every information, that it would have had a directly contrary effect. But if it had this effect, I confess, that I should prefer independency without war, to independency with it; and I have so much trust in the inclinations and prejudices of mankind, and so little in anything else, that I should expect ten times more benefit to this Kingdom from the affection of America, though under a separate establishment, than from her perfect submission to the Crown and Parliament, accompanied with her terror, disgust, and abhorrence. Bodies tied together by so unnatural a bound of union, as mutual hatred, are only connected to their ruin.[1]

In other words goodwill and affection between mother country and colony are crucial and might of themselves hold the empire together when all methods of coercion have failed. To Burke there could be only one government—a just government which to all appearances was rooted in the opinion of its people. In his estimation the ensuring that government should be good and wise so that the people could hold it in awe was a huge responsibility which those who were born to lead had inherited and for which they ultimately were answerable not to men but to God himself.

Take care that when you waste the blood and Treasure of your Country to *no End*, what answer can be given to an all seeing judge for Such conduct? Take care, that when we act in this manner because we mean to *support Government* that it may not be found to be *anarchy and confusion* we are supporting. There is no *Lawful Government* but the Government of *Wisdom and justice*. Every

---

[1] See below, p. 323.

46

thing else is usurpation. They who cannot resist or traverse it, can at best give it only a passive obedience, but if [I] lift one hand or assent with my Voice to it I am an accomplice in this most unnatural and criminal rebellion against every principle of Government. We are indeed by this particular constitution renderd unaccountable to *men* for our Conduct. With how much more awe we ought to stand before the Supreme Ruler to whom no human constitution can abstract us from perfect responsibility. How shall we stand at that audit when we are accused of opening the wounds and tearing out the Bowels of our Country, by carrying on a cruel civil War rather than quieting the minds of an enraged people by an assurance of conceding what you do not value and you do not mean to keep. I wash my hands from that blood—I clear myself from that Crime.[1]

In these words is the secret to understanding why Burke took so many impolitic or seemingly apolitical positions during his career. He angered many of his constituents by voicing concerns on behalf of the Irish, Africans, and Roman Catholics; he fought for lenient treatment of unsavoury people including rioters, mutineers,[2] and, on one occasion, even sodomists;[3] and he spent more than a decade and a half in the political wilderness with a group of relatively lethargic and unambitious but principled country aristocrats, because he wanted Britain to have the kind of enlightened, morally just and therefore glorious government which people could love and worship. The achievement of that end was in Burke's philosophy of preservation through conciliation, the best means to attain a career-long crusade to defend the British constitution and tradition both at home and overseas.

[1] See below, p. 209.   [2] See below, pp. 586–8.
[3] See below, pp. 583–6.

SOURCES

The material in this volume is of three kinds: speeches made in the House of Commons, writings which were published in pamphlet or other form in order to reach an out-of-doors audience, and writings which were unpublished (except, in some cases, later in Burke's *Works*) such as resolutions, petitions, essays, reflections, and thoughts relating to specific subjects.

The Writings

Six of Burke's published works appear in this volume: (1) *Mr. Edmund Burke's Speeches at his Arrival at Bristol and at the Conclusion of the Poll*, (2) *The Speech of Edmund Burke Esq; On Moving his Resolutions for Conciliation with the Colonies, March 22, 1775*, (3) *A letter from Edmund Burke, Esq; One of the Representatives in Parliament for the City of Bristol, to John Farr and John Harris, Esqrs. Sheriffs of that City, on the Affairs Of America*, (4) *Substance of the Speeches made in the House of Commons, on Wednesday, the 15th of December, 1779, on Mr. Burke's giving Notice of his Intention to propose a Plan of Public Œconomy after the Christmas Recess*, (5) *Speech of Edmund Burke on presenting to the House of Commons (on the 11th of February, 1780,) a Plan for the better Security of the Independence of Parliament and the Œconomical Reformation of the Civil and Other Establishments*, (6) *A Speech of Edmund Burke, Esq. at the Guildhall, in Bristol, Previous to the late Election in that City, upon certain Points Relative to his Parliamentary Conduct*. As well, the portion of Admiral Keppel's defence for which Burke was responsible is taken from the published transcript of the *Minutes of the Proceedings at a Court Martial*. Copy text, as specified in the source-note to these pieces, has been selected according to principles discussed fully in volume i. Briefly it may be stated here that the text reproduced is the first edition if not thereafter revised, or the last revised edition if subject to authorial emendation, and in either event the present text essentially is a direct reprint, free of eclectic treatment. Among these eight pieces accidental variants later entered by the printer receive no further notice, but substantive readings eventually introduced by Burke's editors in the collected *Works*, along with all other relevant textual matters, are presented in Appendix B of this volume.

Three letters to Burke's electors at Bristol in 1774 and two advertisements, a letter and a speech relative to the election of 1780 also appear here. These are printed from copies currently in Bristol City Library. Also, some twenty-five unpublished writings including parliamentary addresses and petitions, the Sketch of a Negro Code, the Articles for the impeachment of Government ministers, the draft address for the Catholics, and the resolutions relating to the Gordon riots are reproduced from MSS. copies which are relatively polished and legible in comparison to most of Burke's drafts for speeches.

The Speeches

Burke's speeches present a much more serious editorial problem than his writings. Only a selection of his speeches appears in the form of texts printed in this volume, but the business of choosing and presenting a particular text offers none of the certainties which can be achieved in the case of the writings. For two very important speeches, the second conciliation with America speech and the speech on the duration of Parliament, a variety of sources is used and a number of drafts in Burke's own hand are transcribed in part to demonstrate the difficulty of establishing an authentic version.[1] In the case of the drafts, it is often impossible to determine which one Burke actually used in the House of Commons or, indeed, if any, or even any combination, was used. The only thing that can be said for certain is that whether Burke spoke directly from them or not, the drafts present a unique opportunity for the reader to view the workings of his mind with respect to an enormous number of matters ranging from the duration of Parliament, to the impeachment of Government ministers,[2] to the sanctity of traditional conventions and institutions.[3] Unfortunately, however, it is not practical to present more than one draft of the vast majority of the speeches. Normally only that which in the editor's

---

[1] See below, pp. 201–20, 362–7.
[2] See below, pp. 454–63.
[3] As, for instance, in the statement quoted on p. 20 above. It is taken from a draft of the second conciliation speech.

opinion is the most authoritative text has been selected. Following is a short description of the principal sources from which Burke's parliamentary speeches have been produced.

CONTEMPORARY PUBLISHED REPORTS

By 1774 the practice of reporting the parliamentary debates by the newspapers had been firmly established.[1] Since 1771 the newspapers had learnt to organize their efforts in a more systematic manner than before and some employed several reporters on their parliamentary staff. Burke, as one of the foremost public figures of his time, received a good deal of attention in the press and in fact, as has been seen, appears to have co-operated at least on some occasions in making his speeches available to particular newspapers.[2] Therefore, it is not difficult to find a number of accounts of the majority of his important performances. It is noteworthy as well that in most cases the various versions of his speeches, though presumably significantly altered for the sake of brevity, usually do not radically disagree with each other in the general interpretation of the substance if not the exact wording of his expressed views. Therefore, in absence of anything resembling a modern Hansard, the newspapers are extremely useful for determining the stands which Burke took on the subjects debated in the House of Commons in these years.

Of the sixty-nine speeches reproduced in this volume forty-nine are transcribed from the newspapers.[3] The papers used most frequently are *London Evening Post*, which was published by John Miller,[4] and *St James's Chronicle*, published by Henry Baldwin.[5] Each of these papers has supplied the version selected for transcription for eleven of Burke's speeches. *St James's Chronicle* is particularly useful as a source of the debates between 1774 and 1776 but it is much less so after that. *London Evening Post*, however, is relatively consistent throughout the

---

[1] For an account of this critical period in the history of parliamentary reporting, see P. D. G. Thomas, 'The Beginning of Parliamentary Reporting in Newspapers, 1768–1774', *English Historical Review*, lxxiv (1959), 623–36, and id., 'John Wilkes and the Freedom of the Press (1771)', *Bulletin of the Institute of Historical Research*, xxxiii (1960), 86–98.

[2] See above, p. 7.

[3] i.e. 69 speeches on 63 occasions, since on some days Burke spoke more than once; see Appendix A.

[4] (d. 1782?).

[5] (d. 1810); see J. Grant, *The Newspaper Press: Its Origins, Progress and Present Position*, 2 vols., London, 1871, i. 210–11.

entire 1774–80 Parliament. For the later years of the Parliament the
two best sources are the *Morning Chronicle* and the *General Advertiser*.
The former had been founded in 1769 and was operated for twenty
years by William Woodfall.[1] It increasingly specialized in parliamentary
reporting and it 'developed into London's leading political journal'.[2]
Woodfall was known to his contemporaries as 'Memory' Woodfall for
his ability to reproduce the debates from his own mind sometimes
hours after hearing them. The *Morning Chronicle* is a source for eight
of the debates in this volume. The *General Advertiser* which was edited
by William Cooke,[3] the author of *Memoirs of C. Macklin*, is a source for
seven. It is followed closely by the *General Evening Post* (six) and the
Gazetteer (five). In each case the particular choice has been made on
the basis of the length and thoroughness of the report and its apparent
accuracy when compared with unpublished accounts.

COMPILATIONS

Two major collections of parliamentary debates cover Burke's years in
the House of Commons as a representative for Bristol. John Almon's
Parliamentary Register, was based largely on Almon's own reports. The
editorial work is superficial and is in no major respects any better than
that found in the versions in the contemporary press. However, the
Parliamentary Register is used in this volume where suitable reports
have not been found in the newspapers. The *Parliamentary History*
which began in 1806 under William Cobbett's[4] direction was somewhat more ambitious in its editorial policy. Some of the material was
reproduced from the *Parliamentary Register*, some from other newspapers of the time, and a good deal from the monthly papers, the
London Magazine and *Gentleman's Magazine*. The standard edition of
Burke's speeches,[5] compiled by Cobbett's assistant on the *Parliamentary History*, John Wright,[6] drew entirely on this source, except where it

---

[1] (1746–1803); see H. Hurd, *The March of Journalism: The Story of the British Press from 1672
to the Present Day*, London, 1957, p. 73.
[2] S. Morison, *The English Newspapers: Some Account of the Physical Development of Journals
Printed in London between 1621 and the Present Day*, Cambridge, 1932, p. 167.
[3] (d. 1824).
[4] (1762–1835).
[5] *The Speeches of the Right Honourable Edmund Burke, in the House of Commons, and in Westminster-
Hall*, 4 vols., London, 1816.
[6] (c.1770–1844).

depended on the *Works* themselves, and has no standing in point of scholarship. Neither of these compilations provides an independent record of Burke's speeches in the period 1774–80, and for textual purposes the original versions in the press have been preferred. However, for reference purposes, the *Parliamentary History*, is generally indicated as the collection most accessible to modern readers and as providing more material than is found elsewhere. In addition, for debates on America, there is now the authoritative *Proceedings and Debates of the British Parliaments Respecting North America, 1754–1783*, ed. R. C. Simmons and P. D. G. Thomas, 6 vols., New York, 1982–7, a work published while this volume was in course of preparation.

THE BURKE PAPERS

The vast majority of Burke's surviving papers, excluding his correspondence, directly or indirectly pertain to his parliamentary speeches. For the most part this large collection remains unpublished. However, the speeches which are to be found in the *Works* (1792–1827), are all represented here, though not necessarily in the form in which they appear in the *Works*. Throughout the object has been to reproduce that version which, in the editor's opinion, is the most reliable and instructive account. The main problem with Burke's papers as sources for his speeches is that, unlike other parliamentary reports, most of them (that is, except for a few which he prepared for the press himself after the fact)[1] are not transcriptions of what was actually said in debate but rather records of what Burke intended to include in his speeches. Most of the drafts and notes were probably composed before delivery, and as such they do not reflect any last-minute changes which Burke might have made immediately before or in the course of presentation. Moreover, as noted in volume ii, they

vary enormously in almost every respect. Some are the briefest of jottings, some skeletal arguments, some useful phrases or images, some summaries of information or evidence. Even those which apparently constituted a systematic attempt to prepare for a particular debate are often incomplete and in parts incomprehensible or incoherent. Frequently Burke would leave a draft uncompleted only to return to his theme with a fresh draft later on. Sometimes he repeated himself and sometimes he leaped stages in his argument, amended

[1] See below, p. 229.

the order of delivery, or in other ways modified the original tendency of his notes. At their most perfect his drafts were polished and extended papers for delivery more or less as they stood; but the great majority were defective in one respect or another, and almost all present considerable editorial difficulties.[1]

For all their problems, however, Burke's papers are invaluable. They not only are quite obviously more authentic than other sources but they present insights into the workings of Burke's mind which cannot be found anywhere else. In the privacy of his own study, insulated from public evaluation, Burke could express his feelings on all the important subjects of his day with total anonymity and perfect honesty. Therefore, before being refined for public consumption, his musings, in many cases on bits and scraps of paper, can be interesting indeed. For instance, in the course of composing a speech against shortening the duration of Parliaments in the spring of 1780 he gave vent without reservation to his distaste for election campaigns in general.

To govern according to the Sense and agreeably to the interests of the People is a great and glorious Object of Government [he wrote]. This Object[2] cannot be obtaind but through the Medium of popular Election; and Popular Election is a mighty Evil. It is such, and so great an Evil; that there are few Nations whose Monarch was not originally elective ...
They are the distempers of elections that have destroyd all free States. To cure these distempers difficult if not impossible; the only thing therefore left to save the commonwealth is to prevent their return too frequently.[3]

For the 1774–80 period such statements, many but unfortunately not all of which are reproduced here, help to illuminate some of Burke's most salient principles and prejudices and his feelings with regard to numerous public and private events.

---

[1] pp. 39–40.
[2] In margin: 'Another distemper besides the corruption of the Representative, the corruption of the constituent.'
[3] See below, p. 592.

NOTES ON TRANSCRIPTION

A guide to the principles of textual transcription adopted for this edition will be found in volume i. The main points bearing on this volume are as follows:

The spelling, capitalization, punctuation, and paragraphing of original MSS. are reproduced exactly, subject to the following exceptions:

1. Standard eighteenth-century abbreviations (e.g. wch for which, tho for though) are expanded, as are abbreviations commonly used by those involved in parliamentary affairs (e.g. h.g. for honourable gentleman, H. of C. for House of Commons).

2. Punctuation presents problems. In many cases a sentence break was plainly intended but not properly indicated. Consequently missing stops and capital letters have occasionally been supplied where the presence of one clearly implies the necessity for the other.

3. Angle brackets ⟨...⟩ are used to indicate words or phrases which are illegible, or to enclose uncertain readings.

4. Square brackets [ ] are used sparingly, to supply obvious gaps and omissions where the sense would otherwise be seriously affected.

Burke's Papers

i. *Structure*

Burke's normal practice was to prepare his work in two columns, one representing the main body of the text, the other reserved for insertions, corrections, and key words or headings evidently meant to remind him of the development of his argument. Unfortunately the unfinished nature of these papers makes it difficult, in many instances, to be certain as to the placing of some marginal annotations. Notes which cannot readily be fitted into the text have generally been recorded in footnotes.

ii. *Paragraphing*

Burke used various devices to indicate new paragraphs—indentations, ruled lines, square brackets; his apparent intention has always been followed but there is necessarily a considerable element of editorial discretion in interpreting his directions.

iii. *Cancellations*

Burke was in the habit of heavily revising his notes. In reproducing the MSS. regard has always been had to his final intention. No attempt has been made to record cancelled phrases or words, whatever their potential interest. Uncertainties such as occur frequently with punctuation marks, and, for example, half-deleted phrases in the text are, where appropriate, accompanied by an explanatory footnote. As far as possible, interference with the text by Burke's successive editors and annotators, has been eliminated and ignored.

Speech at Arrival at Bristol
13 October 1774

Source: *Mr. Edmund Burke's Speeches at his Arrival at Bristol, and at the Conclusion of the Poll*, 2nd edn., J. Dodsley, London, 1774

Dodsley's edition of the two 1774 Bristol speeches of 13 October and 3 November contains an introduction ('Editor's Advertisement') not reproduced here.

Burke had to find a new seat at the General Election of 1774 because his former patron, Lord Verney,[1] needed to make a profit out of his pocket borough of Wendover.[2] He first considered Westminster. However, John Wilkes and the City radicals insisted that candidates should subscribe to a 'test' or statement of principles.[3] Burke was also in touch with admirers in Bristol where Henry Cruger was about to challenge the sitting members, Matthew Brickdale[4] and Robert Nugent, Viscount Clare.[5] Cruger's friends were not willing to join with Burke, partly because of differences in outlook, but partly because it was felt that only one seat could be captured by the Opposition.[6] Burke therefore accepted Lord Rockingham's offer of a seat at Malton in Yorkshire.[7] Richard Champion, a Bristol merchant and a staunch Whig, nominated Burke when Lord Clare withdrew.[8] Burke received notification that he had been nominated at Bristol on the same day that he was declared duly elected at Malton. Because of the 'weight and importance of Bristol as a commercial town', and because of their desire to demonstrate support among the 'considerable body of merchants there',[9] Rockingham and Burke were anxious to take advantage of the nomination. Consequently, Burke set out at once to contest the election.

In the following speech to the electors of Bristol, Burke outlined an important constitutional and moral dilemma with which he struggled throughout his career—the need to reconcile liberty with law and order both at home and in America. With respect specifically to the American dispute this dilemma was becoming particularly discomforting, partly as a result of the previous ambivalent actions of his own party. Burke always found it necessary to justify the respect for colonial aspirations which the Rockinghams had demonstrated by repealing the Stamp Act during their first brief administra-

---

[1] Ralph Verney, 2nd Earl Verney (*c.*1712–91), M.P. 1753–84, 1790–1.
[2] *Corr.* iii. 32–3.   [3] Ibid. 58.
[4] (1735–1831), M.P. 1768–74, 1780–90.
[5] Robert Nugent, 1st Viscount Clare (1709–88), later (1776) 1st Earl Nugent, M.P. 1741–84, Joint Vice-Treasurer of Ireland.
[6] P. T. Underdown, 'Henry Cruger and Edmund Burke', *William and Mary Quarterly*, xv (1958), 14–34.
[7] *Corr.* iii. 61.   [8] Ibid. 64.   [9] Ibid. 68.

tion of 1765–6. However, he also had to enunciate the party's belief in the supremacy of Parliament as expressed in their Declaratory Act.[1] In the 1770s he would learn increasingly to emphasize the former position, as the Government led the nation into a war to crush colonial resistance. In 1774, however, he understood public resentment of the Americans' recent behaviour in the Boston Tea Party, which he and the rest of the Rockingham leaders themselves found distasteful.[2] Therefore, in his first election speech to Britain's second most important trading city, he found it appropriate to stress his belief in British superiority and respect for law and order as the foundation of colonial rights and liberty.

Mr. EDMUND BURKE'S SPEECH

GENTLEMEN,

I am come hither to solicit in person, that favour which my friends have hitherto endeavoured to procure for me, by the most obliging, and to me the most honourable, exertions.

I have so high an opinion of the great trust which you have to confer on this occasion; and, by long experience, so just a diffidence in my abilities, to fill it in a manner adequate even to my own ideas, that I should never have ventured of myself to intrude into that awful situation. But since I am called upon by the desire of several respectable fellow-subjects, as I have done at other times, I give up my fears to their wishes. Whatever my other deficiencies may be, I do not know what it is to be wanting to my friends.

I am not fond of attempting to raise public expectation by great promises. At this time, there is much cause to consider, and very little to presume. We seem to be approaching to a great crisis in our affairs, which calls for the whole wisdom of the wisest among us, without being able to assure ourselves, that any wisdom can preserve us from many and great inconveniences. You know I speak of our unhappy contest with America. I confess, it is a matter on which I look down as from a precipice. It is difficult in itself, and it is rendered more intricate by a great variety of plans of conduct. I do not mean to enter into them. I will not suspect a want of good intention in framing them. But however pure the intentions of their authors may have been, we all know that the event has been unfortunate. The means of recovering

---

[1] See vol. ii, p. 46.

[2] For the Rockinghams' attitude towards the American dispute in late 1774, see the Marquess of Rockingham's letter to George Dempster (1732–1818, M.P. 1761–8, 1769–90), on 13 September 1774 (*Rockingham Memoirs*, ii. 252–6).

our affairs are not obvious. So many great questions of commerce, of finance, of constitution, and of policy, are involved in this American deliberation, that I dare engage for nothing, but that I shall give it, without any predilection to former opinions, or any sinister bias whatsoever, the most honest and impartial consideration of which I am capable. The publick has a full right to it; and this great city, a main pillar in the commercial interest of Great-Britain, must totter on its base by the slightest mistake with regard to our American measures.

Thus much, however, I think it not amiss to lay before you; That I am not, I hope, apt to take up or lay down my opinions lightly. I have held, and ever shall maintain, to the best of my power, unimpaired and undiminished, the just, wise, and necessary constitutional superiority of Great-Britain. This is necessary for America, as well as for us. I never mean to depart from it. Whatever may be lost by it, I avow it. The forfeiture even of your favour, if by such a declaration I could forfeit it, though the first object of my ambition, never will make me disguise my sentiments on this subject.

But,—I have ever had a clear opinion, and have ever held a constant correspondent conduct, that this superiority is consistent with all the liberties a sober and spirited American ought to desire. I never mean to put any colonist, or any human creature, in a situation, not becoming a freeman. To reconcile British superiority with American liberty shall be my great object, as far as my little faculties extend. I am far from thinking that both, even yet, may not be preserved.

When I first devoted myself to the public service, I considered how I should render myself fit for it; and this I did by endeavouring to discover what it was, that gave this country the rank it holds in the world. I found that our prosperity and dignity arose principally, if not solely, from two sources; our constitution and commerce. Both these I have spared no study to understand, and no endeavour to support.

The distinguishing part of our constitution is its liberty. To preserve that liberty inviolate, seems the particular duty and proper trust of a member of the House of Commons. But the liberty, the only liberty I mean, is a liberty connected with order; that not only exists along with order and virtue, but which cannot exist at all without them. It inheres in good and steady government, as in its substance and vital principle.

The other source of our power is commerce, of which you are so large a part, and which cannot exist, no more than your liberty, without a connection with many virtues. It has ever been a very particular and a very favorite object of my study, in its principles, and in its details. I think many here are acquainted with the truth of what I say. This I know, that I have ever had my house open, and my poor services ready, for traders and manufacturers of every denomination. My favorite ambition is to have those services acknowledged. I now appear before you to make trial, whether my earnest endeavors have been so wholly oppressed by the weakness of my abilities, as to be rendered insignificant in the eyes of a great trading city; or whether you chuse to give a weight to humble abilities, for the sake of the honest exertions with which they are accompanied. This is my trial to-day. My industry is not on trial. Of my industry I am sure, as far as my constitution of mind and body admitted.

When I was invited by many respectable merchants, freeholders, and freemen of this city, to offer them my services, I had just received the honour of an election at another place, at a very great distance from this. I immediately opened the matter to those of my worthy constituents who were with me, and they unanimously advised me not to decline it. They told me, that they had elected me with a view to the public service; and as great questions relative to our commerce and colonies were imminent, that in such matters I might derive authority and support from the representation of this great commercial city; they desired me therefore to set off without delay, very well persuaded that I never could forget my obligations to them, or to my friends, for the choice they had made of me. From that time to this instant I have not slept; and if I should have the honour of being freely chosen by you, I hope I shall be as far from slumbering or sleeping when your service requires me to be awake, as I have been in coming to offer myself a candidate for your favour.

Appeal to Bristol Electors
13 October 1774

Source: Bristol Public Library Handbill

This appeal was presumably drafted immediately after Burke's initial speech at Bristol. It was issued as a handbill, but also printed in the Bristol newspapers.

To the Gentlemen, Clergy, Freeholders, *and* Freemen, *of the City of* Bristol

Gentlemen,

I have been called upon by a numerous and respectable Part of your Body, to offer you my Services as your Representative in Parliament. I should not have presumed to make that Offer without such an Invitation. The Motive to it has probably been my public Conduct. My Friends perceived in it a great Deal of good Intention; and they were so generous as to look upon the rest with a very partial Indulgence. In Conformity to their Wishes, I now request the Favor of your Votes and Interest; and, if I should have the Honor of becoming one of the Objects of your Choice, you may be assured, that my future Conduct in Parliament, encouraged by that flattering Mark of your Approbation, will continue exactly the same in Principle, and certainly not less active in Exertion. The Welfare of Commerce, in which the most essential Interests of this great City in particular, and of the Kingdom in general are involved, will be the principal Object of my Attention. I feel the whole Importance of the Trust which you may confer upon me, and I shall therefore ever feel the warmest Affection, Respect, and Gratitude towards those who shall think me not wholly unworthy of it.

I have the Honor to be, Gentlemen, *Your most obedient, obliged, and most humble Servant,*

Edmund Burke

Bristol, October 13, 1774

Thanks to Bristol Voters
3 November 1774

Source: Bristol Public Library Handbill

Burke was elected M.P. for Bristol on 2 November 1774. His thanks to the electors was issued as a handbill and published in the local newspapers. His right to the seat was, however, to be challenged. Cruger and Brickdale also published addresses of thanks in the newspapers and the latter announced that he would petition against '*the admissibility* of Candidates and the legality of votes'.[1]

To the Gentlemen, Clergy, Freeholders *and* Freemen, *of the City of* Bristol

Gentlemen,

I Humbly request your acceptance of my most hearty thanks, for the high honor I have this day received, in being elected one of your Representatives in Parliament.

Whatever advantage my public character may derive from the weight of so respectable a representation, you may be assured, shall be employed in promoting to the best of my judgment, the true interests of those from whom it is derived. I hope, that by your frequent advice and seasonable assistance, I may be enabled to execute the great Trust you have reposed in me, in a manner in some degree, equal to its importance and your wishes.

To my particular friends I owe the sincerest affection; to this city the most inviolable duty, to the Sheriffs,[2] who presided, my full testimony, that they have conducted themselves, through the whole of this long election, with the most liberal impartiality; with all the dignity of Magistrates; with all the politeness of gentlemen.

It is natural, that an object, so important as the honor of representing this great city, should not be abandoned without reluctance. The Gentleman, who has been unsuccessful in his pursuit, threatens a petition.[3] I submit, with great chearfulness, my pretensions, and

---

[1] G. E. Weare, *Edmund Burke's Connection with Bristol, from 1774 till 1780; with a Prefatory Memoir of Burke*, Bristol, 1894, pp. 93–4.

[2] John Durbin (1734–1814), knighted in 1778, and James Hill (d. 1802).

[3] Brickdale petitioned on the grounds that Burke had been nominated after Lord Clare's withdrawal—when the Sheriffs ought to have declared Cruger and Brickdale returned—and that freemen had been admitted after the writ had been issued. There were also less important

what are more important, your rights to the Committee of Election; the clearest cause to the justest tribunal.[1] That tribunal, I am confident, will never authorize an attempt to render, contrary to the clear and express law of the land, the original, inherent, corporate rights of those entitled to freedom in this great city, dependent for their valid exercise, on the occasional pleasure of a Minister, by dating their effect from the issuing of the writ. The time for issuing the writ is entirely in the power of a Minister; and he may communicate his intentions to those, and those only, whom he is inclined to favor; and upon this new doctrine enable them and disable all others, from taking advantage of the right of freedom.

No care of mine shall be wanting to support the rights, even of those freemen, whom the Gentleman who threatens a petition, was the first to produce and encourage, and when they can no longer serve his purpose, now endeavors to disfranchise by a retrospect.

I have the honor to be, with the highest veneration, esteem and gratitude.

Gentlemen, *Your most obedient and ever obliged humble Servant,*

Edmund Burke

Bristol, Nov. 3, 1774

Speech at the Conclusion of the Poll
3 November 1774

Source: *Mr. Edmund Burke's Speeches at his Arrival at Bristol, and at the Conclusion of the Poll,* 2nd edn., J. Dodsley, London, 1774

The Bristol election ended on 3 November when Cruger had 3,656, Burke 2,707, Brickdale 2,456, and Lord Clare 283 votes. Much of what follows is Burke's response to the challenge to his seat by Brickdale. However, of more

grounds for challenging Burke's election. See S. Douglas, *The History of the Cases of Controverted Elections,* 4 vols., London, 1775–7, i. 241–89.

[1] The Controverted Elections Act (10 Geo. III, c. 16) introduced by George Grenville (1712–70, M.P. 1741–70) in 1770 and made perpetual in 1774, had significantly reformed parliamentary procedure for dealing with disputed elections. It had replaced the traditional partisan decisions of the whole House with those of a small, more impartial committee of M.P.s chosen by lot. Burke and the Rockingham party had strongly supported the Act both in 1770 and 1774 (see vol. ii, pp. 396–401).

interest and importance is his celebrated argument about the responsibilities of M.P.s to their electors. His insistence upon the need for representatives to use their own judgement on important matters rather than blindly following the will of the electorate was consistent with traditional opinion which considered the bulk of the electors ill-equipped to grapple with the affairs of state.[1] The 'people', wrote one pundit in the mid-1770s 'are much ... as a person under age, who must have guardians to manage his estate, not according to his particular inclination, but his real interest'. Through our constitution, 'the wisdom and virtue of a few, are put in place of the levity and weakness of the many'.[2] In the 1770s, of course, this view was frequently being challenged particularly in reformist literature, which placed a great emphasis on the importance of the people (and the need for their regular intervention) in the government process.[3] It was a view, moreover, which would help to create substantial difficulties for Burke in Bristol where it could clearly be contrasted with the ideas of Cruger. 'It has ever been my opinion that the electors have a right to instruct their members,' the latter had proclaimed when thanking his voters. 'For my part, I shall always think it my duty in Parliament to be guided by your counsels and instructions: I shall consider myself the servant of my constituents, not their master—subservient to their will, not superior to it.'[4] Ultimately, Burke's attitude was to play an important role in his decision not to contest the election in the city in 1780.[5]

Mr. EDMUND BURKE's SPEECH
November 3, 1774

Gentlemen,

I Cannot avoid sympathizing strongly with the feelings of the Gentleman who has received the same honour that you have conferred on

---

[1] See C. S. Emden, *The People and the Constitution*, 2nd edn., Oxford, 1956, pp. 22–5; B. Kemp, 'Patriotism, Pledges, and the People', in *A Century of Conflict 1850–1950: Essays for A. J. P. Taylor*, ed. M. Gilbert, London, 1966, pp. 37–46; Dame Lucy Sutherland, 'Edmund Burke and the Relations between Members of Parliament and their Constituents', *Studies in Burke and his Time*, x (1968–9), 1005–21; W. M. Elofson, 'The Rockingham Whigs and the Country Tradition', *Parliamentary History*, viii (1989), 103–9. Burke was probably himself responsible for a review in the *Annual Register* for 1765 of *Spiritual and Temporal Liberty of Subjects in England* by Anthony Ellys (1690–1761), which quotes a long passage from Ellys similar to the view which Burke expresses in this speech (T. W. Copeland, *Edmund Burke: Six Essays*, London, 1950, pp. 132–3). There is an extract from Ellys in Mrs. Burke's hand at Northampton (A.xxxi.7), the source noted by Burke.
[2] 'A General View of the Excellence of the British Constitution. With a Short Refutation of Doctor Price's Republican View', *London Chronicle*, 9 May 1776.
[3] See, for instance, John Cartwright, *Take Your Choice*, London, 1776; James Burgh, *Political Disquisitions*, 2 vols., London, 1774; Richard Price, *Observations on the Nature of Civil Liberty, the Principles of Government and the Justice and Policy of the War with America*, London, 1776.
[4] *Felix Farley's Bristol Journal*, 5 November 1774.
[5] See below, pp. 620–3.

me. If he, who was bred and passed his whole Life amongst you; if he, who, through the easy gradations of acquaintance, friendship, and esteem, has obtained the honour, which seems of itself, naturally and almost insensibly, to meet with those, who, by the even tenour of pleasing manners and social virtues, slide into the love and confidence of their fellow-citizens;—if he cannot speak but with great emotion on this subject, surrounded as he is on all sides with his old friends; you will have the goodness to excuse me, if my real, unaffected embarrassment prevents me from expressing my gratitude to you as I ought.

I was brought hither under the disadvantage of being unknown, even by sight, to any of you. No previous canvass was made for me. I was put in nomination after the poll was opened. I did not appear until it was far advanced. If, under all these accumulated disadvantages, your good opinion has carried me to this happy point of success; you will pardon me, if I can only say to you collectively, as I said to you individually, simply and plainly, I thank you—I am obliged to you—I am not insensible of your kindness.

This is all that I am able to say for the inestimable favour you have conferred upon me. But I cannot be satisfied, without saying a little more in defence of the right you have to confer such a favour. The person that appeared here as counsel for the Candidate, who so long and so earnestly solicited your votes,[1] thinks proper to deny, that a very great part of you have any votes to give.[2] He fixes a standard period of time in his own imagination, not what the law defines, but merely what the convenience of his Client suggests, by which he would cut off, at one stroke, all those freedoms, which are the dearest privileges of your Corporation; which the common law authorizes: which your Magistrates are compelled to grant; which come duly authenticated into this Court; and are saved in the clearest words, and with the most religious care and tenderness, in that very act of Parliament, which was made to regulate the Elections by Freemen, and to prevent all possible abuses in making them.[3]

I do not intend to argue the matter here. My learned Counsel[4] has supported your Cause with his usual Ability; the worthy Sheriffs have

---

[1] Henry Hobhouse was Brickdale's counsel.
[2] Brickdale petitioned against the return of Cruger and Burke.
[3] 3 Geo. III, c. 15.
[4] Thomas Symons or Symonds.

acted with their usual equity, and I have no doubt, that the same equity, which dictates the return, will guide the final determination. I had the honour, in conjunction with many far wiser men, to contribute a very small assistance, but however some assistance, to the forming the Judicature which is to try such questions.[1] It would be unnatural in me, to doubt the Justice of that Court, in the trial of my own cause, to which I have been so active to give jurisdiction over every other.

I assure the worthy Freemen, and this Corporation, that, if the Gentleman perseveres in the intentions, which his present warmth dictates to him, I will attend their cause with diligence, and I hope with effect. For, if I know any thing of myself, it is not my own Interest in it, but my full conviction, that induces me to tell you—*I think there is not a shadow of doubt in the case.*

I do not imagine that you find me rash in declaring myself, or very forward in troubling you. From the beginning to the end of the election, I have kept silence in all matters of discussion. I have never asked a question of a voter on the other side, or supported a doubtful vote on my own. I respected the abilities of my managers; I relied on the candour of the court. I think the worthy sheriffs will bear me witness, that I have never once made an attempt to impose upon their reason, to surprize their justice, or to ruffle their temper. I stood on the hustings (except when I gave my thanks to those who favoured me with their votes) less like a Candidate, than an unconcerned Spectator of a public proceeding. But here the face of things is altered. Here is an attempt for a general *massacre* of Suffrages; an attempt, by a promiscuous carnage of *friends* and *foes*, to exterminate above two thousand votes, including *seven hundred polled for the Gentleman himself, who now complains*, and who would destroy the Friends whom he has obtained, only because he cannot obtain as many of them as he wishes.

How he will be permitted, in another place, to stultify and disable himself, and to plead against his own acts, is another question. The law will decide it. I shall only speak of it as it concerns the propriety of public conduct in this city. I do not pretend to lay down rules of decorum for other Gentlemen. They are best judges of the mode of proceeding that will recommend them to the favour of their fellow-citizens. But I confess, I should look rather awkward, if I had been the *very first to produce the new copies of freedom*, if I had persisted

---

[1] Under Grenville's Controverted Elections Act.

in producing them to the last; if I had ransacked, with the most unremitting industry, and the most penetrating research, the remotest corners of the kingdom to discover them; if I were then, all at once, to turn short, and declare, that I had been sporting all this while with the right of election: and that I had been drawing out a Poll, upon no sort of rational grounds, which disturbed the peace of my fellow-citizens for a month together—I really, for my part, should appear awkward under such circumstances.

It would be still more awkward in me, if I were gravely to look the sheriffs in the face, and to tell them, they were not to determine my cause on my own principles; nor to make the return upon those votes, upon which I had rested my election. Such would be my appearance to the court and magistrates.

But how should I appear to the *Voters* themselves? If I had gone round to the citizens intitled to Freedom, and squeezed them by the hand—"Sir, I humbly beg your Vote—I shall be eternally thankful—may I hope for the honour of your support?—Well!—come—we shall see you at the Council-house."—If I were then to deliver them to my managers, pack them into tallies, vote them off in court, and when I heard from the Bar—"Such a one only! and such a one for ever!—he's my man!"—"Thank you, good sir—Hah! my worthy friend! thank you kindly—that's an honest fellow—how is your good family?"—Whilst these words were hardly out of my mouth, if I should have wheeled round at once, and told them—"Get you gone, you pack of worthless fellows! you have no votes—you are Usurpers! you are intruders on the rights of real freemen! I will have nothing to do with you! you ought never to have been produced at this Election, and the sheriffs ought not to have admitted you to poll."

Gentlemen, I should make a strange figure, if my conduct had been of this sort. I am not so old an acquaintance of yours as the worthy Gentleman. Indeed I could not have ventured on such kind of free-doms with you. But I am bound, and I will endeavour, to have justice done to the rights of Freemen; even though I should, at the same time, be obliged to vindicate the former part of my antagonist's conduct* against his own present inclinations.

I owe myself, in all things, to *all* the freemen of this city. My particular friends have a demand on me, that I should not deceive their

* Mr. *Brickdale* opened his poll, it seems, with a tally of those very kind of freemen, and voted many hundreds of them.

expectations. Never was cause or man supported with more constancy, more activity, more spirit. I have been supported with a zeal indeed and heartiness in my friends, which (if their object had been at all proportioned to their endeavours) could never be sufficiently commended. They supported me upon the most liberal principles. They wished that the members for Bristol should be chosen for the City, and for their Country at large, and not for themselves.

So far they are not disappointed. If I possess nothing else, I am sure I possess the temper that is fit for your service. I know nothing of Bristol, but by the favours I have received, and the virtues I have seen exerted in it.

I shall ever retain, what I now feel, the most perfect and grateful attachment to my friends—and I have no enmities; no resentment. I never can consider fidelity to engagements, and constancy in friendships, but with the highest approbation; even when those noble qualities are employed against my own pretensions. The Gentleman, who is not fortunate as I have been in this contest, enjoys, in this respect, a consolation full of honour both to himself and to his friends. They have certainly left nothing undone for his service.

As for the trifling petulance, which the rage of party stirs up in little minds, though it should shew itself even in this court, it has not made the slightest impression on me. The highest flight of such clamorous birds is winged in an inferior region of the air. We hear them, and we look upon them, just as you, Gentlemen, when you enjoy the serene air on your lofty rocks, look down upon the Gulls, that skim the mud of your river, when it is exhausted of its tide.

I am sorry I cannot conclude, without saying a word on a topick touched upon by my worthy Colleague. I wish that topick had been passed by; at a time when I have so little leisure to discuss it. But since he has thought proper to throw it out, I owe you a clear explanation of my poor sentiments on that subject.

He tells you, that "the topick of Instructions has occasioned much altercation and uneasiness in this City;" and he expresses himself (if I understand him rightly) in favour of the coercive authority of such instructions.

Certainly, Gentlemen, it ought to be the happiness and glory of a Representative, to live in the strictest union, the closest correspondence, and the most unreserved communication with his constituents. Their wishes ought to have great weight with him; their opinion high respect; their business unremitted attention. It is his duty to sacrifice his repose, his pleasures, his satisfactions, to theirs; and, above all, ever, and in all cases, to prefer their interest to his own. But, his unbiassed opinion, his mature judgement, his enlightened conscience, he ought not to sacrifice to you; to any man, or to any sett of men living. These he does not derive from your pleasure; no, nor from the Law and the Constitution. They are a trust from Providence, for the abuse of which he is deeply answerable. Your Representative owes you, not his industry only, but his judgement; and he betrays, instead of serving you, if he sacrifices it to your opinion.

My worthy Colleague says, his Will ought to be subservient to yours. If that be all, the thing is innocent. If Government were a matter of Will upon any side, yours, without question, ought to be superior. But Government and Legislation are matters of reason and judgement, and not of inclination; and, what sort of reason is that, in which the determination precedes the discussion; in which one sett of men deliberate, and another decide; and where those who form the conclusion are perhaps three hundred miles distant from those who hear the arguments?

To deliver an opinion, is the right of all men; that of Constituents is a weighty and respectable opinion, which a Representative ought always to rejoice to hear; and which he ought always most seriously to consider. But *authoritative* instructions; *Mandates* issued, which the Member is bound blindly and implicitly to obey, to vote, and to argue for, though contrary to the clearest conviction of his judgement and conscience; these are things utterly unknown to the laws of this land, and which arise from a fundamental Mistake of the whole order and tenour of our Constitution.

Parliament is not a *Congress* of Ambassadors from different and hostile interests; which interests each must maintain, as an Agent and Advocate, against other Agents and Advocates; but Parliament is a *deliberative* Assembly of *one* Nation, with *one* Interest, that of the whole; where, not local Purposes, not local Prejudices ought to guide, but the general Good, resulting from the general Reason of the whole. You chuse a Member indeed; but when you have chosen him, he is not Member of Bristol, but he is a Member of *Parliament*. If the local Constituent should have an Interest, or should form an hasty Opinion, evidently opposite to the real good of the rest of the Community, the Member for that place ought to be as far, as any other, from any endeavour to give it Effect. I beg pardon for saying so much on this subject. I have been unwillingly drawn into it; but I shall ever use a respectful frankness of communication with you. Your faithful friend, your devoted servant, I shall be to the end of my life: A flatterer you do not wish for. On this point of instructions, however, I think it scarcely possible, we ever can have any sort of difference. Perhaps I may give you too much, rather than too little trouble.

From the first hour I was encouraged to court your favour to this happy day of obtaining it, I have never promised you any thing, but humble and persevering endeavours to do my duty. The weight of that duty, I confess, makes me tremble; and whoever well considers what it is, of all things in the world will fly from what has the least likeness to a positive and precipitate engagement. To be a good Member of Parliament, is, let me tell you, no easy task; especially at this time, when there is so strong a disposition to run into the perilous extremes of servile compliance, or wild popularity. To unite circumspection with vigour, is absolutely necessary; but it is extremely difficult. We are now Members for a rich commercial *City*; this City, however, is but a part of a rich commercial *Nation*, the Interests of which are various, multiform, and intricate. We are Members for that great *Nation*, which however is itself but part of a great *Empire*, extended by our Virtue and our Fortune to the farthest limits of the East and of the West. All these wide-spread Interests must be considered; must be compared; must be reconciled if possible. We are Members for a *free* Country; and surely we all know, that the machine of a free Constitution is no simple thing; but as intricate and as delicate, as it is valuable. We are Members in a great and ancient *Monarchy*; and we must preserve religiously, the true legal rights of the Sovereign, which form the Key-stone that binds together the noble and well-constructed Arch of our Empire and our Constitution. A Constitution made up of balanced Powers must ever be a critical thing. As such I mean to touch that part of it which comes within my reach. I know my Inability, and I wish for support from every Quarter. In particular I shall aim at the friendship, and shall cultivate the best Correspondence, of the worthy Colleague you have given me.

I trouble you no farther than once more to thank you all; you, Gentlemen, for your Favours; the Candidates for their temperate and polite behaviour; and the Sheriffs, for a Conduct which may give a Model for all who are in public Stations.

A Farewell to Bristol Voters
16 November 1774

Source: Bristol Public Library Handbill

Burke left Bristol on 16 November and published his thanks to the electors.

To the Gentlemen, Clergy, Freeholders, *and* Freemen, *of the City of* Bristol

Gentlemen,

I feel the most sincere concern in being obliged to leave this city, where I have received obligations, which form the greatest honor, and principal satisfaction of my life, without waiting on every one of those worthy persons, to whose partiality I have been indebted for them. I had made an attempt for the discharge of this most pleasing duty: But business of a very urgent nature, both public and private, has prevented me from the completion of my design, by calling me suddenly from among you.[1] I hope my worthy friends will be made sensible, that nothing but the idea of serving this city, by following where the general concern of the public leads, could possibly have prevented me from the most minute and circumstantial attention to my friends, to whom, and to all the worthy citizens of Bristol, I shall ever be

A most faithful, a most dutiful, and a most affectionate Servant,

Edmund Burke

November 16, 1774

---

[1] Burke appeared in London on the 24th. The 'business of a very urgent nature' was almost certainly the defence of his election against Brickdale's petition; see *Corr.* iii. 77–9.

Draft Protest
30 November 1774

Source: MS. at Sheffield, Bk 6.144.

There are slight differences between this draft and the final version entered on the *Journals* (xxxiv. 270) of the House of Lords.

The House of Lords met on 30 November 1774. The Address of Thanks for the King's Speech proposed by the ministry expressed the same tough attitude towards American resistance to British taxation as that which had produced the coercive Acts of the previous session. It included a stern condemnation of the 'daring spirit of resistance' in America, expressed unqualified support for 'the supreme authority of the legislature', and offered 'the strongest assurances that we will cheerfully co-operate in all such measures, as shall be necessary to maintain the dignity, safety, and welfare of the British empire'. The Duke of Richmond who was a regular Rockingham supporter, countered with an amendment. It sought 'an early communication of the accounts which have been received concerning the state of the colonies, that we may not proceed to the consideration of this most critical and important matter, but upon the fullest information'. It was defeated by 63 votes to 13 and the Opposition peers entered a protest on the Journals which had been drafted for them by Burke.

The protest does not openly advocate lenient measures but vaguely attacks the ministry for precipitous behaviour and affirms the Opposition's support for the authority of Parliament. At this stage in the conflict propertied opinion in Britain continued to be decidedly anti-American and the men Burke followed in politics including Rockingham himself, were still very concerned about the threat to the supremacy of Parliament which American resistance represented. Therefore, as in his first Bristol address, Burke did not speak out strongly on behalf of American liberties.

Because

We cannot agree to commit ourselves in expressions, which may in the Event prove fatal to the Lives, properties and Liberties of a very great part of our fellow Subjects, with the careless facility of a common address of compliment. We conceive, that an address of this Nature, and at this time, must necessarily have a considerable influence on our future proceedings, and must impress the publick with an Idea of the general Spirit of the measures which we mean to support. Whatever methods we shall think it advisable to pursue either for the support of the mere authority of Parliament, which seems the sole Consideration of some, or for reconciling that Authority with the peace and satisfaction of the whole Empire which has ever been our object, it will certainly add to the weight and efficacy of our proceedings, if they seem to be the result of full information, mature deliberation, and temperate Enquiry. No proper materials for such Enquiry have been laid before us; nor have any such been promised in the Speech from the Throne, or even in any Verbal assurance from Ministers. In this situation we are called upon to make an address, arbitrarily imposing Qualities and descriptions upon acts done in the Colonies, of the true nature of which we are as yet in a great measure unapprised: a proceeding, which appears to us by no means consonant to that Purity which we ought ever to preserve in our Judicial, and, to that caution which ought always to guide us in our deliberative Capacity.

Because, This address does in Effect imply an approbation of the System adopted with regard to the Colonies in the Last Parliament. This unwise and unfortunate System conceived with so little Prudence and pursued with so little temper, consistency, or foresight, we were in hopes would be abandon'd from our Experience of those Mischiefs which it had produced in proportion to the time it was continued, and the diligence with which it has been pursued. A System which has created the utmost confusion in the Colonies without any rational hope of advantage to the Revenue, and with certain detriment to the Commerce of the mother Country. And It affords us a melancholy prospect of the disposition of Lords in the present Parliament when we see the house, under the pressure of so severe and uniform an Experience, again ready without any enquiry to countenance, if not to adopt the spirit of the former fatal proceedings. But whatever may be the mischievous designs, or the inconsiderate temerity, which leads others to this desperate Course, we wish to be known, as persons, who have ever disapproved of measures so pernicious in their past Effects, and future tendency; and who are not in haste, without enquiry or information, to commit ourselves in declarations which may precipitate our Country into all the Calamities of a Civil War.

Speech on Land Tax
20 December 1774

Sources: 1. *St James's Chronicle*, 22 December 1774
          2. *Lloyd's Evening Post*, 21 December 1774

Burke spoke twice on the land tax on 20 December 1774. The versions here printed were those followed by *Parl. Reg.* i. 27–9, 29 and by *Parl. Hist.* xviii. 71–3, 74. In addition an alternative version of the second speech is printed from *Lloyd's Evening Post*, 21 December (also available in other newspapers). There are two more versions of the first speech in *General Evening Post*, 22, 27 December and elsewhere. See also Simmons and Thomas, v. 258–60. There is a MS. at Sheffield (Bk 6.115) which appears to be a rough draft for the debate.

On 19 December Lord North had moved a resolution in the Committee of Ways and Means that the land tax for the ensuing year should be three shillings in the pound, the rate at which it had been levied since 1767. When the resolution was reported to the House on the following day, Opposition M.P.s expressed their astonishment that the ministry should maintain a peacetime level of taxation when the country was on the brink of open war in America. In every war since the beginning of the century the land tax had sooner or later been raised to four shillings in the pound. Burke spoke twice in the debate. The second version of the second speech is the first known public assertion by Burke that he might be willing to consider relinquishing the Declaratory Act in the cause of peace with America. Hitherto, the Declaratory Act like all other past Rockingham accomplishments had been considered virtually sacrosanct by the party leaders.[1] It is difficult to know whether or not this version of the speech is accurate. However, it is clearly compatible with the basic philosophy Burke was soon to be advocating on a regular basis in American affairs. Simply stated, that philosophy was that the mother country should try to win the affection of the colonies through conciliation and give up all thought of overpowering them with harsh laws or force. Eventually, it would prompt Burke to call for the abandonment not only of the Declaratory Act but of all the laws, statutes, and regulations which the Americans found distasteful.

(1) ST JAMES'S CHRONICLE

Mr. Burke I did not mean to rise in this Debate, if I had not heard the Moderation of one Gentleman, (Mr. Fuller)[2] and the Precipitation of another, (Mr. Hartley)[3] stated as if militating against each other.

[1] See, for instance, vol. ii, pp. 443, 444.

[2] Rose Fuller (*c.*1708–77), M.P. 1756–77. He had condemned the Coercive Acts of 1774 but pleaded for cool and mature deliberation before any further steps were taken.

[3] David Hartley (1732–1813), M.P. 1774–80, 1782–4. He was M.P. for an important commercial town (Hull), a writer on diverse subjects, and a particular friend of the Rockinghams' best-known independent friend, Sir George Savile. He had expressed his alarm at the deteriorating situation in Boston and offered to attend on Christmas Day rather than go into recess without the adoption of further measures.

Now, Sir, I who see Matters in another Light from the Right Hon. Gentleman on the Floor,[1] can easily perceive them to be exactly correspondent. The former, from his Experience of what has been already done, is cautious, and willing to avoid repeating our former Blunders, or adopting others of a similar Nature, but is for having Matters coolly considered, fully investigated, and wisely and effectually determined; the latter aiming at the same Point, considering the Circumstances in the most urgent and pressing Light, is more eager to arrive at the Completion of his Wishes, not perhaps contemplating or foreseeing the Obstructions that may retard him in his Progress. The Right Hon. Gentleman's confessed Ignorance of what is proper to be done, or the Measures his Friends mean to adopt, I am extremely ready to believe;[2] and I have no Reason to doubt but their present Knowledge and Foresight may be nearly on a Par. He certainly mistakes the Matter, if he supposes that we at this Side of the House wish for a War Establishment in Time of Peace;[3] No, Sir, what we object to is, that a Speech[4] which breathed nothing but War, and accompanied with the Motives of such a Declaration, should, without any Cause whatever assigned, at once sink into a tranquil Silence; a Peace Establishment formed on the lowest Scale. I am not now contending what the Establishment ought to be; but I contend, that that already voted by no Means corresponds with the Intimations given to this House by Authority. I know that a heavy Peace Establishment is ruinous and destructive to any Country where it is kept up. I remember very well too, that I, among others on these Benches, have long been dinning that in the Ears of the Minister. I remember likewise, that for so doing we were called factious and discontented. And I am now happy in the flattering Idea, that factious and discontented as we are, we happened for once to be right; for the great Man who conducts the public Affairs of this Country,[5] hath given ample Testimony to our Wisdom, by adopting what he and his Friends for three successive Sessions charitably imputed to ignorance or disappointed Ambition. Nor am I less happy in another Instance of the same Kind. The Noble

---

[1] Richard Rigby. The report of Rigby's speech includes no reference to Fuller's remarks, only to those of Hartley, and those of another Opposition M.P. who had spoken, Thomas Townshend (1733–1800) later (1783) 1st Baron Sydney, M.P. 1754–83.

[2] Rigby had disclaimed speaking on behalf of North or with any information of his own, while supporting the minister's proposal.

[3] Rigby had been commenting on Townshend's speech.

[4] The Speech from the Throne of 30 November 1774.   [5] Lord North.

Lord below me on the Floor, (Lord Beauchamp)[1] being requested
to know from the Minister, if he had any Information to lay before
us, or Measures to propose, came posting to the House with the
Halcyon Tidings, that all was Peace and Tranquillity; and that he had
none.[2] Here again the same factious Spirit obtruded, and broke the
calm Enjoyments which might be derived from such a happy State of
Things; for some of us, who are never to be satisfied, relapsed into
our former Turbulence and Discontent. What was the Consequence?
Why, it seems Turbulence and Discontent once more had Reason at
their Side, and the Minister came forward and assured us himself,
that he had Information to lay before the House, and Measures to
propose.[3] I cannot sit down without saying a Word or two on the
Solicitude the Honourable Member on my left Hand (Mr. Hartley)
has expressed for the Situation of General Gage,[4] and the Troops
under his Command. It is, I confess, most humiliating and mortifying;
and it is difficult to say, whether those who have put them into it,
deserve most our Compassion or our Ridicule. It is, indeed, an
Absurdity without Parallel; a warlike Parliament, and a patient for-
bearing General. I would not be understood to reflect on the Gentleman, who I understand is a very worthy, intelligent, deserving Man;
no, Sir, it is those who have sent him on such an Errand, that are to
blame. The Order of Things is reversed in this new System. The Rule
of Government now is to determine hastily, violently, and without
Consideration, and execute indecisively, or rather not execute at all.
And have not the Consequences exactly corresponded with such a
Mode of Proceeding? They have been Measures, not practicable in
themselves in any Event, nor has one Step been taken to put them
into Execution. The Account we have is, that the General is besieging and besieged; that he had Cannon sent to him, but they were
stolen; that he himself has made Reprisals of a similar Nature on
the Enemy;[5] and, that his Straw has been burnt and his Brick and

---

[1] Francis Seymour Conway (1743–1822), styled Viscount Beauchamp, later (1794) 2nd
Marquess of Hertford, M.P. 1766–94.
[2] On 13 December 1774; see *Parl. Reg.* i. 13.
[3] On 16 December 1774; North had explained that he had information which he would lay
before the House after the Christmas holidays; see *Parl. Reg.* i. 16–17.
[4] Thomas Gage (1721–87), Governor of Massachusetts and Commander-in-Chief.
[5] This does not seem to have been reported by General Gage, although he had informed
Dartmouth on 17 October 1774 that 'twelve Pieces of Cannon' were thought to have been sent
(*The Correspondence of General Thomas Gage with the Secretaries of State 1763–1775*, ed. C. E.
Carter, 2 vols., New Haven, Conn., 1931–3, i. 379).

Mortar destroyed.[1] It is painful to dwell on such monstrous absurd Circumstances, which can be only a Subject of Ridicule, if it did not lead to Consequences of a very serious and alarming Nature. In fine, Sir, your Army is turned out to be a mere Army of Observation; and is of no other Use but as an Asylum for Magistrates of your own creating.

Burke was answered by Sir William Meredith,[2] who asserted that the present troubles were due to the Declaratory Act. General Gage had ful-filled the purposes for which he had been sent. 'The troops, he said, were for the protection of the magistrates, the protection of the property and trade of the merchants, and the enforcing of the acts, all which had been fully accomplished.'[3]

Mr. Burke rose, and complimented Sir William on his great Wisdom, and the Sagacity of Administration, in discovering of which, if they had applied to him, he could have long since informed them. He once more returned to the Asylum of Magistrates. He said he had often heard of such Places for Thieves, Rogues, Robbers and female Orphans; but it was the first Time he had ever heard of an Asylum of Magistrates. As to the Protection of Trade, in a Place where all Sort of Trade or Commerce was prohibited, the Task was a glorious, but not a difficult one. And as to the blocking up an Harbour, it might be very true, but to him, this Mode of Blockade seemed rather novel. Such an Expression it is certain, says he, might come with great Propriety from me; but I must confess I never heard such a Bull in my own Country. At the Entrance of Dublin Harbour, there is a North and a South Bull, but even there or elsewhere, such a Bull as this I never heard.

(2) LLOYD'S EVENING POST

Mr. Burke retorted, that if the Declaratory Act was the accursed thing that had caused all the mischief, they had nothing to do but toss it overboard. For his part, he was ready to sacrifice every thing for peace with America; but he still was of opinion Gen. Gage and his Troops had no business at Boston: That the Magistrates of Boston were said to be in an asylum; he had heard of asylums for thieves, but never of

---

[1] Gage had reported the 'burning the straw and sinking boats with bricks, coming for the use of the troops, and overturning our wood carts' (*Parl. Reg.* i. 58).

[2] 3rd Baronet (*c.*1725–90), M.P. 1754–80, a former supporter of Rockingham who had defected to North in 1773.

[3] *Parl. Reg.* i. 29.

asylums for Magistrates; nor could he conceive how they could be said to be protected, while they could not officiate, but were only in an asylum: That the Troops had been sent to protect the Commerce of the Merchants after all trade was at an end; and that as to the execution of the Acts of Parliament, General Gage could not be said to have enforced them, since the Americans had not yet submitted to them. His severe sarcasms on the Ministry were more proper for the ears of the Members than the Public.

Speech on Petitions on America
26 January 1775

Source: *London Evening Post*, 7 February 1775

This report is followed by *Parl. Reg.* i. 119–21 and *Parl. Hist.* xviii. 187–90. Other versions are in the *Public Ledger*, 28 January; *St James's Chronicle*, 28 January; a brief report, *Morning Post*, 27 January; and *Middlesex Journal*, 28 January. See Simmons and Thomas, v. 309, 310, 311–13, 315, 317–18.

After the Christmas recess the House was presented with some twenty-four petitions on American affairs.[1] Eighteen of them called upon Parliament to end the dispute through conciliation. While Burke believed that Members of Parliament were not bound blindly to follow the will of their electors, he firmly believed in the right of the electorate to express the common will in an effort to influence Parliament. Ideally, he felt that natural leaders in society— 'the few'—had an important role to play in moulding or giving 'direction' to such expressions.[2] Therefore, he worked vigorously to promote the conciliatory campaign.[3] He attempted to get Rockingham to lend party support, but his efforts brought little response and he proceeded independently. He drafted the 'heads' of the petition to Parliament for the Society of Merchant Venturers in Bristol[4] as well as a petition to the Crown from that city;[5] he worked closely with William Baker[6] to promote the London Merchant's petition; and, in conjunction with a local committee in Bristol, he helped to encourage other boroughs and towns to get involved.[7] He received a letter of

---

[1] See J. E. Bradley, *Popular Politics and the American Revolution in England: Petitions, the Crown and Public Opinion*, Macon, Ga., 1986, pp. 17–36.
[2] See above, p. 23.
[3] Bradley, *Popular Politics*, pp. 53–4.
[4] See *Corr.* iii. 101.
[5] See below, pp. 174–5.
[6] (1743–1824), M.P. 1768–74, 1777–84, 1790–1802, 1805–7.
[7] Bradley believes Burke was influential in the petitions from Westbury, Abingdon, Berkshire, Leeds, and possibly Nottingham and Bridgwater (*Popular Politics*, p. 54).

thanks from the Merchants and Manufacturers of Birmingham and one from
the Committee of Manufacturing Hosiers of Nottingham for his efforts in the
House of Commons to promote their conciliatory petitions.[1]

On 26 January a second petition from the London Merchants was presented
to the House of Commons requesting that their first petition be referred to
the Committee of the Whole House which was to consider the American
papers on that day rather than to a separate Committee of the Whole House.
Burke had already labelled the latter the 'Coventry Committee'[2] and the
'Committee of Oblivion'[3] because its apparent purpose was to see that the
petitions could have no direct effect on the American debate.[4] The discussion
of this petition was general. Burke replied to speakers and then he turned to
the real issue. When he did so he very effectively voiced the argument which
would provide the central theme for his speeches on American affairs in the
near future—Britain's major concern in her relationship with America should
be neither principle nor 'dignity' but the immense and lucrative trade carried
on by her merchants.

Mr. Burke followed Mr. Jenkinson.[5] He treated the talk of Paper
Currency with very little respect, and shewed that Mr. Jenkinson's
discourse had not even the most remote tendency to prove this, or
indeed any other point. For what argument (said he) can be drawn
from the instance of an act to prevent Paper Currencies, to prove that
the merchants of London ought not to be heard in the American
Committee? The most depreciated Paper Currency ever issued by
Rhode Island, in its worst times, was not (said he) more different from
good money than this talk of ours from sound argument.

He then turned to Mr. Lewis,[6] and with the greatest good humor
laughed at his petition, of which he exposed the absurdity by taking Mr.
Lewis's own case as an instance. This gentleman was (said Mr. Burke)
sitting Member last parliament.[7] I thought he had a good right to his

---

[1] *Corr.* iii. 121 and n., 122 and n., 123.

[2] 'in allusion to a well known practice, by which a troublesome person is voted to be sent to
Coventry, whereby, without turning him out of company, he is wholly excluded from all attention;
he may be ridiculed and laughed at, and cannot interfere in his own defence' (*Parl. Hist.* xviii.
171).

[3] Ibid.

[4] The first one was presented with two from Bristol on 23 January 1775 (ibid. 168–81).

[5] Charles Jenkinson. He had argued that since the colonies had accepted the Act to regulate
their paper currency (4 Geo. III, c. 34), 'they *ought* to submit to every act of English legislature.'

[6] John Lewis (1738–97), M. P. 1768–9, 1774–5. He had suggested that the merchants 'came
too late; that they ought not to have been silent so long; and that having so long confided in
parliament, they ought to continue that confidence'.

[7] Lewis had been returned for the constituency of New Radnor Boroughs in 1768, only to be
unseated on petition. Though elected in 1774 he was to be unseated once again, on 20 February

seat. I lamented that the public had for seven years been deprived of the benefit of talents; but suppose this had been the same parliament whose acts he defends, and of whose injustice he was the protomartyr, and that he had till the last session been silent, and that his modesty had persuaded him to defraud the House of the benefit of his talents to the last hour, would that septennial silence of his argue, that he ought not to be heard at the end of the seven years, when he at last chose to interfere in the debates? then we would have heard him patiently and calmly, nay, if his argument had required an answer, we would have answered him. He then turned to Sir Gilbert Elliot,[1] who on the former debate had argued that the House was already perfectly acquainted in *general* with the trade and its importance, and admitted in its full extent whatever the merchants could alledge.[2] He said that this gentleman was rather too ready to take the measure of mankind from himself; and because he was so very knowing, did not sufficiently condescend to the ignorance of others. But whatever the knowledge of any gentleman, or of any individual in the House might be, there was a great difference between knowing and feeling. That the honourable gentleman could easily abstract and generalize his ideas even to the *genus generalissimum*; but the nature of mankind was such, that general observations affected their minds in a slight and indistinct manner, when the detail of particulars, and the actual substance of things, made a most forcible impression. He illustrated this by a story of a learned Prince, who was of the same part of the island to which we owe the honourable gentleman. James the First, who, as Osborn tells the story, having ordered a present of 20,000l. for one of his favourites, his Treasurer, a wary and prudent Minister, well read in human nature, and knowing how little the general expression of things operates, and that the word 20,000l. were as easily sounded as twenty thousand farthings, contrived to place the whole sum in a vast heap before the King's eyes as he passed to his levee in good Jacobus's; when the King was taken out of his *generals*, and saw the money itself spread out before his eyes, he was frightened at what he was about, and threw himself in great agony on the mass of gold, and scrambling up a

---

1775. In 1780 the returning officer made a double return, and for the third and final time the Commons ruled against John Lewis. The electoral qualifications at New Radnor had been the subject of repeated dispute.

[1] Sir Gilbert Elliot, 3rd Baronet (1722–77), M.P. 1753–77.

[2] He had spoken in the debate on the first London petition on 23 January (*Parl. Reg.* i. 108), though he is not recorded as making this point.

handful or two, there, says he, 'Ge'en that, that's enough.'[1] Now, said he, if we are to be generous in sacrificing our trade to our dignity, let us know what the value of the sacrifice is that we make; let us not be generous in the dark; true generosity is to give, and see, and know whatever we give. Let us then see this thing, this trade, we are to give up for our dignity. Your dignity may be worth it *all*, but let us be informed by the merchants what *all* really is. To be generous, without knowing what we give, is not liberality but negligence; and fearlessness arising from ignorance, is not courage but insensibility. He said that the reason given by those who sent the petitions to the *Coventry Committee*, for not referring them to that of American papers, was of a most extraordinary and unheard of nature; it was, that the resolutions of that committee were to be solely on the grounds of Policy, and that the commercial examination would delay the measures necessary for the coercion of America.[2] This (he said) was to anticipate and pre-determine the future proceedings in a committee, as a reason for keeping information from it; how did they know what measures would be pursued there, and on what principles? Was there any instruction to the committee so to confine itself? or was it that the Ministry had already not only solved what the committee was to do, but reckoned upon it so much as a certainty, and as a matter so justifiable, that they did not scruple to avow it, and to make it a ground of argument for what the House ought, or ought not to have brought before its committee. This proceeding he thought no less alarming than unprecedented. That if they meant hostility, the reason they gave for not hearing was the strongest for it. But as their War ever must be dependent upon their Finances, and their Finances must depend upon their Commerce, the true State of that Commerce was necessary to be known, especially as Colonies and Commerce are inseparably connected.

He then lamented the Miseries of a Civil War, incurred by the precipitate ignorance of Administration. Trade destroyed—the revenue impoverished—the Poor starving—Manufactures stagnating—the Poor-Rate running into the Land-Tax, and both devouring the Estates. The colouring was very strong, but not over-

---

[1] The story is told by Francis Osborne (1593–1659) of James I, Robert Cecil, 1st Earl of Salisbury (1593–1612) and Robert Carr, 1st Earl of Somerset (*c.*1587–1645). See Osborne's *Works*, 8th edn., London, 1682, pp. 457–8.

[2] On 23 January 1774 Sir William Meredith had argued that the petitions should be referred to a separate committee so as not to lengthen the American debate and prevent decisive Government action to end the dispute (*Parl. Hist.* xviii. 171–2).

charged. He said, he would convict them of such a Chain of Blunders and Neglects, as, though it would not bring Vengeance on their Heads, yet would call Blushes into their Cheeks, and shew them utterly unfit for the great part they had under them. But the Ministry were so confident of the little avail of any pretence that aimed at touching the Feelings of their majority, that they laughed at his Representation of the miserable State of their Country, and the Effects of their Misconduct. He concluded with drawing the picture of the archer who was going to draw his bow against his adversary, but saw that in the enemy's arms was enfolded his own child.[1] Let your Commerce (said he) come before you, and see whether it be your Child that America has in its arms; see of what Value that Child is, and examine whether you ought to shoot, and if you must, to shoot so as to avoid wounding what is dearest to you in the world. Without examining your trade you cannot do this.

Burke spoke again in the debate in defence of Charles Fox but 'was obliged to sit down unheard; to use his own words, in a "torrent of candour, and a storm of moderation". The attempt to get the petition referred to the Committee on American papers failed by 250 votes to 89.[2]

Speech on American Disturbances
6 February 1775

Source: *London Evening Post*, 14 February 1775

The report printed here was used for *Parl. Reg.* i. 167–8 and *Parl. Hist.* xviii. 262–4. There is a brief additional report in the *Morning Post*, 8 February and in *Middlesex Journal*, 9 February. See also Simmons and Thomas, v. 358, 359, 360–1, 378.

The Committee of the Whole House on the American papers had proposed an Address to the King which declared that a rebellion existed in Massachusetts and beseeched the King to take 'the most effectual measures to inforce due obedience to the laws and authority of the supreme legislature'. The Address was agreed to on 7 February and presented jointly by both Houses.[3] On 6 February Lord John Cavendish moved that the Address should be recommitted to the committee. Burke supported the motion and

[1] Burke had urged the need to view the colonies as the 'child' of the mother country before. See, for instance, his speech on American taxation on 19 April 1774 (vol. ii, p. 459).
[2] *Parl. Hist.* xviii. 193.
[3] Ibid. 297–8.

exhorted the members to consider the importance of the American trade and the potential disruption which would accompany more coercive measures.

Mr. Burke applied his argument to that prevalent Idea, which alone can make one honest man the advocate for ministerial measures, viz. *that the Americans attack the Sovereignty of this country.*—

Mr. Burke shewed that they do not attack the *Sovereignty itself,* but *a certain exercise and use of that Sovereignty.*

He stated, that no tyranny itself found a justification of their tyranny in the mere plea of their unlimited authority. He stated seven acts of Tyranny, which justified resistance. He shewed, that the cause of the late rebellions at home,[1] and those disturbances in America, differed widely; that the trade of the country was little affected by those rebellions; that our trade at present is the primary object; that the object of that rebellion was to set an unnatural Tyrant on the throne; that he feared the Americans were *now* what we were then; and they were struggling that an insufferable Tyranny should not be established over them.

Mr. Burke shewed the delusion practiced by Ministry, who in all speeches argue that Boston *alone* was in rebellion, and that it was an affair with Boston *only*; but he shewed that *all* America was concerned, from clear and positive facts. He proved, that from one end of the continent to the other, the like resistance had been found; and he pressed the independent members to consider that; for he said, if people were once convinced that the mischief was so wide, they would think a little more seriously what *might* have been the *causes* of so general discontent, and might wish to apply other remedies than fire or sword.

He said, that their definition of Rebellion was the oddest he had ever heard; it must be the destruction of tea; but burning tea was not in their definition rebellion, for such a place had burnt it; that spoiling it in[2] damp vaults was not in their definition, for it had been so treated in such a place.[3] Now to answer their definition of Rebellion, tea must be drowned like a puppy dog; and even that was not quite enough; it must *be drowned*, and drowned *at Boston*. This was their definition of Rebellion.[4]

---

[1] The Jacobite rebellions of 1715 and 1745.
[2] *London Evening Post*: 'in it'
[3] Tea had been burnt in Maryland and stored in South Carolina.
[4] A reference to the ministry's justification for the Boston Port Bill of 1774.

He exerted himself to deprecate the shameless Tyranny we exercised. He abhorred political as much as he did religious persecution. His heart seemed engaged. He mentioned with Horror the idea of tearing a man from his family and friends the other side of the Atlantic,[1] and tearing his heart out in Smithfield, stiling it the heart of a traitor, because he would not believe in—Virtual Representation, and because he would not believe that America—was part of the Manor of Greenwich.[2]

He said he had two years before called their attention to Virginia, the mother colony; and shewed that in all their proceedings Virginia had taken the lead;[3] and that therefore it was plain it was not Boston, but America; and if you meant a war with the whole, you ought with your eyes open to prepare for that, and not for a skuffle with Boston. He also put it on its true bottom; you have, says he, your option— AMERICA or THIS MINISTRY, and he exposed, with all his wit, the absurdity of balancing in such a choice.

We cannot do justice to this gentleman's great exertions that day; but men surely do not know the effects of that law of Hen. VIII.[4] or of the act we have passed, or they would not support such a tyranny.

Address to the Bristol Electors
20 February 1775

Source: *Felix Farley's Bristol Journal*, 25 February 1775

The committee considering the Bristol election reported to the House of Commons on 20 February that Burke and Cruger had been duly elected. Presumably this address had been drawn up in advance of the decision. For the issues involved, see above, pp. 62–3 and n.

[1] If the statute of Henry VIII had been enforced; see below, n. 4.

[2] In some colonial charters (e.g. Massachusetts 1629) the colony was 'holden of us, our heirs and successors, as of our manor of East Greenwich, in the county of Kent, in full and common socage, and not *in capite*, nor by knight's service'.

[3] No record of this has been found. There is ample evidence, of course, that Burke was correct in stating the importance of Virginia in providing leadership. On 12 March 1773, for instance, the Virginia colonial legislature established the first committee of correspondence and invited other colonial legislatures to do the same. The Declaration of Independence was first to be proposed at the Virginia Convention on 15 May 1776 (M. Jensen, *American Colonial Documents to 1776*, London, 1955, pp. 763, 866–8).

[4] The statute of 1543 (35 Hen. VIII, c. 2) regulating treasons committed outside the realm of England, which the administration in the 1768–9 session had obtained parliamentary support for using to bring colonial opponents to England for trial.

To the Gentlemen, Clergy, Freeholders *and* Freemen *of the City of* Bristol

Gentlemen,

The Justice of the Committee of Elections has confirmed to me, that Seat in Parliament, which originally I owe to your Favour.

I have the greater Pleasure in this equitable and enlightened Determination, because it has connected with my Success, the Security of the Rights of every Elector in this Kingdom. Every such Elector ought undoubtedly to possess, independently of any other, the Power of nominating the Person he wishes to represent him. This important Right is now established by the highest Authority; nor can it by any possible Collusion among Candidates, be hereafter defeated.

It is no less a Matter of Satisfaction to me, that the Exercise of the original Rights of the Freemen of this Corporation, is not made to depend upon the Date of the Writ of Summons to Parliament; which of all Limitations of the Right of Election, would be the most dangerous, partial, and arbitrary.

I am indeed happy in the Prospect that it may be a Means of restoring Concord and Repose to this City; as by this Judgment, the conduct of all the Candidates, and of their Friends, in the late Election is perfectly vindicated.

To the indefatigable Zeal and Constancy of those worthy Citizens who have honour'd me with their Support in the late Election, we owe the Confirmation of Rights so essential to public Liberty. You may be assured, that it shall be my Endeavour, by my whole Conduct, to show myself attentive to that material Object; grateful to those who have given me the Opportunity of defending it; and tenacious to the best of those Principles, to which I am indebted, for the distinguished Honour of being your Representative.

I am, with the highest Respect and most Perfect Regard and Attachment,

> GENTLEMEN, *your most obedient,*
> *most obliged and faithful humble Servant,*
> Edmund Burke

Westminster, Feb. 20, 1775

Speech on North's Conciliatory Proposition
20 February 1775

Source: *Parl. Reg.* i. 211–13

No newspaper source for Almon's report of this speech has been found, but some sentences at the end are in the *London Evening Post*, 25 February. *Parl. Hist.* xviii. 335–7 reproduces the Almon report. See also Simmons and Thomas, v. 437, 439, 448–50, 451. There is a MS. at Northampton (A.xxxvii.26) which appears to be a rough draft of this speech.

On 20 February, the House being in the Committee of the Whole House on North American affairs, Lord North moved a resolution which would have allowed any of the colonies to avoid parliamentary taxation by raising its share—to the imperial Government's satisfaction—of the cost of its own civil government and of the common defence. The resolution also promised to impose no new taxes on the colonists except for the regulation of commerce and to allow any revenues arising out of the latter to be credited to the account of the province in which it was collected. This proposal aroused controversy within North's own Cabinet, and in Parliament it was opposed by some Government supporters.[1] However, to many in Britain it seemed a genuine attempt at reconciliation. North was commended for striking 'the only Medium between the Humanity and Justice of this Kingdom',[2] and the colonies were challenged to 'return to their Duty, in consequence of... receiving so unmerited a Proof of the Tenderness yet remaining in the Mother Country'.[3] The measure thus threatened the credibility of the Opposition's charges that the Government was being harsh and intransigent. Burke spoke for 'above an Hour'[4] in an effort to counteract the favourable impression the motion would make. He had strong evidence to suggest that the Americans would reject the proposal. He was currently involved in a controversy over a similar offer which was thought by some to have been made a decade earlier by the founder of the Stamp Act, George Grenville. In the course of that controversy a former acting colonial agent, Israel Mauduit,[5] had published a letter from the House of Representatives which employed the same argument against Grenville's proposal which Burke now used with respect to North's.

Mr. Burke. He declared he came to the House this day, upon the report of a change of measures, with a full resolution of supporting any thing, which might lead any way towards conciliation—but that he

---

[1] Its object remains a matter for dispute; see B. Donoughue, *British Politics and the American Revolution*, London, 1964, pp. 248–51, and P. D. G. Thomas, *Tea Party to Independence: The Third Phase of the American Revolution, 1773–6*, Oxford, 1991, pp. 178–9, 198–205, 216–18.

[2] *Public Advertiser*, 25 February 1775.

[3] Ibid. 28 February 1775.

[4] *St James's Chronicle*, 21 February 1775.

[5] (1708–87).

found the proposition altogether insidious in its nature, and therefore purposely rendered to the last degree obscure and perplexed in its language. Instead of being at all fitted to produce peace, it was calculated to increase the disorders and confusions in America;—and therefore that he never could consent to it. He readily admitted with Mr. Ellis, and with the Solicitor General of Scotland, that the proposition was a contradiction to every thing that parliament had declared; a shameful prevarication in ministers; and a mean departure from every declaration they had made.[1] He was however willing to purchase peace by any humiliation of ministers, and by what was of more moment, even by the humiliation of parliament. But the measure was mean indeed, but not at all conciliatory. The mode of argument, on the side of administration, he said, was the most ridiculous that ever had been known in parliament. They attempted to prove to one side of the House, that the measure was a concession; and to the other, that it was a strong assertion of authority—just on the silly principles of the Tea Act, which to Great Britain was to be a duty of supply, to the Americans a tax of regulation. He was equally surprised, he said, by another extraordinary phaenomenon. To this day, during the whole course of the American debates, the ministry have daily and hourly denied their having any sort of contest about an American revenue. That the whole was a dispute for obedience to trade-laws, and to the general legislative authority. Now they turn short—and to console our manufacturers and animate our soldiers, they tell them for the first time, "the dispute is put on its true footing, and that the grand contest is, not for empty honour, but substantial revenue." But manufacturers and soldiers will not be so consoled, or so animated; because the revenue is as much an empty phantom, as the honour; and the whole scheme of the resolution is oppressive, absurd, and impracticable—and what indeed the ministers confess the Americans will not accept; nay, what indeed they own America has already rejected. It is oppressive; because, it was never the complaint of the Americans that the mode of taxation was not left to themselves; but that neither the amount and *quantum* of the grant, nor the application, was in their free choice. This was their complaint, and their complaint was just. What else is it to be

[1] Welbore Ellis and Henry Dundas (1742–1811), later (1802) 1st Viscount Melville, M.P. 1774–1802, had both spoken strongly against North's proposal though they were both ministers, Ellis as Joint-Vice Treasurer of Ireland, Dundas as Scottish Solicitor General. It is notable that Dundas's speech on this occasion, characteristically forthright, was his first since entering the Commons in 1774.

taxed by act of parliament in which they are not represented, but for parliament to settle the proportion of the payment, and the application of the money? This is the purport of the present resolution. If an act of parliament compelled the city of Amsterdam, to raise an hundred thousand pounds, is not Amsterdam as effectually taxed without its consent, as if duties to that amount were laid upon that city? To leave them the mode may be of some ease as to the collection; but it is nothing to the freedom of granting; in which the colonies are so far from being relieved by this resolution, that their condition is to be ten-times worse than ever. He contended, that it is far a more oppressive mode of taxing than that hitherto used: for here no determinate demand is made. The colonies are to be held in durance by troops, fleets, and armies, until singly and separately they shall do—what? Until they shall offer to contribute to a service which they cannot know, in a proportion which they cannot guess, on a standard which they are so far from being able to ascertain, that parliament which is to hold it, has not ventured to hint what it is they expect. They are to be held prisoners of war, unless they consent to a ransom, by bidding at an auction against each other and against themselves, until the King and parliament shall strike down the hammer, and say, "enough."

This species of auction, to be terminated not at the discretion of the bidder, but at the will of the sovereign power, was a kind of absurd tyranny, which he challenged the ministers to produce any example of, in the practice of this or of any other nation. What was said to be most like this method of setting the colony assemblies at guessing what contribution might be most agreeable to us in some future time, was the tyranny of Nebuchadnezzar, who having forgot a dream of his, ordered the assemblies of his wise men, on pain of death, not only to interpret his dream, but to tell him what his dream was.[1] To set, he said, the impracticability and absurdity of this scheme in the stronger light, he asked, in case an assembly made an offer which should not be thought sufficient by parliament, was not the business to go back again to America? and so on backwards and forwards as often as the offer displeased parliament? and thus instead of obtaining peace by this proposition, all our distractions and confusions will be encreased tenfold, and continue for ever. It is said indeed by the minister, that

[1] Dan. 11: 1–5.

this scheme will disunite the colonies. Tricks in government have sometimes been successful; but never, when they are known, avowed, and hackneyed. The Boston port-bill was a declared cheat, and accordingly far from succeeding; it was the very first thing that united all the colonies against us, from Nova Scotia to Georgia. The idea of deducting the value of goods supposed to be taken by the colonists, because we sold cheap, at a time when we did not suffer the colonies to make a trial, and by such arithmetic to deduce the propriety of their paying in nearly an equal proportion with the people of England, was of a piece, he said, with the rest of the policy and the argument of this profound project. He strongly declared against any scheme, which began by any mode of extorting revenue. Every benefit, natural or political, must be had in the order of things, and in its proper season. Revenue from a free people must be the consequence of peace, not the condition on which it is to be obtained. If we attempt to invert this order, we shall have neither peace nor revenue. If we are resolved to eat our grapes crude and sour, instead of obtaining nourishment, we shall only set an edge on our own teeth, and those of our posterity for ever. Therefore he was for the reconsideration until it could be brought, he said, to some agreement with common sense.

North's motion was approved by the committee by 274 votes to 88. The resolution was agreed to by the whole House on 27 February.

Reply to Mauduit
February 1775

Sources: MSS. at Sheffield, Bk 6.148–153

Burke's reply to a handbill of Israel Mauduit survives in a draft in his hand (Bk 6.151, 152), and a fair copy made by his clerk, Clement Nevile Zouch (d. 1792), (Bk 6.148, 149, 150), the first half of which has extensive corrections and additions by Burke. The last paragraph is in Burke's hand, on a separate sheet of paper (Bk 6.153), and was not copied by Zouch. Use has been made of the draft where Zouch was not clear about Burke's intentions or misread his handwriting. A copy of Mauduit's handbill is preserved with the manuscripts (Bk 6.147). Burke has underlined portions of the handbill and made comments in the margin. Against the word 'raise' he has written: 'The word raise in Mr. G.'s [Grenville's] Language here and elsewhere always signifies being taxed.' On Grenville's assertion that a stamp duty 'would fall only upon Property', Burke has commented: 'where else can any Tax fall'; and finally on Grenville's statement that 'all would bear their Share of the Publick Burthen', Burke remarks: 'very fallacious a Bond for 10,000 pounds and one for ten shillings bear the same Stamp'. The handbill was printed in the newspapers (e.g. *Gazetteer*, 22 February 1775).

In February 1775 Israel Mauduit printed a handbill[1] bitterly attacking Burke's *Speech on American Taxation*, which had been published on 10 January. In that speech Burke denied a claim that the founder of the Stamp Act, George Grenville, had initially offered to allow the colonies the opportunity to avoid the stamp duty, by taxing themselves and making an appropriate contribution to imperial expenses. In his handbill Mauduit, who had been the acting Agent for Massachusetts in 1764, claimed that other Agents supported his assertion that Grenville had made such an offer and that the colonies had refused to take advantage of it.[2] Burke wrote the following reply in order to refute this claim, but his work was never completed or published.

While evidence does suggest that Burke's interpretation was correct,[3] his views of Grenville and the events leading up to the Stamp Act can hardly be considered objective. Ever since the Rockinghams had repealed the Stamp Act they had been criticized for encouraging the Americans to believe that they could avoid any British laws and regulations which they deemed distasteful. Such criticism invariably evoked Burke's ire: 'Whenever the repeal of the Stamp Act is objected to, or his own or his party's intentions traduced,' it was reported, 'it seems to rouse his whole soul ... [and] to give double spirit, fire or force, to his faculties.'[4] In his concern to demonstrate the wisdom and justness of the Rockinghams' decision to discard the stamp duty, Burke had often condemned its founder for fanning the initial flames of discontent in the colonies and for intransigence.[5] Grenville's supposed offer need not have been seen as a major concession to the Americans. As Mauduit's handbill demonstrates,[6] it suffered from the same major deficiencies in American eyes as North's recent conciliatory proposals. However, the offer made Grenville appear reasonable, indulgent, and flexible.[7] It was that which made Burke uncomfortable because it seemed indirectly to cast doubt on the propriety of the Rockinghams' actions. If the founder of the Stamp Act could in any sense be judged liberal in American matters, the Act

---

[1] The handbill is entitled, *Mr. Grenville's Offer to the Colony Assemblies to raise the Supply themselves, instead of having it done by a Parliamentary Stamp Act.*

[2] See vol. ii, p. 435.

[3] Grenville has been accused of deliberately misleading the colonial Agents by pretending that he would allow the colonies to tax themselves (E. S. and H. M. Morgan, *The Stamp Act Crisis*, New York, 1963, pp. 75–84; E. S. Morgan, 'The Postponement of the Stamp Act', *William and Mary Quarterly*, 3rd series, vii (1950), 353–92.). However, it appears that some of the Agents misunderstood what he said (P. D. G. Thomas, *British Politics and the Stamp Act Crisis*, Oxford, 1975, pp. 72–7; I. R. Christie and B. W. Labaree, *Empire or Independence 1760–1776*, Oxford, 1976, pp. 38–9).   [4] *Parl. Hist.* xvi. 1124.

[5] For Burke's published views of the Grenville administration, see *Observations on a Late State of the Nation* (vol. ii, pp. 102–219).

[6] Mauduit had quoted the reply from the Massachusetts House of Representatives stating that the offer 'amounts to no more than this. That if the Colonies will not Tax themselves, as they may be directed, the Parliament will Tax them'. In other words, it makes little difference who collects it; a tax imposed by the imperial Government is simply that.

[7] See below, p. 95 n. 1.

itself seemed to be less clearly contemptible (and, therefore, its repeal less well vindicated) than Burke liked.

The Colony of Massachusetts Bay is now suffering very heavily under the weight of parliamentary indignation by various penal Statutes; and is likely to suffer still more by various others now in contemplation. The late *Agent* of that Colony Mr. Israel Mauduit,[1] thinks this a seasonable time to pay a debt to Mr. Grenville's memory, by loading that province, to which he had been confidential Trustee, with the odium of having refused a previous offer to Tax itself before a Parliamentary Tax was laid upon it.

Without making any reflexion on this Conduct, I pass to the paper in which he pays this debt. It is apostyled "Mr. Grenville's offer to the Colony Assemblies to raise the Supply themselves, instead of having it done by a Parliamentary Stamp Act". The writer takes his Ground for this attack on the Colonies from a paragraph of a printed Speech which he inserts in his paper and is as follows

"There is also another Circulation abroad (spread with a malignant Intention, which I cannot attribute to those who say the same Thing in this House) that Mr. *Grenville* gave the Colony-Agents an Option for their Assemblies to Tax themselves; which they had refused. I find that much Stress is laid on this, as a Fact. However, it happens neither to be true nor possible. I will observe first, that Mr. *Grenville* never thought fit to make this Apology for himself in the innumerable Debates that were had upon this Subject. He might have proposed to the Colony-Agents, that they should agree in some *Mode* of Taxation, as the Ground of an Act of Parliament: but he never could have proposed that they should Tax themselves on Requisition; which is the Assertion of the Day. Indeed Mr. *Grenville* well knew, that the Colony-Agents could have no general Powers to consent to it; and they had no Time to consult their Assemblies for particular Powers before he passed his first Revenue Act. If you compare Dates you will find it impossible."[2]

The person supposed to have spoken this Speech, is esteemed tolerably careful and accurate with regard to facts, however he may be unfortunately obscure in his manner of stating them. Mr. Israel Mauduit, declares himself "utterly at a loss to guess the meaning of the

---

[1] He was not the official Agent. His brother Jasper Mauduit held that post.
[2] This paragraph is from Burke's *Speech on American Taxation* (see vol. ii, p. 435).

above paragraph. After a careful perusal he cannot determine what it is the writer means to affirm or deny" and "he will not attempt to penetrate into the meaning of a sentence worded with such well chosen Terms of Ambiguity."

This Gentleman, who is extremely *well informed*, cannot guess at the meaning of the Paragraph, but he thinks, "that what the *uninformed* Reader will be led to conclude from it is obvious enough."

Whether I am one of the uninformed, who can, or the informed, who cannot penetrate into the meaning of this wonderfully ambiguous sentence, I shall not determine. But to my understanding it conveys, substantially, and in the clearest manner, "that Mr. Grenville had made an Act for *raising a Revenue* in America *before* any option was or could be given to[1] the Colonies to Tax themselves."

This position in the Speech seems to me exceedingly *clear*. Whether it be equally *true*, is next to be examined; and very happily We have a short and satisfactory Method of determining this question by an Application to the Journals of the House of Commons for the dates, and to the Statute Book for the Act.

We shall there see, that an Act was made upon resolutions passed in March 1764 to[2] tax the Colonies. This act is the 15th of the 4th of George the third entitled "an Act for *granting certain Duties in the British Colonies and Plantations*" and for many other purposes recited in a large Title.[3] This act sets forth in the Preamble "That it is *just and necessary*, that a Revenue be raised in his Majesties dominions in America" and then it proceeds with the words "giving and granting" to the imposition of several and these no inconsiderable duties. This act the ambiguous Speech calls Mr. Grenville's *first* revenue Act.

Whether this be an Act for raising a Revenue, the Reader will judge; whether the Colonies had or could have an option upon the Act before it passed, lies upon Mr. Mauduit to prove. He was in the *confidence* of his constituents of Massachusetts Bay; he is furnished with *matter*, and he has no objection to being a *Witness*.

Instead of doing this he tells a story, of little use, in my opinion, either to elucidate or to contradict the paragraph in the printed

---

[1] Zouch's copy: 'given by'
[2] Burke has written above: 'on a string of'
[3] Usually now called the Sugar Act, 4 Geo. III, c. 5.

Speech. But it is of some use in misleading the publick judgment on very material and interesting points. Observe in what manner this is effected.

"In the beginning (says he) of *March 1764* a Number of Resolutions, relative to the *Plantation TRADE*, were proposed by Mr. Grenville and passed in the House of Commons.

The fifteenth of these was: That towards the further defraying of the said expences, it may be proper to charge certain Stamp Duties in the said Colonies and Plantations.

The *other* Resolutions [that is the first fourteen[1]], were formed into the *Plantation Act*: but the fifteenth was put off till the next Session. Mr. Grenville declaring, that he was willing to give time to the Colonies to consider of it, and to make their option of raising *that* or some other *Tax*."

By this language of Mr. Mauduit no man living could divine, that any *Tax* upon the Colonies had been the object of any of the first 14 Resolutions. He only states them as *relative* to the plantation *trade*— and he calls the Act formed out of them, the *Plantation Act*.

I am willing to suppose there was no intentional concealment in this State of the Case; and that it was merely the effect of haste in Mr. Israel Mauduit arising from a laudable promptitude in discharging, at the expence of his constituents, the Debt he owed to Mr. Grenville's memory.

But the reader not having that Debt to pay, nor that fund to pay it from, may be less in an hurry and will be at the pains to turn to the Journal. If he does he will see that it was out of the first 14 Resolutions the above Act arose, which Mr. M. calls the *plantation* Act; but which calls itself, as the very first in the Roll of its Titles, "An Act for granting certain Duties in the British Colonies".

It is necessary to clear up this point because in the docket on Mr. M.'s paper the expression is remarkable Mr. G.'s "offer to the Colonies to raise *the Supply* themselves *instead* of having *it* done by a Parliamentary Stamp act." These words "the supply" and "it" seem to be universals; and not stating any other supply or part of a supply, seem as if this proposed Stamp Act were the *whole* of the Supply, whereas other and very considerable duties were laid on by the preceding resolutions

---

[1] The square brackets are in the MS.

concerning which there is no pretence of any previous offer having been made in any way or by any person whatsoever.

But this[1]

So far as to the Story—of the first Tax Act,[2] which I conceive perfectly supports the Assertion in the Speech, and vindicates the supposed Speaker. But his vindication is of little moment in comparison to that of two Millions of people who are the principal Objects of accusation in the paper. Mr. Mauduit asserts[3] that *they refused to raise the supply*, and he[4] refers to their Letter to him as their Agent.[5] I have read that Letter again and again with no small astonishment, and I find not one Word of such refusal.

They complain indeed of the resolutions—they desire not to be taxed by Parliament;[6] and they instruct him to sollicit the repeal of the Sugar Act—not a single Syllable of a refusal to raise a supply when applied to by the usual requisition.

Nothing appears by that Letter but that they did not instantly comply with Mr. Grenvilles private Mandate. They are desired to raise the Supply—For what? How much and in what proportion? Nothing could be more Vague, idle, and unofficial[7] than this discourse. Were the Colonies to raise £370,000 Per Annum? Was the Single Colony of Massachusetts to raise it?

When a Charge is made upon any free people of their having refused to raise a Supply, before such refusal can be imputed to them as any sort of Offence, it must appear[8] that it is asked upon due consideration of their Circumstances; that they are permitted to state these Circumstances; that a Judgment is formed upon a fair hearing of that State; that the demand is made in the usual and constitutional manner, and without Menaces.

If these conditions are not observed, it does not,[9] nor will it, I suppose to any fair man appear a Ground of Taxing the Colony of

[1] Burke has not completed this paragraph, and the rest of the copy has not been altered by him.

[2] Zouch's copy: 'Tax'd Act'; the draft: 'Tax Act'

[3] In the draft there is a comma after 'asserts'.

[4] The 'he' is in the draft but not in the copy.

[5] The letter to Jasper Mauduit (dated 14 June 1764, but probably of 13 June) is quoted in the handbill. See also J. M. Sosin, *Agents and Merchants*, Lincoln, Nebr. 1965, p. 56 n. 43.

[6] Supplied from the draft.

[7] In Zouch's copy 'official'; in the draft 'unofficial'

[8] There is a comma after 'appear' in the draft.

[9] There is a gap here in the copy, and in the draft an unclear phrase, which may be 'to me'.

Massachusetts Bay without their consent as a body, which is supposed to have voluntarily and obstinately renounced its Share of the publick burthen.

Mr. Grenville's harangue to the Colony Agents which is solemnly set down in Mr. Mauduits paper as a matter of some importance, is the most notorious that ever was heard. It amounts to no more than this; that he did not propose to tax the Colonies until he thought it absolutely necessary, and perfectly just;[1] and I suppose no financier ever spoke another Language. But it is mere general Language. The question is,[2] whether the Circumstances of Massachusetts Bay were such as to prove his assertion at all applicable to them.

This writer tells just as much of a story as he likes. He tells you what Mr. Grenville said, and he tells you nothing more; so that for any thing which appears from this *plain* narrative, the Colonies by their Agents[3] were like Sheep before their Sheerers that Open'd not their Mouths. It does not appear from thence that they had any pretext to colour their delay in obeying the Closet demand of a Minister. But as I must suppose that at that time Mr. Mauduit did his Duty as Agent to the Colony, must have told the Minister what he does not tell in his present paper that the Language held[4] of the necessity of taxing the Colonies from the great military establishment brought upon them was not a necessity of their making. That even the propriety of such an encrease of Establishment might well be doubted; and as to the Debt contracted, the Colonies had likewise contracted a Debt of their own, by which they were burthen'd very heavily and until it was discharged they could not without absolute ruin contribute further.[5] That the

---

[1] Mauduit's work quotes Grenville as having used the following reasonable sounding words: 'That the late War had found us Seventy Millions, and left us more than One hundred and forty Millions in Debt. He knew that all Men wished not to be taxed: But that in these unhappy Circumstances, it was his Duty, as a Steward for the Publick, to make use of every just Means of improving the Publick Revenue: That he never meant, however, to charge the Colonies with any Part of the Interest of the National Debt. But, besides that Publick Debt, the Nation had incurred a great Annual Expence in the Maintaining of the several new Conquests, which we had made during the War, and by which the Colonies were so much benefited. That the American Civil and Military Establishment, after the Peace of *Aix-la-Chapelle*, was only £70,000 per Ann. It was now increased to £350,000. This was a great Additional Expence incurred upon an *American* Account: And he thought, therefore, that *America* ought to contribute towards it. He did not expect that the Colonies should raise the Whole; but some Part of it he thought they ought to raise.'

[2] The comma is omitted in the copy.

[3] 'Agent' in the copy; 'Agents' in the draft.

[4] The copy omits 'held'.

[5] From 'they' to 'further' is taken from the draft, in which Burke has accidentally deleted 'could'.

commercial Regulations and the other Duties attending this Stamp Duty, which Parliament came to a Resolution of imposing disabled them from the paying that or any other Tax, as they apprehended the total ruin of their Fisherys ⟨distillery⟩[1] and indeed of their whole commerce from thence; that the taking of their Frontier fort[2] by the French in the late War was not considered an Event more alarming. This[3] the Agents must have represented to Mr. Grenville, or they were then as basely betrayed as now they are unjustly accused. Governour Barnard stated[4] all this at that time, and in a much stronger manner than I do.[5] Is it not material when a Ministers *motives* for a demand of Taxes are Stated; and a refusal to comply alledged, to state the grounds of the refusal as well as those of the demand? This is what equity would have required of a Stranger.

I must ask did not the house after taxing them come to a resolution, that it may be proper to lay a Stamp duty upon the Colonies?—was not this a previous [act] to any application to the Colonies? did not the Colony of Massachusetts Bay by petition desire that the execution of this resolution should "be referred until they in conjunction with the other Colonies might have an opportunity to make a more full representation of the State and condition of the Colonies and of the Interest of Great Britain with regard to them."[6] Is a desire to be heard concerning the propriety of being taxed a *refusal* to contribute? But is not a *refusal* to hear or to receive petitions a denial of Justice and an act of the most manifest and atrocious Tyranny? did not they make such a petition, and receive such a rejection and were they not taxed without any parliamentary enquiry to know whether they had or had not refused, were or were not able to contribute. Is it justice that a province which refuses an instant[7]

---

[1] Supplied from the draft.
[2] Fort William Henry, on Lake George, surrendered to the French on 9 August 1757.
[3] 'This' in the draft; 'Thus' in the copy.
[4] In the copy 'states'.
[5] Francis Bernard (*c.*1711–79, 1st Baronet, Governor of Massachusetts 1760–71), had written: 'the publication of orders for the strict execution of the Molasses Act has caused greater alarm in this country than the taking of Fort William Henry did in 1757 ... the Merchants say, There is an end of the trade in this Province' (Morgan, *The Stamp Act Crisis*, p. 43).
[6] The petition, of 3 November 1764, is printed in M. Jensen, *American Colonial Documents to 1776*, pp. 664–7.
[7] The draft stops at this point.

Speech on Restraining Bill
6 March 1775

Source: *London Evening Post*, 11 March 1775

This report was reproduced in *Parl. Reg.* i. 295–8 and *Parl. Hist.* xviii. 389–92. A different report is in *St James's Chronicle*, 7 March, and *London Chronicle*, 9 March. Walpole gives an extensive report (*Last Journals*, i. 442–3). See also Simmons and Thomas, v. 500, 501, 505–7, 508.

On 10 February, Lord North renewed his campaign of coercion when he obtained leave to bring in a Bill to restrain the commerce of the four New England provinces and prohibit them from carrying on any fishery on the Banks of Newfoundland. On 6 March it was moved that the Bill be engrossed. Burke's speech marks a distinct change in his response to the American conflict. After delivering his standard warning about the harmful effects of the dispute with respect to British trade, he went on to make a long, highly charged, humanitarian appeal on behalf of the Americans. From this point on he would reverse the position he had taken during the election. He would express significantly less concern for the supremacy of Parliament and he would increasingly and openly champion the cause of the American colonies, their rights, and their liberties.

Mr. Burke then rose, and said, that he was afraid debate on this subject was to little purpose. When this Parliament, originally disengaged to any system, and free to choose among all, had, previous to any examination whatsoever, began by adopting the proceedings of the *last*; the whole line of our public conduct was then determined.

[Here the majority raised a great cry of approbation].[1] He said the cry was natural, and the inference from what he had said just; that the road by penitence to amendment was, he knew, humiliating and difficult—and that most of mankind were disposed like Macbeth to think

> "I am in blood
> Stept in so far, that should I wade no more,
> Returning were as tedious as go o'er;"[2]

and thus they pass towards the further bank, be the channel ever so wide, or the flood ever so deep and rapid. That as this measure was in

---

[1] The square brackets are in the newspaper.
[2] *Macbeth*, III. iv. 135–7.

the same spirit, as all the former, he did not doubt but that it would be productive of the very same consequence.

This was in effect the Boston Port Bill, but upon infinitely a larger scale. That evil principles are prolific; this Boston Port Bill begot this New England Bill; that this New England Bill, will beget a Virginia Bill; that again, a Carolina Bill, and that will beget a Pennsylvania Bill; till one by one Parliament ruins all its colonies, and roots up all its commerce; until the statute book becomes nothing but a black and bloody roll of proscriptions, a frightful code of rigour and tyranny, a monstrous digest of acts of penalty, incapacity, and general attainder; and that open it where you will, you will find a title for destroying some trade, or ruining some province.

That the scheme of Parliament was new and unheard of in any civilized nation, "to preserve your authority by destroying your dominions." It was rather the idea of hostility between independent states, where one, not being able to conquer another, thinks to reduce its strength gradually, by destroying its trade and cutting off its resources. That this mode was never used by princes towards their subjects in rebellion; the maxim in such cases always was to cut off the *rebels* but to *spare the country*, because its strength is the strength of the Sovereign himself. Here the principle was reversed, the force used against the rebels was trifling (though very expensive) but the *trade*, which was the wealth of the country, was to be destroyed.

He then entered into the difference of expence and loss between the two modes, and proved in detail, that these bills would, in all probability, cost the nation more than the maintenance of an army of 40,000 men.

That when things are come to violence, he thought the *sword* much the most effectual, and though severe, *not so unjust as these universal proscriptions*, because it will fall only on those who resist. But this act confounds all kinds of people; all sexes, all ages in one common ruin. That nothing could be at once more foolish, more cruel, and more insulting, than to hold out, as a resource to the starving fishermen, ship-builders, and the infinite number of other mechanicks employed in trade and fishery, and ruined by this act, that after the plenty of the ocean, they may poke into the brooks, and rake in the puddles of their respective countries, and diet on what we consider as husks and draft for hogs.

It was, he said, foolish and insulting, because when you deprive a man of his trade and occupation, you deprive him of the means of his livelihood, if there were ever so much fish in the streams, or corn in the fields. That a shoemaker's livelihood goes, when the fisherman can no longer pay him for his shoes. He has no resource in other peoples plenty. How is he to get at horse-beans of Indian corn, or at the worst of food, for himself and his starving family? Then he shewed, that the ruin of the staple trade of a people involved it in the ruin of the whole community, and proved, by entering minutely into its nature and employment, that the British capital employed in the New England trade could not possibly be turned to the British fishery;[1] and (treating very lightly the demonstration of Euclid) he shewed, that but one year's intermission of the course of the New England foreign trade, would be the certain loss of the whole debt now due to the English merchants.[2]

But the point of which he rested most, was this—The sentence was (in the mildest way) beggary, if not famine on four great provinces. The condition of their redemption was *"when it should be made appear* to the Governors, and the majority of the council in *two* of these provinces, that the laws would be obeyed." *By what evidence* (said he) is this to be made to appear? Who is to produce it? What facts are to be proved? What *rule* has the person who is to make it appear, to go by? What *rule* have the two Governors to determine so as to acquit them— in *complying* or in *refusing*, either to government here, or to the people there? You sentence (said he) to famine at least 300,000 people in two provinces, at the mere arbitrary will and pleasure of two men whom you do not know, for you do not know who will be Governors when this act takes place. And lest[3] these two should risque an act of mercy, you add, as a controul to them, the majority of two councils whom you do not know, and one of them at present has no existence![4] And as to the other provinces (Connecticut and Rhode Island) the act has not left a man in these two provinces, who, by the exertion even of an *arbitrary discretion*, can relieve 200,000 people more, or any innocent or re- penting individual, let their behaviour be what it will. A Governor of

---

[1] For the American whale-fishing industry, see below, p. 118 and n. 2.

[2] The Solicitor General for Scotland, Henry Dundas had said in the same debate that 'the part of the capital stock of England, which was now employed in carrying on the fisheries of New England, would be employed in carrying on our own, and thus our merchants could suffer no loss . . . whatsoever. This was as clear as any demonstration of Euclid' (*Parl. Hist.* xviii. 388).

[3] *London Evening Post*: 'least'.

[4] The Council of Massachusetts.

another province, who can never regularly and officially know their true state, can alone be *arbitrary* in favour of justice.

This (said he) is because, in those two ill-starred[1] provinces, the people chuse their Governor:[2] But is that a crime in individuals which is the legal constitution of the country? If it be a bad one, *England* has given it to them, and has not taken even a step towards altering it.

On this point, of the unheard of power given to Governors, of starving so many hundreds of thousands at their mere pleasure, of which (he said) no history of real, and even no fabulous invention of fictitious tyranny, had ever furnished an example, he dwelt a long time, and placed it in an infinite variety of lights, and kindled into such warmth, that he was at length called to order. But he continued to repeat the strong terms, as he said, he had a right to give such epithets to the bill as he pleased, until it has passed the House. If that should be the case, he would then be silent, because it would be against *order* to speak of it as it deserved; and against *prudence* to offend a body of men who had so much power, and would shew, by passing that bill, how harsh an use they were disposed to make of it.

He said, however, he was convinced, by the whole tenour of the debate, as well as his private conversation, that most of those who should vote for this bill had never read it; that what they did was not out of malice, but out of respect to the opinions of others, who, by presenting them such a bill, shewed how little they deserved this unlimited confidence. He said, that if any were in that situation, he hoped they would have the benefit of the prayer made for those who alone had done an act worse than this, "Forgive them, they know not what they do".[3]

The speech, of which many heads of argument, and many illustrations, are of necessity wholly omitted, lasted above an hour, and it was thought that he never spoke with so much power and animation.

The Bill was engrossed by 215 votes to 61.

[1] *London Evening Post*: 'ill-starved'.
[2] The Governors and magistrates had been elected by the 'freemen' of both provinces from the earliest days—even before the provinces were granted Charters by Charles II; see R. J. Taylor, *Colonial Connecticut: A History*, Millwood, NY, 1979, pp. 21–48; W. G. McLoughlin, *Rhode Island: A Bicentennial History*, New York, 1978, pp. 3–49.
[3] Luke 23: 34.

Speech on Restraining Bill
8 March 1775

Source: *Parl. Reg.* i. 303

No newspaper report has been found of Burke's speech. The Almon report is reproduced in *Parl. Hist.* xviii. 396. See also Simmons and Thomas, v. 513.

Only a brief report of Burke's speech on the third reading of the New England Restraining Bill survives. His friend David Hartley proposed the addition of a clause to the Bill, permitting inter-colonial trade in 'fuel, corn, meal, flour, or other victual' on humanitarian grounds. North opposed the clause and was immediately followed by Burke who took the opportunity to continue the type of argument he had used on 6 March.

Mr. *Burke* was warm against the bill. It was not, he said, sanguinary, it did not mean to shed blood, but to suit some gentlemen's humanity, it only meant to starve five hundred thousand people, men, women, and children at the breast. Some gentlemen had expressed their approbation of famine in preference to fire and sword.[1] This bill not only had taken from these people the means of subsisting themselves by their own labour, but, rejecting the clause now proposed, took from them the means of being subsisted by the charity of their friends. You had reduced the poor people to beggary, and now you take the beggar's scrip from them. You even dash from the mouth of hunger the morsel which the hand of charity would stretch out to it. On the subject of famine he was fine and pathetick.

The clause was defeated by 188 votes to 58; the Bill duly passed into law.[2]

---

[1] Burke is probably referring in particular to Henry Dundas. See his speeches on 6 March 1775 (*Parl. Reg.* i. 294, 306).
[2] 15 Geo. III, c. 10.

Speech on Conciliation with America
22 March 1775

Source: *The Speech of Edmund Burke Esq; on moving his Resolutions for Conciliation with the Colonies, March 22, 1775*, 3rd edn., J. Dodsley, London, 1775

As the gallery of the House of Commons was closed to the general public, the newspaper accounts are brief and inaccurate. Burke himself had not intended to publish the speech. William Burke, who heard it, wrote that Edmund was being 'pressed by friends and foes I had almost said, to print it. I took such notes, and some remember such parts that He may do it, and I think will' (O'Hara MSS., printed by R. J. S. Hoffman, *Edmund Burke, New York Agent . . .*, Philadelphia, 1956, pp. 576–7). James Prior (*Memoir of Edmund Burke*, London, 1824, pp. 186–9), prints a contemporary abbreviated version. See also Simmons and Thomas, v. 594, 595, 596–7, 598–631.

Burke had been contemplating introducing a plan to settle the American question for some time and at the beginning of the session he had announced his intention to present a Bill.[1] His party, as the largest Opposition group in Parliament, must have felt rather intense pressure to offer a solution. In late 1774 and early 1775 a plethora of ideas had been propagated from a variety of sources both friendly and hostile towards the colonists.[2] Out of doors, the press had been bringing forth one proposal after another and, in Parliament, not only had Lord North offered his controversial measure, but the ever contentious Lord Chatham[3] had also submitted a scheme. It would have repealed all the obnoxious Acts and announced that Britain would never again impose taxation for revenue on 'British freemen in America' without the consent of representatives of the provincial assemblies meeting in a general congress at Philadelphia.[4] In return, all British subjects in the colonies were to acknowledge the 'supreme legislative authority and superintending power' of Parliament.

Burke had originally planned to introduce his Bill on 16 March, but on that day it was postponed until 22 March.[5] He rose to speak at 3.30.[6] What followed represented a landmark in his career for several reasons. First, he laid out a detailed scheme for ending the American dispute. Previously he had always been content merely to eulogize the stand adopted by the Rockingham Whigs in 1765–6; that is, to insist that the imperial Parliament had the right to legislate for the colonists as it chose, but should, for practical reasons show restraint in using that right.[7] Now he made the case for suspending all the legislation which the colonists disliked, including not only all the coercive measures of recent years and all Acts which imposed taxes for revenue

---

[1] See his explanation of events in the text of his speech below, pp. 106–8.
[2] See p. 103, nn. 1–5. There are many other pamphlets on this subject as well.
[3] William Pitt, 1st Earl of Chatham (1708–78).
[4] *Parl. Hist.* xviii. 198–216.
[5] *Morning Chronicle*, 17 March 1775.
[6] *Corr.* iii. 139; *St James's Chronicle*, 23 March 1775.
[7] See, in particular, vol. ii, pp. 406–63.

purposes, but also the Quebec Act of 1774. This was also the first time he had ever suggested that England ask the colonies to 'grant' money to the Crown or that he had proposed changes in the Judicature and Courts of Admiralty to make them more responsive to American needs.

In laying out his plan Burke also publicly endorsed certain important principles which had recently gained acceptance amongst particular interests in Britain. Thus he came very close to advocating without qualification the maxim being promulgated by noted American sympathizers, including Granville Sharp,[1] Richard Price,[2] and John Cartwright,[3] that Parliament could not tax the Americans because they were not satisfactorily represented in the House of Commons. This was something of a retreat from the Rockinghams' earlier position, and it helped to cast doubts on their own Declaratory Act, which had announced in 1766 that Parliament could legislate for the American colonies 'in all cases whatsoever'.[4] Burke's discourse also demonstrates the influence of the 'free trade' school which, under the leadership of intellectuals like David Hume and Adam Smith, was becoming increasingly vocal. That influence in part accounts for Burke's central message, that Britain should not fear the natural growth of America nor enforce taxation but should build goodwill on the prosperity which would result both at home and in America, from the relatively unimpeded development of colonial society, commerce, and industry.[5] An 'Empire' he argued

is the aggregate of many States, under one common head . . . I can scarcely conceive any thing more compleatly imprudent, than for the Head of the Empire to insist, that, if any privilege is pleaded against his will, or his acts, that his whole authority is denied . . . Will not this . . . very soon teach the provinces to make no distinctions on their part? Will it not teach them that the Government, against which a claim of Liberty is tantamount to high-treason, is a Government to which submission is equivalent to slavery?[6]

In Burke's career, perhaps the greatest significance of the speech was its impact on the British public. The performance was loudly applauded by spokesmen of virtually every political persuasion. Rockingham himself was so

---

[1] (1735–1813); see *A Declaration of the People's Natural Right to a Share in the Legislature, which is the Fundamental Principle of the British Constitution of State*, London, 1774.

[2] *Observations on the Nature of Civil Liberty , the Principles of Government and the Justice and Policy of the War with America*, London, 1776.

[3] *American Independence, The Interests and Glory of Great Britain*, London, 1774.

[4] The Declaratory Act was regularly being attacked by many Americans and friends of America; see [Arthur Lee], *An Appeal to the Justice and Interests of the People of Great Britain, in the present Dispute with America* . . . , London, 1774, pp. 27–8. Chatham had challenged the wisdom of the measure in the House of Lords on 20 January (*Parl. Hist.* xviii. 156–7).

[5] For an example of the free-trade argument in the early 1770s, see [William Knox (1732–1810)] *Principles of Trade*, London, 1774. For the use of a version of it in the American debate, see Cosmopolite [pseud.], *A Plan to Reconcile Great Britain and her Colonies and Preserve the Dependency of America*, London, 1774.

[6] See below, pp. 132–3.

impressed that he began a letter of commendation. 'I never felt more . . . satisfaction on hearing any speech,' he said, 'than I did on hearing yours this day, the matter and the manner were equally perfect, and in spite of envy and malice and in spite of all politicks, I will venture to prognosticate that there will be but one opinion, in regard to the wonderful ability of the performance.'[1] 'He spoke for nearly three hours,' commented an observer who was unconnected with the party, 'during which time the attention of the house was riveted to him. The most interesting information was afforded the most exquisite entertainment.'[2] *St James's Chronicle*, proclaimed the speech 'a most masterly and comprehensive Investigation and general View of the Trade and Commerce of North America' which had proved

in the best chosen Words, the most solid Reasoning, the clearest and most extensive and familiar Knowledge of the Subject in every possible Light of Commerce, Policy, and Finance, . . . that nothing but Folly and Injustice in the Extreme could tempt the People of this Country to rule America in an Arbitrary, oppressive and tyrannical Manner.[3]

Burke was already a recognized master of parliamentary debate. This performance, however, raised him to the very highest level in almost everyone's estimation. Over the years to follow no member of the House of Commons would receive more acclaim in the newspapers for eloquence, general knowledge, and the ability to present complex issues in a clear and compelling manner. It should be said that there is little of substance in the presentation which might be called novel or original. Virtually every important idea from no taxation without adequate representation, to taxation by grant and the proposed changes in the system of justice, had been enunciated earlier by others.[4] The speech also cannot be considered a product just of Burke's views. A number of the leading members of the Rockingham party discussed the important principles it embraced, as well as the specific resolutions offered to Parliament, well in advance of 22 March.[5] What makes the speech so distinctive is not originality but the immense wealth of information; the apparently extensive understanding of the American economy, government, systems of religion, and society in general; the success with which a huge amount of material is woven together into central theses; and, as always in Burke's better performances in these years, the strength of feeling.

---

[1] *Corr.* iii. 139.

[2] *Gentleman's Magazine*, xlv (1775), 201.

[3] 25 March 1775.

[4] Cosmopolite, *Plan to Reconcile Great Britain and her Colonies*; [Arthur Lee], *Appeal to the Justice and Interests of the People*. Chatham's proposal would also have called upon the Americans to *grant* financial assistance.

[5] On 12 March 1775 Richmond mentioned the resolutions and the need to stress the call for an end to taxation for revenue and 'the advantages of commerce' which could be lost from cramping American trade (MS. at Sheffield, R1.1559). He informed Rockingham that he had discussed these matters with Lord John Cavendish and it is clear that Rockingham was well aware of the resolutions himself.

The end result is an imaginative and extremely absorbing compendium of the most reasoned pro-American ideas to come out of England in the pre-Revolution years. As such, this is simply Burke at his very best.

SPEECH OF EDMUND BURKE, Esq.

I HOPE, Sir, that, notwithstanding the austerity of the Chair, your good-nature will incline you to some degree of indulgence towards human frailty. You will not think it unnatural, that those who have an object depending, which strongly engages their hopes and fears, should be somewhat inclined to superstition. As I came into the house full of anxiety about the event of my motion, I found to my infinite surprize, that the grand penal Bill, by which we had passed sentence on the trade and sustenance of America, is to be returned to us from the other House.* I do confess, I could not help looking on this event as a fortunate omen. I look upon it as a sort of providential favour; by which we are put once more in possession of our deliberative capacity, upon a business so very questionable in its nature, so very uncertain in its issue. By the return of this Bill, which seemed to have taken its flight for ever, we are at this very instant nearly as free to chuse a plan for our American Government, as we were on the first day of the Session. If, Sir, we incline to the side of conciliation, we are not at all embarrassed (unless we please to make ourselves so) by any incongruous mixture of coercion and restraint. We are therefore called upon, as it were by a superior warning voice, again to attend to America; to attend to the whole of it together; and to review the subject with an unusual degree of care and calmness.

Surely it is an awful subject; or there is none so on this side of the grave. When I first had the honour of a seat in this House, the affairs of that Continent pressed themselves upon us, as the most important and most delicate object of parliamentary attention.[1] My little share in

---

* The Act to restrain the Trade and Commerce of the Provinces of Massachuset's Bay and New Hampshire, and Colonics of Connecticut and Rhode Island, and Providence Plantation, in North America, to Great Britain, Ireland, and the British Islands in the West Indies; and to prohibit such Provinces and Colonies from carrying on dry Fishery on the Banks of Newfoundland, and other places therein mentioned, under certain Conditions and Limitations.[2]

[1] Burke had been elected for Wendover on 23 December 1765, when the question of repealing the Stamp Act was the leading issue.

[2] The House of Lords had amended the Bill so that it would also affect the colonies of New Jersey, Pennsylvania, Maryland, Virginia, and South Carolina (*Parl. Hist.* xviii. 455–7). The Commons did not accept these amendments, but later in a separate Act (15 Geo. III, c. 18), achieved the same effect.

this great deliberation oppressed me. I found myself a partaker in a very high trust; and having no sort of reason to rely on the strength of my natural abilities for the proper execution of that trust, I was obliged to take more than common pains, to instruct myself in every thing which relates to our Colonies. I was not less under the necessity of forming some fixed ideas, concerning the general policy of the British Empire. Something of this sort seemed to be indispensable; in order, amidst so vast a fluctuation of passions and opinions, to concenter my thoughts; to ballast my conduct; to preserve me from being blown about by every wind of fashionable doctrine.[1] I really did not think it safe, or manly, to have fresh principles to seek upon every fresh mail which should arrive from America.

At that period, I had the fortune to find myself in perfect concurrence with a large majority in this House. Bowing under that high authority, and penetrated with the sharpness and strength of that early impression, I have continued ever since, without the least deviation, in my original sentiments. Whether this be owing to an obstinate perseverance in error, or to a religious adherence to what appears to me truth and reason, it is in your equity to judge.

Sir, Parliament having an enlarged view of objects, made, during this interval, more frequent changes in their sentiments and their conduct, than could be justified in a particular person upon the contracted scale of private information. But though I do not hazard any thing approaching to a censure on the motives of former parliaments to all those alterations, one fact is undoubted; that under them the state of America has been kept in continual agitation. Every thing administered as remedy to the public complaint, if it did not produce, was at least followed by, an heightening of the distemper; until, by a variety of experiments, that important Country has been brought into her present situation;—a situation, which I will not miscall, which I dare not name; which I scarcely know how to comprehend in the terms of any description.

In this posture, Sir, things stood at the beginning of the session. About that time, a worthy member* of great parliamentary experience,

---

* Mr. Rose Fuller.[2]

[1] Burke's adaptation of St Paul (Eph. 4: 14).

[2] Fuller was a prominent ironmaster in Sussex and one of the wealthiest planters in Jamaica. In 1766 he had been an active member of the committee of West India merchants and planters and had worked closely with the North American committee. He had been on good terms with the Rockinghams while his friend the Duke of Newcastle (Thomas Pelham-Holles, 1st Duke, 1693–1768) had been active but before the latter's death in 1768 he appears to have become a Government supporter except on the subject of America.

who, in the year 1766, filled the chair of the American committee with much ability, took me aside; and, lamenting the present aspect of our politicks, told me, things were come to such a pass, that our former methods of proceeding in the house would be no longer tolerated. That the public tribunal (never too indulgent to a long and unsuccessful opposition) would now scrutinize our conduct with unusual severity. That the very vicissitudes and shiftings of ministerial measures, instead of convicting their authors of inconstancy and want of system, would be taken as an occasion of charging us with a predetermined discontent, which nothing could satisfy; whilst we accused every measure of vigour as cruel, and every proposal of lenity as weak and irresolute. The publick, he said, would not have patience to see us play the game out with our adversaries: we must produce our hand. It would be expected, that those who for many years had been active in such affairs should shew, that they had formed some clear and decided idea of the principles of Colony Government; and were capable of drawing out something like a platform of the ground, which might be laid for future and permanent tranquillity.[1]

I felt the truth of what my Hon. Friend represented; but I felt my situation too. His application might have been made with far greater propriety to many other gentlemen. No man was indeed ever better disposed, or worse qualified, for such an undertaking than myself. Though I gave so far into his opinion, that I immediately threw my thoughts into a sort of parliamentary form, I was by no means equally ready to produce them. It generally argues some degree of natural impotence of mind, or some want of knowledge of the world, to hazard Plans of Government, except from a seat of Authority. Propositions are made, not only ineffectually, but somewhat disreputably, when the minds of men are not properly disposed for their reception; and for my part, I am not ambitious of ridicule; not absolutely a candidate for disgrace.

Besides, Sir, to speak the plain truth, I have in general no very exalted opinion of the virtue of Paper Government; nor of any Politicks, in which the plan is to be wholly separated from the execution. But when I saw, that anger and violence prevailed every day more and more; and that things were hastening towards an incurable alienation of our Colonies; I confess, my caution gave way. I felt this,

---

[1] Burke had been attacking the North Government since its inception for failing to establish a clear American policy. See, for instance, his speech in the House of Commons on 9 May 1770 (vol. ii, pp. 323–34).

as one of those few moments in which decorum yields to an higher duty. Public calamity is a mighty leveller; and there are occasions when any, even the slightest, chance of doing good, must be laid hold on, even by the most inconsiderable person.

To restore order and repose to an Empire so great and so distracted as ours, is, merely in the attempt, an undertaking that would ennoble the flights of the highest genius, and obtain pardon for the efforts of the meanest understanding. Struggling a good while with these thoughts, by degrees I felt myself more firm. I derived, at length, some confidence from what in other circumstances usually produces timidity. I grew less anxious, even from the idea of my own insignificance. For, judging of what you are, by what you ought to be, I persuaded myself, that you would not reject a reasonable proposition, because it had nothing but its reason to recommend it. On the other hand, being totally destitute of all shadow of influence, natural or adventitious, I was very sure, that, if my proposition were futile or dangerous; if it were weakly conceived, or improperly timed, there was nothing exterior to it, of power to awe, dazzle, or delude you. You will see it just as it is; and you will treat it just as it deserves.

The proposition is Peace. Not Peace through the medium of War; not Peace to be hunted through the labyrinth of intricate and endless negociations; not Peace to arise out of universal discord, fomented, from principle, in all parts of the Empire; not Peace to depend on the Juridical Determination of perplexing questions; or the precise marking the shadowy boundaries of a complex Government. It is simple Peace; sought in its natural course, and its ordinary haunts.—It is Peace sought in the Spirit of Peace; and laid in principles purely pacific.[1] I propose, by removing the Ground of the difference, and by restoring the *former unsuspecting confidence of the Colonies in the Mother Country*,[2] to give permanent satisfaction to your people; and (far from a scheme of ruling by discord) to reconcile them to each other in the

---

[1] Josiah Tucker (1712–99), Dean of Gloucester, commented: 'What a pompous description is here! ... For after all, what is this Heaven-born pacific Scheme, of which we have heard so laboured an Encomium? Why truly; if we will grant the colonies all that they shall require, and stipulate for nothing in Return; then they will be at Peace with us. I believe it; and on these simple Principles of simple peace-making I will engage to terminate every Difference throughout the World' (*A Letter to Edmund Burke*, Gloucester, 1775, p. 73).

[2] Burke in his *Letter to the Sheriffs of Bristol* on 3 April 1777 would attribute this phrase to the Continental Congress (below, p. 321).

same act, and by the bond of the very same interest, which reconciles them to British Government.

My idea is nothing more. Refined policy ever has been the parent of confusion; and ever will be so, as long as the world endures. Plain good intention, which is as easily discovered at the first view, as fraud is surely detected at last, is, let me say, of no mean force in the Government of Mankind. Genuine Simplicity of heart is an healing and cementing principle. My Plan, therefore, being formed upon the most simple grounds imaginable, may disappoint some people, when they hear it. It has nothing to recommend it to the pruriency of curious ears. There is nothing at all new and captivating in it. It has nothing of the Splendor of the Project, which has been lately laid upon your Table by the Noble Lord in the Blue Ribband.* It does not propose to fill your Lobby with squabbling Colony Agents, who will require the interposition of your Mace, at every instant, to keep the peace amongst them. It does not institute a magnificent Auction of Finance, where captivated provinces come to general ransom by bidding against each other, until you knock down the hammer, and determine a proportion of payments, beyond all the powers of Algebra to equalize and settle.

The plan, which I shall presume to suggest, derives, however, one great advantage from the proposition and registry of that Noble Lord's Project. The idea of conciliation is admissible. First, the House, in accepting the resolution moved by the Noble Lord, has admitted, notwithstanding the menacing front of our Address,[1] notwithstanding our heavy Bill of Pains and Penalties—that we do not think ourselves precluded from all ideas of free Grace and Bounty.

The House has gone farther; it has declared conciliation admissible,

---

* "That when the Governor, Council, or Assembly, or General Court, of any of his Majesty's Provinces or Colonies in America, shall *propose* to make provision, *according to the condition, circumstances*, and *situation*, of such Province or Colony, for contributing their *proportion* to the *Common Defence* (such *proportion* to be raised under the Authority of the General Court, or General Assembly, of such Province or Colony, and disposable by Parliament) and shall *engage* to make Provision also for the Support of the Civil Government, and the Administration of Justice, in such Province or Colony, it will be proper, *if such Proposal shall be approved by his Majesty, and the two Houses of Parliament*, and for so long as such Provision shall be made accordingly, to forbear, *in respect of such Province or Colony*, to levy any Duty, Tax, or Assessment, or to impose any farther Duty, Tax, or Assessment, except such Duties as it may be expedient to continue to levy or impose, for the Regulation of Commerce; the Nett Produce of the Duties last mentioned to be carried to the account of such Province or Colony respectively." Resolution moved by Lord North in the Committee; and agreed to by the House, 27 Feb. 1775.

[1] Agreed to on 7 February and presented to the King by both Houses (*Parl. Hist.* xviii. 297–8).

previous to any submission on the part of America. It has even shot a
good deal beyond that mark, and has admitted, that the complaints of
our former mode of exerting the Right of Taxation were not wholly
unfounded. That right thus exerted is allowed to have had something
reprehensible in it; something unwise, or something grievous: since, in
the midst of our heat and resentment, we, of ourselves, have proposed
a capital alteration; and, in order to get rid of what seemed so very
exceptionable, have instituted a mode that is altogether new; one that
is, indeed, wholly alien from all the ancient methods and forms of
Parliament.[1]

The *principle* of this proceeding is large enough for my purpose.
The means proposed by the Noble Lord for carrying his ideas into
execution, I think indeed, are very indifferently suited to the end; and
this I shall endeavour to shew you before I sit down. But, for the
present, I take my ground on the admitted principle. I mean to give
peace. Peace implies reconciliation; and where there has been a
material dispute, reconciliation does in a manner always imply concession on the one part or on the other. In this state of things I make
no difficulty in affirming, that the proposal ought to originate from us.
Great and acknowledged force is not impaired, either in effect or in
opinion, by an unwillingness to exert itself. The superior power may
offer peace with honour and with safety. Such an offer from such a
power will be attributed to magnanimity. But the concessions of the
weak are the concessions of fear. When such a one is disarmed, he is
wholly at the mercy of his superior; and he loses for ever that time and
those chances, which, as they happen to all men, are the strength and
resources of all inferior power.

The capital leading questions on which you must this day decide,
are these two. First, whether you ought to concede; and secondly, what
your concession ought to be. On the first of these questions we have
gained (as I have just taken the liberty of observing to you) some
ground. But I am sensible that a good deal more is still to be done.
Indeed, Sir, to enable us to determine both on the one and the other of
these great questions with a firm and precise judgement, I think it may
be necessary to consider distinctly the true nature and the peculiar
circumstances of the object which we have before us. Because after

[1] Burke is referring here to the resolution North got passed through the House as part of his
own conciliatory plan on 27 February 1775; see Burke's speech of 20 February 1775, above, p.
86.

all our struggle, whether we will or not, we must govern America, according to that nature, and to those circumstances; and not according to our own imaginations; not according to abstract ideas of right; by no means according to mere general theories of government, the resort to which appears to me, in our present situation, no better than arrant trifling. I shall therefore endeavour, with your leave, to lay before you some of the most material of these circumstances in as full and as clear a manner as I am able to state them.

The first thing that we have to consider with regard to the nature of the object is—the number of people in the Colonies. I have taken for some years a good deal of pains on that point. I can by no calculation justify myself in placing the number below Two Millions of inhabitants of our own European blood and colour; besides at least 500,000 others, who form no inconsiderable part of the strength and opulence of the whole. This, Sir, is, I believe, about the true number.[1] There is no occasion to exaggerate, where plain truth is of so much weight and importance. But whether I put the present numbers too high or too low, is a matter of little moment. Such is the strength with which population shoots in that part of the world, that state the numbers as high as we will, whilst the dispute continues, the exaggeration ends. Whilst we are discussing any given magnitude, they are grown to it. Whilst we spend our time in deliberating on the mode of governing Two Millions, we shall find we have Millions more to manage. Your children do not grow faster from infancy to manhood, than they spread from families to communities, and from villages to nations.

I put this consideration of the present and the growing numbers in the front of our deliberation; because, Sir, this consideration will make it evident to a blunter discernment than yours, that no partial, narrow, contracted, pinched, occasional system will be at all suitable to such an object. It will shew you, that it is not to be considered as one of those *Minima*[2] which are out of the eye and consideration of the law; not a paltry excrescence of the state; not a mean dependant, who may be neglected with little damage, and provoked with little danger. It will prove, that some degree of care and caution is required in the handling such an object; it will shew, that you ought not, in reason, to trifle with so large a mass of the interests and feelings of the human race. You

---

[1] Burke's estimates are roughly in line with modern calculations.
[2] The legal maxim and a favourite of Burke's: 'De minimis non curat lex', 'The law takes no account of very trifling matters.'

could at no time do so without guilt; and be assured you will not be able to do it long with impunity.

But the population of this country, the great and growing population, though a very important consideration, will lose much of its weight, if not combined with other circumstances. The commerce of your Colonies is out of all proportion beyond the numbers of the people. This ground of their commerce indeed has been trod some days ago, and with great ability, by a distinguished person,[1] at your bar.[2] This gentleman, after Thirty-five years[3]—it is so long since he first appeared at the same place to plead for the commerce of Great Britain—has come again before you to plead the same cause, without any other effect of time, than, that to the fire of imagination and extent of erudition, which even then marked him as one of the first literary characters of his age, he has added a consummate knowledge in the commercial interest of his country, formed by a long course of enlightened and discriminating experience.

Sir, I should be inexcusable in coming after such a person with any detail; if a great part of the members who now fill the House had not the misfortune to be absent, when he appeared at your bar. Besides, Sir, I propose to take the matter at periods of time somewhat different from his. There is, if I mistake not, a point of view, from whence if you will look at this subject, it is impossible that it should not make an impression upon you.

I have in my hand two accounts; one a comparative state of the export trade of England to its Colonies, as it stood in the year 1704, and as it stood in the year 1772. The other a state of the export trade of this country to its Colonies alone, as it stood in 1772, compared with the whole trade of England to all parts of the world (the Colonies included) in the year 1704. They are from good vouchers; the latter period from the accounts on your table,[4] the earlier from an original manuscript of Davenant,[5] who first established the Inspector General's office,[6] which has been ever since his time so abundant a source of parliamentary information.

---

[1] Richard Glover (1712–85). He was well known as a poet as well as a merchant.
[2] He had summed up the evidence on 16 March (*Parl. Hist.* xviii. 461–78).
[3] Strictly speaking after thirty-three years. He had appeared at the Bar on 2 March 1742.
[4] Reviewed by the House on 18 May 1774 (*Parl. Hist.* xvii. 1330).
[5] Charles Davenant (1656–1714). The MS. referred to appears to be in the MSS. at Sheffield (R.61.25).
[6] He was in fact the second Inspector-General, appointed in 1705, and had nothing to do with the creation of the office.

The export trade to the Colonies consists of three great branches. The African, which, terminating almost wholly in the Colonies,[1] must be put to the account of their commerce; the West Indian; and the North American. All these are so interwoven, that the attempt to separate them, would tear to pieces the contexture of the whole; and if not entirely destroy, would very much depreciate, the value of all the parts. I therefore consider these three denominations to be, what in effect they are, one trade.

The trade to the Colonies taken on the export side, at the beginning of this century, that is, in the year 1704, stood thus:

Exports

To North America, and the West Indies,	£483,265
To Africa,	86,665
	569,930

In the year 1772,[2] which I take as a middle year between the highest and lowest of those lately laid on your table, the account was as follows:

To North America, and the West Indies,	£4,791,734
To Africa,	866,398
To which if you add the export trade from Scotland, which had in 1704 no existence,[3]	364,000
	6,022,132[4]

From Five Hundred and odd Thousand, it has grown to Six Millions. It has increased no less than twelve-fold. This is the state of the Colony trade, as compared with itself at these two periods, within this century;—and this is matter for meditation. But this is not all. Examine my second account. See how the export trade to the Colonies

---

[1] i.e. the slave trade.

[2] In the Dodsley edition of the speech the year is given as '1722'. However, the trade figures quoted make it clear that Burke is referring to 1772.

[3] i.e. no legal existence before the union between England and Scotland in 1707; its actual existence was one of the forces which led to that union.

[4] Sir C. Whitworth, *State of the Trade of Great Britain in its Imports and Exports, Progressively, from the Year 1697*, London, 1776, pp. lxiii–lxiv, puts the total figure for North America and the West Indies at just over £4,791,750. Whitworth's figure, however, includes the exports from Scotland and, therefore, it indicates a lower total than Burke's figure. The discrepancy appears in part to be the result of the fact that Burke's figure for Scotland includes exports to the foreign West Indies as well as the British West Indies.

alone in 1772 stood in the other point of view, that is, as compared to the whole trade of England in 1704.

The whole export trade of England, including ⎫
    that to the Colonies, in 1704,   ⎬   £6,509,000[1]
Export to the Colonies alone, in 1772,   6,022,132

Difference,   487,868[2]

The trade with America alone is now within less than 500,000*l.* of being equal to what this great commercial nation, England, carried on at the beginning of this century with the whole world! If I had taken the largest year of those on your table, it would rather have exceeded. But, it will be said, is not this American trade an unnatural protuberance, that has drawn the juices from the rest of the body? The reverse. It is the very food that has nourished every other part into its present magnitude. Our general trade has been greatly augmented; and augmented more or less in almost every part to which it ever extended; but with this material difference; that of the Six Millions which in the beginning of the century constituted the whole mass of our export commerce, the Colony trade was but one twelfth part; it is now (as a part of Sixteen Millions) considerably more than a third of the whole. This is the relative proportion of the importance of the Colonies at these two periods: and all reasoning concerning our mode of treating them must have this proportion as its basis; or it is a reasoning weak, rotten, and sophistical.

Mr. Speaker, I cannot prevail on myself to hurry over this great consideration. It is good for us to be here.[3] We stand where we have an immense view of what is, and what is past. Clouds indeed, and darkness, rest upon the future.[4] Let us however, before we descend from this noble eminence, reflect that this growth of our national prosperity has happened within the short period of the life of man. It has happened within Sixty-eight years. There are those alive whose memory might touch the two extremities. For instance, my Lord

---

[1] Given in the MS. as 6,552,019.18.4, and also in Burke's *Observations on a Late State of the Nation* (vol. ii, p. 143). It is also the figure given by Whitworth.

[2] This figure is incorrect. The difference is actually 486,868.

[3] Mark 9: 5.

[4] 'The wide, th'unbounded prospect lies before me, But shadows, clouds, and darkness rest upon me' (Addison, *Cato*, v. i. 13–14).

Bathurst[1] might remember all the stages of the progress. He was in 1704 of an age, at least to be made to comprehend such things. He was then old enough *acta parentum jam legere, et quæ sit poterit cognoscere virtus*[2]—Suppose, Sir, that the angel of this auspicious youth, fore-seeing the many virtues, which made him one of the most amiable, as he is one of the most fortunate men of his age, had opened to him in vision, that, when, in the fourth generation,[3] the third Prince of the House of Brunswick had sat Twelve years on the throne of that nation, which (by the happy issue of moderate and healing councils) was to be made Great Britain, he should see his son, Lord Chancellor of England, turn back the current of hereditary dignity to its fountain, and raise him to an higher rank of Peerage, whilst he enriched the family with a new one[4]—If amidst these bright and happy scenes of domestic honour and prosperity, that angel should have drawn up the curtain, and unfolded the rising glories of his country, and whilst he was gazing with admiration on the then commercial grandeur of England, The Genius should point out to him a little speck, scarce visible in the mass of the national interest, a small seminal principle, rather than a formed body, and should tell him—"Young man, There is America—which at this day serves for little more than to amuse you with stories of savage men, and uncouth manners; yet shall, before you taste of death,[5] shew itself equal to the whole of that commerce which now attracts the envy of the world. Whatever England has been growing to by a progressive increase of improvement, brought in by varieties of people, by succession of civilizing conquest and civilizing settlements in a series of Seventeen Hundred years, you shall see as much added to her by America in the course of a single life!" If this state of his country had been foretold to him, would it not require all the sanguine credulity of

[1] Allen Bathurst, 1st Earl Bathurst (1684–1775) was a close friend of Lord North. He had been made an Earl in 1772 and enjoyed a pension of £2,000 per year. He was known for his Tory principles. He had been a regular critic of Sir Robert Walpole and had been made a privy councillor upon Walpole's fall. The Bathursts were a long-lived family. Bathurst's grandfather had been born in 1529 and his son Baron Apsley (see n. 4 below) was in the North ministry.

[2] 'He was able to examine the deeds of his ancestors and learn what virtue is'; Virgil, *Eclogues*, iv. 26–7.

[3] George III was the grandson of George II.

[4] Bathurst's son, Henry Bathurst (1714–94), was created Baron Apsley in 1771 when he became Lord Chancellor. In 1775 he succeeded his father as 2nd Earl Bathurst. Burke is making a direct dig at the Tories whom he is shrewdly insinuating had done very well by the Brunswick line which of course they were known originally to have opposed.

[5] e.g. Matt. 16: 28.

youth, and all the fervid glow of enthusiasm, to make him believe it? Fortunate man, he has lived to see it! Fortunate indeed, if he lives to see nothing that shall vary the prospect, and cloud the setting of his day![1]

Excuse me, Sir, if turning from such thoughts I resume this comparative view once more. You have seen it on a large scale; look at it on a small one. I will point out to your attention a particular instance of it in the single province of Pensylvania. In the year 1704 that province called for 11,459*l.* in value of your commodities, native and foreign. This was the whole. What did it demand in 1772? Why nearly Fifty times as much; for in that year the export to Pensylvania was 507,909*l.* nearly equal to the export to all the Colonies together in the first period.

I choose, Sir, to enter into these minute and particular details; because generalities, which in all other cases are apt to heighten and raise the subject, have here a tendency to sink it. When we speak of the commerce with our Colonies, fiction lags after truth; invention is unfruitful, and imagination cold and barren.

So far, Sir, as to the importance of the object in the view of its commerce, as concerned in the exports from England. If I were to detail the imports, I could shew how many enjoyments they procure, which deceive the burthen of life; how many materials which invigorate the springs of national industry, and extend and animate every part of our foreign and domestic commerce. This would be a curious subject indeed—but I must prescribe bounds to myself in a matter so vast and various.

I pass therefore to the Colonies in another point of view, their

---

[1] Hester Thrale, née Lynch (1741–1823), praised this passage to Dr. Samuel Johnson, (1709–84). Johnson said he would have answered it as follows: 'Suppose Mr. Speaker, that to Wharton or Marlborough, or some of the most eminent Whigs in the last Age—the Devil had—not with any great Impropriety consented to appear, he would perhaps in these words have commenced the Conversation.

"You seem my Lord to be concerned at the judicious Apprehension, that while you are sapping the Foundations of Royalty, and Propagating the Doctrines of Resistance here at home, the distance of America may secure its Inhabitants from your Arts though active; but I will unfold to you the gay Prospects of Futurity: the People now so innocent, so harmless, shall draw their Sword upon their Mother Country and brake its Point in the blood of their Benefactors: this people now contented with a little; shall then refuse to spare what they themselves they could not miss; and these Men, now so honest and so grateful shall in return for Peace and for Protection *see their vile* Agents in the house of Parliament, there to sow the seeds of Sedition, and propagate Confusion Perplexity and Pain. Be not dispirited then at the Contemplation of their present happy state; I promise you that Anarchy Poverty and Death shall carry even across the spacious Atlantick—and settle even in America the consequences of Whiggism"' (*Thraliana*, ed. K. C. Balderson, 2 vols., Oxford, 1942, i. 194).

agriculture. This they have prosecuted with such a spirit, that, besides feeding plentifully their own growing multitude, their annual export of grain, comprehending rice, has some years ago exceeded a Million in value. Of their last harvest, I am persuaded, they will export much more. At the beginning of the century, some of these Colonies imported corn from the mother country. For some time past, the old world has been fed from the new. The scarcity which you have felt would have been a desolating famine; if this child of your old age, with a true filial piety, with a Roman charity,[1] had not put the full breast of its youthful exuberance to the mouth of its exhausted parent.[2]

As to the wealth which the Colonies have drawn from the sea by their fisheries, you had all that matter fully opened at your bar.[3] You surely thought those acquisitions of value; for they seemed even to excite your envy; and yet the spirit, by which that enterprizing employment has been exercised, ought rather, in my opinion, to have raised your esteem and admiration. And pray, Sir, what in the world is equal to it? Pass by the other parts, and look at the manner in which the people of New England have of late carried on the Whale Fishery. Whilst we follow them among the tumbling mountains of ice, and behold them penetrating into the deepest frozen recesses of Hudson's Bay, and Davis's Streights, whilst we are looking for them beneath the Arctic circle, we hear that they have pierced into the opposite region of polar cold, that they are at the Antipodes, and engaged under the frozen serpent of the south.[4] Falkland Island, which seemed too remote and romantic an object for the grasp of national ambition,[5] is but a stage and resting place in the progress of their victorious industry. Nor is the equinoctial heat more discouraging to them, than the accumulated winter of both the poles. We know that whilst some of them draw the line and strike the harpoon on the coast of Africa, others run the longitude, and pursue their gigantic game along the coast of Brazil. No

[1] A reference to the story of Xanthippe and Cimon as told by Hyginus (*Fabulae*, cliv).

[2] It was in this period that Britain became an importer of grain. British imports increased from a trickle in the 1730s to over 50,000 quarters in 1754 to over 1,000,000 quarters in 1775 (E. B. Schumpeter, *English Overseas Trade Statistics, 1697–1808*, Oxford, 1960, pp. 54–7).

[3] On 28 February (*Parl. Reg.* i. 257–79).

[4] Burke is referring to Hydrus, which in astronomy is the water serpent, a small southern constellation far to the south within the Antarctic between Eridanus and Octans.

[5] A British expedition had been sent to the Falkland Islands by the Rockingham Administration in 1765. The resulting settlement had been expelled by the Spanish authorities. The North administration successfully negotiated the restoration of the settlement, but there was probably a secret promise to withdraw (J. Goebel, *The Struggle for the Falkland Islands: A Study in Legal and Diplomatic History*, New Haven, 1927, pp. 274–407). Withdrawal took place in 1774.

sea but what is vexed by their fisheries. No climate that is not witness to their toils.[1] Neither the perseverance of Holland, nor the activity of France, nor the dextrous and firm sagacity of English enterprize, ever carried this most perilous mode of hardy industry to the extent to which it has been pushed by this recent people;[2] a people who are still, as it were, but in the gristle, and not yet hardened into the bone of manhood. When I contemplate these things; when I know that the Colonies in general owe little or nothing to any care of ours, and that they are not squeezed into this happy form by the constraints of watchful and suspicious government, but that through a wise and salutary neglect, a generous nature has been suffered to take her own way to perfection: when I reflect upon these effects, when I see how profitable they have been to us, I feel all the pride of power sink, and all presumption in the wisdom of human contrivances melt, and die away within me. My rigour relents. I pardon something to the spirit of Liberty.

I am sensible, Sir, that all which I have asserted in my detail, is admitted in the gross; but that quite a different conclusion is drawn from it. America, Gentlemen say, is a noble object. It is an object well worth fighting for. Certainly it is, if fighting a people be the best way of gaining them. Gentlemen in this respect will be led to their choice of means by their complexions and their habits. Those who understand the military art, will of course have some predilection for it. Those who wield the thunder of the state, may have more confidence in the efficacy of arms. But I confess, possibly for want of this knowledge, my opinion is much more in favour of prudent management, than of force; considering force not as an odious, but a feeble instrument, for preserving a people so numerous, so active, so growing, so spirited as this, in a profitable and subordinate connexion with us.

First, Sir, permit me to observe, that the use of force alone is but

---

[1] A Virgilian echo: 'Quae regro in terris nostris non plena laboris' (*Aeneid*, i. 460).

[2] In the eighteenth century the position of the whaling industry was as follows: Davis Strait was reached in 1732, Baffin Bay in 1751, Hudson's Bay in 1761, Guinea in 1763, the Western and Cape Verde Islands, the West Indies, and Caribbean Sea by 1765, and the Coast of Brazil in 1774. Just prior to the Revolution the colonial whaling fleet, of which just under half operated out of Nantucket, numbered some 360 vessels employing 4,700 men and producing 45,000 barrels of sperm oil, 8,500 barrels of whale oil, and 75,000 tons of whale bone annually. This produce was worth some £300,000 sterling. During the American war virtually the entire industry was destroyed (E. P. Hohman, *The American Whalemen*, Clifton, 1972, pp. 23–35).

temporary. It may subdue for a moment; but it does not remove the necessity of subduing again: and a nation is not governed, which is perpetually to be conquered.

My next objection is its *uncertainty*. Terror is not always the effect of force; and an armament is not a victory. If you do not succeed, you are without resource; for, conciliation failing, force remains; but, force failing, no further hope of reconciliation is left. Power and authority are sometimes bought by kindness; but they can never be begged as alms, by an impoverished and defeated violence.

A further objection to force is, that you *impair the object* by your very endeavours to preserve it. The thing you fought for, is not the thing which you recover; but depreciated, sunk, wasted, and consumed in the contest. Nothing less will content me, than *whole America*. I do not choose to consume its strength along with our own; because in all parts it is the British strength that I consume. I do not choose to be caught by a foreign enemy at the end of this exhausting conflict; and still less in the midst of it. I may escape; but I can make no insurance against such an event. Let me add, that I do not choose wholly to break the American spirit, because it is the spirit that has made the country.

Lastly, we have no sort of *experience* in favour of force as an instrument in the rule of our Colonies. Their growth and their utility has been owing to methods altogether different. Our ancient indulgence has been said to be pursued to a fault. It may be so. But we know, if feeling is evidence, that our fault was more tolerable than our attempt to mend it; and our sin far more salutary than our penitence.

These, Sir, are my reasons for not entertaining that high opinion of untried force, by which many Gentlemen, for whose sentiments in other particulars I have great respect, seem to be so greatly captivated. But there is still behind a third consideration concerning this object, which serves to determine my opinion on the sort of policy which ought to be pursued in the management of America, even more than its Population and its Commerce, I mean its *Temper and Character*.

In this Character of the Americans, a love of Freedom is the predominating feature, which marks and distinguishes the whole: and as an ardent is always a jealous affection, your Colonies become suspicious, restive, and untractable, whenever they see the least attempt to wrest from them by force, or shuffle from them by chicane, what they think the only advantage worth living for. This fierce spirit of Liberty is stronger in the English Colonies probably than in any other people of the earth; and this from a great variety of powerful causes; which, to understand the true temper of their minds, and the direction which this spirit takes, it will not be amiss to lay open somewhat more largely.

First, the people of the Colonies are descendents of Englishmen.[1] England, Sir, is a nation, which still I hope respects, and formerly adored, her freedom. The Colonists emigrated from you, when this part of your character was most predominant; and they took this biass and direction the moment they parted from your hands. They are therefore not only devoted to Liberty, but to Liberty according to English ideas, and on English principles. Abstract Liberty, like other mere abstractions, is not to be found. Liberty inheres in some sensible object; and every nation has formed to itself some favourite point, which by way of eminence becomes the criterion of their happiness. It happened, you know, Sir, that the great contests for freedom in this country were from the earliest times chiefly upon the question of Taxing. Most of the contests in the ancient commonwealths turned primarily on the right of election of magistrates; or on the balance among the several orders of the state. The question of money was not with them so immediate. But in England it was otherwise. On this point of Taxes the ablest pens, and most eloquent tongues, have been exercised; the greatest spirits have acted and suffered. In order to give the fullest satisfaction concerning the importance of this point, it was not only necessary for those who in argument defended the excellence of the English constitution, to insist on this privilege of granting money as a dry point of fact, and to prove, that the right had been acknowledged in ancient parchments, and blind usages, to reside in a certain body called an House of Commons. They went much further; they attempted to prove, and they succeeded, that in theory it ought to be so, from the particular nature of a House of Commons, as an immediate representative of the people; whether the old records had delivered this oracle or not. They took infinite pains to inculcate, as a fundamental principle, that, in all monarchies, the people must in effect themselves mediately or immediately possess the power of granting their own money, or no shadow of liberty could subsist. The

---

[1] In 1790, 60.9% of the colonists were of English descent, 8.3% were Scottish, and 9.7 were Irish (*Historical Statistics of the United States, Colonial Times to 1970*, United States Bureau of Census, Washington, DC, 1975, pt. 2, p. 1168).

Colonies draw from you as with their life-blood, these ideas and principles. Their love of liberty, as with you, fixed and attached on this specific point of taxing. Liberty might be safe, or might be endangered in twenty other particulars, without their being much pleased or alarmed. Here they felt its pulse; and as they found that beat, they thought themselves sick or sound. I do not say whether they were right or wrong in applying your general arguments to their own case. It is not easy indeed to make a monopoly of theorems and corollaries. The fact is, that they did thus apply those general arguments; and your mode of governing them, whether through lenity or indolence, through wisdom or mistake, confirmed them in the imagination, that they, as well as you, had an interest in these common principles.

They were further confirmed in this pleasing error by the form of their provincial legislative assemblies. Their governments are popular in an high degree; some are merely popular; in all, the popular representative is the most weighty; and this share of the people in their ordinary government never fails to inspire them with lofty sentiments, and with a strong aversion from whatever tends to deprive them of their chief importance.

If any thing were wanting to this necessary operation of the form of government, Religion would have given it a complete effect. Religion, always a principle of energy in this new people, is no way worn out or impaired; and their mode of professing it is also one main cause of this free spirit. The people are protestants; and of that kind, which is the most adverse to all implicit submission of mind and opinion. This is a persuasion not only favourable to liberty, but built upon it. I do not think, Sir, that the reason of this averseness in the dissenting churches from all that looks like absolute Government is so much to be sought in their religious tenets, as in their history. Every one knows, that the Roman Catholick religion is at least coeval with most of the governments where it prevails; that it has generally gone hand in hand with them; and received great favour and every kind of support from authority. The Church of England too was formed from her cradle under the nursing care of regular government. But the dissenting interests have sprung up in direct opposition to all the ordinary powers of the world; and could justify that opposition only on a strong claim to natural liberty. Their very existence depended on the powerful and unremitted assertion of that claim. All protestantism, even the most cold and passive, is a sort of dissent. But the religion most prevalent in

121

our Northern Colonies[1] is a refinement on the principle of resistance; it is the dissidence of dissent; and the protestantism of the protestant religion. This religion, under a variety of denominations, agreeing in nothing but in the communion of the spirit of liberty, is predominant in most of the Northern provinces; where the Church of England, notwithstanding its legal rights, is in reality no more than a sort of private sect, not composing most probably the tenth of the people. The Colonists left England when this spirit was high; and in the emigrants was the highest of all: and even that stream of foreigners, which has been constantly flowing into these Colonies, has, for the greatest part, been composed of dissenters from the establishments of their several countries, and have brought with them a temper and character far from alien to that of the people with whom they mixed.

Sir, I can perceive by their manner, that some Gentlemen object to the latitude of this description; because in the Southern Colonies the Church of England forms a large body, and has a regular establishment. It is certainly true. There is however a circumstance attending these Colonies, which in my opinion, fully counterbalances this difference, and makes the spirit of liberty still more high and haughty than in those to the Northward. It is that in Virginia and the Carolinas, they have a vast multitude of slaves. Where this is the case in any part of the world, those who are free, are by far the most proud and jealous of their freedom. Freedom is to them not only an enjoyment, but a kind of rank and privilege. Not seeing there, that freedom, as in countries where it is a common blessing, and as broad and general as the air,[2] may be united with much abject toil, with great misery, with all the exterior of servitude, Liberty looks amongst them, like something that is more noble and liberal. I do not mean, Sir, to commend the superior morality of this sentiment, which has at least as much pride as virtue in it; but I cannot alter the nature of man. The fact is so; and these people of the Southern Colonies are much more strongly, and with an higher and more stubborn spirit, attached to liberty than those to the Northward. Such were all the ancient commonwealths; such were our Gothick ancestors; such in our days

---

[1] In 1761 a study had estimated the numbers in the major New England Faiths as follows: Episcopalians 12,600, Society of Friends 16,000, Baptists 22,000, Congregationalists 440,000; see E. Stiles, *A Discourse on the Christian Union*, Boston, 1761, cited in C. Bridenbaugh, *Mitre and Sceptre, Transatlantic Faiths, Ideas, Personalities and Politics, 1689–1775*, New York, 1962, p. 12.
[2] *Macbeth*, III. iv. 21.

were the Poles;[1] and such will be all masters of slaves, who are not slaves themselves. In such a people the haughtiness of domination combines with the spirit of freedom, fortifies it, and renders it invincible.[2]

Permit me, Sir, to add another circumstance in our Colonies, which contributes no mean part towards the growth and effect of this untractable spirit. I mean their education. In no country perhaps in the world is the law so general a study. The profession itself is numerous and powerful; and in most provinces it takes the lead. The greater number of the Deputies sent to the Congress were Lawyers.[3] But all who read, and most do read, endeavour to obtain some smattering in that science. I have been told by an eminent Bookseller,[4] that in no branch of his business, after tracts of popular devotion, were so many books as those on the Law exported to the Plantations. The Colonists have now fallen into the way of printing them for their own use. I hear that they have sold nearly as many of Blackstone's Commentaries in America as in England.[5] General Gage marks out this disposition very particularly in a letter on your table. He states, that all the people in his government are lawyers, or smatterers in law; and that in Boston they have been enabled, by successful chicane, wholly to evade many parts of one of your capital penal constitutions.[6] The smartness of debate

---

[1] i.e. before the Partition of 1772.

[2] Burke's analysis of the effects of slavery is famous and has been generally accepted. He may well have taken it from Andrew Burnaby, *Travels through the Middle Settlements in North America in the Years 1759 and 1760. With Observations upon the State of the Colonies.* This had been published in February 1775. Speaking of the Virginians, Burnaby wrote: 'Their authority over their slaves renders them vain and imperious... they are haughty and jealous of their liberties, impatient of restraint, and can scarcely bear the thought of being controlled by any superior power. Many of them consider the Colonies as independent states, unconnected with Great Britain, otherwise than by having the same common king, and being bound to her with natural affection' (pp. 18–20).

[3] Of the fifty-six men who signed the Declaration of Independence, twenty-five were lawyers; thirty-one of the fifty-five members of the Constitutional Convention in Philadelphia were lawyers; in the first Congress, ten of twenty-nine Senators and seventeen of sixty-five Representatives were lawyers (D. J. Boorstin, *The Americans: The Colonial Experience*, New York, 1958, p. 205). In Britain from 1734 to 1831 an average of 13.9% of the M.P.s were lawyers (i.e. barristers or solicitors) (D. Podmore, *Solicitors and the Wider Community*, London, 1980, p. 47).

[4] Not identified but probably James Dodsley (1724–97), Burke's publisher.

[5] The *Commentaries* of Sir William Blackstone (1723–80, M.P. 1761–70), were printed in Philadelphia in 1771–2. 'Nearly 2500 copies of Blackstone's *Commentaries* were absorbed by the colonies on the Atlantic seaboard before they declared their independence. James Kent (1763–1847), aged fifteen, found a copy, and (to use his own words) was "inspired with awe"; John Marshall (1755–1855) found a copy in his father's library; and the common law went straight to the Pacific' (F. W. Maitland, *Historical Essays*, ed. H. M. Cam, Cambridge, 1957, p. 147).

[6] General Gage explained in a letter of 27 August 1774, laid before the House on 19 January 1775, that the Town Meeting of Boston kept itself alive by adjournment. The new Council

will say, that this knowledge ought to teach them more clearly the rights of legislature, their obligations to obedience, and the penalties of rebellion. All this is mighty well. But my honourable and learned friend on the floor,* who condescends to mark what I say for animadversion, will disdain that ground. He has heard as well as I, that when great honours and great emoluments do not win over this knowledge to the service of the state, it is a formidable adversary to government. If the spirit be not tamed and broken by these happy methods, it is stubborn and litigious. *Abeunt studia in mores.*[1] This study renders men acute, inquisitive, dextrous, prompt in attack, ready in defence, full of resources. In other countries, the people, more simple and of a less mercurial cast, judge of an ill principle in government only by an actual grievance; here they anticipate the evil, and judge of the pressure of the grievance by the badness of the principle. They augur misgovernment at a distance; and snuff the approach of tyranny in every tainted breeze.

The last cause of this disobedient spirit in the Colonies is hardly less powerful than the rest, as it is not merely moral, but laid deep in the natural constitution of things. Three thousand miles of ocean lie between you and them. No contrivance can prevent the effect of this distance, in weakening Government. Seas roll, and months pass, between the order and the execution; and the want of a speedy explanation of a single point is enough to defeat an whole system. You have, indeed, winged ministers of vengeance,[2] who carry your bolts in their pounces to the remotest verge of the sea. But there a power steps in, that limits the arrogance of raging passions and furious elements, and says, "So far shalt thou go, and no farther."[3] Who are you, that

---

unwilling to give advice, terming the matter 'a point of law, which ought to be referred to the Crown lawyers' (*Parl. Reg.* i. 45). Similarly the Council avoided the question of the removal of sheriffs. Referring to the Opposition in general, Gage wrote: 'They chicane, elude, openly violate, or passively resent the laws, as opportunity serves' (ibid. 47).

* The Attorney General.[4]

[1] 'One's usual pursuits pass over into character' (Ovid, *Herodias*, xv. 53).

[2] *Paradise Lost*, i. 170; iii. 229.

[3] Burke is presumably referring to the version of David Hume of Canute and the waves. Hume in his turn was recalling Job 28: 11.

[4] Edward Thurlow (1731–1806), later (1778) 1st Baron Thurlow, M.P. 1765–78. The Attorney-General's speech in the ensuing debate, is not reported in any detail. He was 'strongly for the Right of the Supreme Legislature, and the Propriety and expedience of enforcing it. He asserted it was absurd and ridiculous to the last Degree to talk of the Right, and when the Right was disputed, not to assert it' (*St James's Chronicle*, 23–25 March 1775).

should fret and rage, and bite the chains of Nature?—Nothing worse happens to you, than does to all Nations, who have extensive Empire; and it happens in all the forms into which Empire can be thrown. In large bodies, the circulation of power must be less vigorous at the extremities. Nature has said it. The Turk cannot govern Ægypt, and Arabia, and Curdistan, as he governs Thrace; nor has he the same dominion in Crimea and Algiers, which he has at Brusa and Smyrna. Despotism itself is obliged to truck and huckster. The Sultan gets such obedience as he can. He governs with a loose rein, that he may govern at all; and the whole of the force and vigour of his authority in his centre, is derived from a prudent relaxation in all his borders. Spain, in her provinces, is, perhaps, not so well obeyed, as you are in yours. She complies too; she submits; she watches times. This is the immutable condition; the eternal Law, of extensive and detached Empire.

Then, Sir, from these six capital sources; of Descent; of Form of Government; of Religion in the Northern Provinces; of Manners in the Southern; of Education; of the Remoteness of Situation from the First Mover of Government, from all these causes a fierce Spirit of Liberty has grown up. It has grown with the growth of the people in your Colonies, and encreased with the encrease of their wealth; a Spirit, that unhappily meeting with an exercise of Power in England, which, however lawful, is not reconcileable to any ideas of Liberty, much less with theirs, has kindled this flame, that is ready to consume us.

I do not mean to commend either the Spirit in this excess, or the moral causes which produce it. Perhaps a more smooth and accommodating Spirit of Freedom in them would be more acceptable to us. Perhaps ideas of Liberty might be desired, more reconcileable with an arbitrary and boundless authority. Perhaps we might wish the Colonists to be persuaded, that their Liberty is more secure when held in trust for them by us (as their guardians during a perpetual minority) than with any part of it in their own hands. But the question is, not whether their spirit deserves praise or blame;—what, in the name of God, shall we do with it? You have before you the object; such as it is, with all its glories, with all its imperfections on its head.[1] You see the magnitude; the importance; the temper; the habits; the disorders. By all these considerations, we are strongly urged to determine something concerning it. We are called upon to fix some rule and line for our future conduct, which may give a little stability to our politics, and

[1] *Hamlet*, I. v. 79.

prevent the return of such unhappy deliberations as the present. Every such return will bring the matter before us in a still more untractable form. For, what astonishing and incredible things have we not seen already. What monsters have not been generated from this unnatural contention? Whilst every principle of authority and resistance has been pushed, upon both sides, as far as it would go, there is nothing so solid and certain, either in reasoning or in practice, that has not been shaken. Until very lately, all authority in America seemed to be nothing but an emanation from yours. Even the popular part of the Colony Constitution derived all its activity, and its first vital movement, from the pleasure of the Crown. We thought, Sir, that the utmost which the discontented Colonists could do, was to disturb authority; we never dreamt they could of themselves supply it; knowing in general what an operose business it is, to establish a Government absolutely new. But having, for our purposes in this contention, resolved, that none but an obedient Assembly should sit, the humours of the people there, finding all passage through the legal channel stopped, with great violence broke out another way.[1] Some provinces have tried their experiment, as we have tried ours; and theirs has succeeded. They have formed a Government sufficient for its purposes, without the bustle of a Revolution, or the troublesome formality of an Election. Evident necessity, and tacit consent, have done the business in an instant. So well they have done it, that Lord Dunmore (the account is among the fragments on your table) tells you, that the new institution is infinitely better obeyed than the antient Government ever was in its most fortunate periods.[2] Obedience is what makes Government, and not the names by which it is called: not the name of Governor, as formerly; or Committee, as at present. This new Government has originated directly from the people; and was not transmitted through any of the ordinary artificial media of a positive constitution. It was not a manufacture ready formed, and exported to them in that condition from England. The evil arising from hence is this; that the Colonists

[1] The Bill for Regulating the Government of Massachusetts Bay (14 Geo. III, c. 45) passed by the Commons on 2 May 1774, removed the appointment of Council from popular to royal control and strengthened the powers of the executive. This enabled the Governor to dissolve a disobedient assembly whenever he felt it was necessary and to operate for considerable periods without it; see vol. ii, p. 463.

[2] The letter dated 24 December of John Murray, 4th Earl of Dunmore (1732–1809), Governor of Virginia, was laid before the House on 15 February. In it he referred to the laws of Congress 'which they talk of in a stile of respect, and treat with marks of reverence, which they never bestowed on their legal government, or the laws proceeding from it' (*Parl. Reg.* i. 187).

having once found the possibility of enjoying the advantages of order, in the midst of a struggle for Liberty, such struggles will not henceforward seem so terrible to the settled and sober part of mankind, as they had appeared before the trial.

Pursuing the same plan (of punishing disorders by the denial of Government) to still greater lengths, we wholly abrogated the antient Government of Massachuset. We were confident, that the first feeling, if not the very prospect of anarchy, would instantly enforce a compleat submission. The experiment was tried. A new, strange, unexpected face of things appeared. Anarchy is found tolerable. A vast province has now subsisted, and subsisted in a considerable degree of health and vigour, for near a twelve-month, without Governor, without public Council, without Judges, without executive Magistrates. How long it will continue in this state, or what may arise out of this unheard-of situation, how can the wisest of us conjecture? Our late experience has taught us, that many of those fundamental principles, formerly believed infallible, are either not of the importance they were imagined to be; or that we have not at all adverted to some other far more important, and far more powerful principles, which entirely over-rule those we had considered as omnipotent. I am much against any further experiments, which tend to put to the proof any more of these allowed opinions, which contribute so much to the public tranquillity. In effect, we suffer as much at home, by this loosening of all ties, and this concussion of all established opinions, as we do abroad. For, in order to prove, that the Americans have no right to their Liberties, we are every day endeavouring to subvert the maxims, which preserve the whole Spirit of our own. To prove that the Americans ought not to be free, we are obliged to depreciate the value of Freedom itself; and we never seem to gain a paltry advantage over them in debate, without attacking some of those principles, or deriding some of those feelings, for which our ancestors have shed their blood.

But, Sir, in wishing to put an end to pernicious experiments, I do not mean to preclude the fullest enquiry. Far from it. Far from deciding on a sudden or partial view, I would patiently go round and round the subject, and survey it minutely in every possible aspect. Sir, if I were capable of engaging you to an equal attention, I would state, that, as far as I am capable of discerning, there are but three ways of proceeding relative to this stubborn Spirit, which prevails in your Colonies, and disturbs your Government. These are—To change that

Spirit, as inconvenient, by removing the Causes. To prosecute it as criminal. Or, to comply with it as necessary. I would not be guilty of an imperfect enumeration; I can think of but these three. Another has indeed been started, that of giving up the Colonies;[1] but it met so slight a reception, that I do not think myself obliged to dwell a great while upon it. It is nothing but a little sally of anger; like the frowardness of peevish children; who, when they cannot get all they would have, are resolved to take nothing.

The first of these plans, to change the Spirit as inconvenient, by removing the causes, I think is the most like a systematic proceeding. It is radical in its principle; but it is attended with great difficulties, some of them little short, as I conceive, of impossibilities. This will appear by examining into the Plans which have been proposed.

As the growing population in the Colonies is evidently one cause of their resistance, it was last session mentioned in both Houses, by men of weight, and received not without applause, that, in order to check this evil, it would be proper for the crown to make no further grants of land.[2] But to this scheme, there are two objections. The first, that there is already so much unsettled land in private hands, as to afford room for an immense future population, although the crown not only withheld its grants, but annihilated its soil. If this be the case, then the only effect of this avarice of desolation, this hoarding of a royal wilderness, would be to raise the value of the possessions in the hands of the great private monopolists, without any adequate check to the growing and alarming mischief of population.

But, if you stopped your grants, what would be the consequence? The people would occupy without grants. They have already so occupied in many places. You cannot station garrisons in every part of these deserts. If you drive the people from one place, they will carry on their annual Tillage, and remove with their flocks and herds to

[1] This was the view of Josiah Tucker (see above, p. 108). 'My scheme', he later wrote, '(which Mr. Burke, in his last Speech of *March* 22, 1775, is pleased to term a *childish* one) is,—To separate totally from the Colonies and to reject them from being Fellow-Members, and joint Partakers with us in the Privileges and Advantages of the *British* empire; because they refuse to submit to the Authority and Jurisdiction of the *British* Legislature—offering at the same Time to enter into Alliances of Friendship, and Treaties of Commerce with them, as with any other sovereign independent States' (*An Humble Address and Earnest Appeal*, Gloucester, 1775, p. 5).

[2] Burke had informed the New York Committee of Correspondence on 2 August 1774 that this view had been expressed (*Corr.* iii. 15). An order of the Privy Council had stipulated that the Crown would make no more grants of land (Bernard Bailyn, *Voyagers to the West*, Cambridge, Mass., 1991, pp. 55–6).

another. Many of the people in the back settlements are already little attached to particular situations. Already they have topped the Apalachian mountains. From thence they behold before them an immense plain, one vast, rich, level meadow; a square of five hundred miles. Over this they would wander, without a possibility of restraint; they would change their manners with the habits of their life; would soon forget a government, by which they were disowned; would become Hordes of English Tartars; and, pouring down upon your unfortified frontiers a fierce and irresistible cavalry, become masters of your Governors and your Counsellors, your collectors and comptrollers, and of all the Slaves that adhered to them. Such would, and, in no long time, must be, the effect of attempting to forbid as a crime, and to suppress as an evil, the Command and Blessing of Providence, "Encrease and Multiply."[1] Such would be the happy result of an endeavour to keep as a lair of wild beasts, that earth, which God, by an express Charter, has given to the children of men.[2] Far different, and surely much wiser, has been our policy hitherto. Hitherto we have invited our people by every kind of bounty, to fixed establishments. We have invited the husbandman, to look to authority for his title. We have taught him piously to believe in the mysterious virtue of wax and parchment. We have thrown each tract of land, as it was peopled, into districts; that the ruling power should never be wholly out of sight. We have settled all we could; and we have carefully attended every settlement with government.

Adhering, Sir, as I do, to this policy, as well as for the reasons I have just given, I think this new project of hedging-in population to be neither prudent nor practicable.

To impoverish the Colonies in general, and in particular to arrest the noble course of their marine enterprizes, would be a more easy task. I freely confess it. We have shewn a disposition to a system of this kind; a disposition even to continue the restraint after the offence; looking on ourselves as rivals to our Colonies, and persuaded that of course we must gain all that they shall lose. Much mischief we may certainly do. The power inadequate to all other things is often more than sufficient for this. I do not look on the direct and immediate power of the Colonies to resist our violence, as very formidable. In this however, I may be mistaken. But when I consider, that we have

---

[1] Gen. 1: 22 via *Paradise Lost*, ix. 730.   [2] Ps. 115: 16.

Colonies for no purpose but to be serviceable to us, it seems to my poor understanding a little preposterous, to make them unserviceable, in order to keep them obedient. It is, in truth, nothing more than the old, and, as I thought, exploded problem of tyranny, which proposes to beggar its subjects into submission. But, remember, when you have compleated your system of impoverishment, that Nature still proceeds in her ordinary course; that discontent will encrease with misery; and that there are critical moments in the fortune of all states, when they, who are too weak to contribute to your prosperity, may be strong enough to complete your ruin. *Spoliatis arma supersunt.*[1]

The temper and character which prevail in our Colonies, are, I am afraid, unalterable by any human art. We cannot, I fear, falsify the pedigree of this fierce people, and persuade them that they are not sprung from a nation, in whose veins the blood of freedom circulates. The language in which they would hear you tell them this tale, would detect the imposition; your speech would betray you.[2] An Englishman is the unfittest person on earth, to argue another Englishman into slavery.

I think it is nearly as little in our power to change their republican Religion, as their free descent; or to substitute the Roman Catholick, as a penalty; or the Church of England, as an improvement. The mode of inquisition and dragooning, is going out of fashion in the old world; and I should not confide much to their efficacy in the new. The education of the Americans is also on the same unalterable bottom with their religion. You cannot persuade them to burn their books of curious science;[3] to banish their lawyers from their courts of law; or to quench the lights of their assemblies, by refusing to choose those persons who are best read in their privileges. It would be no less impracticable to think of wholly annihilating the popular assemblies, in which these lawyers sit. The army, by which we must govern in their place, would be far more chargeable to us; not quite so effectual; and perhaps, in the end, full as difficult to be kept in obedience.

With regard to the high aristocratic spirit of Virginia and the Southern Colonies, it has been proposed, I know, to reduce it, by declaring a general enfranchisement of their slaves. This project has had its advocates and panegyrists; yet I never could argue myself into

---

[1] Juvenal, *Satires*, viii. 124: 'The robbed have recourse to arms.'
[2] Matt. 26: 73.   [3] Acts 19: 19.

any opinion of it.[1] Slaves are often much attached to their masters. A general wild offer of liberty, would not always be accepted. History furnishes few instances of it. It is sometimes as hard to persuade slaves to be free, as it is to compel freemen to be slaves; and in this auspicious scheme, we should have both these pleasing talks on our hands at once. But when we talk of enfranchisement do we not perceive that the American master may enfranchise too; and arm servile hands in defence of freedom? A measure to which other people have had recourse more than once, and not without success, in a desperate situation of their affairs.

Slaves as these unfortunate black people are, and dull as all men are from slavery, must they not a little suspect the offer of freedom from that very nation which has sold them to their present masters? From that nation, one of whose causes of quarrel with those masters, is their refusal to deal any more in that inhuman traffick?[2] An offer of freedom from England, would come rather oddly, shipped to them in an African vessel, which is refused an entry into the ports of Virginia or Carolina, with a cargo of three hundred Angola negroes.[3] It would be curious to see the Guinea captain attempting at the same instant to publish his proclamation of liberty, and to advertise his sale of slaves.

But let us suppose all these moral difficulties got over. The Ocean remains. You cannot pump this dry; and as long as it continues in its present bed, so long all the causes which weaken authority by distance will continue. "Ye gods, annihilate but space and time, and make two lovers happy!"[4]—was a pious and passionate prayer;—but just as reasonable, as many of the serious wishes of very grave and solemn politicians.

If then, Sir, it seems almost desperate to think of any alterative course, for changing the moral causes (and not quite easy to remove

---

[1] Lord Dunmore on 7 November 1775 proclaimed freedom to all slaves who should rally to his standard.

[2] Over the years, Virginia's laws restraining the importation of slaves through import duties had been disallowed by the Crown (A. Calder, *Revolutionary Empire: The Rise of the English Speaking Empires from the Fifteenth-Century to the 1780s*, London, 1981, pp. 503–4). In April 1772 the Virginia House of Burgesses petitioned the King against the slave trade, but without success (B. Fladeland, *Men and Brothers, Anglo-American Antislavery Cooperation*, Urbana, 1972, pp. 22, 25).

[3] The Articles of Association of the Continental Congress, adopted on 20 October 1774, prohibited the slave trade after 1 December 1774.

[4] From *Peri Bathous: or, Martinus Scriblerus his Treatise of the Art of Sinking in Poetry*—in fact principally the work of Alexander Pope. See *The Art of Sinking in Poetry*, ed. E. L. Steeves, New York, 1952, pp. 52, 155. The original source has not been found for these lines.

the natural), which produce prejudices irreconcileable to the late exercise of our authority; but that the spirit infallibly will continue; and, continuing, will produce such effects, as now embarrass us; the second mode under consideration is, to prosecute that spirit in its overt-acts, as *criminal*.

At this proposition, I must pause a moment. The thing seems a great deal too big for my ideas of jurisprudence. It should seem, to my way of conceiving such matters, that there is a very wide difference in reason and policy, between the mode of proceeding on the irregular conduct of scattered individuals, or even of bands of men, who disturb order within the state, and the civil dissensions which may, from time to time, on great questions, agitate the several communities which compose a great Empire. It looks to me to be narrow and pedantic, to apply the ordinary ideas of criminal justice to this great public contest. I do not know the method of drawing up an indictment against an whole people. I cannot insult and ridicule the feelings of Millions of my fellow-creatures, as Sir Edward Coke insulted one excellent individual (Sir Walter Raleigh) at the bar.[1] I am not ripe to pass sentence on the gravest public bodies, entrusted with magistracies of great authority and dignity, and charged with the safety of their fellow-citizens, upon the very same title that I am. I really think, that for wise men, this is not judicious; for sober men, not decent; for minds tinctured with humanity, not mild and merciful.

Perhaps, Sir, I am mistaken in my idea of an Empire, as distinguished from a single State or Kingdom. But my idea of it is this; that an Empire is the aggregate of many States, under one common head; whether this head be a monarch, or a presiding republick. It does, in such constitutions, frequently happen (and nothing but the dismal, cold, dead uniformity of servitude can prevent its happening) that the subordinate parts have many local privileges and immunities. Between these privileges, and the supreme common authority, the line may be extremely nice. Of course disputes, often too, very bitter disputes, and much ill blood, will arise. But though every privilege is an exemption (in the case) from the ordinary exercise of the supreme authority, it is no denial of it. The claim of a privilege seems rather, *ex vi termini*,[2] to imply a superior power. For to talk of the privileges of a

---

[1] Sir Edward Coke (1552–1634), as Attorney-General conducted the prosecution of Sir Walter Ralegh (1552–1618) in 1603 with notorious rancour.

[2] From the very meaning of the word.

State or of a person, who has no superior, is hardly any better than speaking nonsense. Now, in such unfortunate quarrels, among the component parts of a great political union of communities, I can scarcely conceive any thing more compleatly imprudent, than for the Head of the Empire to insist, that, if any privilege is pleaded against his will, or his acts, that his whole authority is denied;[1] instantly to proclaim rebellion, to beat to arms, and to put the offending provinces under the ban. Will not this, Sir, very soon teach the provinces to make no distinctions on their part? Will it not teach them that the Government, against which a claim of Liberty is tantamount to high-treason, is a Government to which submission is equivalent to slavery? It may not always be quite convenient to impress dependent communities with such an idea.

We are, indeed, in all disputes with the Colonies, by the necessity of things, the judge. It is true, Sir. But, I confess, that the character of judge in my own cause, is a thing that frightens me. Instead of filling me with pride, I am exceedingly humbled by it. I cannot proceed with a stern, assured, judicial confidence, until I find myself in something more like a judicial character. I must have these hesitations as long as I am compelled to recollect, that, in my little reading upon such contests as these, the sense of mankind has, at least, as often decided against the superior as the subordinate power. Sir, let me add too, that the opinion of my having some abstract right in my favour, would not put me much at my ease in passing sentence; unless I could be sure, that there were no rights which, in their exercise under certain circumstances, were not the most odious of all wrongs, and the most vexatious of all injustice. Sir, these considerations have great weight with me, when I find things so circumstanced; that I see the same party, at once a civil litigant against me in a point of right; and a culprit before me, while I sit as a criminal judge, on acts of his, whose moral

---

[1] Burke's views here compare interestingly with those he had expressed when helping Rockingham defeat the proposed Irish absentee tax in 1773 (*Corr.* ii. 474–5). At first glance the two views appear inconsistent for in the earlier issue he denied the right of 'subordinate' parts of the empire to special privileges while here he insists that the colonies must have them. On closer examination, however, it is evident that the inconsistency is more apparent than real. In the Irish absentee tax issue he had been concerned about the assumption by the subordinate states of the 'right to the imperial legislature ... that law which regulates the polity and economy of the several parts, as they relate to one another and to the whole.' This, he felt, should only be the domain of the mother country. Here, on the other hand, he was concerned about 'local privileges and immunities' which he clearly felt the colonies must be allowed if they were to be expected to stay within the empire.

quality is to be decided upon the merits of that very litigation. Men are every now and then put, by the complexity of human affairs, into strange situations; but Justice is the same, let the Judge be in what situation he will.

There is, Sir, also a circumstance which convinces me, that this mode of criminal proceeding is not (at least in the present stage of our contest) altogether expedient; which is nothing less than the conduct of those very persons who have seemed to adopt that mode, by lately declaring a rebellion in Massachuset's Bay,[1] as they had formerly addressed to have Traitors brought hither under an act of Henry the Eighth, for Trial.[2] For though rebellion is declared, it is not proceeded against as such; nor have any steps been taken towards the apprehension or conviction of any individual offender, either on our late or our former address; but modes of public coercion have been adopted, and such as have much more resemblance to a sort of qualified hostility towards an independant power than the punishment of rebellious subjects. All this seems rather inconsistent; but it shews how difficult it is to apply these juridical ideas to our present case.

In this situation, let us seriously and coolly ponder. What is it we have got by all our menaces, which have been many and ferocious? What advantage have we derived from the penal laws we have passed, and which, for the time, have been severe and numerous? What advances have we made towards our object, by the sending of a force, which, by land and sea, is no contemptible strength? Has the disorder abated? Nothing less.—When I see things in this situation, after such confident hopes, bold promises, and active exertions, I cannot, for my life, avoid a suspicion, that the plan itself is not correctly right.

If then the removal of the causes of this Spirit of American Liberty be, for the greater part, or rather entirely, impracticable; if the ideas of Criminal Process be inapplicable, or, if applicable, are in the highest degree inexpedient, what way yet remains? No way is open, but the third and last—to comply with the American Spirit as necessary; or, if you please, to submit to it, as a necessary Evil.

If we adopt this mode; if we mean to conciliate and concede; let us see of what nature the concession ought to be? To ascertain the nature of our concession, we must look at their complaint. The Colonies complain, that they have not the characteristic Mark and Seal of

---

[1] In the Address of 7 February; see Burke's speech of 20 February 1775, printed above.
[2] The Address presented on 13 February 1769. The statute is 35 Hen. VIII, c. 2.

British Freedom. They complain, that they are taxed in a Parliament, in which they are not represented. If you mean to satisfy them at all, you must satisfy them with regard to this complaint. If you mean to please any people, you must give them the boon which they ask; not what you may think better for them, but of a kind totally different. Such an act may be a wise regulation, but it is no concession: whereas our present theme is the mode of giving satisfaction.

Sir, I think you must perceive, that I am resolved this day to have nothing at all to do with the question of the right of taxation. Some gentlemen startle—but it is true: I put it totally out of the question. It is less than nothing in my consideration. I do not indeed wonder, nor will you, Sir, that gentlemen of profound learning are fond of displaying it on this profound subject. But my consideration is narrow, confined, and wholly limited to the Policy of the question. I do not examine, whether the giving away a man's money be a power excepted and reserved out of the general trust of Government; and how far all mankind, in all forms of Polity, are intitled to an exercise of that Right by the Charter of Nature. Or whether, on the contrary, a Right of Taxation is necessarily involved in the general principle of Legislation, and inseparable from the ordinary Supreme Power? These are deep questions, where great names militate against each other; where reason is perplexed; and an appeal to authorities only thickens the confusion. For high and reverend authorities lift up their heads on both sides; and there is no sure footing in the middle. This point is the *great Serbonian bog, betwixt Damiata and Mount Casius, old, where armies whole have sunk.*[1] I do not intend to be overwhelmed in that bog, though in such respectable company. The question with me is, not whether you have a right to render your people miserable; but whether it is not your interest to make them happy? It is not, what a lawyer tells me, I *may* do; but what humanity, reason, and justice, tell me, I ought to do. Is a politic act the worse for being a generous one? Is no concession proper, but that which is made from your want of right to keep what you grant? Or does it lessen the grace or dignity of relaxing in the exercise of an odious claim, because you have your evidence-room full of Titles, and your magazines stuffed with arms to enforce them? What signify all those titles, and all those arms? Of what avail are they, when the reason of the thing tells me, that the assertion of my title is the loss

---

[1] *Paradise Lost*, ii. 592–4.

of my suit; and that I could do nothing but wound myself by the use of my own weapons?

Such is stedfastly my opinion of the absolute necessity of keeping up the concord of this empire by a Unity of Spirit,[1] though in a diversity of operations, that, if I were sure the Colonists had, at their leaving this country, sealed a regular compact of servitude; that they had solemnly abjured all the rights of citizens; that they had made a vow to renounce all Ideas of Liberty for them and their posterity, to all generations; yet I should hold myself obliged to conform to the temper I found universally prevalent in my own day, and to govern two million of men, impatient of Servitude, on the principles of Freedom. I am not determining a point of law; I am restoring tranquillity; and the general character and situation of a people must determine what sort of government is fitted for them. That point nothing else can or ought to determine.

My idea therefore, without considering whether we yield as matter of right, or grant as matter of favour, is *to admit the people of our Colonies into an interest in the constitution*; and, by recording that admission in the Journals of Parliament, to give them as strong an assurance as the nature of the thing will admit, that we mean for ever to adhere to that solemn declaration of systematic indulgence.

Some years ago, the repeal of a revenue act, upon its understood principle, might have served to shew, that we intended an unconditional abatement of the exercise of a Taxing Power. Such a measure was then sufficient to remove all suspicion; and to give perfect content.[2] But unfortunate events, since that time, may make something further necessary; and not more necessary for the satisfaction of the Colonies, than for the dignity and consistency of our own future proceedings.

I have taken a very incorrect measure of the disposition of the House, if this proposal in itself would be received with dislike. I think, Sir, we have few American Financiers. But our misfortune is, we are too acute; we are too exquisite in our conjectures of the future, for men oppressed with such great and present evils. The more moderate among the opposers of Parliamentary Concession freely confess, that they hope no good from Taxation; but they apprehend the Colonists have further views; and if this point were conceded, they would instantly attack the Trade-laws. These Gentlemen are convinced, that this was the intention from the beginning; and the quarrel of the

---

[1] I Cor. 12: 4; Eph. 4: 3.   [2] The repeal of the Stamp Act.

Americans with Taxation was no more than a cloke and cover to this design. Such has been the language even of a Gentleman of real moderation,* and of a natural temper well adjusted to fair and equal Government. I am, however, Sir, not a little surprized at this kind of discourse, whenever I hear it; and I am the more surprized, on account of the arguments which I constantly find in company with it, and which are often urged from the same mouths, and on the same day.

For instance, when we alledge, that it is against reason to tax a people under so many restraints in trade as the Americans, the Noble Lord in the blue ribband[†] shall tell you, that the restraints on trade are futile and useless; of no advantage to us, and of no burthen to those on whom they are imposed; that the trade to America is not secured by the acts of navigation, but by the natural and irresistible advantage of a commercial preference.

Such is the merit of the trade laws in this posture of the debate. But when strong internal circumstances are urged against the taxes; when the scheme is dissected; when experience and the nature of things are brought to prove, and do prove, the utter impossibility of obtaining an effective revenue from the Colonies; when these things are pressed, or rather press themselves, so as to drive the advocates of Colony taxes to a clear admission of the futility of the scheme; then, Sir, the sleeping trade laws revive from their trance; and this useless taxation is to be kept sacred, not for its own sake, but as a counter-guard and security of the laws of trade.

Then, Sir, you keep up revenue laws which are mischievous, in order to preserve trade laws that are useless. Such is the wisdom of our plan in both its members. They are separately given up as of no value; and yet one is always to be defended for the sake of the other. But I cannot agree with the Noble Lord, nor with the pamphlet from whence he seems to have borrowed these ideas, concerning the inutility of the

---

* Mr Rice.[1]

[†] Lord North.[2]

[1] George Rice (*c.*1724–79), M.P. 1754–79, had said on 6 March: 'He was satisfied from a careful comparison of all the parts of the proceedings of the Americans with each other, that independency was their object; that they intended to throw off the commercial restrictions, as well as the taxes: on which latter point he was as much inclined to relax as any other gentleman, if he could be tolerably assured that such relaxation would not be introductory to a further, and a worse opposition on their parts' (*Parl. Reg.* i. 294–5). The tribute to Rice was a graceful gesture to the Chairman of the Committee which had decided the disputed Bristol election in Burke's favour.

[2] George III had conferred the Garter on him in 1772. No report has been found of North expressing the point of view Burke mentions here.

trade laws.[1] For without idolizing them, I am sure they are still, in many ways, of great use to us; and in former times, they have been of the greatest.[2] They do confine, and they do greatly narrow, the market for the Americans. But my perfect conviction of this, does not help me in the least to discern how the revenue laws form any security whatsoever to the commercial regulations; or that these commercial regulations are the true ground of the quarrel; or, that the giving way in any one instance of authority, is to lose all that may remain unconceded.

One fact is clear and indisputable. The public and avowed origin of this quarrel, was on taxation. This quarrel has indeed brought on new disputes on new questions; but certainly the least bitter, and the fewest of all, on the trade laws. To judge which of the two be the real radical cause of quarrel, we have to see whether the commercial dispute did, in order of time, precede the dispute on taxation? There is not a shadow of evidence for it. Next, to enable us to judge whether at this moment a dislike to the Trade Laws be the real cause of quarrel, it is absolutely necessary to put the taxes out of the question by a repeal. See how the Americans act in this position, and then you will be able to discern correctly what is the true object of the controversy, or whether any controversy at all will remain? Unless you consent to remove this cause of difference, it is impossible, with decency, to assert that the dispute is not upon what it is avowed to be. And I would, Sir, recommend to your serious consideration, whether it be prudent to form a rule for punishing people, not on their own acts, but on your conjectures? Surely it is preposterous at the very best. It is not

[1] Josiah Tucker had written in *Four Tracts, Together with Two Sermons, on Political and Commercial Subjects*, Gloucester, 1774, 'were the whole Trade of North America to be divided into two Branches, *viz.* the *Voluntary*, resulting from a free choice of the Americans themselves, pursuing their own Interest, and the *Involuntary*, in consequence of *Compulsory* Acts of the *British* Parliament;—this latter would appear so very small and inconsiderable, as hardly to deserve a Name in an Estimate of National Commerce' (p. 201). Tucker was critical not only of the laws of trade and navigation but the entire mercantile system which they had helped to foster. He like Burke was influenced by the free-trade school and the belief, which Adam Smith was about to avow so compellingly in his *Wealth of Nations*, that self-interest rather than government regulation was the central moving force in the economy. However, he differed radically with Burke about the American problem, arguing that Britain and America should separate and that self-interest would bring them back together as trading partners.

[2] The trade laws had helped to deprive the Dutch of the carrying trade. While the importance of the trade laws was being down played by people like Tucker, Smith, and David Hume, the vast majority in Britain, including North and his colleagues in the ministry, thought them crucial to the British economy; see V. T. Harlow, *The Founding of the Second British Empire, 1763–1793*, 2 vols., London, 1952–64, i. 180–210. Though Burke had accepted much of the free-trade argument he appears from his words here to have been somewhere between the two sides with respect to the specific issue of the laws of trade and navigation.

justifying your anger, by their misconduct; but it is converting your ill-will into their delinquency.

But the Colonies will go further.—Alas! alas! when will this speculating against fact and reason end? What will quiet these panic fears which we entertain of the hostile effect of a conciliatory conduct? Is it true, that no case can exist, in which it is proper for the sovereign to accede to the desires of his discontented subjects? Is there any thing peculiar in this case, to make a rule for itself? Is all authority of course lost, when it is not pushed to the extreme? Is it a certain maxim, that, the fewer causes of dissatisfaction are left by government, the more the subject will be inclined to resist and rebel?

All these objections being in fact no more than suspicions, conjectures, divinations; formed in defiance of fact and experience; they did not, Sir, discourage me from entertaining the idea of a conciliatory concession, founded on the principles which I have just stated.

In forming a plan for this purpose, I endeavoured to put myself in that frame of mind, which was the most natural, and the most reasonable; and which was certainly the most probable means of securing me from all error. I set out with a perfect distrust of my own abilities; a total renunciation of every speculation of my own; and with a profound reverence for the wisdom of our ancestors, who have left us the inheritance of so happy a constitution, and so flourishing an empire, and what is a thousand times more valuable, the treasury of the maxims and principles which formed the one, and obtained the other.

During the reigns of the kings of Spain of the Austrian family,[1] whenever they were at a loss in the Spanish councils, it was common for their statesmen to say, that they ought to consult the genius of Philip the Second.[2] The genius of Philip the Second might mislead them; and the issue of their affairs shewed, that they had not chosen the most perfect standard. But, Sir, I am sure that I shall not be misled, when, in a case of constitutional difficulty, I consult the genius of the English constitution. Consulting at that oracle (it was with all due humility and piety) I found four capital examples in a similar case before me: those of Ireland, Wales, Chester, and Durham.

Ireland, before the English conquest, though never governed by a despotic power, had no Parliament. How far the English Parliament

---

[1] i.e. the Habsburgs beginning with Charles V, King of Spain 1516–1556 and Holy Roman Emperor 1519–56.
[2] Charles V's successor as King of Spain, 1556–98.

itself was at that time modelled according to the present form, is
disputed among antiquarians. But we have all the reason in the world
to be assured, that a form of Parliament, such as England then
enjoyed, she instantly communicated to Ireland; and we are equally
sure that almost every successive improvement in constitutional liberty,
as fast as it was made here, was transmitted thither. The feudal
Baronage, and the feudal Knighthood, the roots of our primitive
constitution, were early transplanted into that soil; and grew and
flourished there. Magna Charta, if it did not give us originally the
House of Commons, gave us at least an House of Commons of weight
and consequence. But your ancestors did not churlishly sit down
alone to the feast of Magna Charta. Ireland was made immediately a
partaker. This benefit of English laws and liberties, I confess, was
not at first extended to *all* Ireland. Mark the consequence. English
authority and English liberties had exactly the same boundaries. Your
standard could never be advanced an inch before your privileges. Sir
John Davis[1] shews beyond a doubt, that the refusal of a general
communication of these rights, was the true cause why Ireland was five
hundred years in subduing; and after the vain projects of a Military
Government, attempted in the reign of Queen Elizabeth, it was soon
discovered, that nothing could make that country English, in civility
and allegiance, but your laws and your forms of legislature. It was not
English arms, but the English constitution, that conquered Ireland.
From that time, Ireland has ever had a general Parliament, as she had
before a partial Parliament. You changed the people; you altered the
religion; but you never touched the form or the vital substance of free
government in that kingdom. You deposed kings; you restored them;
you altered the succession to theirs, as well as to your own crown;
but you never altered their constitution; the principle of which was
respected by usurpation; restored with the restoration of Monarchy,
and established, I trust, for ever, by the glorious Revolution. This has
made Ireland the great and flourishing kingdom that it is; and from a
disgrace and a burthen intolerable to this nation, has rendered her a
principal part of our strength and ornament. This country cannot be
said to have ever formally taxed her. The irregular things done in the
confusion of mighty troubles, and on the hinge of great revolutions,

[1] Sir John Davies (1569–1626), author of *A Discoverie of the True Cause why Ireland was never
entirely subdued, nor brought under obedience of the Crowne of England untill the beginning of his
Majesties happie raigne*, [London], 1612. For Burke's treatment of Irish history, see vol. ix, pp.
469–75, 615–19.

even if all were done that is said to have been done, form no example. If they have any effect in argument, they make an exception to prove the rule. None of your own liberties could stand a moment, if the casual deviations from them, at such times, were suffered to be used as proofs of their nullity. By the lucrative amount of such casual breaches in the constitution, judge what the stated and fixed rule of supply has been in that Kingdom. Your Irish pensioners would starve, if they had no other fund to live on than taxes granted by English authority. Turn your eyes to those popular grants from whence all your great supplies are come; and learn to respect that only source of public wealth in the British empire.

My next example is Wales. This country was said to be reduced by Henry the Third. It was said more truly to be so by Edward the First. But though then conquered, it was not looked upon as any part of the realm of England. Its old constitution, whatever that might have been, was destroyed; and no good one was substituted in its place. The care of that tract was put into the hands of Lords Marchers—a form of Government of a very singular kind; a strange heterogeneous monster, something between Hostility and Government; perhaps it has a sort of resemblance, according to the modes of those times, to that of commander in chief at present, to whom all civil power is granted as secondary. The manners of the Welsh nation followed the Genius of the Government: The people were ferocious, restive, savage, and uncultivated; sometimes composed, never pacified. Wales within itself was in perpetual disorder; and it kept the frontier of England in perpetual alarm. Benefits from it to the state, there were none. Wales was only known to England, by incursion and invasion.

Sir, during that state of things, Parliament was not idle. They attempted to subdue the fierce spirit of the Welsh by all sorts of rigorous laws. They prohibited by statute the sending all sorts of arms into Wales, as you prohibit by proclamation (with something more of doubt on the legality) the sending arms to America.[1] They disarmed the Welsh by statute, as you attempted (but still with more question on the legality) to disarm New England by an instruction.[2] They made

---

[1] An Order in Council of 19 October 1774 prohibited the export of arms and ammunition (*Acts of the Privy Council of England, Colonial Series*, ed. J. Mungo, 6 vols., London, 1911, v. 401).
[2] Burke appears to be referring to the fact that on 2 November 1774 General Gage had given an 'order to the store-keeper not to deliver out any powder from the magazine where the merchants deposit it' (*Parl. Hist.* xviii. 104). No formal instruction on this subject appears to have been issued by the British Government.

an act to drag offenders from Wales into England for trial, as you have done (but with more hardship) with regard to America. By another act, where one of the parties was an Englishman, they ordained, that his trial should be always by English. They made acts to restrain trade, as you do; and they prevented the Welsh from the use of fairs and markets, as you do the Americans from fisheries and foreign ports. In short, when the statute-book was not quite so much swelled as it is now, you find no less than fifteen acts of penal regulation on the subject of Wales.

Here we rub our hands—A fine body of precedents for the authority of Parliament and the use of it!—I admit it fully; and pray add likewise to these precedents, that all the while, Wales rid this kingdom like an *incubus*; that it was an unprofitable and oppressive burthen; and that an Englishman travelling in that country, could not go six yards from the high road without being murdered.

The march of the human mind is slow. Sir, it was not, until after Two Hundred years, discovered, that by an eternal law, Providence had decreed vexation to violence; and poverty to rapine. Your ancestors did however at length open their eyes to the ill husbandry of injustice. They found that the tyranny of a free people could of all tyrannies the least be endured; and that laws made against an whole nation were not the most effectual methods for securing its obedience. Accordingly, in the Twenty-seventh year of Henry VIII. the course was entirely altered. With a preamble stating the entire and perfect rights of the crown of England, it gave to the Welsh all the rights and privileges of English subjects.[1] A political order was established; the military power gave way to the civil; the marches were turned into counties. But that a nation should have a right to English liberties, and yet no share at all in the fundamental security of these liberties, the grant of their own property, seemed a thing so incongruous; that Eight years after, that is, in the Thirty-fifth of that reign, a complete and not ill-proportioned representation by counties and boroughs was bestowed upon Wales, by act of Parliament.[2] From that moment, as by a charm, the tumults subsided; obedience was restored; peace, order, and civilization, followed in the train of liberty—When the day-star of

[1] 27 Hen. VIII, c. 26.
[2] Burke is mistaken here. 27 Hen. VIII. c. 26 provided the Welsh with representation as well. He is referring to 34 and 35 Hen. VIII, c. 8, which did significantly clarify and extend their representation.

the English constitution had arisen in their hearts,[1] all was harmony within and without—

> *Simul alba nautis*
> *Stella refulsit,*
> *Defluit saxis agitatus humor:*
> *Concidunt venti, fugiuntque nubes:*
> *Et minax (quod sic voluere) ponto*
> *Unda recumbit.*[2]

The very same year the county palatine of Chester received the same relief from its oppressions, and the same remedy to its disorders.[3] Before this time Chester was little less distempered than Wales. The inhabitants, without rights themselves, were the fittest to destroy the rights of others; and from thence Richard II. drew the standing army of Archers, with which for a time he oppressed England. The people of Chester applied to Parliament in a petition penned as I shall read to you:

"To the King our Sovereign Lord, in most humble wise shewn unto your Excellent Majesty, the inhabitants of your Grace's county palatine of Chester; That where the said county palatine of Chester is and hath been always hitherto exempt, excluded and separated out and from your high court of parliament, to have any knights and burgesses within the said court; by reason whereof the said inhabitants have hitherto sustained manifold disherisons, losses and damages, as well in their lands, goods, and bodies, as in the good, civil, and politick governance and maintenance of the commonwealth of their said country: (2.) And for as much as the said inhabitants have always hitherto been bound by the acts and statutes made and ordained by your said highness, and your most noble progenitors, by authority of the said court, as far forth as other counties, cities, and boroughs have been, that have had their knights and burgesses within your said court of parliament, and yet have had neither knight ne burgess there for the said county palatine; the said inhabitants, for lack thereof, have been oftentimes touched and grieved with acts and statutes made within the said court, as well derogatory unto the most antient jurisdictions, liberties, and privileges of your said county palatine, as prejudicial unto the common wealth, quietness, rest, and peace of your grace's most bounden subjects inhabiting within the same."

---

[1] 2 Pet. 1: 19.
[2] Horace, *Odes*, I, xii. 27–32. 'As soon as whose clear effulgent star, amid the tempest's war, gleams upon the shipmen, the spray subsides from the weltering rocks, the wind creeps in zephyrs, the clouds disperse that veiled the cheerful day, and on the wild and wasteful sea, such is their power [Castor and Pollux], the menacing waves are lulled to sleep.'
[3] 34 and 35 Hen. VIII, c. 13.

What did Parliament with this audacious address?—reject it as a libel? Treat it as an affront to government? Spurn it as a derogation from the rights of legislature? Did they toss it over the table? Did they burn it by the hands of the common hangman?—They took the petition of grievance, all rugged as it was, without softening or temperament, unpurged of the original bitterness and indignation of complaint; they made it the very preamble to their act of redress; and consecrated its principle to all ages in the sanctuary of legislation.

Here is my third example. It was attended with the success of the two former. Chester, civilized as well as Wales, has demonstrated that freedom and not servitude is the cure of anarchy; as religion, and not atheism, is the true remedy for superstition. Sir, this pattern of Chester was followed in the reign of Charles II. with regard to the county palatine of Durham,[1] which is my fourth example. This county had long lain out of the pale of free legislation. So scrupulously was the example of Chester followed, that the style of the preamble is nearly the same with that of the Chester act; and without affecting the abstract extent of the authority of Parliament, it recognizes the equity of not suffering any considerable district in which the British subjects may act as a body, to be taxed without their own voice in the grant.

Now if the doctrines of policy contained in these preambles, and the force of these examples in the acts of Parliament, avail any thing, what can be said against applying them with regard to America? Are not the people of America as much Englishmen as the Welsh? The preamble of the act of Henry VIII. says, the Welsh speak a language no way resembling that of his Majesty's English subjects. Are the Americans not as numerous? If we may trust the learned and accurate Judge Barrington's account of North Wales, and take that as a standard to measure the rest, there is no comparison. The people cannot amount to above 200,000; not a tenth part of the number in the Colonies.[2] Is America in rebellion? Wales was hardly ever free from it. Have you attempted to govern America by penal statutes? You made Fifteen for Wales. But your legislative authority is perfect with regard to

---

[1] 25 Car. II, c. 9.
[2] The estimate by Daines Barrington (1727–1800), appointed a judge for the counties of Merioneth, Carnarvon, and Anglesey in 1757, of the population of these counties is to be found in *Archaeologia*, i (1770), 281. He estimated their population to be 50,000 in 1767, but in fact it probably amounted to 94,000 and the population of Wales (including Monmouthshire) to about 482,000 (*Bulletin of the Board of Celtic Studies*, viii (1935–7), 359–61). In 1801 the population of Wales and Monmouthshire was 587, 245.

America; was it less perfect in Wales, Chester, and Durham? But America is virtually represented. What! does the electric force of virtual representation more easily pass over the Atlantic, than pervade Wales, which lies in your neighbourhood; or than Chester and Durham, surrounded by abundance of representation that is actual and palpable? But, Sir, your ancestors thought this sort of virtual representation, however ample, to be totally insufficient for the freedom of the inhabitants of territories that are so near, and comparatively so inconsiderable. How then can I think it sufficient for those which are infinitely greater, and infinitely more remote?

You will now, Sir, perhaps imagine, that I am on the point of proposing to you a scheme for a representation of the Colonies in Parliament. Perhaps I might be inclined to entertain some such thought; but a great flood stops me in my course. *Opposuit natura*[1]—I cannot remove the eternal barriers of the creation. The thing in that mode, I do not know to be possible. As I meddle with no theory, I do not absolutely assert the impracticability of such a representation. But I do not see my way to it; and those who have been more confident, have not been more successful.[2] However, the arm of public benevolence is not shortened; and there are often several means to the same end. What nature has disjoined in one way, wisdom may unite in another. When we cannot give the benefit as we would wish, let us not refuse it altogether. If we cannot give the principal, let us find a substitute. But how? Where? What substitute?

Fortunately I am not obliged for the ways and means of this substitute to tax my own unproductive invention. I am not even obliged to go to the rich treasury of the fertile framers of imaginary common wealths; not to the Republick of Plato, not to the Utopia of More; not to the Oceana of Harrington. It is before me—It is at my feet, *and the rude swain treads daily on it with his clouted shoon.*[3] I only wish you to recognize, for the theory, the ancient constitutional policy of this kingdom with regard to representation, as that policy has been declared in acts of parliament; and, as to the practice, to return to that mode which an uniform experience has marked out to you, as best; and in

---

[1] Juvenal, *Satires*, x. 152: 'Nature is opposed.'
[2] James Otis (1725–83) and Benjamin Franklin (1706–90) had advocated colonial representation in Parliament. Burke had attacked the idea—on grounds of its impracticability—in *Observations on a Late State of the Nation* (vol. ii, pp. 178–80).
[3] Milton, *Comus*, 634–5.

which you walked with security, advantage, and honour, until the year 1763.[1]

My resolutions therefore mean to establish the equity and justice of a taxation of America, by *grant*, and not by *imposition*. To mark the *legal competency* of the Colony assemblies for the support of their government in peace, and for public aids in time of war. To acknowledge that this legal competency has had a *dutiful and beneficial exercise*; and that experience has shewn the *benefit of their grants*, and the *futility of parliamentary taxation as a method of supply*.

These solid truths compose six fundamental propositions. There are three more resolutions corollary to these. If you admit the first set, you can hardly reject the others. But if you admit the first, I shall be far from sollicitous whether you accept or refuse the last. I think these six massive pillars will be of strength sufficient to support the temple of British concord.[2] I have no more doubt than I entertain of my existence, that, if you admitted these, you would command an immediate peace; and with but tolerable future management, a lasting obedience in America. I am not arrogant in this confident assurance. The propositions are all mere matters of fact: and if they are such facts as draw irresistible conclusions even in the stating, this is the power of truth, and not any management of mine.

Sir, I shall open the whole plan to you together, with such observations on the motions as may tend to illustrate them where they may want explanation. The first is a resolution—"That the Colonies and Plantations of Great Britain in North America, consisting of Fourteen separate Governments, and continuing Two Millions and upwards of free inhabitants, have not had the liberty and privilege of electing and sending any Knights and Burgesses, or others to represent them in the high Court of Parliament"—This is a plain matter of fact, necessary to be laid down, and (excepting the description) it is laid down in the language of the constitution; it is taken nearly *verbatim* from acts of Parliament.

The second is like unto the first[3]—"That the said Colonies and Plantations have been liable to, and bounden by, several subsidies, payments, rates, and taxes, given and granted by Parliament, though

---

[1] Burke is referring to the attempt by the mother country substantially to increase revenues in the American colonies in particular through George Grenville's Sugar Act (4 Geo. III, c. 15) and the disastrous Stamp Act (5 Geo. III, c. 12), which the Rockinghams repealed in 1766.

[2] A reference to the Temple of Concord at Rome.

[3] Matt. 22: 39.

the said Colonies and Plantations have not their Knights and Burgesses, in the said high Court of Parliament, of their own election, to represent the condition of their country; by lack whereof they have been often-times touched and grieved by subsidies given, granted, and assented to, in the said court, in a manner prejudicial to the common wealth, quietness, rest, and peace of the subjects inhabiting within the same."

Is this description too hot, or too cold, too strong, or too weak? Does it arrogate too much to the supreme legislature? Does it lean too much to the claims of the people? If it runs into any of these errors, the fault is not mine. It is the language of your own ancient acts of Parliament. *Non meus hic sermo, sed quae praecepit. Ofellus, rusticus, abnormis sapiens.*[1] It is the genuine produce of the ancient rustic, manly, home-bred sense of this country—I did not dare to rub off a particle of the venerable rust that rather adorns and preserves, than destroys the metal.[2] It would be a profanation to touch with a tool the stones which construct the sacred altar of peace.[3] I would not violate with modern polish the ingenuous and noble roughness of these truly constitutional materials. Above all things, I was resolved not to be guilty of tamper-ing, the odious vice of restless and unstable minds. I put my foot in the tracks of our forefathers; where I can neither wander nor stumble. Determining to six articles of peace, I was resolved not to be wise beyond what was written;[4] I was resolved to use nothing else than the form of sound words,[5] to let others abound in their own sense; and carefully to abstain from all expressions of my own. What the law has said, I say. In all things else I am silent. I have no organ but for her words. This, if it be not ingenious, I am sure is safe.

There are indeed words expressive of grievance in this second resolution, which those who are resolved always to be in the right, will deny to contain matter of fact, as applied to the present case; although Parliament thought them true, with regard to the counties of Chester and Durham. They will deny that the Americans were ever "touched and grieved" with the taxes. If they consider nothing in taxes but their

---

[1] Horace, *Satires*, ii. 2–3: 'This is not my own discourse, but consists of the wisdom of the present Ofellus, an untrained philosopher.'
[2] Compare Juvenal, Satires, xiii. 147–8: 'grandia templi pocula adorandae rubiginis', 'antique temple venerable for rust'.
[3] Compare Exod. 20: 25.
[4] 1 Cor. 4: 6.
[5] 2 Tim. 1: 13.

weight as pecuniary impositions, there might be some pretence for this denial.[1] But men may be sorely touched and deeply grieved in their privileges, as well as in their purses. Men may lose little in property by the act which takes away all their freedom. When a man is robbed of a trifle on the highway, it is not the Two-pence lost that constitutes the capital outrage. This is not confined to privileges. Even ancient indulgences withdrawn, without offence on the part of those who enjoyed such favours, operate as grievances. But were the Americans then not touched and grieved by the taxes, in some measure, merely as taxes? If so, why were they almost all, either wholly repealed or exceedingly reduced? Were they not touched and grieved, even by the regulating Duties of the Sixth of George II? Else why were the duties first reduced to one Third in 1764, and afterwards to a Third of that Third in the year 1766?[2] Were they not touched and grieved by the Stamp Act? I shall say they were, until that tax is revived. Were they not touched and grieved by the duties of 1767,[3] which were likewise repealed, and which, Lord Hillsborough tells you (for the ministry) were laid contrary to the true principle of commerce? Is not the assurance given by that noble person to the Colonies of a resolution to lay no more taxes on them, an admission that taxes would touch and grieve them?[4] Is not the resolution of the noble Lord in the blue ribband, now standing on your Journals, the strongest of all proofs that parliamentary subsidies really touched and grieved them? Else, why all these changes, modifications, repeals, assurances, and resolutions?

The next proposition is—"That, from the distance of the said Colonies, and from other circumstances, no method hath hitherto been devised for procuring a representation in Parliament for the said Colonies." This is an assertion of a fact. I go no further on the paper; though in my private judgement, an useful representation is

---

[1] On 2 February Lord North—estimating American population at 3 million—calculated that an Englishman paid 25s. annually in taxes and an American only 6d. (*Parl. Reg.* i. 133).

[2] By the Molasses Act 1733 (6 Geo. II, c. 13) the duty on foreign molasses was six pence a gallon. This duty was reduced by the Sugar Act of 1764 (4 Geo. III, c. 15) to 3d., and by the Revenue Act of 1766 (6 Geo. III, c. 52) to 1d. Burke appears to have confused the molasses duty with the 9d. duty on rum in the 1733 Act.

[3] The Townshend Duties, 7 Geo. III, c. 46.

[4] Wills Hill, 1st Earl of Hillsborough (1718–93), Secretary of State, informed the colonial governors in May 1769 that the ministry had no intention of asking Parliament to lay further taxes on America and would remove the duties on glass, paper, and colours which had been levied 'contrary to the true principles of commerce' (*Autobiography and Political Correspondence of Augustus Henry, Third Duke of Grafton*, ed. W. R. Anson, London, 1898, p. 232). On 20 February 1775 Lord North made a similar promise in his conciliation proposal (above, p. 86).

impossible; I am sure it is not desired by them; nor ought it perhaps by us; but I abstain from opinions.[1]

The fourth resolution is—"That each of the said Colonies hath within itself a body, chosen in part, or in the whole, by the freemen, freeholders, or other free inhabitants thereof, commonly called the General Assembly, or General Court, with powers legally to raise, levy, and assess, according to the several usage of such Colonies, duties and taxes towards defraying all sorts of public services."

This competence in the Colony assemblies is certain. It is proved by the whole tenour of their acts of supply in all the assemblies, in which the constant style of granting is, "an aid to his Majesty;" and acts granting to the Crown have regularly for near a century passed the public offices without dispute. Those who have been pleased paradoxically to deny this right, holding that none but the British parliament can grant to the Crown,[2] are wished to look to what is done, not only in the Colonies, but in Ireland, in one uniform unbroken tenour every session. Sir, I am surprized, that this doctrine should come from some of the law servants of the Crown.[3] I say, that if the Crown could be responsible, his Majesty—but certainly the ministers, and even these law officers themselves, through whose hands the acts pass, biennially in Ireland, or annually in the Colonies, are in an habitual course of committing impeachable offences. What habitual offenders have been all Presidents of the Council, all Secretaries of State, all First Lords of Trade, all Attornies and all Sollicitors General! However, they are safe; as no one impeaches them; and there is no ground of charge against them, except in their own unfounded theories.

The fifth resolution is also a resolution of fact—"That the said General Assemblies, General Courts, or other bodies legally qualified as aforesaid, have at sundry times freely granted several large subsidies and public aids for his Majesty's service, according to their abilities, when required thereto by letter from one of his Majesty's principal Secretaries of State; and that their right to grant the same, and their

---

[1] The Continental Congress in its resolves of 14 October 1774 asserted that the colonists 'from their local and other circumstances cannot properly be represented in the British Parliament'. This had also been the view of the Stamp Act Congress.

[2] George Grenville in particular held the view that Burke criticizes.

[3] The ministerial side is not reported as having expressed this view in the period immediately before Burke's speech, but the issue was discussed in the debate which followed it, when the ministerial side repeated and reinforced 'their general arguments' (*Parl. Reg.* i. 368).

chearfulness and sufficiency in the said grants, have been at sundry times acknowledged by Parliament." To say nothing of their great expences in the Indian wars;[1] and not to take their exertion in foreign ones, so high as the supplies in the year 1695;[2] not to go back to their public contributions in the year 1710;[3] I shall begin to travel only where the Journals give me light; resolving to deal in nothing but fact, authenticated by parliamentary record; and to build myself wholly on that solid basis.

On the 4th of April 1748,* a Committee of this House came to the following Resolution:

"Resolved,

That it is the opinion of this Committee, *that it is just and reasonable* that the several Provinces and Colonies of Massachuset's Bay, New Hampshire, Connecticut, and Rhode Island, be reimbursed the expences they have been at in taking and securing to the crown of Great Britain, the Island of Cape Breton, and its dependencies."

These expences were immense for such Colonies. They were above 200,000*l.* sterling; money first raised and advanced on their public credit.

On the 28th of January 1756,† a message from the King came to us, to this effect—"His Majesty, being sensible of the zeal and vigour with which his faithful subjects of certain Colonies in North America have exerted themselves in defence of his Majesty's just rights and possessions, recommends it to this House to take the same into their consideration, and to enable his Majesty to give them such assistance as may be a proper reward and encouragement."

On the 3d of February 1756,‡ the House came to a suitable resolution, expressed in words nearly the same as those of the message: but with the further addition, that the money then voted was as an *encouragement* to the Colonies to exert themselves with vigour. It will not

---

* Journals of the House, vol. xxv.[4]
† Ibid. vol. xxvii.[5]
‡ Ibid.[6]
[1] Burke is referring to the part the colonists took in defending British North America against the French and the Indians just prior to and during the Seven Years War. See W. J. Eccles, *The Canadian Frontier, 1534–1760*, New York, 1969, pp. 164–85.
[2] During the Nine Years War (1689–97) the American colonists became heavily involved in the fight against the French and their Indian allies in New France and Acadia (ibid. pp. 121–31).
[3] In 1710 a combined American and English expedition captured Port Royal from the French (ibid. 141).
[4] p. 614.
[5] p. 415.
[6] pp. 424–5.

be necessary to go through all the testimonies which your own records have given to the truth of my resolutions. I will only refer you to the places in the Journals:

Vol. XXVII.—16th and 19th May 1757.

Vol. XXVIII.—June 1st, 1758—April 26th and 30th, 1759—March 26th and 31st, and April 28th, 1760—Jan. 9th and 20th, 1761.

Vol. XXIX.—Jan. 22d and 26th, 1762—March 14th and 17th, 1763.[1]

Sir, here is the repeated acknowledgement of Parliament, that the Colonies not only gave, but gave to satiety. This nation has formally acknowledged two things; first, that the Colonies had gone beyond their abilities, Parliament having thought it necessary to reimburse them; secondly, that they had acted legally and laudably in their grants of money, and their maintenance of troops, since the compensation is expressly given as reward and encouragement. Reward is not bestowed for acts that are unlawful; and encouragement is not held out to things that deserve reprehension. My resolution therefore does nothing more than collect into one proposition, what is scattered through your Journals. I give you nothing but your own; and you cannot refuse in the gross, what you have so often acknowledged in detail. The admission of this, which will be so honourable to them and to you, will, indeed, be mortal to all the miserable stories, by which the passions of the misguided people have been engaged in an unhappy system. The people heard, indeed, from the beginning of these disputes, one thing continually dinned in their ears, that reason and justice demanded, that the Americans, who paid no Taxes, should be compelled to contribute. How did that fact of their paying nothing, stand when the Taxing System began? When Mr. Grenville began to form his system of American Revenue, he stated in this House, that the Colonies were then in debt two millions six hundred thousand pounds sterling money; and was of opinion they would discharge that debt in four years.[2] On this state, those untaxed people were actually subject to the payment of taxes to the amount of six hundred and fifty thousand a year. In fact, however, Mr. Grenville was mistaken. The funds given for sinking the debt did not prove quite so ample as both the Colonies and he

---

[1] pp. 894, 901, 263, 560, 564, 834, 847, 894, 1009, 1032; 113, 123, 555, 572.

[2] No record of any such statement has been found in the surviving accounts of Grenville's speech of 9 March 1764 (Simmons and Thomas, i. 188–92). On 6 February 1765 Grenville did refer to the debts being paid off in four years (L. B. Namier, 'Charles Garth Agent for South Carolina', Part II, *English Historical Review*, liv (1939), 649–50).

expected. The calculation was too sanguine: the reduction was not compleated till some years after, and at different times in different Colonies.[1] However, the Taxes after the war, continued too great to bear any addition, with prudence or propriety; and when the burthens imposed in consequence of former requisitions were discharged, our tone became too high to resort again to requisition. No Colony, since that time, ever has had any requisition whatsoever made to it.

We see the sense of the Crown, and the sense of Parliament, on the productive nature of a *Revenue by Grant*. Now search the same Journals for the produce of the *Revenue by Imposition*—Where is it?—let us know the volume and the page?—what is the gross, what is the nett produce?—to what service is it applied?—how have you appropriated its surplus?—What, can none of the many skilful Index-makers,[2] that we are now employing, find any trace of it?—Well, let them and that rest together.—But are the Journals, which say nothing of the Revenue, as silent on the discontent?—Oh no! a child may find it. It is the melancholy burthen and blot of every page.

I think then I am, from those Journals, justified in the sixth and last resolution, which is—"That it hath been found by experience, that the manner of granting the said supplies and aids, by the said General Assemblies, hath been more agreeable to the said Colonies, and more beneficial, and conducive to the public service, than the mode of giving and granting aids in Parliament, to be raised and paid in the said Colonies." This makes the whole of the fundamental part of the plan. The conclusion is irresistible. You cannot say, that you were driven by any necessity, to an exercise of the utmost Rights of Legislature. You cannot assert, that you took on yourselves the task of imposing Colony Taxes, from the want of another legal body, that is competent to the purpose of supplying the Exigences of the State without wounding the prejudices of the people. Neither is it true that the body so qualified, and having that competence, had neglected the duty.

The question now, on all this accumulated matter, is;—whether you will chuse to abide by a profitable experience, or a mischievous theory; whether you chuse to build on imagination or fact; whether you prefer enjoyment or hope; satisfaction in your subjects, or discontent?

If these propositions are accepted, every thing which has been made to enforce a contrary system, must, I take it for granted, fall along with

[1] In general the debts were not a great burden by 1764.

[2] A general index was being prepared at this time (D. Menhemet, *The Journal of the House of Commons*, London, 1971, pp. 30–2).

it. On that ground, I have drawn the following resolution, which, when it comes to be moved, will naturally be divided in a proper manner: "That it may be proper to repeal an act, made in the seventh year of the reign of his present Majesty, intituled, An act for granting certain duties in the British Colonies and Plantations in America; for allowing a drawback of the duties of customs upon the exportation from this Kingdom, of coffee and cocoa-nuts of the produce of the said Colonies or Plantations; for discontinuing the drawbacks payable on China earthen-ware exported to America; and for more effectually preventing the clandestine running of goods in the said Colonies and Plantations.— And that it may be proper to repeal an act, made in the fourteenth year of the reign of his present Majesty, intituled, An act to discontinue, in such manner, and for such time, as are therein mentioned, the landing and discharging, lading or shipping, of goods, wares, and merchandize, at the town and within the harbour of Boston, in the Province of Massachuset's Bay in North America.—And that it may be proper to repeal an act, made in the fourteenth year of the reign of his present Majesty, intituled, An act for the impartial administration of justice, in the cases of persons questioned for any acts done by them, in the execution of the law, or for the suppression of riots and tumults, in the province of Massachuset's Bay in New England.—And that it may be proper to repeal an act, made in the fourteenth year of the reign of his present Majesty, intituled, An act for the better regulating the Government of the province of the Massachuset's Bay in New England.—And also that it may be proper to explain and amend an act, made in the thirty-fifth year of the reign of King Henry the Eighth, intituled, An act for the Trial of Treasons committed out of the King's Dominions."[1]

I wish, Sir, to repeal the Boston Port Bill, because (independently of the dangerous precedent of suspending the rights of the subject during the King's pleasure) it was passed, as I apprehend, with less regularity, and on more partial principles, than it ought. The corporation of Boston was not heard, before it was condemned. Other towns, full as guilty as she was, have not had their ports blocked up. Even the Restraining Bill of the present Session does not go to the length of the Boston Port Act. The same ideas of prudence, which induced you not to extend equal punishment to equal guilt, even when you were

---

[1] Burke here advocates the repeal of the tea duty and the 'Intolerable' Acts (except the Quebec Act) and a modification of 35 Hen. VIII, c. 2.

punishing, induce me, who mean not to chastise, but to reconcile, to be satisfied with the punishment already partially inflicted.

Ideas of prudence, and accommodation to circumstances, prevent you from taking away the Charters of Connecticut and Rhode-island, as you have taken away that of Massachuset's Colony, though the Crown has far less power in the two former provinces than it enjoyed in the latter; and though the abuses have been full as great, and as flagrant, in the exempted as in the punished. The same reasons of prudence and accommodation have weight with me in restoring the Charter of Massachuset's Bay. Besides, Sir, the Act which changes the Charter of Massachuset's is in many particulars so exceptionable, that, if I did not wish absolutely to repeal, I would by all means desire to alter it; as several of its provisions tend to the subversion of all public and private justice. Such, among others, is the power in the Governor to change the sheriff at his pleasure; and to make a new returning officer for every special cause. It is shameful to behold such a regulation standing among English Laws.

The act for bringing persons accused of committing murder under the orders of Government to England for Trial, is but temporary. That act has calculated the probable duration of our quarrel with the Colonies; and is accommodated to that supposed duration. I would hasten the happy moment of reconciliation; and therefore must, on my principle, get rid of that most justly obnoxious act.

The act of Henry the Eighth, for the Trial of Treasons, I do not mean to take away, but to confine it to its proper bounds and original intention; to make it expressly for Trial of Treasons (and the greatest Treasons may be committed) in places where the jurisdiction of the Crown does not extend.[1]

Having guarded the privileges of Local Legislature, I would next secure to the Colonies a fair and unbiassed Judicature; for which purpose, Sir, I propose the following resolution: "That, from the time when the General Assembly or General Court of any Colony or Plantation in North America, shall have appointed by act of Assembly, duly confirmed, a settled salary to the offices of the Chief Justice and other Judges of the Superior Court, it may be proper, that the said Chief Justice and other Judges of the Superior Courts of such Colony, shall hold his and their office and offices during their good behaviour;

---

[1] In other words people charged with treason in the colonies, or any other part of the empire where the jurisdiction of the Crown did extend, would no longer be subject to the law.

and shall not be removed therefrom, but when the said removal shall be adjudged by his Majesty in Council, upon a hearing on complaint from the General Assembly, or on a complaint from the Governor, or Council, or the House of Representatives severally, of the Colony in which the said Chief Justice and other Judges have exercised the said offices."

The next resolution relates to the Courts of Admiralty.

It is this: "That it may be proper to regulate the Courts of Admiralty, or Vice Admiralty, authorized by the 15th Chap. of the 4th of George the Third, in such a manner as to make the same more commodious to those who sue, or are sued, in the said Courts, and to provide for the more decent maintenance of the Judges in the same."[1]

These Courts I do not wish to take away; they are in themselves proper establishments. This Court is one of the capital securities of the Act of Navigation. The extent of its jurisdiction, indeed, has been encreased; but this is altogether as proper, and is, indeed, on many accounts, more eligible, where new powers were wanted, than a Court absolutely new. But Courts incommodiously situated, in effect, deny justice; and a Court, partaking in the fruits of its own condemnation, is a robber. The congress complain, and complain justly, of this grievance.*

These are the three consequential propositions. I have thought of two or three more; but they come rather too near detail, and to the province of executive Government, which I wish Parliament always to superintend, never to assume. If the first six are granted, congruity will carry the latter three. If not, the things that remain unrepealed, will be, I hope, rather unseemly incumbrances on the building, than very materially detrimental to its strength and stability.

Here, Sir, I should close; but that I plainly perceive some objections remain, which I ought, if possible, to remove. The first will be, that, in resorting to the doctrine of our ancestors, as contained in the

* The Solicitor-general[2] informed Mr. B. when the resolutions were separately moved, that the grievance of the judges partaking of the profits of the seizure had been redressed by office; accordingly the resolution was amended.

[1] The Revenue Act of 1764 authorised the creation of a new 'Court of Vice Admiralty . . . over all America' (4 Geo. III, c. 15). The new court was subsequently located at Halifax, Nova Scotia, and the salary of its judge was to come in the first instance from the Crown's share of forfeitures. In 1768 three additional courts were created with a similar arrangement. Burke's proposal did not meet American objections to the principle of Admiralty courts trying offences against the Navigation Acts without juries.

[2] Alexander Wedderburn.

preamble to the Chester act, I prove too much; that the grievance from a want of representation, stated in that preamble, goes to the whole of Legislation as well as to Taxation. And that the Colonies grounding themselves upon that doctrine, will apply it to all parts of Legislative Authority.

To this objection, with all possible deference and humility, and wishing as little as any man living to impair the smallest particle of our supreme authority, I answer, that *the words are the words of Parliament, and not mine*; and, that all false and inconclusive inferences, drawn from them, are not mine; for I heartily disclaim any such inference. I have chosen the words of an act of Parliament, which Mr. Grenville, surely a tolerably zealous and very judicious advocate for the sovereignty of Parliament, formerly moved to have read at your table, in confirmation of his tenets. It is true that Lord Chatham considered these preambles as declaring strongly in favour of his opinions. He was a no less powerful advocate for the privileges of the Americans.[1] Ought I not from hence to presume, that these preambles are as favourable as possible to both, when properly understood; favourable both to the rights of Parliament, and to the privilege of the dependencies of this crown? But, Sir, the object of grievance in my resolution, I have not taken from the Chester, but from the Durham act, which confines the hardship of want of representation, to the case of subsidies; and which therefore falls in exactly with the case of the Colonies. But whether the unrepresented counties were *de jure*, or *de facto*, bound, the preambles do not accurately distinguish; nor indeed was it necessary; for, whether *de jure*, or *de facto*, the Legislature thought the exercise of the power of taxing, as of right, or as of fact without right, equally a grievance and equally oppressive.

I do not know, that the Colonies have, in any general way, or in any cool hour, gone much beyond the demand of immunity in relation to taxes. It is not fair to judge of the temper or dispositions of any man, or any set of men, when they are composed and at rest, from their conduct, or their expressions, in a state of disturbance and irritation. It is besides a very great mistake to imagine, that mankind follow

---

[1] Burke is referring to the speeches of Grenville and Chatham (then William Pitt) on 14 January 1766 (*Parl. Hist* xvi. 101–8). They had argued over the meaning of the preambles of two Acts—one in the reign of Henry VIII and the other in the reign of Charles II. The latter Act was probably 25 Car. II, c. 7. It is clear from the wording of the preamble that it was designed exclusively for the regulation of trade and prevention of fraud, not for the raising of a revenue.

up practically any speculative principle, either of government or of freedom, as far as it will go in argument and logical illation. We Englishmen, stop very short of the principles upon which we support any given part of our constitution; or even the whole of it together. I could easily, if I had not already tired you, give you very striking and convincing instances of it. This is nothing but what is natural and proper. All government, indeed every human benefit and enjoyment, every virtue, and every prudent act, is founded on compromise and barter. We balance inconveniencies; we give and take; we remit some rights, that we may enjoy others; and, we chuse rather to be happy citizens, than subtle disputants. As we must give away some natural liberty, to enjoy civil advantages; so we must sacrifice some civil liberties, for the advantages to be derived from the communion and fellowship of a great empire. But in all fair dealings the thing bought must bear some proportion to the purchase paid. None will barter away the immediate jewel of his soul.[1] Though a great house is apt to make slaves haughty,[2] yet it is purchasing a part of the artificial importance of a great empire too dear, to pay for it all essential rights, and all the intrinsic dignity of human nature. None of us who would not risque his life, rather than fall under a government purely arbitrary. But, although there are some amongst us who think our constitution wants many improvements, to make it a complete system of liberty, perhaps none who are of that opinion, would think it right to aim at such improvement, by disturbing his country, and risquing every thing that is dear to him. In every arduous enterprize, we consider what we are to lose, as well as what we are to gain; and the more and better stake of liberty every people possess, the less they will hazard in a vain attempt to make it more. These are *the cords of man*.[3] Man acts from adequate motives relative to his interest; and not on metaphysical speculations.[4] Aristotle, the great master of reasoning, cautions us, and with great weight and propriety, against this species of delusive geometrical accuracy in moral arguments,[5] as the most fallacious of all sophistry.

---

[1] *Othello*, III. iii. 160.
[2] Juvenal, *Satires*, v. 66.
[3] Hos. 11: 4.
[4] A central argument in Aristotle's *Nicomachean Ethics*, Book I. Aristotle argues that man's actions are motivated by a desire for happiness and therefore he constantly works for what he considers to be the good of himself and/or his society. It is this objective which Burke is referring to when he speaks of 'the cords of man', i.e. the common quality which links all men together.
[5] *Nicomachean Ethics*, iii. 1–4, vii. 17–19.

The Americans will have no interest contrary to the grandeur and glory of England, when they are not oppressed by the weight of it; and they will rather be inclined to respect the acts of a superintending legislature, when they see them the acts of that power, which is itself the security, not the rival, of their secondary importance. In this assurance, my mind most perfectly acquiesces; and I confess, I feel not the least alarm, from the discontents which are to arise, from putting people at their ease; nor do I apprehend the destruction of this empire, from giving, by an act of free grace and indulgence, to two millions of my fellow citizens, some share of those rights, upon which I have always been taught to value myself.

It is said indeed, that this power of granting vested in American assemblies, would dissolve the unity of the empire; which was preserved, entire, although Wales, and Chester, and Durham, were added to it. Truly, Mr. Speaker, I do not know what this unity means; nor has it ever been heard of, that I know, in the constitutional policy of this country. The very idea of subordination of parts, excludes this notion of simple and undivided unity. England is the head; but she is not the head and the members too. Ireland has ever had from the beginning a separate, but not an independent, legislature; which, far from distracting, promoted the union of the whole. Every thing was sweetly and harmoniously disposed through both Islands for the conservation of English dominion, and the communication of English liberties. I do not see that the same principles might not be carried into twenty Islands, and with the same good effect. This is my model with regard to America, as far as the internal circumstances of the two countries are the same. I know no other unity of this empire than I can draw from its example during these periods, when it seemed to my poor understanding more united than it is now, or than it is likely to be by the present methods.

But since I speak of these methods, I recollect, Mr. Speaker, almost too late, that I promised, before I finished, to say something of the proposition of the Noble Lord* on the floor, which has been so lately received, and stands on your Journals. I must be deeply concerned, whenever it is my misfortune to continue a difference with the majority of this House. But as the reasons for that difference are my apology for thus troubling you, suffer me to state them in a very few words. I

---

* Lord North.[1] 'Burke is referring to North's own conciliatory propositions (above, p. 86).

shall compress them into as small a body as I possibly can, having already debated that matter at large, when the question was before the Committee.

First, then, I cannot admit that proposition of a ransom by auction;— because it is a meer project. It is a thing new; unheard of; supported by no experience; justified by no analogy; without example of our ancestors, or root in the constitution. It is neither regular parliamentary taxation, nor Colony grant. *Experimentum in corpore vili;*[1] is a good rule, which will ever make me adverse to any trial of experiments on what is certainly the most valuable of all subjects; the peace of this Empire.

Secondly, it is an experiment which must be fatal in the end to our constitution. For what is it but a scheme for taxing the Colonies in the antichamber of the Noble Lord and his successors? To settle the quotas and proportions in this House, is clearly impossible. You, Sir, may flatter yourself, you shall sit a state auctioneer with your hammer in your hand, and knock down to each Colony as it bids. But to settle (on the plan laid down by the Noble Lord) the true proportional payment for four or five and twenty governments, according to the absolute and the relative wealth of each, and according to the British proportion of wealth and burthen, is a wild and chimerical notion. This new taxation must therefore come in by the back-door of the constitution. Each quota must be brought to this House ready formed; you can neither add nor alter. You must register it. You can do nothing further. For on what grounds can you deliberate either before or after the proposition? You cannot hear the counsel for all these Provinces, quarrelling each on its own quantity of payment, and its proportion to others. If you should attempt it, the Committee of Provincial Ways and Means, or by whatever other name it will delight to be called, must swallow up all the time of Parliament.

Thirdly, it does not give satisfaction to the complaint of the Colonies. They complain, that they are taxed without their consent; you answer, that you will fix the sum at which they shall be taxed. That is, you give them the very grievance for the remedy. You tell them indeed, that you will leave the mode to themselves. I really beg pardon: it gives me pain to mention it; but you must be sensible that you will not perform this part of the compact. For, suppose the Colonies

---

[1] 'Let the experiment be performed upon a worthless body.' Apparently from Antoine Du Verdier (1544–1600); see T. B. Harbottle, *Dictionary of Quotations (Classical)*, London, 1902, p. 64.

were to lay the duties which furnished their Contingent, upon the importation of your manufactures; you know you would never suffer such a tax to be laid. You know too, that you would not suffer many other modes of taxation. So that, when you come to explain yourself, it will be found, that you will neither leave to themselves the quantum nor the mode; nor indeed any thing. The whole is delusion from one end to the other.

Fourthly, this method of ransom by auction, unless it be *universally* accepted, will plunge you into great and inextricable difficulties. In what year of our Lord are the proportions of payments to be settled? To say nothing of the impossibility that Colony agents should have general powers of taxing the Colonies at their discretion; consider, I implore you, that the communication by special messages, and orders between these agents and their constituents on each variation of the case, when the parties come to contend together, and to dispute on their relative proportions, will be a matter of delay, perplexity, and confusion, that never can have an end.

If all the Colonies do not appear at the outcry, what is the condition of those assemblies who offer, by themselves or their agents, to tax themselves up to your ideas of their proportion? The refractory Colonies, who refuse all composition, will remain taxed only to your old impositions; which, however grievous in principle, are trifling as to production. The obedient Colonies in this scheme are heavily taxed; the refractory remain unburthened. What will you do? Will you lay new and heavier taxes by Parliament on the disobedient? Pray consider in what way you can do it? You are perfectly convinced that in the way of taxing, you can do nothing but at the ports. Now suppose it is Virginia that refuses to appear at your auction, while Maryland and North Carolina bid handsomely for their ransom, and are taxed to your quota? How will you put these Colonies on a par? Will you tax the tobacco of Virginia? If you do, you give its death-wound to your English revenue at home, and to one of the very greatest articles of your own foreign trade. If you tax the import of that rebellious Colony, what do you tax but your own manufactures, or the goods of some other obedient, and already well-taxed Colony? Who has said one word on this labyrinth of detail, which bewilders you more and more as you enter into it? Who has presented, who can present you, with a clue, to lead you out of it? I think, Sir, it is impossible, that you should not recollect that the Colony bounds are so implicated in one another (you know it by your other experiments in the Bill for prohibiting the New-England fishery) that you can lay no possible restraints on almost any of them which may not be presently eluded, if you do not confound the innocent with the guilty, and burthen those whom, upon every principle, you ought to exonerate. He must be grossly ignorant of America, who thinks, that, without falling into this confusion of all rules of equity and policy, you can restrain any single Colony, especially Virginia and Maryland, the central, and most important of them all.

Let it also be considered, that, either in the present confusion you settle a permanent contingent, which will and must be trifling; and then you have no effectual revenue: or you change the quota at every exigency; and then on every new repartition you will have a new quarrel.

Reflect besides, that when you have fixed a quota for every Colony, you have not provided for prompt and punctual payment. Suppose one, two, five, ten years arrears. You cannot issue a treasury extent against the failing Colony. You must make new Boston port bills, new restraining laws, new Acts for dragging men to England for trial. You must send out new fleets, new armies. All is to begin again. From this day forward the Empire is never to know an hour's tranquility. An intestine fire will be kept alive in the bowels of the Colonies, which one time or other must consume this whole empire. I allow indeed that the empire of Germany raises her revenue and her troops by quotas and contingents; but the revenue of the empire, and the army of the empire, is the worst revenue, and the worst army, in the world.

Instead of a standing revenue, you will therefore have a perpetual quarrel. Indeed the noble Lord, who proposed this project of a ransom by auction, seemed himself to be of that opinion. His project was rather designed for breaking the union of the Colonies, than for establishing a Revenue. He confessed, he apprehended that his proposal would not be to *their taste*. I say, this scheme of disunion seems to be at the bottom of the project; for I will not suspect that the noble Lord meant nothing but merely to delude the nation by an airy phantom which he never intended to realize.[1] But whatever his views

---

[1] In replying to Colonel Isaac Barré (1726–1802, M.P. 1761–90), on 20 February Lord North had said it was very probable that his proposal would not be acceptable to the Americans in general. The gentleman has charged me with mean, low, and foolish policy, in measures on that maxim *divide et impera*. Is it foolish, is it mean, when a people heated and misled by evil councils, are running into unlawful combinations, to hold out those terms which will sift the reasonable

may be; as I propose the peace and union of the Colonies for the very foundation of my plan, it cannot accord with one whose foundation is perpetual discord.

Compare the two. This I offer to give you is plain and simple. The other full of perplexed and intricate mazes. This is mild; that harsh. This is found by experience effectual for its purposes; the other is a new project. This is universal; the other calculated for certain Colonies only. This is immediate in its conciliatory operation; the other remote, contingent, full of hazard. Mine is what becomes the dignity of a ruling people; gratuitous, unconditional, and not held out as matter of bargain and sale. I have done my duty in proposing it to you. I have indeed tired you by a long discourse; but this is the misfortune of those to whose influence nothing will be conceded, and who must win every inch of their ground by argument. You have heard me with goodness. May you decide with wisdom! For my part, I feel my mind greatly disburthened, by what I have done to-day. I have been the less fearful of trying your patience, because on this subject I mean to spare it altogether in future. I have this comfort, that in every stage of the American affairs, I have steadily opposed the measures that have produced the confusion, and may bring on the destruction, of this empire. I now go so far as to risque a proposal of my own. If I cannot give peace to my country; I give it to my conscience.

But what (says the Financier) is peace to us without money? Your plan gives us no Revenue. No! But it does—For it secures to the subject the power of REFUSAL; the first of all Revenues. Experience is a cheat, and fact a liar, if this power in the subject of proportioning his grant, or of not granting at all, has not been found the richest mine of Revenue ever discovered by the skill or by the fortune of man. It does not indeed vote you £152,750: 11: 2¾ths, nor any other paltry limited sum.—But it gives the strong box itself, the fund, the bank, from whence only revenues can arise amongst a people sensible of freedom: *Posita luditur arca.*[1] Cannot you in England; cannot you at this time of day; cannot you, an House of Commons, trust to the principle which has raised so mighty a revenue, and accumulated a debt of near 140 millions in this country? Is this principle to be true in England, and

---

from the unreasonable; that will distinguish those who act upon principles from those who wish only to profit of the general confusion?' Only Nova Scotia accepted North's propositions.

[1] Juvenal, *Satires*, i. 90: 'The treasure chest is staked upon the game.'

false every where else? Is it not true in Ireland? Has it not hitherto been true in the Colonies? Why should you presume that, in any country, a body duly constituted for any function, will neglect to perform its duty, and abdicate its trust? Such a presumption would go against all government in all modes. But, in truth, this dread of penury of supply, from a free assembly, has no foundation in nature. For first observe, that, besides the desire which all men have naturally of supporting the honour of their own government; that sense of dignity, and that security to property, which ever attends freedom, has a tendency to increase the stock of the free community. Most may be taken where most is accumulated. And what is the soil or climate where experience has not uniformly proved, that the voluntary flow of heaped-up plenty, bursting from the weight of its own rich luxuriance, has ever run with a more copious stream of revenue, than could be squeezed from the dry husks of oppressed indigence, by the straining of all the politic machinery in the world.

Next we know, that parties must ever exist in a free country. We know too, that the emulations of such parties, their contradictions, their reciprocal necessities, their hopes, and their fears, must send them all in their turns to him that holds the balance of the state. The parties are the Gamesters; but Government keeps the table, and is sure to be the winner in the end. When this game is played, I really think it is more to be feared, that the people will be exhausted, than that Government will not be supplied. Whereas, whatever is got by acts of absolute power ill obeyed, because odious, or by contracts ill kept, because constrained; will be narrow, feeble uncertain, and precarious. *"Ease would retract vows made in pain, as violent and void."*[1]

I, for one, protest against compounding our demands: I declare against compounding, for a poor limited sum, the immense, evergrowing, eternal Debt, which is due to generous Government from protected Freedom. And so may I speed in the great object I propose to you, as I think it would not only be an act of injustice, but would be the worst œconomy in the world, to compel the Colonies to a sum certain, either in the way of ransom, or in the way of compulsory compact.

But to clear up my ideas on this subject—a revenue from America transmitted hither—do not delude yourselves—you never can receive it—No, not a shilling. We have experience that from remote countries

---

[1] *Paradise Lost*, iv. 96–7.

it is not to be expected. If, when you attempted to extract revenue from Bengal, you were obliged to return in loan what you had taken in imposition; what can you expect from North America?[1] for certainly, if ever there was a country qualified to produce wealth, it is India; or an institution fit for the transmission, it is the East-India company. America has none of these aptitudes. If America gives you taxable objects, on which you lay your duties here, and gives you, at the same time, a surplus by a foreign sale of her commodities to pay the duties on these objects which you tax at home, she has performed her part to the British revenue. But with regard to her own internal establishments; she may, I doubt not she will, contribute in moderation. I say in moderation; for she ought not to be permitted to exhaust herself. She ought to be reserved to a war; the weight of which, with the enemies that we are most likely to have, must be considerable in her quarter of the globe. There she may serve you, and serve you essentially.

For that service, for all service, whether of revenue, trade, or empire, my trust is in her interest in the British constitution. My hold of the Colonies is in the close affection which grows from common names, from kindred blood, from similar privileges, and equal protection. These are ties, which, though light as air, are as strong as links of iron.[2] Let the Colonies always keep the idea of their civil rights associated with your Government;—they will cling and grapple to you;[3] and no force under heaven will be of power to tear them from their allegiance. But let it be once understood, that your Government may be one thing, and their Privileges another; that these two things may exist without any mutual relation; the cement is gone; the cohesion is loosened; and every thing hastens to decay and dissolution. As long as you have the wisdom to keep the sovereign authority of this country as the sanctuary of liberty, the sacred temple consecrated to our common faith, wherever the chosen race and sons of England worship freedom, they will turn their faces towards you.[4] The more they multiply, the more friends you will have; the more ardently they love liberty, the more perfect will be their obedience. Slavery they can have any where. It is a weed that grows in every

---

[1] A reference to the attempt of Chatham to extract a revenue from the East India Company in 1767, which helped to put the Company in a difficult financial position and necessitated a loan from Parliament in 1773 (L. S. Sutherland, *The East India Company in Eighteenth-Century Politics*, Oxford, 1952, pp. 182–268).

[2] *Julius Caesar*, I. iii. 93–5.

[3] *Hamlet*, I. iii. 62–3.

[4] 1 Kgs. 8: 44–5.

soil. They may have it from Spain, they may have it from Prussia. But until you become lost to all feeling of your true interest and your natural dignity, freedom they can have from none but you. This is the commodity of price, of which you have the monopoly. This is the true act of navigation, which binds to you the commerce of the Colonies, and through them secures to you the wealth of the world. Deny them this participation of freedom, and you break that sole bond, which originally made, and must still preserve, the unity of the empire. Do not entertain so weak an imagination, as that your registers and your bonds, your affidavits and your sufferances, your cockets and your clearances, are what form the great securities of your commerce. Do not dream that your letters of office, and your instructions, and your suspending clauses, are the things that hold together the great contexture of this mysterious whole. These things do not make your government. Dead instruments, passive tools as they are, it is the spirit of English communion that gives all their life and efficacy to them. It is the spirit of the English constitution, which, infused through the mighty mass, pervades, feeds, unites, invigorates, vivifies, every part of the empire, even down to the minutest member.[1]

Is it not the same virtue which does every thing for us here in England? Do you imagine then, that it is the land tax act which raises your revenue? that it is the annual vote in the committee of supply, which gives you your army? or that it is the Mutiny Bill which inspires it with bravery and discipline? No! surely no! It is the love of the people; it is their attachment to their government from the sense of the deep stake they have in such a glorious institution, which gives you your army and your navy, and infuses into both that liberal obedience, without which your army would be a base rabble, and your navy nothing but rotten timber.

All this, I know well enough, will sound wild and chimerical to the profane herd of those vulgar and mechanical politicians, who have no place among us;[2] a sort of people who think that nothing exists but what is gross and material; and who therefore, far from being qualified to be directors of the great movement of empire, are not fit to turn a wheel in the machine. But to men truly initiated and rightly taught,

---

[1] Compare Virgil, *Aeneid*, vi. 726 ff. Dryden (lines 984–5) translates the passage as follows: 'The Active Mind infus'd through all to space Unites and Mingles with the mighty Mass.'
[2] Compare Horace, *Odes*, III, i. 1: 'Odi profanum vulgus et arceo', 'The uninitiate crowd I ban and spurn.'

these ruling and master principles, which, in the opinion of such men as I have mentioned, have no substantial existence, are in truth every thing, and all in all. Magnanimity in politicks is not seldom the truest wisdom; and a great empire and little minds go ill together. If we are conscious of our situation, and glow with zeal to fill our place as becomes our station and ourselves, we ought to auspicate all our public proceedings on America, with the old warning of the church, *Sursum corda!*[1] We ought to elevate our minds to the greatness of that trust to which the order of Providence has called us. By adverting to the dignity of this high calling, our ancestors have turned a savage wilderness into a glorious empire; and have made the most extensive, and the only honourable conquests; not by destroying, but by promoting, the wealth, the number, the happiness, of the human race. Let us get an American revenue as we have got an American empire. English privileges have made it all that it is; English privileges alone will make it all it can be.

In full confidence of this unalterable truth, I now (*quod felix faustumique sit*)[2]—lay the first stone of the Temple of Peace; and I move you,

"That the Colonies and Plantations of Great Britain in North America, consisting of Fourteen separate governments, and containing Two Millions and upwards of free inhabitants, have not had the liberty and privilege of electing and sending any Knights and Burgesses, or others, to represent them in the high Court of Parliament."

Upon this Resolution, the previous question was put, and carried;—for the previous question 270,—against it 78.

As the Propositions were opened separately in the body of the Speech, the Reader perhaps may wish to see the whole of them together, in the form in which they were moved for.

MOVED

"That the Colonies and Plantations of Great Britain in North America, consisting of Fourteen separate Governments, and containing two Millions and upwards of Free Inhabitants, have not had the liberty and privilege of electing and sending any Knights and Burgesses, or others, to represent them in the High Court of Parliament.

[1] 'Lift up your hearts.'
[2] 'May it be happy and prosperous.' A common literary phrase; see e.g. Livy, *Ab urbe condita*, III. liv. 8.

"That the said Colonies and Plantations have been made liable to, and bounden by, several subsidies, payments, rates, and taxes, given and granted by Parliament; though the said Colonies and Plantations have not their Knights and Burgesses, in the said High Court of Parliament, of their own election, to represent the condition of their country; *by lack whereof, they have been oftentimes touched and grieved by subsidies given, granted and assented to, in the said Court, in a manner prejudicial to the common wealth, quietness, rest and peace, of the subjects inhabiting within the same.*

"That, from the distance of the said Colonies, and from other circumstances, no method hath hitherto been devised for procuring a Representation in Parliament for the said Colonies.

"That each of the said Colonies hath within itself a Body, chosen, in part or in the whole, by the Freemen, Freeholders, or other Free Inhabitants thereof, commonly called the General Assembly, or General Court; with powers legally to raise, levy, and assess, according to the several usage of such Colonies, duties and taxes towards defraying all sorts of public services.*

"That the said General Assemblies, General Courts, or other bodies, legally qualified as aforesaid, have at sundry times freely granted several large subsidies and public aids for his Majesty's service, according to their abilities, when required thereto by letter from one of his Majesty's Principal Secretaries of State; and that their right to grant the same, and their chearfulness and sufficiency in the said grants, have been at sundry times acknowledged by Parliament.

"That it hath been found by experience, that the manner of granting the said supplies and aids, by the said General Assemblies, hath been more agreeable to the inhabitants of the said Colonies, and more beneficial and conducive to the public service, than the mode of giving and granting aids and subsidies in Parliament to be raised and paid in the said Colonies.

"That it may be proper to repeal an act made in the 7th year of the reign of his present Majesty, intituled, An Act for granting certain duties in the British Colonies and Plantations in America; for allowing a draw-back of the duties of Customs, upon the exportation from this

---

* The first Four Motions and the last had the previous question put on them. The others were negatived.

The words in Italics were, by an amendment that was carried, left out of the motion: which will appear in the Journals, though it is not the practice to insert such amendments in the Votes.

kingdom, of coffee and cocoa-nuts, of the produce of the said Colonies or Plantations; for discontinuing the draw-backs payable on China earthen ware exported to America; and for more effectually preventing the clandestine running of goods in the said Colonies and Plantations.

"That it may be proper to repeal an Act, made in the 14th year of the reign of his present Majesty, intituled, An Act to discontinue, in such manner, and for such time, as are therein mentioned, the landing and discharging, lading or shipping of goods, wares, and merchandize, at the Town, and within the Harbour, of Boston, in the province of Massachuset's Bay, in North America.

"That it may be proper to repeal an Act made in the 14th year of the reign of his present Majesty, intituled, An Act for the impartial adminis- tration of justice, in cases of persons questioned for any acts done by them in the execution of the law, or for the suppression of riots and tumults, in the province of Massachuset's Bay, in New England.

"That it is proper to repeal an Act made in the 14th year of the reign of his present Majesty, intituled, An Act for the better regulating the government of the province of the Massachuset's Bay in New England.

"That it is proper to explain and amend an Act made in the 35th year of the reign of King Henry VIII, intituled, An Act for the trial of treasons committed out of the King's dominions.

"That, from the time when the General Assembly, or General Court, of any Colony or Plantation, in North America, shall have appointed, by act of Assembly duly confirmed, a settled salary to the offices of the Chief Justice and Judges of the superior Courts, it may be proper that the said Chief Justice and other Judges of the superior Courts of such Colony shall hold his and their office and offices during their good behaviour; and shall not be removed therefrom, but when the said removal shall be adjudged by his Majesty in Council, upon a hearing on complaint from the General Assembly, or on a complaint from the Governor, or Council, or the House of Representatives, severally of the Colony in which the said Chief Justice and other Judges have exercised the said office.

"That it may be proper to regulate the Courts of Admiralty, or Vice-admiralty, authorized by the 15th chapter of the 4th of George III, in such a manner, as to make the same more commodious to those who sue, or are sued, in the said courts; *and to provide for the more decent maintenance of the Judges of the same.*"

Burke sat down between 6.00 and 6.30. He was seconded by Lord John Cavendish, and a lengthy debate ensued which lasted apparently until about midnight. The speech was first published on 22 May 1775.

Speech on Somerset House
28 April 1775

Source: *Morning Post*, 29 April 1775

The same reports are in *Middlesex Journal*, 29 April, and different reports in *London Chronicle*, 29 April; *St James's Chronicle*, 29 April; and *Gazetteer*, 29 April (and other papers).

The King had agreed that Somerset House, where he had founded and helped to fund the Royal Academy of Arts,[1] should be pulled down and the site used for public offices. In 1775 Buckingham House became the Queen's official dower house in place of Somerset House, and the King was compensated for the cost of purchasing and improving the former. Burke spoke in the Committee of Supply on a resolution to grant £100,000 to the King. His opinion of the type of building which should be erected in place of Somerset House demonstrates his belief that public edifices, like the system of government and the constitution they serve, should be awe inspiring and suggest stability and permanency.[2]

Mr. Burke. I do not rise to oppose a motion which I think very reasonable; and I would not have it thought that we ought to grudge an expense which may add to the convenience of a great Princess who forms so large a part of the happiness of our Sovereign: But, Sir, I would speak more particularly to the latter part of the noble Lord's proposition, not to oppose it, but merely to throw out an idea by way of a hint to those who will have the conduct of this business, not to let the new building be such a disgrace to the public, as so many of the public buildings of the present are. When we go to a great expence of 100,000l. or more, do not let us sordidly save a few thousands and disgrace ourselves by such ill-timed parsimony. There are few opportunities of doing any thing of this sort; this is one of them, and I would wish the new edifice may be rendered an ornament to this great,

---

[1] J. Brooke, *King George III*, London, 1972, pp. 283, 301. For the history of Somerset House, see L. M. Bates, *Somerset House: Four Hundred Years of History*, London, 1967.
[2] See above, p. 36.

wealthy, and luxurious metropolis. When the public money is spent on
public works, the public spend it on themselves; they enjoy those works
when elegant and magnificent; they pride themselves on the glory of
their country possessing such. I never walk thro' Westminster Abbey
but I think it mine; it is every man's; and when such works are erected,
they do honour to the age. If we were upon an oeconomical system
only, and the old offices were to serve, I should admit oeconomy but if
we are to go to a great expense, in the name of national liberality, let it
be compleat. There will be two fronts to decorate, one to the River, the
other to the Strand; the latter is contracted by private houses so much,
that if you would have your building an ornament to that part of
the town, those private houses should be purchased. The additional
expense will be amply made up by the advantages you will gain in the
plan.[1]

Thomas Townshend[2] advocated economy in the construction of the new
building. Burke replied to him.

Though I must certainly differ from my honourable friend in his
principles of œconomy, yet I shall certainly agree with him in those of
humanity, so tenderly exerted against disturbing a roost of old women;
but the same humanity which dictates this should have operated with
the Gentleman to consider the probability, that if Somerset-house is
left unrepaired, or rather not rebuilt, instead of being the hospital for
old women it will prove their tomb, for they must be very old indeed if
they do not find it e'er long tumbling about their ears. Now having
dispatch'd the business of the old women, and no one can dispatch that
of old and young better, than my honourable friend; (*Here the House
was in a roar of laughter*) let us consider whether it is worth while in so
wealthy and luxurious an age, to lay out a large sum in a public
structure, and render it an object of disgust instead of pleasure, for
want of a farther small one. Our freedom, Sir, ought to dictate the
magnificence of our public works—common wealths have ever shewn
their glory and their liberality by these splendid expenses. Reflect on
the edifices of the common wealths of antiquity more magnificent than
those of emperors, as the buildings of the Republic of Holland exceed

[1] Lord North said that the principal front would be to the river and the Strand front left 'as
little expressive as may be' because of the cost of buying private houses.
[2] See above, p. 75, n. 1.

the efforts of Kings. The Stadthouse of Amsterdam[1] is a greater and better work than Versailles; but, Sir, this country has been niggardly throughout the present age—we have done nothing. Let this age come in for a share of that fame which attends the exertion of these laudable and useful expences. Who is it will say that Westminster Abbey and St Paul's are not an honour and glory to this country? If our building had been raised with equal magnificence the kingdom would have been paid their expense by the concourse of foreigners to see them. See Rome supported by this alone—Sir, I do not contend for original expense; but I say when you necessarily do much, and go to a great expense do not stop short, and lose all elegance and magnificence for want of a few thousands more. This is my argument: as you must build—as there must be fronts and ornaments of some sort, let them be beautiful—let them really decorate this great capital—let them in some degree partake of the splendor of the people to whom they belong, and by whom they are raised. Do this, though the expence be consequently greater.

The resolution was approved and embodied in the resulting statute (15 Geo. III, c. 33); work started on the new building, designed by Sir William Chambers (1772–93), in 1776.

Speech on New York Remonstrance
15 May 1775

Source: *Parl. Reg.* i. 467–8

There is no newspaper report of this speech. 'The contents of his Speech upon the occasion', *Lloyd's Evening Post*, 17 May, notes, 'have not transpired.' *Parl. Hist.* xviii. 643–4 differs slightly from *Parl. Reg.* Burke himself described the parliamentary proceedings in a letter to New York (*Corr.* iii. 164–7). See also Simmons and Thomas, vi. 34–5.

Burke, as Agent for the General Assembly of New York, presented to the Commons the Colony's Representation and Remonstrance.[2] This document

---

[1] Jacob van Campen (1595–1657) began the Town House, now the Royal Palace, in Amsterdam, in 1648.
[2] Burke moved that it be brought up, Henry Cruger actually read it (*Parl. Reg.* i. 473–8).

reviewed the legislation affecting America in recent years, condemning it in strong terms. In particular, it objected to the Declaratory Act of 1766, and claimed 'an exemption from internal taxation, and the exclusive right of providing for the support of our own civil government, and administration of justice in this colony'. It also stressed the colonists' 'undoubted and inalienable rights, as Englishmen'. This put Burke in a difficult position because the unyielding stance, in comparison to that of a previous measure in which he had also played a role, was clearly not going to help the cause of peace. On 23 May the Secretary of State for the colonies, Lord Dartmouth,[1] wrote to an official in America about the contrast between the remonstrance and a recent petition to the King from New York. He said,

Mr. Burke having delivered to me the Petition to the King, I had the honour to present it to His Majesty, who was pleased to receive it with the most gracious expressions of regard and attention to the humble requests of his faithful subjects in New York, who have on this occasion manifested a duty to His Majesty and a regard for the authority of the parent state.

Dartmouth added somewhat sourly that had their expressions in that measure not 'been unfortunately blended' with unacceptable declarations in expedients such as the remonstrance, they 'might have laid the foundation of that conciliation we have so long and so ardently wished for'.[2]

Obviously, Burke's feelings were also affected by the direct attack on the Rockinghams' Declaratory Act. It is apparent that Burke was drawing to the conclusion himself that that Act was too strong in the present crisis, since he was no longer convinced that Britain should insist upon Parliament's right to tax people for revenue who could not be represented in the House of Commons.[3] However, his second conciliation speech in November 1775 would demonstrate, that while he was prepared to give up some of the rights enshrined in that Act he was not yet prepared to discard the Act itself, or to allow that it had been responsible for the present unrest in the colonies.[4] After presenting the remonstrance he informed the Committee of Correspondence of the General Assembly of New York that 'I shewed that although your opinion concerning the universality of the Legislative power of Great Britain might not meet with the Approbation of the house, yet as that opinion, however erronious, was expressed in Terms proper and decent' it should be heard.[5] The following words seem to evince his discomfort in presenting a document which denounced this former Rockingham measure in such straightforward terms.

---

[1] As Secretary of State Dartmouth was also the President of the Board of Trade and Foreign Plantations.

[2] *Documents of the American Revolution, 1770–1783*, ed. K. G. Davies, 21 vols., Dublin, 1975, ix. 141.

[3] See above, pp. 74 and 103.

[4] See below, p. 198.

[5] *Corr.* iii. 164.

Mr. *Burke* said, he had in his hand a paper of importance. That it was from the general assembly of the province of New York, a province which yielded to no part of his Majesty's dominions in its zeal for the prosperity and unity of the empire, and which had ever contributed as much as any, in its proportion to the defence and wealth of the whole.

That it was a complaint in the form of a remonstrance, of several acts of parliament, some of which (as they affirmed) had established *principles*, and others had made *regulations* subversive of the rights of English subjects. That he did not know whether the House would approve of every opinion contained in that paper; but as nothing could be more decent and respectful than the whole tenor and language of the remonstrance, a mere mistake in opinion upon any one point, ought not to hinder them from receiving it, and granting redress on such other matters as might be really grievous, and which were not necessarily connected with that erroneous opinion. They never had before them so fair an opportunity of putting an end to the unhappy disputes with the colonies as at present; and he conjured them, in the most earnest manner, not to let it escape, as possibly the like might never return. He thought this application from America so very desirable to the House, that he could have made no sort of doubt of their entering heartily into his ideas, if lord North some days before, in opening the budget, had not gone out of his way, to make a panegyrick on the last parliament; and in particular to commend as acts of lenity and mercy, those very laws which the remonstrance considers as intolerable grievances.[1] This circumstance indeed did somewhat abate the sanguine hopes of success which he had entertained from this dutiful procedure of the colony of New York. That he was so ill as not to be able to trouble them, if he were willing, with a long speech.[2] He had several times in the session expressed his sentiments very fully upon every thing contained in that remonstrance; as for the rest it spoke so strongly for itself that he did not see how people in their senses could refuse at least the consideration of so reasonable and decent an address.

[1] Lord North's speeches as reported in *Parl. Reg.* (i. 446–50, 452) do not express these sentiments. Presumably the laws were the Coercive Acts of 1774.
[2] On 7 June 1774 Burke informed the Committee of Correspondence of the General Assembly of New York that 'I offered your remonstrance in my place' even though 'I found myself in no very good state of Health and Spirits' (*Corr.* iii. 164).

He then stated the heads of the remonstrance, which he moved for leave to bring up.

Burke moved for leave to bring up the remonstrance. Lord North carried (by 186 votes to 67) an amendment so that the motion would read: 'That the said representation and remonstrance (in which the said assembly claim to themselves rights derogatory to, and inconsistent with, the legislative authority of Parliament as declared by the said act [the Declaratory Act]) be brought up.' As amended the motion was defeated.

Bristol Petition
27 September 1775

Source: P.R.O. HO 55/11/64

Richard Champion sent hastily made copies of this petition to Portland (MS. PwF 2,717) and to Rockingham (MS. at Sheffield, R1.1603b). The petition was printed in *Morning Chronicle*, 13 October, *Middlesex Journal* and *General Evening Post*, 14 October, and other papers.

In the spring and summer of 1775 the American war had in all practical respects begun. The initial battles were fought at Lexington in April and Bunker Hill in June and the Second Continental Congress assembled at Philadelphia to assume the functions of a national government. One of its first duties was to select George Washington[1] of Virginia 'to command all the continental forces, raised, or to be raised, for the defence of American liberty'.[2] In Britain the Crown received a large number of loyal addresses, during the summer and autumn, promising support against the rebellion in America. The addresses were encouraged and in part promoted by a matching campaign of petitions to the King, pleading for a policy of conciliation. In a number of places, the conciliatory petition was a direct response to a coercive address. But in Bristol the meeting held on 27 September in the guild-hall by opponents of the North Administration, preceded the meeting called to support coercion.[3] However, Burke had had considerable difficulty garnering support for the measure. 'The principal difficulty I found among well affected people', he told Rockingham, 'was this. What should they do? The Business of Petitions had hitherto proved so ineffectual that they altogether despaird.' At one point, this had compelled him to tell them that 'if they could not

---

[1] (1732–99).
[2] *Journals of the Continental Congress 1774–1789*, eds. W. C. Ford et al., 34 vols., Washington, 1904–37, i. 69–71, 73, 80, 83.
[3] J. E. Bradley, *Popular Politics and the American Revolution in England: Petitions, the Crown, and Public Opinion*, Macon, Ga., 1986, pp. 73–4.

prevail on themselves to follow up their Petition by a regular sollicitation, pursued through all the modes of civil resistance, and legal opposition, that they should not present it at all'.[1] Burke was almost certainly the author of the petition. Champion wrote to Rockingham on 27 September: 'The excellence of it will soon convince your Lordship whose it is.'[2]

To the King's most excellent Majesty

The humble Petition of the Merchants, Traders, Manufacturers, and others, Citizens of BRISTOL

May it please your Majesty:

We your Majesty's most dutiful and loyal Subjects, the Merchants, Traders, Manufacturers, and others, Citizens of Bristol, humbly beg leave to approach the Throne with the most respectful assurances of our unalterable attachment and affection to your Majesty's Royal Person and Family, and of our unfeigned Zeal for the support of your Government, the Glory of your Reign, and the peace and prosperity of your once united and flourishing, but now most unhappily distracted Empire.

It is with an affliction, not to be express'd, and with the most anxious apprehensions for ourselves and our posterity, that we behold the growing distractions in America threaten, unless prevented by the timely interposition of your Majesty's Wisdom and Goodness, nothing less than a lasting and ruinous civil War. We are apprehensive, that, if the present measures are adhered to, a total alienation of the affections of our fellow-Subjects, in the Colonies will ensue; to which affection, much more than to a dread of any power, we have been hitherto indebted for the inestimable Benefits which we have derived from those Establishments. We can foresee no good effects to the Commerce or Revenues of this Kingdom, at a future period, from any victories which may be obtained by your Majesty's arms over desolated Provinces and an exasperated People. From the consequences of a reverse of things, in the course of human events not impossible, we chuse to avert our Eyes. We apprehend that none can profit by the continuance of this War, and therefore we hope, none can wish it, except those Nations who, envious of the diffusive liberty and consequent power

---

[1] *Corr.* iii. 208.
[2] MS. at Sheffield, R1.1603.

and prosperity of your Dominions, are the natural Enemies of Great Britain.

We owe a testimony of Justice to your Colonies, which is, that in the midst of the present distractions, we have received many unequivocal proofs, that our fellow-Subjects in that part of the World are very far from having lost their ancient affection and regard to their Mother Country, or departed from the principles of commercial honour and private Justice. Notwithstanding the cessation of the powers of Government throughout that vast Continent, we have reason to think, judging by the imports into this City, and by our extensive correspondencies, that the Commodities of American growth, enumerated by Acts of Parliament, have been as regularly brought to Great Britain as in the most quiet times. We assure your Majesty, that the trade of this Port, and the subsistence of a great part of your Kingdom, have depended very much on the honourable, and, in this instance, amicable behaviour of your American Subjects. We have in this single City received, within one year, from the first of September 1774, more than one million Bushells of Wheat,[1] to say nothing of the great quantity of other valuable Commodities, essential to our Navigation and Commerce. These Circumstances, we humbly beg leave with the utmost deference, to submit to your Majesty's consideration, in order to shew that, whenever your Royal Clemency shall exert itself in behalf of your Colonies, the dispositions on their part to peace and reconciliation are by no means so unfavourable, as many Persons, from passion or misinformation, may possibly suggest.

No part of your Majesty's Subjects can wish more earnestly to preserve the Constitutional Superiority of the British Legislature over all parts of your Dominions than the Citizens of Bristol. But they are convinced, from clear reason and severe experience, that this superiority can hardly be preserved by mere force, nor without acquiring the confidence, and cultivating the affections of the great and numerous people who inhabit the British Plantations. We humbly conceive that this Authority would suffer no diminution in the least prejudicial to it by healing concessions; by the relaxation of penal statutes which have been found ineffectual for their purposes, and by relinquishing the pursuit of an Object, the possible attainment of which, under any circumstances of fortune, may admit of the most serious doubt. On the

---

[1] See above, p. 117.

contrary we have reason, altho' things have been carried to unfortunate lengths of hostility on both sides, to hope the most salutary effects from a return, under your Majesty's provident and sagacious direction, to the antient, indulgent. and happy usage of this Kingdom, with regard to its Colonies.

We find ourselves under an indispensable necessity of making, with respectful plainness, this dutiful and most faithful representation of our sentiments to your Majesty, lest it might be supposed, that by our silence, we were consenting to the opinions and wishes for coercive proceedings, express'd in the late addresses to your Majesty. We assure your Majesty, that we are Men of peaceful dispositions; that we detest the thought of obtruding on your Majesty's Wisdom and Clemency any sort of recommendation of force and rigour against any part of your people. That we who have long flourish'd by an amicable intercourse with the Colonies should call for coercive measures, as the probable means of future Commerce, would not only be arrogant and presumptuous, but unnatural and ungrateful. No experience has hitherto taught us the good effects of such measures; and it little becomes us to recommend violent and hazardous proceedings. We must always look back with Satisfaction and Gratitude to that period of your Majesty's reign, when a prudent concession restored tranquillity and commerce to all your Majesty's Dominions. We trust, that after having humbly intreated the exertion of your Majesty's Wisdom for reconciling amicably the differences which unhappily subsist among your Subjects, we have cleared ourselves to our own Consciences, and acquitted ourselves in the Eyes of Almighty God, of our Sovereign, and of our Country, from any share whatsoever, in producing the Calamities which the present proceedings so inauspiciously begun, may yet bring upon this Nation.

The petition was presented on 11 October 1775.[1]

---

[1] Bradley, *Popular Politics*, p. 65.

Draft Petition on America
[1775]

Source: MS. at Sheffield, Bk 6.109

This rough draft of a petition to the Commons can be dated autumn 1775 from matters to which it refers. 'The Merchants who humbly supplicated to be heard' were almost certainly those of Bristol and other places who presented petitions during the 1774–5 session (see above, p. 73). Consideration of those petitions was, as indicated here, put off until after North had brought forward other measures relative to the growing conflict. The 'Correspondence' laid before Parliament appears to be that which was brought forward at the beginning of the same session (see above, p. 79).

This draft serves as an indication of Burke's frame of mind after the initial battles in the American war. However, it appears never to have been put into final form and it was not used.

[1]That your Petitioners amidst the great Calamities they suffer and the ⟨yet⟩ greater they apprehend had the natural and just expectation that Parliament, convinced by experience of the fatal consequences arising from the measures of coercion, would have at length abandond so injudicious and so fatal a System.

As British Subjects we have the most serious interest in the reputation of the publick Councils of this Kingdom. We find that in the last Session a very imperfect and avowedly garbled Correspondence was laid before you here. The true state of America was designedly conceald from you. Establishments were proposed to you with a knowledge that they were inadequate to their purposes.[2] The Kings Ministers conceald even from their own Collegues the true State of their affairs. The Merchants who humbly supplicated to be heard before you had determined on Measures of the most unhappy tendency, and who from their correspondences were capable of supplying the premeditated deficiency of Official information, were with every mark of contempt postpond until the house had come to violent resolutions upon the imperfect matter before them.[3] Time and bitter experience have shewn, that they ought to have been heard that there was no occasion for

---

[1] At the top: 'One years more experiment—if it cost nothing I agree. But when the success is not probable the Object disproportiond. This experiment absurd.'

[2] On 20 December 1774 Burke had joined others in challenging North on his proposal to maintain a peacetime level of taxation when the country was on the brink of war; see his speech of 20 December 1774 on the land tax, above, pp. 74–8.

[3] A reference to the 'Coventry Committee'; see above, p. 79.

precipitating Measures which could, they have had, no other tendency than to exasperate the minds of men already inflamed, and to kindle discontent and dissatisfaction into decided hostility and open War. That they added no

Your Petitioners observe, that the Ministers in consequence of this miserable plan for the delusion of themselves and of Parliament sent over an army which through the very flower of the British Military and[1]

Draft Petition on Use of Indians
[1775]

Source: MS. at Sheffield, Bk 6.174

This piece was probably also written in the autumn of 1775. An erased passage refers to the presentation of a petition to the House of Commons 'in the beginning of the last Session of Parliament' from 'the Merchants and Manufacturers of this City'. The Merchants and Manufacturers of Bristol petitioned the House of Commons on 23 January 1775 and Burke gave them his full support (see above, p. 78).

Burke was concerned about the barbarities of the American war and thus about the use by the British of Indians and Black slaves which he firmly considered inhumane.[2] He undoubtedly knew of rumours which were circulating in the colonies by late 1775 that the 'Wild and barbarous savages of the wilderness have been sollicited by gifts to take up the hatchet against us, and instigated to deluge our settlements with the blood of innocent and defenceless women and children.'[3] He also knew that the Governor of Virginia, Lord Dunmore, had issued a proclamation promising freedom to Negro slaves who would take the British side in the conflict. Though it was never used, the following rough draft of a petition largely on the Indian question, underscores the depth of Burke's concern for what he considered acceptable standards of behaviour even in warfare.

To the Honourable the Commons of G. B. in Parliament assembled, the humble Petition of the Mayor, Sheriffs, Merchants Manufacturers, and others Freemen of the City of Bristol.

[1] At the end: 'An Enemy from principle independent of Events. I constant and uniform that such a conquest as proposed would produce the total lasting, ruin of this Country instead of adding to its strength and would fix a wasting cancer in its vitals that would turn to so destruction every Cause of its prosperity and all its food in to poison.' Endorsed: 'Genl Am. Draft of Petn. one way if a Coup de main another if a Systematick War.'
[2] See below, pp. 308, 354–67.
[3] *Universal Magazine*, lvii (September 1775), 145.

Your Petitioners touched with the sentiments of humanity which naturally arise in the hearts of all those not perfect Strangers [to] the present most miserable State of the British dominions now labouring under the horrors of an unnatural Civil War in all the humility which can be inspired by the most ⟨   ⟩ beg leave to prostrate themselves before this honourable house, and to supplicate the restoration of peace to their Country.

The means by which this War has been[1] attempted—to call from that Wilderness, which is not yet reclaimed [by] the spirited Enterprise of our American brethren and which they looked to as the present ⟨provision⟩ ⟨object⟩ for the growing industry of future generations, every Class of savages and Cannibals the most cruel and ferocious ever ⟨known⟩ to lay Waste with fire hatchet with Murders, and Sanguinary Tortures of the Inhabitants, the most beautiful Work of Skill and Labour by which the creation and name of God was ever glorified by his Creatures. Publick assemblies of the Savages have been held for this horrid purpose. Messengers have been dispatched to every Tribe to incite them to ravage and destroy the English. Even the Agents which were maintain'd[2] at the Charge and out of the labours of those unfortunate people in order to conciliate their minds to the English Inhabitants [and] soften their ferocity, have as we are credibly informed by an horrid and unnatural breach of Trust, endeavourd to direct the fury of these Barbarians against your Majesties people.[3] These are not ways of making War like the generous open and humane procedure which formerly even in its hostilities distinguishd this gallant Nation. And we wish to acquit ourselves in this publick and solemn manner, before the representatives of the people, and before the world from any sort of encouragement whatsoever to a War which must be carried on upon such a degenerate manner. We know of no concession so humiliating as this mode of enforcement.[4]

---

[1] MS.: been been

[2] In the margin: 'and lay in reserve'.

[3] The superintendants of the Indian districts had been instructed to enlist Indian support.

[4] Burke intended to insert a paragraph on Bristol's loss of trade, but has not indicated where it was to come. It reads: 'Your Petitioners feel them[selves] as capable and not influenced by sordid or selfish consideration. They know themselves to be actuated by the purest Motives as capable and of their Trade and Commerce, which are however the most serious Interest to them [and] to the whole Kingdom. Whenever they are called to ⟨make so great a⟩ sacrifice [to the] Dignity of their Sovereign, and the honour of their Country; But they are thoroughly convinced that the present War can add nothing to the glory of the King, or for the advantage of reputation or greatness of the State.'

Your Petitioners conceive, that they are fully entitled by the constitution and strictly bound by their Duty humbly to request a redress of Grievances from the house of Commons. They therefore beg leave to represent this War as an heavy Grievance. From the unfeigned deference to the Judgment of [the] house they will not assert, what they greatly fear, that it were better it never had been undertaken. But as the house is not concernd in the Conduct of this unhappy, Measure, they beg leave to represent that Hostilities carried on though with great and ruinous expense yet weakly and ineffectively; so as to reflect no Credit upon the Counsels and arms of this Country; and they humbly pray, that an enquiry may be made to discover by what means it has happend, and by whose Neglect or Crimes that when those hostilities which they had formerly deprecated and now deplore, had been resolved upon, preparations correspondent to the magnitude of so arduous and dangerous an undertaking were not made; by which violent resolve and feeble execution the means of Lenity have been rejected, and the Effects of Terrour not Obtaind; That America is for the present lost to this Kingdom, and that the ways of recovering it, otherwise than by reestablishing the antient affection of the Colonies, is as uncertain as it is mischievious and dishonourable.

Speech on Militia Bill
2 November 1775

Source: *Morning Chronicle*, 3 November 1775

The same report is in the *London Evening Post* and *Middlesex Journal* of 4 November. It was also used by *Parl. Reg.* iii. 98–9 and *Parl. Hist.* xviii. 853–4. Another report is in *Lloyd's Evening Post*, 3 November (and other papers). See also Simmons and Thomas, vi. 167.

On 30 October Lord North presented a Bill for enabling the King to call out and assemble the militia, in cases of rebellion in any part of the dominions belonging to the Crown of Great Britain. The debate on the second reading on 2 November ranged widely, one of the subjects discussed being the recent addresses to the Crown.

Mr. Burke then rose, and observed, that the Manchester Address[1] was not singular in the indecency of its language, but that all the ministerial

---

[1] *London Gazette*, 16 September 1775.

Addresses spoke of those who had endeavoured to prevent the civil war in which this country was unhappily now plunged through the ruinous and destructive measures pursued by Administration, in the most scurrilous and illiberal manner, That the Gentleman who defended Manchester[1] stood in the same predicament with many others who had signed what they never read, and therefore wondered when they afterwards heard of the language of the Addresses; language, he said, which disgraced the name of Britons, in which the good-nature of Englishmen and the manners of gentlemen were totally forgot, and which, though procured by courtiers, contained nothing characteristic of them but the most ignoble servility, and the most unmerciful encouragement of barbarous blood-thirsty measures. There were two Addresses Mr. Burke declared, which called loudly for the censure of that House—the Address from the first battalion of the Devonshire Militia,[2] and the Address from the University of Oxford.[3]—These he termed the Addresses Military and Ecclesiastic;—Addresses from persons who, at all times, and on all occasions, were debarred constitutionally from meddling with the politics of the country. He descanted largely on the first, shewing the impropriety of the Militia, or any armed body's soliciting to be employed against their fellow-subjects. With regard to the latter, he directly charged Lord North with having not only seen it before it was presented to the King, but with having altered the composition of it[4]—and he thundered out, that if Lord North avowed the propriety of the University of Oxford (a body of learned, religious men, whose fervent wishes and pious prayers for the good of their country ought to be their only notice of her government) interfering with the politics of Great Britain, advising a civil war, and calling those that opposed it Rebels and Traitors, *the Freedom of this country was dead,—her Liberty was no more*. He painted in strong colours, the situation of the heads of an University, who he declared ought by no means to instil political principles into the minds of those who were

---

[1] Sir Thomas Egerton, 7th Baronet (1749–1814), M.P. 1772–84. He was the first signer of the Manchester Address and had presented it to the King. The Address referred to the 'artful design of a discontented faction'.

[2] *London Gazette*, 14 October 1775.

[3] Ibid., 31 October 1775.

[4] John Dunning, a leading spokesman for the Chathamite Opposition and a member of the Shelburne connection, had made a similar claim about the Devonshire address but was compelled to withdraw it. Lord North agreed that as Chancellor of the University he had seen the Oxford address before it was presented, but denied that he had altered the language (*Parl. Reg.* iii. 102–3).

not sufficiently matured,—who knew too little of the world to be able to judge of their propriety, and to distinguish between sound policy and destructive expedients. Every man, he observed, must feel the violent error of such a conduct; he had himself a son[1] at the University, and he could not approve of his son's being told by grave men, that his father was an abettor of Rebels. He concluded with declaring that Lord North ought not only to have abstained from taking part in the formation of that Address, but that he ought to have rejected it when it was sent to him, and prevented it from being presented.

The debate ended with a division on the Militia Bill, which obtained a second reading by 259 votes to 50.

Second Speech on Conciliation
16 November 1775

Sources: *Parl. Reg.* iii. 170–86; MSS. at Sheffield, Bk 6.202, 196, 197a, 200, 192, 203, 191, 194

The text of this speech was presumably prepared by someone close to Burke. The gallery was closed for the speech so that the immediate newspaper reports are poor. Two instalments of the text printed by Almon had been printed in the newspapers (e.g. *London Evening Post*, 18, 23 November; see also Simmons and Thomas, vi. 260–7, 273–4, 275), but the final part or parts did not appear in the press. There is a MS. of the Bill which is appended to the speech at Sheffield (Bk 6.205–6), and a few omissions in the Almon text are supplied from it. A considerable number of overlapping drafts also survive (MSS. at Sheffield, Bk 6.190–203), some of them made after the delivery of the speech (*Corr.* iii. 246). The more coherent of these are reproduced here; others are quoted in annotation.

Burke prepared a new plan of conciliation for the parliamentary session of 1775–6. By the time he presented it to the Commons the hope of achieving peace had grown slim indeed. On 7 November a petition to the Crown from the General Congress in America calling for 'a happy and permanent reconciliation' was presented to the House of Lords by Richard Penn.[2] It was greeted 'only with silence' by Lord Dartmouth, the Secretary of State for the colonies, and the Duke of Richmond's motion to use it as 'Grounds of Conciliation' failed.[3] The North Government was now in the process of preparing the American Prohibitory Act[4] which, while it would provide for the

---

[1] Richard Burke (1758–94), at Christ Church.
[2] (1736–1811), grandson of William Penn (1644–1718), the founder of Pennsylvania.
[3] *Parl. Hist.* xviii. 919–35. The petition was also published in the newspapers. See, for instance, *Gentleman's Magazine*, xlv (1775), 433.
[4] 16 Geo. III, c. 5.

formation of a commission to negotiate conciliation with the colonies,[1] would also end all trade and intercourse between Britain and America and empower the officers and crews on ships of the British navy to make 'lawful prize' of colonial shipping. Burke gave notice on 2 November that he would propose his plan on 10 November, but it was twice postponed: first because of other parliamentary business (and also because Charles Fox would not be present); and again from 13 to 16 November because of the death of Dr. Christopher Nugent,[2] Burke's father-in-law.[3]

The second conciliation speech represents a further modification of Burke's position. This may in part reflect growing anxiety resulting from the realization that Britain could not win the war, since her erstwhile enemies France and Spain would eventually become involved.[4] The Bill Burke presented would not only have made it clear that Britain would never again tax America for revenue purposes, but in order to demonstrate the imperial Government's sincerity, it would have employed a variation of North's earlier plan by giving the assemblies in the colonies access to any duties arising from taxes imposed for the regulation of trade and commerce.[5] Like Chatham's proposal of 20 February it would also have provided official British recognition of an American congress.

The public had eagerly awaited this speech and on 13 November people had so packed the gallery of the House of Commons that officials felt compelled to clear it and lock the doors.[6] Burke's performance did not make quite the same impact on those who did hear it, however, that his first conciliatory speech had. The response from members of the press and others, though certainly positive, was somewhat less eulogistic. Part of the reason appears to have been that Burke himself was less animated than he had been earlier. Listeners were most impressed with the clarity and strength of his logic, but they made very few comments about the passion behind his words or the entertainment value. Typical newspaper coverage respectfully acknowledged that 'his arguments were irresistible ... those who did not approve could not oppose'.[7] Burke was now a recognized champion of American liberty and there was no longer any need for him to convince either himself or the public of where his real sentiments lay. He was able, therefore, simply to present the studied and well-deliberated views of a seasoned fighter in what for him was a rather straightforward and subdued manner. His

---

[1] 16 Geo. III, c. 18.

[2] (1698–1775).

[3] *Lloyd's Evening Post*, 6 November; *Morning Chronicle*, 11 November; *London Chronicle*, 14 November; R. J. S. Hoffman, *Edmund Burke New York Agent*, New York, 1973, p. 607.

[4] See below, pp. 300, 440. This view is to be compared with those expressed in his first conciliation speech (above, pp. 118–9).

[5] North offered to credit the accounts of the colonial assemblies with any monies accrued through the regulation of trade and thereby reduce the amount owed for the payment of the tax which they were to be allowed to collect themselves.

[6] *Corr.* ii. 236.

[7] *Gentleman's Magazine*, xlvi (1776), 8.

arguments were relatively well received by M.P.s as well as the press; the minority on the motion to bring on the Bill rose to 105—at that point the largest of the session.

As a preliminary to the speech Burke presented a petition from Wiltshire clothiers on the decline of trade which called for the adoption of

such lenient measures as may restore to this great kingdom and her colonies that affectionate intercourse with each other, which alone can prevent the Manifold evils with which they are now threatened, and establish the national greatness on the broad foundation of equal rule, and the genuine happiness of a free, loyal, and united people.

(1) PARLIAMENTARY REGISTER

Mr. *Burke*, who presented this petition, said, that the signers were all men who manufactured for themselves; and he was authorized to say that they possessed more than 500,000l. of English property.

He wished the prayer of that petition to be considered as the exordium of what he had to say to the House. He complained of the difficulties which in civil wars lay upon moderate men, who advised lenient measures; that their moderation was attributed to a want of zeal, and their fears for the public safety, to a want of spirit; that on this particular occasion whatever they said to incline the House to lenity, was construed into a countenance of rebellion; and so many arts, and so many menaces had been used, that if they had not been opposed with a good share of firmness by the friends to the peace of their country, all freedom of debate, and indeed all public deliberation, would have been put an end to.

He said, that for his part he was no way intimidated by all these machinations from doing his duty; and that nothing that could be threatned by those whose measures had brought this country into so deplorable a situation, should hinder him from using his best endeavours to deliver it from its distresses.

The first step for this purpose, was to get out of general discourses, and vague sentiments, which he said had been one of the main causes of our present troubles; and to appreciate the value of the several plans that were, or might be proposed, by an exact detail of particulars.

He stated, that there were three plans afloat. First, simple war, in order to a perfect conquest. Second, a mixture of war and treaty. And thirdly, peace grounded on concession.

As to the first plan, that of mere war, he observed, that it was proposed in two ways; the one *direct* by conquest, the other *indirect* by distress. In either of these ways he thought it his duty before he voted for a war, to know distinctly that the means of carrying it on were adequate to the end. It did not satisfy his conscience to say, that the resources of this nation were great; he must see them. That before he could trust to those resources, on the credit of what had been formerly done, he must find the situation of the country to be what it formerly was.

He then examined what the ministers had laid before the House as the means of carrying on the ensuing campaign. That as to the forces which they had made the House expect from his Majesty's allies, all discourse of them had, for some time, entirely subsided: he could, therefore, take credit for nothing more on that account, than a handful of Hanoverians, which only answered the purpose of an imperfect security to some of our foreign garrisons. That our national forces to be employed in America, by the account on the table, amounted to no more than 26,000 men. In this, credit was taken for the army now in America at full numbers. He could not allow that estimate; as supposing that if the reduction of the troops in future was to be estimated by the past, they must be reduced to little or nothing, by the beginning of next campaign. That the troops here are only upon paper, and the difficulty of recruiting was acknowledged. On the whole, he saw reason to apprehend that we should not be very materially stronger at the beginning of the next year, than we were at the beginning of the last. He said, the probable number of troops, whether national or foreign, weighed very little in his judgment; as he thought the circumstances of the country were such, as would disable them from effecting any thing like a conquest of it.

That as to the *predatory*, or war by distress (on the nature of which he greatly enlarged) he observed, that it might irritate a people in the highest degree; but such a war had never yet induced any one people to receive the government of another. That it was a kind of war adapted to distress an independent people, and not to coerce disobedient subjects.

But his great objection to it was, that it did not lead to a speedy decision. The longer our distractions continued, the greater chance there was for the interference of the Bourbon powers, which in a long protracted war, he considered not only as probable, but in a manner certain. That he was very sure this country was utterly incapable of carrying on a war with America and these powers acting in conjunction. He entered into a long and particular enumeration of all the dangers and difficulties which must attend such a war.

He stated the condition of France at the beginning of this century, and even within a few years; and compared it with her present situation. He observed, that from being the *first*, she was, with regard to effective military power, only the *fifth* state in Europe. That she was fallen below her former rank, solely from the advantages we had obtained over her; and that if *she* could humble *us*, she would certainly recover her situation. There was now an opportunity for her making herself, with very little hazard or difficulty, the first maritime power in the world; and to invest herself with every branch of trade, necessary to secure her in that pre-eminence. He admitted, that at present there were circumstances (which he mentioned) that *might* prevent her from availing herself of this opportunity. But, he said, we must be mad to trust such an interest as ours to such a chance; and that they who presumptuously trust to the *extraordinary* Providence of God, by acting without prudence or foresight, deserve to be abandoned by his *ordinary* protection.[1]

He then observed that, as he saw no probability of success in the *detail* of any of the arrangements[2] that were proposed, neither did he see any thing of *authority* to induce him to believe that they would succeed; not one military or naval officer having given an opinion in its favour; and many of the greatest in both services, having given their opinion directly against it.

That as no man of *military experience* had vouched for the *sufficiency* of the force, so no man in the *commissariate* would answer for its *subsistence* from the moment it left the sea coast; that therefore its subsistence[3] and its operation were become incompatible.

To the objection, that at this rate the Americans might always bring us to unreasonable terms, by the supposed impossibility of reducing them by force, he said that he could not help the difficulties which arose from nature and the constitution of things; that he could not make America nearer to us than it is; or a country of another nature than what God has made it. That people who cannot contrive to reconcile their quarrels, must suffer the evils that happen to a divided

[1] Burke placed Russia, Austria, and Prussia above France (see below, p. 212). Britain presumably was first.

[2] *Parl. Reg.*: 'arrangement'.

[3] *Parl. Reg.*: 'subsistance'.

nation. That he was of opinion, there was no dishonour at all in any kind of amicable adjustment of domestic quarrels; and he would rather yield an hundred points; when it was Englishmen that gave and received, than a single point to a foreign nation; and we were in such circumstances that we must yield to either one or the other.

After an examination of the merits of the first plan, that of reducing the colonies to obedience by *simple war, in order to a perfect conquest*, he entered into a discussion of the second, viz. *That of the mixture of war and treaty*.

Among the great and manifest diversity of sentiments which prevailed on the treasury-bench, he thought he could discern that this plan had been the most generally adopted by ministers, or by those who acted as such. That no light, however, had been let in upon the *particulars* of the scheme, except in the speech from the throne. It was indeed very little, and that little very fallacious. One would be inclined to think from that speech, that nothing had retarded the restoration of peace, but a doubt, whether those in arms might, upon laying them down, obtain a speedy pardon. However, the fact was, no pardon had been ever applied for. If nothing had been wanting to conclude the peace but such a power, the commander in chief might be authorised to hold out mercy to all those who should submit; and then there would be no need of the laborious, expensive, uncertain, and dilatory process of a commission.

It was impossible to pass by the very exceptionable manner in which this power of pardoning was to be delegated: "they shall have authority (says the speech from the throne) to grant general or *particular* pardons or indemnities, in *such manner*, and *to such persons, as they shall think fit*." A shocking, arbitrary power, not to be trusted to any persons, as giving encouragement to *dangerous partialities*, and tending rather to distract than to quiet the country. That the rule of pardon, when delegated to subjects, ought not to be their *pleasure* or *displeasure*, but the compliance or non-compliance of the guilty, with certain *fixed conditions*. That some such discretionary power as that mentioned in the speech, seems to be given already, and to have produced the mischiefs which might be expected from it. For that general Gage had already, whether by himself, or by order from ministers, made a very indiscreet use of it, by offering mercy to those who were openly in arms, and actually besieging him in his station, and excluding from mercy those who were five hundred miles from him,* and then sitting in an assembly never declared by authority to be illegal; an assembly, from which the ministers in the House of Commons had at one time declared they were not without hopes of proposals, which might lead to accommodation.[1] On this part of the speech from the throne he animadverted with great severity.

He said he understood, that instead of the Americans waiting for pardons, they were to be persuaded by negotiation to accept them. Therefore it would be necessary to examine what *body* of men it was that administration proposed to negotiate with, and what the *objects* of the negotiation were to be.

That if he did not mistake the discourses of ministers, they did not now propose to negotiate with the present, or with any other *General Congress* or meeting, but with the *several assemblies* distinctly. In this scheme, he said, they knew that they could not succeed. Because there was one principal province, that of Massachuset's bay, whose assembly, under their charter, was destroyed by act of Parliament. That no assembly would sit in that province under the new constitution; because if it should, the inhabitants must, as a preliminary, yield the principal object for which they had taken up arms; and thus turn the negotiation against themselves, even before it should be opened. That this province was the actual seat of war, as its sufferings had been the cause of the war itself. Treaty must therefore stumble upon the threshold.

That besides this objection, (which was fundamental) a negotiation with so many provinces, of such different constitutions, tempers, and opinions, never could come to an end. In the mean time our hostile operations with their whole train of disasters, accidents, and ruinous expences would be continued, to the destruction of this country and of that. That the hope of *dividing* the colonies, on which this part of the plan was founded, and which was even avowed as a reason for adopting it, would be the most unfortunate thing that could happen; as it would protract the war, and complicate its horrors and miseries, without a

---

* Messrs. Hancock and Adams, who were excepted in the general pardon offered by general Gage on submission, whilst Ward, Putnam, &c. besieging him, were *not* excepted.[2]

[1] If ministers made such a statement, it does not seem to have been recorded.

[2] General Gage had issued a proclamation on 12 June offering pardon to all who laid down their arms except John Hancock (1737–93) and Samuel Adams (1722–1803), both members of the Continental Congress (*Corr.* iii. 179–80). Gage was besieged in Boston by Artermas Ward (1727–1800) and Israel Putnam (1718–90).

possibility of ending it. It was, he said, a vain imagination, that any of the colonies would take up arms in favour of ministry, for the execution of any of their plans; and that a *part* of the colonies was sufficient, at least to keep this war alive, until the interference of foreign powers should render it utterly destructive.

That with regard to the *objects* of the treaty,—they must be concessions on the side of the colonies; or upon ours or upon both. That upon their side they must be either *speculative* recognitions of rights upon *as large a scale as we had claimed them*; and this it was absolutely certain they never would submit to; or upon a *lesser, excluding taxation*, and its *consequences*, and this they had submitted to already; so that there seemed to be no object of the speculative kind, which made it necessary to postpone peace by a protracted negotiation.

That the other object of treaty might be a *practical* recognition of our right of taxing for a revenue; that this revenue was to be either nominal or beneficial; if only *nominal*, it amounted to nothing more than that speculative acknowledgment of right, which we knew they would for ever refuse to make. If *beneficial* and productive, it was to be either by submitting to lord North's proposition, namely, that of forcing them to furnish a *contingent* by authority of Parliament; or according to their ancient mode, by a *voluntary grant* of their own assemblies.

If the former, we know, said he, they have already rejected that proposition; and never can submit to it, without abandoning that point, for the maintenance of which they have risked their all. If it only requires, that they should resort to their ancient mode of granting by their assemblies, they have declared again and again, from the beginning of this contest to the end, that they were willing to contribute according to their ability, *as estimated by themselves*, who were the best judges of what their ability was.[1] That ability would be lessened, if not totally be destroyed, by the continuance of those troubles. This armed negotiation for taxes would therefore inevitably defeat its own purposes; and prevent for ever the possibility of raising any revenue, either by our authority, or by that of their own assemblies.

That if the ministers treated for a revenue, or for any other purpose, they had but two securities for the performance of the terms: either the

---

[1] The Americans had in fact claimed ever since Grenville's negotiations with them in 1764–5 that they had to be the ones to decide how much if anything they should contribute. See Burke's reply to Mauduit of [February 1775], above, pp. 91–6.

same force which compelled these terms; or the honour, sincerity, and good inclination of the people. If they could trust the people to *keep* the terms without force, they might trust them to *make* them without force. If nothing but force could hold them, and that they meant nothing but *independency*, as the speech from the throne asserted, then the House was to consider how a standing army of 26,000 men, and 70 ships of war, could be constantly kept up in America. A people meaning independency, will not mean it the less, because they have, to avoid a present inconvenience, submitted to treaty. That after all our struggles, our hold on America, is, and must be, her good inclination. If this fails, all fails; and we had better trust to the honesty of the colonies, before we had ruined ourselves, than after; before we had irritated them, than after we had alienated their affections for ever.

That the troops sent for the purpose of *forwarding*, would certainly *impede* the negotiation. That it was impossible the provincials could be mad enough to lay down their arms, whilst a great adverse military power remained in their country, without any assurance whatsoever of their obtaining any one of the points for which they had contended. This would not be to negociate, but to surrender at discretion. All the grievances they had complained of, were contained in acts of Parliament. Lord North had declared very truly, that nobody could have power to negociate for the repeal of an act of Parliament.

But if the colonies should incline to put any confidence in the *certain* influence of ministry over Parliament, even that grand confidence must fail them; as they cannot tell whether the same ministers will continue in power; and that even at this very time no two persons upon the treasury-bench were of the same opinion, on the conduct to be held towards America. Which of those opinions would finally prevail, no man living could divine. That this uncertainty might continue the armed negociation for several years, to the utter ruin of both countries.

He gave many other equally strong reasons against this scheme; and concluded this part of his speech, by observing, that although the mixed plan of war and negotiation could answer no good end in *future*, it might have a *retrospective* operation,—to justify the ministers in the use of their forcible proceedings. For *force* and *concession* going out together, if peace should be the result, ministers would attribute the success, not to the *concession*, but to the *force*, So that all this delay, bloodshed, and expence, was incurred merely to furnish ministers with an excuse in debate.

After going through the two first plans, he spoke to the third (his own) that of a *concession previous to treaty*.

He observed, that as he put no great trust in any negotiation, and none at all in an *armed* negotiation, his idea was, to have very little treaty; and that little as short as possible. The House was therefore at that time to judge, whether it was necessary to make any concession to the colonies: if it should appear to them that such concession was necessary, he was clearly of opinion, that they ought to make it immediately, and of their own free grace. This he thought of more dignity with regard to themselves, and of much more efficacy with regard to the quiet of the colonies, than the *concession upon treaty* which had been proposed.

He said, that the first ground of treaty must be *confidence*; and that the colonies never could confide for the effect of any concession (as he had shewn in examining the foregoing plan) in a less assurance than that of Parliament itself.

He then shewed, by a variety of instances, collected from the public proceedings during the last ten years, how necessary it was that government should be aided by Parliament in re-establishing that confidence which had been shaken by those proceedings, and that some firm ground should be laid as a foundation for future peace.

He was of opinion, that this foundation of confidence was become the more necessary, from the constitution of the present ministry. That in no time or country, or under any form of government, was the power of ministers suffered to survive the success of their counsels; or the same men permitted to inflame a dependent people to arms, and then to appease them by concessions. That the duke of Alva[1] would be a strange plenipotentiary to have sent, for making the concessions, which king Philip the Second proposed to the Netherlands. In concession, the credit of a state is saved by the disgrace of a minister; because it is his *counsel* alone that is discredited. But when the very same ministers do and undo, in consequence of the resistance they meet, it is the *nation* itself that submits. Besides, he alledged that all treaty is more easy, and fewer concessions are required by all men, when they have a confidence in those they treat with.

He was convinced, that the mere removal of the offensive acts would

---

[1] Fernandez Alvarez de Tuledo, Duke of Alva (1508–82), sent by Philip II to suppress the revolt in the Netherlands in 1567.

have given satisfaction in former times, and from amicable hands. But now things are on another footing; and if more concession is required, it is because injudicious coercion has made it necessary. That he had always wished to preserve the legislative power of this kingdom entire in every thing; and that it was with great grief he saw, that even an odious and scarcely ever to be exercised part of it, was to be abandoned. But when the maxims of public councils are not steady, it is necessary that laws should supply the want of prudence. That it was thus, and for this reason, that limits had been set to absolute power in all countries; and that power (though not absolute) had been preserved, not destroyed by such limitations.

That we were now in a *quarrel*; and in putting an end to any quarrel, it is necessary to look to its *origin*; that the origin of this present difference had evidently been upon the subject of *taxation*. That an arrangement of this question, either by enforcement or concession, was a preliminary essential to peace. That the House ought to estimate the full value of the object to be conceded, before they agree to give it up. If they were of opinion, that the taxation of America could repay them their expences, or compensate their risks, they ought to pursue it. If, on the contrary, it was evident beyond all contradiction, and so evident as to force reiterated acknowledgments, that they never could enjoy a moment's quiet as long as that matter of contention continued—it was then altogether as essential to the preservation of their own authority in all other points, as to the liberty of America and the quiet of the whole empire, to give it up, with such limitations in the concession, as the rights of sovereignty required.

That the Parliament of Great Britain were not the *representative*, but (as Lord John Cavendish had said, some days before, with great truth and propriety) the *sovereign* of America.[1] That the sovereignty was not in its nature an idea of abstract unity; but was capable of great complexity and infinite modifications, according to the temper of those who are to be governed, and to the circumstances of things; which being infinitely diversified, government ought to be adapted to them, and to conform itself to the nature of things, and not to endeavour to force them. That although taxation was inherent in the *supreme power* of society, taken as an *aggregate*, it did not follow that it must reside in any *particular* power in that society. That in the society of England, for

---

[1] There is no report in *Parl. Reg.* of Cavendish making such a statement.

instance, the King is the sovereign; but the power of the purse is not in his hands; and this does not derogate from his power in those things, in which our constitution has attributed power to him. If Parliament be the sovereign power of America, Parliament may, by its own act, for wise purposes, put the local power of the purse into other hands than its own, without disclaiming its just prerogative in other particulars.

That formerly, whatever their right might be to it, the Kings of England were in the practice of levying taxes by their own authority, upon the people of England; they contended that the crown, being charged with the public defence must be furnished also with the means of providing for it. That it would be absurd to commit a trust into the hands of one person, and to leave the power of executing it to depend upon the will of another. They therefore held, that this power was inseparable from the crown; and in general they made use of the very arguments in favour of the King's indefeasible right to tax the people of England, that are now used by the Parliament of England, to tax the people of America. Notwithstanding all these arguments, one of the greatest of our Kings, by an express and positive act, cut off from the Sovereign power this right of taxing.

This act which has been the foundation of the unity and happiness of England since that time; that is, the stat. 35 Edward I. called *Statutum de tallagio non concedendo*, Mr. Burke made his pattern; and from thence (if his plan should be adopted) he hoped the same good effects in future. That this pattern statute was absolutely *silent about the right*; but confined itself to giving satisfaction in future; and that it laid down no *general principles* which might tend to affect the royal prerogative in *other* particulars. That in all human probability the preservation of the other branches of the prerogative was owing to the clear and absolute surrender of this.[1]

("He then moved that the statute *de tallagio non concedendo* might be read.")

He observed, that this statute consisted of three capital parts; a renounciation of taxing,—a repeal of all statutes which had been made upon a contrary principle,—and a general pardon.—*He then read his own Bill*, and shewed its conformity to the spirit of that act, supposing Great-Britain to stand in the place of the Sovereign, and America in that of the subject. That the circumstances are not indeed in every

[1] The statute, or parliamentary declaration, is 34 Edw. I. It undertook to levy no tallage or aid without the goodwill and assent of the community.

respect *exactly* parallel, but that they are sufficiently so to justify, his following an example that gave satisfaction and security on the subject of *taxes*, and left all *other* rights and powers whatsoever exactly upon the bottom on which they stood before that arrangement had been made.

He then gave his reasons for not adopting the methods, which (though not proposed in the House) had been frequently suggested in conversation by several friends and well wishers of America.

And first he mentioned the proposal for repealing the *declaratory act* of 1766.[1] On this occasion he entered into the history of that act, the reasons for making of it; and the perfect acquiescence of the colonies under it; until by the renewal of the scheme of actual taxation their apprehensions were roused, and they were taught to look with suspicion and terror upon the unlimited powers of British legislature. That the repeal of a declaratory act was a thing impossible; for it was nothing less, than to make legislature accuse itself of uttering propositions that were false, and making claims that were groundless. That the disgrace of an English Parliament could add nothing to the security of American liberty.—That on the contrary our inconstancy would become a bad ground of trust.—That the declaratory act had been misrepresented, as if it had been the cause of the taxation; whereas the grand scheme of taxation had *preceded* the declaratory act, and not been the *consequence* of it.—That the act has said nothing in *particular* of taxation, but is an affirmation of the *universality* of the legislative power of Great-Britain over the colonies.—That if this act were repealed, it would be a *denial* of legislative power, as *extensive* as the *affirmation* of it in the act so repealed.—That he was averse to doing any thing upon speculations of right. Because when Parliament made a *positive* concession, the bounds of it were clear and precise; but when they made a concession founded in *theory and abstract principles*, the consequences of those principles were things out of the power of any legislature to limit. That this bill gave as effectual a security against future taxation as any declaration of right could possibly do; and that it put American liberty in that point upon just as good a footing as English liberty itself.

[1] The Declaratory Act was widely attacked by pro-American interests as the 'political Hydra of the Colonies' (*Public Advertiser*, 16 November 1775). It is clear from Burke's words here that he still clung to the hope that the Declaratory Act could be salvaged if the policy of taxing the colonies should be abandoned. However, there is no reason to doubt the sincerity of his earlier statement (if in fact that statement was correctly reported) that he was prepared to give the Declaratory Act up if necessary to re-establish peace; see also above, p. 77.

He next considered the proposition for repealing all the acts since 1763. This he shewed to be impossible, without ruining the whole system of the trade laws, and some of those laws also, which are extremely beneficial to America. That all the laws which leaned upon the colonies, and were the cause or consequence of our quarrel, were to be repealed in this bill, which made provision likewise for authorising such a negotiation as might tend to the settlement of all those lesser matters to the mutual advantage of the parties. That the congress did not require this sweeping repeal as a preliminary to peace; but that even if it had, he was for treating of peace with and making concessions to the colonies, and not receiving laws from them. That he did not conceive, that when men come to treat of peace they must of course persevere in demanding every thing which they claimed in the height of the quarrel. That the cause of the quarrel was taxation; that being removed, the rest would not be difficult. For he denied that the desire of absolute independency was or could be general in the colonies. It was so contrary to their clearest interests, provided their liberties were preserved, that so far from disbelieving them, when they denied such a design, he could scarcely credit them if they should assert it. He then stated five or six capital facts, to prove that independency, neither was or could be their object.

He said he was confident, both from the nature of the thing, and from information which did not use to fail him, that this bill would restore immediate peace; and as much obedience as could be expected after so rude a shock had been given to government, and after so long a continuance of public disturbances. That in this bill, a basis was laid for such satisfaction in the minds of all sober people in America, as would enable government to fix and settle, if common prudence were employed in its future construction and management. That in the first operation it would be the *true* means of *dividing* America. Not the dangerous and fallacious method of dividing which had been proposed, and from which nothing but confusion could grow; not the division of province from province, or the rich from the poor; or the landed from the trading interest; but the division of the peaceable from the factious; the quiet from the ambitious; the friends to the unity of the empire, from the projectors of independence. That this would put the standard of American liberty into the hands of the friends to British government; and when this was done, there was no doubt, but that a sense of interest, natural affection, the dread of the horrors of war, and even the love of freedom itself, better secured by such an act, than by any schemes of hazardous speculation, would leave the really factious very few followers or companions.

He then strongly urged the necessity of granting peace to our colonies on terms of freedom; dilated largely on the uncertainty (to say no worse) of obtaining it upon any other; and the utter impossibility of preserving it in future, without setting the minds of the people at rest. He dwelt largely on the mischiefs which we must suffer by the continuance of this quarrel. He rested little on the consideration of trade and revenue; he put that out of the question, as a matter that would require a large discussion by itself; but chiefly aimed at shewing, that in the progress of this business new powers must be daily added to the crown; so that in seeking to destroy the freedom of others we may fail to obtain what we pursue, and in the pursuit may lose our own liberty. On this head he dwelt very largely, and concluded the whole with a warm and earnest address to the consciences of the members, and an exhortation not to trust to general good intention and to an opinion, that what they were doing was for the *support of government*, when it was far from evident, that under the name of government, it was not the ambition, the interest, the ignorance and obstinacy of particular men that they were supporting; that they were bound not to give confidence, where rational grounds of confidence did not appear; and that anarchy instead of government and civil confusion instead of peace and obedience would be the consequence of an encouragement given by that House to a blind perseverance in measures, which were not conceived with wisdom, or conducted with ability.

He moved, "That leave be given to bring in a Bill for composing the present troubles, and for quieting the minds of his Majesty's subjects in America."

The following is a copy of the Bill.[1]

WHEREAS, by the blessing of Almighty God, and the industry, enterprize and courage of several of the people of this realm, extensive and valuable territories have been acquired in America to the crown of Great Britain, which are now inhabited by great multitudes of his Majesty's subjects, who have cultivated and improved the same for the most part at their own charges, to the great encrease of the commerce and naval strength of this kingdom, and have also, of their own free

---

[1] There is also a MS. copy of the Bill at Sheffield; see Bk 6.205–206.

gift, made provision for the support of the civil government within their said plantations, have maintained many expensive wars against the Indian nations, and have at sundry times granted large sums of money, and other very considerable aids to his Majesty, and his royal predecessors, to support them against the enemies of this kingdom, notwithstanding which the inhabitants of the said colonies have been made liable to several taxes given and granted in Parliament, for the purpose of raising a revenue, when they have had no knights or burgesses, or others of their own chusing, to represent them in Parliament; and from the great distance of the said colonies from this land, and other impediments, are not able conveniently to send representatives to the said Parliament, whereby the said inhabitants of the British colonies have conceived themselves to be much aggrieved, and thereby great troubles have arisen, and are likely to continue, if a fitting remedy be not provided. Wherefore, we pray your Majesty that it may be enacted and declared, and it is hereby enacted and declared, by, &c. &c. &c.

That no aid, subsidy, tax, duty, loan, benevolence, or any other burthen or imposition whatsoever, shall be granted, laid, assessed, levied, or collected upon the inhabitants of any colony or plantation in America, by the authority, or in virtue of any act of Parliament, or in any other manner, or by any other authority, than the voluntary grant of the general assembly, or general court of each colony or plantation, and which shall be assented to by his Majesty's governor, and otherwise confirmed according to the usage of each province respectively, any law, statute, custom, right, prerogative, or any other matter whatsoever to the contrary notwithstanding. Saving to his Majesty, his heirs, and successors, his right of reserving and collecting quit-rents, and other his antient dues and revenues, and all other duties and taxes by this act not repealed, and saving and reserving to all proprietories and charter-companies, their antient rights, privileges, and possessions.

Provided always, that nothing in this act contained[1] shall extend, or be construed to extend, to restrain the future imposition, and levy of duties and taxes for the regulation of trade and commerce in all the dominions, to the imperial crown of this realm belonging.

And in order to remove all doubt and uneasiness from the minds of his Majesty's subjects in the colonies, it is hereby further enacted, that

---

[1] 'contained' is supplied from the MS.

if any act of Parliament shall be hereafter made for the purpose of such regulation of[1] trade, the produce of the duties thereby laid, shall be held by the collectors, or receivers of his Majesty's customs, for the disposal of the general assemblies, as if the same had been levied by the authority of the several general assemblies in the said colonies.

And whereas, during these troubles, the assemblies, or inhabitants of the said colonies, have formed a general meeting, which said meeting was not authorised by law to make any order or resolution, or to do any other act of force, to bind his Majesty's subjects. And whereas it may be necessary, that the said colonies should have authority to do certain acts by common consent, which should conclude the whole body of the said colonies. Be it therefore enacted, that it shall and may be lawful for his Majesty, his heirs and successors, to give authority to his governors in America, to require the said several assemblies to send deputies to a general meeting, with full powers to bind their said several provinces, to all acts done by a majority of voices in the said general meeting, which meeting, and the powers thereof, shall cease and determine on ——— if not further continued by Parliament.

And whereas, in consequence of the late troubles several acts of Parliament have been made for the purpose of coercing and restraining the colonies, of which an advantage has been taken to represent the same, as if a design had been formed to deprive the people of the said colonies of several rights, benefits, and advantages of nature, and of the British constitution, which hath greatly encreased the discontents of the colonies, and fomented the troubles in America. In order, therefore, to quiet the minds of his Majesty's subjects in America, and to reclaim the disobedient by that lenity, which ought to have the strongest operation on the minds of free subjects, be it enacted, that an act made in the seventh year of the reign of[2] his present Majesty, intituled "An act for granting certain duties in the British colonies and plantations in America, for allowing a drawback of the duties of customs upon the exportation from this kingdom, of coffee and cocoa nuts, of the produce of the said colonies or plantations; for discontinuing the drawbacks, payable on China earthen ware, exported to America; and for more effectually preventing the clandestine running of goods in said colonies and plantations." Also one other act, made in the fourteenth year of the reign of his present Majesty, intituled "An

---

[1] *Parl. Reg.*: 'or'   [2] 'the reign of' is supplied from the MS.

199

act to discontinue in such manner, and for such time, as are therein mentioned, the landing and discharging, lading or shipping, of goods, wares, and merchandize, at the town, and within the harbour of Boston, in the province of Massachuset's bay, in North America." Also one other act, made in the fourteenth year of his present Majesty, intituled "An act for the impartial administration of justice in cases of persons questioned for any acts done by them in the execution of the law, or for the suppression of riots and tumults in the province of Massachuset's Bay, in New England." And[1] also, one other act made in the fourteenth year of the reign of his present Majesty, intituled "An act for the better regulating the government of the province of the Massachuset's Bay, in New England," be hereby severally and respectively repealed.

And the King's most excellent Majesty taking into his gracious consideration, the great troubles, discords and wars, that have of late been in some of his Majesty's colonies in America, and that divers of his subjects are, by occasion thereof, and otherwise, fallen into, and be obnoxious to great pains and penalties, out of a hearty and pious desire to put an end to all suits and controversies, that by occasion of the late distractions in America, have arisen, or may arise, between his subjects; and to the intent, that no crime whatsoever, committed against his Majesty, shall hereafter rise in judgment, or be brought in question, against any of them, to the least endamagement of them, either in their lives, liberties, or estates, or to the prejudice of their reputations; and to bury all seeds of future discords and remembrance of the former, as well in his own breast, as in the breasts of his subjects, one towards another; is graciously pleased, that it may be enacted, and be it enacted, &c. &c.

That all and all manner of treasons, misprisions of treasons, murders, felonies, offences, crimes, contempts, and misdemeanors, counselled, commanded, acted or done since the ——— by any person or persons in America, before the ——— by virtue, or colour of any command, power, authority, commission, warrant or instruction from his Majesty, or from any other person or persons, deriving or pretending to derive authority, mediately or immediately, from his Majesty, or of or from any assembly, council, general court, convention, congress, or meeting, in any of his Majesty's colonies in America, called or reputed, or taking on them the name of the assembly, council, or general court, of any

---

[1] The 'And' is supplied from the MS.

of his Majesty's colonies in America, or of a general congress, or provincial congress; or any other name or style whatsoever, or by virtue or colour of any writ, commission, or instructions of or from any person or persons, reputed, or taken to be, or claiming or exercising the power of commander in chief of the continental army in America, or of any provincial army, or commander of any army, or body of troops whatsoever, within any of his Majesty's colonies in America, by sea or land, or of any magistrate or reputed magistrate[1] or officer, within any of the said colonies, or by any pretence, warrant, or command whatsoever, from them, or any of them, or their, or any of their respective counsel or counsels, or any member of such counsel or counsels, or from any person or persons whatsoever, deriving, or pretending to derive authority from them, or any of them, be pardoned, released, indemnified, discharged, and put in utter oblivion.

And that all and every the person and persons, acting, advising, assisting, abetting, and counselling the same, they, their heirs, executors, and administrators, be, and are hereby pardoned, released, acquitted, indemnified, and discharged from the same; and of and from all pains of death, and other pains, judgments, indictments, informations, convictions, attainders, outlawries, penalties, escheats, and forfeitures, and every of them, and all grants thereupon made, and all estates derived under the same, be and are hereby declared and enacted to be, from henceforth null and void; extinguishing all actions, suits, demands, and prosecutions, civil, or criminal, public or private, except for the restoration of such estates, as have been or shall be, seized from the owners, during the troubles; and for restoring to the said owners the mean profits of the same. Provided, that arms not taken up by his Majesty's authority, shall be laid down by our subjects in the said provinces, within—.

The motion was defeated by a vote of 210–105.

(2) MS. AT SHEFFIELD, BK 6.202.

This draft sets the background for much of the printed speech.

We had humbled every power which we dreaded—we had established the foundations of a New kind of Empire upon Earth—our Constitution had made and formed the Spirit and the power which conducted

---

[1] 'or reputed magistrate' is supplied from the MS.

us to this greatness. By assisting Prussia we made new ballances in the power of Europe.[1] But the prosperity which all this Success [has brought] has been our Ruin. Proud and insolent to our dependencies fawning and abject to our Government careless and inattentive of our affairs. We have got into our present situation by rashness and it is not inexperience which can bring us out of it.

Great question is what we are to do? To determine this we ought to know precisely in what situation we stand. The account is short. America was:—and the Glory of England has had its day!

1. Worked on an improper principle.
2. took improper methods
3. In these methods conducted ourselves weakly

Why did you blot so much Paper with penal and ⟨insulting⟩ acts of Parliament.[2] The Word *War* contained them all. In the belly of that was contain all your Charters fishery etc.—If they were in Rebellion: That is War it is your force that must subdue it—rebels were never subdued by Laws—The Idea is absurd and ⟨insulting⟩ because it is by setting Laws at naught that They become rebels.

great Success commonly occasions and may therefore in some sort excuse insolence. But the arrogance of disappointment, the pride of defeat, the haughtiness of disgrace, so unnatural and so provoking, these are things which do truly tax the patience of the most callous and enduring mind.

The preventitive charges made on others by conscious guilt. This more ⟨great⟩ to bear because this is natural greatly at a loss how to express myself on this occasion

All the world is agreed, that we meet in a deplorable condition; but the circumstance in my humble opinion the most deplorable in our condition is[3] this. That it is a constant repetition of the same Effects arising from the same faults; with no variation whatever but in the growing greatness of the Evils which attend every repetition. What are

---

[1] The Convention of Westminster, concluded between George II and Frederick II of Prussia in 1756, had precipitated the so-called Diplomatic Revolution, bringing together two historic enemies, the Houses of Bourbon and Habsburg, and terminating the old system of alliance between Britain, the United Provinces, and Austria.

[2] In margin: 'Paper Chains puddling in making dirt pies by turning Legislative powers to improper Objects you not only weakend your own acts—disgracing Legislative but not aiding force'.

[3] MS.: 'is is'.

you ⟨   ⟩ Coals or ⟨   ⟩ Chalks.[1] It is ⟨more⟩ and vigour that you want

if your great scheme could be blown down by the Languid breath of an expiring minority in this house, ⟨would⟩ that all your schemes might be defeated by the vain dissent of those whom you affected to despise— why did you not as a preliminary get the better of this dissent? but if you say that could not be without destroying the freedom of debate, then your complaint amounts to this that you have a publick council which admits of free debate.[2]

The more ⟨you⟩ exaggerate the misbehaviour of the Americans the more you make this condemn yourselves—they are such people— why did you not provide against them as such? Were you ignorant of it. Not to know the Character of those against whom you direct your operations is a Crime in a Minister. But they did know it; and they did not know it just as it served a turn when they persuaded you to[3] deliverd Towns for ever to arbitrary destruction, when you overturned the Charters of Provinces, without hearing. When you answered them the better part was infinitely the lawyer's.

They were deceived by their Trust in this country—and this has been the Cause of all they have and all they can suffer Government.

I am persuaded, that they did not believe the people of England in earnest in their hostility against them. For when they saw so weak a preparation, they could not imagine so decided a Malice. For otherwise, resolving as you see, they have done, not to submit to your penal Laws and having a force as you see, or rather as you feel to defend them in their resistence—they never would have triffled with their danger so long.

If you say it is absurd, it amounts to no more than a most miserable petitio principii[4]—or this that whatever a Minister proposes it is treason to dispute his will. Whenever you intend to make war, and the consequences are pointed out

The sword pleads its own Cause. If that has lost—all other re-scources are ridiculous—Temper its force at its Risque. But the

---

[1] Burke seems to be playing e'n Horacos, 'Sani ut creta, an carbone notati' (marked with chalk as sane or with charcoal; *Satires*, ii. 3. 246)

[2] The MS. suggests that Burke meant to alter this to read 'that you have a publick council and that you have free debate'   [3] MS.: 'to to'.

[4] A standard expression meaning to beg or sidestep the real issue, in this case by substituting an illogical premiss.

making harsh Laws *before* the reduction of a people[1] on whom these are to operate is the arriving at once at[2] the Climax of Folly, to the thence ⟨precipitate⟩ into the yawning Gulph of ruin and despair

Every adverse act of Parliament that was made, became a reason against submission[3] to the power of that malicious and impotent adversary, whose cold meditations were so full of vigour, and who was weak enough to declare and publish to the world the *harsh* Laws[4] of his Conquest, even before he was ready fought his *Battle*.

I never heard of a power who carried manacles and chains and neck yokes to an invasion that was not defeated. Some such shewn in the old armoury.[5]

Davis says of Ireland[6]—a hostile country like a soil must be broke with Iron before it can receive the seed of Laws and institutions.[7] Lord Hardwicke[8] a ⟨maxim⟩ disgraced the Laws and Legislative wisdom of this Country.[9] Alnaschar has the Glassman[10] resolved before hand to kick his Wife and demolishes the materials of all his fortunes. So for the bad plan of Laws. they will hang up acts of Parliament—bad plan of Arms. mistook the people—1. their affections. Their power. Their Spirit.

America gone—how to recover it.

   1. To get it back by Policy.
   2. To conquer it by the way in which we are going on
   3. To change the mode of War.

[1] In margin: 'I wish we could have contrived to fall into less disgrace. What will they do when conquerors'.   [2] In margin: 'arriving—flight'.

[3] In margin: 'committed so many of pledges of your authority to fortune.'

[4] In margin: 'You get the agreements of many but of if you could get the world to approve of weakness and insanity, they would be weakness and insanity still and would in spite of that world Produce their Effects. Took the facility of blotting paper to be the Art of Government.'

[5] In margin: 'to plead weakness and want of information as an extenuation of an Offence, is natural but when were they heard of as titles to Trust and power'. The 'old armoury' was presumably that in the Tower of London.

[6] In 1612 Sir John Davies had written: 'For the Husbandman must first breake the Land, before it bee made capable of good seede: and when it is thoroughly broken and manured, if he do not forthwith cast good seed into it, it will grow wilde againe and beare nothing but Weeds. So a barbarous Country must be first broken buy a warre, before it will be capable of good Government (*A Discoverie of the State of Ireland*, pp. 8–9).

[7] In margin: 'every session begins in a Tone of complaint and ends in exultation.'

[8] Philip Yorke, 1st Earl of Hardwicke, (1690–1764).

[9] In margin: 'did not know their true Situation—The true Character of the Country quid fieri ⟨recusant?⟩'.

[10] In the *Arabian Nights* Alnaschar invests all his money in a basket of glassware, with a view to making his fortune and marrying the Vizier's daughter. Thinking of his future marriage he becomes angry with the wife of his dreams, and takes a kick, overturning the basket and shattering the glass.

They perish by their own success—It is because they have done That murderd Sense and reason and reason which they oppress in this house[1] lays heavy on their soul in the day of Battle

Lay it down as a foundation—that every thing which [has been] done has been wrong. That every thing that has happend in the order of Nature and that weak counsels have produced unhappy Events;[2] and that nothing but a change in Counsels and in Counsellors can restore us.

We have lost a question—you have lost an Empire

France 5th power—well a good distance between them and Prussia—Philosophic—general Nature accident suppose a Minister[3] there should arise like the common run of able Ministers—a man of civil prudence not of speculative wisdom, who would think it necessary to ⟨re-establish⟩ his Country who would think this an opportunity which if once lost is never to be recoverd.

By their such acts they have cut off our retreat; they have burntt their ships and broke up the Roads behind them. They have left us no escape out of the field of danger but through the defiles of infamy.

We should have anticipated the calamities of our Country; and we should have ⟨been⟩ ten years sooner the stain of Council, the shame of War. The ruin of Commerce and the ⟨derision⟩ to the world. It would have been then easy. ⟨Vain talk—⟩ who told you so? You say you think they might easily be reduced. You said so now. You have tried whether the

One of your offences you have attempted to deceive the people Endeavour to pull down all along with the

if you have all the arms, the fleets that ⟨try⟩

the hearts of the people whose is the rescource.

Danger happy if they had thought as to operate tried ways to avoid it, by prudence or to struggle against it, by force because you thought no danger you made no provision

to conquer a Nation you disperse a mob.

Passiveness of the house the Cause

That those who give notice of the danger are the Cause of it—That there is no danger where there is no warning. ⟨utilium tardus

---

[1] MS.: 'house ⟨house⟩'.
[2] In margin: 'Traiterous correspondence is'.
[3] In margin: '⟨Min[istr]y⟩ gone'.

provisor⟩ prodigus aeris, monitoribus asper. Cereus in vitium flecti.[1]

Grand Errour—to think all the Battle here—that made it fought weakly *there*—no ability so small that is not quickend by diligence none so great not lost by want of it.[2] They were much the most anxious for the success of their Battle here, because they imagined that by failing in that they might lose their places for themselves failing in the other they only lost an Empire for their Country. Voila la difference. House cause not only of this But all future inability became a faction. Our Empire like the undrawn dagger—I have thee not, and yet I see thee Still[3]

those who shall write our Elegy and weep over the Wrecks of those Plans[4]

The devil sooner got his nose out of St ⟨Dimetrius⟩ fiery Tongs[5]— than they out of the prison of this dilemma.

did any man ever open a proposition to a Council and said, if nobody contradicts me this will succeed. It amounts to this that it is a bad proposition but what worse can be said of it than that it will not bear discussion. It falls like dead bodies crashes on the touch of a finger.

(3) MSS. AT SHEFFIELD,

BK 6.196, 197(a)

This draft relates some of the general principles underlying the printed speech.

[1] Burke is trying to quote Horace, *Ars Poetica*, 163–4: 'cereus in vitium flecti, monitoribus asper, utilium tardus provisor, prodigus aeris' ('soft as wax for moulding to evil, peevish with his counsellors, slow to make needful provision, lavish of money').

[2] Burke and the anti-war Opposition had been painted as traitors by supporters of the North regime and had been accused actually of encouraging rebellion in the colonies. Burke is pointing out that the American conflict has not been transported from Britain to the colonies but is a very real and dangerous problem which he and his colleagues sincerely want to see resolved. He is also saying that those who want to portray this as a British problem are simply playing politics. They are attempting to discredit the Opposition in order to secure their own places and to that end they are perfectly prepared to sacrifice the American colonies.

[3] *Macbeth*, II. i. 35. In margin: 'Such Simony in Politicks—The Spirit that makes and preserves Empire the Spirit of Wisdom is not Talk of your Riches—they and thy money perish with thee—This miserable rich ⟨Magician⟩ was struck with blindness'.

[4] In margin: 'a work of darkness Errour and illusion—a bad ⟨bottom⟩ it was a work of darkness not a wind was from his prison strayd—and delusion but this ⟨rusted⟩ bark—built in eclipse and rigged with ⟨tresses⟩ dark has sunk so low that raised head of ⟨thine⟩ Oh would to God the Battle had been more equally fought here.'

[5] A common phrase in early and medieval English literature; see, for instance, Samuel Rowlands, *Hell's Broke Loose*, p. 47: 'their flesh torn from their bones with fiery tongs'.

Indeed Sir the publick is in a bad situation. Great difficulties straiten us upon every Side. We are labouring in a mighty Tempest, in a great swell; and in an heavy sea. The Noble person who sits at the Steerage has comforted us with a declaration that he will not quit the Vessel whilst the Storm lasts. It is a pledge of safety I suppose to have him on board.[1] But this is all—for he does not seem to hold the tiller with a very steady and assured hand; nor does he seem by any means to be determined to what points he is to direct his Course.

Decision

We want decision. Those who are defective in other Qualities, may happen to have some share of this. Their very *defects* may give it. A mind more gross, less mercurial, less refined and *productive* less anxious in Stating Objections may, (from a certain coarse robustness of mental constitution) be the more apt than a more comprehensive Genius to come to a fixed determination and to adhere to it.

As I have formed my opinion possibly from the narrowness of my Ideas with a firm persuasion, I shall lay open every part of it to you with great frankness, just as if I were thinking aloud among friends and not guarding myself against the subtility of adverse parties in a debate.

This openness and confidence is not because I am not aware of many, too many difficulties in the understating. Although The first of all my own want of ability and want of importance of that I shall say little, lest under a Sense of that difficulty when I undertake a matter of this Magnitude, there, may appear some[2] sort of contradiction between my professions and my Conduct—Next that it is not right to complain of what it is impossible to correct.

But if I had none in myself great external difficulties arising from the Temper of the house; our former proceedings; and in the subject matter itself.

One thing ever has,[3] and ever will embarrass those who under irritating circumstances advise to a Course of moderation. For besides the unpropitious ⟨opposition and⟩ the unfavourable aspect of the heavens to which this side of the house is exposed, those who in publick counsels advise to a *moderate* use of *power*, seem to entertain some distrust of the ⟨*perfection*⟩ of that *power* whose exercise they would *limit*. It hurts the pride of power not to seem equal to all its Objects. *Moderation* seems to be made for *mediocrity*. It passes with

---

[1] In margin: 'not like trial'.   [2] MS.: 'some some'.   [3] MS.: 'has has'.

many for a poor creeping Virtue. Popular orators therefore who study the Temper of the Assemblies in which they reign, make it their constant Business to exalt and magnifye their power and urge them to enterprises correspondent to the highest Ideas. They fear no dangers, they apprehend no difficulties. They admire all that is at home—They hold themselves out as *Bigots* for their Country &c. I have often felt how heavy this ⟨supposed⟩ distrust of the omnipotence of our power has made all opposition to the late unhappy American measures.

In the next place the office of a *Mediator* by its *nature* is *ticklish and invidious*. In private Life if I interpose in favour of an Offending Son or Servant against a passionate Master or enraged Parent. I must of Course, justifye, their Conduct or at least palliate their faults, and thus I seem *inevitably* to make myself a *party* with those who are under disgrace. In defending the culprit I seem to accuse the Judge. Thus we who have for ten years stood, and still do stand in the way of Violence have been constantly oppressed with an odious cry "of an American faction—favourers of Rebellion. Enemies to the dignity of Parliament" and yet From this ⟨same⟩ scource of passion and prejudice it became extremely difficult for an honest man to know how he was to act.

For if at any time from timidity or despair or[1] reluctance to be always struggling against the Torrent—we were remiss and did not oppose—and mischief followd. Why do you insidiously lye by when the measure is carrying and then meanly attack it when it fails of success? Why did you not kindly give Notice[2] of the danger—If another Course was taken and that Course was most commonly taken that we made a vigorous opposition and pointed out with great precision the Evils which might ensue, then the answer was it was easy to prophesy the mischiefs which you cause.

I who believe from my soul that Government is of divine *institution* and *sacred* authority, and no *arbitrary device of men*, to be modified at their *pleasure* or conducted by their *fancies*, or *feelings*, am persuaded that every one of us shall be called to a solemn and tremendous account for the part we take in it. I have no more right in the Eye of my Creator to place my confidence without the rational and natural grounds of Trust[3] which I and not I have made than I have to pay my debts where they are not due; and neglect to pay ⟨where⟩ I owe them. I have no more right to give away the publick money without a *distinct probable*

---

[1] MS.: 'or or'.
[2] MS.: 'give me Notice give Notice'.
[3] MS.: 'grounds of grounds of Trust'.

view of publick Service, than I have to commit *a robbery*. I have no more right to send out *armies* of my fellow Citizens to *danger* and death, without *probable* Grounds either distinctly known to myself, or where that cannot be, presumed on the best human authority, than I have to *commit murder*. They are all equal violations of the *eternal Law* of human society—but aggravated in us, by a sort of sacriligeous Breach of the highest & holiest Trust. I may be acquitted by the blind Multitude, but what will cover me from ⟨   ⟩. Is morality to have place in paltry transactions and to be excluded from the great ⟨Hour⟩

Good Intentions are no justification of absurd or intemperate actions. No good intentions can justifye me in a fanatical Neglect or defiance of my rational powers. Take care that when you waste the blood and Treasure of your Country to *no End*, what answer can be given to an all seeing judge for Such conduct? Take care, that when we act in this manner because we mean to *support Government* that it may not be found to be *anarchy and confusion* we are supporting. There is no *Lawful Government* but the Government of *Wisdom and justice*. Every thing else is usurpation. They who cannot resist or traverse it, can at best give it only a passive obedience, but if [I] lift one hand or assent with my Voice to it I am an accomplice in this most unnatural and criminal rebellion against every principle of Government. We are indeed by this particular constitution renderd unaccountable to *men* for our Conduct. With how much more awe we ought to stand before the supreme Ruler to whom no human constitution can abstract us from perfect responsibility. How shall we stand at that audit when we are accused of opening the wounds and tearing out the Bowels of our Country, by carrying on a cruel civil War rather than quieting the minds of an enraged people by an assurance of conceding what you do not value and you do not mean to keep. I wash my hands from that blood—I clear myself from that Crime. If concession proper at any time it.[1]

(4) MS. AT SHEFFIELD, BK 6.200

This draft is an outline for much of the printed speech but expands on portions of it.

---

[1] There are two detached sentences on a related fragment, Bk 6.197(b): 'If we trust to miracles and accidents make ourselves outlaws of the Establishment of God and disclaim the protection of his ordinary providence which is great impiety and folly. A weak arrangement is used to lure into an unpolitick War'.

She is. That her old and proud rival England has obtain a manifest and decided superiority over her;[1] and that much of the superiority of all the others depends upon the depression she feels from hence.

Suppose he should consider this not as an opportunity accidentally offerd for replacing her, but dropped as it were, from heaven for raising that Country and Monarchy to her antient eminence. Once Gone never recoverd. If I act as if no such Minister could or would arise I am out of my Senses.

For if this unfortunate War should be continued, and that the Bourbon powers should interfere, the first and direct Effect[2] is on our vital *parts*; it directly [acts] upon our Naval power and transports and all ⟨   ⟩ to France. For does any person imagine, that with the opportunity of the American Ports extending a Line of seacoast that French and American Vessels—the first fall would be the Newfoundland Fishery. 2. next. African Trade—West Indian. And thus the whole Fabrick of British Commerce would tumble to the Ground. Nothing can save us from it but mere chance—probability is against us. Nothing but accident in our favour.[3]

I will put the whole War plan on this Bottom. 1. Our past experience and our future hopes. Hitherto all we have done by 12,000 men a great fleet and such an artillery as never was known to attend that proportion of Troops—is to lose all America except what was just sufficient to be *insulted* in. The History of our experience[4] is very clear and very short.

2. Our hopes are of the very same kind with those which have hitherto been disappointed.[5]

  1. Your army in America in the Clouds[6]

  2. Army to be sent on paper

  3. Army of Allies not so good as on paper.

You declare they mean independence and you offer them pardon.[7] If

---

[1] In margin: 'That under England her Genius is subdued.'

[2] In margin: '1. the Trade of Timber and of Naval Stores which would at once give her an incredible Supply. 2. Seamen the means of manning—Fishery Tobacco Rice'.

[3] In margin: 'It may be otherwise.—France may be no wiser than we—but those who trust to an extraordinary, Ought to be abandond by the Protection of an ordinary Providence and be trans'.

[4] In margin: 'The mischiefs that happen in a civil War quod ⟨hominibus lenissimis ademit misericordiam⟩'; 'stifled compassion in the most tender-hearted men', Cicero, *Pro Sexto Roscio Amerino*, 154.

[5] In margin: 'Plan of intimidation—resolutions of Censure and Warning.'

[6] In margin: 'If a vote was an army you have them—but without Offence to the omnipotent.'

[7] In margin: 'capricious disposition of Pardons most apt to prevent peace—pardon those in open Rebellion—not those whose guilt must have been obscure'.

unconditional submission Generals suffice. Howe[1] and Burgoyne[2] can do it.

If conditions they must relate[3] to grievances and these to acts of Parliament.

drawing Treaty into Length—

If you make an armed Treaty with them—if independency be their Object as that Libel affirms and as Ld N. says—what signifies That paper of that Treaty.

2d Plan conciliation[4]

go to the Origin of the Quarrel—remove the original Ground. Give security whence arises the Necessity of such security.[5]

1. Great charges. 2. Power of Ministry in Parliament. Charges whilst the same ⟨Q⟩ Necessity of treating with an adverse power.[6]

Tax made
Assemblies dissolved.
Petitions rejected
Taxes partially given up.
refused on the whole[7]
Governours to refuse their Salaries.
Troops sent—recalled.

all requires a Stable foundation.

3d. Plan to mix—Army will prevent will lengthen things.

Qu of the Kings Speech.

Ill consequences of refusal, Advantages of France and Spain State of Europe and the E. Indies.

From the very beginning of the dispute to this hour from the first ⟨sound⟩ murmur of discontent, to the sound of Drums and Cannon and the[8] ⟨alarm⟩ of War. I have never been able to turn my Eyes ⟨one Moment⟩ from the Effect of this controversy in our situation

[1] Major General Sir William Howe (1729–1814), M.P. 1758–80. On 10 October 1775 he was appointed to replace Gage as Commander-in-Chief in America.
[2] Major General John Burgoyne (1723–92), M.P. 1761–92.
[3] In margin: 'Genl Gage breach of Parliaments promises ill kept threats ill executed Armed defaulter'.
[4] In margin: 'founded on this that there are conciliating dispositions in both sides.'
[5] In margin: 'ought to know our minds whether give up or not. Ought to make a real decision.'
[6] In margin: '1. War to subdue 2. War to intimidate—into concession'.
[7] In margin: 'sovereign not Parliament'.
[8] In margin: 'mixed plans, perfect or imperfect concession. Whether what you receive is worth the difference.'

relative to foreign powers. The powers of France and Spain glare in my Eyes like frightful Spectres, and haunt me wherever I go. I never considered it to be possible to continue an unmixed civil War. There is the *true* danger. I know that the present State of the Ministry and in some Measure of the people of France is a good deal different[1] from what it had been formerly. A certain ⟨Tener of⟩ Philosophy, a certain System d'oeconomie politique has passed from the closet of ⟨Learned⟩ men to the Cabinets of Princes and has humanized perhaps too relaxed the minds of that people. The King on the Throne too seems not fond of War. But all this is accident. Accidental fashion cannot long suspend general Nature: suppose some Minister should arise in that Country such as great Ministers generally have been,[2] a Man of a vigorous and ambitious mind, a man rather powerful in political prudence, than in speculative Wisdom. Suppose such a Man should behold The great revolution which within our own Memory has happend in France. That from being a Throne formidable to the World and clearly the first she should have sunk in reality and Truth to be no more than a fourth in the Scale of Europe—That Russia, that Austria, that Prussia have all of them more considerable Armies and are able to give them a more considerable operation.

(5) MS. AT SHEFFIELD, BK 6.192

This draft expands on the portion of the printed speech which treats of 'simple war, in order to a perfect conquest' (above, p. 185).

I will talk of this affair with the utmost coldness, without considering it in the Lights in which honour ⟨generosity⟩ and humanity would place it, but merely as a Matter of prudence. To this War of distress and intimidation I have many serious Objections derived from our Late *actual* and our desired *future* relation to America

First,[3] It confesses in the very radical and essential principle of the Scheme, an opinion of *Weakness*. No people will *destroy* what they have

---

[1] MS.: 'different is different'.
[2] In margin: 'obliged to think of this because highly probable and because if less probable ought to be attended to on account of the magnitude of the consequence.'
[3] In margin: '*Weak*'.

an hope to possess. *Piracy* and *wasting* have never yet been considerd as Instruments and means of *dominion*. They have been hitherto the gratifications of *revenge* to those who despair of *Victory* and I believe no people, since the foundation of the world to this day, have ever yet receivd Governours, Garrisons and supreme Legislative authority, from others merely because their Trade was interrupted and their sea coast ravaged and destroyd. These are the ways of weakening a rival and independent States, and not of coercing disobedient Subjects.

Secondly,[1] it is exceedingly *uncertain* in its Effect. The success [of] The attempt of intimidating by distress greatly depends[2] on the Character of mind you mean to *affect*; and the *value* which he sets upon the Objects you mean to *destroy*.

Threats and injuries to a robust and resentful mind tend rather to irritate than intimidate. It may be so far from bringing him under Subjection, that these Violences become a reason against ever submitting to a power capable of such a mode of Hostility.

Next the value they set on the Objects. We are not to presume on human Nature ⟨impassive⟩ from its ordinary State. Men are capable of making great sacrifices to their feelings—take forms ⟨distorted by⟩ servitude or bloated with Luxury for the pattern of the Human kind. Dutch Painters. Heroic Nature is nature as much as the most vulgar. Enthusiasm may decay, I admit it. But enthusiasm gives birth to an order and discipline—which preserve it, direct it, and supply the decay of its fervour.

We know by experience that the burning of Towns and destroying of Trade will not do the Business.

Lastly it will draw the War into length. Whatever does not only wastes the radical vital Substance of this Country gives chances to foreign powers.

NEGOTIATION. Lord North's proposition inadmissible. Do you mean to go on with Hostilities while you treat. Must take it from conversation, what their Objects preliminary to a peace may be. What I hear said in conversations, in this house and collect from the various scatterd remarks of Ministers what they would be at. 1st a speculative recognition of the authority of Parliament by the several seperate assemblies.[3]

---

[1] In margin: 'Uncertain'.   [2] MS.: 'greatly depends greatly'.
[3] In margin: 'Some have no Assemblies such as Mas Bay. either take their assembly or none'.

If you go to the *separate* assemblies you never can get the same recognition from *all*,[1] being of such different Tempers constitutions, views, and situations and will you take more from some and less from others and then you keep the wound open for ever—and this Treaty will be more expensive and ruinous than any war.

But I suppose you get this declaration from all, and get it from all instantaneously Of what Service would it be to you since you declare[2] that you can put no Trust in their declarations?—You revert at last for your Security of peace and Empire to that very *faith* the *want* of which you declare to be the ground of *War*.[3] But if this faith is to be guaranteed by seventy ships and twenty five thousand men then it is on the force, not *faith*, you depend and this is *eternal War*.[4]

But if you satisfye yourselves by an explicit declaration with the exception of Taxes, in all matters almost worth it they acquiesce already and this turns back to faith &c. I have no opinion of speculative recognitions.

Practical either an Effective revenue[5] to answer publick purposes— then we are at war for Taxes;[6] It is our Object then [to] see with what prudence we have chosen by exhausting ourselves and them.[7] If not but only an acknowlegement then this Tribute must be either *voluntary* or involuntary.[8] If *voluntary* already and still decline, if involuntary never—and a ⟨arrow⟩ and Turf or a Barrier of Earth no more. King of Naples—a bloody War for that ⟨horse⟩. He can take

(6) MS. AT SHEFFIELD, BK 6.203

The fifth draft elaborated the portion of the printed speech which deals with the third plan '(his own) that of a *concession previous to treaty*' (above, p. 192).

---

[1] In margin: '1. Parties you treat with 2. Object of Treaty'.

[2] Burke has crossed out 'declare'.

[3] In margin: 'can they Negotiate unarmed in the Eye of a vast army. 1. uncertain Objects of treaty, 2. divided Ministry and 3. an unknown parliamentary ratification.'

[4] In margin: 'addresses if the opinion of the people may send a Parliament totally hostile'.

[5] In margin: 'Lord North says a fixed Revenue best way to keep peace'.

[6] In margin: 'either *Beneficial* or *nominal* and honorary'.

[7] In margin: 'War not for Taxation—if not, say so—permanent revenue best ground of peace. If Beneficial, is it from burnt Cities annihilated fisheries, a desolated Sea Coast and ruind Country you expect them. 1. The meanness of the Object 2. Uncertainty of acquiring it. Turpe est difficiles habere ⟨Nugas et stultus⟩ Labor est ⟨ineptiarum⟩'. See Martial, *Epigrams*, ii. 86, 9.

[8] Burke has continued accidentally 'or voluntary'.

The preference which I give to the method of pure conciliation is grounded upon three principles.

1st that there still remains a disposition to kindness in America. I speak of this remnant of filial Kindness as a thing that *was* true,[1] when the last accounts came away. There is a parenthesis of 3,000 miles of ocean between the beginning and end of every sentence we speak of America. How much still remains of that vast fund remains unconsumed I know not. [1] Much shaken by the savages[2]—but not irritated by them—2. Much Shaken by the application to foreign powers[3] but not irritated by them[4]—3. Much shaken by refusal of Petitions—Not irritated—still renewed—Georgia the other day 4.[5] It is from her mode of carrying on *hostility* that I judge their friendship—They are defensive almost every where—They suffer at present by it. They sufferd you to Land they sufferd you to occupy their Harbours they prepared no Naval force though perfectly in their power.

2 They have an interest in the connection constitutional and political and commercial

3. They must and do suffer in the Contest

These reciprocal notwithstanding the addresses for the folly of which measure there is no name except to shew the publick voice of no Value.[6] made the violent acts in spite of Petitions.

means of

These principles clear the ground for peace.

Peace such as suits our present situation

Which way best to lay a ground here and treat to arrange inferior matters or vice versa. First to avoid Negotiation and to shorten it as much as possible. For Parliament in a truly kingly strain to grant and not to bargain.[7]

---

[1] In margin: 'I am ashamed to preoccupy such Objections but I see them used by the first men in the gravest questions. Let me not be smartly asked if good why are they in arms. When I speak of good dispositions let me not be mistaken, I speak of good dispositions of a people in actual Hostility. Not a disposition which was strong enough to keep them from Arms, but to persuade them a reasonable condition to lay them down.'

[2] In margin: '1st proof'. Burke presumably refers to the British use of Indian auxiliaries.

[3] In margin: '2nd proof'. See below, p. 220.

[4] In margin: 'Paying Debts—Trade.'

[5] For the Address to the King of the Provincial Congress of Georgia, 14 July 1775, see Davies, *Documents of the American Revolution*, xi. 46.

[6] Addresses in support of goverment policy; see below, p. 305.

[7] A short draft (Bk 6.193) expands on some points here: 'A whole Nation cannot be treated as in Rebellion. In contests of this Kind various kinds of men and various dispositions are mixed

In endeavouring to reconcile any quarrel we must go to the ground of it

First universal affirmance universal denial[2] cannot repeal declaratory act upon speculative principles—that is argumentative principles because Legislature even the most perfect is not master of these principles. An act of Parliament to prohibit inference and analogy would be ridiculous.

But I may circumscribe it practically—I will never use my Right. If I had it I give it up, for there no inference follows—I give up one Right; I Limit my power by my will, and do not circumscribe my Right by establishing principles incompe[tent] While with ⟨   ⟩

(7) MS. AT SHEFFIELD, BK 6.191

This draft relates to the portion of the printed speech beginning 'He was of opinion, that this foundation of confidence was become the more necessary, from the constitution of the present ministry' (above, p. 192).

The grand difficulty in the way of proposing any plan of peace is the constitution of the present Ministry and its authority with Parliament. This I know is generally reputed to be an invidious and perilous Topic. I know and feel it—but the clearness of my own intentions which I know and feel as well, and the Obvious necessity of the Case, make it necessary that this difficulty should be stated to you fully, because a considerable part of my future Argument depends upon it.

The Ministry tell us that they are and always have been the true friends to the Liberty [of] America. They have been particularly loud this Session in that Assertion. I do not dispute their intentions—God and they and not I know them. But it has so happened, that they have been the persons to whose lot it has fallen to inflame the house with

---

together. This is a Test truly formed, to discriminate those who enter into Wars from a real Sense of Grievance, Lament these disorders and their consequences, and those, who taking advantage of the general discontent make the honest feelings of others subservient to their own Avarice or ambition.

Those who begin moderate, end violent—In others height risking high thoughts.

Negotiation is admitted; Question whether a previous ground is to be laid here, and to negotiate after on that ground—or whether negotiation first, and then parliament' perform the condition.

[2] In margin: '1. cannot universally 2. cannot partially on speculation'.

strong criminal accusations against that people. That they have this very Session charged them in the face of Europe with such false pretences, in order to cover the most criminal designs. That they have passed heavy penal acts of Parliament against them taking from [them] every right without exception of the constitution and of human nature—That they have incited the Savages to fall upon them in the West and attempted to ⟨buy⟩ the unrelenting fury of the Savages of the North and East: and whatever Ferocity roves the Wilds of Tartary to fall upon them.[1]

These may be just accusations and proper punishments,[2] but the *accusers* of Crimes and the authors of *punishments* never passed with the weakness of human nature for *friends*. Now when peace is to be made[3] and concessions are to follow the trial [of] Violence, it has been the constant Course of all Governments under heaven for their own dignity, ease, and safety to put the their affairs into *other hands*. The counsellors and the measures have gone together. Despotick ⟨Ministry⟩ The same Men have not been sufferd to do and to undo—Duke of Alba[4] sent to negotiate in Antwerp when his Statue trampling. Sovereign thought mad who would send him.

The reason is plain it is for the dignity of the sovereign power whether King or Senate never to be in the wrong in his own person. He may be deceivd by others false representations never can err himself—His arms may be misconducted but he is never vanquished—He has always among his people faithful informers and sound advisers but when the men who have gone to violence because they would not concede, after Trial of Violence make a concession, the nation itself, its wisdom firmness and justice is disgraced. So far the party conceding. On the subject of the party to whom concession is made undoubtedly all men treat with less suspicion with those who they ⟨find⟩ are kindly intentioned towards them.[5] They have less fear less distrust—They require less security, as what may be wanting in strictness of Law may be made up in kindness of inclination—Timeo

[1] Burke is referring to the government's efforts to hire Russian troops.
[2] In margin: 'Fregose and admiral Cusieu.'
[3] In margin: 'not absolutely'.
[4] See above, p. 192.
[5] In margin: 'But I would end a Civil War with some dishonour rather than conduct it with the greatest Glory.'

danaos[1] their very concessions are as much examined—a Trick is suspected in every thing—all things go on dully.

But I have observed two things in the house—Patience and satisfaction on giving up the measures, but force from us our Ministry

therefore conform to this[2]

To remove the ground of the Quarrel—not by conceding as a *Basis everything* thing that ever was asked during the quarrel.

But going to the *Root* of it—and removing all that has been done consequentially to the quarrel. The rest proper subject of Negotiation.

Not Parliament must act as sovereign.[3] Statute de Tallagio an Example.[4]

Not to concede if useful or may be made so

My Idea therefore is to make such a plan as is suited to those who have tried a violent course. Who arrest themselves in the midst from the misfortunes which have arisen from their mistake—whose moderation though a little *unseasonable* does not come *too late*, and to support *concession* in those hands *coercion* has not prospered.

What do you lose, if you throw away a kind act, you have it to spare you have *thrown away* several acts of *severity*—your Boston &tc will be as little executed as this will be accepted. If you succeed and conquer America—every one is satisfied that this Business of taxing[5] must be given up; if you *fail* and lose America, your Right to Tax[6] an independent Country is of small advantage. If you have lost it by violence and hope to recover ⟨Maybe⟩ to subdue[7]

2. War intimidating—depends on the value at which they estimate of the Objects at Stake[8]—Dutch painters Heroic nature. All measure hitherto of that intimidating Nature

3. To enforce the acceptance of Concession—odd—it is because it

---

[1] 'I fear the Greeks [even bearing gifts]'; Virgil, *Aeneid*, ii. 49.

[2] In margin: 'Position of one who has tried Violence—who wishes to go no further and means to support concession in the hands of those who have declared for Violence and misconducted it.
1st Ground of Quarrel Taxation Knows the value of taxation the rest valueless.
2 discriminatory proving not so easy to recover as to keep.'

[3] In margin: 'suppose they have these Evil dispositions'.

[4] See above, p. 194.

[5] In margin: 'every thing used to intimidate a weak mind ⟨   ⟩ imitates a strong one'.

[6] In margin: 'In War calculate the difference between blockade and universal conquest'.

[7] In margin: 'Objections to giving up always thus. even so'.

[8] In margin: '1 To intimidate to ⟨provoke⟩'.

is perfect, or imperfect.[1] If Perfect why odd to reconcile if imperfect, ⟨calculate⟩ the value of what you keep.—

But fear a retrospective operation is meant, first that it should seem, as if the peace accompanied with the Sword concessions[2] was owing to the sword and not the concessions and thus justifye the plan of Violence—Next to justifye suspicion—that they meant further and that your intimidation prevented[3]

Gentlemen who say we have such a strong Party of friends—will they not be strengthend by such an act and much more than if they have[4] no such security. Will they not go better with a *Large* concession really and in *hand*[5] rather than less held out in *hope?*

1. Thus your friends must fight.

2. Your Enemies must fight without their Grand pretence—The Standard will be in the hands of their adversaries.

Have they by refusing to yield lessend their demands.

Not conditions—only clog and of no sort of use but to beget mistrust—this does not clog one Military operation. It strengthens your friends. It weakens your Enemies—It does honour to your own moderation and stability.

(8) MS. AT SHEFFIELD, BK 6.194

This draft cannot be readily attached to any particular part of the printed speech.

By trying how much constancy was to be found in human Nature you made discoveries, which however honourable to our Species was infinitely mischievous to those who held the experiment [and] called out the rescources of Nature.

In New England you have turned a mean shifty peddling Nation into a people of heroes. They rejected the respite which you gave to their Navigation. They cast in your face the stinted shew of Mercy by which

---

[1] In margin: '⟨mean⟩ to ⟨benefits⟩'.
[2] In the MS. 'concessions' is written above 'the sword'.
[3] In margin: 'In concession—what they ask—what fit to yield.'
[4] In margin: 'Act as Americans and on American ground?'
[5] In margin: 'Whoever will go to war without a consideration of its dangers is neither fit for peace or ⟨War⟩'.

your proscription was accompanied—the apostles did not quit their Nets with more alacrity at the Call of Grace than they did at the call of honour. They have realised in Modern days all that we read of antient Spirit.

Predicted that nature could not adhere to the nonimportation agreement so contrary to their interests. this Idea taken from low interested unimpassiond Nature.

By depriving them of all external engagements Virtue was become their sole Enjoyment—It became dearer and dearer to them when it was no longer incumberd by various other meaner subsidiary pleasures. Deprived of common Luxury convenience they consoled themselves with Liberty dignity and honour.

Speech on German Treaties
29 February 1776

Source: *St James's Chronicle*, 5 March 1776

This report (also in *General Evening Post* and *Middlesex Journal*, 7 March) is repeated in *Parl. Reg.* iii. 357–8 and *Parl. Hist.* xviii. 1182–3. See also Simmons and Thomas, vi. 404–13.

On 29 February Lord North moved that the treaties entered into with the Landgrave of Hesse-Cassel, the Duke of Brunswick, and the hereditary Prince of Hesse-Cassel, for obtaining mercenaries, should be referred to the Committee of Supply. Burke spoke in the debate. He and the rest of the Rockingham leaders intensely disliked the idea of employing foreign troops in a dispute between Britain and British subjects in the colonies. Amongst the Rockingham papers at Sheffield there is a sketch of a protest against the treaties which the party submitted in the House of Lords.[1] Significantly, it warned that

when the Colonies come to understand that Great Britain is forming Alliances & hiring foreign Troops for their Destruction they may think they are well justified by the Example in endeavoring to avail themselves of the like assistance; and that France, Spain, Prussia or other Powers of Europe may conceive they have as good a Right as Hesse, Brunswsick and Hanau to interfere in our domestick Quarrels.[2]

---

[1] See above, p. 186, and below, p. 235.
[2] R97.12; the protest was also printed in *Lords Journals*, xxxiv. 577.

Mr. Burke complimented his Lordship highly on his great Talents for Ridicule, his political Witticisms, and well pointed ironical Strictures. He observed, that his Lordship one Day came down to the House with a very grave serious argumentative Air, and told the Country Gentlemen, that they should have a Revenue, for it was the very Point in Issue. The next he changed his Tone, and as gravely affirmed, that nothing was further from his Intentions; for it was the supreme legislative Power of Parliament that employed all his sleeping and waking Thoughts; a paltry trifling Revenue was beneath the Dignity and wise Consideration of a British Parliament. Again, the Dispute only related to the Destruction of the Tea at Boston; neither the Revenue nor Supremacy made any Part of the Controversy. At the Beginning of the Sessions not a single Foreigner was intended to be employed; now nothing is to be effected without the Aid of foreign Mercenaries; but if Necessity should compel us to employ Foreigners, it was only because they could be procured upon cheaper Terms. The Necessity is arrived; but the Pretence of Cheapness is at once abandoned; for it turns out, that for every 1,000 Foreigners we have taken into our Service, we shall pay as much as for 1,500 Natives.[1] If his Lordship was charged with being the Promoter of those Measures, the Fact was denied, he only co-operated with the rest of the King's Servant[s]; if they were attributed to any other Set of Men, he instantly put in his Claim to the whole Merit. If he was reproached with Versatility of Sentiment, or Contrariety of Opinion, he laughed at his Opponents, and turned the Whole into a mere Matter of Ridicule. So that on the Whole, Supremacy or no Supremacy, Revenue or no Revenue, Foreigners or Natives, Cheapness or Dearness, Responsibility or no Responsibility, his Lordship seemed to regard very little, the Whole was made to end in a Joke; Promises, Reasons, and Arguments, were made to yield to ministerial Pleasantry and Good-Humour, the House was made merry, a Laugh was created, and the mere Grumblers were, as they deserved, turned into Ridicule and Contempt.

North's motion was carried by 242 votes to 88.

---

[1] Estimates of the cost of employing foreign troops and of raising troops in Ireland had recently been reviewed in the House of Commons (*Journals*, xxxv. 564–5, 578, 579, 595).

Speech on Scottish Militia Bill
5 March 1776

Source: *St James's Chronicle*, 7 March 1776

This report is repeated in *Parl. Reg.* iii. 396–7 and *Parl. Hist.* xviii. 1229–30.

On 2 November 1775 John Stuart, styled Lord Mountstuart,[1] secured the appointment of a committee to draw up a Bill to provide Scotland with a militia.[2] The Bill proved unpopular and was defeated largely because of the expense and widespread prejudices against the Scots—a people 'tinctured with notions of despotism' as one speaker put it.[3] It was also defeated because of fears of the undue influence of the Crown. A number of speakers observed that the militia had in truth become standing armies as a result of the King's power to call out and disband them at his pleasure. The Rockinghams in general appear to have been strongly swayed by that argument. Over the years the party leaders had learned to blame many of their country's ills on the undue influence of the Crown and by the end of the decade they would propose their celebrated 'economical reform' programme as a means of curtailing it.[4] Burke and his friends may also have been swayed by the fact that Mountstuart was the son of the third Earl of Bute[5], towards whom the Rockinghams had earlier displayed so much animosity.[6] In the 1760s the party leaders had blamed Bute for turning the King's friends against their first administration.[7] In recent years they had given up much of the battle against Bute himself, since it was becoming evident that he was no longer a major player in British politics, but they continued to feel some anxiety at the thought of a group of officeholders sitting in the House of Commons taking orders from a secret adviser to George III.

It would conduce greatly to our acting with some regularity if we knew who the Ministry were ... [Burke wrote in early 1775] I have great reason to suspect that [Charles] Jenkinson governs every thing ... A trusty person set at his door to follow him in his motions, would give great lights ... To follow Jenkinson, will be to discover my Lord Bute, and my Lord Mansfield, and another person [the King] as considerable as either of them.[8]

[1] (1744–1814), later (1776) 2nd Baron Mountstuart and 4th Earl and 1st Marquess of Bute, M.P. 1766–76.
[2] For the Scottish militia issue, see J. Robertson, *The Scottish Enlightenment and the Militia Issue*, Edinburgh, 1985.
[3] See speech by John Sawbridge on 20 March 1776 (*Parl. Reg.* iii. 427–8).
[4] See W. M. Elofson, 'The Rockingham Whigs in Transition: The East India Company Issue, 1772–3', *English Historical Review*, civ (1989), 947–74; and Burke's speech on public expense of 15 December 1779, printed below, pp. 466–76.
[5] John Stuart (1713–92).
[6] See vol. ii, pp. 56, 250, 251, 275, 276, 314, 442.
[7] Langford, *Rockingham Administration*, pp. 236–63, 280–3.
[8] *Corr.* iii. 89–90. Mansfield (William Murray, 1st Baron Mansfield, 1705–93, later, 1776, 1st Earl of Mansfield, M.P. 1746–56) was Lord Chief Justice of the King's Bench and, like Jenkinson, was considered to have much influence in the closet.

The Rockinghams were likely to view anyone who had ever been closely associated with Bute as one of the King's friends and therefore they may well have found it difficult to be objective towards Mountstuart's Bill.

On 5 March Burke spoke on the second reading of the Bill.

Mr. Burke spoke for a considerable Time against the Commitment. He said, in his Opinion Scotland was neither properly taxed, nor fully represented, nor until it was, could it be intitled to the Favour now desired. The Proportion between the Numbers to be embodied in both Kingdoms, was in a Proportion of one to five, whereas Scotland did not pay above 1–40th of the Land-Tax, the very specific Tax out of which the Money for the Pay and Cloathing of the Militia was to be drawn. He therefore could not possibly conceive how the People of that Country could come to Parliament and expect that a Scotch Militia, at least five sixths of the Expense to be incurred by such an Establishment, could be paid by English Land-owners. It was an Absurdity on the very Face of it; it was directly repugnant to the first Principles on which a national Militia was formed or paid.[1] He said he had other Objections against the Bill besides that now mentioned, one of which was, that it threw more Power into the Hands of the Crown than had hitherto been thought consistent with public Liberty.[2] In King William's Time, when one half of the Kingdom were attached to their exiled Prince, and when one of the most powerful and ambitious

[1] The old militia had been supported by charges on land. But the Militia Act of 1757 included a provision financing it from the land tax, a general tax, subject to annual review. This was presented as relieving the landed interest of a potential burden and ensuring regular review of the militia by Parliament (J. R. Western, *The English Militia in the Eighteenth Century: The Story of a Political Issue 1660–1802*, London, 1965, p. 130). So far as Scotland was concerned, Dr. Johnson took the same view as Burke, but characteristically added a criticism of the Scots: 'As Scotland contributes so little land-tax towards the general support of the nation, it ought not to have a militia paid out of the general fund . . . No, Sir; now that the Scotch have not the pay of English soldiers spent among them, as so many troops are sent abroad, they are trying to get money another way, by having a militia paid' (*Boswell's Life of Johnson*, ed. G. B. Hill, rev. L. F. Powell, 6 vols., Oxford, 1934–50, iii. 186–7). By the Union of 1707 the Scottish contribution was fixed permanently at one-fortieth of the English and Welsh. It was much utilized as an anti-Scottish argument in a variety of contexts and usually countered by references to the much larger contribution which Scotland made to the revenues of customs and excise.

[2] For the clause to which Burke probably objected, see *Parl. Reg.* iii. 431–2. 'And be it enacted, That his Majesty's lieutenant, or any three deputy lieutenants of any county or stewartry, is and are hereby authorized, by warrant under his hand and seal, or their hands and seals, to employ such person or persons as he or they shall think fit to seize and remove the arms, clothes and accoutrements, belonging to the militia of such county or stewartry, whenever his Majesty's said lieutenants, or the deputy lieutenants, shall adjudge it necessary to the kingdom, and to deliver the said arms, clothes, and accoutrements, into the custody of such person or persons as his Majesty's said lieutenants, or deputy lieutenants, shall appoint to receive the same, for the purpose of this act.'

Monarchs that ever sat on the French Throne, or on any Throne in Europe for several Centuries, and who besides had a personal Enmity to our new-elected King, even in such a critical Season as that 7,000 standing Forces were thought fully sufficient to protect this Kingdom against all its open Foes and secret Enemies;[1] and will any Man, who wishes to be believed, pretend to tell us, that a standing Force of five Times the Number, in Times of profound Peace, and an English Militia of 32,000 Men, are not, when none of those Causes longer exist, fully adequate to every Purpose of preserving domestic Tranquillity, and of repelling any Attempts of our foreign Enemies?

Speech on Butcher's Meat Bill
26 March 1776

Source: *St James's Chronicle*, 28 March 1776

The same report is in the *General Evening Post* and the *Middlesex Journal* of 30 March.

Burke spoke after John Sawbridge, the Lord Mayor of London, on the third reading of a Bill for regulating the sale of Butcher's meat. The Bill was designed to prevent the slaughtering of livestock 'at too short a time' after the drive to market as it was believed that unless the animals were given time to rest and cool down before they were killed the meat would be 'tainted'. Burke opposed the Bill ostensibly in part because it offended the principles of free trade. Some fifteen years later he would write:

Of all things, an indiscreet tampering with the trade of provisions is the most dangerous, and it is always worst in the time when men are most disposed to it:—that is, in the time of scarcity. Because there is nothing on which the passions of men are so violent, and their judgement so weak, and on which there exists such a multitude of ill-founded popular prejudices.[2]

Mr. Burke observed, that such a Power as that intended to be vested in the Butchers by this Act, would tend to create a Monopoly, as no small Butcher who had not a Way of keeping the Beasts he might purchase,

[1] In 1698 the Commons proposed to reduce the army in England to about 8,000 men. William III regarded 30,000 as an absolute minimum (D. Ogg, *England in the Reigns of James II and William III*, Oxford, 1957, pp. 440–1). For a full discussion of the debate over standing armies, see L. G. Schwoerer, *'No Standing Armies!' The Antiarmy Ideology in Seventeenth-Century England*, Baltimore, 1974.
[2] See *Thoughts and Details on Scarcity*, vol. ix, p. 120.

would venture to buy in warm Weather. He insisted that poor People would buy Meat a little tainted, and that Means might be devised by Salt, Spices, etc. to preserve it from Putrefaction, so as in the End, to render it both wholesome and palatable Food. He said that it was not long since that a general Notion prevailed, that all Wines were of a poisonous Quality, till a Set of venturesome Blades, more hardy than the rest, tried the Experiment; the Effect of which was, not Death, but Chearfulness and good Humour. For the same Reason, he did not doubt, if some of the Beef, Mutton, and Pork, which was described as so unwholesome, were salted or spiced, and made into Sausages, that a Man might eat heartily, without any Consequence but that of filling his Belly.

Sawbridge protested that the Bill in fact took away power from the Butchers' Company. The Bill was defeated.

Speech on Shipwreck Bill
27 March 1776

Source: *St James's Chronicle*, 28 March 1776

The same reports are in *Lloyd's Evening Post*, 29 March; *General Evening Post*, 30 March; and *London Chronicle*, 28 March. They are the reports followed by *Parl. Reg.* iii. 472, 473 and *Parl. Hist.* xviii. 1298.

Burke had introduced a Bill to prevent the plundering of shipwrecks in 1775, but too late in the session for it to be considered.[1] He brought up the matter again on 27 March 1776.[2] The concern to prevent the plundering of wrecked ships was naturally important to the large merchant and trading interest in Burke's Bristol electorate. The Merchant Venturers of Bristol earlier had petitioned in support of Burke's Bill claiming that it was 'necessary for the Protection of the Commerce, on the Prosperity of which the Value of the Lands of this Kingdom must depend, and of the Lives of those brave Men who are the Source of the National Prosperity and natural Defence of this

---

[1] *Commons Journals*, xxxv. 204.
[2] *Corr.* iii. 140, 222, 258. Both the 1775 and 1776 Bills were printed (*Commons Sessional Papers*, xxvii. 107–10, 281–6). For the practice of wrecking, see J. G. Rule, 'Wrecking and Coastal Plunder', in D. Hay et al., *Albion's Fatal Tree: Crime and Society in Eighteenth-Century England* London, 1975, pp. 167–88, though Burke's Bills of 1775 and 1776 are there confused.

Kingdom'.[1] The Bill would have made it compulsory for local authorities to see that the 'Goods & Chattels' of shipwrecks which washed ashore in a particular area be returned to their rightful owners. Anyone who interfered with this process was to be 'liable to the same penalties & forfeitures as persons Feloniously taking & Carrying away Ship Wrecked or Stranded Goods'.[2] The Bill met opposition mainly because by its Provisions, 'if a Ship is plundered, the Hundred is to make good the Damages, although every possible Effort of the Magistracy'[3] may have been employed to prevent it. The principle of hundredal liability was an ancient and recognized one.[4] But compensation to merchants and ship owners would have involved coastal districts in sums far more onerous than those conventionally levied, for instance, to recompense victims of robbery.

Mr. Burke moved for Leave to bring in a Bill "to prevent the inhuman Practice of plundering Ships wrecked on the Coast of Great Britain; and for the further Relief of Ships in Distress on said Coast". He said, he thought something ought to be done to prevent such shameful and horrid Practices as had been frequently committed on the several Coasts of this Kingdom, scarcely a Winter passing, but our public Prints were full of Accounts which were sufficient to disgrace any civilized Country, in which such Matters were permitted to pass un-noticed and unpunished. He said, that commercial Countries, particularly this, which prided itself on its[5] national Honour, should take Care to do every Thing possible in its Power, to discourage and punish such outrageous Proceedings.

The motion was opposed by John Sawbridge, the Lord Mayor of London, and others. It was argued that the laws in existence were sufficient.

Mr. Burke said, it seemed very extraordinary, that the first Magistrate of the first trading City in the World, should oppose a Bill designed to protect the Property of Persons concerned in Trade and commerce. He hoped, however, before the Matter was further pursued, that Gentlemen would rise, declare their Sentiments, and take a decided

[1] On 18 April (*Commons Journals*, xxxv. 705). The city of Poole also petitioned for it on 2 May (ibid. 749).

[2] There is a copy of part of the Bill at Northampton (A.xxxv.25) with minor changes apparently penned by Sir Thomas Clavering (1719–94, M.P. 1753–60, 1768–90).

[3] The hundreds on the sea coast of Carmarthen petitioned against the Bill on the second reading on 30 April 1776 (*Commons Journals*, xxxv. 738).

[4] F. Pollock and F. W. Maitland, *The History of English Law before the Time of Edward I*, 2nd edn., 2 vols., Cambridge, 1952, i. 558.

[5] *Lloyd's Evening Post*: 'prided itself so much on its'.

Part. For his Part, he had no particular Reason for pushing such a Law. It is true, he thought it might be of Service, but if the House disapproved of it, there his Task ended, and he should chearfully acquiesce[1] in whatever it determined. He entreated, therefore, that Gentlemen would speak out, and not permit the Bill to be brought in, merely for affording an Opportunity to throw it out, after Trouble and Time had been spent in framing and bringing it in.

The Bill was ordered in by a vote of 56 to 13.

Speech on Shipwreck Bill
30 April 1776

Source: *St James's Chronicle*, 2 May 1776

The same reports are in the *Middlesex Journal*, 4 May, and are repeated for the second speech in *Parl. Reg.* iii. 502–3 and *Parl. Hist.* xviii. 1301–2.

Mr. Burke then rose, and moved for the Order of the Day, that the Bill for preventing the inhuman Practice of plundering Ships wrecked on the Coast of England and Wales, be read a second Time.

Mr. Burke replied to the several Objections, and was extremely severe on some of his Opposers; said, when he moved for Leave to bring in the Bill, the House seemed to be almost unanimous; but now he perceived that Gentlemen had changed their Minds; he had done, and must submit; for he perceived the Bell had rung, as the departing Knell of his favourite Bill. He then entered into a View of the French Laws, and shewed, in a Variety of Instances, what great Advantages they had over ours, in Respect of Ships wrecked on their Coasts.[2] He was very sarcastical on Mr. Van, for calling the Bill a black Bill,[3] and observed, that the Gentlemen affected great Caution in the present

---

[1] *St James's Chronicle*: 'acquiese'.
[2] Those who supported the Bill argued that 'every other country in Europe had provided a remedy for this terrible calamity but these kingdoms' (*Parl. Hist.* xviii. 1301).
[3] Charles Van (d. 1778, M.P. 1772–8), had called it a 'black Bill', in an apparent allusion to Robert Walpole's Waltham Black Act (9 Geo. I, c. 22). Van had declared the Bill might be 'productive of the grossest fraud and imposition' (*Parl. Hist.* xix. 1301). Ostensibly, he was attempting to bring home a warning to M.P.s who refused to oppose the measure that they might well see their county included 'in a more general law' in the future.

Case, though it was well known we had Laws enacted on the most trivial Occasions. We had some against pulling a Stake out of a Hedge;[1] others against touching Paling;[2] others still more extra-ordinary against disturbing a Thorn.[3] All those, according to the Language held this Day, were, it seems, of more Consequence in the Estimation of some Gentlemen, than the destroying, pillaging, or purloining the Cargo of a Vessel worth several thousand Pounds.

The Bill was defeated by 55 votes to 43.

Speech on Motion on Shipwrecks
1 May 1776

Source: *St James's Chronicle*, 4 May 1776

Burke's Bill having been defeated, he tried to rescue the principle on which it was based.

MR. BURKE moved for a Committee to consider of the several Statutes which provide for raising on certain Districts, and obliging them to answer in Damages for Injuries done to certain Species of Property. He observed that the Principle being once established it would follow that the atrocious disgraceful Custom of plundering Wrecks came within the Description of the general Law of Compensation. He then moved that the 13th of Edward 1. Chap. 46, and the 27th of Elizabeth, Chap. 13. be read, to shew that the Spirit of our Laws was that of Compensation,[4] and at the same Time to apprise the House that he meant to proceed on those Authorities as a Groundwork to bring in a Bill the succeeding Session, to prevent the inhuman

---

[1] 13 Ed. I, Stat. 1, c. 46.
[2] 1 Geo. I, Stat. 2, c. 48, see n. 4 below.
[3] 9 Geo. III, c. 41, sect. viii.
[4] Burke also moved for three other similar statutes to be read: 1 Geo. I, Stat. 2, c. 5, which forced 'Inhabitants of the Hundred' to pay compensation for damage to property from unlawful rioters; 1 Geo. I, Stat. 2, c. 48, which forced the Parish to compensate the owner of trees 'destroyed illegally'; and 9 Geo. I, c. 22, which made the Hundred liable to the maximum of £200 for illegal 'killing or maiming of Cattle, cutting down or destroying trees, or setting fire to any House, Barn or other property.'

Practice of plundering Ships wrecked on the Coast of England and Wales.

Burke's motion for a committee was, after amendment, defeated.

Speech on Loss of Boston
6 May 1776

Source: 1. *St James's Chronicle*, 7 May 1776
2. MS. at Sheffield, Bk 6.176

The newspaper report in the *St James's Chronicle* is truncated in other papers (e.g. *London Chronicle*, 9 May), but is the basis of the report in *Parl. Reg.* iii. 511–12. See also Simmons and Thomas, vi. 515, 517. Burke's draft was evidently written after the debate, since it comments on what Lord North had said during it.

On 6 May 1776 Colonel Isaac Barré[1] moved that an Address be presented to the King asking that the dispatches received from Boston which had been evacuated by Sir William Howe on 17 March, be given to the House. Burke had been relatively inactive in American affairs since his second conciliation speech largely as a result of frustration from ill-success and the deepening of the conflict.[2] The fact that the ministry could now be held to account for a major setback in the war may have helped to reawaken his interest in the parliamentary battle.

(1) *ST JAMES'S CHRONICLE*

Mr. Burke, who has been partly silent for some Time past, resumed his former Ardour. He spoke for a full Hour, and was heard with great Attention. He took a short but comprehensive View of the Conduct of the War from its first Commencement, and jocularly observed, that if he had not the highest Opinion of the Integrity and Probity of the noble Lord and his Colleagues in Office, he should be inclined to suspect that they were secret Friends to America, and had been bribed to betray the Honour and military Reputation of this Country; for from the first Embarkation of Troops from Ireland, to this Instant, every

---

[1] See above, p. 161.   [2] *Corr.* iii. 242.

single Measure which had been adopted or pursued were directed to the impoverishing this Country, and emancipating America. He observed that the noble Lord had disclaimed any Intention of giving false Colours to the Account which appeared in the London Gazette; but there was not Room left for a Possibility of Misrepresentation, for though the Boston Extraordinaries for 8,000 Men, in the Course of twelve Months, had amounted to One Million and a Half, or nearly Two Hundred Pounds a Man, for salt Beef and sour Crout, he would be bold to affirm, and called upon the noble Lord to contradict him, that the Troops could not have remained in that Town, ten Days longer, if the Heavens had not rained down *Manna* and *Quails*; and in a similar Expectation, he presumed, the Troops were embarked for Halifax, a Land flowing with *Milk* and *Honey*.

(2) MS. AT SHEFFIELD, BK 6.176

The N[oble] L[ord] says that the narrative of his Gazette,[1] contains a full, and fair account, and that no false Colours are laid upon it. As to the fullness I readily admit that nothing can be more comprehensive. In one short paragraph it contains the history [of] our total perhaps our final exclusion from twelve great provinces. That no false Colours are laid upon the Narrative can as little be controverted—there is not *space* enough to spread any colour upon it, either true or false. The nicest miniature painter could scarcely contrive to touch this truly geometrical point with the tip of his Pencil. The noble Lord is in the right. Where all is darkness there can be no colour.

But in reality is this the satisfactory account which an injured, despoild, dishonoured Nation, receives of the loss of its dominions? If we have no duty to fulfil have we no curiosity to gratifye?

It is enough for us to know that General Howe had *taken a resolution* of quitting Boston with that army which was sent to reduce all America? Not one particular of the preceding situation of his affairs. No movement of the Enemy; no proceedings of his own. The Noble Lord tells you that we did not retire upon Treaty with General Washington, that the retreat of our Troops was not a capitulation but a successful flight. This is our Comfort. Our conquering army has made its escape

---

[1] The *London Gazette*, 4 May 1776, printed a very brief report from Howe, who wrote that he had 'taken a Resolution on the 7th of March to remove from Boston to Halifax'.

without loss. If we were inclined to acquiesce in that account as true, will not our curiosity be a little interested to know what that situation could be which made an escape from it a circumstance in itself so happy, and the execution a matter of so much glory to the General who conducted it. For my part I feard all along that this favourite war would be fruitful of such sort of glory. But ⟨imagining⟩ if it be matter of Triumph to him who *abandons* a place without loss what must it be his honour who takes it without loss? Washington conveys a very different story to his masters at the Congress from that with which Ministry has chosen to entertain their servants in the House of Commons. But had the Case been reversed, and General Washington written to the Congress that he had effected an happy retreat from Boston without loss I am persuaded it would have met another reception from that impolite and unpractised people new to affairs, and with all the eagerness of their Natural feelings and passions about them.

Our General has *taken a resolution* to quit Boston—Not driven says the Noble Lord by the superiority of the Enemy, by Famine by sickness, by desertion or any calamity of Nature or of War. We are duller than dutchmen. If General Cronstrom had written to their high Mightinesses that he had *taken a resolution* to abandon Bergen op Zoom to the arms of Lowendal,[1] even dutchmen, as dull as we are pleased to suppose them, would certainly have been tempted to ask some sour questions about the why and wherefore of that *resolution*. Had the noble Lord told us, and had it been true that we had been driven from our posts by slaughter or famine—I should have had infinitely better prospects for the future. Men may be recruited; provisions may be supplied, even Courage may be renovated—but what hope is left for those, when armies unimpaird and untouchd as they are represented hold it glorious to abandon the places which they were expressly sent to defend and think it an happy change of position to fly for plenty and security to the regions of famine and desolation? There is in this account a contradiction to all the principles of Reason such a woful perversion of all the human faculties and sensations, that

---

[1] Isaac Kock, Baron Cronstrôm (1661–1751), had defended Bergen-op-Zoom against Ulric-Frédéric-Waldemar, Comte de Lowendal (1700–55), in 1747, but had surrendered the town to him. This was a critical strategic point in the War of the Austrian Succession; see R. Lodge, *Studies in Eighteenth-Century Diplomacy 1740–1748*, London, 1930, pp. 260, 271, 286, 290, 292, 329.

if it contain'd a single Syllable of truth our ruin must be irretrievable. Fortune cannot save us.

But by some means or other probably by having fait[h] in general so much their Enemy every thing seems to the Gentlemen on that Bench, to be more to their advantage than what is true. They tell you steadily that the dereliction of Boston was *voluntary*. Let us examine this point. Boston then was quitted because Boston was not a proper position for the King's forces. Is this really so? Was then the Blood pourd out with such prodigality of Slaughter at Bunkers Hill, shed in order to preserve a place which it was not proper to maintain? Is this the consolation Ministers hold out to the wounded and maimed in their Battles, to the widows and children of those who were miserably slain in their quarrel?—and do those who exposed them to that fire write on their Tombs, "here lie these[1] men who died in defending a situation which Prudence and honour dictated to abandon?" Did they put their country to a charge of 400,000 for artillery service to maintain a place which ought not to be held.

Barré's motion was defeated by 171 votes to 54.

Speech on Conway's Motion
22 May 1776

Sources: MSS. at Northampton, A.xxvii.93; A.xxvi.15

This report was written almost certainly after the debate in a clear hand and a form suitable for publication. The first portion is in Burke's hand, the second in Zouch's hand, corrected in part by Burke—but unfortunately Burke has not filled in the gaps left by Zouch in the major part of his copy. The speech is briefly reported in the newspapers (*St James's Chronicle*, 25 May; *London Chronicle*, 23 May) and in *Parl. Reg.* iv. 125–6 and *Parl. Hist.* xviii. 1360–1. See also Simmons and Thomas, vi. 589, 590, 593–4.

Letters patent issued on 6 May 1776 had appointed the Commanders-in-Chief in America, General Sir William Howe and his brother Viscount Howe,[2] special commissioners for granting pardons and taking other measures for the conciliation of the colonies. On 22 May General Henry Seymour Conway moved that the instructions given to the Howes should be com-

---

[1] MS.: 'this'.

[2] Richard, 4th Viscount Howe (1726–99), M.P. 1757–82, Commander-in-Chief of the British naval forces in America, was Sir William's older brother.

municated to the House. Conway had been Rockingham's Secretary of State for the South when Burke entered Parliament at the end of 1765. He was a consistent opponent of the American war but exasperated his old friends in the Rockingham party by dissociating himself from the parliamentary opposition. At one point in his speech Conway had said: 'What shall I say, Sir, there is but one moment between this great country and destruction! I wish to seize it—The urgencies of this crisis will be my apology to the House. I am no partizan, nor indiscriminate opposer of government, except in this point.'[1]

Great expectations were entertaind, that General Conways motion for laying the [instructions to the Howes, as Commissioners, before the House] would have drawn out something concerning the designs of Ministry in the Negotiation which the two Brothers[2] are to open with the Congress in America. These expectations were compleatly disappointed. The Commission does not expressly direct them to treat with that body; but as it authorises them to treat *with any persons whatsoever*, a power of Treaty with the Congress is included within the Limits of that authority. As The Congress are now the sole ruling power which is acknowledged in any part of the thirteen united Colonies it is therefore that power which alone can be treated with. Accordingly it was acknowledged that the Commissioners might treat with the Congress but denied that they had been instructed to do it *openly*.

At first the Ministry seemd to decline all explanation on the Subject. After the proposition had been moved with great ability by General Conway, and seconded with equal force and eloquence by Lord J. Cavendish—it was sometime before any of the Treasury Bench thought proper to speak; and a loud Cry for the Question was raised near the Bar. At length Lord North arose, and professing great Candour and calmness, recited the heads of the *Commission* which he said he should have had no Objection to laying before them. But denied the propriety of producing *instructions* whilst a Negotiation was depending which he said might be a means of defeating the whole and was contrary to all precedent. That although the Romans had made a rule to themselves not to treat cum *armato hoste*,[3] and that he was not desirous of such a treaty if it could possibly be helped; yet Rules were to be varied according to circumstances, and that he would now treat with any Colony even before they had laid down their arms. He said

---

[1] *Parl. Reg.* iv. 119.   [2] The Howes.   [3] 'With an armed enemy'.

that he had been always desirous of taking hold of any opportunity of putting a Stop to the effusion of blood and never had held the doctrine of unconditional Submission. The Commissioners were accordingly provided with the most ample powers of hearing reporting and redressing Grievances; and thereby of restoring peace; But it would be highly improper, that the Terms should be divulged, because the Terms were to be varied according to Events; and if the highest that might be obtaind, should be known at once, nothing would be left to[1] concede when the Exigency of affairs might require it. He thought that in *all reason* we ought to get peace on the best Terms for the authority of Parliament that we could, and therefore was against divulging the ultimatum of concession.

Mr. Burke answered him with great Energy and earnestness and spoke for a long time. He said that the motion had drawn a very proper Line of distinction between what ought and what ought not to be divulged in the present Negotiation. That Mr. Conway did not ask where, nor with whom, nor in what manner this Negotiation was to be conducted—all these questions might be improper—first because It was well known that Ministry had already delayed[2] this Treaty [until] we had not a foot of Land in the 13 Colonies where we could invite any persons to treat with us—That the Congress could hardly be expected to[3] meet in the Cabbin of Lord Howes ship. They would not go to Nova Scotia, until they had security against famine—publick opinion supposed they were to land at New York, where he had then ⟨known⟩ General Lee[4] commanded. He did not ask what their mode of address would be to General Lee whom they had abused without measure in[5] order to obtain his protection and safe Conduct to the Congress. When there, he did not ask what kind of submission they were to make to Mr. Handcock whom they had destined to the Cord and excepted by proclamation from their offers of General pardon.[6] He did not ask what arguments they were to use.[7]

---

[1] MS.: 'to to'.
[2] MS.: 'to delay'.
[3] MS.: 'to to'.
[4] Charles Lee (1731–82), an Englishman by birth, appointed early in 1776 to superintend the defence of New York, but on 1 March sent to the South.
[5] MS.: 'without measure hoping'.
[6] See above, p. 188, n. 2.
[7] The report in Burke's hand ceases at this point.

He does not enquire how a Secretary for the Colonies,[1] who came into Office with those whom he had long opposed, and left those whom he had long supported[2] for no other reason than to enforce the highest claims of Parliament by Acts of wiser and better conducted hostility, is able to manage his Style, in authorising an individual to an absolute disposal of those Rights—see the motion aims at is to know whether these are rights, or Claims, or whatever they may be, are[3] to be given up, or suspended, or qualified in the exercise by this Treaty: Yea or no?

This motion has nothing to do with private, personal, or occasional instructions for the Management of so difficult an Affair. It relates solely to the *Basis* of the Treaty. It relates, not to the *Conduct*, but to the *Object*, of the Negotiation. This Treaty with our Colonies in Arms bears no sort of resemblance to a Treaty with a foreign power; wherein as the parties are independent, the Objects are all merely *political*. In that Case Parliament cannot[4] question the *Legality* of the power, but only the *abuse* of it; and they can not presume the abuse until it has happened. To *political Treaty* the Kings power is perfectly competent. But the Royal power is not competent to negotiate away the *Constitution*. Such a power is not within the federative Trust reposed in the Crown.

If the Crown had conferred such powers either by Commission or instruction, they are illegal and usurped powers; if not this Negotiation is nothing but a foolish uncoverd attempt at fraud for the purpose of cheating the provincials into a suspension of hostilities, until subsistence could be secured for the foreign Army of Mercenaries we were introducing amongst them. What success we might have in such a fraudulent attempt in a military light he could not undertake to say. But he was sure that it was mean and[5] unworthy in itself and never could lead to a speedy, much less to a Solid peace.

The Noble Lord at the head of the Treasury had said indeed that the Commissioners were sent to enquire into the Grievances of the

---

[1] Lord George Germain (1716–85), later (1782) 1st Viscount Sackville, M.P. 1741–82.

[2] There was no real inconsistency in Germain's political conduct at this time. He had always been an advocate of firm measures against America and in party terms essentially independent. Though he had collaborated with the Rockinghams in the early 1770s, he was never truly one of their number. He joined North in November 1775 as Secretary of State for the Colonies specifically to strengthen the ministry's direction of the war.

[3] MS.: 'are are'.   [4] MS.: 'cannot not'.   [5] MS.: 'and and'.

Americans and to report them. This could not be true in any part of it; because we were already perfectly acquainted with every Grievance the Colonies feel or pretend to feel, by the means of innumerable, and (as we once seemed to think) very troublesome representations. If then the Grievances are known in England in their fullest extent it[1] is perfectly ridiculous to send into America to enquire what they are.

But let us suppose there was any Sense in this Voyage for discovery of Grievances, how can the Commissioners *redress* them? We know that all the demands of the Colonies however they may branch out, are reducible to three heads. 1st. The repeal of Revenue Laws 2d. The Repeal of Laws relative to Charters. 3d. Some parliamentary Security against future Taxation. The objects of the Complaint and the objects of redress are all, and in every part, parliamentary. What inducements then can Lord Howe hold out to the Colonists, to persuade them to lay down their Arms? Has he authority from Parliament to do anything but to grant Pardons? and to open Ports? His attempting to promise on the part of Parliament, without powers from this house, would only serve to detract from the little Credit he may have in other things. Because no security can be given for the performance of any Terms he may choose to make except such a security as is grounded on the Supposed Notoriety of the servile and passive disposition of Parliament, and the certainty that we will either assert Rights with a barbarous fury, or give them up with an abject tameness, just as we are required by our Ministerial Masters. When we are incited to war we are always told that it is for the Rights of Parliament we are to fight and the Crown justifies itself on the advice and authority of the two houses. But when peace is to be made, we are told that this right and the disposal of it is in the Crown; and we are not, even so much as to know, what Ministers mean to do with those constitutional Objects.

The Commission therefore being without powers can produce no Effect. But the deficiency which may be in powers the Noble Lord seems to think will be made up by the Zeal and abilities of the Commissioners. Nobody, he said, could dispute the Zeal or the general abilities of the two excellent Brothers. To them he paid many very high Compliments. But he took exception to their being the sole Commissioners for the following among other Reasons.

1st That they Admiral and General were *merely Military Men,*

---

[1] MS.: '*or It*'.

and though high in professional Merit, were perhaps, even by that Merit as having turned their whole minds that one way, but the more disqualified to treat with men of the first civil Abilities, there, in questions of such Magnitude, and intricacy; and so involved in Law, and in parliamentary practice, and precedent, as to have divided the first Men of Civil abilities in both houses here. The appointment of such persons *exclusively* to such a business; he believes did at first view astonish every Body; he thought it impeachable matter, and most highly Criminal.

2dly That in an attempt towards Reconciliation, where a friendly disposition of Mind is supposed to go a great way, some persons supposed to be friendly to America, or at least Neutral in these unhappy Contests, ought to have been appointed. But in the present Commission all was exclusively put into the hands of the Admiral and the Commander in Chief, who were in those Characters, to carry fire and Sword into the heart of the Country—and who in their Parliamentary Capacity had been universally known, to have voted (very conscientiously he believed) but had certainly Voted for all, or most of the measures, that had produced the very confusion which they were now appointed to put an End to.

3dly[1] That the American prize Act[2] had given a lucrative interest in the Captures to the Marine Officers employed in the Service, and that nothing could do more to impede the Effect of Negotiation than that the Admiral being Commissioner was himself to profit of the prizes which would be[3] daily made, perhaps the property of the very men he was in Treaty with; and if the Admiral should be willing from Generosity to give up his own share, it might be honorable to himself personally, it would   lessen the Odium of that hostile and
        situation so contrary to the lenient Character of a Negotiator, instead of reconciling the people, and which furnished daily and hourly matter of suspicion and

The whole ill effect of this plan he[4] removed from the Commander and threw it upon the Ministry. Nothing can be so disgraceful to Parliament or so disreputable to the National Character, or so little

---

[1] In the margin: '[The Time]'.
[2] The Prohibitory Act, 16 Geo. III, c. 5.
[3] There are no corrections by Burke after this point.
[4] MS.: 'he I'.

likely to forward peace as the Scheme opened by Lord North, if a Scheme it could be called that of having no fixed principle to proceed upon, but give leave to Officers to vary our Claims and concessions according to the Event of war. It was publishing to the World that we were not to govern our Colonies by a natural disposition of moderation and   but according to the Vigour of their Rebellion. That reason and justice could get nothing; but   famine, Cannonade, Bombardment, was the only way to dispose the Parliament of Great Britain to the   of a prudent and moderate Government. The high Spirit of this Nation (so much vaunted in the Speech from the Throne) was it seems too high, to yield to anything but the heaviest blows, and the most ignominious defeats.

This mode of proceeding had brought us Step by Step into our present misfortunes. Having refused to receive the most decent petitions, when they were humbly brought here from legal Assemblies, we were now reduced to go ourselves into America, in effect to petition illegal Assemblies in hopes of cheating those whom we despair of bullying. He then by a recapitulation of Events shewed the mischiefs which had arisen from tricks and cunning, and the want of an open and sincere mode of proceeding from the beginning, from all which he inferred That it was absolutely necessary for Parliament no longer to trust its honour to others, but to lay a Basis for Treaty, by procuring security from its own Authority. They ought to consider how much they can yield with safety to the Empire, that ought to be declared as soon as possible, and no Events of war ought to alter it. He began from Lord Hillsboroughs Letter and pursued it through the instructions to Governours, the Cheat put upon the Assembly of New York, Lord North's conciliatory proposition, and the breach of faith in the Navigation Revenue, on all which he would not dilate having a few days before spoke at large on that Subject.[1]

---

[1] For Hillsborough's letter to the Governors in 1768, see vol. ii. p. 97 and P. D. G. Thomas, *The Townshend Duties Crisis: The Second Phase of the American Revolution, 1767–1773*, Oxford, 1987, p. 81. For Lord North's conciliatory proposition, see Burke's speech on 20 February 1775, printed above pp. 86–9. The 'cheat put upon the Assembly of New York', refers to the dispute between that colony and the home government in 1766–7 over the Mutiny Act of 1765, which called on the colonists to make provisions for British troops stationed among them. The 'Navigation Revenue' refers to the 'Townshend duties' imposed in 1767.

He said the Country Gentlemen who voted such Taxes and those who promoted addresses either within or without the house, ought to look for being severely responsible for having given those constitutional Rights and that national dignity to which they had incited hot and unthinking Men to make such declarations and such valuable sacrifices, to be disposed of merely at the discretion of two Gentlemen according to their Ideas of the fortune of War. That the same facility could not be found on their side. The Congress had too much Wisdom, Honesty, and dignity to trust such powers to their Generals; or to suffer them to dispose at their discretion of any of their constitutional Rights, or those privileges dearer to them than their Lives. One Reason (it does not appear how applicable) for not revealing the instructions, is least it should abate the Terrour, which is to be a principle in the American Government, and which is to be affected by an armed Negotiator, with unknown powers. This is a poor illusion like the rest. The Americans know that Noble Lord condescends to treat because he does not hope to conquer. He has over and over examined the alledged Grievances of America and has as often declared they were no Grievances at all. For what does he give up points which he has said a thousand times have been demanded against reason and justice. Is it because he has 70,000 Men to enforce reason and justice. The true one is obvious. That his Army cannot conquer America. If he treats with them he must still leave them Armed; the Idea of disarming an unconquered people is ridiculous. It is not possible to disarm that continent, if it were conquered, what then will he do? Does he mean to keep a great standing Army there?

Lord North   No—No—I never meant it.

Why then you leave them with some concessions in their favour, armed and yourself disarmed. In that condition what hold have you of them, but that very kindred love and common affection, which you now reprobate and have so often reprobated as a principle of Government? You are obliged to return to it late and disgraced—but on this you must rest at last.

Therefore you must acquire affection and confidence the only way in which it can be acquired by kind intention and open dealing.

He ended with saying; he had day after day so often combated this matter in the house that he would not have trouble[d] them at all that time but to shew a mark of personal regard and attention to the Gentleman who made the Motion.

That he had been happy in beginning his first Parliamentary attempts under His auspices. That Gentleman[1] was as willing to continue and   them in the same humble support, as long as he continued animated by those Sentiments, which he was happy to see he still entertained, and had enforced with such distinguished abilities this day. But as to his general Politicks they were past his comprehension. On what principle could he value himself on a general support of Ministry whose power and influence he declared in the very same breath to be employed for the destruction of his Country? If there is a Word of that Gentlemans Speech grounded upon fact or reason, no honest Man can consistently suffer such a set of people to Administer the affairs or direct the Councils of the Nation for a Single Moment. No Man can support the power of Guilty Men without becoming an accomplice in their Guilt. For his part   he hoped he had not been negligent to Oppose, to traverse, to disturb, to   them in every possible way and will continue the same Course until they abandon their Schemes or all attempts against them shall become manifestly impracticable and ridiculous.

Much mischief he said had been done by this   of general support of Government, which was a thing subversive of the constitution of the House of Commons and directly contrary to its End. That it had its colour from confounding two things perfectly different; Namely—the support of Government, and the support of any certain Junto in Administration. A thousand sets of Politicians might be alternately made and destroyed, and Government remain just where it was. It might even be necessary for the very being of Government itself to oppose and to change the Governors. The Great fundamental points of Government and which gives it its name and essence the administration of justice, the conservation of Order, the preservation of religion and manners, and the security and improvement of the commercial revenues and force of the Country, he appealed to the Treasury Bench whether in all matters relative to these points and seperated from particular ministerial politicks, he had not always instead of obstructing, given Government the fullest support, full as much though not so able as the Gentleman that made the Motion. But that it was abusing the sacred name of Government to confound it with the power of every miserable faction.

---

[1] MS.: 'Gentlemas'.

Nothing could be so destructive to its Ends. To strengthen the hands of Men whose Conduct and principles are ruinous, and then to hope to arrest them on the Moment of executing the Mischief, was a project not conformable to the general experience and wisdom of the Gentleman who made the motion.

He admitted indeed that Great Men by keeping themselves reserved from the Tasks of daily opposition drew a kind of personal dignity and reverence to themselves which frequently gave the greatest weight and effect to their occasional interference at a great political or constitutional Crisis. That Mr. Conway of whose good intentions, publick spirit, honour and integrity he said the highest things had never in any instance failed his Country at such a Crisis, but the event of this day was to shew how far such a conduct was to be preferred in the whole to that of the plain regular and obvious mode of opposing a dangerous System in the administration.

When Mr. Burke who spoke a long time and with much Vehemence had sat down, the debate seemed again on the point of expiring. Nobody on the Treasury side rose to answer him. The question was again called for. The Majority not having expressed the least desire of information on a Subject which had cost the Nation so much. Mr. Viner[1] then rose. He seemed not a little affected. This Gentleman is of that description commonly known by the Name of Tories; a man of honour and spirit, strongly attached to his party, a fast friend to Ministry, a sanguine promoter of the American War. It was he who distinguished himself by saying he would covenant to pay thirteen Shillings in the pound rather than suffer any abatement in the Claims of this Country.[2]

Conway's motion was defeated by 171 votes to 85.

[1] Robert Vyner (1717–99), M.P. 1754–61, 1774–84, 1785–96, was a respected country gentleman known for his disinterested approach to politics and his independence. He had been a staunch supporter of North's authoritarian American policy. He is said to have had an income of £8,000 or £10,000.

[2] On 3 May 1775 he had said 'he was willing to pay not only 4s. but 14s. in the pound' (*Parl. Reg.* i. 451). He now declared that the landed gentlemen had supported North's coercive policy 'in expectation of a revenue from America . . . But he now found they had been amused; that they had been led into a fine scrape; for all these were now to be given up without consulting, without even communication with Parliament.' North hastily explained that taxation was not to be given up but that the Commissioners would determine whether it should be enforced 'at present, as hereafter' (*Parl. Reg.* iv. 126). Vyner's remonstrance was particularly damning to the ministry, coming, as it did, from one of North's leading supporters among the country gentlemen. It is unfortunate that Burke's version of it stops at this point.

On Education
[June 1776]

Sources: MSS. at Sheffield, Bk 27.108–10.

Burke describes the change in the household of the Prince of Wales, which took place on 28 May 1776, as having occurred 'three weeks since'.

On 28 May George III entirely changed the households of the Prince of Wales and his brother, Prince Frederick.[1] He removed their Governor, the Earl of Holdernesse,[2] their Preceptor, William Markham the Bishop of Chester,[3] their sub-Governor, Leonard Smelt,[4] and their sub-Preceptor, Cyril Jackson.[5] The King did this because Holdernesse had lost his influence over his pupils and apparently because there were major differences of opinion between Holdernesse and Smelt on the one hand and Markham and Jackson on the other, connected with their divergent political views.[6] Lord Bruce[7] was appointed to head a new establishment, but he accepted the responsibility with reluctance and resigned it almost at once. Bruce's brother Lord Montagu[8] was then appointed in his place. He too was hesitant, but the King's offer of an earldom in remainder to his daughter persuaded him. Burke was prompted by this event to write briefly on the history of educational theory and on the reasons for the change. In Burke's words the animosity which he and the Rockinghams felt towards George III for turning the Whigs out of power in the 1760s is clearly visible. Like them, Holdernesse 'was bred a Whigg' and had to be removed because he might 'give the Prince an Idea of the obnoxious doctrine ... called the rights of Mankind'.

There are very few things which have engaged the thoughts of ingenious men in all ages and Countries, so much as the Subject of Education. Quintilian wrote on the Education of an orator;[9] The Marquis of Halifax on the Education of a daughter.[10] Montaigne has left us an Essay upon it which without method and perhaps for that reason, contains a prodigious deal of excellent matter.[11] Rabelais

[1] Frederick, Duke of York and Bishop of Osnaburg (1763–1827); see J. Brooke, *King George III*, London, 1972, pp. 242–3.
[2] Robert D'Arcy, 4th Earl (1718–78).
[3] (1719–1807).
[4] (*c*.1719–1800), Captain Royal Engineers.
[5] (1745–1819).
[6] See Walpole, *Last Journals*, ii. 49, 53.
[7] Thomas Brudenell, 2nd Baron Bruce (1729–1814), later (1776) 1st Earl of Aylesbury.
[8] George Brudenell, 1st Duke of Montagu (1712–90).
[9] Marcus Fabius Quintilianus (AD *c*.35–95) was the author of *Institutio Oratoria*.
[10] *The Lady's New-Year's Gift; or, Advice to a Daughter*, by George Savile, 1st Marquess of Halifax (1633–95), was first printed in 1688. There was a copy of Halifax's *Works* in Burke's library.
[11] Michel Eyquem de Montaigne (1533–92), *Essais*, Book I, xxvi: 'De l'Institution des Enfans'. His works were well represented in Burke's library.

notwithstanding the wildness and almost Phrensy of his Style and manner has some chapters on this Subject that are ever worth studying.[1] Milton who was himself a great Scholar wrote upon it in a scholastick Spirit.[2] The famous archbishop of Cambray with that gracious mildness and benignity that mellows and sweetens whatever he puts his hand to wrote for the Education of a King.[3] Locke has wrote an express Treatise.[4] It is not equal to his great reputation. But it shews he thought it worthy of the anatomist of the Human understanding. Rollin[5] has treated it like a careful and religious head of a French college. Mr Fordyce in the Style of a university Fine Gentleman, a Character peculiar to North Britain.[6] Madame La Marquise de Lambert[7] has written about it with much good sense but with little Novelty or force. Lord Bullinbroke[8] in his Idea of a Patriot King has not neglected His Education.[9] This piece was wrote *at* the late Prince of Wales[10] and *for* his present Majesty. Lord Bullinbroke has not indeed enterd minutely into the Subject. His touches are few and masterly. He knew that a great deal of precept and discussion is saved when he recommended a Scotch Governour[11] to form the mind and manners of his pattern of ideal perfection. The excellence of Lord Chesterfields Plan is at present a Subject of discussion.[12] It proposes to form a Compleat Courtier and perfect man of the World at a

[1] The views of François Rabelais (*c.*1494–*c.*1533) on education were advanced for his time; see especially *Gargantua et Pantagruel*, Book I, chap. xxiii.

[2] Milton's *Of Education* was published in 1644.

[3] François de Salignac de la Mothe-Fénélon (1651–1715), Archbishop of Cambrai, wrote *Télémaque* for his pupil Louis, Duc de Bourgogne (1681–1712), grandson of Louis XIV.

[4] John Locke (1632–1704) published *On Education* in 1693.

[5] Charles Rollin (1661–1741), the celebrated French educator. See, H. Ferte, *Rollin sa vie, ses oeuvres et l'univiersité de son temps*, Paris, 1902.

[6] David Fordyce (1711–51) was the author of *Dialogues Concerning Education* (1745–8). There was a copy in Burke's library.

[7] Anne-Thérèse de Lambert, Marquise de Lambert, née Marguenat de Courcelles (1647–1733), author of several educational works.

[8] The name is repeated as 'Lord Bolingbroke'.

[9] Henry St John, 1st Viscount Bolingbroke (1658–1751), wrote *On the Idea of a Patriot King* in 1738. It was published in 1749.

[10] Frederick Lewis, Prince of Wales (1707–51).

[11] Presumably Burke is referring to Lord Bute. He is plainly scoring party points by insinuating that George III had been influenced by Bolingbroke, the Tory enemy of both the Whigs and the House of Brunswick, in promoting Bute and other favourites in the 1760s. This Burke and the Rockinghams believed, had been responsible for the fall of the Whigs in the present reign and for the political instability, which had characterized the first decade of the reign; see *Thoughts on the Cause of the Present Discontents*, in vol. ii, pp. 253–87.

[12] Philip Dormer Stanhope, 4th Earl of Chesterfield (1694–1773). His controversial letters to his son were published in 1774.

very easy expense of Learning and at a minimum of Morality and is likely therefore to make its fortune. Rousseau with his exuberant and vehement torrent of Style and imagination that disdains all ⟨Bounds⟩ has hurried it down the precipices of Paradox.[1] But this flighty madman enters at the same time so profoundly into Human Nature, that the solemn mind may collect points of infinite value from the ⟨treasury⟩ of his fine Phrensy. After him nobody could imagine that any thing at least very unexpected and astonishing could appear upon that Subject.

Within a few days however the world has been surprised with a new *practical Essay* upon Education infinitely exceeding all the Visions of Rousseau. Nothing could be better calculated to elevate and surprise. And I defy any man to shew in this or in all these authors and many more I ought [to] have mentiond any thing like it. I cannot help congratulating Mr. Walpole[2] on this accession to his valuable collection of Noble and Royal Authors.[3] He is too liberal to exclude him from that character because he does not load the Shelves of Libraries; Socrates without writing has been considerd as the first of publick instructors and in every well understood Sense an Author of the highest Class.

We all recollect how well we were pleased when his Majesty a few years ago (without the slightest consultation with one of his Ministers) made the arrangement for the Education of the Prince of Wales.[4] We feel how much we are delighted when, three weeks since (with the same just contempt of the opinion of those to whom he inadvisedly commits the affairs of his Empire,) he destroyd every part and particle [of] that arrangement. We exulted, when with as little notice taken of his grave Cabinet Counsel, he appointed a new establishment with Lord Bruce at the head of the System. But whilst we stood gazing in silent wonder at this brilliant phœnomenon a flash struck across that entirely confounded our miserable mortal of his obliqua [perstringens] lumina flamma[5]—So—the Scene passes—Lord Bruce disappears as

---

[1] Jean-Jacques Rousseau (1712–78), whose *Émile* was probably reviewed by Burke himself for the *Annual Register* for 1762. There were copies of the French text and English translation in Burke's library.

[2] Horace Walpole (1717–97), later (1791) 4th Earl of Orford, M.P. 1741–68. He published *A Catalogue of the Royal and Noble Authors of England* in 1758.

[3] Presumably Burke means the King himself.

[4] The household had been established in 1771.

[5] 'dazzling the eyes with slanting flame'; Lucan, *Phasalia*, i. 154.

soon as he was noticed above the horison. He shone only as precursor to the full Day that broke upon us in the Duke of Montague. Three Systems of publick Education without the Knowledge of those who receive the pay of publick advisers,[1] has taken place in about as many weeks. I am sure these deep Statesmen and shrewd Courtiers know nothing of the changes with which the long period of the next week is pregnant. But his Majesty is indulgent to his Ministers as well as his people. He would confine their errours to their own Generation; The Prince of Wales may when late he begins to Govern not have another Empire to spare.

It was matter of Enquiry for what the Earl of Holderness The Bishop of Chester, Colonel Smelt—and Mr. Jackson are removed. We hear that His Majesty has expressed the highest Satisfaction in them all; and the only difference in the Stories told on every side[2] is this; is with which he is the most perfectly pleased—I am told that the inferior ⟨teachers⟩ of subordinate accomplishments as well all those who attended the ⟨convenience⟩ or decoration of the young Princes who were all removed in this complete change even to the valet de chambre and Friseur had the consolation in their[3] fall with the gracious assurance[4] that when he turned them off no persons in the world could have deserved it less. Though poorly provided with the kings of this world, they were set down to the Banquet of a good Conscience—which as it has been well observed is a perpetual Feast.[5]

It could not in truth be a crime in such a Court to have deserved well; and we must look for other causes of this important Change, and it will not be hard to find them; if we reason from facts and not from Speculation; and form our[6] judgements of the nature of the work by the qualities of the workmen. The Prince of Wales has passed through the ordinary preliminary parts of Education. He is a good proficient in Greek and Latin; He has a[7] tolerable Notion of ⟨Poetry⟩ [and] antient History. But the great Education, that Education which is to regulate his opinions in the fundamental parts of government; and to

---

[1] The King considered his sons' household a matter strictly for himself to determine. North was taken as much by surprise as anyone.

[2] MS.: 'sides'.

[3] MS.: 'their their'.

[4] MS.: 'and at the ⟨assurance⟩ with a gracious assurance'.

[5] See G. L. Apperson, *English Proverbs and Proverbial Phrases*, London, 1929, p. 111: 'A good conscience is a continual feast' and 'For a good conscience being a perpetual feast.'

[6] MS.: 'and and form'.   [7] MS.: 'and He has a has a'.

mark out objects for his imitation; to give a proper Bias to his politicks and to direct the[1] proper choice of men This important period is just now commencing. The Preceptor[2] becomes every day of less importance the Governour of more. With whom he reads whatever remains to be read of Classics is of no great moment, nor does it signifye whether such a preceptor has had breeding has been with Tories who are passive on Opinion or whiggs who are passive for Interest.[3]

Lord Holdernesse is without doubt a very pretty Gentleman. He has formed the heir of the Crown to a great deal of that Species Liberalis[4] without which the greatest Prince can only be a clown out of his Place. But here was an End of his Services.[5] Lord Hold. was bred a Whigg.[6] If he retains Whigg principles he may be dangerous. If he forgot them he is good for nothing. At some odd moment something by inadvertence might slip out that might give the Prince an Idea of the obnoxious doctrine of what is falsely called the rights of Mankind. He could not say

Amendment to Address
31 October 1776

Sources: MSS. at Sheffield, Bk 27.197–8

Printed from Burke's original draft which appeared in *Corr.* (1844), ii. 121–6. Corrections, most of them in Burke's hand, which are made on copies at Sheffield (R101) are noted, except for deletions not clearly by Burke. The omission of words which are in the draft Bk 27.197–8 in

[1] MS.: 'direct and the'.
[2] The new Preceptor was Richard Hurd (1720–1808) Bishop of Lichfield and Coventry. Like Markham, he was associated with Mansfield. He was also particularly congenial to the King.
[3] Tories as believing in the doctrine of passive obedience or non-resistance and Whigs who had deserted Rockingham to preserve their places at Court.
[4] Higher, more noble, respectable and engaging quality.
[5] In margin: 'a daring master of an higher Order. A quality in which the Tories'.
[6] Smelt, who was later to help the Rockinghams oppose Christopher Wyvill and the association movement in Yorkshire (see below, pp. 466–7), was also known as a Whig of independent cast of mind; Markham and Jackson were regarded as pawns of Mansfield and 'Prerogative' men, though their Whiggish credentials were no less impeccable. Holdernesse's Whiggism had nothing whatever to do with his retreat; he admitted his inability to control two headstrong princes of the blood.

R101.8(1-2), which is docketed 'To make the other copies agreeable to the corrections to this' are recorded. In another version, the first part was almost entirely rewritten—see R101.8(10). The completed amendment to the Address is printed on *Commons Journals*, xxxvi. 4–5 and *Lords Journals*, xxxv. 7–8.

The King's speech at the opening of the 1776–7 session reported the Declaration of Independence, the recovery of Canada and the prospect of further success at New York. Because of the mother country's seemingly strong position many members of both Houses of Parliament were in a particularly unyielding frame of mind. The ministry's draft of the Address of Thanks supported by large majorities congratulated the King on his success and strongly condemned the rebels. In this climate the Rockinghams had decided upon a secession from Parliament as the most appropriate way to make a general statement against the actions of the Government and the majority.[1] However, some of their following, including their irrepressible new friend Charles James Fox, considered secession too tepid.[2] It was now 'more necessary than ever', Fox had argued, 'to produce some manifest petition or public instrument upon the present situation of affairs ... to exhort his Majesty to make the only proper use of his Victory'[3] by seeking a resolution of the dispute. The party leaders thus decided that before seceding they should take specific steps publicly to clarify their position. An amendment to the Address was written by Burke and revised by his friends. It was moved in the Commons and the Lords and was used as the basis of a formal protest signed in the Upper House by the Marquess and thirteen other peers.[4]

To assure his Majesty, that animated, as we are and ever have been, with the most earnest and sincere Zeal for his Majesties true interest and the real glory of his Reign, we behold with inexpressible concern the minds of a very large, and lately loyal and affectionate part of his people entirely alienated from his Government.

That nothing but gross ignorance of human nature,[5] or a spirit of adulation, that would be unacceptable to the dignity of his Majesties Sentiments, unworthy of his faithful Commons, and utterly unsuitable to the serious circumstances of this critical time, could induce us to represent to his Majesty, that the revolt of a whole people could possibly happen without some considerable Errors in the Conduct which has been held towards them.

---

[1] It is first mentioned in a letter and in specific comments by William Baker of 23 November 1776 (MS. at Sheffield, R1.1690–1).

[2] *Corr.* iii. 294.

[3] MS. at Sheffield, R1.1686: C. J. Fox to Rockingham, 13 October 1776.

[4] *Parl. Hist.* xviii. 1392–5.

[5] MS.: 'of human and nature' [corrected in the copies].

As of ourselves we know, so of your Majesty we are fully persuaded,[1] that these Errors could in no Sort be owing to any thing like an ill intention in his Majesty,[2] or in the great publick Councils of this Kingdom. But we are apprehensive that the true origin of the most important and most dangerous of them, has been in misinformation given to, and true and perfect information of facts withheld from Parliament and his Majesty by his Majesties Ministers, and the principal Servants of the Crown. On this imperfect and mistaken State of things, Measures have been pursued for the reduction and chastisement of a supposed inconsiderable party of factious men which have driven thirteen great Provinces to despair. Every act, which has been proposed as a[3] means of procuring peace and submission has become a new cause of War and revolt. We trusted that as his Majesties Ministers were from their Duty obliged, and from their official situation enabled, to know most perfectly the Temper, Character, and disposition of the people in the British Colonies in America, they would be the best able to point out such measures as might produce a salutary effect. From this principle, full Credit has been given to all the plans proposed by them,[4] until this house by continuing this confidence[5] we find ourselves almost inextricably involved in a bloody and chargeable civil War; which besides exhausting, for the present, the strength of all his Majesties Dominions, and[6] exposing our Allies to the designs of their Enemies,[7] and leaving this Kingdom in a perilous[8] situation, threatens, in its issue, the most deplorable Calamaties to the whole British Race.

That we cannot avoid Lamenting that in consequence of the Credit afforded to the Delusive representations of his Majesties Ministers, no hearing has been given to the reiterated petitions and complaints of the Colonies. We lament too, that no ground has been laid for removing the original Cause of these unhappy differences; which, as they have arisen on questions relative to Parliamentary proceeding, so none but

---

[1] Rockingham has suggested in the margin that the beginning of this sentence should be changed to: 'That we are fully persuaded that these Errors.' R101.8(1) changes it to: 'That, as our own part we know, so of his Majesty's part we are fully persuaded'.

[2] MS.: 'your Majesty' [corrected in copies].

[3] R101.8(1) omits 'a'.

[4] R101.8(1): 'by these Ministers'.

[5] R101.8(1): 'until by a continuance of the Confidence of the house'.

[6] R101.8(1) omits 'and'.

[7] R101.8(1): 'of their and our Enemies'.

[8] R101.8(1): 'Kingdom itself in a most perilous'.

Parliament could give any authority to settle. By this fatal omission the Commissioners sent into, or nominated in America, for the pretended[1] purpose of making peace,[2] were furnished with no other[3] legal powers, but that of giving or withholding pardons at their pleasure, and for relaxing the severities of a single penal act of Parliament; Leaving the whole foundation of this unhappy controversy just as it stood in the beginning.

To represent to his Majesty, that in addition to this Neglect, solely owing to the representation of his Ministers, his said[4] Ministers, in direct violation of publick faith held out from the Throne itself, when in the beginning of the last Session, his Majesty in his gracious speech to both houses of Parliament declared his resolution of sending out Commissioners for the purpose[5] therein expressed, *as speedily as possible*,[6] no such Commissioners were sent until near seven Months afterwards; and until the Nation was alarmed by the Evacuation of the only Town[7] then held for his Majesty in the thirteen united Colonies. By this intentional delay, acts of the most critical Nature, the Effect of which must as much depend on the power of immediately relaxing them on Submission, as in enforcing them upon disobedience, had only an operation to enflame and exasperate. But if any Colony, Town, or place had been induced to submit by the operation of the Terrors of these Acts, there were none on the place, of power to restore the people so submitting to the common Rights of Subjection. The Inhabitants of the Colonies therefore apprised that they were put out of the protection of Government and seeing no means provided for their entering into it, were furnished with reasons but too colourable for breaking off their dependency on the Crown of this Kingdom.

To assure his Majesty, that removing[8] our confidence from those who in so many instances have so grossly[9] abused it, we shall endeavour to restore to parliament the confidence of all his People.[10]

---

[1] R101.8(1): 'the Commissioners nominated for the pretended'. In R101.8(3) 'pretended' is changed to 'apparent'.
[2] The commission given to the Howe brothers.
[3] R101.8(1): omits 'other'.
[4] R101.8(1): omits 'said'.
[5] R101.8(1): 'purposes'.
[6] The King's Speech of 26 October 1775; see *Parl. Hist.* xviii. 695–7.
[7] Boston.
[8] Rockingham has written in the margin: 'Quae to alter'.
[9] R101.8(2): 'so' is deleted.
[10] MS.: 'your people' [corrected in copy].

To this end it may be advisable to make a more minute enquiry into the Grievances of the Colonies, as well as into the Conduct of Ministers with regard to them; for the redress of the one; and, if cause should appear, for animadversion on the other. We may think it proper, particularly to enquire how it has happened, that the Commerce of this Kingdom has been left exposed to the reprisals of the Colonies, at the very time when their Seamen and Fishermen, being indiscriminately prohibited from the peaceable exercise of their occupations, and declared open Enemies, must be expected, with a certain assurance, to betake themselves to Plunder, and to wreak their Revenge on the Commerce of Great Britain.

That We understand, that amidst the many disasters and disgraces, attendant on[1] his Majesties arms in many Parts of America, a signal advantage has been gained by his Majesties British and[2] foreign mercenary forces, in the Province of New York.[3] That if a Wise, moderate, and provident Use be made of this advantage, it is not improbable that happy Effects may result from it.[4] And we assure his Majesty, that nothing shall be wanting on our part to enable his Majesty to take full advantage of any dispositions to reconciliation which may be the consequence of the late Victory,[5] by laying down real[6] permanent grounds of connection between Great Britain and the Colonies, on principles of well ascertained Dependence, and well secured Liberty.[7]

That whilst we lament this effusion of English blood which we hope has not been greater or other than Necessity required and honour justified we should most heartily congratulate his Majesty on any Event leading to this great desirable End of such a peace as might promise[8] to last, that is a peace founded upon Terms of mutual advantage.[9] Any other would necessarily require even in Case of a Total conquest an army to maintain, ruinous to the finances and incompatible with the freedom of his Majestys people. We should look

---

[1] R101.8(2): 'which have attended on'.
[2] R101.8(4): 'British Troops and'.
[3] The Battle of Long Island.
[4] R101.8(2): 'from that use'.
[5] R101.8(4): 'miseries of War'.
[6] R101.8(2): 'down on our part real'.
[7] R101.8(4): 'on principles of Liberty and Terms of mutual advantage'.
[8] R101.8(2): 'to the great desirable end of settling a Peace, which might promise'.
[9] R101.8(4): 'to last, and by the restoration of the antient affection which has happily subsisted in former Times between this Kingdom and its Colonies'.

with the utmost shame and horrour, on any Events of what Nature so ever, that should tend to break the Spirit of any large part of the British Nation; to Cow them to an Abject unconditional submission to any power whatsoever; to annihilate their Liberties; and to subdue them to servile principles and passive habits, by the mere force of foreign mercenary Arms, because we cannot help, amidst the excesses and abuses which have happend, to respect the Spirit and principles operating in these commotions. Our wish is to regulate not to destroy them. For, though differing in some Circumstances, these very principles[1] evidently bear so close a resemblance and exact an analogy,[2] with those which support the most valuable part of our own Constitution that we cannot, with any appearance of Justice, think[3] of wholly extirpating them by the sword in any part of his Majesties dominions, without admitting consequences, and establishing precedents, the most dangerous to the Liberties of this Kingdom.

In the Commons the amendment to the Address was defeated by a vote of 242 to 87. Burke seems not to have spoken in the debate. In the Lords, where Rockingham led the Opposition's attack, it was voted down by 82 votes (92 including proxies) to 26.

Speech on Cavendish's Motion on America
6 November 1776

Source: *Parl. Reg.* v. 58–62

Burke seconded Lord John Cavendish's motion as well as making a (second) speech on it. His speech seconding the motion is in *Parl. Reg.* v. 51 and *Parl. Hist.* xviii. 1434, and is presumably taken from *Gazetteer*, 8 November. It is not reprinted here. His second speech has no known newspaper source. It is taken from *Parl. Reg.* and is also in *Parl. Hist.* xviii. 1441–5. Other reports of the second speech are in *London Chronicle*, 7 November; *London Evening Post*, 7 November; *St James's Chronicle*, 8 November; *Public Advertiser*, 7 November; *Gazetteer*, 9 November; and *London Packet*, 8 November.

On 6 November 1776, the day before the Rockinghams began a partial secession,[4] Lord John Cavendish read to the Commons the Declaration

---

[1] Rockingham has written in the margin: 'Quae and which place ['called' written above] Your Majesty's Family on the throne.'

[2] R101.8(2): 'a resemblance to and so exact an analogy'.

[3] R101.8(2): 'that it is impossible with any appearance of justice to think'.

[4] See above, p. 247, and *Corr.* iii. 309.

of Lord Howe and General Howe which stated that the King was 'most graciously pleased . . . to concur in the revisal of all his acts by which his subjects . . . [in America] may think themselves aggrieved'. Lord John moved that the House resolve itself into a committee 'to consider the revisal of all acts of Parliament by which his Majesty's subjects in America think themselves aggrieved'. Burke seconded the motion principally asking for ministerial clarification of the Declaration. Later in the debate he spoke more fully.

Mr. *Burke.* Rejoiced I am, that the learned gentleman[1] has regained, if not his talent, at least his voice; that as he would not, or could not reply the other night, to my honourable friend, charmed as he must have been with the powerful reasoning of that eloquent speech, he had the grace to be silent.[2] On that memorable occasion he lay prostrate, on the *oblivious pool*,[3] confounded and *astounded*,[4] though called upon by the whole satanic host: he lay prostrate, dumb-founded and unable to utter a single syllable, and suffered the goads of the two noble Lords[5] to prick him till he scarcely betrayed a single sign of animal or mental sensibility. Why, Sir, would he not be silent now,—instead of attempting to answer, what in truth was unanswerable? But the learned gentleman has now called to his assistance, the bayonets of 12,000 Hessians;[6] and as he thinks it absurd to reason at present with the Americans, he tells us, that by the healing, soothing, merciful measures of foreign swords, at the breasts of those unhappy people, their understandings would be enlightened, and they would be enabled to comprehend the subtlities of his logic. It was well said, on another occasion, that your speech demands an army![7]—and I may say, that the learned gentleman demands blood; reasoning he says is vain;—the

---

[1] Alexander Wedderburn, Solicitor-General, had spoken immediately before Burke.

[2] In the debate on 31 October on the Address of Thanks for the Speech from the Throne, when he had been expected to reply to Charles Fox.

[3] *Paradise Lost*, i. 266.

[4] *Parl. Reg.*: 'astouned'.

[5] Lord North and Lord George Germain.

[6] Burke is exploiting the looseness of Wedderburn's wording. He had expressed a hope that the 'hand tying' of Congress would soon be 'dissolved, from the difference of the troops on both sides'. Wedderburn had intended this remark as a comment on the superiority of English troops; Burke deliberately interpreted it as a reference to the Hessian forces under Howe's command.

[7] In the King's Speech at the opening of the session on 31 October 1776 the ministry had used tough language with respect to the 'indignity and insult' done to the mother country and had made it clear that the colonists' 'treason' could not be tolerated. During the debate on the Address of Thanks, Lord John Cavendish had moved an amendment which among other things had pointed out that the failure of conciliation 'would necessarily require, even in case of a total conquest, an army to maintain, ruinous to the finances and incompatible with the freedom of his

sword must *convince* America, and clear up their clouded apprehensions. The learned gentleman's abilities surely desert him, if he is obliged to call such a coarse argument as an army to his assistance;—not that I mean any thing reflecting on his parts—I always esteem, and sometimes dread, his talents. But has he told you why commissioners were not sent sooner to America? Has he explained that essential point? Not a jot. Why, after the act pass'd for them,[1] why were they delayed full seven months, and not permitted to sail till May; and why was the commission appointing them delayed till the 6th of that month?— Answer this. The blood and devastation that followed, was owing to this delay; upon your conscience it ought to lay a heavy load. If the measure was right, and necessary in order for conciliation, as the King declared in his speech at the opening of that session, why was it not executed at a time, in which it could be effectual; instead of being *purposely deferred* to one, when it could not possibly answer any end but that of adding hypocrisy to treachery, and insult and mockery to cruelty and oppression. By this delay you drove them into the declaration of independency; *not* as a matter of *choice*, but *necessity*;—and now they have declared it, you bring it as an argument to prove, that there can be no other reasoning used with them, but the sword: what is this but declaring, that you were originally determined not to *prevent*, but to *punish* rebellion; not to use conciliation, but an army: *not* to *convince*, but to *destroy*!—Such were the effects of those seven months cruelly lost, to which every mischief that has happened since, must be attributed.

But still the learned gentleman persists, that nothing but the commissioners can give peace to America;—it is beyond the power of this House. What was the result of the conference with the delegates from the Congress? Why, we are told, that they met in order to be convinced, that taxation is no grievance;—no tyranny used to be the phrase; but that is out of fashion now.[2] Then, Sir, what an insult to all America, was it to send as commissioners, none but the commanders of the fleet and army to negociate peace.—Did it not shew how much you were determined, that the only arguments you meant to use,

Majesty's people' (*Parl. Hist.* xviii. 1401). Also, on 20 December 1774 Burke himself had used virtually the same words he refers to here during his speech on the land tax, printed above.

[1] Burke refers to the Howe Commission, authorized by the American Prohibitory Act, 16 Geo. III, c.5.

[2] The title of Dr. Johnson's tract of 1774 was *Taxation no Tyranny*.

were your broad-swords and broad-sides. Let me assert, Sir, that the doctrines to be laid down in America, would not have been too trivial an occasion, even for the reasoning abilities of the learned gentleman himself,—But, Sir, you may think to carry these doctrines into execution, and be mistaken too;—the battle is not yet fought; but if it was fought, and the wreath of victory adorned your brow, still is not that continent conquered; witness the behaviour of one miserable woman, who with her single arm, did that, which an army of a hundred thousand men could not do—arrested your progress, in the moment of your success. This miserable being was found in a cellar, with her visage besmeared and smutted over, with every mark of rage, despair, resolution, and the most *exalted heroism, buried* in combustibles, in order to fire New-York, and perish in its *ashes*;—she was brought forth, and knowing that she would be condemned to die, upon being asked her purpose, said, *to fire the city!* and was determined to omit no opportunity of doing what her country called for.[1] Her train was laid and fired; and it is worthy of your attention, how Providence was pleased to make use of those humble means to serve the American cause, when open force was used in vain.—In order to bring things to this unhappy situation, did not you pave the way, by a succession of acts of tyranny;—for this, you shut up their ports;—cut off their fishery;—annihilated their charters;—and governed them by any army. Sir, the recollection of these things, being the evident causes of what we have seen, is more than what *ought* to be *endured.* This it is, that has *burnt* the noble city of New-York; that has planted the bayonet in the bosoms of my principals;—in the bosom of the city, where alone your wretched government once boasted the only friends she could number in America.—If this was not the only succession of events you determined, and therefore looked for, why was America left without any power in it, to give security to the persons and property of those who were and wished to be loyal;—this was essential to government; you did not, and might therefore be well said to have abdicated the government.

I have been reading a work given us by a country, that is perpetually employed in productions of merit.—I believe it is not published yet;—

---

[1] The fire which destroyed about a quarter of New York took place on the night of 20–1 September. It has not been established that it was caused by incendiaries. For the sources, see D. S. Freeman, *George Washington*, 6 vols., New York, 1948–57, iv. 205.

the History of Philip the Second,[1] and I there find, that that tyrannical monarch never dreamt of the tyranny exerted by this administration.— Gods! Sir, shall we be told, that you cannot analyze[2] grievances?— that you can have no communication with rebels, because they have declared for independency!—Shall you be told this, when the tyrant Philip did it after the same circumstance in the Netherlands.—By edict he allowed their ships to enter their ports, and suffered them to depart in peace;—he treated with them;—made them propositions;—and positively declared that he would redress all their grievances. And James II. when he was sailing from France, at the head of a formidable force, assisted like you by foreign troops, and having a great party in the kingdom, still offered specific terms;—while his exceptions of pardon were few, among the rest my honourable friend's ancestor, Sir Stephen Fox:[3]—But you will offer none;—you simply tell them to lay down their arms, and then you will do just as you please. Could the most cruel conqueror say less? Had you conquered the Devil himself in hell, could you be less liberal? No! Sir, you would offer no terms;— you meant to drive them to the declaration of independency:—and even after it was issued, ought by your offers to have reversed the effect. You would not receive the remonstrance which I brought you from New-York, because it denied your rights to certain powers;—yet the late King of France received the remonstrances from his parliaments, that expressly denied his right to the powers he was in the constant exercise of—answered them, and even redressed some of the grievances, which those very remonstrances complained of, though he refused to grant, what he thought more peculiarly entrenched upon his own authority.[4]

In this situation, Sir, shocking to say, are we called upon by another proclamation[5] to go to the altar of the Almighty, with war and vengeance in our hearts, instead of the peace of our blessed Saviour;— he said, "My peace I give you;"[6]—but we are on this fast, to have war

---

[1] *The History of the Reign of Philip the Second King of Spain*, by Robert Watson (c.1730–81). It was published in London in 1777, and reviewed in the *Annual Register* for 1776 (pp. 243–59). There was a copy in Burke's library.

[2] *Parl. Reg.*: 'annalize'.

[3] (1627–1716), grandfather of Charles Fox. He was excepted from pardon by James II in a declaration issued at La Hogue in 1692.

[4] Burke is probably referring particularly to the *séance de la flagellation* of 3 March 1766 (J. Flammeront, *Les Remonstrances du Parlement de Paris au XVIIIe siècle*, 11 vols., Paris, 1888–98, ii. 554–60).

[5] For a General Fast on 13 December.

[6] John 14: 27.

only in our hearts and mouths; war against our brethren.—Till our churches are purified from this abominable service, I shall consider them, not as the temples of the Almighty, but the synagogues of Satan. An act not more *infamous*, respecting its political purposes, than *blasphemous* and *profane* as a pretended act of national devotion, when the people are called upon, in the most solemn and awful manner, to repair to church, to partake of a sacrament, and at the foot of the altar, to commit sacrilege, to perjure themselves publicly by charging their American bretheren with the horrid crime of rebellion, with propagating *"specious falsehoods,"*[1] when either the charge must be *notoriously false*, or those who make it, not knowing it to be true, call Almighty God to witness to not a *specious*, but a most *audacious* and *blasphemous* falsehood.

Lord John Cavendish's motion was defeated by 109 votes to 47.

Petition for Bristol
[January 1777]

Source: MS. at Sheffield, Bk 16.3

The MS. is in Zouch's hand, corrected by Burke and endorsed by him: 'Sketch of Petition for some Corporation. As I remember Bristol.' It can be dated from Burke's letter to Champion of [21 January 1777] (*Corr.* iii. 320–1).

This petition was drafted for the opponents of the ministry to sign at a time when its supporters in Bristol were organizing an address.[2] The petition was never presented.

The humble Petition of
  We your Majesties most dutiful and loyal Subjects,
  sensibly touched with the Miseries of the Civil War which now sorely afflicts your Majesties formerly flourishing and happy dominions beg leave, on occasion of the late success of The German Troops in conjunction with some of your Majesties standing National Army, in all humility to renew our supplications to your Majesty, for your powerful

---

[1] A quotation from the proclamation of the Fast.
[2] *Corr.* iii. 317–21.

and benevolent interposition towards restoring to all your people the blessings of peace, Liberty, and unanimity.

Whatever may have been the Conduct[1] of our English Brethren in the Colonies (a great and arduous question which we wish had not been put to the decision of the Sword) we can conceive no joy in hearing of their blood being spilled, or their persons brought into Captivity by foreigners, who have no concern in the Cause, but who seem to have a very ample Share in the quarrel. They, Sir, being only military instruments, can know nothing, but how to Slaughter those who resist, or how to receive those who are not able to withstand them, to servile unconditional Submission. They can neither have any feeling for the value, or any knowledge of the reason of these inestimable principles of the British Constitution, on the discussion of which this unhappy War had its origin. They may derive some military Glory from accomplishing the purposes for which they are kept up; but we cannot think, that any honour is or can be acquired to your Majesties Government, by subduing with a foreign mercenary Sword, an English people, without the offer of any sort of Terms for the Security of their Libertys; especially in that important point on which those who settled your Majesties illustrious family on the Throne of these Kingdoms, had taught us, (we hope not erroniously) to believe was the birthright of all Englishmen; constituted all their happiness and dignity, and made it an advantage to them to be the Members of this, rather than of any other community.

We therefore most humbly entreat your majesty by that innate goodness, with which providence has favoured you, and on which we daily pray for increase, and blessing, that you will be most graciously pleased, to find some method of previously holding out to your unhappy Subjects in America distinct Terms of accomodation, which we do not presume to dictate to your wisdom. We see but too evidently that the mere offer of pardon, or laying down Arms; and dispersing before a victorious Army composed for the greater part of foreigners, drives your people of your Colonies to despair of obtaining in future any reasonable Terms of subjection. We had flattered ourselves that the Commanders of your Majesties Fleets and Armies, had been furnished with much more satisfactory powers of accomodation. The want of these pacific powers, we are sorry to see supplyed by the

---

[1] Burke may have intended to replace 'conduct' with 'Grounds'.

257

plenitude of the Sword[1]—and we wish not to be numbered with those, who, for interested or party purposes, from an adherence to arbitrary principles, or a Lust of War and blood, are stimulating your Majesty to the unconditional Subjection of their fellow Creatures to the yoke of standing armies, without receiving any kind of security for their rights as Men or as Citizens.

Address to the King
[January 1777]

Source: MS. at Sheffield, R155.9

The MS. from which this *Address to the King* is here printed is not the MS. on which the version printed in *Works* (1792–1827) is based. It has alterations in Burke's hand which are not reproduced in *Works*. (The *Works* version also has some minor editing done to it which is not reproduced here.) There are two earlier versions of the *Address*. The immediately preceding version exists in a copy in the hand of C. N. Zouch (R101.6) and also in a clerk's copy (R155.4), which has a few variant readings from the Zouch copy, most of which are copying errors. The earliest version (R101.5), also in a clerk's hand (but corrected by Burke), differs markedly from the later texts: it is this version which was pirated (Todd, 68). Differences between the Zouch copy and the version here printed are noted, and some use has been made of the other versions. It is not absolutely certain that the final version is that sent to Rockingham on 9 January 1777 (*Corr.* iii. 308–15): it was probably the result of subsequent discussions.

The Rockinghams' policy of secession was never whole-heartedly embraced by all members of the group.[2] The failure of the party to establish a 'settled Plan . . . of action or inaction'[3] left Burke feeling frustrated in early 1777 and filled with anxieties at the potential negative consequences of a 'weak, irregular, desultory, peevish opposition'.[4] As a means of helping to rectify that situation, he accepted a request to prepare a manifesto to justify the principles and actions of his political associates. The result was an Address to the King. In the end, it probably did little to lift Burke's spirits, since the party never managed to present it.

The Address is instructive, however, as a concise and precise elaboration of the Rockinghams' opposition to the ministry's entire American policy. It is also one of the most successful attempts Burke ever made to blend the

---

[1] Burke wrote to Champion on [21 January 1777]: 'I will send you tomorrow the Petition somewhat corrected. If you should not receive it time enough only alter the words "plenitude of the Sword" to "arms and violence"' (*Corr.* iii. 320).

[2] See the headnote to Burke's amendment to the address of 31 October 1776, above, p. 247.

[3] *Corr.* iii. 311.

[4] Ibid. 313.

concept of no taxation without representation with the principle of parliamentary supremacy. Here the role of the imperial Parliament is to watch out for the interests of all the various dominions within the empire and implement the spirit rather than the letter of the British constitution. Authority can only properly be established, Burke believed, 'in the minds, affections, and Interests of the People'.[1] Therefore, it is necessary for the mother country to do not only what is likely to be beneficial for the colonists but what the colonists earnestly perceive to be grounded in their own ultimate good.

AN ADDRESS TO THE KING

We your Majesties most dutiful and loyal Subjects, several of the Peers of the Realm, and several Members of the House of Commons chosen by the[2] People to represent them in Parliament,[3] do in our individual capacity, but with hearts fill'd with a warm affection[4] to your Majesty, with a strong attachment[5] to your Royal House, and with the most unfeigned[6] devotion to your true Interest, beg leave at this Crisis[7] of your affairs, in all humility to approach your Royal presence.

Whilst we lament the measures adopted by the Public Councils of the Kingdom, we do not mean to question the legal validity of their proceedings. We do not desire to appeal from them to any person whatsoever. We do not dispute the conclusive authority of the bodies in which we have a place, over all their Members. We know, that it is our ordinary Duty to submit ourselves to the determinations of the Majority in everything, except what regards the just defence of our honour and reputation. But the situation into which the British Empire has been brought, and the conduct to which we are reluctantly driven in that situation, are such that we hold ourselves bound by the relation in which we stand both to the Crown and the People, clearly to explain them to your Majesty and our Country.[8]

---

[1] See below, p. 263.
[2] In the Zouch text (R101.6): 'your'.
[3] In the Zouch text: 'in your Parliament'.
[4] In the Zouch text: 'the warmest affection'.
[5] In the Zouch text: 'the most inviolable attachment'.
[6] In the Zouch text, presumably a misreading: 'unsigned'.
[7] In the Zouch text: 'awful crisis'.
[8] In the Zouch text this sentence reads: 'A Situation without example necessitates a conduct without precedent. We are driven, in this mode of addressing your Majesty, reluctantly to supersede those forms, which in other circumstances we shoud highly respect; and to regulate ourselves by no other rules, than those of our Laws, our Rights, and the profound Reverence we bear to our Sovereign.'

We have been called upon in the Speech from the Throne,[1] at the opening of this Session of Parliament[2] in a manner peculiarly mark'd, singularly emphatical, and from a place, from whence anything implying censure falls with no trivial weight,[3] to concur in unanimous approbation of those measures which have produced our present distresses, and threaten us in future with others far more grievous. We trust therefore, that we shall stand justified in offering to our Sovereign and the public, our reasons for persevering inflexibly in our uniform dissent from every part of those measures. We lament them, from an experience of their mischief, as originally We opposed them, from a sure foresight of their unhappy and inevitable tendency.[4]

We see nothing in the present events, in the least degree sufficient to warrant an alteration in our opinion. We were always steadily averse to this Civil war; not because we thought it impossible that it should be attended with Victory; but because we were fully persuaded that in such a contest, Victory would only vary the mode of our ruin; and by making it less immediately sensible, would render it the more lasting and the more irretrievable. Experience had but too fully instructed us in the possibility of the reduction of a free people to Slavery by Foreign mercenary armies: But we had an horror of becoming the instruments in a design, of which, in our turn, we might become the Victims. Knowing the inestimable value of Peace, and the contemptible value of what was sought by War, we wished to compose the distractions of our Country not by the use of foreign arms, but by prudent regulations in our own domestick policy.[5] We deplored as your Majesty has done in your Speech from the Throne, the disorders which[6] prevail in your Empire;[7] but we are convinced, that the disorders of the people in the

---

[1] 'in the Speech from the Throne' is not in the Zouch text.

[2] Of 31 October 1776. 'One great advantage, however, will be derived from the object of the rebels being openly avowed, and clearly understood [through the Declaration of Independence]; we shall have unanimity at home, founded on the general conviction of the justice and necessity of our measures'.   [3] In the Zouch text: 'falls with a decisive weight'.

[4] After 'grievous' the Zouch text continues: 'We hold ourselves therefore bound, for the preservation of our honour, and of what stands next in our estimation, your Majesties good opinion, to represent at the foot of your Throne, to your Majesty and our Country, our humble apology for inflexibly persevering in our dissent from every part of those proceedings, on the experience of their mischief, which we originally gave from a sure foresight of their unhappy and inevitable tendency.'

[5] The Zouch text starts the paragraph at this point.

[6] In the Zouch text: 'We deplore along with your Majesty the distractions and disorders which'.

[7] The King's Speech of 31 October 1776 referred to the 'troubles' 'which have so long distracted my colonies in North America'.

present time, and in the present place,[1] are owing to the usual and natural cause of such disorders at all times and in all places[2] where such have prevail'd,—The Misconduct of Government; That they are owing to plans, laid in Error; pursued with obstinacy; and conducted without Wisdom.

We cannot attribute so much to the power of faction at the expense of human nature, as to suppose, that in any part of the World,[3] a combination of men, few in number, not considerable in rank, of no natural hereditary dependencies,[4] should be able by the efforts of their policy alone, or the mere exertion of any Talents, to bring the People into the disposition which has produced the present troubles[5] in your American dominions. We cannot conceive, that without some powerful concurring cause, any management should prevail on some Millions of People, dispersed over an whole Continent, in Thirteen provinces, not only unconnected, but in many particulars of Religion, Manners, Government; and local Interest totally different and adverse, voluntarily to submit themselves to a suspension of all the profits of Industry, and all the comforts of Civil Life, added to all the Evils of an unequal War, carried on with circumstances of the greatest asperity and rigour. This Sir, we conceive[6] cou'd never have happen'd but from a general Sense of some grievance, so radical in its nature, and so spreading in its effects, as to poison all the ordinary satisfactions of Life, to discompose[7] the frame of Society, and to convert into fear and hatred, that habitual reverence ever paid by Mankind to an Ancient and venerable Government.

That grievance is as simple in its nature, and as level to the most Ordinary understanding, as it is powerful in affecting the most languid Passions—

"It is an attempt, to dispose of the property of a whole People without their consent."

Your Majesties English Subjects in the Colonies, possessing the

---

[1] The Zouch text does not have 'and in the present place'.

[2] The Zouch text does not have 'and in all places'.

[3] The Zouch text does not have 'in any part of the World'.

[4] The Zouch text has after 'dependencies': 'of talents, which however respectable, appear to be no way uncommonly imposing'.

[5] The Zouch text has: 'should, by the efforts of their Policies alonone [alone], be able to bring the people of your American Dominions into the disposition which has produced the present troubles.'

[6] The Zouch text does not have 'we conceive'.

[7] In the Zouch text: 'to dislocate'.

ordinary faculties of Mankind, know, that to live under such a plan of Government is not to live in a state of Freedom. Your English Subjects in the Colonies still impressed with the ancient feelings of the people from whom they are derived,[1] cannot live under a Government which does not establish Freedom as its Basis.

This Scheme being therefore set up in direct opposition to the rooted and confirmed Sentiments and habits of thinking of an whole People,[2] has produced the Effects[3] which ever must result from such a collision of power and opinion. For we beg leave, with all duty and humility to represent to your Majesty (what we fear[4] has been industriously conceald from you) that it is the opinion not only[5] of a very great number, or even of the Majority, but the universal sense of the whole Body of the People in those Provinces, that the practice of taxing, in the mode and on the principles, which have been lately contended for, and enforced, is subversive of all their rights.

This sense, has been declared, (as we understand on good information)[6] by the unanimous voice of all their Assemblies; each Assembly also, on this point,[7] perfectly unanimous within itself. It has been declared as fully by the actual voice of the people without these Assemblies, as by the constructive voice within them; as well by those in that Country[8] who addressed, as by those who remonstrated; and it is as much the avowed opinion[9] of those who have hazarded their all rather than take up arms against Your Majestys forces, as of those who have run the same risk to oppose them. The difference among them is, not on the grievance, but on the mode of redress; and we are sorry to say, that they who have conceived hopes from the placability of the Ministers who influence the public Councils of this Kingdom, disappear, in the multitude of those, who conceive, that passive compliance only confirms and emboldens oppression.

The sense of a whole people, most gracious Sovereign, never ought to be contemned by wise and beneficent rulers; whatever may be the abstract claims, or even rights of *the Supreme Power*. We have been too

[1] In the Zouch text: 'sympathising with the antient feelings of your Subjects here.'
[3] In the Zouch text: 'to the rooted and inveterate prejudices of an whole people'.
[3] R155.4: 'all the Effects'.
[4] In the Zouch text: 'what we are persuaded'.
[5] In the Zouch text the 'not' comes before 'the opinion'.
[6] The phrase in brackets is not in the Zouch text.
[7] 'on this point' is not in the Zouch text.
[8] 'in that Country' is not in the Zouch text.
[9] The Zouch text has 'sense'.

early instructed, and too long habituated to believe, that the only firm seat of all authority is in the minds, affections, and Interests of the People, to change our opinion,[1] on the Theoretick reasonings of speculative men, or for the convenience of a mere temporary arrangement of State. It is not consistent with Equity or Wisdom to set at defiance the general feelings of great Communities, and of all the orders which compose them. Much power is tolerated and passes unquestioned where much is yielded to opinion. All is disputed where everything is enforced.

Such are our Sentiments[2] on the Duty and Policy of conforming to the prejudices of a whole people, even where the foundation of such prejudices may be false or disputable. But permit us to lay at your Majesties feet, our deliberate judgment on the real merits of that principle, the violation of which is the known ground and origin of these troubles. We assure your Majesty, that on our part we shou'd think ourselves unjustifiable as good Citizens, and not influenced by the true spirit of Englishmen, if, with any effectual means of prevention in our hands, we were to submit to Taxes to which we did not consent either directly; or by a representation of the People, securing to us the substantial benefit of an absolutely free disposition of our own property in that important[3] case. And we add Sir, that if fortune instead of blessing us with a situation where we may have daily access to the propitious presence of a Gracious Prince had fixed us in Settlements[4] on the remotest part of the Globe, we must carry these Sentiments with us, as part of our being; persuaded that the distance of Situation would only render this privilege in the disposal of property, but the more necessary. If no provision had been made for it such provision ought to be made, or permitted.[5] Abuses of subordinate authority increase, and all means of redress lessen, as the distance of the Subject removes him from the Seat of the Supreme power. What, in those circumstances can save him from the last extremes of indignity and oppression, but something left *in his own hands*, which may enable him

---

[1] The Zouch text has 'sentiments' and continues 'for the convenience of a temporary arrangement of State'.

[2] In the Zouch text the paragraph begins: 'This is the Tenet we invariably hold'.

[3] In the Zouch text this sentence reads: 'We assure your Majesty, that on our parts, we should think ourselves unworthy of Life, which we only value for the means of spending it in honour and virtue, if we ever submitted to Taxes to which we did not consent, either directly, or by a representation satisfactory to the body of the people.'

[4] The Zouch text has: 'in a Settlement'.

[5] This sentence is not in the Zouch text.

to conciliate the favor and controul the excesses of Government? When no means are possessed, of power to awe or to oblige, the strongest ties, which connect mankind in every relation Social and Civil, and which teach them mutually to respect each other are broken.— Independency from that moment virtually exists. Its formal declaration will quickly follow. Such must be our feelings for ourselves. We are not in possession of another rule for our brethren.

When the late attempt practically to annihilate that inestimable privilege, was made great disorders and tumults very unhappily and very naturally[1] arose from it.[2] In this state of things, we were of opinion that satisfaction ought instantly to be given; or that at least the punishment of the disorder might be[3] attended with the redress of the grievance;[4] We were of opinion, if our dependencies had so outgrown the positive institutions made for the preservation of Liberty in this Kingdom, that the operation of their powers was become rather a pressure than a relief to the Subject in the Colonies, that wisdom dictated, that the spirit of the Constitution should rather be applied to their circumstances, than its authority enforced with violence in those very parts, where its reason became wholly inapplicable.[5]

Other methods were then recommended and followed, as infallible means of restoring Peace and order. We looked upon them to be, what they have since proved to be, the cause of inflaming discontent into disobedience, and resistance into revolt.

The Subversion of Solemn, fundamental Charters on a suggestion of abuse, without citation, Evidence, or hearing;—The total suspension of the Commerce of a great Maritime City, the Capital of a great Maritime Province during the pleasure of the Crown; The establishing of a military force not accountable to the ordinary Tribunals of the Country in which it was kept up;[6] Those and other proceed-

---

[1] The Zouch text has 'very unnaturally'; R155.4 has 'very naturally'.
[2] The Tea Act (13 Geo. III, c. 44) had given the East India Company concessions on the export of its huge stocks of tea in England and thus made more objectionable to the colonists the tax on tea which they had been required to pay as a result of the Revenue Act (7 Geo. III, c. 46) and a further Act (7 Geo. III, c. 56). This had brought on the Boston Tea Party and ignited the movement to war; see vol. ii, pp. 28, 95, 404, 407, 413–14, 417 n., 418.
[3] The Zouch text has: 'ought to be'.
[4] The Zouch text has: 'of Grievance'.
[5] After 'Grievance' the Zouch text continues: 'Because whenever a disorder arises from, and is directly connected with a grievance, to confine ourselves to the punishment of the disorder, is to declare against the reason and justice of the Complaint.'
[6] Burke is referring to three of Lord North's original coercive measures which had substantially contributed to a revolutionary atmosphere in America after the Boston Tea Party:

ings at that time, if no previous cause of dissention had subsisted were sufficient to produce great troubles. Unjust at all times, they were then irrational.[1]

We could not conceive, when disorders had arisen from the complaint of one violated right, that to violate every other was the proper means of quieting an exasperated People.[2] It seem'd to us absurd and preposterous, to hold out as the means of calming a people, in a state of extreme inflammation and ready to take up arms, the austere Law, which a rigid Conqueror would impose as the sequel of the most decisive Victories.[3]

Recourse indeed[4] was, at the same time, had to Force; and we saw a Force sent out, enough to menace Liberty, but not to awe opposition;[5] tending to bring odium on the Civil Power, and contempt on the Military; at once to provoke and encourage resistance. Force was sent out not sufficient to hold one Town;[6] Laws were passed to inflame Thirteen Provinces. This mode of proceeding by harsh Laws, and feeble armies could not be defended on the principle of Mercy and Forbearance. For Mercy, as we conceive, consists not in the weakness of the means, but in the benignity of the ends. We apprehend that mild measures may be powerfully enforced; and that acts of extreme rigour and injustice may be attended with as much feebleness in the execution as severity in the formation.

In consequence of these terrors, which falling upon some, threaten'd all, the Colonies made a common cause with the sufferers; and proceeded

---

the Massachusetts Bay Regulating Act (14 Geo. III, c. 45), see vol. ii, pp. 463; the Boston Port Act (14 Geo. III, c. 10), see vol. ii, pp. 404–6; and the Justice Act (14 Geo. III, c. 39).

[1] The Zouch text, after the first sentence of the previous paragraph, reads: 'We could not consider these methods at all adapted to the End. On the contrary we looked upon them to be, what they have proved to be, the cause of inflaming discontent into disobedience, and resistance into revolt. The principal instruments in that unfortunate plan; were the three following. 1st The infringement of the Charter of Massachusets Bay in many of its most essential points, upon a suggestion of abuse, without citation, evidence, or hearing. 2d. The putting a stop (also without hearing) to the Commerce of a great Maritime City [Boston], during the pleasure of the Crown. 3d. The establishment of a Military Force not accountable to the ordinary criminal Tribunals in the Country in which they reside.'

[2] The Zouch text here has two sentences omitted in the final version: 'If there had been no disobedience, these severe Laws could not have been proposed as necessary. Disobedience prevailing, it was Evident, that nothing but force, or concession could restore authority.'

[3] The Zouch text adds: 'The Frame and principle of these Acts implied the strongest disposition to disobedience in those who were the objects of them. The possibility of their execution must have presupposed, the most perfect and passive submission.'

[4] 'indeed' is not in the Zouch text.

[5] The Zouch text has 'resistance'.   [6] i.e. Boston.

on their part, to acts of resistance. In that alarming Situation We besought your Majesties Ministers to entertain some distrust of the operation of coercive measures, and to profit of their experience. Experience had no effect. The modes of Legislative rigour were construed[1] not to have been erroneous in their Policy, but too limited in their extent. New severities were adopted. The Fisheries of your People in America followed their Charters; and their mutual combination to defend what they thought their common rights, brought on a total[2] prohibition of their mutual commercial intercourse. No distinction of Persons or merits was observed—the Peaceable and the Mutinous; Friends and Foes were alike involved, as if the rigour of the Laws had a certain tendency to recommend the authority of the Legislator.

Whilst the penal Laws increased in rigour and extended in application over all the Colonies, the direct force was still applied but to one part. Had the great Fleet and Foreign Army since employed been at that time called for, the greatness of the preparation would have declared the magnitude of the danger. The Nation would have been alarmed, and taught the necessity of some means of reconciling with our Countrymen in America, who, whenever they are provoked to resistance demand a force to reduce them to obedience full as destructive to us as to them. But Parliament and the People, by a premeditated concealment of their real situation were drawn into perplexities, which furnished excuses for further armaments; and whilst they were taught to believe themselves preparing to suppress a Riot, they found themselves involved in a mighty war.[3]

At length British blood was spilld by British hands. A fatal Aera! which we must ever deplore, because your Empire will forever feel it. Your Majesty was touched with a sense of so great a disaster. Your Paternal breast was affected with the suffering of your English Subjects in America. In your Speech from the Throne in the beginning of the Session of 1775, you were graciously pleased to declare yourself inclined to relieve their distresses, and to pardon their errors.[4] You

---

[1] The Zouch text has: 'was construed'.
[2] 'total' is not in the Zouch text.
[3] This whole paragraph is not in the Zouch text.
[4] The King's Speech had referred to the fact that he had acted in the 'same temper' as Parliament—'anxious to prevent if it had been possible the effusion of the blood' of his subjects 'and the calamities which are inseparable from a state of war' and promising to 'be ready to receive the misled with tenderness' and 'to remove as soon as possible the calamities which they suffer'.

felt their sufferings under the late penal acts of Parliament. But your
Ministry felt differently. Not discouraged by the pernicious Effects
of all they had hitherto advised, and notwithstanding the gracious
declaration of your Majesty, They obtain'd another act of Parliament in
which the rigours of all the former were consolidated, and imbitter'd
by circumstances of additional severity and outrage. The whole trading
property of America (even unoffending Shipping in Port) was[1] indiscriminately and irrecoverably given as the plunder of Foreign
Enemies to the Sailors of your Navy.[2] This property was put out of the
reach of your mercy. Your People were dispoiled; and your Navy by a
new dangerous and prolific[3] example corrupted with the plunder of
their Countrymen. Your people in that part of your dominions were
put, in their general and political, as well as their personal capacity,
wholly[4] out of the protection of your Government.[5]

Though unwilling to dwell on all the improper modes of carrying on
this unnatural and ruinous war, and which have led directly to the
present unhappy seperation of Great Britain and its Colonies, We must
beg leave to represent two particulars, which we are sure must have
been entirely contrary to your Majestys Order or approbation. Every
course of action in hostility, however that hostility may be just or
merited, is not justifiable or excusable. It is the duty of those who claim
to rule over others, not to provoke them beyond the necessity of the
Case; nor to leave stings in their minds, which must long rankle;
even when the appearance of tranquillity is restored. We therefore
assure your Majesty, that it is with Shame and sorrow we have seen
several acts of hostility, which could have no other tendency than
incurably to alienate the minds of your American Subjects. To excite
by a Proclamation issued by your Majesty's Governor, an universal
insurrection of Negro Slaves in any of the Colonies, is a measure
full of complicated horrors; absolutely illegal; suitable neither to the
practice of War, or to the Laws of Peace.[6] Of the same quality we look
upon all attempts to bring down upon your Subjects an irruption of
those fierce and cruel Tribes of Savages[7] in whom the Vestiges of

---

[1] In the Zouch text: 'were'.
[2] By the Prohibitory Act.
[3] Perhaps Burke meant 'profligate'.
[4] 'wholly' is not in the Zouch text.
[5] By the American Prohibitory Act.
[6] See Burke's Petition on the Use of Indians [autumn 1775], above, pp. 179–81.
[7] The Zouch text adds: 'and Cannibals'.

human nature are nearly effaced by ignorance and barbarity. They are not fit Allies for your Majesty in a[1] War with your People. They are not fit instruments of an English Government. These and many other Acts we disclaim as having advised, or approved when done; and we clear ourselves to your Majesty and to all civilized Nations from any participation whatever before or after the fact, in such unjustifiable and horrid proceedings.

But there is one weighty Circumstance, which we lament equally with the Causes of the War and the modes[2] of carrying it on. That no disposition whatsoever towards Peace or Reconciliation has ever been shewn by those who have directed the Public Councils of this Kingdom, either before the breaking out of these hostilities, or during the unhappy continuance of them. Every proposition made in your Parliament to remove the Original cause of these troubles, by taking off Taxes obnoxious for their principle or their design, has been overruled. Every Bill brought in for quiet; rejected, even on the first proposition. The Petitions of the Colonies have not been admitted, even to an hearing. The very possibility of Public Agency, by which such Petitions cou'd authentically arrive at Parliament has been evaded and chicaned away. All the public declarations, which indicate any thing *resembling* a disposition to reconcile, seem to us,[3] loose, general, equivocal, capable of various meanings, or of none; and are accordingly construed differently at different times by those on whose recommendation, they have been made; being wholly unlike the precision and stability of public faith; and bearing no mark of that ingenuous simplicity, and native candour and integrity, which formerly characterised the English Nation.

Instead of any relaxation of the claims of Taxing at the discretion of Parliament, Your Ministers have devised a new mode of enforcing that claim, much more effectual for the oppression of the Colonies, though not for your Majestys service, both as to the quantity and application, than any of the former methods;[4] and this mode has been expressly[5] held out by Ministers, as a Plan not to be departed from by the House

---

[1] Not in the Zouch text.
[2] Zouch text: 'and with the modes'.
[3] 'seem to us' is not in the Zouch text.
[4] In the Zouch text: 'much more effectual both as to the quantity and application than any of the former methods'.
[5] In the Zouch text: 'earnestly'.

of Commons, and as the very condition on which the Legislature is to accept the dependence of the Colonies.

At length, when after repeated refusals to hear or to conciliate, an act dissolving your Government by putting your People in America out of your protection was passed, Your Ministers suffered several months to elapse, without affording to them, or any Community, or any individual amongst them the means of entering into that protection, even on unconditional submission, contrary to Your Majestie's gracious declaration from the Throne;[1] and in direct violation of the public faith.

We cannot therefore agree to unite in new severities against the Brethren of our blood for asserting[2] an Independency, to which, we know in our conscience, they have been necessitated by the conduct of those very Persons who now make use of that Argument to provoke us to a continuance and repetition of the acts which in a regular series have led to this great misfortune.

The reasons,[3] dread Sir, which have been used to justify this perseverance in a refusal to hear or conciliate, have been reduced into a sort of Parliamentary maxims which we do not approve. The first of these maxims is "that the two Houses ought not to receive (as they have hitherto refused to receive) petitions containing matter derogatory to any part of the authority they claim." We conceive this maxim, and the consequent practice, to be unjustifiable by reason or the practice of other Sovereign Powers, and must be productive, if adhered to, of a total seperation between this Kingdom and its dependencies. The supreme power, being in ordinary cases the ultimate judge, can as we conceive, suffer nothing in having any part of his rights excepted to, or even discussed, before himself. We know, that Sovereigns, in other Countries, where the assertion of absolute regal Power is as high, as the assertion of absolute power in any Politick body can possibly be here, have received many petitions in direct opposition to many of their claims of prerogative; have listen'd to them; condescended to discuss and to give answers to them. This refusal to admit even the discussion of any Part of an undefined prerogative, will naturally tend to annihilate any privilege that can be claimed by every inferior dependent Community, and every subordinate order in the state.

The next maxim, which has been put as a bar to any plan of

[1] The Zouch text does not have 'from the Throne'.
[2] The Zouch text does not have 'asserting'.
[3] The Zouch text has 'reason'.

269

accommodation, is "that no offer of terms of Peace ought to be made before Parliament is assured that those terms will be accepted." On this we beg leave to represent to your Majesty, that, if in all events, the policy of this Kingdom is to govern the people in your Colonies as a free people, no mischief can possibly happen from a declaration to them and to the world of the manner and form in which Parliament proposes that they shall enjoy the Freedom it protects. It is an encouragement to the innocent and meritorious, that they at least, shall enjoy those advantages which they patiently expected rather from the benignity of Parliament than their own Efforts. Persons more contumacious may also see, that they are resisting terms of perhaps greater freedom and happiness than they are now in arms to obtain. The glory and propriety of offer'd mercy is neither tarnished or weaken'd by the folly of those who refuse to take advantage of it.

We cannot think that the declaration of Independency makes any natural difference in the reason and policy of the offer. No Prince out of the possession of his dominions, and become a Sovereign *de jure* only, ever thought it derogatory to his rights or his Interests, to hold out to his former Subjects a distinct prospect of the advantages to be derived from his readmission, and a security for some of the most fundamental of those popular privileges in vindication of which he had been deposed. On the contrary such offers have been almost uniformly made under similar circumstances. Besides as Your Majesty has been graciously pleased in your speech from the Throne[1] to declare your intention of restoring your People in the Colonies to a state of Law and Liberty,[2] no objection can possibly lie against defining what that Law and Liberty are; because, those who offer and those who are to receive terms frequently differ most widely and most materially in the signification of these very important words.[3]

To say[4] that we do not know at this day what the grievances of the

[1] The Zouch text does not have 'in your speech from the Throne'.

[2] The King's Speech of 31 October 1776 concluded: 'My desire is to restore to them the blessings of law and liberty, equally enjoyed by every British subject, which they have fatally and desperately exchanged, for all the calamities of war, and the arbitrary tyranny of their chiefs.'

[3] The Zouch text reads: 'differ in the objects to which they apply such words.'

[4] The earliest text (R101.5.6) has the following version of this paragraph: 'To say that we do not know at this day what the grievances of the Colonies are, be they real or pretended, would be unworthy of us; but by waiting under this pretext untill their grievances are transmitted to us by certain Commissioners we weaken their powers of Treaty and we delay the hour of Peace. In the mean time we are wasting the substance of both Countries; We are continuing the Effusion of Human of Christian of English Blood; a consideration too serious to suffer us to trifle by a pretended ignorance of the origin of this quarrel and of the measure of concession which may be

Colonies are, (be they real or pretended) would be unworthy of us. But whilst we are thus[1] waiting to be informed of what we perfectly know, We weaken the powers of the Commissioners;[2] We delay, perhaps we lose,[3] the happy hour of Peace; We are wasting the Substance of both Countries, We are continuing the Effusion of human, of Christian, of English Blood.

We are sure, that we must[4] have your Majesties heart along with us, when we declare in favor of mixing something conciliatory with our force. Sir[5] we abhor the Idea of making a conquest of our Countrymen. We wish that they may yield to well ascertain'd, well authenticated, and well secured Terms of reconciliation; not that Your Majesty should owe the recovery of your Dominions to their total waste and destruction. Humanity will not permit us to entertain such a desire; nor will the reverence we bear to the Civil Rights of Mankind, make us even wish, that Questions of great difficulty, of the last importance, and lying deep in the vital principles of the British Constitution, should be solved by the arms of foreign Mercenary Soldiers.[6]

It is not, Sir, from a want of[7] the most inviolable duty to your Majesty, not from[8] a want of a partial and passionate regard to that part of your Empire in which we reside, and which we wish to be supreme, that we have hitherto withstood all attempts to render the Supremacy of one part of your Dominions inconsistent with the Liberty and safety of all the rest. The motives of our opposition are found in those very sentiments which we are supposed to violate. For we are convinced beyond a doubt, that a System of dependence, which leaves no security to the people for any part of their freedom in their

---

made with the greatest probability of putting an end to it. We are sure we have your Majesty's heart along with us when we declare in favour of mixing something conciliatory with our force; and had rather they should yield to well and ascertained and well authenticated terms of reconciliation than that your Majesty should owe the recovery of your Dominions to their total waste and destruction, or suffer difficult Questions lying deep in the vital principles of the British Constitution, to be solved by the coarse Barbarian and venal military Conduct of German mercenarys.'

[1] 'thus' is not in the Zouch text.
[2] The Howe brothers.
[3] The Zouch text omits 'perhaps we lose'.
[4] 'must' is not in the Zouch text.
[5] The Zouch text has: 'To speak plainly, Sir,'.
[6] The Zouch text reads: 'solved by the coarse Barbarian, and venal military Conduct of foreign Mercenaries.'
[7] The Zouch text reads: 'for want of'.
[8] The Zouch text reads: 'nor from'.

own hands, cannot be established in any inferior Member of the British Empire, without consequentially destroying the freedom of that very body, in favor of whose boundless pretensions such a scheme is adopted. We know and feel, that Arbitrary Power over distant Regions is not within the competence, nor to be exercised agreeably to the forms, or consistently with the spirit of great popular Assemblys. If such Assemblys are called to a nominal share in the exercise of such Power, in order to screen under general participation the guilt of desperate measures, it tends only the more deeply to corrupt the deliberative Character of those Assemblys, in training them to blind obedience; in habituating them to proceed upon grounds of fact, with which they can rarely be sufficiently acquainted and in rendering them executive instruments of designs, the bottom of which they cannot possibly fathom.

To leave any real freedom to Parliament, much Freedom[1] must be left to the Colonies. A Military government[2] is the only substitute for Civil Liberty. That the establishment of such a power in America[3] will utterly ruin our finances, though its certain effect, is the smallest part of our Concern. It will become an apt, powerful, and certain Engine for the destruction of our Freedom here.[4] Great Bodies of armed Men, trained to a contempt of Popular Assemblys representative of an English People; kept up for the purpose of exacting impositions without their consent, and maintain'd by that exaction; Instruments in subverting, without any process of Law, great Ancient establishments; and respected forms of Governments; set free from,[5] and therefore above the ordinary English Tribunals of the Country where they serve, these Men cannot so transform themselves, merely by crossing the Sea, as to behold with Love and Reverence, and to submit with profound obedience, to the very same things in Great Britain, which in America they had been taught to despise, and been accustom'd to awe, and humble. All Your Majesties Troops in the Rotation of Service, will pass through this discipline, and contract these habits. If we could flatter ourselves that this would not happen we must be the weakest of men: We must be the worst, if we were indifferent whether it happen'd

---

[1] The Zouch text does not have 'Freedom'.
[2] The Zouch text has 'Military Power' as the beginning of the sentence.
[3] The Zouch text does not have 'in America'.
[4] The Zouch text reads: 'of our own Freedom'.
[5] The Zouch text does not have 'from'.

or not. What, Gracious Sovereign, is the Empire of America to us or the Empire of the World, if we lose our own[1] Liberties? We deprecate this last of Evils.

We depricate the effect of the Doctrines, which must support and countenance the Government over conquered Englishmen. As it will be impossible[2] long to resist the powerful and equitable arguments in favor of the freedom of these unhappy people, that are to be drawn from[3] the principle of our own Liberty; Attempts will be made, attempts have been made, to ridicule and to argue away this principle; and to inculcate into the minds of your People, other maxims of government and other grounds of obedience, than those which have prevail'd at and since the glorious revolution. By degrees these doctrines, by being convenient may grow prevalent. The consequence is not certain; but a general change of principles rarely happens among a People without leading to a change of Government.

Sir, Your Throne cannot stand secure upon the principles of un-conditional submission and passive obedience; on powers exercised without the concurrence of the People to be governed; on Acts made in defiance of their prejudices and habits; on acquiescence procured by foreign Mercenary Troops, and secured by standing Armies. These may possibly be the foundation of other Thrones; they must be the subversion of yours. It was not to passive principles in our Ancestors, that we owe the honour of appearing before a Sovereign, who cannot feel that he is a Prince, without knowing that we ought to be free. The revolution is a departure from the ancient course of the descent of this Monarchy. The People at that time[4] reenter'd into their original rights; and it was not because a positive Law authorized what was then done, but because the freedom and safety of the Subject, the origin and cause of all Laws, required a proceeding paramount and superior to them. At that ever memorable and instructive period, the Letter of the Law was superseded in favour of the substance of Liberty. To the free choice therefore of the People, without either King or Parliament, we owe that happy establishment out of which both King and Parliament were regenerated. From that great principle of Liberty

---

[1] The Zouch text does not have 'own'.
[2] The Zouch text begins: 'It will be impossible'.
[3] The Zouch text reads: 'unhappy people, to be drawn from'.
[4] The Zouch text does not have 'at that time'. The reference is to the Revolution of 1688.

have originated the Statutes confirming and ratifying the establishment from which your Majesty derives your right to rule over us.[1]

Those Statutes have not given us our Liberties; Our Liberties have produced them. Every hour of your Majesties Reign, your title stands upon the very same foundation on which it was at first laid; and we do not know a better on which it can possibly be placed.

Convinced Sir, that you cannot have different rights and a different security in different parts of your Dominions, we wish to lay an even platform for your Throne; and to give it an immovable[2] stability, by laying it on the general freedom of your People; and by securing to your Majesty, that confidence and affection in all parts of your Dominions, which makes your best security and dearest Title in this the chief Seat of your Empire.

Such, Sir, being amongst us the foundation of Monarchy itself, much more clearly and much more peculiarly is it the ground of all Parliamentary power. Parliament is a security provided for the protection of Freedom and not a subtil fiction contrived to amuse the People, in its place. The Authority of both Houses, can, still less than that of the Crown, be supported upon different principles in different places; so as to be for one part of your Subjects, a Protector of Liberty; and for another a fund of Despotism, through which Prerogative is extended by occasional powers, whenever an Arbitrary Will finds itself streigthen'd by the restrictions of Law. Had it seem'd good to Parliament to consider itself as the indulgent Guardian and strong protector of the freedom of the Subordinate Popular Assemblies, instead of exercising its powers to their utter annihilation, there is no doubt that it never could be their inclination, because not their Interest, to have raised questions[3] on the Extent of Parliamentary Rights; or to have enfeebled privileges, which were the security of their own. Powers, evident from necessity and not suspicious from an alarming mode or purpose in the execution;[4] would, as formerly they were, be cheerfully submitted to; and these would have been fully sufficient for conservation of unity in the Empire, and for directing its wealth to one common centre. Another use has produced other consequences;

---

[1] The Bill of Rights 1689 (1 Will. and Mary, sess. 2, c. 2) and the Act of Settlement 1701 (12 and 13 Will. III, c. 2).
[2] Zouch text: 'unmoveable'.
[3] In the Zouch text: 'captious questions'.
[4] In the Zouch text: 'exertion'.

and a Power which refuses to be limited by moderation,[1] must either be lost or find other more distinct and satisfactory Limitations.

As for us, a supposed, or if it could be, a real participation in arbitrary Power, would never reconcile our minds to its establishment. We should be ashamed to stand before your Majesty, boldly asserting in our own favor, inherent rights which bind and regulate the Crown itself, and yet insisting on the exercise in our own persons, of a more arbitrary sway over our fellow of Citizens and fellow of freemen.[2]

These, most[3] gracious Sovereign, are the Sentiments which we consider ourselves as bound in justification of our present Conduct, in the most serious and solemn manner, to lay at your Majesties feet. We have been called by your Majesties Writts and Proclamations, and we have been authorized either by Hereditary Privilege, or the Choice of your People, to confer and treat with your Majesty in your highest Councils upon the Arduous Affairs of your Kingdom. We are sensible of the whole importance of the Duty which this Constitutional summons[4] implies. We know the religious punctuality of attendance, which in the ordinary course it demands. It is no light cause which even for a time, could persuade us to relax in any part of that attendance. The British Empire[5] is in convulsions which threaten its dissolution. Those particular proceedings which cause and inflame this disorder after many years incessant struggle, we find ourselves wholly unable to oppose, and unwilling to behold.[6] All our endeavors having

---

[1] The Zouch text reads: 'limited by its own moderation'.

[2] From this point to the end of the *Address* the earliest text (R01.5.8) reads: 'These most gracious Sovereign are our sentiments on this most important Subject, on this most Critical of all occasions. Whenever the day shall arrive, which promises the least disposition to act on these principles, we shall attend to support and perfect with the same clear intentions with which we formerly attended to oppose those of a contrary tendency or as we now relax our Attendance, from a dread of countenancing by the false appearance of a free discussion, proceedings fatal to the Liberty and Unity of the Empire; proceedings which exhaust the strength of all your Majestys dominions, and leave us exposed to the suspicious mercy and uncertain politics of our Neighbouring and rival Powers. If such dispositions should not appear, we have the satisfaction of having given faithful notice to your Majesty of those Evils; and however few in Number, or overborne by the prevalence of corrupt practices, or the misguided Zeal of arbitrary factions, to stand forth and record our names in assertion of those principles, whose operation here in better times made your Majesty a Great Prince and the British Dominions a mighty Empire.'

[3] The Zouch text does not have 'most'.

[4] In the Zouch text: 'invitation'.

[5] In the Zouch text: 'Your Empire'.

[6] The Zouch text concludes this paragraph as follows: 'We are in dread of countenancing any longer by the false ⟨appearance⟩ of a free discussion, proceedings fatal to the Liberty and unity of the Empire; proceedings which exhaust the Strength of all your Majesties dominions; destroy all Trust and dependance of our Allies; and leave us at home exposed to the suspicious mercy, and uncertain inclinations of our Neighbour and rival powers.'

proved fruitless, we are fearful at this time, of irritating by contention those passions, which we have found it impracticable to compose by Reason. We cannot permit ourselves to countenance by the appearance of a silent assent proceedings fatal to the liberty and unity of the Empire; Proceedings which exhaust the strength of all your Majesties dominions; destroy all Trust and dependance of our Allies, and leave us, both at home and abroad, exposed to the suspicious mercy, and uncertain inclinations of our neighbor and rival powers, to whom by this desperate Course, We are driving even our own Countrymen for protection, and with whom we have forced them into connections and may bind them by habits and by interests. An Evil which no Victories that may be obtain'd and no severities which may be exercised ever will or can remove.

If but the smallest hope should from any circumstances[1] appear, of a return to the Ancient Maxims and true policy of this Kingdom, We shall with Joy and readiness return to our attendance, in order to give our hearty support to whatever means may be left for alleviating the complicated Evils which oppress this[2] Nation.

If this should not happen we have discharged our Consciences by this faithful representation to your Majesty and our Country; and however few in number, or however We may be overborne by practices whose operation is but too powerful, by the revival of servile exploded principles,[3] or by the misguided Zeal of such arbitrary factions as in some periods have formerly prevail'd in this Kingdom, and always to its detriment and disgrace, we have the satisfaction of standing forth, and recording our names in assertion of those principles, whose operation hath, in better times, made your Majesty a great Prince, and the British Dominions a mighty Empire.[4]

---

[1] The Zouch text does not have 'from any circumstances'.

[2] The Zouch text reads: 'left of snatching our Country from the complicated Evils which oppress it.'

[3] Divine right and passive obedience.

[4] The Zouch text of the final paragraph reads: 'If this should not happen, we have discharged our Consciences by giving faithful Notice to your Majesty and our Country of those Evils, and however few in Number, or however overborne by the prevalence of corrupt practices, or the misguided Zeal of Arbitrary factions; we have the satisfaction, at least of standing forth, and recording our names in assertion of those principles, whose operation hath, in better time, made your Majesty a great Prince, and the British Dominions a mighty Empire.'

Address to the Colonists
[January 1777]

Source: *Works* (1792–1827), v. 141–52

This Address to the Colonists was printed in *Works* and associated with Burke's letter to Rockingham of 6 January 1777 and the Address to the King. No additional information appears to be available about the date or circumstances of its composition.

Professor Ross Hoffman has suggested that this 'Address to the British Colonists in North America' may have been written when Burke was thinking of going to Paris to see Benjamin Franklin.[1] Whatever the case, the document demonstrates Burke's efforts to convince the colonists that a harmonious relationship with the mother country can indeed be for their own ultimate good particularly in the form of military protection from enemies outside the empire and from civil war within. The address also helps to document the Rockinghams' acceptance of the moderate reform ideology, which would eventually culminate in their celebrated 'economical reform' campaign. It is the first public declaration by Burke and the party that some sort of modification might well be necessary in order to adapt the constitution to the needs of an increasingly diffuse and complex empire as it spreads across the face of the earth. If we have 'outgrown the limits of a Constitution made for a contracted object,' it proclaims, 'we ought to bless God, who has furnished us with this noble occasion for displaying our skill and beneficence in enlarging the scale of rational happiness, and of making the politick generosity of this Kingdom as extensive, as its fortune.'[2]

The very dangerous crisis, into which the British Empire is brought, as it accounts for, so it justifies, the unusual step we take in addressing ourselves to you.

The distempers of the State are grown to such a degree of violence and malignity, as to render all ordinary remedies vain and frivolous. In such a deplorable situation, an adherence to the common forms of business appears to us, rather as an apology to cover a supine neglect of duty, than the means of performing it in a manner adequate to the exigency that presses upon us. The common means we have already tried, and tried to no purpose. As our last resource, we turn ourselves to you. We address you merely in our private capacity; vested with no other authority, than what will naturally attend those, in whose declara-

---

[1] *Corr.* iii. 310–11; R. J. S. Hoffman, *The Marquess: A Study of Lord Rockingham 1730–1782*, New York, 1973, p. 340.
[2] Below, p. 285.

tions of benevolence you have no reason to apprehend any mixture of dissimulation or design.

We have this title to your attention: we call upon it in a moment of the utmost importance to us all. We find, with infinite concern, that arguments are used to persuade you of the necessity of separating yourselves from your antient connection with your parent Country, grounded on a supposition, that a general principle of alienation and enmity to you had pervaded the whole of this Kingdom; and that there does no longer subsist between you and us any common and kindred principles, upon which we can possibly unite, consistently with those ideas of Liberty, in which you have justly placed your whole happiness.

If this fact were true, the inference drawn from it would be irresistible. But nothing is less founded. We admit, indeed, that violent addresses have been procured, with uncommon pains, by wicked and designing men, purporting to be the genuine voice of the whole people of England; that they have been published by authority here; and made known to you by proclamations;[1] in order by despair and resentment incurably to poison your minds against the origins of your race, and to render all cordial reconciliation between us utterly impracticable. The same wicked men, for the same bad purposes, have so far surprised the justice of Parliament, as to cut off all communication betwixt us, except what is to go in their own fallacious and hostile channel.

But we conjure you by the invaluable pledges, which have hitherto united, and which we trust will hereafter lastingly unite us, that you do not suffer yourselves to be persuaded, or provoked into an opinion, that you are at war with this Nation. Do not think, that the whole, or even the uninfluenced majority of Englishmen in this Island, are enemies to their own blood on the American Continent. Much delusion has been practised; much corrupt influence treacherously employed. But still a large, and we trust the largest and soundest part of this Kingdom, perseveres in the most perfect unity of sentiments, principles, and affections, with you. It spreads out a large and liberal platform of common Liberty, upon which we may all unite for ever. It abhors the hostilities, which have been carried on against you, as much as you, who feel the cruel effect of them. It has disclaimed in the

---

[1] Presumably, Burke is referring in particular to 'A Proclamation by the King for the Suppressing Rebellion and Sedition', 23 August 1775. See *Documents of American History*, ed. H. S. Commager, 2nd edn., New York, 1942, p. 96.

most solemn manner, at the foot of the Throne itself, the addresses, which tended to irritate your Sovereign against his Colonies. We are persuaded, that even many of those, who unadvisedly have put their hands to such intemperate and inflammatory addresses, have not at all apprehended to what such proceedings naturally lead; and would sooner die, than afford them the least countenance, if they were sensible of their fatal effects on the Union and Liberty of the Empire.

For ourselves, we faithfully assure you, that we have ever considered you as rational creatures; as free agents; as men willing to pursue, and able to discern, your own true interest. We have wished to continue united with you, in order, that a people of one origin and one character should be directed to the rational objects of Government by joint Counsels, and protected in them by a common force. Other subordination in you we require none. We have never pressed that argument of general union to the extinction of your local, natural, and just privileges. Sensible of what is due both to the dignity and weakness of Man, we have never wished to place over you any Government, over which, in great fundamental points, you should have no sort of check or control in your own hands; or which should be repugnant to your situation, principles, and character.

No circumstances of fortune, you may be assured, will ever induce us to form, or tolerate any such design. If the disposition of Providence (which we deprecate) should even prostrate you at our feet, broken in power and in spirit, it would be our duty and inclination to revive, by every practicable means, that free energy of mind, which a fortune unsuitable to your virtue had damped and dejected; and to put you voluntarily in possession of those very privileges, which you had in vain attempted to assert by arms. For we solemnly declare, that although we should look upon a separation from you as an heavy calamity, (and the heavier because we know you must have your full share in it,) yet we had much rather see you totally independent of this Crown and Kingdom, than joined to it by so unnatural a conjunction, as that of Freedom with Servitude:—a conjunction, which if it were at all practicable, could not fail, in the end, of being more mischievous to the peace, prosperity, greatness, and power of this Nation, than beneficial, by any enlargement of the bounds of nominal empire.

But because, Brethren, these professions are general, and such as even enemies may make, when they reserve to themselves the

279

construction of what Servitude and what Liberty are, we inform you, that we adopt your own standard of the blessing of free Government. We are of opinion, that you ought to enjoy the sole and exclusive right of freely granting, and applying to the support of your Administration, what God has freely granted as a reward to your industry. And we do not confine this immunity from exterior coercion, in this great point, solely to what regards your local Establishment, but also to what may be thought proper for the maintenance of the whole Empire. In this resource we cheerfully trust and acquiesce; satisfied by evident reason, that no other expectation of revenue can possibly be given by freemen; and knowing from an experience, uniform both on yours and on our side of the Ocean, that such an expectation has never yet been disappointed. We know of no road to your coffers, but through your affections.

To manifest our sentiments the more clearly to you and to the world on this subject; we declare our opinion, that if no revenue at all, which however we are far from supposing, were to be obtained from you to this Kingdom, yet as long as it is our happiness to be joined with you in the bonds of fraternal charity and freedom, with an open and flowing commerce between us, one principle of enmity and friendship pervading, and one right of War and Peace directing the strength of the whole Empire, we are likely to be, at least, as powerful as any nation, or as any combination of nations, which in the course of human events may be formed against us. We are sensible that a very large proportion of the wealth and power of every Empire, must necessarily be thrown upon the presiding State. We are sensible that such a State ever has borne, and ever must bear the greatest part, and sometimes the whole, of the public expences: and we think her well indemnified for that (rather apparent than real) inequality of charge, in the dignity and preeminence she enjoys, and in the superior opulence, which after all charges defrayed, must necessarily remain at the center of affairs. Of this principle we are not without evidence in our remembrance (not yet effaced) of the glorious and happy days of this Empire. We are, therefore, incapable of that prevaricating style, by which, when taxes without your consent, are to be extorted from you, this Nation is represented as in the lowest state of impoverishment and public distress; but when we are called upon to oppress you by force of arms, it is painted as scarcely feeling its impositions, abounding with wealth, and inexhaustible in its resources.

We also reason and feel, as you do, on the invasion of your Charters. Because the Charters comprehend the essential forms, by which you enjoy your liberties, we regard them as most sacred, and by no means to be taken away or altered without process, without examination, and without hearing, as they have lately been. We even think, that they ought by no means to be altered at all, but at the desire of the greater part of the people, who live under them. We cannot look upon men as delinquents in the mass; much less are we desirous of lording over our Brethren, insulting their honest pride, and wantonly overturning establishments, judged to be just and convenient by the public wisdom of this Nation at their institution; and which long and inveterate use has taught you to look up to with affection and reverence. As we disapproved of the proceedings with regard to the forms of your Constitution, so we are equally tender of every leading principle of free Government. We never could think with approbation of putting the military power out of the coercion of the civil justice in the country where it acts.[1]

We disclaim also any sort of share in that other measure, which has been used to alienate your affections from this Country, namely, the introduction of foreign mercenaries.[2] We saw their employment with shame and regret, especially in numbers so far exceeding the English forces, as in effect to constitute vassals, who have no sense of freedom, and strangers, who have no common interest or feelings, as the arbiters of our unhappy domestic quarrel.

We likewise saw with shame the African slaves, who had been sold to you on public faith, and under the sanction of Acts of Parliament, to be your servants and your guards, employed to cut the throats of their masters.[3]

You will not, we trust, believe, that born in a civilized country, formed to gentle manners, trained in a merciful religion, and living in enlightened and polished times, where even foreign hostility is softened from its original sternness, we could have thought of letting loose upon you, our late beloved Brethren, these fierce tribes of Savages and Cannibals, in whom the traces of human nature are

---

[1] Burke is referring here to the Act for the Impartial Administration of Justice in Massachusetts Bay (14 Geo. III, c.39). It gave the Governor of the American colonies the right to send at his discretion, military and other officials to another colony or to Britain to be tried for indictable offences.

[2] See Burke's speech of 29 February 1776 on the German treaties, above, p. 221.

[3] See Burke's petition of [1775] on the use of Indians, above, pp. 179–81.

effaced by ignorance and barbarity. We rather wished to have joined with you, in bringing gradually that unhappy part of mankind into civility, order, piety, and virtuous discipline, than to have confirmed their evil habits, and encreased their natural ferocity, by fleshing them in the slaughter of you, whom our wiser and better ancestors had sent into the Wilderness, with the express view of introducing, along with our holy religion, its humane and charitable manners. We do not hold that all things are lawful in war. We should think, that every barbarity, in fine, in wasting, in murders, in tortures, and other cruelties too horrible and too full of turpitude for Christian mouths to utter or ears to hear, if done at our instigation (by those, who, we know, will make war thus if they make it at all) to be, to all intents and purposes, as if done by ourselves. We clear ourselves to you our Brethren, to the present age and to future generations, to our King and our Country, and to Europe, which, as a spectator, beholds this tragic scene, of every part or share in adding this last and worst of evils to the inevitable mischiefs of a Civil War.

We do not call you Rebels and Traitors. We do not call for the vengeance of the Crown against you. We do not know how to qualify millions of our Countrymen, contending, with one heart, for an admission to privileges, which we have ever thought our own happiness and honour, by odious and unworthy names. On the contrary, we highly revere the principles, on which you act, though we lament some of their effects. Armed as you are, we embrace you as our friends, and as our brethren, by the best and dearest ties of relation.

We view the establishment of the English Colonies on principles of Liberty, as that which is to render this Kingdom venerable to future ages. In comparison of this, we regard all the victories and conquests of our warlike ancestors, or of our own times, as barbarous, vulgar distinctions, in which many nations, whom we look upon with little respect or value, have equalled, if not far exceeded us. This is the peculiar and appropriated glory of England. Those, who *have and who hold* to that foundation of common Liberty, whether on this or on your side of the Ocean, we consider as the true and the only true Englishmen. Those, who depart from it, whether there or here, are attainted, corrupted in blood, and wholly fallen from their original rank and value. They are the real rebels to the fair constitution and just supremacy of England.

We exhort you, therefore, to cleave for ever to those principles, as being the true bond of union in this Empire; and to shew, by a manly perseverance, that the sentiments of honour and the rights of mankind are not held by the uncertain events of war, as you have hitherto shewn a glorious and affecting example to the world, that they are not dependant on the ordinary conveniences and satisfactions of life.

Knowing no other arguments to be used to men of liberal minds, it is upon these very principles, and these alone, we hope and trust, that no flattering and no alarming circumstances shall permit you to listen to the seductions of those, who would alienate you from your dependance on the Crown and Parliament of this Kingdom. That very Liberty, which you so justly prize above all things, originated here; and it may be very doubtful, whether without being constantly fed from the original fountain it can be at all perpetuated or preserved in its native purity and perfection. Untried forms of Government may, to unstable minds, recommend themselves even by their novelty. But you will do well to remember, that England has been great and happy under the present limited Monarchy (subsisting in more or less vigour and purity) for several hundred years. None but England can communicate to you the benefits of such a Constitution. We apprehend you are not now, nor for ages are likely to be capable of that form of Constitution in an independent State. Besides, let us suggest to you our apprehensions, that your present union (in which we rejoice, and which we wish long to subsist) cannot always subsist without the authority and weight of this great and long respected Body, to equipoise, and to preserve you amongst yourselves in a just and fair equality. It may not even be impossible, that a long course of war with the Administration of this Country, may be but a prelude to a series of wars and contentions among yourselves, to end, at length (as such scenes have too often ended) in a species of humiliating repose, which nothing but the preceding calamities would reconcile to the dispirited few, who survived them. We allow, that even this evil is worth the risque to men of honour, when rational Liberty is at stake, as in the present case we confess and lament that it is. But if ever a real security, by Parliament, is given against the terror or the abuse of unlimited power, and after such security given you should persevere in resistance, we leave you to consider, whether the risque is not incurred without an object; or incurred for an object infinitely diminished, by such concessions, in its importance and value.

As to other points of discussion, when these grand fundamentals of your Grants and charters are once settled and ratified by clear Parliamentary authority, as the ground for peace and forgiveness on our side, and for a manly and liberal obedience on yours, treaty and a spirit of reconciliation will easily and securely adjust whatever may remain. Of this we give you our word, that so far as we are at present concerned, and if by any event we should become more concerned hereafter, you may rest assured, upon the pledges of honour not forfeited, faith not violated, and uniformity of character and profession not yet broken, we at least, on these grounds, will never fail you.

Respecting your wisdom, and valuing your safety, we do not call upon you to trust your existence to your enemies. We do not advise you to an unconditional submission. With satisfaction we assure you, that almost all, in both Houses (however unhappily they have been deluded, so as not to give any immediate effect to their opinion) disclaim that idea. You can have no friends, in whom you cannot rationally confide. But Parliament is your friend from the moment, in which, removing its confidence from those, who have constantly deceived its good intentions, it adopts the sentiments of those, who have made sacrifices (inferior indeed to yours) but have, however, sacrificed enough to demonstrate the sincerity of their regard and value for your liberty and prosperity.

Arguments may be used to weaken your confidence in that publick security; because from some unpleasant appearances, there is a suspicion, that Parliament itself is somewhat fallen from its independent spirit. How far this supposition may be founded in fact, we are unwilling to determine. But we are well assured, from experience, that even if all were true, that is contended for, and in the extent too, in which it is argued, yet as long as the solid and well disposed forms of this Constitution remain, there ever is within Parliament itself a power of renovating its principles, and effecting a self-reformation, which no other plan of Government has ever contained. This Constitution has therefore admitted innumerable improvements, either for the correction of the original scheme, or for removing corruptions, or for bringing its principles better to suit those changes, which have successively happened in the circumstances of the nation, or in the manners of the people.

We feel, that the growth of the Colonies is such a change of circumstances; and that our present dispute is an exigency as pressing, as any which ever demanded a revision of our Government. Public

284

troubles have often called upon this Country to look into its Constitution. It has ever been bettered by such a revision. If our happy and luxuriant encrease of dominion, and our diffused population, has outgrown the limits of a Constitution made for a contracted object, we ought to bless God, who has furnished us with this noble occasion for displaying our skill and beneficence in enlarging the scale of rational happiness, and of making the politick generosity of this Kingdom as extensive, as its fortune. If we set about this great work on both sides, with the same conciliatory turn of mind, we may now, as in former times, owe even to our mutual mistakes, contentions and animosities, the lasting concord, freedom, happiness, and glory of this Empire.

Gentlemen, the distance between us, with other obstructions, has caused much misrepresentation of our mutual sentiments. We, therefore, to obviate them as well as we are able, take this method of assuring you of our thorough detestation of the whole War; and particularly the mercenary and savage War, carried on or attempted against you; our thorough abhorrence of all addresses adverse to you, whether public or private; our assurances of an invariable affection towards you; our constant regard to your privileges and Liberties; and our opinion of the solid security you ought to enjoy for them, under the paternal care and nurture of a protecting Parliament.

Though many of us have earnestly wished, that the authority of that august and venerable body, so necessary in many respects to the union of the whole, should be rather limited by its own equity and discretion, than by any bounds described by positive laws and public compacts; and though we felt the extreme difficulty, by any theoretical limitations, of qualifying that authority, so as to preserve one part and deny another; and though you (as we gratefully acknowledge) had acquiesced most cheerfully under that prudent reserve of the Constitution, at that happy moment, when neither you nor we apprehended a further return of the exercise of invidious powers, we are now as fully persuaded, as you can be, by the malice, inconstancy, and perverse inquietude of many men, and by the incessant endeavours of an arbitrary faction, now too powerful, that our common necessities do require a full explanation and ratified security for your liberties and our quiet.

Although His Majesty's condescension in committing the direction of his affairs into the hands of the known friends of his family, and of the liberties of all his People, would, we admit, be a great means of giving repose to your minds, as it must give infinite facility to reconciliation, yet we assure you, that we think, with such a security, as we recommend, adopted from necessity and not choice even by the unhappy authors and instruments of the public misfortunes, that the terms of reconciliation, if once accepted by Parliament, would not be broken. We also pledge ourselves to you, that we should give even to those unhappy persons an hearty support in effectuating the peace of the Empire; and every opposition in an attempt to cast it again into disorder.

When that happy hour shall arrive, let us in all affection recommend to you the wisdom of continuing, as in former times, or even in a more ample measure, the support of your Government, and even to give to your Administration some degree of reciprocal interest in your freedom. We earnestly wish you not to furnish your Enemies here or elsewhere, with any sort of pretexts for reviving quarrels, by too reserved and severe or penurious an exercise of those sacred rights, which no pretended abuse in the exercise ought to impair, nor, by overstraining the principles of freedom, to make them less compatible with those haughty sentiments in others, which the very same principles may be apt to breed in minds not tempered with the utmost equity and justice.

The well wishers of the liberty and union of this Empire salute you, and recommend you most heartily to the Divine protection.

Speech on Birmingham Playhouse Bill
26 March 1777

Source: *Aris's Birmingham Gazette*, 31 March 1777

This report may be copied from a missing London newspaper. The first part of it is also in the *Morning Post*, 27 March. There are two additional reports in *St James's Chronicle*, 27 March, and in the *Public Advertiser* and *General Evening Post*, 27 March, and in *Lloyd's Evening Post*, 28 March).

The performance of plays outside Westminster (and places where the sovereign resided) was forbidden by the Licensing Act.[1] Nevertheless, illegal theatres continued to exist in provincial towns. A number of towns, however,

---

[1] 10 Geo. II, c. 28.

had obtained Acts of Parliament which exempted them from the Licensing Act and allowed the King to issue Letters Patent to establish a theatre or playhouse. Birmingham had two illegal playhouses. The manager of one of them, Richard Yates,[1] sought a similar Act of Parliament.[2] Burke gave him cautious support.

Mr. Burke. I am sure, Mr. Speaker, that if the Play-house in Question produces Pieces with half as much Wit in them as the honourable Gentleman[3] has exerted against the Bill, in what I may call the Prologue to the Play, the Town of Birmingham will be most admirably entertained;—but, Sir, the Honourable Member's Wit stops short even of the *Denoument* of the Piece:—Let us see something more of it; let us hear the Piece before we declare against it. He has brought ancient History to tell you the Circumstances of the City where Iron and Steel were first wrought:—but I will likewise tell him, that we are indebted to the same Deity for Amusement[4] and theatrical Representation, consequently what he said is an Argument for the Bill.[5]—But, Sir, to be more serious;—I do not know that Theatres are Schools of Virtue; I would rather call them Nurseries of Idleness;—but then, Sir, of the various Means which Idleness will take for its Amusement, in Truth I believe the Theatre is the most innocent:—The Question is not, Whether a Man had better be at Work than go to the Play?—it is simply this.—Be Idle; shall he go to the Play or some Blacksmith's Entertainment? why, I shall be free to say, I think the Play will be the best Place, that it is probable a Blacksmith's Idle Moments will carry him to. The Honourable Gentleman informs the House, that great Inconveniences, have been found from the licensed Houses at Liverpool and Manchester—the Case is not parallel between those Towns and Birmingham—they have a *General* Licence—Birmingham asks for a *Four Months Licence only*—their Theatres are under the Direction of some strolling Manager, who when he once enters the Town, never quits it, whilst by any Arts, he can force Company to

---

[1] (c.1706–96), a comic actor of considerable reputation.
[2] The Bill is printed in *Aris's Birmingham Gazette*, 10 March. For this whole affair, see J. Money, *Experience and Identity: Birmingham and the West Midlands 1760–1800*, Manchester, 1977, pp. 86–91, and the article by P. T. Underdown cited below.
[3] Sir William Bagot, 6th Baronet (1728–98), M.P. 1754–80.
[4] *Morning Post*: 'musical'.
[5] The report of Bagot's speech does not help to elucidate Burke's allusions to it.

his Theatre.—Birmingham Theatre will be under the Direction of a Man very Eminent in his profession as a Comedian; who in London conducts the most elegant Entertainment in Europe, and who never has, or wishes to be there, but during the Time the Theatres of Drury-Lane and Covent-Garden are shut up in the Summer.[1]

I look upon *Birmingham* to be the *great Toy Shop of Europe*, and submit it to the members of this Honourable House, to consider if Birmingham *on that Account*, is not the *most proper Place* in England to have *a licensed Theatre*.

The Question before us turns upon this Point—there are already two Playhouses unlicensed; now the Bill proposes, that instead of *two in Defiance of Law*, the People of Birmingham should have *one according to Law*—therefore, let us proceed, and send the Bill to a Committee; when we shall hear the Evidence of Inhabitants of the first Reputation; and if they can prove, *that one legal Playhouse* will check Industry, promote Idleness, and do other Mischiefs to Trade, which *two Theatres contrary to Law, do not*—then it will be Time to throw out the Bill.

The Bill was given a first reading and referred to a committee by a vote of 48 to 28.

Letter to the Sheriffs of Bristol
3 April 1777

Source: *A Letter from Edmund Burke, Esq; One of the Representatives in Parliament for the City of Bristol, to John Farr and John Harris, Esqrs. Sheriffs of that City, on the Affairs of America*, 3rd edn., J. Dodsley, London, 1777

The policy of secession from Parliament adopted by the Rockingham party attracted adverse comment in Bristol. Burke himself received particular criticism for his failure to appear in the Commons actively to oppose the American Treasons Act[2] which suspended the Habeas Corpus Act[3] for persons charged or suspected of committing high treason out of the realm or of piracy against British subjects on the high seas.[4] Burke decided, about 21 February 1777, to write a public letter to explain his own and his party's

---

[1] This was an attempt to buy off local opposition (P. T. Underdown, 'Religious Opposition to Licensing the Bristol and Birmingham Theatres', *University of Birmingham Historical Journal*, vi (1957–8), 154–5).
[2] 17 Geo. III, c. 9.   [3] 31 Car. II, c. 2.   [4] *Corr.* iii. 332.

actions.[1] It was addressed to John Farr[2] and John Harris,[3] the Sheriffs of Bristol, and it was despatched on 3 April, though alterations in the course of printing it were made when the Rockinghams resumed attendance in Parliament on 16 April.

At the point of writing this letter Burke was in a deeply dejected state of mind. He was upset primarily by the fact that the American war had continued to go very well for the mother country and, therefore, to receive immense public support.[4] Misguided enthusiasm amongst the propertied classes, he believed, was reducing the empire to ashes and promoting a tragic carnage in which an horrific amount of English blood was being shed. To make matters worse Burke's own party had failed of late to agree on an appropriately ambitious parliamentary strategy for ending the war. Secession had still not been accepted by some of the leading members of the connection, and Burke had believed from the beginning that a partial measure would be perceived as timidity by the public.[5] Thus he appears to have felt powerless and depressed and he poured out his feelings to his readers in truly ominous tones. In his writing the world seems to be suffering from a fatal disease which is spreading like a cancer. Every where 'designing men are labouring with . . . malignant industry' to destroy the empire, and 'the malignity of an evil principle' or 'the malignant credulity of envy and ignorance'[6] are shown constantly to be at work.

Despite his obvious pessimism Burke did manage to elaborate what had become the central pillar in his imperial philosophy. The empire and the supremacy of the mother country can be sustained only in the confidence and security which the subordinate member states feel in them.[7] That confidence can only be gained through demonstrated concern in Britain for American rights and liberties. This makes it necessary for the Crown and Parliament, however reluctantly, ultimately to yield to virtually all colonial demands. The mother country must learn now and again to part with a particular power 'as with a limb: but as with a limb to save the body; . . . Anything rather than a fruitless, hopeless, unnatural civil war'.[8] It was this philosophy which would eventually encourage Burke publicly to sacrifice the Declaratory Act and even to accept American independence.[9]

A LETTER, &c.

GENTLEMEN,

I HAVE the honour of sending you the two last acts which have been passed with regard to the troubles in America.[10] These acts are similar

---

[1] Ibid. iii. 330–4.   [2] d. 1787.   [3] c.1726–1801.   [4] See e.g. *Corr.* iii. 293.
[5] See above, p. 258.   [6] See below, pp. 363, 398, 326.
[7] See, in particular, pp. 309, 314–15.   [8] See below, p. 323.
[9] See below, pp. 374–6.
[10] The American Treason Act and the Letters of Marque Act (17 Geo. III, c. 7). The latter passed by the House of Commons on 6 February, enabled 'the commissioners for executing the

to all the rest which have been made on the same subject. They operate by the same principle; and they are derived from the very same policy. I think they complete the number of this sort of statutes to nine.[1] It affords no matter for very pleasing reflection, to observe, that our subjects diminish, as our laws encrease.

If I have the misfortune of differing with some of my fellow-citizens on this great and arduous subject, it is no small consolation to me, that I do not differ from you. With you, I am perfectly united. We are heartily agreed in our detestation of a civil war. We have ever expressed the most unqualified disapprobation of all the steps which have led to it, and of all those which tend to prolong it. And I have no doubt that we feel exactly the same emotions of grief and shame on all its miserable consequences; whether they appear, on the one side or the other, in the shape of victories or defeats; of captures made from the English on the continent, or from the English in these islands; of legislative regulations which subvert the liberties of our brethren, or which undermine our own.

Of the first of these statutes (that for the letter of marque) I shall say little. Exceptionable as it may be, and as I think it is in some particulars, it seems the natural, perhaps necessary result of the measures we have taken, and the situation we are in. The other (for a partial suspension of the *Habeas Corpus*[2]) appears to me of a much deeper malignity. During its progress through the House of Commons, it has been amended, so as to express more distinctly than at first it did, the avowed sentiments of those who framed it:[3] and the main ground of my exception to it is, because it does express, and does carry into execution, purposes which appear to me so contradictory to all the principles, not only of the constitutional policy of Great Britain, but even of that species of hostile justice, which no asperity of war wholly extinguishes in the minds of a civilized people.

---

office of lord high admiral of Great Britain to grant commissions, or letters of marque, to the commanders of private ships and vessels to take and make prize of all ships or vessels, and their cargoes, belonging to or possessed by any of the inhabitants of the colonies' (*Parl. Hist.* xix. 3).

[1] The four Coercive Acts of 1774, the new England Restraining Act (15 Geo. III, c. 10), the provisions of which were extended to other colonies (15 Geo. III, c. 18), and the American Prohibitory Act (16 Geo. III, c. 5). Burke did not include the Quebec Act.

[2] Introduced in the Commons on 7 February and passed by the Lords on 24 February (*Parl. Hist.* xix. 4–6, 33, 51, 52).

[3] A Government amendment had been moved on 13 February, and it was further amended on 17 February (*Parl. Reg.* vi. 230, 240–1). The reason for amending the Bill was to make clear that it would operate only as far as offences committed in America or on the high seas.

If seems to have in view two capital objects; the first, to enable administration to confine, as long as it shall think proper, (within the duration of the act) those, whom that act is pleased to qualify by the name of *Pirates*. Those so qualified, I understand to be, the commanders and mariners of such privateers and ships of war belonging to the colonies, as in the course of this unhappy contest may fall into the hands of the crown. They are therefore to be detained in prison, under the criminal description of piracy, to a future trial and ignominious punishment, whenever circumstances shall make it convenient to execute vengeance on them, under the colour of that odious and infamous offence.

To this first purpose of the law, I have no small dislike. Because the act does not (as all laws, and all equitable transactions ought to do) fairly describe its object. The persons, who make a naval war upon us, in consequence of the present troubles, may be *rebels*; but to call and treat them as *pirates*, is confounding, not only the natural distinction of things, but the order of crimes; which, whether by putting them from a higher part of the scale to the lower, or from the lower to the higher, is never done without dangerously disordering the whole frame of jurisprudence. Though piracy may be, in the eye of the law, a *less* offence than treason; yet as both are, in effect, punished with the same death, the same forfeiture, and the same corruption of blood, I never would take from any fellow-creature whatever, any sort of advantage, which he may derive to his safety from the pity of mankind, or to his reputation from their general feelings, by degrading his offence, when I cannot soften his punishment. The general sense of mankind tells me, that those offences, which may possibly arise from mistaken virtue, are not in the class of infamous actions. Lord Coke,[1] the oracle of the English law, conforms to that general sense, where he says, that "those things which are of the highest criminality may be of the least disgrace." The act prepares a sort of masqued proceeding, not honourable to the justice of the kingdom, and by no means necessary for its safety. I cannot enter into it. If lord Balmerino,[2] in the last rebellion, had driven off the cattle of twenty clans, I should have thought it a scandalous and low juggle, utterly unworthy of the

---

[1] Sir Edward Coke. 'Lord Coke' used here probably because of his eminence.
[2] Arthur Elphinstone, 6th Baron Balmerinoch (1688–1746), executed 18 August 1746 for his participation in the 'forty-five' rebellion.

manliness of an English judicature, to have tried him for felony, as a stealer of cows.

Besides, I must honestly tell you, that I could not vote for, or countenance in any way, a statute, which stigmatizes with the crime of piracy, those men, whom an act of parliament had previously put out of the protection of the law.[1] When the legislature of this kingdom had ordered all their ships and goods, for the mere new-created offence of exercising trade, to be divided as a spoil among the seamen of the navy,—for the same legislature afterwards to treat the necessary reprisal of an unhappy, proscribed, interdicted people, as the crime of piracy, seems harsh and incongruous. Such a procedure would have appeared (in any other legislature than ours) a strain of the most insulting and most unnatural cruelty and injustice. I assure you, I do not remember to have heard of any thing like it in any time or country.

The second professed purpose of the act is to detain in England for trial, those who shall commit high treason in America.

That you may be enabled to enter into the true spirit of the present law, it is necessary, gentlemen, to apprise you, that there is an act, made so long ago as the reign of Henry the eighth, before the existence or thought of any English colonies in America, for the trial in this kingdom of treasons committed out of the realm.[2] In the year 1769, parliament thought proper to acquaint the crown with their construction of that act, in a formal address, wherein they intreated his Majesty, to cause persons, charged with high treason in America, to be brought into this kingdom for trial.[3] By this act of Henry the eighth, *so construed and so applied,* almost all that is substantial and beneficial in a trial by jury is taken away from the subject in the colonies. This is however saying too little; for to try a man under that act is, in effect, to condemn him unheard. A person is brought hither in the dungeon of a ship's hold: thence he is vomited into a dungeon on land; loaded with irons, unfurnished with money, unsupported by friends, three thousand miles from all means of calling upon, or confronting evidence, where no one local circumstance that tends to detect perjury, can possibly be judged of;—such a person may be executed according to form, but he can never be tried according to justice.

---

[1] By the American Prohibitory Act.
[2] By the Treason Act (35 Hen. VIII, c. 2).
[3] The Address was sent by the Lords to the Commons on 15 December 1768 and agreed to by the Commons on 8 February 1769. It was presented on 13 February.

I therefore could by no means reconcile myself to the bill I send you; which is expressly provided to remove all inconveniences from the establishment of a mode of trial, which has ever appeared to me most unjust and most unconstitutional. Far from removing the difficulties which impede the execution of so mischievous a project, I would heap new difficulties upon it, if it were in my power. All the ancient, honest juridical principles, and institutions of England, are so many clogs to check and retard the headlong course of violence and oppression. They were invented for this one good purpose;—that what was not just should not be convenient. Convinced of this, I would leave things as I found them. The old, cool-headed, general law, is as good as any deviation dictated by present heat.

I could see no fair justifiable expedience pleaded to favour this new suspension of the liberty of the subject. If the English in the colonies can support the independency to which they have been unfortunately driven, I suppose nobody has such a fanatical zeal for the criminal justice of Henry the eighth, that he will contend for executions which must be retaliated tenfold on his own friends; or who has conceived so strange an idea of English dignity, as to think the defeats in America compensated by the triumphs at Tyburn. If, on the contrary, the colonies are reduced to the obedience of the crown, there must be, under that authority, tribunals in the country itself, fully competent to administer justice on all offenders. But if there are not, and that we must suppose a thing so humiliating to our government, as that all this vast continent should unanimously concur in thinking, that no ill fortune can convert resistance to the royal authority into a criminal act, we may call the effect of our victory peace, or obedience, or what we will; but the war is not ended: The hostile mind continues in full vigour; and it continues under a worse form. If your peace be nothing more than a sullen pause from arms; if their quiet be nothing but the meditation of revenge, where smitten pride, smarting from its wounds, festers into new rancour, neither the act of Henry the eighth,[1] nor its handmaid of this reign, will answer any wise end of policy or justice. For if the bloody fields, which they saw and felt, are not sufficient to subdue the reason of Americans (to use the expressive phrase of a great lord in office)[2] it is not the judicial slaughter, which is made in

---

[1] The original Treason Act was reinstated in 1777; see below, p. 295, n. 1.

[2] No record has been found of any members of the ministry using this phrase during the preceding debates of the session.

another hemisphere against their universal sense of justice, that will ever reconcile them to the British government.

I take it for granted, gentlemen, that we sympathize in a proper horror of all punishment further than as it serves for an example. To whom then does the example of an execution in England for this American rebellion apply? Remember, you are told every day, that the present is a contest between the two countries; and that we in England are at war for *our own* dignity against our rebellious children. Is this true? If it be, it is surely among such rebellious children that examples for disobedience should be made. For who ever thought of instructing parents in their duty by an example from the punishment of a dis-obedient son? As well might the execution of a fugitive negro in the plantations, be considered as a lesson to teach masters humanity to their slaves. Such executions may indeed satiate our revenge; they may harden our hearts: and puff us up with pride and arrogance. Alas! this is not instruction.

If any thing can be drawn from such examples by a parity of the case, it is to shew, how deep their crime, and how heavy their punish-ment will be, who shall at any time dare to resist a distant power actually disposing of their property, without their voice or consent to the disposition; and overturning their franchises without charge or hearing. God forbid, that England should ever read this lesson written in the blood of *any* of her off-spring!

War is at present carried on, between the king's natural and foreign troops, on one side, and the English in America, on the other, upon the usual footing of other wars; and accordingly an exchange of prisoners has been regularly made from the beginning. If, notwith-standing this hitherto equal procedure, upon some prospect of ending the war with success (which however may be delusive), administra-tion prepares to act against those as *traitors* who remain in their hands at the end of the troubles, in my opinion we shall exhibit to the world as indecent a piece of injustice as ever civil fury has produced. If the prisoners who have been exchanged have not by that exchange been *virtually pardoned*, the cartel (whether avowed or understood) is a cruel fraud: for you have received the life of a man; and you ought to return a life for it, or there is no parity of fairness in the transaction.

If, on the other hand, we admit, that they, who are actually ex-changed are pardoned, but contend that we may justly reserve for vengeance, those who remain unexchanged; then this unpleasant and unhandsome consequence will follow; that you judge of the delinquency of men merely by the time of their guilt, and not by the heinousness of it; and you make fortune and accidents, and not the moral qualities of human action, the rule of your justice.

These strange incongruities must ever perplex those, who confound the unhappiness of civil dissention, with the crime of treason. Whenever a rebellion really and truly exists, (which is as easily known in fact, as it is difficult to define in words) government has not entered into such military conventions; but has ever declined all intermediate treaty, which should put rebels in possession of the law of nations with regard to war. Commanders would receive no benefits at their hands, because they could make no return for them. Who has ever heard of capitulation, and parole of honour, and exchange of prisoners, in the late rebellions in this kingdom? The answer to all demands of that sort was, "we can engage for nothing; you are at the king's pleasure." We ought to remember, that if our present enemies be, in reality and truth, rebels, the king's generals have no right to release them upon any conditions whatsoever; and they are themselves answerable to the law, and as much in want of a pardon for doing so, as the rebels whom they release.

Lawyers, I know, cannot make the distinction, for which I contend; because they have their strict rule to go by. But legislators ought to do what lawyers cannot; for they have no other rules to bind them, but the great principles of reason and equity, and the general sense of mankind. These they are bound to obey and follow; and rather to enlarge and enlighten law by the liberality of legislative reason, than to fetter and bind their higher capacity by the narrow constructions of subordinate artificial justice. If we had adverted to this, we never could consider the convulsions of a great empire, not disturbed by a little disseminated faction, but divided by whole communities and provinces, and entire legal representatives of a people, as fit matter of discussion under a commission of oyer and terminer.[1] It is as opposite to reason and prudence, as it is to humanity and justice.

This act, proceeding on these principles, that is, preparing to end the present troubles by a trial of one sort of hostility, under the name of piracy, and of another by the name of treason, and executing the act

---

[1] By the Treason Act (17 Geo. III, c. 17, sec. 2) magistrates were empowered to commit persons charged with treason in America to special places of confinement.

of Henry the eighth according to a new and unconstitutional interpretation, I have thought evil and dangerous, even though the instruments of effecting such purposes had been merely of a neutral quality.

But it really appears to me, that the means which this act employs
are, at least, as exceptionable as the end. Permit me to open myself a
little upon this subject, because it is of importance to me, when I am
obliged to submit to the power without acquiescing in the reason of an
act of legislature, that I should justify my dissent, by such arguments as
may be supposed to have weight with a sober man.

The main operative regulation of the act is to suspend the common
law, and the statute *Habeas Corpus*, (the sole securities either for liberty
or justice,) with regard to all those who have been out of the realm or
on the high seas, within a given time. The rest of the people, as I
understand, are to continue as they stood before.

I confess, gentlemen, that this appears to me, as bad in the principle,
and far worse in its consequence, than an universal suspension of the
Habeas Corpus act; and the limiting qualification, instead of taking out
the sting, does in my humble opinion sharpen and envenom it to a
greater degree. Liberty, if I understand it at all, is a *general* principle,
and the clear right of all the subjects within the realm, or of none.
Partial freedom seems to me a most invidious mode of slavery. But,
unfortunately, it is the kind of slavery the most easily admitted in times
of civil discord. For parties are but too apt to forget their own future
safety in their desire of sacrificing their enemies. People without much
difficulty admit the entrance of that injustice of which they are not to
be the immediate victims. In times of high proceeding, it is never the
faction of the predominant power that is in danger; for no tyranny
chastises its own instruments. It is the obnoxious and the suspected
who want the protection of law; and there is nothing to bridle the
partial violence of state factions, but this great, steady, uniform principle; "that whenever an act is made for a cessation of law and justice,
the whole people should be universally subjected to the same suspension of their franchises." The alarm of such a proceeding would then
be universal. It would operate as a sort of *call of the nation*. It would
become every man's immediate and instant concern, to be made very
sensible of *the absolute necessity* of this total eclipse of liberty. They
would more carefully advert to every renewal, and more powerfully
resist it. These great determined measures are not commonly so
dangerous to freedom. They are marked with too strong lines to slide

into use. No plea or pretence of mere *inconvenience or evil example* (which must in their nature be daily and ordinary incidents) can be admitted as a reason for such mighty operations. But the true danger is, when liberty is nibbled away, for expedients, and by parts. The *Habeas Corpus* act supposes (contrary to the genius of most other laws) that the lawful magistrate may see particular men with a malignant eye; and it provides for that identical case. But when men, *under particular descriptions, marked out by the magistrate himself,* are delivered over by parliament to this possible malignity, it is not the *Habeas Corpus* that is occasionally suspended, but its spirit that is mistaken, and its principle that is subverted. Indeed nothing is security to any individual but the common interest of all.

This act, therefore, has this distinguished evil in it, that it is the first *partial* suspension of the *Habeas Corpus* which has been made. The precedent, which is always of very great importance, is now established. For the first time a distinction is made among the people within this realm. Before this act, every man putting his foot on English ground, every stranger owing only a local and temporary allegiance, even a negro slave, who had been sold in the colonies and under an act of parliament, became as free as every other man who breathed the same air with him.[1] Now a line is drawn, which may be advanced farther and farther at pleasure, on the same argument of mere expedience, on which it was first described. There is no equality among us; we are not fellow-citizens, if the mariner who lands on the quay does not rest on as firm legal ground, as the merchant who sits in his comptinghouse. Other laws may injure the community; this tends to dissolve it. It destroys *equality*, which is the essence of community. As things now stand, every man in the West Indies, every one inhabitant of three unoffending provinces on the continent,[2] every person coming from the East Indies, every gentleman who has travelled for his health or education, every mariner who has navigated the seas, is, for no other offence, under a temporary proscription. Let any of these facts (now become presumptions of guilt) be proved against him, and the bare suspicion of the crown puts him out of the law. It is even by no means

---

[1] A reference to the case of James Somerset, a slave brought to England, who was released in 1772 by Lord Mansfield on a writ of *Habeas Corpus*.

[2] There were more than three: Quebec, Nova Scotia, the Island of St John (later Prince Edward Island), Newfoundland, East and West Florida.

clear to me, whether the negative proof does not lie upon the person apprehended on suspicion, to the subverson of all justice.

I have not debated against this bill in its progress through the House; because it would have been vain to oppose, and impossible to correct it. It is some time since I have been clearly convinced, that in the present state of things, all opposition to any measures proposed by ministers, where the name of America appears, is vain and frivolous. You may be sure, that I do not speak of my opposition, which in all circumstances must be so; but that of men of the greatest wisdom and authority in the nation. Every thing proposed *against* America is supposed of course to be *in favour* of Great Britain. Good and ill success are equally admitted as reasons for persevering in the present methods. Several very prudent, and very well-intentioned persons were of opinion, that during the prevalence of such dispositions, all struggle tended rather to inflame than to abate the distemper of the public counsels. Finding such resistance to be considered as factious by most within doors, and by very many without, I could not conscientiously support what is against my opinion, nor prudently contend with what I know is irresistible.

Preserving my principles unshaken, I reserve my activity for rational endeavours; and I hope my past conduct has given sufficient evidence, that if I am a single day from my place, it is not owing to indolence or love of dissipation. The slightest hope of doing good is sufficient to recal me to a station which I quitted with regret. In declining my usual strict attendance, I do not in the least condemn the spirit of those gentlemen, who, with a just confidence in their abilities, (in which I claim a sort of share from my love and admiration of them) were of opinion that their exertions in this desperate case might be of some service. They thought, that by contracting the sphere of its application, they might lessen the malignity of an evil principle. Perhaps they were in the right. But when my opinion was so very clearly to the contrary, for the reasons I have just stated, I am sure *my* attendance would have been ridiculous.

I must add, in further explanation of my conduct, that, far from softening the features of such a principle, and thereby removing any part of the popular odium or natural terrors attending it, I should be sorry, that any thing framed in contradiction to the spirit of our constitution did not instantly produce in fact, the grossest of the evils, with which it was pregnant in its nature. It is by lying dormant a long time, or being at first very rarely exercised, that arbitrary power steals upon a people. On the next unconstitutional act, all the fashionable world will be ready to say—Your prophecies are ridiculous, your fears are vain, you see how little of the mischiefs which you formerly foreboded are come to pass. Thus, by degrees, that artful softening of all arbitrary power, the alledged infrequency or narrow extent of its operation, will be received as a sort of aphorism—and Mr. *Hume* will not be singular in telling us, that the felicity of mankind is no more disturbed by it, than by earthquakes, or thunder, or the other more unusual accidents of nature.[1]

The act of which I have said so much is among the fruits of the American war; a war, in my humble opinion, productive of many mischiefs of a kind, which distinguish it from all others. Not only our policy is deranged, and our empire distracted, but our laws and our legislative spirit are in danger of being totally perverted by it. We have made war on our Colonies, not by arms only, but by laws. As hostility and law are not very concordant ideas, every step we have taken in this business, has been made by trampling on some maxim of justice, or some capital principle of wise government. What precedents were established, and what principles overturned, (I will not say of English privilege, but of general justice), in the Boston Port, the Massachusets Charter, the Military Bill,[2] and all that long array of hostile acts of parliament, by which the war with America has been begun and supported? Had the principles of any of these acts been first planted on English ground, they would probably have expired as soon as they touched it. But by being removed from our persons, they have rooted in our laws; and the latest posterity will taste the fruits of them.

Nor is it the worst effect of this unnatural contention, that our *laws* are corrupted. Whilst *manners* remain entire, they will correct the vices of law, and soften it at length to their own temper. But we have to

---

[1] 'Private property seems to me almost as secure in a Civilized European monarchy as in a republic; nor is danger much apprehended, in such a government, from the violence of the sovereign, more than we commonly dread harm from thunder, or earth-quakes, or any accident the most unusual or extraordinary ('Of Civil Liberty', *David Hume, The Philosophical Works*, ed. T. H. Green and T. H. Grose, 4 vols, London, 1878 iii. 160).

[2] The Quartering Act of 1774 (14 Geo. III, c. 54).

lament, that in most of the late proceedings we see very few traces of that generosity, humanity, and dignity of mind, which formerly characterized this nation. War suspends the rules of moral obligation; and what is long suspended is in danger of being totally abrogated. Civil wars strike deepest of all into the manners of a people. They vitiate their politicus; they corrupt their morals; they pervert even the natural taste and relish of equity and justice. By teaching us to consider our fellow-citizens in an hostile light, the whole body of our nation becomes gradually less dear to us. The very names of affection and kindred, which were the bonds of charity whilst we agreed, become new incentives to hatred and rage, when the communion of our country is dissolved. We may flatter ourselves that we shall not fall into this misfortune. But we have no charter of exemption, that I know of, from the ordinary frailities of our nature.

What but that blindness of heart which arises from the phrenzy of civil contention, could have made any persons conceive the present situation of the British affairs as an object of triumph in themselves, or of congratulation to their sovereign? Nothing surely could be more lamentable to those who remember the flourishing days of this kingdom, than to see the insane joy of several unhappy people, amidst the sad spectacle which our affairs and conduct exhibit to the scorn of Europe. We behold (and it seems some people rejoice in beholding) our native land, which used to fit the envied arbiter of all her neighbours, reduced to a servile dependence on their mercy; acquiescing in assurances of friendship which she does not trust; complaining of hostilities which she dares not resent; deficient to her allies; lofty to her subjects; and submissive to her enemies; whilst the liberal government of this free nation is supported by the hireling sword of German boors and vassals; and three millions of the subjects of Great-Britain are seeking for protection to English privileges in the arms of France!

These circumstances appear to me more like shocking prodigies, than natural changes in human affairs. Men of firmer minds may see them without staggering or astonishment.—Some may think them matters of congratulation and complimentary addresses; but I trust your candour will be so indulgent to my weakness, as not to have the worse opinion of me for my declining to participate in this joy; and my rejecting all share whatsoever in such a triumph. I am too old, too stiff in my inveterate partialities, to be ready at all the fashionable evolutions of opinion. I scarcely know how to adapt my mind to the feelings with which the Court Gazettes mean to impress the people. It is not instantly that I can be brought to rejoice, when I hear of the slaughter and captivity of long lists of those names which have been familiar to my ears from my infancy; and to rejoice that they have fallen under the sword of strangers, whose barbarous appellations I scarcely know how to pronounce. The glory acquired at the *White Plains* by *Colonel Raille*,[1] has no charms for me; and I fairly acknowledge, that I have not yet learned to delight in finding *Fort Kniphausen*[2] in the heart of the British dominions.

It might be some consolation for the loss of our old regards, if our reason were enlightened in proportion as our honest prejudices are removed. Wanting feelings for the honour of our country, we might then in cold blood be brought to think a little of our interests as individual citizens, and our private conscience as moral agents.

Indeed our affairs are in a bad condition. I do assure those Gentlemen who have prayed for war, and obtained the blessing they have sought, that they are at this instant in very great straits. The abused wealth of this country continues a little longer to feed its distemper.[3] As yet they, and their German allies of twenty hireling states, have contended only with the unprepared strength of our own infant colonies. But America is not subdued. Not one unattacked village, which was originally adverse, throughout that vast continent, has yet submitted from love or terror. You have the ground you encamp on; and you have no more. The cantonments of your troops and your dominions are exactly of the same extent. You spread devastation, but you do not enlarge the sphere of authority.

The events of this war are of so much greater magnitude than those who either wished or feared it, ever looked for, that this alone ought to fill every considerate mind with anxiety and dissidence. Wise men often tremble at the very things which fill the thoughtless with security. For many reasons I do not choose to expose to public view, all the

---

[1] Colonel Johann Gottlieb Rahl (d. 1776). His name is given in the *London Gazette* as Raille. It is also sometimes spelt Rall. The Battle of White Plains had taken place on 28 October 1776.

[2] Previously Fort Washington, on Manhattan Island. It was renamed in honour of Lieutenant General Wilhelm, Freiherr von Kniphausen (1730–89).

[3] It is indicative of Burke's disenchantment with what he clearly considered the disorderly state of public and political affairs that he used this particular word over and over again in 1777. In his Address to the Colonists, for instance, he argued that 'The distempers of the State are grown to such a degree of violence and malignity, as to render all ordinary remedies vain and frivolous' (above, p. 277). In the *Letter to the Sheriffs* itself he used the word (or the derivative) 'distemper' four times (above, p. 298, below, pp. 308, 319).

particulars of the state in which you stood with regard to foreign powers, during the whole course of the last year. Whether you are yet wholly out of danger from those powers, is more than I know, or than your rulers can divine. But even if I were certain of my safety, I could not easily forgive those who had brought me into the most dreadful perils, because by accidents, unforeseen by them or me, I have escaped.

Believe me, gentlemen, the way still before you is intricate, dark, and full of perplexed and treacherous mazes. Those who think they have the clue, may lead us out of this labyrinth. We may trust them as amply as we think proper. But as they have most certainly a call for all the reason which their stock can furnish, why should we think it proper to disturb its operation by inflaming their passions? I may be unable to lend an helping hand to those who direct the state; but I should be ashamed to make myself one of a noisy multitude to halloo and hearten them into doubtful and dangerous courses. A conscientious man would be cautious how he dealt in blood. He would feel some apprehension at being called to a tremendous account for engaging in so deep a play, without any sort of knowledge of the game. It is no excuse for presumptuous ignorance, that it is directed by insolent passion. The poorest being that crawls on earth, contending to save itself from injustice and oppression, is an object respectable in the eyes of God and man. But I cannot conceive any existence under heaven, (which, in the depths of its wisdom, tolerates all sorts of things) that is more truly odious and disgusting, than an impotent helpless creature, without civil wisdom or military skill, without a consciousness of any other qualification for power but his servility to it, bloated with pride and arrogance, calling for battles which he is not to fight, contending for a violent dominion which he can never exercise, and satisfied to be himself mean and miserable, in order to render others contemptible and wretched.

If you and I find our talents not of the great and ruling kind, our conduct at least is conformable to our faculties. No man's life pays the forfeit of our rashness. No desolate widow weeps tears of blood over our ignorance. Scrupulous and sober in our well-grounded distrust of ourselves, we would keep in the port of peace and security: and perhaps in recommending to others something of the same diffidence, we shew ourselves more charitable to their welfare, than injurious to their abilities.

302

There are many circumstances in the present zeal for civil war, which seem to discover but little of real magnanimity. The addressers offer their own persons; and they are satisfied with hiring Germans. They promise their private fortunes, and they mortgage their country. They have all the merit of volunteers, without risque of person or charge of contribution; and when the unfeeling arm of a foreign soldiery pours out their kindred blood like water, they exult and triumph, as if they themselves had performed some notable exploit. I am really ashamed of the fashionable language which has been held for some time past; which, to say the best of it, is full of levity. You know, that I allude to the general cry against the cowardice of the Americans, as if we despised them for not making the King's soldiery purchase the advantages they have obtained, at a dearer rate. It is not, Gentlemen, it is not to respect the dispensations of Providence, not to provide any decent retreat in the mutability of human affairs. It leaves no medium between insolent victory and infamous defeat. It tends to alienate our minds further and further from our natural regards, and to make an eternal rent and schism in the British nation. Those who do not wish for such a separation, would not dissolve that cement of reciprocal esteem and regard, which can alone bind together the parts of this great fabrick. It ought to be our wish, as it is our duty, not only to forbear this style of outrage ourselves, but to make every one as sensible as we can of the impropriety and unworthiness of the tempers which gave rise to it, and which designing men are labouring with such malignant industry to difuse amongst us. It is our business to counter-act them, if possible; if possible to awaken our natural regards; and to revive the old partiality to the English name. Without something of this kind I do not see how it is ever practicable really to reconcile with those, whose affections, after all, must be the surest hold of our government; and which are a thousand times more worth to us, than the mercenary zeal of all the circles of Germany.

I can well conceive a country completely over-run, and miserably wasted, without approaching in the least to settlement. In my apprehension, as long as English government is attempted to be supported over Englishmen by the sword alone, things will thus continue. I anticipate in my mind the moment of the final triumph of foreign military force. When that hour arrives, (for it may arrive) then it is, that all this mass of weakness and violence will appear in its full light. If we should be expelled from America, the delusion of the partizans of military government might still continue. They might still feed their imaginations with the possible good consequences which might have attended success. Nobody could prove the contrary by facts. But in case the sword should do all that the sword can do, the success of their arms and the defeat of their policy will be one and the same thing. You will never see any revenue from America. Some increase of the means of corruption, without any ease of the public burthens, is the very best that can happen. Is it for this that we are at war; and in such a war?

As to the difficulties of laying once more the foundations of that government, which, for the sake of conquering what was our own, has been voluntarily and wantonly pulled down by a court faction here, I tremble to look at them. Has any of these Gentlemen, who are so eager to govern all mankind, shewed himself possessed of the first qualification towards government, some knowledge of the object, and of the difficulties which occur in the tasks they have undertaken?

I assure you, that on the most prosperous issue of your arms, you will not be where you stood, when you called in war to supply the defects of your political establishment. Nor would any disorder or disobedience to government, which could arise from the most abject concession on our part, ever equal those which will be felt after the most triumphant violence. You have got all the intermediate evils of war into the bargain.

I think I know America. If I do not, my ignorance is incurable, for I have spared no pains to understand it; and I do most solemnly assure those of my constituents who put any sort of confidence in my industry and integrity, that every thing that has been done there has arisen from a total misconception of the object: that our means of originally holding America, that our means of reconciling with it after quarrel, of recovering it after separation, or keeping it after victory, did depend, and must depend, in their several stages and periods, upon a total renunciation of that unconditional submission which has taken such possession of the minds of violent men. The whole of those maxims, upon which we have made and continued this war, must be abandoned. Nothing indeed (for I would not deceive you) can place us in our former situation. That hope must be laid aside. But there is a difference between bad and the worst of all. Terms relative to the cause of the war ought to be offered by the authority of parliament. An arrangement at home promising some security for them ought to be made. By doing this, without the least impairing of our strength, we add to the credit of our moderation, which, in itself, is always strength more or less.

I know many have been taught to think, that moderation, in a case like this, is a sort of treason: and that all arguments for it are sufficiently answered by railing at rebels and rebellion, and by charging all the present or future miseries which we may suffer, on the resistance of our brethren. But I would wish them, in this grave matter, and if peace is not wholly removed from their hearts, to consider seriously, first,—that to criminate and recriminate never yet was the road to reconciliation, in any difference amongst men. In the next place, it would be right to reflect, that the American English (whom they may abuse, if they think it honourable to revile the absent) can, as things now stand, neither be provoked at our railing, or bettered by our instruction. All communication is cut off between us. But this we know with certainty; that though we cannot reclaim them, we may reform ourselves. If measures of peace are necessary, they must begin somewhere; and a conciliatory temper must precede and prepare every plan of reconciliation. Nor do I conceive that we suffer any thing by thus regulating our own minds. We are not disarmed by being disencumbered of our passions. Declaiming on Rebellion never added a bayonet, or a charge of powder, to your military force; but I am afraid that it has been the means of taking up many a musket against you.

This outrageous language, which has been encouraged and kept alive by every art, has already done incredible mischief. For a long time, even amidst the desolations of war, and the insults of hostile laws daily accumulated on one another, the American leaders seem to have had the greatest difficulty in bringing up their people to a declaration of total independence. But the Court Gazette accomplished what the abettors of independence had attempted in vain.[1] When that disingenuous compilation, and strange medley of railing and flattery, was adduced, as a proof of the united sentiments of the people of Great Britain, there was a great change throughout all America. The tide of popular affection, which had still set towards the parent country, began immediately to turn; and to flow with great rapidity in a contrary course. Far from concealing these wild declarations of enmity, the author of the celebrated pamphlet which prepared the minds of the

---

[1] A flood of addresses in support of governmental policy was presented to the King in the autumn and winter of 1775. The addresses were printed in the *London Gazette*.

people for independence, insists largely on the multitude and the spirit of these Addresses; and he draws an argument from them, which (if the facts were as he supposes) must be irresistible.[1] For I never knew a writer on the theory of government, so partial to authority, as not to allow, that the *hostile mind* of the rulers to their people, did fully justify a change of government. Nor can any reason whatever be given, why one people should voluntarily yield any degree of pre-eminence to another, but on a supposition of great affection and benevolence towards them. Unfortunately your rulers, trusting to other things, took no notice of this great principle of connexion. From the beginning of this affair, they have done all they could to alienate your minds from your own kindred; and if they could excite hatred enough in one of the parties towards the other, they seemed to be of opinion that they had gone half way towards reconciling the quarrel.

I know it is said, that your kindness is only alienated on account of their resistance; and therefore if the colonies surrender at discretion all sort of regard, and even much indulgence, is meant towards them in future. But can those who are partizans for continuing a war to enforce such a surrender, be responsible (after all that has passed) for such a future use of a power, that is bound by no compacts, and restrained by no terrors? Will they tell us what they call indulgences? Do they not at this instant call the present war and all its horrors, a lenient and merciful proceeding?

No conqueror, that I ever heard of, has *professed* to make a cruel, harsh, and insolent use of his conquest. No! The man of the most declared pride, scarcely dares to trust his own heart, with this dreadful secret of ambition. But it will appear in its time; and no man who professes to reduce another to the insolent mercy of a foreign arm, ever had any sort of good-will towards him. The profession of kindness, with that sword in his hand, and that demand of surrender, is one of the most provoking acts of his hostility. I shall be told, that all this is lenient, as against rebellious adversaries. But are the leaders of their faction more lenient to those who submit? Lord Howe and General Howe have powers under an Act of Parliament,[2] to restore to the King's peace and to free trade any men, or district, which shall

---

[1] Thomas Paine (1737–1809) in *Common Sense* (1776) wrote: 'The last cord is now broken, the people of England are presenting addresses against us' (Paine, *Common Sense*, ed. I. Kramnick, London, 1976, p. 99).

[2] The American Prohibitory Act.

submit. Is this done? We have been over and over informed by the authorised Gazette, that the city of New York and the countries of Staten and Long Island have submitted voluntarily and cheerfully, and that many in these places are full even of zeal to the cause of Administration.[1] Were they instantly restored to trade? Are they yet restored to it? Is not the benignity of two commissioners, naturally most humane and generous men, some way fettered by instructions, equally against their dispositions and the spirit of parliamentary faith, when Mr. Tryon,[2] vaunting of the fidelity of the City in which he is Governor, is obliged to apply to ministry for leave to protect the King's loyal subjects, and to grant to them (not the disputed rights and privileges of freedom) but the common rights of men, by the name of *Graces*?[3] Why do not the commissioners restore them on the spot? Were they not named as commissioners for that express purpose? But we see well enough to what the whole leads. The trade of America is to be dealt out in *private indulgences and graces*; that is, in jobbs to recompence the incendiaries of war. *They* will be informed of the proper time in which to send out their merchandise. From a national, the American trade is to be turned into a personal monopoly: and one set of Merchants are to be rewarded for the pretended zeal, of which another set are the dupes; and thus between craft and credulity, the voice of reason is stifled; and all the misconduct, all the calamities of the war are covered and continued.

If I had not lived long enough to be little surprized at any thing, I should have been in some degree astonished at the continued rage of several Gentlemen, who, not satisfied with carrying fire and sword into America, are animated nearly with the same fury against those neighbours of theirs, whose only crime it is, that they have charitably and humanely wished them to entertain more reasonable sentiments, and not always to sacrifice their interest to their passion. All this rage against unresisting dissent, convinces me, that at bottom they are far from satisfied they are in the right. For what is it they would have? A war? They certainly have at this moment the blessing of something that

---

[1] Letters from William Tryon (1729–88, Royal Governor of New York) to Germain were printed in the *London Gazette* of 22 February and 20 March. In the first letter written on 24 December 1776, Tryon had spoken of 'a general Satisfaction expressed at my coming among . . . [the inhabitants of Long Island] and to judge from the Temper and Disposition I perceivd in them, there is not the least Apprehension of any farther Commotion'.

[2] See previous footnote.

[3] See the letter of Tryon in the *London Gazette*, 20 March 1777.

is very like one; and if the war they enjoy at present be not sufficiently hot and extensive, they may shortly have it as warm and as spreading as their hearts can desire. Is it the force of the Kingdom they call for? They have it already; and if they choose to fight their battles in their own person, nobody prevents their setting sail to America in the next transports. Do they think, that the service is stinted for want of liberal supplies? Indeed they complain without reason. The table of the House of Commons will glut them, let their appetite for expence be never so keen. And I assure them further, that those who think with them in the House of Commons are full as easy in the control, as they are liberal in the vote of these expences. If this be not supply or confidence sufficient, let them open their own private purse-strings, and give from what is left to them, as largely and with as little care as they think proper.

Tolerated in their passions, let them learn not to persecute the moderation of their fellow-citizens. If all the world joined them in a full cry against rebellion, and were as hotly inflamed against the whole theory and enjoyment of freedom, as those who are the most factious for servitude, it could not in my opinion answer any one end what-soever in this contest. The leaders of this war could not hire (to gratify their friends) one German more, than they do; or inspire him with less feeling for the persons, or less value for the privileges, of their revolted brethren. If we all adopted their sentiments to a man, their allies the savage Indians could not be more ferocious than they are: They could not murder one more helpless woman or child, or with more exquisite refinements of cruelty torment to death one more of their English flesh and blood, than they do already. The public money is given to purchase this alliance;—and they have their bargain.

They are continually boasting of unanimity, or calling for it. But before this unanimity can be matter either of wish or congratulation, we ought to be pretty sure, that we are engaged in a rational pursuit. Phrensy does not become a slighter distemper on account of the number of those who may be infected with it. Delusion and weak-ness produce not one mischief the less, because they are universal. I declare, that I cannot discern the least advantage, which could accrue to us, if we were able to persuade our Colonies that they had not a single friend in Great Britain. On the contrary, if the affections and opinions of mankind be not exploded as principles of connexion, I conceive it would be happy for us, if they were taught to believe, that there was even a formed American party in England, to whom they could always look for support! Happy would it be for us, if in all tempers they might turn their eyes to the parent state; so that their very turbulence and sedition should find vent in no other place than this. I believe there is not a man (except those who prefer the interest of some paltry faction to the very being of their country) who would not wish that the Americans should from time to time carry many points, and even some of them not quite reasonable, by the aid of any denomination of men here, rather than they should be driven to seek for protection against the fury of foreign mercenaries, and the waste of savages, in the arms of France.

When any community is subordinately connected with another, the great danger of the connexion is the extreme pride and self-complacency of the superior, which in all matters of controversy will probably decide in its own favour. It is a powerful corrective to such a very rational cause of fear, if the inferior body can be made to believe, that the party inclination or political views of several in the principal state, will induce them in some degree to counteract this blind and tyrannic partiality. There is no danger that any one acquiring consideration or power in the presiding state should carry this leaning to the inferior too far. The fault of human nature is not of that sort. Power in whatever hands is rarely guilty of too strict limitations on itself. But one great advantage to the support of authority attends such an amicable and protecting connexion, that those who have conferred favours obtain influence; and from the foresight of future events can persuade men who have received obligations sometimes to return them. Thus, by the mediation of those healing principles, (call them good or evil) troublesome discussions are brought to some sort of adjustment; and every hot controversy is not a civil war.

But, if the Colonies (to bring the general matter home to us) could see, that in Great Britain the mass of the people is melted into its Government, and that every dispute with the Ministry must of necessity be always a quarrel with the nation; they can stand no longer in the equal and friendly relation of fellow-citizens to the subjects of this Kingdom. Humble as this relation may appear to some, when it is once broken, a strong tie is dissolved. Other sort of connexions will be sought. For, there are very few in the world, who will not prefer an useful ally to an insolent master.

Such discord has been the effect of the unanimity into which so many have of late been seduced or bullied, or into the appearance of which they have sunk through mere despair. They have been told that their dissent from violent measures is an encouragement to rebellion. Men of great presumption and little knowledge will hold a language which is contradicted by the whole course of history. *General* rebellions and revolts of an whole people never were *encouraged*, now or at any time. They are always *provoked*. But if this unheard-of doctrine of the encouragement of rebellion were true, if it were true, that an assurance of the friendship of numbers in this country towards the colonies, could become an encouragement to them to break off all connexion with it, what is the inference? Does any body seriously maintain, that, charged with my share of the public councils, I am obliged not to resist projects which I think mischievous, lest men who suffer should be encouraged to resist? The very tendency of such projects to produce rebellion is one of the chief reasons against them. Shall that reason not be given? Is it then a rule, that no man in this nation shall open his mouth in favour of the Colonies, shall defend their rights, or complain of their sufferings? Or, when war finally breaks out, no man shall express his desires of peace? Has this been the law of our past, or is it to make the terms of our future, connexion? Even looking no further than ourselves, can it be true loyalty to any government, or true patriotism towards any country, to degrade their solemn councils into servile drawing-rooms, to flatter their pride and passions, rather than to enlighten their reason, and to prevent them from being cautioned against violence, lest others should be encouraged to resistance! By such acquiescence great Kings and mighty nations have been undone; and if any are at this day in a perilous situation from rejecting truth, and listening to flattery, it would rather become them to reform the errors under which they suffer, than to reproach those who have forewarned them of their danger.

But the rebels looked for assistance from this country. They did so in the beginning of this controversy most certainly; and they sought it by earnest supplications to Government, which dignity rejected, and by a suspension of commerce, which the wealth of this nation enabled you to despise. When they found that neither prayers nor menaces had any sort of weight, but that a firm resolution was taken to reduce them to unconditional obedience by a military force, they came to the last extremity. Despairing of us, they trusted in themselves. Not strong enough themselves, they sought succour in France. In proportion as all encouragement here lessened, their distance from this country encreased. The encouragement is over; the alienation is compleat.

In order to produce this favourite unanimity in delusion, and to prevent all possibility of a return to our antient happy concord, arguments for our continuance in this course are drawn from the wretched situation itself into which we have been betrayed. It is said, that being at war with the Colonies, whatever our sentiments might have been before, all ties between us are now dissolved; and all the policy we have left is to strengthen the hands of Government to reduce them. On the principle of this argument, the more mischiefs we suffer from any administration, the more our trust in it is to be confirmed. Let them but once get us into a war, their power is then safe, and an act of oblivion past for all their misconduct.

But is it really true, that Government is always to be strengthened with the instruments of war, but never furnished with the means of peace? In former times ministers, I allow, have been sometimes driven by the popular voice to assert by arms the national honour against foreign powers. But the wisdom of the nation has been far more clear, when those ministers have been compelled to consult its interests by treaty. We all know that the sense of the nation obliged the court of King Charles the 2d, to abandon the *Dutch war*;[1] a war next to the present the most impolitic which we ever carried on. The good people of England considered Holland as a sort of dependency on this Kingdom; they dreaded to drive it to the protection, or to subject it to the power of France, by their own inconsiderate hostility. They paid but little respect to the court jargon of that day: They were not inflamed by the pretended rivalship of the Dutch in trade; by their Massacre at Amboyna,[2] acted on the stage to provoke the public vengeance;[3] nor by declamations against the ingratitude of the United Provinces for the benefits England had conferred upon them in their infant state. They were not moved from their evident interest by all these arts; nor was it enough to tell them, they were at war; that they must go through with it; and that the cause of the dispute was lost in the consequences. The people of England were then, as they are now,

---

[1] The Third Dutch War of 1672–4.
[2] Of English merchants at Amboina in the Moluccas in 1623.
[3] Dryden's play, *Amboyna, or the Cruelties of the Dutch to the English Merchants*, was first performed in 1672 and published in 1673.

called upon to make government strong. They thought it a great deal better to make it wise and honest.

When I was amongst my constituents at the last Summer Assizes, I remember that men of all descriptions did then express a very strong desire for peace, and no slight hopes of attaining it from the commission sent out by my lord Howe. And it is not a little remarkable, that in proportion as every person shewed a zeal for the court measures, he was at that time earnest in circulating an opinion of the extent of the supposed powers of that commission. When I told them that lord Howe had no powers to treat, or to promise satisfaction on any point whatsoever of the controversy, I was hardly credited; so strong and general was the desire of terminating this war by the method of accommodation. As far as I could discover, this was the temper then prevalent through the kingdom. The king's forces, it must be observed, had at that time been obliged to evacuate Boston. The superiority of the former campaign rested wholly with the Colonists. If such powers of treaty were to be wished, whilst success was very doubtful; how came they to be less so, since his Majesty's arms have been crowned with many considerable advantages? Have these successes induced us to alter our mind, as thinking the season of victory not the time for treating with honour or advantage? Whatever changes have happened in the national character, it can scarcely be our wish, that terms of accommodation never should be proposed to our enemy, except when they must be attributed solely to our fears. It has happened, let me say, unfortunately, that we read of his Majesty's commission for making peace, and his troops evacuating his last town in the thirteen colonies, at the same hour, and in the same Gazette.[1] It was still more unfortunate, that no commission went to America to settle the troubles there, until several months after an act had been passed to put the colonies out of the protection of this government, and to divide their trading property without a possibility of restitution, as spoil among the seamen of the navy. The most abject submission on the part of the colonies could not redeem them. There was no man on that whole continent, or within three thousand miles of it, qualified by law to follow allegiance with protection, or submission with pardon. A proceeding of this kind has no example in history. Independency, and independency with an enmity (which putting ourselves out of the

[1] The *London Gazette* of 4 May 1776.

question would be called natural and much provoked) was the inevitable consequence. How this came to pass, the nation may be one day in an humour to enquire.

All the attempts made this session to give fuller powers of peace to the commanders in America, were stifled by the fatal confidence of victory, and the wild hopes of unconditional submission. There was a moment, favourable to the king's arms, when if any powers of concession had existed, on the other side of the Atlantick, even after all our errors, peace in all probability might have been restored. But calamity is unhappily the usual season of reflexion; and the pride of men will not often suffer reason to have any scope until it can be no longer of service.

I have always wished, that as the dispute had its apparent origin from things done in Parliament, and as the acts passed there had provoked the war, that the foundations of peace should be laid in Parliament also. I have been astonished to find, that those whose zeal for the dignity of our body was so hot, as to light up the flames of civil war, should even publickly declare, that these delicate points ought to be wholly left to the Crown. Poorly as I may be thought affected to the authority of Parliament, I shall never admit that our constitutional rights can ever become a matter of ministerial negociation.

I am charged with being an American. If warm affection, towards those over whom I claim any share of authority, be a crime, I am guilty of this charge. But I do assure you (and they who know me publickly and privately will bear witness to me) that if ever one man lived, more zealous than another, for the supremacy of Parliament, and the rights of this imperial Crown, it was myself. Many others indeed might be more knowing in the extent, or in the foundation of these rights. I do not pretend to be an Antiquary, or a lawyer, or qualified for the chair of Professor in Metaphysics. I never ventured to put your solid interests upon speculative grounds. My having constantly declined to do so has been attributed to my incapacity for such disquisitions; and I am inclined to believe it is partly the cause. I never shall be ashamed to confess, that where I am ignorant I am diffident. I am indeed not very sollicitous to clear myself of this imputed incapacity; because men, even less conversant than I am, in this kind of subtleties, and placed in stations to which I ought not to aspire, have, by the mere force of civil discretion, often conducted the affairs of great nations with distinguished felicity and glory.

313

When I first came into a publick trust, I found your Parliament in possession of an unlimited legislative power over the Colonies. I could not open the Statute-Book, without seeing the actual exercise of it, more or less, in all cases whatsoever. This possession passed with me for a title. It does so in all human affairs. No man examines into the defects of his title to his paternal estate, or to his established government. Indeed common sense taught me, that a legislative authority, not actually limited by the express terms of its foundation, or by its own subsequent acts, cannot have its powers parcelled out by argumentative distinctions, so as to enable us to affirm, that here they can, and there they cannot bind. Nobody was so obliging as to produce to me any record of such distinctions, by compact or otherwise, either at the successive formation of the several Colonies, or during the existence of any of them. If other Gentlemen were able to see, how one power could be given up, (merely on abstract reasoning) without giving up the rest, I can only say, that they saw further than I could; nor did I ever presume to condemn any one for being clear-sighted, when I was blind. I praise their penetration and learning; and hope that their practice has been correspondent to their theory.

I had indeed very earnest wishes to keep the whole body of this authority perfect and entire as I found it, and to keep it so, not for our advantage solely, but principally for the sake of those, on whose account all just authority exists; I mean, the people to be governed. For I thought I saw, that many cases might well happen, in which the exercise of every power, comprehended in the broadest idea of legislature, might become, in its time and circumstances, not a little expedient for the peace and union of the Colonies amongst themselves, as well as for their perfect harmony with Great-Britain. Thinking so, (perhaps erroneously) but being honestly of that opinion, I was at the same time very sure, that the authority of which I was so jealous, could not, under the actual circumstances of our Plantations, be at all preserved in any of its members, but by the greatest reserve in its application; particularly in those delicate points, in which the feelings of mankind are the most irritable. They who thought otherwise, have found a few more difficulties in their work, than (I hope) they were thoroughly aware of, when they undertook the present business.

I must beg leave to observe, that it is not only the invidious branch of taxation that will be resisted, but that no other given part of legislative rights can be safely exercised, without regard to the general opinion of those who are to be governed. That general opinion is the vehicle, and organ of legislative omnipotence. Without this, the extent of legislative power may be a theory to entertain the mind, but it is nothing in the direction of affairs. The compleatness of the legislative authority of Parliament *over this kingdom* is not questioned; and yet there are many things indubitably included in the abstract idea of that power, and which carry no absolute injustice in themselves, which, being contrary to the opinions and feelings of the people, can as little be exercised, as if Parliament in such cases had been possessed of no right at all. I see no abstract reason, which can be given, why the same power that made and repealed the High Commission Court and the Star Chamber, might not revive them again; and these courts, warned by their former fate, might possibly exercise their powers with some degree of justice. But the madness would be as unquestionable, as the competence, of that Parliament, which should make such attempts. If any thing can be supposed out of the power of human legislature, it is Religion: I admit however that the established religion of this country has been three or four times altered by act of parliament; and therefore that a statute binds even in that case. But we may very safely affirm, that notwithstanding this apparent omnipotence, it would be now found as impossible for King and Parliament to change the established religion of this country, as it was to King *James* alone, when he attempted to make such an alteration without a parliament. In effect, to follow, not to force the publick inclination; to give a direction, a form, a technical dress and a specifick sanction, to the general sense of the community, is the true end of legislature. When it goes beyond this, its authority will be precarious, let its rights be what they will.

It is so with regard to the exercise of all the powers, which our constitution knows in any of its parts, and indeed to the substantial existence of any of the parts themselves. The King's negative to bills is one of the most indisputed of the royal prerogatives; and it extends to all cases whatsoever.[1] I am far from certain, that if several laws, which I know, had fallen under the stroke of that sceptre, that the publick would have had a very heavy loss. But it is not the *propriety* of the exercise which is in question. The exercise itself is wisely forborne. Its repose may be the preservation of its existence; and its existence may

---

[1] The royal veto had not been employed since 1708.

be the means of saving the constitution itself, on an occasion worthy of bringing it forth.

As the disputants, whose accurate and logical reasonings have brought us into our present condition, think it absurd that powers, or members of any constitution should exist, rarely if ever to be exercised, I hope, I shall be excused in mentioning another instance that is material. We know, that the Convocation of the Clergy had formerly been called and sat with nearly as much regularity to business as Parliament itself. It is now called for form only. It sits for the purpose of making some polite ecclesiastical compliments to the King; and when that grace is said, retires and is heard of no more. It is however *a part of the Constitution*, and may be called out into act and energy, whenever there is occasion; and whenever those, who conjure up that spirit, will choose to abide the consequences. It is wise to permit its legal existence; it is much wiser to continue it a legal existence only. So truly has Prudence (constituted as the God of this lower world) the entire dominion over every exercise of power, committed into its hands; and yet I have lived to see prudence and conformity to circumstances, wholly set at naught in our late controversies, and treated as if they were the most contemptible and irrational of all things. I have heard it a hundred times very gravely alledged, that in order to keep power in wind, it was necessary, by preference, to exert it in those very points in which it was most likely to be resisted, and the least likely to be productive of any advantage.

These were the considerations, Gentlemen, which led me early to think, that in the comprehensive dominion which the divine Providence had put into our hands, instead of troubling our understandings with speculations concerning the unity of empire, and the identity or distinction of legislative powers, and inflaming our passions with the heat and pride of controversy, it was our duty, in all soberness, to conform our Government to the character and circumstances of the several people who compose this mighty and strangely diversified mass. I never was wild enough to conceive, that one method would serve for the whole; I could never conceive that the natives of *Hindostan* and those of *Virginia* could be ordered in the same manner; or that the *Cutchery*[1] Court and the grand Jury of *Salem* could be regulated on a

---

[1] Cutchery comes from the Hindi word 'Kachari' meaning in this case a court house with facilities for a public audience.

similar plan. I was persuaded that Government was a practical thing, made for the happiness of mankind, and not to furnish out a spectacle of uniformity, to gratify the schemes of visionary politicians. Our business was, to rule, not to wrangle; and it would have been a poor compensation that we had triumphed in a dispute, whilst we lost an empire.

If there be one fact in the world perfectly clear, it is this; "That the disposition of the people of America is wholly averse to any other than a free Government;" and this known character of the people is indication enough to any honest statesman, how he ought to adapt whatever power he finds in his hands to their case. If any ask me what a free Government is? I answer, that, for any practical purpose, it is what the people think so;[1] and that they, and not I, are the natural, lawful, and competent judges of this matter. If they practically allow me a greater degree of authority over them than is consistent with any correct ideas of perfect freedom, I ought to thank them for so great a trust, and not to endeavour to prove from thence, that they have reasoned amiss, and that having gone so far, by analogy, they must hereafter have no enjoyment but by my pleasure.

If we had seen this done by any others, we must have concluded them far gone in madness. It is melancholy as well as ridiculous, to observe the kind of reasoning with which the public has been amused, in order to divert our minds from the common sense of our American policy. There are people, who have split and anatomised the doctrine of free Government, as if it were an abstract question concerning metaphysical liberty and necessity; and not a matter of moral prudence and natural feeling. They have disputed, whether liberty be a positive or a negative idea; whether it does not consist in being governed by laws, without considering what are the laws or who are the makers; they have questioned whether man has any rights by nature; and whether all the property he enjoys, be not the alms of his government, and his life itself their favour and indulgence. Others corrupting religion, as these have perverted philosophy, contend, that Christians are redeemed into captivity; and the blood of the Saviour of mankind

---

[1] James Boswell (1740–95) reports Dr. Johnson's views on this phrase: 'Mr. Burke's "letter to the Sheriffs of Bristol on the affairs of America" being mentioned, Johnson censured the composition much, and he ridiculed the definition of a free government, *viz.* "For any practical purpose, it is what the people think so." "I will let the King of France govern me on those conditions, (said he,) for it is to be governed just as I please" '(*Boswell's Life of Johnson*, iii. 281).

has been shed to make them the slaves of a few proud and insolent sinners. These shocking extremes provoking to extremes of another kind, speculations are let loose as destructive to all authority, as the former are to all freedom. In this manner the stirrers up of this contention, not satisfied with distracting our dependencies and filling them with blood and slaughter, are corrupting our understandings: they are endeavouring to tear up, along with practical liberty, all the foundations of human society, all equity and justice, religion and order.

Civil freedom, gentlemen, is not, as many have endeavoured to persuade you, a thing that lies hid in the depths of abstruse science. It is a blessing and a benefit, not an abstract speculation; and all the just reasoning that can be upon it, is of so coarse a texture, as perfectly to suit the ordinary capacities of those who are to enjoy, and of those who are to defend it. Far from any resemblance to those propositions in Geometry and Metaphysics, which admit no medium, but must be true or false in all their latitude, social and civil freedom, like all other things in common life, are variously mixed and modified, enjoyed in very different degrees, and shaped into an infinite diversity of forms, according to the temper and circumstances of every community. The *extreme* of liberty (which is its abstract perfection, but its real fault) obtains no where, nor ought to obtain any where. Because extremes, as we all know, in every point which relates either to our duties or satisfactions in life, are destructive both to virtue and enjoyment. Liberty too must be limited in order to be possessed. The degree of restraint it is impossible in any case to settle precisely. But it ought to be the constant aim of every wise publick counsel, to find out by cautious experiments, and rational, cool endeavours, with how little, not how much of this restraint, the community can subsist. For liberty is a good to be improved, and not an evil to be lessened. It is not only a private blessing of the first order, but the vital spring and energy of the state itself, which has just so much life and vigour as there is liberty in it. But whether liberty be advantageous or not, (for I know it is a fashion to decry the very principle) none will dispute that peace is a blessing; and peace must in the course of human affairs be frequently bought by some indulgence and toleration at least to liberty. For as the Sabbath (though of divine institution) was made for man, not man for the Sabbath[1], government, which can claim no higher origin or

---

[1] Mark, 2. 27.

authority, in its exercise at least, ought to conform to the exigencies of the time and the temper and character of the people, with whom it is concerned; and not always to attempt violently to bend the people to their theories of subjection.[1] The bulk of mankind on their part are not excessively curious concerning any theories, whilst they are really happy; and one sure symptom of an ill conducted state, is the propensity of the people to resort to them.

But when subjects, by a long course of such ill conduct, are once thoroughly inflamed, and the state itself violently distempered, the people must have some satisfaction to their feelings, more solid than a sophistical speculation on law and government. Such was our situation; and such a satisfaction was necessary to prevent recourse to arms; it was necessary towards laying them down; it will be necessary to prevent the taking them up again and again. Of what nature this satisfaction ought to be, I wish it had been the disposition of Parliament seriously to consider. It was certainly a deliberation that called for the exertion of all their wisdom.

I am, and ever have been, deeply sensible, of the difficulty of reconciling the strong presiding power, that is so useful towards the conservation of a vast, disconnected, infinitely diversified empire, with that liberty and safety of the provinces, which they must enjoy, (in opinion and practice at least) or they will not be provinces at all. I know, and have long felt, the difficulty of reconciling the unwieldy haughtiness of a great ruling nation, habituated to command, pampered by enormous wealth, and confident from a long course of prosperity and victory, to the high spirit of free dependencies, animated with the first glow and activity of juvenile heat, and assuming to themselves as their birth-right, some part of that very pride which oppresses them. They who perceive no difficulty in reconciling these tempers (which however to make peace must some way or other be reconciled) are much above my capacity, or much below the magnitude of the business. Of one thing I am perfectly clear, that it is not by deciding the suit, but by compromising the difference, that peace can be restored or kept. They who would put an end to such quarrels, by declaring roundly in favour of the whole demands of either party, have mistaken, in my humble opinion, the office of a mediator.

The war is now of full two years standing; the controversy of many more. In different periods of the dispute, different methods of reconciliation were to be pursued. I mean to trouble you with a short state of things at the most important of these periods, in order to give you a more distinct idea of our[1] policy with regard to this most delicate of all objects. The Colonies were from the beginning subject to the legislature of Great-Britain, on principles which they never examined; and we permitted to them many local privileges, without asking how they agreed with that legislative authority. Modes of administration were formed in an insensible, and very unsystematick manner. But they gradually adapted themselves to the varying condition of things.— What was first a single kingdom stretched into an empire; and an imperial superintendency of some kind or other became necessary. Parliament, from a mere representative of the people, and a guardian of popular privileges for its own immediate constituents, grew into a mighty sovereign. Instead of being a control on the Crown on its own behalf, it communicated a sort of strength to the Royal authority; which was wanted for the conservation of a new object, but which could not be safely trusted to the Crown alone. On the other hand, the Colonies advancing by equal steps, and governed by the same necessity, had formed within themselves, either by royal instruction, or royal charter, assemblies so exceedingly resembling a parliament, in all their forms, functions, and powers, that it was impossible they should not imbibe some opinion of a similar authority.

At the first designation of these assemblies, they were probably not intended for anything more, (nor perhaps did they think themselves much higher) than the municipal corporations within this Island, to which some at present love to compare them. But nothing in progression can rest on its original plan. We may as well think of rocking a grown man in the cradle of an infant. Therefore, as the Colonies prospered and encreased to a numerous and mighty people, spreading over a very great tract of the globe; it was natural that they should attribute to assemblies, so respectable in their formal constitution, some part of the dignity of the great nations which they represented. No longer tied to bye-laws, these assemblies made acts of all sorts and in all cases whatsoever. They levied money, not for parochial purposes, but upon regular grants to the Crown, following all the rules and principles of a Parliament, to which they approached every day more and more nearly. Those who think themselves wiser than Providence and stronger than the course of nature, may complain of all this variation, on the one side

---

[1] Due to faulty inking, or a broken sort, this word appears to be 'cur'.

or the other, as their several humours and prejudices may lead them. But things could not be otherwise; and English Colonies must be had on these terms, or not had at all. In the mean time neither party felt any inconvenience from this double legislature, to which they had been formed by imperceptible habits, and old custom, the great support of all the governments in the world. Though these two legislatures were sometimes found perhaps performing the very same functions, they did not very grossly or systematically clash. In all likelyhood this arose from mere neglect: possibly from the natural operation of things, which, left to themselves, generally fall into their proper order. But whatever was the cause, it is certain, that a regular revenue by the authority of Parliament, for the support of civil and military establishments, seems not to have been thought of until the Colonies were too proud to submit, too strong to be forced, too enlightened not to see all the consequences which must arise from such a system.

If ever this scheme of taxation was to be pushed against the inclinations of the people, it was evident, that discussions must arise, which would let loose all the elements that composed this double constitution; would shew how much each of their members had departed from its original principles; and would discover contradictions in each legislature, as well to its own first principles, as to its relation to the other, very difficult if not absolutely impossible to be reconciled.

Therefore at the first fatal opening of this contest, the wisest course seemed to be, to put an end as soon as possible to the immediate causes of the dispute; and to quiet a discussion, not easily settled upon clear principles, and arising from claims, which pride would permit neither party to abandon, by resorting as nearly as possible to the old successful course. A mere repeal of the obnoxious tax, with a declaration of the legislative authority of this kingdom, was then fully sufficient to procure peace to *both sides*. Man is a creature of habit; and the first breach being of very short continuance, the Colonies fell back exactly into their antient state. The Congress has used an expression with regard to this pacification which appears to me truly significant. After the repeal of the Stamp Act, "the Colonies fell," says this assembly, "into their antient state of *unsuspecting confidence in the Mother Country*."[1] This unsuspecting confidence is the true center of gravity

---

[1] Burke appears to be referring to a passage in the 'Memorial to the Inhabitants of the British Colonies': 'After the repeal of the Stamp Act, having again resigned ourselves to our antient unsuspicious affection for the parent state' (*Journals of the Continental Congress*, i. 92).

amongst mankind, about which all the parts are at rest. It is this *unsuspecting confidence* that removes all difficulties, and reconciles all the contradictions which occur in the complexity of all antient puzzled political establishments. Happy are the rulers which have the secret of preserving it!

The whole empire has reason to remember with eternal gratitude, the wisdom and temper of that man and his excellent associates, who, to recover this confidence, formed the plan of pacification in 1766.[1] That plan, being built upon the nature of man, and the circumstances and habits of the two countries, and not on any visionary speculations, perfectly answered its end, as long as it was thought proper to adhere to it. Without giving a rude shock to the dignity (well or ill understood) of this Parliament, it gave perfect content to our dependencies. Had it not been for the mediatorial spirit and talents of that great man, between such clashing pretensions and passions, we should then have rushed headlong (I know what I say) into the calamities of that civil war, in which, by departing from his system, we are at length involved; and we should have been precipitated into that war, at a time, when circumstances both at home and abroad were far, very far, more unfavourable unto us than they were at the breaking out of the present troubles.

I had the happiness of giving my first votes in Parliament for that pacification. I was one of those almost unanimous members, who, in the necessary concessions of Parliament, would as much as possible have preserved its authority, and respected its honour.[2] I could not at once tear from my heart prejudices which were dear to me, and which bore a resemblance to virtues. I had then, and I have still, my partialities. What Parliament gave up I wished to be given, as of grace, and favour, and affection, and not as a restitution of stolen goods. High dignity relented as it was soothed; and an act of benignity from old acknowledged greatness had its full effect on our dependencies. Our unlimited declaration of legislative authority produced not a single murmur. If this undefined power has become odious since that time, and full of horror to the Colonies, it is because the *unsuspicious*

---

[1] Burke is clearly referring here to the Marquess of Rockingham and to the Rockingham party's handling of the Stamp Act issue during the 1765–6 administration; see Langford, *Rockingham Administration*, pp. 109–198; P. D. G. Thomas, *British Politics and the Stamp Act Crisis*, pp. 131–252.

[2] Burke is referring here to his support for the Declaratory Act in 1766; see vol. ii, pp. 45–51.

confidence is lost; and the parental affection, in the bosom of whose boundless authority they reposed their privileges, is become estranged and hostile.

It will be asked, if such was then my opinion of the mode of pacification, how I came to be the very person who moved, not only for a repeal of all the late coercive states, but for mutilating, by a positive law, the entireness of the legislative power of Parliament, and cutting off from it the whole right of taxation?[1] I answer, because a different state of things requires a different conduct. When the dispute had gone to the last extremities (which no man laboured more to prevent than I did) the concessions which had satisfied in the beginning, could satisfy no longer; the violation of tacit faith required explicit security. The same cause, which has introduced all formal compacts and covenants among men, made it necessary: I mean, habits of soreness, jealousy, and distrust. I parted with it, as with a limb: but as with a limb to save the body; and I would have parted with more, if more had been necessary. Anything rather than a fruitless, hopeless, unnatural civil war. This mode of yielding would, it is said, give way to independency, without a war. I am persuaded from the nature of things, and from every information, that it would have had a directly contrary effect. But if it had this effect, I confess, that I should prefer independency without war, to independency with it; and I have so much trust in the inclinations and prejudices of mankind, and so little in anything else, that I should expect ten times more benefit to this Kingdom from the affection of America, though under a separate establishment, than from her perfect submission to the Crown and Parliament, accompanied with her terror, disgust, and abhorrence. Bodies tied together by so unnatural a bond of union, as mutual hatred, are only connected to their ruin.

One hundred and ten respectable Members of Parliament voted for that concession.[2] Many, not present when the motion was made, were of the sentiments of those who voted. I knew it would then have made peace. I am not without hopes that it would do so at present, if it were adopted. No benefit, no revenue, could be lost by it. For be fully assured, that, of all the phantoms that ever deluded the fond hopes of a credulous world, a parliamentary revenue in the Colonies is the most perfectly chimerical. Your breaking them to any subjection, far from

---

[1] In his second conciliation speech, see above, pp. 190–5.
[2] Actually it was 105 (107 with the two tellers); see *Parl. Hist.* xviii. 992.

relieving your burthens, (the pretext for this war,) will never pay that military force which will be kept up to the destruction of their liberties and yours. I risque nothing in this prophecy.

Gentlemen, you have my opinion on the present state of public affairs. Mean as these opinions may be in themselves, your partiality has made them of some importance. Without troubling myself to enquire whether I am under a formal obligation to it, I have a pleasure in accounting for my conduct to my Constituents. I feel warmly on this subject, and I express myself as I feel. If I presume to blame any public proceeding, I cannot be supposed to be personal. Would to God I could be suspected of it. My fault might be greater, but the public calamity would be less extensive. If my conduct has not been able to make any impression on the warm part of that ancient and powerful party, with whose support, I was not honoured at my election; on my side, my respect, regard, and duty to them is not at all lessened. I owe the Gentlemen who compose it my most humble service in every thing. I hope that whenever any of them were pleased to command me, that they found me perfectly equal in my obedience. But flattery and friendship are very different things; and to mislead is not to serve them. I cannot purchase the favour of any man by concealing from him what I think his ruin.

By the favour of my fellow-citizens, I am the representative of an honest, well-ordered, virtuous City; of a people, who preserve more of the original English simplicity, and purity of manners, than perhaps any other. You possess among you several men and magistrates of large and cultivated understandings, fit for any employment in any sphere. I do, to the best of my power, act so as to make myself worthy of so honourable a choice. If I were ready, on any call of my own vanity or interest, or to answer any election purpose, to forsake principles, (whatever they are) which I had formed at a mature age, on full reflexion, and which have been confirmed by long experience, I should forfeit the only thing which makes you pardon so many errors and imperfections in me.

Not that I think it fit for any one to rely too much on his own understanding; or to be filled with a presumption, not becoming a Christian man, in his own personal stability and rectitude. I hope I am far from that vain confidence, which almost always fails in trial. I know my weakness in all respects, as much at least as any enemy I have; and I attempt to take security against it. The only method which has ever been found effectual to preserve any man against the corruption of nature and example, is an habit of life and communication of councils with the most virtuous and public-spirited men of the age you live in. Such a society cannot be kept without advantage, or deserted without shame. For this rule of conduct I may be called in reproach a *party man*; but I am little affected with such aspersions. In the way which they call party, I worship the constitution of your fathers; and I shall never blush for my political company. All reverence to honour, all idea of what it is, will be lost out of the world, before it can be imputed as a fault to any man, that he has been closely connected with those incomparable persons, living and dead, with whom for eleven years I have constantly thought and acted. If I have wandered out of the paths of rectitude, into those of interested faction, it was in company with the Saviles,[1] the Dowdeswells,[2] the Wentworths,[3] the Bentincks;[4] with the Lennoxes,[5] the Manchesters,[6] the Keppels,[7] the Saunders's;[8] with the temperate, permanent, hereditary virtue of the whole house of Cavendish;[9] names, among which, some have extended your fame and empire in arms, and all have fought the battle of your liberties in fields not less glorious.—These, and many more like these, grafting public principles on private honour, have redeemed the present age, and would have adorned the most splendid period in your history. Where could a man, conscious of his inability to act alone, and willing to act as he ought to do, have arranged himself better? If any one thinks this kind of society to be taken up as the best method of gratifying low personal pride, or ambitious interest, he is mistaken; and knows nothing of the world.

Preferring this connexion; I do not mean to detract in the slightest degree from others. There are some of those, whom I admire at something of a greater distance, with whom I have had the happiness also perfectly to agree, in almost all the particulars, in which I have

[1] Sir George Savile.
[2] William Dowdeswell.
[3] Charles Watson Wentworth, the Marquess of Rockingham.
[4] William Henry Cavendish Bentinck, the Duke of Portland.
[5] Charles Lennox, 3rd Duke of Richmond. At this point Richmond was still a Rockingham supporter though he was to leave the fold over the question of reform in 1780.
[6] Manchester was really more a Chathamite than a Rockingham, but he had been on good terms with the Marquess and others for many years.
[7] Admiral Augustus Keppel (1725–1806), later (1783) Viscount Keppel, M.P. 1755–82.
[8] Sir Charles Saunders (*c.*1713–75), M.P. 1750–75.
[9] Lord John Cavendish, the head of the family, his brothers Lord Frederick (1729–1803), M.P. 1751–80, and Lord George Augustus (1727–94), M.P. 1751–80, 1781–94, their cousins Lord George Augustus Henry (1754–84), M.P. 1775–96, 1797–1831, and Lord Richard (1752–81), M.P. 1773–81, and their nephew William, 5th Duke of Devonshire (1748–1811).

differed with some successive administrations; and they are such, as it never can be reputable to any government to reckon among its enemies.[1]

I hope there are none of you, corrupted with the doctrine taught by wicked men for the worst purposes, and greedily received by the malignant credulity of envy and ignorance, which is, that the men who act upon the public stage are all alike; all equally corrupt; all influenced by no other views than the sordid lucre of salary and pension. The thing, I know by experience to be false. Never expecting to find perfection in men, and not looking for divine attributes in created beings, in my commerce with my contemporaries, I have found much human virtue. I have seen not a little public spirit; a real subordination of interest to duty; and a decent and regulated sensibility to honest fame and reputation. The age unquestionably produces (whether in a greater or less number than in former times, I know not) daring profligates, and insidious hypocrites. What then? Am I not to avail myself of whatever good is to be found in the world, because of the mixture of evil that will always be in it? The smallness of the quantity in currency only heightens the value. They, who raise suspicions on the good on account of the behaviour of ill men, are of the party of the latter. The common cant is no justification for engaging in such a party. I have been deceived, say they, by *Titius* and *Mævius*.[2] I have been the dupe of this pretender or of that mountebank; and I can trust appearances no longer. But my credulity and want of discernment cannot, as I conceive, amount to a fair presumption against any man's integrity. A conscientious person would rather doubt his own judgment, than condemn his species. He would say, I have observed without attention, or judged upon erroneous maxims; I trusted to profession, when I ought to have attended to conduct. Such a man will grow wise, not malignant, by his acquaintance with the world. But he that accuses all mankind of corruption ought to remember that he is sure to convict only one. In truth I should much rather admit those, whom at any time I have disrelished the most, to be patterns of perfection, than seek a consolation to my own unworthiness in a general communion of depravity with all about me.

---

[1] Burke almost certainly means the Chathamites with whom the Rockinghams had been allies on numerous issues over the years though the relationship had seldom been an easy one; see headnote to Burke's speech on the funeral of Lord Chatham on 21 May 1778, below, pp. 380–2.
[2] i.e. John Doe and Richard Roe.

That this ill-natured doctrine should be preached by the missionaries of a court, I do not wonder. It answers their purpose. But that it should be heard among those who pretend to be strong assertors of liberty, is not only surprising, but hardly natural. This moral levelling is a *servile principle*. It leads to practical passive obedience far better, than all the doctrines, which the pliant accommodation of Theology to power has ever produced.[1] It cuts up by the roots, not only all idea of forcible resistance, but even of civil opposition. It disposes men to an abject submission, not by opinion, which may be shaken by argument or altered by passion, but by the strong ties of public and private interest. For if all men who act in a public situation are equally selfish, corrupt, and venal, what reason can be given for desiring any sort of change, which, besides the evils which must attend all changes, can be productive of no possible advantage? The active men in the state are true samples of the mass. If they are universally depraved, the commonwealth itself is not sound. We may amuse ourselves with talking as much as we please of the virtue of middle or humble life; that is, we may place our confidence in the virtue of those who have never been tried. But if the persons who are continually emerging out of that sphere, be no better than those whom birth has placed above it, what hopes are there in the remainder of the body which is to furnish the perpetual succession of the state?[2] All who have ever written on government, are unanimous, that among a people generally corrupt, liberty cannot long exist. And indeed how is it possible? when those who are to make the laws, to guard, to enforce, or to obey them, are, by a tacit confederacy of manners, indisposed to the spirit of all generous and noble institutions.

I am aware that the age is not what we all wish. But I am sure, that the only means of checking its precipitate degeneracy, is heartily to concur with whatever is the best in our time; and to have some more correct standard of judging what that best is, than the transient and uncertain favour of a court. If once we are able to find, and can prevail on ourselves to strengthen an union of such men, whatever accidentally

---

[1] This might be compared with Hume's short essay 'Of Passive Obedience' (*David Hume, Essays Moral, Political and Literary*, ed. E. Miller, Indianapolis, 1985, pp. 488–92).

[2] This statement helps to demonstrate Burke's belief that a few men were born to lead and the rest to follow. It was this view which had governed his declaration about the proper relationship between M.P.s and their constituents in his first speech to his electors in Bristol in 1774, printed above. For a discussion of this view and the problems it created for Burke in Bristol, see below, pp. 621–2, and above, pp. 23–5.

becomes indisposed to ill-exercised power, even by the ordinary operation of human passions, must join with that society; and cannot long be
joined, without in some degree assimilating to it. Virtue will catch as
well as vice by contact; and the public stock of honest manly principle
will daily accumulate. We are not too nicely to scrutinize motives
as long as action is irreproachable. It is enough, (and for a worthy
man perhaps too much) to deal out its infamy to convicted guilt and
declared apostacy.

To act on the principles of the constitution, with the best men the
time affords, has been from the beginning the rule of my conduct; and
I mean to continue it, as long as such a body as I have described, can
by any possibility be kept together. For I should think it the most
dreadful of all offences, not only towards the present generation but to
all the future, if I were to do any thing which could make the minutest
breach in this great conservatory of free principles. Those who perhaps
have the same intentions, but are separated by some little political
animosities, will, I hope, discern at last, how little conducive it is to any
rational purpose, to lower its reputation. For my part, Gentlemen, from
much experience, from no little thinking, and from comparing a great
variety of things, I am thoroughly persuaded, that the last hopes of
preserving the spirit of the English Constitution, or of re-uniting the
dissipated members of the English race upon a common plan of
tranquillity and liberty, does entirely depend on the firm and lasting
union of such men;[1] and above all on their keeping themselves from
that despair, which is so very apt to fall on those, whom a violence of
character, and a mixture of ambitious views, do not support through a
long, painful, and unsuccessful struggle.

There never, Gentlemen, was a period in which the stedfastness of
some men has been put to so sore a trial. It is not very difficult for
well-formed minds to abandon their interest; but the separation of
fame and virtue is an harsh divorce. Liberty is in danger of being made

---

[1] This is the view Burke had been propagating since the late 1760s and early 1770s in
attempting to bring the various parties in opposition into a general union under the Rockinghams'
banner. This statement might be compared to that in the *Thoughts*, in 1770: 'If the reader believes
that there really exists such a Faction as I have described; a Faction ruling by the private
inclinations of a Court, against the general sense of the people...; he will believe also, that
nothing but a firm combination of public men against this body, and that, too, supported by the
hearty concurrence of the people at large, can possibly get the better of it' (vol. ii, p. 321). For a
discussion of the Rockinghams' desire for a union in opposition, see W. M. Elofson, 'The
Rockingham Whigs and the Country Tradition', *Parliamentary History*, viii (1989), 90–115.

unpopular to Englishmen. Contending for an imaginary power, we begin to acquire the spirit of domination, and to lose the relish of honest equality. The principles of our forefathers become suspected to us, because we see them animating the present opposition of our children. The faults which grow out of the luxuriance of freedom, appear much more shocking to us, than the base vices which are generated from the rankness of servitude. Accordingly the least resistance to power appears more inexcuseable in our eyes than the greatest abuses of authority. All dread of a standing military force is looked upon as a superstitious panick. All shame of calling in foreigners and savages in a civil contest is worn off. We grow indifferent to the consequences inevitable to ourselves from the plan of ruling half the empire by a mercenary sword. We are taught to believe, that a desire of domineering over our countrymen, is love to our country; that those who hate civil war abet rebellion; and that the amiable and conciliatory virtues of lenity, moderation, and tenderness to the privileges of those who depend on this kingdom, are a sort of treason to the state.

It is impossible that we should remain long in a situation, which breeds such notions and dispositions, without some great alteration in the national character. Those ingenuous and feeling minds, who are so fortified against all other things, and so unarmed to whatever approaches in the shape of disgrace, finding the principles, which they considered as sure means of honour, to be grown into disrepute, will retire disheartened and disgusted. Those of a more robust make, the bold, able, ambitious men, who pay some part of their court to power through the people, and substitute the voice of transient opinion in the place of true glory, will give into the general mode. The superior understandings, which ought to correct vulgar prejudice, will confirm and aggravate its errors. Many things have been long operating towards a gradual change in our principles. But this American war has done more in a very few years than all the other causes could have effected in a century. It is therefore not on its own separate account, but because of its attendant circumstances, that I consider its continuance, or its ending in any way but that of an honourable and liberal accommodation, as the greatest evils which can befal us. For that reason I have troubled you with this long letter. For that reason I intreat you again and again, neither to be perswaded, shamed, or frighted out of the principles that have hitherto led so many of you to abhor the war, its cause, and its consequences. Let us not be amongst the first who renounce the maxims of our forefathers.

> *I have the honour to be,* GENTLEMEN,
> *Your most obedient, and faithful humble Servant,*
> EDMUND BURKE

Beaconsfield, *April* 3, 1777

P.S. You may communicate this Letter in any manner you think proper to my Constituents.

FINIS

Speech on Civil List Debts
16 April 1777

Source: *Parl. Reg.* vi. 83–4

Reprinted in *Parl. Hist.* xix. 125–7. There is a MS. at Sheffield (Bk 14.25) which appears to be a rough draft for this speech.

On 9 April 1777 a message from the King was delivered to the House of Commons asking for help in the payment of debts on the Civil List amounting to more than £600,000.[1] A motion was carried to refer the message to the Committee of Supply on 16 April. This brought strong reaction from the Opposition press in the City of London which generally blamed the arrears on ministerial incompetence, political bribery and corruption, and an unjust war. The 'extraordinary requisition, particularly at a crisis, when the strictest economy is absolutely necessary, to counteract ruinous expences of the desperate war, prosecuting against our fellow subjects in North America' was denounced over and over again.[2]

For Burke and the Rockingham party in general the issue was of special interest. It should be seen as a relatively important step in the development of their economical reform programme in which their primary concern would be to limit the Crown's powers of patronage.[3] Ever since the East India Company affair of 1772–3, the Rockinghams had been attempting to paint themselves

---

[1] For a thorough discussion of the civil list in the eighteenth century, see E. A. Reitan, 'The Civil List in 18th Century British Politics, Parliamentary Supremacy versus the Independence of the Crown', *Historical Journal*, ix (1966), 318–37; 'Edmund Burke and the Civil List 1769–82', *The Burke News Letter*, viii (1966), 604–18; 'The Civil List, 1766–77: Problems of Finance and Administration', *Bulletin of the Institute of Historical Research*, xlvii (1974), 686–701.

[2] *London Evening Post*, 15 April 1777.

[3] See Burke's speech of 15 December 1779 on public expenses, below, pp. 467–76.

to the world as the champions of resistance to the undue influence of the Crown. They considered it not only the foundation of all government corruption but also the reason for the subservience of Parliament and the people to ministerial measures.[1] This issue gave them a perfect opportunity to take that stand, and they were determined not to miss it. On 16 April Rockingham, himself, who had otherwise largely given up challenging the seemingly unbeatable North regime, made a long and impassioned appeal in the House of Lords against 'vesting such large sums without accounts in the hands of Ministers, when an opinion is known to prevail . . . that your Majesty's Civil List revenues are employed in creating undue influence in Parliament'.[2] On the same day Lord John Cavendish moved the discharge of the reference in the House of Commons. Burke spoke on this motion.

Mr. *Burke* was severe upon the noble Lord who spoke last.[3] He said, that the time of bringing in this demand was full of indecency and impropriety; that when we were going to tax every gentleman's house in England, even to the smallest domestic accommodation,[4] and to accumulate burthen upon burthen, nothing but a confidence in the servility of the House, and an experience in our carelessness, with regard to all affairs, could make the ministry desperate enough to tell us, 'tis in such a time we had not provided sufficiently for the splendour of the crown. That the main argument on which the demand stood, was the experience of the whole reign, that 800,000l. was not sufficient for the civil list expences.[5] To this ground of argument he objected; because if it were once admitted, the propriety of every man's practice would be judged by the practice itself; a man's extravagance

---

[1] See W. M. Elofson, 'The Rockingham Whigs in Transition: The East India Company Issue, 1772–3', *English Historical Review*, civ (1989), 947–74.

[2] *London Evening Post*, 17 April 1777.

[3] Lord North.

[4] A new Act, 18 Geo. III, c. 26, would establish a tax 'upon all the inhabited houses within the Kingdom of Great Britain'. This tax was to be more equitable than the one which had been levied since 1428. It was to be assessed not by reference to the hearths or the windows in the house, but upon a rate, this time charged upon the householder by reference to the annual value of the house (S. Dowell, *History of Taxation and Tax in England from the Earliest Times to the Present Day*, 4 vols, London, 1884, i. 119).

[5] By the Civil List Act of 1760 (1 Geo. III, c. 1), a sum of £800,000 had been provided for the annual expenditure of the Crown. This settlement differed from that of 1727 in one important respect. It transferred surpluses on the revenues directed to the Civil List from the King to the Exchequer. In 1727 George II had been permitted to enjoy any surpluses, however much they exceeded the sum of £100,000. In 1769 George III had been compelled to seek parliamentary payment of his debts; by 1777 he was forced to do so once again. Ironically, the arrangement of 1760 had been part of the new regime's demonstration of its public-spiritedness in declining to claim the privilege enjoyed by its predecessor (see vol. ii, pp. 262, 303–8).

would become the measure of his supply, and because he had actually spent a great deal, he ought in reason to be furnished with a great deal to spend. That this would be to establish a principle of public profusion, which could never cease to operate, whilst we had a shilling to spend. That it would even make it the interest of ministers to be prodigal, since their extravagance, instead of lessening their income, would be the certain means of increasing their estate.

Having refuted this kind of argument; taking for granted the very point in question, which was, whether the ministers had managed well or ill; whether they had incurred the debt properly or improperly, he said, that the only way of judging of this matter, was to proceed as wise men ought to do in all their private affairs, viz. to try whether the object obtained was equal to the consideration paid.

The object to be obtained was the royal dignity, the consideration paid was 800,000l. a year. The sum has been paid; has the object been attained? Is the court great, splendid, and magnificent? To know whether the royal dignity might have been attained for that sum, and to discover whether the not obtaining it was owing to the scantiness of the supply, and not to the mismanagement of what was given, it was proper to see how other kings had maintained the royal dignity; what their charge, and what their incomes were. For this purpose, he took a comparative view of the income and stile of living of his present Majesty, and King George the Second, and of King William. That George the Second had a more extensive family for a great part of his reign; that his income was not larger, nor so large, as that of the present King;[1] that he appeared in a more princely manner than the ministers suffered the present King to live. That King William had but 700,000l. a year, yet that all his expences were great and royal; and if it should be objected, that all means of living in splendour were cheaper in that age, he answered, first by doubting the fact, and saying, that though some of the same articles might be cheaper, others were much dearer. Next he said, that this argument of the price of things could serve no purpose in the present question, because King William not

---

[1] Burke is being a little unfair in his comparison of the finances of the two kings. Since George II's reign inflation had made it very difficult to manage on the sums which would have been sufficient in the past. One estimate is that George III needed £1,000,000 per annum in 1780 to match the £800,000 that George II had been guaranteed since 1727. Moreover, at the end of his reign George II's civil list income had considerably exceeded £800,000. The surpluses he had been allowed to keep. George III on the other hand had given up all surpluses in 1760 (Reitan, 'The Civil List in 18th Century British Politics').

only did more, but paid more; that his charges in all articles, in which royal dignity properly consists, were higher than the correspondent articles of the King's expences; larger not only in effect but in account. That King William was censured for being expensive; he was so; but he was magnificent. He attained his object, which appeared in the number and stateliness of his buildings, his furniture, pictures, &c. &c. King George the Second was accused of parsimony, not wholly without reason; but he attained his object, he was rich. His present Majesty, to whom no one imputes either extravagance or penury, is, by the mismanagement of his ministers, neither magnificent nor wealthy. That King William's magnificence was useful to the public; it added to the splendour of the crown and the dignity of the nation, and we have the monuments of it still. King George the Second's œconomy added 170,000l. into his Majesty's civil list at his accession. He did more and better. King George the Second maintained a year's war in Germany, against the whole power of France, in a quarrel wholly British, at his own expence.[1] He spent about a million sterling for this nation, and after all he died not poor, but left a large sum, besides a surplus of civil list cash to his present Majesty.

From all these circumstances he concluded, that the debt incurred could not be for the royal dignity, but in ways not fit to be avowed by ministry, and therefore very fit to be inquired into by this House. He dwelt long upon the above heads, on which, and other topics, as well in answer to the ministerial arguments, as shewing the ill consequence of payments of all debts on the proof of their mere existence.

Lord John Cavendish's motion was defeated by 281 to 114, and the House went into Committee of Supply and resolved to pay the debt and increase the Civil List by £100,000 a year.

---

[1] Presumably during the War of the Austrian Succession. George II personally had led the 'Pragmatic Army' in the Battle of Dettingen in 1743; see R. Lodge, *Great Britain and Prussia in the Eighteenth Century*, Oxford, 1923, p. 44.

Speeches on Civil List Debts
18 April 1777

Sources: *Parl. Reg.* vii. 116, 120; *Public Advertiser*, 21 April 1777

The reports of the first and second speeches are reprinted in *Parl. Hist.* xix. 151–2, 155–6. For these there is no newspaper report. The third speech is in the *Public Advertiser* of 21 April and the *Whitehall Evening Post* of 22 April.

On 18 April the Speaker put the question that the report of the Committee of Supply of 16 April should be received. This was opposed. During the debate John Sawbridge said that the deficiency in the Civil List could be accounted for 'without having recourse to the encreased price of the necessaries of life; it had been employed in corrupting both houses'. The result of this assertion was 'a great confusion'.

Mr. *Burke* rose, and endeavoured to still the uproar, by jocularly observing, that the words "influence the members" and "encrease the influence of the crown" were the current and fashionable expressions used in the former debate, as well as the present, which substantially imported the same with the words which had now given such high offence. For his part, he could see little difference, if any, between influence and corrupt influence; and corrupt influence and downright plain corruption. He confessed however, that the sound of the latter was coarse and impolite, when compared with the former. On this ground therefore, the whole matter might be explained to the entire satisfaction of all parties: those who liked, and those who disliked the word corruption; for though it should be given up by one side, the sense would be still retained, and it would compleatly satisfy such as disapprove of it, that it was to be discarded forever out of the Parliamentary vocabulary. The honourable gentleman was a citizen,[1] and had not attained to that height of polite phraseology, for which such as happily reside at the other end of the town are so justly distinguished; for which reason what a courtier or an inhabitant of the west end of the town called influence, the worthy alderman, according to his gross mode of expression, very improperly called corruption.

Burke spoke later in the debate on the substantive issue before the House.

---

[1] i.e. of London.

Mr. *Burke* entered into a detail of the civil list expenditure; compared it with that of every reign since the revolution, particularly the late reign; and proved from a variety of documents, that the civil list revenue, as it now stood, if properly managed, was amply sufficient to maintain the Royal Household in dignity, splendour, and affluence; and all the expences of the civil government, upon the most generous and liberal scale: from which he drew this natural deduction, that the excess of expenditure arose from a want of œconomy; or was employed to carry into execution a system of bribery and corruption, which had become for several years past the great engine of government in this country. Though it was nine o'clock when he rose, he was heard with great attention.

At the end of the debate Sir James Lowther[1] moved an amendment that the additional £100,000 of the Civil List for the 'better support of his Majesty's Household' should also be used 'for the different branches of the royal family' in reference to the situation of the Dukes of Cumberland and Gloucester.[2]

Mr. Burke expressed his Satisfaction that a Motion should be made for a better Provision than has hitherto been made for his Majesty's Brothers, and that such a Motion could not come with more Propriety than from the first Commoner of England, as he believed the Honourable Member payed more Taxes, from the Extent of his Property, than any other Member of the House.[3] He thought his Majesty was now fully enabled to provide for his Brothers, and that it was a Disgrace to this Country to suffer them to live in Indigence and Obscurity: That Rome was an improper Place for the Princes of the Brunswick Line.[4] He wished however that the Honourable Member would agree with the House to separate the Motion from the Report of the Committee of Supply.

---

[1] 5th Baronet (1736–1802), later (1784) 1st Earl of Lonsdale, M.P. 1757–68, 1769–84.

[2] The King's relationship with his brothers, William Henry, Duke of Gloucester (1743–1805) and Henry Frederick, Duke of Cumberland (1745–90), had been strained since 1772 when the King had become aware that both had entered into controversial marriages. This had helped to prevent the establishment of a satisfactory financial settlement for the Princes and their families. Some Opposition politicians had tended to take the side of the Princes for political reasons (J. Brooke, *King George III*, pp. 272–82).

[3] Lowther's fortune, the accidental amalgamation of the property of three distinct branches of his family, was certainly immense. Whether he paid more taxes than any other M.P. is less certain; the rate of land taxation was extremely low in the north-west, where most of Lowther's property lay. Lowther, an old enemy of the Rockingham party, had been collaborating with them in opposition since 1775 but the relationship was never a very easy one.

[4] The Duke and Duchess of Gloucester had been living at Rome.

Consideration of Lowther's amendment was postponed. The resolution for the payment of the debt was approved; that increasing the Civil List by £100,000 was carried on a division by 231 votes to 109.

Speech on British Museum
28 April 1777

Source: *Parl. Reg.* vii. 131

Reprinted in *Parl. Hist.* xix. 192. Other reports are in *St James's Chronicle*, *General Evening Post*, and *Whitehall Evening Post*, 29 April.

In the Committee of Supply on 28 April Sir Grey Cooper moved for a grant of £3,000 for the British Museum.

Mr. *Burke* observed, that the House had of late shewn a most generous and giving disposition, both of their own, and the public money; probably they remained still in the same good temper. To make a trial of that, he begged leave to amend the honourable gentleman's motion, and instead of 3,000l. insert 5,000l. Parliament had been liberal of late, not of single thousands, or hundreds of thousands, but millions, granted for slaying their brethren and fellow-subjects in America; and surely they would not be more backward to encourage and protect the liberal and polite arts, than to forward the destruction of their species, and effect all those horrid mischiefs which are the inevitable consequences of civil war.

John Wilkes seconded Burke's motion, but the proposal of Sir Grey Cooper was carried by 74 votes to 60.

Speech on Birmingham Playhouse Bill
29 April 1777

Source: *General Evening Post*, 1 May 1777

Another report is in the *Public Advertiser*, 1 May and *Lloyd's Evening Post*, 2 May and was reprinted in *Parl. Reg.* vii. 140–1 and *Parl. Hist.* xix. 202–3. A briefer report is in *Morning*

Chronicle, 1 May. A pamphlet report of the debate (*A Full and Authentic Account of what passed in the House of Commons on the Second Reading of the Birmingham Playhouse Bill*) conflates, for Burke's speech, the reports of the *General Evening Post* and *Morning Chronicle*.

Opponents of the Birmingham Playhouse Bill persuaded some of Burke's Bristol constituents to bring pressure on their M.P. to vote against the Bill. Burke decided to yield to this pressure on the second reading of the Bill.[1]

Mr. Burke spoke in a very liberal and handsome manner respecting Mr. Yates and the profession of an actor; he said that the disappointment of not having a petition granted, was to any man sufficiently mortifying, without having the additional misfortune of being treated harshly, and sent from Parliament with a worse opinion of himself than he had entertained before his application. He justified Mr. Yates for having applied, and declared that there was no impropriety in his conduct on the occasion; that he had, as appeared from the evidence heard at the bar, proceeded on a supposition, that his application was agreeable to the majority of the inhabitants of Birmingham; that he believed Mr. Yates had been mistaken, and therefore he should now vote against the Bill; but that Mr. Yates was not at all censurable for his mistake, nor did his application deserve the epithets that had been given it; that every Member was liable to such a mistake, when he declared himself a Candidate for a seat in Parliament; and that when a gentleman presented a petition against a sitting Member, it was not to be deemed a petition against the opinion of the majority of the electors, for that every man, by the very act of applying to Parliament, presumed the majority was in his favour: this clearly had been the case with Mr. Yates, and there surely could be nothing deserving of blame in his asking legislature to legitimate that entertainment, which not only almost every Member of the House admired, but which the inhabitants of Birmingham had, as it appeared, encouraged for a series of years. Mr. Burke dwelt a considerable time on the profession of actors, and lamented exceedingly that in consequence of a severe and an ill-judged act, passed in barbarous times, and founded on a false enthusiasm, men of a profession so liberal and noble as that of an Actor, should be disgraced with epithets by no means applicable to Englishmen, in almost any station, much less[2] to men who essentially contributed to the reformation of manners, and to the rational entertainment of the

---

[1] *Corr.* iii. 335–6; P. T. Underdown, 'Religious Opposition to Licensing the Bristol and Birmingham Theatres', *University of Birmingham Historical Journal*, vi (1958), 149–60.
[2] 'less' supplied from *Morning Chronicle* report.

public.[1] He gave his opinion strongly in favour of Theatres, but declared, that as he thought it extremely hard to measure other mens inclinations by his own habits and passions, and as he understood the majority of the town of Birmingham were against having a licensed Theatre, he must, though contrary to his own wish, vote against the motion.

In the course of Mr. Burke's speech he was extremely witty on Sir William Baggot's calling Birmingham a village;[2] he said it was a *chopping* village, and quoted the speech of Major Oldfox in Wycherly's Plain-Dealer, to the Widow Blackacre, where she calls her tall son, Jerry, her *minor*.[3]—Mr. Burke also took occasion to aim a stroke at modern politics, observing, that one man had formerly boasted of converting small villages into great towns,[4] and wishing that he might not live to see the day when great towns were reduced to little villages.

The Bill was defeated by 69 votes to 18.

Notes for Speech on Capital Punishment
[*ante* 14 May 1777]

Source: MS. at Sheffield, Bk 8.200

The occasion for which Burke made these notes is uncertain. The reference to 'John the Painter' makes a debate on the Bill for Better Securing of Dockyards a possibility—a Bill presented on 18 March 1777, but abandoned after it had been ordered to be engrossed on 14 May. Burke moved for leave to bring in the Bill on 13 March—'apologizing to the House and the public for being instrumental in increasing our criminal laws'[5]—and spoke on its commitment on 13 May.[6] The speech itself provides another excellent

---

[1] Actors had been classed as rogues, vagabonds, and sturdy beggars in 39 Eliz. I, c. 4.

[2] Bagot had remarked, 'that Birmingham was a village; that it had, for the industry & abilities of the inhabitants grown into a large town; its glory, however, was in its village situation, and he wished to retain it; he wanted not to see it ornamented with any royal trinkets, no royal charters, no royal incorporation, no royal theatres' (*Parl. Hist.* xix. 199).

[3] See *The Complete Plays of William Wycherley*, ed. G. Weales, New York, 1966, pp. 404 ff.

[4] i.e. Bagot.

[5] *St James's Chronicle*, 15 March 1777.

[6] See L. Radzinowicz, *A History of the English Criminal Law and its Administration from 1760*, 4, vols., London, 1948–68, i. 473–6.

example of Burke's respect for tradition (i.e. 'the antient Law and institutions of our Country') working in conjunction with his concern for humanity and civilized standards.

If I thought that capital punishments, were the only sure mode of preventing Crimes, no misplaced Lenity should make me step between the *Life* of an offender; and the safety of the *innocent*.

But if we know anything by experience it is; that *capital* punishments are not more certain to prevent Crimes than *inferior* penalties; and then, when we use punishments which are at *once heavy and ineffectual*, we incur a reproach upon our *Wisdom*, without any excuse from our *humanity*.

great difference in this Case between repealing an *old Law*—and making a *new* one.

The Crime in itself may deserve that punishment abstractedly speaking.

But the question now is, whether the Law of the Land, *not* having made that Offence capital, we have so strong and urgent a reason as to make us depart from the *Classes* of Crimes which the antient Law and institutions of our Country have fixed by encreasing the Number of Capital punishments.

The mischiefs which have happend already from disordering them. Whenever an inferior offence is once raised to an higher penalty; it becomes a reason for raising all others and on this Analogy all Crimes will become Capital. This Act grounded on that reasoning—Cabbages Turnips—

eternal differences
injury to person and to property
To an house that guards person and property.

All the mistake here—that we suppose the Gallows the only force; and what is not guarded by Capital punishment is abandon'd—

John the Painter[1] committed almost every species of capital Offense.

---

[1] James Aitken (1752–77)—'John the Painter'—was tried, convicted, and executed on 10 March 1777 for arson at Portsmouth. He was also guilty of causing a serious fire at Bristol (*Corr.* iii. 320–1, 324, 325–7).

Speeches on African Slave Trade
5 June 1777

Sources: *Parl. Reg.* vii. 260, 262–3; *London Chronicle,* 7 June 1777

The first two of Burke's speeches on 5 June 1777 relative to the African slave trade, are transcribed below from *Parl. Reg.* They are also recorded in *Parl. Hist.* xix. 315. The third speech is taken from the *London Chronicle.* Versions of the speeches are also reported in *Gazetteer, Lloyd's Evening Post,* and *Public Advertiser,* 6 June; and *General Evening Post, Morning Chronicle,* and *Westminster Evening Post,* 7 June.

The following speeches provide a record of Burke's second public criticism of the slave trade during the 1774–80 Parliament. Even though Burke supported the African Company itself, the fact that he disliked the trade, and that this was recorded in the newspapers, must have done his cause some damage among many Bristol constituents who were either involved in the trade or who, as businessmen, supported it just as they would virtually any commercial activity. The first time Burke had criticized the trade had been during his first speech on conciliation with America when he had briefly referred to it as 'that inhuman traffick'.[1] In the last of the following speeches he seems rather to have equivocated (ostensibly out of concern for his constituents' views)[2] before directly attacking the trade. The *London Evening Post,* 7 June, noted that Burke 'as an advocate for liberty, appeared somewhat awkward in the fetters, which he actually put on, as well as in the defence of the use of them'.

At the time Burke made his speeches the Commons was involved in an enquiry into the management of the Company of Merchant Adventurers trading to Africa as a result of charges that, among other things, it was using its annual grants from Parliament to maintain a monopoly.[3] On 5 June North successfully attempted to end the enquiry by presenting a motion that the usual 'sum of 13,000l. . . . be issued to the African Company, for the maintenance of their garrisons, and . . . forts, &c. on the coast of Africa'. Burke replied to attacks on the company and its servants by Temple Simon Luttrell.[4]

Mr. *Burke* spoke in favour of the African committee, and defended the conduct of the Company's affairs in general, and the necessity of granting them a still farther parliamentary aid.

Mr. *Burke.* I shall not follow the honourable gentleman in the detail he has given of what might be done; I believe he is very right in a part of what he has told, but I can by no means agree with him, or with any man, that the servants of the Company have behaved themselves wrong;

---

[1] See above, p. 131.   [2] *Corr.* iii. 340–2, 345–6.
[3] See *Parl. Hist.* xix. 291–313.   [4] (?1738–1803), M.P. 1775–80.

instead of having been wanting in œconomy, they have excerted such an œconomy as this House has not been used to; they have supported eleven forts, ten governors, and the establishments necessary for them, and treaties with the country powers; yet with all this, they are not accusd of contracting a greater debt in so many years than 16,000l.

Mr. *Gascoyne*[1] seemd to rejoice at Mr. Burke's mentioning the debt as 16,000l. and ridiculed the idea of the servants being such faithful ones while contracting such a debt.

Mr. *Burke* retorted upon Mr. Gascoyne's speaking in the stile of accusation, when he was the judge, which he said was such a perversion of the distinctions of judge, jury, and party, that he congratulated his feelings on it. "Nature had made him the accuser, an Act of Parliament the judge;[2] but I hope the gentleman is not my accuser: I thank my God he is not my judge."

Mr. *Hartley*[3] went upon the cruelties of slavery, and urging the Board of Trade to take some means of mitigating it; he produced a pair of hand-cuffs, which he said was a manufacture they were now going to establish. . . .

Mr. Burke did not disapprove Mr. Luttrell's motion,[4] but he still defended the present management of the company's affairs, and with respect to Mr. Hartley's notions about slavery, he observed, that he had brought a convincing proof in his hand of the hardships of it, and it certainly was a proper object of enquiry, whether it might not be softened; but Africa, time out of mind, had been in a state of slavery, therefore the inhabitants only changed one species of slavery for another; however, he was sorry to say, that in changing from African to European slavery, they generally changed much for the worse, which certainly was a matter of reproach somewhere, and deserved serious consideration.

[1] Bamber Gascoigne (1725–91), M.P. 1761–3, 1765–8, 1770–86.
[2] Gascoyne was a member of the Commission for Trade and Plantations, which had laid before the House a report critical of the African Company.
[3] David Hartley.
[4] Luttrell had called upon Parliament to request 'a general information'.

Speech on Address on King's Speech
20 November 1777

Source: *London Evening Post*, 22 November 1777

This is the report also to be found in *Parl. Reg.* viii. 18–19 and *Parl. Hist.* xix. 431. In both cases it is incorrectly dated 18 November. The same report is in *St James's Chronicle* and *General Evening Post* of 22 November, but truncated. A different and substantial report is in the *Morning Post* of 22 November and *Morning Chronicle*, and *Lloyd's Evening Post*, 24 November. The *Public Advertiser* has three brief reports in its issues of 21, 22, and 24 November. MSS. at Sheffield (Bk 6.63, 6.113) appear to be rough drafts for this speech.

Just prior to the beginning of the 1777–8 session of Parliament many in Britain had started to realize that victory in America was not close at hand. This seemed to a degree to justify the Rockinghams' years of opposition to the conflict. Those 'who have always abominated the violent measures against America', the Marquess told Burke, 'are not looked upon with quite so angry eyes, as they were some time ago.'[1] Still, for a period, this brought little new life or enthusiasm to a party which had opted for much of the previous session to withdraw from the parliamentary arena. News of the major defeats at Philadelphia and Saratoga had not yet arrived,[2] and Rockingham himself felt unsure that reports from overseas would continue to be bad. 'I am very apt to believe', he continued in the same letter, 'that if any thing, like what is called *good news* from America should come, the generality of the publick will be ready to relapse and begin again to entertain *hopes*'. Thus Burke found himself forced once more to urge activity from an aristocratic leadership whose natural inclination was to avoid it. When Howe's victory over Washington at the Brandywine was reported he told Rockingham 'as the few who are not to be moved, want comfort; it will be necessary not to carry the appearance of too much despondency; but to appear to be doing something, lest they should conclude, perhaps sooner than they ought, that nothing can be done.'[3] Finally after much dithering and after considerable coaxing from Burke and others[4] the Marquess, the Duke of Portland, and their friends began slowly to make the trek to the capital.

The King's Speech at the start of the new session offered no hope of an early end to the war, nor did the Address moved in response to it. The Opposition submitted an amendment demanding a cessation of hostilities and some attempt at an accommodation with the rebels. Burke spoke after Lord North had replied to some of the points raised in the debate.

Mr. Burke replied to his Lordship, and expressed a great concern that the matters urged by so many respectable members as spoke before him, should be treated so lightly, and took a very proper opportunity

[1] *Corr.* iii. 392.   [2] Ibid. 405, 406.
[3] Ibid. 399.   [4] Ibid. 398–9.

of complimenting the several honourable persons we have already mentioned,[1] and ridiculed the haughtiness of the Minister in terms of the most pointed satire. If the shortness of time did not prevent us, we should be happy to give the detail of a speech, which, in the course of two hours, commanded the attention, excited the laughter, and some times drew tears from the sympathising few who were not hardened by prejudice in the sentiments of any party. We shall omit all those changes of ridicule which were rung by his ingenuity upon the defence which Lord North made in answer to the charge against General Burgoyne's proclamation.[2] We are obliged to pass over his unanswerable proofs of the *futility*, not to say the *injury* of our conquests in the Colonies, and touch only on that pathetic supplication which he made to the House, to seize the present happy moment to attempt an accommodation, when neither elated with *insolent victory*, nor debased with *abject defeat*, we could with honour to ourselves make such proposals to our colonists, as they could, without dishonours accept. He apostrophised with a degree of honest enthusiasm upon the noble spirit of MEN, who, *if they had not been rebels*, he could have been lavish in praising; of WOMEN who, reduced by the ruin of civil discord, to the most horrible situation of distress and poverty, had constancy, generosity, and public spirit, to strip the blankets, in a freezing season, from themselves and their infants, to send to the camp, and preserve that army which they had sent out to fight for their liberty. And shall Britons, said he, overlook such virtue? and will they persist in oppressing it? Shall we give them no alternative but UNCONDITIONAL SUBMISSION? A three years war has not terrified them, distressed as they are, from their great purpose. Let us try the power of lenity over those generous bosoms. To follow him all through, we must have omitted the rest of the debate and to do him justice would be impossible.

The amendment was defeated by 243 votes to 86.

---

[1] The amendment to the Address had been moved by Charles Manners, styled Marquess of Granby (1754–87), M.P. 1774–9, and seconded by Lord John Cavendish. George Johnstone (1730–87), M.P. 1768–84, 1786–7, John Wilkes, Frederick Bull (*c.*1714–84), M.P. 1773–84, Lord Mayor of London 1773–4, Sir Philip Jennings Clerke (1772–88), M.P. 1768–88, and James Adair (?1743–98), M.P. 1775–80, 1793–8, had spoken for it.

[2] See *Parl. Reg.* viii. 17–18 for Lord North's speech, and below, p. 358, for Burgoyne's proclamation.

Speech on Fox's Motion
2 December 1777

Source: *General Advertiser*, 4 December 1777

This report, also in *London Evening Post*, 6 December, is followed by *Parl. Reg.* viii. 77–9 and *Parl. Hist.* xix. 515–17.

On 2 December 1777 Charles Fox moved that the House should resolve itself into a Committee of the Whole House on 2 February 1778 'to consider the state of the nation'. This was agreed to. He then moved for papers. Lord North opposed:

He said he must object to it from the reason that papers produced during the existence of a negotiation, if any had taken place, must be very injurious to the cause. He was ready and willing to grant every reasonable information in his power; but he could not consent that discoveries should be made prejudicial to government, and to the true interests of this country.

Mr. Burke observed, that he never heard the noble Lord (Lord North) behave with so much candour, generosity, and spirit, as to-day; he had agreed to every tittle of his friend's request; he had published a bond wherein he granted all; but in the end was inserted a little defeasance, with a power of revocation, by which he preserved himself from the execution of every grant he had made. His conduct, he said, reminded him of a certain Governor, who, when he arrived at his place of appointment, sat down to a table covered with profusion, and abounding with every dainty and delicacy that art, nature, and a provident steward could furnish; but a pigmy Physician, who watched over the health of the Governor, excepted to one dish, because it was disagreeable; to another because it was hard of digestion; to a third, because it was unhealthy; and in this progressive mode[1] robbed the Governor of every dish on table, and left him without a dinner.[2] He answered minutely the arguments of Mr. Stanley,[3] exposed the folly of the idea, that we must not negociate with the Americans until they had renounced their claim of independance. Are they not, he observed, in possession? are they not independent *de facto*? They possess the

---

[1] *General Advertiser*: 'made'.
[2] *Parl. Reg.* adds: 'alluding to Cervantes humorous account of Sancho Panza, in his government of Barataria' (*Don Quixote*, Book 11, chap. xlvii).
[3] Hans Stanley (1721–80), M.P. 1743–7, 1757–80; he had urged the impossibility of negotiating with armed rebels who demanded independence.

whole country of America. What we have, we have gained by arms. If we have a Government in America, it is founded upon conquest since they set up their independance; and as they enjoy the right, *de facto*, and we alone *de jure*, we must and ought to treat with them on the terms of a foederal union. He instanced the supposition of a treaty with France. The King of Britain enjoys the right de jure to the Kingdom of France.[1] The French King enjoys it *de facto*; he is merely a Congress usurper; and yet would it be argued, that no treaty of peace could take place with him until he had renounced his claim. He begged to have leave to consider the effects that would arise from a renunciation of their independance. By renouncing their independance, they acknowledged their rebellion, by acknowledging their rebellion, they acknowledged their crime; by their crime they were deprived of their rights, and obnoxious to punishment. In[2] such case, no conciliation nor treaty could be made consistent with the honour of the British name; so that terms of negociation must be entered into during their independance. He said that the act on which Lord and Sir William Howe were vested with their commissions, proposes two methods to be prosecuted to bring about a peace; the one by force of arms, and the other by terms of conciliation.[3] It would be necessary, he said, to inquire if both these methods had been practised; the first he was sensible, and all must know had been indeed practised, but he was afraid the second had not, else why were not New York, Staten and Long Islands, with any other territory we are in possession of, restored to the King's peace. Governor Tryon, he said, had written to General Howe for the purpose of restoring New York to the King's peace. General Howe answered that he could not do it without the concurrence of the Secretary of State, and there it stopped.[4] This, he hoped, would be particularly inquired into. He made several other defences of the propriety of his honourable friend's motion, and

[1] Since the Hundred Years War the Kings of England and Great Britain had included the Kingdom of France among their titles.

[2] *General Advertiser*: 'I'sn'.

[3] The Prohibitory Act prohibited trade with the thirteen colonies on the one hand and gave the King power, on the other, to appoint commissioners able to grant pardons and issue proclamations for the purpose of conciliation.

[4] On 13 December 1775, Tryon had written to Howe, 'the spirit of rebellion in this colony especially the city of New York is abated, and we now wait only for five thousand regulars in this critical moment to open our commerce and restore our valuable constitution' (*Documents of the American Revolution, 1770–1783*, ed. Davies, xi. 210). On 11 January 1776 Howe replied that he could not at present send the troops or arms (ibid. x. 189).

concluded with saying, that he hoped his friend would not depart from a tittle of his proposition.

The motion for papers was defeated by 178 votes to 89.

Speech on Subscriptions
22 January 1778

Sources: *General Advertiser*, 23 January 1778; *Parl. Reg.* viii. 259–62

The report in *General Advertiser*, 23 January, differs slightly at the beginning from *Parl. Reg.* and has a curtailed conclusion. The text printed here follows first the *General Advertiser* and then *Parl. Reg. Parl. Hist.* xix. 617–20 reproduces *Parl. Reg.* Burke made a second speech in the debate which is reported in *Parl. Reg.* viii. 268. Other reports are in *Gazetteer*, 23 and 24 January; *Craftsman*, 24 January; *Morning Chronicle*, 24 January; *Morning Post*, 23 January; *General Evening Post*, 24 January; *Whitehall Evening Post*, 24 January; and *Public Advertiser*, 23 January.

On 10 December the House of Commons had adjourned for six weeks; the adjournment, coming soon after news of Burgoyne's surrender at Saratoga, and in a plainly deteriorating situation, was strongly opposed by Burke and other opponents of the ministry. When the recess ended Sir Philip Jennings Clerke moved for an address requesting information about the intense military recruitment which had proceeded while Parliament was up. His motion was substantially approved, and Lord North informed the House of the subscription 'lately set on foot in several parts of the kingdom' to raise forces for the Crown.

Mr. Burke expatiated, with pointed severity, on the *zeal* of the noble Lord, and the *warmth* and ardour of his bosom for the public weal.

He supposed it to be that *zeal*, warmth, and ardour, that had induced him to *assist*, if not to *devise*, the raising of men without the knowledge of Parliament, and by that means acting *unconstitutionally* for the *good* of his country. He remembered that the noble Lord voted for an adjournment of Parliament for six weeks, for two several reasons; the one, to give him an opportunity of digesting an equitable plan of conciliation, founded on concession; and the other, to guard him from being shot through and through with the long arrows of militant opposition. It had turned out, he said, however, that another more substantial reason existed for the adjournment of Parliament—not of contriving propositions of peace, but of securing force towards war, in an illegal, unconstitutional, and extravagant way.

He observed on the present crisis of Britain, that it was lamentable in the extreme. He said, he had the same day examined the state of our funds, and found that the three per cents consolidated stood at $71\frac{1}{4}$; and he begged leave to contrast that with the state of the same fund in January 1760, the fifth year of a war with the united House of Bourbon, when they were 79. In the latter instance they were 79, when we had funded 23,000,000l[1] and in the first they are 71, when we have funded 5,000,000l.[2] He continued to observe on the present mode of raising supplies, that he would consider its propriety in two separate points of view; 1st, whether it was in respect of expence the most œconomical; and 2dly, whether it was in respect of strength, the most effectual. He considered the first expence of raising a regiment to be about 5,000l. So much we receive, supposing that the supplies flow from the voluntary gift of the subscribers. They are embodied in separate corps, habited, maintained for the war, discharged, and placed upon the half pay list, all which, calculating the amount of halfpay at ten years purchase, would cost us 30,000l. so that we in reality received 60,000l. as there are 16 regiments offered, to pay 480,000. That this is œconomy worthy the people who contrived it he was well convinced; the offer received was a seeming advantage, but an actual loss; for where there [was] ever occasion for multiplying the supplies granted by Parliament, it was most œconomical to raise[3] them in separate corps, while the battalions already raised want more than one half of their war establishments, as it brings a double charge of officers both on full and half pay, which charge constitutes the expence, amounting, as said before, to 30,000l. for each 5,000l. So far as to the *œconomy*. As to the *efficacy*, he would only observe, that in our former wars, it was held prudent and expedient to advance the battalions from their peace to their war establishment, which was nearly double, mingling thereby the new with the veteran troops, and adding to the strength of the one the experience of the other. This, he said, was the practice of former

---

[1] *General Advertiser:* ' l.'
[2] For statistics on the funded debt, see B. R. Mitchell and P. Deane, *Abstract of British Historical Statistics*, Cambridge, 1962, p. 402, and on the price of 3 per cent consolidated stock, see Sir John Sinclair, *The History of the Public Revenue of the British Empire*, London, 1790, repr. 1970, Appendix, pp. 58, 63, where the price is given as 82 in January 1760 (79 in June 1759) and 72 in January 1778.
[3] *General Advertiser:* 'raise arise'.

times; it was so done last war, and, as we were crown'd with conquest, he would not believe that it was wrong, nor would he adopt any other mode[1] in preference to it. He observed, that of all the expedients used by a *skillful*[2] ministry towards redeeming public credit, none was ever more truly deserving of attention, or more worthy of applause, than the present. A charitable subscription was begun for the relief of the distressed American prisoners,[3] and the Ministry nobly caught at the contrivance, envied the small contributions made to relieve the distress themselves had occasioned, and opened the strings and the mouth of a subscription bag for the Treasury. Convinced as they were, that the country would no longer be induced by interest, to hazard their money in subscribing towards loans, secured by government, they applied to their benevolence, and, like a beggar asking a boon, received charitable donations from the pity-disposed people of this country. He said the noble Lord in the blue ribbon reminded him of *Pericles*, who, exhausted with misfortune, wasted with disease, and lingering with pain, walked abroad, bedecked with amulets, charms, and saws of old women.[4] The loan now unfilled up and unpaid, was his disease; and the charitable contributions of his friends were his amulets and charms.[5] He was ready to grant, that voluntary donations might be fairly interpreted, as proofs of a people's affection, but they were no less so of their real poverty. Private and public life exhibited pregnant proofs, that solicitations on one hand, or benevolences on the other, were the common effects of pride, poverty and pity. Persons might be mean from choice, naked from madness; but rags discovered an involuntary madness, or a poverty willing to be concealed. It was true, that France, during the late war, in the midst of her national distresses, was assisted by the people, who delivered their plate for the public service.[6] This was a glorious instance of national patriotism, but it was likewise a proof of national poverty. The mention of the last war must recal to the ideas of every person present, the most disagreeable and humiliating ideas, and fill the House, as well as nation, with regret. He

---

[1] *General Advertiser*: 'modde'.   [2] *General Advertiser*: 'skilful'.

[3] In which the Opposition was prominent (*Corr.* iii. 411).

[4] Burke extends Plutarch, *Pericles*, xxxviii.

[5] The *General Advertiser* closes: 'He concluded with several observations on the futility of the plans before adopted towards the *reduction* and the impotence of this new measure, avowedly adopted, as the Minister had said, for the conciliation of America.'

[6] See the *Annual Register* for 1759, p. 55.

then contrasted the state of this country at present, and the period alluded to, in the most striking point of view; and said, what added a particular aggravation to the nature of our misfortunes was, that every wicked, weak, or blundering measure was sanctioned under the name of the constitution; every thing that was transacted in Parliament, cabinet, or elsewhere, was sheltered under that venerable name. The use this word was lately employed in, brought to his recollection, Dean Swift's application of Whitshed, a prostitute Irish crown lawyer's motto on his coach, *libertas et natale solum*, which would be applied by every man according to his own ideas, or as his interests led him.[1] Just so with the noble Lord; the idea annexed to the word *constitution* by him was very different to its true import in a limited monarchy. He might mention it as often as he pleased, and ring the changes upon constitution, constitutional, etc. but he might as well vainly expect that his garter would preserve him from the gout, or his ribbon expel a fever, as to imagine, that to prostitute the word *constitution*, would prevent an investigation into his conduct at some future period.

The papers supplied to the House as a result of the motion revealed that the equivalent of twelve regiments of volunteers had been raised, one in Wales, nine in Scotland, and two from Liverpool and Manchester.

Petition for Bristol
[January 1778]

Source: MS. at Sheffield, Bk 16.1–2

The MS. is in Zouch's hand and endorsed by Burke: 'Bristol Subscription for the American War'. There is an earlier version in Zouch's hand with extensive corrections and additions by Burke (MS. at Sheffield, Bk 16.7–9). It can be dated by the subscription movement which was launched in early 1778.

On 19 January a meeting was held in Bristol which decided to raise a subscription 'to strengthen the hands of Government'.[2] Apparently a good deal of enthusiasm was displayed as some £14,000 was raised in less than a

[1] The motto ('Liberty and my native country') of William Whitshed (c.1656–1727), Lord Chief Justice of the King's Bench of Ireland, was commented on by Swift in the *Drapier's Letters* and 'Whitshed's Motto on his Coach'.
[2] J. Latimer, *The Annals of Bristol in the Eighteenth Century*, Bristol, 1893, pp. 431–2.

half hour.[1] Burke, who spoke in the House against subscriptions, presumably composed this petition in order to demonstrate that many in the city opposed the war effort. No use was made of it.

To the Honourable the Commons of Great Britain in Parliament Assembled.

The humble Petition of several of the Merchants, Traders, Freeholders and Freemen of the City of Bristol and others.

Most humbly Sheweth

That your Petitioners, though not without an early and anxious foreboding of the Calamities of the present unhappy Civil War, (which they earnestly but fruitlessly deprecated, at the Bar of this Honourable House,[2] and at the foot of the Throne[3]) find at this day with inexpressible grief, that their worst apprehensions have fallen Short of the real distresses which that War has brought upon their Country. If they are not permitted to lament that part of the suffering which has fallen to the share of the English Race in America, it will, they most humbly hope, be looked upon as no mark of disaffection if they dutifully express their Sense of what they endure themselves.

It is in various ways announced to the people, that his Majesties Government is under great difficulties. In consequence, or under pretext thereof, projects are set on foot in this City, and in other places, as obviously inadequate to the relief of the present distress, as they conceive they will be found irreconcileable to the principles of the Law and Constitution of this Kingdom.

Your Petitioners do not look upon themselves to be of Ability for entering into the Subtilties of positive Law;—but there are certain broad and obvious principles of the Constitution, which, as they are not above their Comprehension, or remote from their Interest, they hold themselves bound to understand, to love, and to assert.

Among those principles they humbly conceive this to be fundamental; that the House of Commons has within this Realm the Sole and exclusive Right of granting Supplies, either compulsory[4] or Voluntary, to the Crown, for the raising or maintenance of Military forces, or for any other purpose of Government.

[1] *London Chronicle*, 22 January 1778.
[2] Presented on 23 January 1775.
[3] See Bristol petition of 27 September 1775, above, pp. 175–7.
[4] MS.: 'cumpulsory'.

If the house of Lords, for whose most respectable body your Petitioners entertain the highest reverence, has not a right even to originate a grant of Money to the Crown, (as your Petitioners, part of the Commons of England, for themselves assert and claim that they have not) much less can any combination of private Men have a Title to supercede the Authority, and usurp the functions of this Honourable House, so as to Vote Money to his Majesty to be disposed of as to his Majesty's Wisdom shall seem fit.[1] How much may be allowed to the urgent strong necessities of a Rebellion raging within the Kingdom, or of an actual or[2] imminent invasion from abroad your Petitioners will not undertake to determine, but they are perswaded, that such a practice without such a cause, may establish a precedent subversive of the very being of Parliament, from whose Authority it is in all cases a considerable derogation. Your Petitioners therefore humbly beg leave to clear themselves to this Honourable House of any Share whatsoever in this most dangerous and unconstitutional practice; and they complain thereof to this Honourable House, as of a publick Grievance.

That your Petitioners entertaining the greatest Reverence for the Wisdom by which the Constitution of Parliament was framed, are fully convinced, that as no other body is competent to, so no other is capable of its high and important functions. No other is in a situation to judge of the publick wants, of the Supply which they require; the special Services to which that Supply is to be directed; and the measure and proportion in which it ought to be distributed—No other has the means to detect or the power to punish fraud, abuse, and[3] misapplication; or to prevent the appearance of pretended want, or delusive opulence; deceptions which are always scandalous, and may be frequently mischievous to Government. The unenlightened officiousness of private Zeal may even injure the service it means to promote. We wish it may not be found, that Ideas of a Standard Price of enlisting, excited by the enormous Bounties now given will continue when the miserable resource of private Subscriptions has passed away

---

[1] This statement might be compared to that Burke was to make in his *Third Letter on a Regicide Peace* published posthumously in 1797. 'My opinion', he was to write, 'is that publick contributions ought only to be raised by the publick will. By the judicious form of our constitution, the publick contribution is in it's name and substance a grant. In it's origin it is truly voluntary; not voluntary, according to the irregular, unsteady, capricious will of individuals, but according to the will and wisdom of the whole popular mass, in the only way in which will and wisdom can go together' (vol. ix, p. 351.).

[2] The 'or' is supplied from the earlier version.

[3] The 'and' is in the earlier version; the MS. has 'or'.

with the delusions which have given rise to it; and thus leave the publick charged with an heavy and lasting usury[1] for a precarious and short-lived supply.

Your Petitioners have borne with silence, and submission, the Burthen of accumulated Taxes, on a Trade reduced in Demand limited in its objects, and wasted by Captures; and they wish to collect, what they are sure they shall want, all the strength which self-denial, frugality, and patient fortitude can furnish, to bear the much greater which are unavoidably imminent. They have seen with the same reverential silence in the midst of so expensive a War, instead of any reduction, very large additions made to the charge of Ordinary Government; they have also seen the great Revenue of the Customs of England decrease five hundred thousand pounds, (about one fifth of its Net produce) in a Single year.[2] They have seen profitable Loans, the former Objects of desire and competition become a Load upon the Subscriber. Yet in this State of disgraceful War, harassed Trade, and prostrate Credit, they have never chosen to trouble the House with their griefs and apprehensions, untill they saw, at the expence of the very foundation of Parliament, attempts made, and encouraged by authority, to form a Test of Zeal in favour of the very cause of all our miseries.

Instead of these vain devices suggested, by what they are meant to cover, the great Indiscretion and Mismanagement of executive Government, we trust we demonstrate our Zeal for our Country with more propriety, by flying for succour to the collected and constitutional Wisdom of the Nation—most humbly imploring, that you will enquire by what management our resources are become so short, as to call for such irregular and unparliamentary Aids? Upon what conception or representation of the Temper, Intentions, and strength of the British Colonies we have been animated to this War? Upon what solidity of principle we have been engaged in it? With what sagacity the difficulties attending it have been foreseen? And by what provident Care they have been anticipated and Lightened?[3] What previous

---

[1] Zouch had difficulty with this word. In the earlier version it appears as 'army'. Burke rewrote the passage. Zouch then read it as 'injury'. Burke appears to have intended 'usury'.

[2] Burke is correct in stressing the loss of trade and revenues to the mother country. The annual average value of exports to the thirteen colonies dropped from £1,825,000 in the 1766–70 period to £264,000 in the 1776–80 period. Imports fell from an annual average of £1,452,000 in the 1771–5 period to £35,000 in the 1776–80 period (E. Schumpeter, *English Overseas Trade Statistics, 1697–1808*, Oxford, 1960, pp. 17–18).

[3] 'and Lightened' is from the earlier version.

security was provided for our Trade whilst that of our Colonies was given to Sailors as the Spoil of War? What plans have been pursued for carrying on that War with Success? And what Measures have been taken for ending it with Security and Advantage? From such an Enquiry impartially, faithfully and diligently pursued by you, and not by a wild Zeal for War, regardless of means and consequences, in us the affairs of this Nation may possibly[1] be saved from the last ill Effects of the measures which have been pursued.

Any appearance on the part of your Petitioners of Unanimity, for the purpose of supporting imbecility in power, and delusion in Credit, can have no other Effect than to sink the Errors of Administration in the Madness of the people; to disculpate others by criminating ourselves; and to make us appear the Authors or Abettors of the Measures under which we suffer.

Resting in the most unreserved confidence in the Wisdom and Justice of this Honourable House, and with Hearts touched with the miserable waste and slaughter of our more immediate Countrymen indicated by[2] the strained Efforts which have occasioned this Petition. Your Petitioners do most humbly and fervently supplicate this House, that it will be pleased to interpose its healing Mediation and powerful Assistance in Aid of his Majesties Clemency and goodness, to enable him to restore peace to us all. Your Petitioners are perswaded, that Humanity has always *some* degree of Policy in it; that its Errors are always the most light, the most pardonable, and the most retrievable. It is the excuse of your Petitioners for presuming to hope, that the Terms of Peace will be such, as you have solid reason to believe will be effectual for that one great End—Terms calculated, not for justifying a continuance, but for substantially putting an End to the Calamities of War—Not for dividing the Colonies amongst themselves, but for uniting them in affection and interest with the Mother Country. Experiments for Treaties of Peace (as we were informd) for collateral purposes have been tried already, and the Issue has not furnished any good reason for repeating them.[3]

Your Petitioners, with whom (as a part of the publick) no pains have

---

[1] 'Possibly' is from the earlier version.

[2] Zouch could not read this sentence: 'immediate' and 'indicated', for which gaps are left, have been supplied from the earlier version.

[3] Offers to persuade individual colonies to come to terms had produced no significant response.

[been] spared in other respects, have never been given to understand, how any difference between (what are called) the highest and Lowest Terms, upon which the British Nation can be restored to concord, can possibly compensate to this Kingdom the duration of a War, which every moment of its continuance tends to carry our Colonies further from us and nearer to our Rival Nations.

Your Petitioners hold the most successful Termination of the War to be that which is most effectual to keep the Colonies and us from the last and most ruinous of all Calamities,[1] a discontented People under an Armed Government. They hold that those are the best Terms of Peace, which promise the soonest to bring on, and the longest to preserve affection, confidence, and mutual interest, which produce a more lasting Union than any Laws, conventions, or forms of[2] Government. Such a plan, your prudence, taking its rule and direction from our actual situation, will we humbly hope clearly and explicitly express; whilst you provide, that nothing in political arrangements shall be suffered to contradict the declarations and offers of amity that are made, or to afford a ground of future fear and suspicion. The People in the Colonies are said to be greatly deceived and deluded. The directness and manly simplicity of your superior Wisdom, will take away all opportunities of such misrepresentation; and disarm the Enemies of Peace. The only hope which remains for the return of confidence, we humbly conceive, lies in steadily pursuing the plain, open, strait forward policy of Truth, Justice, candour, and humanity, which, as they are the glory of our Nature and the truest Wisdom are sure to conciliate the affections of Men, and to draw down a blessing from heaven.

Speech on the Use of Indians
6 February 1778

Sources: *Parl. Reg.* viii. 347–52; Walpole, *Last Journals*, ii. 104–5; MSS. at Sheffield, Bk 27.245, 244

The gallery of the House of Commons was closed for this speech and the newspaper reports are brief. Presumably Almon obtained his report from Burke himself or somebody in close contact with him. There are drafts at Sheffield in addition to the two presented here (Bk 6.33, 60, 143; Bk 27.246).

[1] The comma is supplied from the earlier version.
[2] The MS. has 'convention' and 'form of'; the earlier version 'conventions' and 'forms of'.

Burke raised the question of the employment of Indians and slaves as a separate issue on 6 February 1778.[1] He obviously spoke with a great deal of feeling. 'It was universally thought the very best [speech] Mr. Burke had ever delivered.'[2] The *Public Advertiser* of 7 February reported that the

shocking cruelties generally exercised by Savages on their Foes, and particularly since the commencement of this war . . . were described with a Pathos which melted the Auditory almost to tears and filled them with the utmost Horror . . . [Burke's] metaphors were Bold, his Expressions nervous . . . , his Stile in general pathetic, eloquent, and sublime. But his Colourings we hope, for the Honour of Human Nature, were too High, and the Act of an undisciplined Individual perhaps exaggerated and . . . attributed to a whole people. When Mr. Burke had wound up the Feelings of his Auditors as high as he thought necessary, he moved . . .

(1) *PARLIAMENTARY REGISTER*

Mr. *Burke* moved, 'That an humble address be presented to his Majesty, that he will be graciously pleased to give directions, that there be laid before this House copies of all papers that have passed between any of his Majesty's ministers, and the generals of his armies in America, or any person acting for government in Indian affairs, relative to the military employment of the Indians of America, in the present civil war, from the first of March, 1774, to the first day of January, 1778.'

Mr. Burke began by observing, that one of the grand objects in the enquiry into the state of the nation, was the condition and quality of the troops employed in America. That an account of the King's regular forces, and those of his European allies, were upon the table. That hitherto no account had appeared of his irregular forces, those in particular of his savage allies; although there had been great dependence upon them, and that they were obtained at a great expence. That it was necessary to examine into this point; because an extention of their mode of making war had been lately strenuously recommended. The prevailing idea was, that in the next campaign, the plans hitherto pursued were to be abandoned; and a war of distress

---

[1] He appears to have taken some trouble to study the history of the Indians. The drafts refer to Cadwallader Colden (1688–1776), Pierre-François-Xavier de Charlevoix (1682–1761), Louis Hennepin (1640–*c.*1700), Joseph-François Lafitau (1681–1746), and Louis-Armand de Lom d'Arce, Baron de Lahontan (1666–*c.*1713). For other expressions of Burke's own attitude on this subject, see above, pp. 179–81.

[2] *Parl. Reg.* viii. 352.

and intimidation was to take place of a war of conquest, which had been found impracticable.

He observed, that this mode of war had been hitherto tried upon a large scale; and the success which hitherto had attended it would best prove, how far it would be proper to extend it to all our troops, and all our operations. That if it did not promise to be very decisive, as a plan merely military, it could be attended with no collateral advantages to our reputation as a civilized people, or to our policy in reconciling the minds of the colonies to his Majesty's government.[1]

He then stated what a war by Indians was. That the fault of employing them did not consist in their being of one colour or another; in their using one kind of weapon or another; but in their way of making war; which was so horrible, that it shocked not only the manners of all civilized people, but far exceeded the ferocity of all barbarians mentioned in history.[2]

That the Indians in North America never have but two principal objects for going to war: the glory of destroying, or, when opportunity offered, of exterminating their enemies; the other, which always depended on the former, the glory of procuring the greatest number of scalps, which they hung up in their huts as trophies of victory, conquest, and personal prowess, much in the same manner that standards, kettle-drums, and colours, are deposited in public places in civilized nations, in token of some signal overthrow of a powerful and dangerous enemy. The Indians of America had no titles, sine-cure places, lucrative governments, pensions, or red ribbons, to bestow on those who signalized themselves in the field; their rewards were generally received in human scalps, in human flesh, and the gratifications arising from torturing, mangling, scalping, and sometimes eating their captives in war. He then repeated several instances of this diabolical mode of war, scarcely credible, and, if true, improper to be repeated.

He went largely into the proofs of this their mode of making war in all times. He proved, that they had not altered that mode of mak-

---

[1] In a draft: 'This plan if only peace is sought might not be amiss for a good deal may be yielded to save from an Enemy—but if Government another thing for it never can be imagined that a fierce and mercenary and cruel Enemy ever will make a mild and gracious Governour' (Bk 6.60).
[2] In a draft: 'Whether it is Lawful in a Rebellion to employ persons to waste burn and destroy the Country and with a promiscuous carnage to murder men women and children, and to torture to death with every cruelty as many as fall into their hands—He that employs Indians employs them to do that' (Bk 6.60).

ing war; and that no possible means could prevail on them to alter it. He then took a view of the employment of these savages in the wars between France and England; and shewed, that it had been the inevitable consequence of the connection of the two nations with the several Indian tribes; who, on the first European settlements, were, comparatively, great and powerful states; that alliances had been formed with them, and all our affairs became necessarily entangled with theirs.[1] But now no European nation but the English colonies remained in North America; and the savages were so reduced in number, that there was no necessity of any connection with them as nations. They were only formidable from their cruelty; and to employ them was merely to be cruel ourselves in their persons; and to become chargeable with all the odious and impotent barbarities, which they would certainly commit, whenever they were called into action.

On all these points he dwelt a long time, explaining and illustrating every particular with great clearness and precision. He then considered the apologies which had been made for employing them; such as, 1st, 'That if his Majesty had not employed them the rebels would; 2d, and that great care had been taken to prevent the indiscriminate murder of men, women, and children, according to their savage custom. 3d, That they were never employed but in the company of disciplined troops, in order to prevent their irregularities.'

To the first, he answered, that no proof whatever had been given of the Americans having attempted an offensive alliance with any one tribe of savage Indians. Whereas, the imperfect papers already before that House demonstrated, that the King's ministers had negotiated and obtained such alliances from one end of the continent of America to the other. That the Americans had actually made a treaty on the footing of neutrality with the famous Five Nations;[2] which the King's ministers had bribed them to violate, and to act offensively against the Colonies. That no attempt had been made in a single instance on the part of the King's ministers to procure a neutrality. That if the fact had been that the Americans had actually employed those savages, yet

---

[1] In a draft: 'They [Britain and France] did not employ Indians, but were themselves involved in the Wars of great Indian Nations whom they could neither destroy nor control. They became entangled in the System of America as you are in that of Europe' (Bk 27.246).

[2] The Five Nations were the Cayuga, the Oneida, the Seneca, the Onondaga, and the Mohawk—all members of the Iroquois Confederacy. Congress would certainly have liked to have obtained such a treaty but was not successful. See above, p. 180.

the difference of employing them against armed and trained soldiers, embodied and encamped, and employing them against the unarmed and defenceless men, women, and children of a country, dispersed in their houses, was manifest; and left those who attempted so inhuman and unequal a retaliation without excuse.

To the second defence, 'That care had been taken to prevent mischief,' he answered, that he did not doubt the humanity of General Burgoyne and our other officers. They endeavoured it indeed, but in vain. He even stated the attempt itself as perfectly ridiculous. Here he entered into the consideration of General Burgoyne's famous speech to the savages, which he painted in a ludicrous light; not condemning the speech in itself; he said, it was rational and proper, if applied to any other; but as applied to savages, to whom it must be perfectly unintelligible and without the least effect, it might as well have been applied to the wild beasts of the forest.[1] He then entered into many particulars of that General's expedition, as well as Colonel St Leger's,[2] to shew, that the savages, did in effect, indiscriminately murder men, women, and children, friends and foes; and that particularly the slaughter fell mostly upon those who were best affected to the King's government, and who for that reason had been lately disarmed by the provincials. Here he painted in very strong colours the horrid story of Miss Mac Ray, murdered by the savages on the day of her marriage with an officer of the King's troops.[3]

As to the third head of defence, 'That they had always regular troops to restrain and direct them,' this he positively denied, and shewed, that whole nations of savages had been bribed to take up the hatchet, without a single regular officer or soldier amongst them. This he instanced in the case of the Cherokees, who were bribed and betrayed into war, upon promise of being assisted by a large regular force; that they accordingly had invaded Carolina in their usual manner, and for want of the support promised, were nearly exterminated, and the remains

[1] Burgoyne's speech of June 1777 was reported in *Gentleman's Magazine*, xlviii. 122–3.
[2] Barry St Leger (1737–89) had supported Burgoyne's campaign by advancing from Oswego to Fort Stanwix.
[3] Jane McCrea (1754–77) was engaged to one of Burgoyne's troops. On 27 July 1777 she was captured at Fort Edward by a band of Indians who were working for the British forces. She was subsequently murdered and scalped though the details are not entirely clear. The tragedy was exploited to whip up popular indignation against the British. Some historians have credited the incident with helping to turn the tide of the war. See H. Nickerson, *Turning Point of the Revolution; or, Burgoyne in America*, Boston, 1928, pp. 470–2.

of that people now lived in a state of servitude to the Carolinians.[1]

He then shewed the monstrous expence of that kind of ally. That one Indian soldier cost as much as five of the best regular, or irregular European troops. The ministers thought that inhumanity and murder could not be bought too dear. That the expence of these Indians had not been less than 150,000l. and yet there never had been more than seven or eight hundred of them in the field; and that for a very short time. That on the least appearance of ill success, they deserted; and often even turned their arms on their friends. That by falling upon all the inhabitants without distinction, they made every man a soldier; and that the greatest part of the army (as it were conjured up against General Burgoyne) was raised by indignation and horror at the use of the savages; and to them the loss of a gallant European army under an accomplished general, was principally owing.

After this he touched upon the burning of the towns of Falmouth and Norfolk,[2] as well as private gentlemen's and farmers' houses, and other ravages of the King's troops, as parts of the war of distress; and the ill effects which such barbarities had produced.

He lastly entered upon Lord Dunmore's attempt to incite an insurrection of negroes. He stated his proclamation[3] as contrary to the common and statute law of this kingdom, as well as to the law of nations. He stated what an insurrection of negroes was; the number of that sort of men in Virginia and Maryland; the mischiefs of setting a crew of fierce, foreign barbarians and slaves to judge which of their masters were in rebellion, and which of their acts were or were not rebellious: the utter impossibility of containing them and keeping them in order was stated in a strong manner. He appealed to all who knew the southern colonies, and the West Indies, what murders, rapes, and enormities of all kinds, were in the contemplation of all negroes who meditated an insurrection. He lastly asked what means were proposed for governing these negroes, who were 100,000 at least; when they had reduced the province to their obedience, and made themselves masters of the houses, goods, wives and daughters of their murdered lords?

---

[1] The Cherokees had attacked in 1776 against the advice of the British Agent. See J. R. Alden, *The South in the Revolution*, Baton Rouge, 1957, pp. 268–73.

[2] Falmouth (now Portland, Maine) was destroyed on 18 October 1775, and Norfolk, Virginia, on 1 January 1776.

[3] Of 7 November 1775.

Another war must be made of them; and another massacre, adding confusion to confusion, and destruction to destruction. He said, that providentially the English white civilized inhabitants had so strengthened themselves, as to keep under his Majesty's negro allies; that not above one thousand or thereabouts were able to escape, and put themselves under the banners of Lord Dunmore, and that the end of these wretches, seduced into an insurrection, in which they were not supported, was truly deplorable; not above one or two, as he heard, having escaped a miserable death by disease or famine; but he promised to move for papers to clear up, and ascertain this point.[1]

Then he dwelt on the affair of Lord Dunmore, because his proceedings were evident by his proclamation, and by the negro army which he had collected. But that there was very strong reason to believe, that the governors of both the Carolinas, and one at least of the Floridas, had been concerned in designs of the same sort. That one of these governors had been accused of it, who did not deny, that in case of rebellion he would avail himself of such a resource. That this was the grand cause of the greater resentment which appeared in the southern, than in many of the northern Colonies; as they had been the first to abjure the King: and one of them, Virginia, to declare, that if the rest should submit, they would hold out to the last: for what security could they receive, that if they admitted an English governor, he would not raise their negroes on them, whenever he thought it good to assert any given disturbances should amount to a rebellion, and declare martial law.

The only remedy he conceived there could be for the alienation of affections, and distrust and terror of our government, brought on by these measures; was for Parliament to enquire seriously into them; and to shew their disapprobation of practices as contrary to all true policy, as to the dictates of feeling and humanity: for otherwise the colonies

---

[1] In a draft (Bk 27.246) there are two comments on the position of the slaves: (1) 'There the acute understanding of a Negro Slave was to distinguish who was in rebellion and who not—and to aid that refined understanding He had the greatest interest in the world to find his Master a rebel. He was to have liberty—arms, pay, and to become a Lord over those he had served—the condition of a Soldier is no great dignity to a freeman but to a Slave it is the greatest advancement which can be conceived'; (2) 'The ferocity of a wild african to judge of the Law and Liberty of England. The ferocity the revenge, the fear of returning to servitude of an emancipated Slave. A negro serves a Loyal Master—he is to be a slave—will he be satisfied that another of his Kind should be free and happy because his Master is a bad subject. That his misery is to depend on others good behaviour. Will they be slaves who are the support of Government. How long are they to be in repairing to the K.'s Standard before they lose the Slave will the Slave wait.'

would never believe, that those who were capable of carrying on so cruel and dishonourable a war, could ever be trusted for a sound and cordial peace; much less be safely trusted with power and dominion.

The speech lasted for more than three hours. It was universally thought the very best Mr. Burke had ever delivered.

(2) WALPOLE, *LAST JOURNALS*

The 6*th* was memorable for the chef-d'oeuvre of Burke's orations. He called Burgoyne's Talk with the Indians, the 'sublimity of bombast absurdity,' in which he demanded the assistance of seventeen Indian nations, by considerations of *our Holy Religion*, by regard for our constitution; and though he enjoined them not to scalp men, women, or children alive, he promised to pay them for any scalps of the dead, and required them to repair to the King's standard, which— where was it? said Burke,—on board Lord Dunmore's ships, whose practices with the Indians he severely stigmatized. Seventeen inter-preters from the several nations, said he, could not have given them any ideas of his reasons—but, added Burke, the invitation was just as if, at a riot on Tower Hill, the keeper of the wild beasts had turned them loose, but adding, 'my gentle lions, my sentimental wolves, my tender-hearted hyenas, go forth,[1] but take care not to hurt men, women, or children.'[2] He then grew serious; and as the former part had excited the warmest and most continued bursts of laughter even from Lord North, Rigby, and the Ministers themselves, so he drew such a pathetic picture of the cruelties of the King's Army, particularly in the alleged case of a young woman[3] on whose ransom, not beauty, they quarrelled, and murdered her,—*that he drew iron tears* down Barre's cheek.[4]

---

[1] In a letter to William Mason (1724–97) Walpole records this phrase as 'My gentle lions, my humane bears, my sentimental wolves, my tender-hearted hyenas, go forth' (*The Correspondence of Horace Walpole*, ed. W. S. Lewis, 48 vols., New Haven, 1937–83, xxviii. 354–5). It is expanded in another draft (Bk 27.246): 'Indians—would recommend them to the Enemy errorem hostibus illum [Virgil, *Georgics*, iii. 513] my gentle lions, my tender heart[ed] tygers, my meek well orderd famished wolves, my discriminatory clear headed Bears—go forth—speech as well understood and like to be as effective with one or with the other' (Bk 27.246).

[2] The Royal Menagerie was in the Tower.

[3] Jane McCrea.

[4] Milton, *Il Penseroso*, 107.

(3) MS. AT SHEFFIELD, BK 27.245

I have been so long used to have everything[1] that I *know* to be done from conscience attributed to *faction* and treated accordingly, not what I am now going to offer relative to some part of His Majesties forces will be rather as an *apology for proposing* than as *reasons* for *accepting* them.

It is to have an account brought before you, in order 1. that you of a part of his Majesties forces may form a judgment of the propriety of *their* past or future employment. 2. *that you may* judge of the Efficacy of making war at all upon the principle—on which they were employd.

Indians and savages employd from one End of Am[erica] to the other. Notorious as a fact—stated in Letters of our Generals—appear on account. 2 Negroes

In an insurrection let the Lions out of the Tower—good Lyons— dear Lyons they are my subjects.

Propriety of employing them. History of our connexion—They a great we a little people[2] involved and entangled in their affairs—by a course of Events reduced—Now only bodies of bandittis of the most cruel and atrocious Kind. Laws of War Might then be less considerd. 1. The faults were equal. 2. The Nations foreign.[3]

Now the question is whether a just and merciful Providence and being possessed of other powerful forces rich resources his subjects inclining to rebellion or actually in it, can lawfully and honourably use these Instruments.

Laws in War as well as peace[4]—these Laws of Limitation—if our Virtues limited how much more our violence[5]—Great Laws 1. as short as possible—2 as little a party as possible, during the continuance 2 these two must stand together—not the second swallowd up in the first.[6]

1st Objection[7]—that Instead of selected it is indiscriminate, friends and foes, friends though weaker not to be killed. in New York actually

---

[1] In margin: 'thought at first to have said nothing'.

[2] In margin: 'rather grew into it than chose it'.

[3] In margin: 'their vices ⟨ours⟩—never without some Stigma equality of Evil a kind of Justice.'

[4] In margin: 'Stands on the same Ground as all Laws'.

[5] In margin: 'Mercy arising out of Cruelty reprobated'.

[6] In margin: 'now let us see whether it be more defensive in reason than reconcilable to humanity.'

[7] In margin: 'a resource odious to humanity—feeble—dangerous If you had not taken them the Americans would—first a most authentic document that they did not. The Congress talk.

did a murder. 2. That it is making war on domestick unprepared Life. 3. That it is cruel. You ⟨are⟩ not to condemned numberless innocent

1st Southern Colonies back settlers most exposed—2d No guard sufficient—Officers Letter—Case of Mrs. MacRea.[1] he does—what should you do. a Parent—

Urge the Necessity at—to weep over it—Necessity—Egyptian King—if 60,000 cannot—this will not—Event.

Principle of *Terror*—Nature of Terror[2] if it does not extinguish all powers it calls them out—succeeding or failing it leaves hatred and gall political consequence of Indians—after peace restored must be extirpated.[3]

domestick Security Negroes. Those who know a Negro insurrection. Number of Negroes in Virginia. Suppose the ⟨Scheme⟩ had taken place

Suppose they had vanquished the Whites—Can they ever forgive what would become of your Government of them and their Masters.

Suppose a Virgin of an honourable place, that had grown up the delight and comfort of a family that paid

In that moment of blessing that God who meant the union the relation and continuance of his Creatures has made the highest point of human felicity and is indeed a part of pleasure and innocence which Angels might look down and Envy, when this poor Creature dressed up in those pretty[4] little ornaments which ingenious poverty with which we make the most of our condition[5] of a Country new to Luxury ⟨proudest⟩ on what it has most valuable,[6] surrounded with tender parents, and sympathising kindred, and holy Priests and happy Lovers just in that moment ⟨of momentary⟩ anxiety of love—and those with that hair dressed for other purposes that morning torn from her head to decorate the infernal habitation of cruelty and barbarism and there

---

⟨   ⟩—No reason they would be an incumbrance they could give no aid against a regular army which they had to oppose but very fit to destroy a country which they had to protect'.

[1] In margin: '⟨mem the copies⟩ was inspection all the politicks of the Earth not worth it'.

[2] In margin: 'has several points of weakness—If according to the Minds which applied. King of Spain or Portugal—'.

[3] In margin: 'attacked within and without by savages. smallest objection flatly illegal. 1. could he restrain them in Victory. 2. Who would be the Masters wild illiterate savages—with all the rage of new got freedom—resentment against Masters would be keep faith—'.

[4] In margin: 'who for her beauty was the pride and boast of this rude Country'.

[5] In margin: 'and decorate what we love'.

[6] In margin: 'Hideousyells shrieks and ⟨screams⟩ and war hoops that would have appalled the stoutest heart and seized the half dead victim'.

left[1] a naked and ⟨foul scale⟩ her body a mangled ghastly spectacle of blood and horrour, crying through an hundred mouths to that whose image was defaced for Vengeance. Is it to be wondered that the whole Country with a general insurrection[2] rose to exterminate the ⟨savages⟩

They who have ordered have done it. It is he that is answerable to God and men for this cruel murder this good humored person who seems so full entertains you ⟨upon⟩ the subject of the publick misfortunes that is guilty of this unparalleled act of Horrour.

Some days ago I had prepared, a few motions for papers[3] relative to a part of the force which his Majesty had been advised to employ in America—I found to my surprise (as I believe it will be to that of the House)[4] that these papers would be refused—I am therefore under the necessity of saying a little more to you on the Subject than I really wished.

The wisdom of appointing a Government to administer justice which could not support itself and then a military power that could not receive justice from the Civil power it was to support. Transfers a port from Boston to Salem without any reason to think Salem more obedient than Boston. The length of time given to Boston gave the whole continent time to know and weigh their course and to find it their own.

America independent—what so great Evil is at that at three thousand miles distance. a people should be found agreeing in everything. It is not America independent but America hostile.

If dependent, what security that she should not be hostile.

(4) MS. AT SHEFFIELD, BK 27.244

All hitherto wrong[5]—plan of War to be changed from a War of conquest to a war of *intimidation and distress*.[6]

---

[1] MS.: 'left left'.

[2] In margin: 'Suppose they had got room. Suppose they had the blessing of a people burthensome and unworthy on the Camp useless in the field; contributing nothing to their success and turning their checks into the most ruinous defeats—falling on them when they most not want their assistance.—what is in all that to Envy—yet this reason the only reason given.'

[3] In margin: 'with the greatest frankness communicated'.

[4] MS.: 'that of the House that of the house'.

[5] In margin: 'did not suspect a ⟨refuser⟩ had used ⟨both⟩ European and Indian and were to judge of the effect and economy of both'.

[6] In margin: 'Therefore necessary to judge of a War of Intimidation and distress
You are now between the failure of your first project and your Trial of a second.'

To show that you have *tried* this already—that you have tried it in a great extent—at a boundless expense[1] and to see whether the advantage countervails the *odium, injustice, horror,* and even *charge,* attending it for in the œonomy? of Mischief and destruction—it is a *rule* not to *squander* it away, nor to *employ* more of it than answers the ⟨immediate⟩ interest of the employer.[2]

The things I intend to bring before you, are the operations of your Allies the Savage Indians and the insurgent Negroes.[3] Which as Gross facts are matters of Public Notoriety. As to the former, as I know that the propriety of using them is justified (as wrong things are generally justified, not by[4] principle but by precedent and example) by the reciprocal use made of them by France and us in all our Wars on that continent—it may not be amiss to take a short View of our connexion with them. When the French began a little Settlement on the Banks of the river St Lawrence[5] They a great we a little people—we were *protected* by one of those Nations against another—we entered into alliances offensive and defensive. We did not employ them[6] in War; but were *involved* in their Wars.

We were entangled in the ⟨affairs of⟩ Indian Nations whose *manners* we could not alter and whose *power* we could not control. We were entangled in their affairs,[7] we became involved in the System of America, as we are in the system of Europe—until at length [we] grew upon that people we have overspread the Country and they faded away— with their vices and ours[8] until at length there is but one single Nation in America—and that is The English—The Indians are no longer a *people* in any proper acceptation of the Word—but several gangs of Banditti scattered along a wild of a great civilized empire[9]—a Banditti of the most cruel and atrocious kind such as infest many such empires

[1] In margin: 'Confess if they go on in this way there is no hope that if they should continue to act as they have acted to plan as they have planned; and to direct as they have directed the destruction of the Empire'.
[2] In margin: 'to commit great Crimes for small advantages—what goes to waste is ⟨gone⟩ was lost try Not to commit great Horrors for little purposes'.
[3] In margin: 'Justice and policy'.
[4] MS.: '(not by)'.
[5] In margin: 'little struggling Settlements on the ⟨banks⟩ of brooks and the mouths of rivers. innumerable Nations of which now no trace remains—great Empires—now shrunk to nothing'.
[6] In margin: '⟨   ⟩ did not employ them—they employd you'.
[7] In margin: 'two great Empires—The Hurons and Iroquois. The French would not subsist without the One nor we without the other.' [Burke here insets the phrase 'We enterd into alliances offensive and defensive' already inserted above.]
[8] In margin: 'a fatal union the manners of savages were the Luxury of Civilized'.
[9] In margin: 'no matter whether justifiable or no formerly'.

[1]Question of employing Indians is therefore this *whether* a just and merciful prince being under the unhappy *Necessity* of War with his subjects can Lawfully burn, waste and destroy a country;—murder man woman and child—friend and foe in one promiscuous carnage—and by cruel and lingering tortures slaughter the prisoners which fall into his hands—for all this is the very thing expressed in the Terms of employing Indians. Would not condemn to death.[2]

Their mode of War can be no other.—proved not to be alterd or alterable mode of War—not from Henepin and Lahontan but authors of the first Magnitude and Credit—Lafitau—Charlevoix—Governor Colden—for natural purposes go—Mode of *individual* War on individuals. great Principle—to weaken—with women and children answers as well—so is Revenge—torture and revenge—Left to Women. Objects of greatest compassion most exposed—Individual War.

Not alterd—Gardiner[3]—cadres—Manuscript Letter—Claus Letter on the Table[4]—Miss MacRea on Topics they dont understand and motives they do ⟨not⟩ feel.

Effects.—Expence—must maintain the whole Tribe. Little advantage—quit you in good from inconstancy. In Evil from ill fortune. Cause of General Burgoines destination.

1. Could not obtain neutrality—not fact. They did and from

Int. suppose they did what did they gain for your Case. most necessary Lord North—Aegyptain King.[5]

State of the Southern your laws

People What must feel on the offer to subdue them by their own Negroes—How restraind how reclaimed—Numbers, ⟨turn⟩ it into—how to distinguish when all have freedom.[6]

---

[1] In margin at head of paragraph: 'in sum—assistance got little—precarious—useless—dangerous—expence—odious and horrible'.

[2] In the margin against this and succeeding paragraphs: 'No polity—civil—or military. In the rudest and most ferocious state of human Society if it may [be] at all call'd so—making war 1. commencement. War feast. 2. To kill the first glory to revenge the first Virtue, not in the writer but the What is there ridiculous in this? Is it not this that you address motives to those to whom it is ridiculous to apply them show that it is not—attempts made through ineffectual—General Burgoines Speech. 1st they never obey command either foreign or domestick may seem to do it. Eloquence *to 17* Nations ⟨to the Alleghenies⟩—never mens manners alterd by a speech do or not understand his Terms. Lieut of the Tower—finding a Riot—pretend to obey orders.'

[3] Captain Henry Farington Gardiner, Burgoyn's *aide-de-camp*, had returned to Britain.

[4] Daniel Claus, Indian agent. For his letter, see *Parl Reg*, viii. 234.

[5] '...a new king over Egypt which knew not Joseph'; Ex. 1: 8.

[6] In margin: against this and two preceding paragraphs: 'Cause of Zeal. every Man threatned every man a Soldier Gatess proclamation—They receive not a paper return. Massachusets ⟨province⟩ approbation of the Wise distinguished soldiers from minister Friends and foes—

On the whole Laws of War
Mischief of Independency what

Burke's motion was defeated by 223 votes to 137. He put five further motions for related papers concerning the employment of Indians and slaves. All were negatived without a division.

Speech on North's Conciliatory Bill
23 February 1778

Source: *General Advertiser*, 25 February 1778

This report is also in *London Chronicle*, 26 February. It is repeated in *Parl. Reg.* viii. 392–3 and *Parl. Hist.* xix. 778–9. There is an alternative report in the *Gazetteer* of 26 February and in *Westminster Journal*, 28 February. There is at Sheffield a MS. (Bk 6.96) which appears to be a draft for this speech. It is not refined enough for transcription.

On 17 February Lord North introduced a plan of conciliation with America. This change of approach was the result of two circumstances—the recent loss at Saratoga and rumours 'that a treaty of alliance and guarantee [had been] ... signed between France and America'.[1] North's plan was to renounce the power to tax America and to appoint a commission to negotiate a settlement of other differences. Commissioners were to be appointed under a Bill, presented to the Commons on 19 February, which received the Royal Assent on 11 March.[2] The Commission was headed by Frederick Howard, 5th Earl of Carlisle,[3] who accepted his appointment on 22 February.[4] Burke spoke on 23 February on a motion to instruct the Committee of the Whole House to make provision for nominating the commissioners.

Mr. Burke said, that the present was a question of *men*; that the measure was decided upon, which was to give a full power to dispose of all the legislative acts, and all the legislative powers of Parliament, so far as they concerned America.

That there never had been such a trust delegated to men, and that therefore nothing ever was more important than the proper choice of them;—that if Ministers had hitherto shown, in any one instance, that

---

Tryon County discovered would Left savages to ruin offer them pardon at the hand of their Aegyptain King.'
[1] *General Evening Post*, 19 February 1778.
[2] 18 Geo. III, c. 13.   [3] (1748–1825).
[4] Historical Manuscripts Commission, *Carlisle MSS.*, p. 322.

they had formed a right judgement on men, he would admit, that they ought to be trusted with the nomination of men upon this occasion.

Next to honesty (which he would not dispute with the Ministers) the ground of confidence in men was founded on two things;—that they were incapable of deceiving others; and were alike incapable of being deceived themselves.

That the Ministers had been publicly charged in that House, by those who had all along supported their measures, with having *deceived them*;—and their justification had been, that they were *themselves deceived* in every particular relating to America.

Now, take it which way you please, whether they were deceivers, as their friends assert, or deceived, as themselves alledge, they are not fit, on either ground to be trusted;—and they, who had judged so ill of the men they had credited, in all their information concerning America, would not judge better in the choice of the men whom they nominated to get rid of the fatal consequences of that ill information.

That their constant defence, with regard to the ill success of their army in America, was the incapacity, error, or neglect of the Generals they had appointed;—that though he did not believe this was the cause, yet, on their own confession, they had made a wrong judgement of the persons they had employed; and if they were so unhappy in their choice of Generals, they would not prove more fortunate in their choice of negotiators.

He apprehended, that no good could come of any negotiation whatsoever intrusted to their hands;—that the affair was not too little to be undertaken by Parliament itself. If parliamentary rights must be negotiated upon, it was fit to be done by a Committee of the two Houses of Parliament.

In order to settle India affairs, a Committee of the House had sat in Leaden hall-street;[1] they might as well sit in America, the object is more important, if the distance be greater;—that he saw the drift of the whole;—[t]he Ministers thought to pay their court, by extending the prerogative, in proportion as they had lessened the empire;—and that this war (which was pretended to be made to prevent the King's having a revenue in America independent of Parliament, and to assert the power of the House of Commons, to tax all the British dominions)

---

[1] Where the headquarters of the East India Company were. The Secret Committee of 1772 met there.

now terminated in a surrender of our right of taxation, and of all our other parliamentary rights to the Crown.

The motion was rejected without a division.

Petition for Bristol
[February 1778]

Source: MS. at Sheffield, Bk 16.4–5

The MS. is in Zouch's hand, with corrections and additions by Burke, who endorsed it: 'Sketch of a Petition I think for Bristol'. It was written after the introduction of the Bill to appoint commissioners to treat with America (presented to the Commons on 19 February), but before the actual commissioners were known.

Burke presumably drafted this document in connection with a project in Bristol to petition Parliament to make peace with America.[1] The papers reported that a meeting was held at Bristol on 10 February 'at the Bush Tavern . . . to consider a petition to the House of Commons, to promote a speedy peace . . . and to shew that the Citizens in general were far from being unanimous in their wishes to promote the present war.'[2] It was 'unanimously agreed to present such a petition'. None was presented.

To the Honourable the Commons of Great Britain in Parliament Assembled.
    The humble Petition of
Sheweth
    That your Petitioners are alarmed at the present State and condition of the Kingdom.
    As Men they must feel for their situation. As Englishmen they have a right to express their feelings. As persons paying to the publick a very large proportion of the product of their Industry, they have a just Title to expect a due return in the advantage of a vigilant, a wise, and a provident Government.
    They have every reason to apprehend that they have been disappointed in that expectation. Whilst they submit as they ought to the unsearchable dispensation of Providence, they cannot avoid an opinion,

---

[1] *Bonner and Middleton's Bristol Gazette*, 14 February 1778.
[2] *London Chronicle*, 14 February 1778.

that Great Calamaties cannot happen to great prosperity, nor great humiliation to mighty power, without giving rise to a natural and necessary presumption of Misconduct.

They see with satisfaction and Gratitude, that this House, sympathising with its Constituents, has enter'd into an Enquiry into the State of the Nation:[1] And relying as they do, on the honour, Virtue, and publick Spirit, of the representatives of the Commons of Great Britain, they abhor from the bottom of their hearts, the most remote suspicion, of what has been suggested by wicked and factious persons, that this House could be so much wanting to itself, so lost to all sense of its Duty, and so dead to all regard for the common interest, as to close an Enquiry, (voluntarily and unanimously enter'd into,) of that most important and urgent kind, and in such critical Circumstances, without some resolutions consolatory to the Publick; either by shewing that their uneasiness be ill founded, or by such a decision on the Cause of their calamity, as to afford hope of better management and better fortune in future.

Your Petitioners assure this Honourable House that it has required a full exertion of all that confidence which good Citizens are willing to repose in the constitutional powers that are over them, to acquiesce, in what they are so little able to reconcile, as the continuance of the affairs of this Kingdom under the care of the present Ministers and advisers (who ever they are), with the evident tokens that appear of want of knowledge, ability, or integrity in the management of those affairs. To see an Empire dismemberd; thirteen great Provinces lost; a Military establishment kept up of more than four score thousand Land forces, and of Sixty thousand Seamen; The greatest part of that Force transported and maintained at the other side of the Atlantick Ocean at an expence unheard of, and without any serious advantage in possession or prospect; thirty Millions spent or certainly incurred; six hundred of our Ships taken; whole branches of Trade almost cut off;[2] and others greatly impaired; publick Credit prostrate, publick Burthens accumulating; Our Arms dishonoured; our Policy dispised; a necessity of bearing insults with the utmost disgrace, or resenting them with the utmost peril; A foreign War imminent over us with our antient and

[1] On 2 December 1777 the House resolved that it would go into a Committee of the Whole House to consider the state of the nation on 2 February 1778. The House did so on 2 and 9 February, 11 and 19 March, and 9 and 10 April.
[2] In the margin: '[African]'.

powerful Rivals and Enemies,[1] at the time when we are exhausted by a civil contention with our antient friends and Brethren. In this situation, to behold with indifference the Authors, advisers, and contrivers of these evils in Credit and power, and by being so in a condition to perpetuate and agravate our Calamities, would argue in us rather a stupid and degenerate insensibility to all publick interest, than that decent deference which is due, and which we have ever willingly paid, to just and constitutional Authority.

Your Petitioners in praying the particular attention of this Honourable House to the material Objects of Enquiry now before it, most humbly trust, that they will not suffer Ministers to avail themselves of their usual resource, of attributing the blame of their mistaken policy to the brave Men whose valour and capacity has been thrown away in unworthy designs, or impracticable Attempts. We have no reason to doubt the Bravery or skill of our Officers by Sea or Land more at this than at any other time. But we have abundant reason to think the very project of the American War to have been so erroneous in its principle as to induce a perpetual series of Mistakes in its Conduct. If your Petitioners had been of Opinion, that the objects of this war were properly chosen, they must feel with a sharp resentment the measures which induced the necessity of giving them up in the way in which they are now surrender'd. But as your Petitioners have ever thought, that the publick councils of the Kingdom were led into the adoption of that fatal Scheme by misinformation; and that the credulity and passions of the people at large were excited and abused by the Arts of wicked and mercenary Men, they are obliged to look much farther back. They are obliged to lament, that Objects (comparatively of little value) were not given up, at such a time, and in such circumstances as would have bestowed Grace and effect on concession; and might make it appear the free gift of favour and kindness, and not a sacrifice offerd by necessity and distress.

If those persons are to be entrusted with the direction of the further concessions to be made by this Country, and with the Appointment of those who are to negotiate, your Petitioners are under the greatest apprehensions, that the concessions, (which are in themselves enfeebled by being delayd) will be renderd yet more precarious, by being entirely in the hands of those who can shew no other Title to the

---

[1] France signed treaties with the United States on 6 February.

confidence of our late fellow Subjects, than (according to their Ideas) that of constant and impotent Hatred; and who in appointing to the Commission will naturally choose those who are most like themselves, and most in their confidence;—namely those, whom, from their voluntary Hostility, and forced reconciliation, America can neither love, respect nor trust.

Impressed with these Ideas your Petitioners place their last hope in a British House of Commons. If the control of your Honourable House over the Ministers or Councillors of the Crown has any foundation in the constitution, or is at any time fit to be used—we cannot conceive any occasion that can possibly demand that control if the present does not urgently call for it. Your Petitioners therefore in consideration of the burthens they have borne, and are yet to bear, humbly implore this Honourable House to have compassion on human suffering and human Infirmity, and not to forget that old principle of the Constitution, not lost we hope by disuse, that the redress of Grievances ought sometimes to precede or at least to accompany the grant of Supplies.[1]

Speech on Budget
10 March 1778

Source: *London Chronicle*, 12 March 1778

This report is also in the *Public Advertiser* of 11 March and, with slight differences, in *General Evening Post*, 12 March.

On 9 March Thomas Gilbert,[2] a Government supporter and the Controller of the Great Wardrobe and Paymaster of the Charity for the Relief of Widows of Naval Officers, proposed a tax on places and pensions. The proposal was approved in committee by 100 votes to 82. Gilbert who was probably best known for his efforts to reform the poor laws, claimed to be deeply concerned about 'the expenditure of public money, particularly the exorbitant contracts and abuses of office'.[3] The following day Burke spoke on this proposal when it was reported to the House. Interestingly, though Gilbert's objectives were essentially the same as some which would prompt Burke to propagate

[1] Lord North opened his budget on 9 March.
[2] (?1719–98), M.P. 1763–94.
[3] *Parl. Reg.* viii. 421.

economical reform, he was unable to give his wholehearted approval to the idea. Two years later he would explain his reluctance on the basis of the difficulty of putting a real and realistic value on offices.[1] The following speech suggests that perhaps his disapproval was also grounded in his lifelong concern for the dignity and respectability of all the highest and most important traditional offices and officers of government.[2] It is worthy of note that when he propagated his economical reform legislation he would be attacked for leaving all the most considerable places under the Crown untouched in his programme to reduce government expenditure.[3]

Mr. Burke spoke very ably in opposition to it, observing that he thought the profits of the several offices under government were by no means too well paid; that men of ability, who devoted their whole time to such laborious employments, ought to be enabled to provide for their families, and that he believed no government in Europe was so cheaply administered. After he had delivered his opinion, in which our correspondent says he wishes his memory would enable him to do him justice, he left the house not choosing to vote on either side.

The proposal was defeated by 147 votes to 141.

Speech on Repeal of Declaratory Act
6 April 1778

Source: *London Evening Post*, 7 April 1778

The same report is in the *General Advertiser* of 7 April. An alternative report is in the *Morning Post*, 7 April, *St James's Chronicle*, 7 April, and *Lloyd's Evening Post*, 8 April. The report in *Parl. Hist.* xix. 1012 has no known newspaper source. A MS. at Sheffield (Bk 6.2) appears to be a rough draft for this speech.

On 6 April Sir William Meredith moved for leave to bring in a Bill to repeal the Declaratory Act. There appears to have been considerable support for the removal of that Act amongst Opposition interests anxious to pacify the Americans and end the war. There also appears to have been some concern about how the Rockingham party would react to attacks on an important statute which they themselves had drafted. Earlier in the session John Wilkes

[1] See below, pp. 493–4.
[2] See above, pp. 35–6.
[3] See below, pp. 581–3.

had introduced a Bill similar to Meredith's, and he had taken the precaution to assure the Rockinghams that his 'wishes were very far from being hostile' to them.[1] In the following speech Burke clarified his position. One year earlier he had claimed publicly that he was prepared to cast off virtually any specific measure to hold the empire together—'a limb to save the body'[2]—and in this speech he declared himself absolutely loyal to that principle. His presentation followed a motion to adjourn the debate for two months. North had pointed out that the Declaratory Act applied to the West Indies as well as America and the repealing it was 'a consequential matter'.

Mr. Burke in the course of the debate, observed, that tho' he was well convinced the declaratory law, in its original intention, was a wise and politic measure, necessary to the existence of the supremacy of the mother-country, and productive of salutary effects; yet in the present state of affairs, he thought it wise to give it up, if thereby the minds of the Americans could be conciliated, and their affections regained.[3]

The debate was adjourned two months in order to avoid a division on Meredith's motion.

Speech on Powys's Motion on American Commission
10 April 1778

Source: *General Advertiser*, 14 April 1778

This report also appears in the *Whitehall Evening Post* of 16 April. Another report is in the *St James's Chronicle*, 11 April, and other papers; it is also in *Parl. Hist.* xix. 1088.

On 10 April Thomas Powys[4] moved to enlarge the power of the Commissioners going to America, so that they might grant unconditional independence. Burke supported him and, in so doing, made his first unequivocal public declaration that American independence was inevitable and must be accepted. This placed him in a small minority in the House at this time. The propertied

---

[1] MS. at Sheffield, R1.1763: James Adair to Rockingham, [25 January 1778]. Wilkes presented his motion for the repeal of the Declaratory Act on 10 December 1777 (*Parl. Hist.* xix. 563–89).

[2] See above, p. 289.

[3] The *Parl. Hist.* report might appear to be in conflict—though it is probably merely incomplete. It concludes: 'That the House had already formally renounced the obnoxious power in question, which was supposed to be involved in that Act; and that, therefore, this repeal would be only for parliament to give itself the lie, for no manner of purpose.'

[4] (1734–1800), later (1797) 1st Baron Lilford, M.P. 1774–97.

classes were presumably now growing significantly less pleased with the war, but many M.P.s appear to have felt that to 'begin by acknowledging . . . [American] Independence—Exclusive of the humiliating Circumstances of being bullied into it by the House of Bourbon' would be a distinctly distasteful and 'unpopular' approach.[1]

Mr. Burke, very pointedly and conclusively refuted the arguments of Governor Johnstone.[2]—Was there ever, he observed, a more incompetent, or a more contradictory reason advanced than that he meant to use to bring back the Americans to dependency. "You will, says he, by independency, perhaps, in some future period, rise to naval grandeur and importance, and compare with the European powers for superiority and opulence. This, however, must be at some distant period; but by returning to dependency, you will enjoy the protection of Britain, and live a happy and a quiet people; and this, forsooth, is to be the argument that is to prevail on their good sense and their common understandings, and persuade them that it is their interest to return to the embrace of Britain; you will be rich and powerful, though dangerously independent, and therefore you ought to return to abject, miserable, though secure dependency."[3] He hoped the honourable Commissioner was possessed of more solid arguments, more reasonable pretences, for if not, their plain understandings might bring back to his recollection a fable from the ancient moralist, Aesop, that would refute every tittle of what he had said. 'A dog and a wolf had entered into a friendly conversation, as they passed along; when the dog, with many eulogiums on his master's munificence, intreated the wolf to come and live with him; telling him at the same time, that there were many sinecures, pensions, and gifts; that is, many bones, scraps, and dinners to be met with, much more comfortable than a precarious living in the woods. The wolf agreed readily to partake of so comfortable a situation, and travelled with him homewards, till observing that the dog's neck was fretted and callous, he begged to know the cause: the dog replied it, was the *frettings* of the *collar* which his master enjoined him to wear. Is it so, replies the wolf, then enjoy the comforts of your life singly, for I will rather prowl for my prey, as usual, in the woods, and be free to range the fields as I list, tho'

---

[1] MS. at Sheffield, R1.1774: Sir John Griffin to Rockingham, 11 April 1778.
[2] George Johnstone was one of the Commissioners; he had opposed the motion.
[3] The second quotation mark is supplied.

pinched with hunger, than submit to wear any man's collar for the sake of his scraps'.[1] It was not to be expected, that men blest with the light of reason, would prefer slavery to freedom, or inferiority to domination. And he thought it the duty of the Committee to prevent the further waste of treasure and expence of blood, by enlarging the terms of concession; and making the Americans, by an act of our legislature, what they had irrevocably, by the force of arms, made themselves—a free people.

The motion was lost without a division.

Draft Address for the Catholics
[April 1778]

Source: MS. at Sheffield, Bk 8.27

There are many stylistic differences between this draft, which survives in Burke's hand, of an Address for the Catholics and the Address as presented to the King on 1 May (*London Gazette*, 2 May; E. H. Burton, *The Life and Times of Bishop Challoner*, 2 vols., London, 1909, ii. 195–6).

Burke had always believed in widespread toleration for all the non-established faiths in Britain,[2] indeed, even for 'Pagans'.[3] Throughout his life he supported efforts to promote religious freedom when to do so did not in his mind threaten the position of the Church of England.[4] Amongst the papers at Sheffield is a quotation from Blackstone's *Commentaries* penned by Burke which rather succinctly sums up his position on the question of Catholic relief in 1778. It reads as follows:

But if a time should ever arrive, and *perhaps it is not very distant*, when all fears of a *pretender* shall have vanished, and the power and influence of the *pope* shall become *feeble, ridiculous* and *despicable*, not only in England, but in *every Kingdom in Europe*, it probably would then not be amiss to revise and soften these rigorous Edicts . . . For it ought not to be left in the Breast of *every merciless Bigot* to drag down the vengeance of these occasional Laws upon inoffensive though mistaken Subjects, in opposition to the lenient inclination of the civil magistrate, and to the destruction of every principle of toleration and religious Liberty.[5]

---

[1] Aesop, *Fables*, ed. E. Chambury, Paris, 1927, p. 100.
[2] See above, pp. 38–42.
[3] *Corr.* iii. 112.
[4] See vol. ii, pp. 368–70.
[5] Bk 27.205. See *Commentaries on the Laws of England*, 4 vols., London, 1765–9, iv. 57.

Burke's sympathy for the Catholic cause was particularly strong because it was entwined with his concern for his native Ireland where obsolete penal laws brought hardship to the vast majority of the people. In England and Scotland only some 110,000 out of a total population of some 7,200,000 were Catholic, but in Ireland about 75 per cent of some 4,000,000 people were Catholic. Generally the penal laws outlawed their clergy and the mass and denied them the right to vote and hold political office. They also restricted Catholic education and landowning, closed the legal and academic professions to them, restricted their use of arms and forbade them military service. The laws were not normally enforced but, as Blackstone's words suggest, they were always a threat and of course of symbolic importance.

The American war, which made the question of the enlistment of Catholics in the armed forces important,[1] combined with a growing fear that disaffected Irishmen could take up arms to support the American side,[2] provided an opportunity for modifying the restrictions. Burke worked for both the English[3] and Irish[4] Relief Bills in 1778, and he told a friend in Ireland that he understood them to be 'intended ultimately for you. Indeed [he said] you had the unhappy Title to preference, on account of the nature of the oppression and the Multitude of the oppressed. The whole was laid together for that purpose.'[5] It was thought appropriate for the Catholics in England at the start of the parliamentary campaign to present a loyal address to the King to relax the penal laws—and Burke provided a draft for them.

Your Majesties dutiful and Loyal Subjects the Roman Catholick Peers and Commoners of your Kingdom most humbly trust, that it can at no time be offensive to the Clemency of your Majesties Nature, or to the Maxims of your just and wise Government, that any part of your subjects should approach your Royal presence, respectfully to assure your Majesty of the affectionate reverence which [they] feel for your person and their true attachment to a civil constitution, which has been perpetuated through all changes of religious opinions, and establishments, and perfected by that revolution, which for the general happiness of your Subjects has placed your Majesties illustrious house on the Throne of these Kingdoms; and for ever inseperably uniting

---

[1] See R. K. Donovan, 'The Military Origins of the Roman Catholic Relief Programme of 1778', *Historical Journal*, xxviii (1985), 79–102; T. Bartlett, The *Fall and Rise of the Irish Nation*: *The Catholic Question 1690–1830*, Dublin, 1992.

[2] See Burke's resolutions on Ireland of 11 May 1779, printed below.

[3] See Burke's preamble for a Catholic Relief Bill of [May 1778], below, pp. 384–5.

[4] 17 and 18 Geo. III, c.49. Like the English Catholic Relief Act it allowed Catholics to take land leases up to 999 years and repealed a provision under which Catholic landowners sons who conformed could take title to their fathers' land.

[5] *Corr.* iii. 455. For further discussion, see A. P. Levack, 'Edmund Burke, his Friends, and the Dawn of Irish Catholic Emancipation', *Catholic Historical Review*, xxxvii (1951–2), 405.

your Title to the Crown, with the Laws and Liberties of your people.

Our[1] exclusion from many of the Benefits of that constitution, has not taken away our Love and admiration of its perfection which we contemplate without Envy in the felicity of our fellow subjects. The heat of antient contentions is in us perfectly coold, and the prejudices of former times are worn from our Minds. We have patiently submitted to discouragements which by the National Wisdom [have] been deemd necessary to the safety of the whole; and they have thankfully received such relaxations in the Execution of the Laws, as the mildness of this enlightend age and the benignity[2] [of] your Majesties Government has produced; and they submissively wait without prescribing time or measure for such other indulgence as these principles will, they hope, naturally effect.

They do assure your Majesty, that their dissent from the established church is purely conscientious, wholly unmixed with faction, or with any political consideration whatsoever; that they hold no opinions, with regard to church or to state which engage them to a disaffection to your Majesties Government, or which unfit them for the Duties of good Citizens in any relation of Life. And they trust that this has been more unequivocally shown by their irreproachable Conduct as subjects and as men, under circumstances of displeasure and distrust, for severall years, than it can be manifested by any declarations whatsoever.

They have, with the modesty which suited the situation of men excluded from the commonwealth, for a long time abstaind from meddling in any of the party disputes which have agitated the Nation, and have generally forborn to intrude any opinion of theirs upon publick affairs. But when we are threatned with a foreign War in which your Majesties Subjects can have but one Interest and ought to have but one wish and one Sentiment and in which a perfect unanimity may possibly add something to the Spirit and Security of the Nation, We think it may be proper to assure your Majesty of our entire devotion to your Government, of our unalterable affection to the Cause and welfare of our Country, and our utter abhorrence [of] the prevalence of any foreign power against the dignity of your Majesties Crown or the common good of our fellow Subjects.

---

[1] In this draft Burke gets confused between the first and third person.
[2] MS.: 'benigtity'.

The delicacy of our Situation is such that we are at a loss to know what service it is we can offer but we faithfully assure your Majesty, that we are ready on this Critical occasion, or on any occasion to give such proofs of our fidelity and the clearness of our Intentions as your Majesties Wisdom and the Sense of the Nation shall think expedient.

Speech on Vote of Credit
6 May 1778

Source: *General Advertiser*, 8 May 1778

Other reports are *in the Public Advertiser*, 8 May, and *Whitehall Evening Post*, 9 May, repeated in *Parl. Reg.* ix. 173–4 and *Parl. Hist.* xix. 1136; and *London Chronicle*, 7 May (and other papers).

On 5 May Lord North had delivered a message from the King asking the House to 'enable him to defray any extraordinary expenses incurred, or to be incurred, on account of military services, for the service of the year 1778'. The vote of credit for £1,000,000 was debated the following day.

Mr. Burke, in one of the most able and conclusive speeches we ever heard in that House, took a very extended view of the subject. The noble Lord, he said, instead of *watching* over the interests of the state, like a pious and worthy christian, *prayed* over them; and indeed the situation of the state was so deplorable, that we stood in need of the prayers of all good and pious men. It was however a sign of our imbecility, that we trusted in hopes and prayers for protection. It was ever the language of despair, and spake the mind incapable of acting, to pour forth their feeble hopes of Fortune's interference. Such was the desperate crisis of the nation, that nothing now but *Fortune* could save us. They had reduced us to the extremity of trusting to the caprice of the fickle deity, instead of commanding, as wise men at all times do, success. They blamed the uncertainty of winds, and dared to say it was impossible for wisdom to foresee such a prevention. Wisdom at all times, and in every case, can foresee, and the winds themselves are subjected to her controul. Could not prudence and wisdom foresee an event natural in the course of the seasons, and which is accounted for by causes within human knowledge. That the wind would change, about the beginning of May, from the East to West, and continue nearly as long in that quarter as it usually does in the other. The return of every season tells us, that, during the months of March and April, the wind generally stands easterly for six weeks; and after that time turns to a contrary quarter. It was the business of foresight and experience to take advantage of this circumstance, and not reduce us to the miserable dilemma in which we now stand. Such is the consequence of this neglect, that Monsieur d'Estaing will, in all human probability, accomplish the purpose on which he is sent. The place of his destination is too evident to require concealment. He is gone to America;[1] and the fleet of Lord Howe, and the army, consisting of the best 36,000 troops in the universe, will fall a prey to his superiority. We know that he has on board Monsieur Girard,[2] as Plenipotentiary to the Thirteen United States, as well as many passengers and American pilots. It is impossible that bravery can save our fleet and army. Even Fortune herself can hardly overtake him. He adverted, in a particular manner, to what fell from the noble Lord, and marked, with the strongest energy, the expression he had used, That the situation of a Minister was no longer an object of envy, or a mark for ambition. Such was their success, that they had even rendered grandeur, power, the ability of doing good, and the service of their country, objects unworthy of ambition.

The vote of credit was approved without division.

Speech on Funeral of Lord Chatham
21 May 1778

Source: *Morning Chronicle*, 23 May 1778

The same report is in the *General Evening Post, London Chronicle*, and (abbreviated) *St James's Chronicle* for 23 May. It is reported in *Parl. Hist.* xix. 1232–3. Other reports are in *Lloyd's Evening Post*, 22 May; *Morning Post*, 22 May; *Gazetteer*, 23 May; *General Advertiser*, 22 May; *London Evening Post*, 23 May; and *Whitehall Evening Post*, 23 May.

[1] Jean-Baptiste-Charles-Henri-Hector, Comte d'Estaing (1729–94) had sailed from Toulon in April. He arrived off Delaware on 8 July and off Sandy Hook, New York, on 11 July. Ministers had been compelled to explain that the fleet at Spithead had not received an order to intercept d'Estaing in time to escape contrary winds.
[2] Conrad-Alexandre Gérard (1729–90), the first French Minister to the United States.

Lord Chatham died on 11 May. Throughout the 1760s and 1770s the relationship between him and the Rockingham party had virtually never been an easy one. The Rockinghams had oscillated between rather desperately seeking his approval and friendship[1] to despising him almost totally. Burke, himself, had often demonstrated a strong animosity towards him for what he believed to be his duplicity in dealing with the party. In 1766, after watching the Rockingham leaders pursue Chatham during much of their first administration, Burke had claimed that 'by looking for a support exterior to themselves, and leaning on it, they have weakened themselves, rendered themselves triffling, and at length have had drawn away from them that prop upon which they have leaned.'[2] Now, however, this important public figure was gone and Burke was prepared to forget the past. The House had accepted unanimously a resolution requesting the King to give directions for his burial at public expense, and that a monument be erected to him in Westminster Abbey. On 21 May a petition from the City of London was presented requesting that Chatham be buried in St Paul's.[3] Burke supported it wholeheartedly.

Mr. Burke joined with those who wished that Lord Chatham's remains might be buried in St. Paul's; that spacious Cathedral was particularly calculated for monuments; it was now a mere desart; while Westminster-abbey was over crouded. He dwelt much upon the virtues of the noble Lord; and though he knew that there had been some shades in his character,[4] for it was in some degree impossible to be in nature a great character without faults, yet they were so brightened by the resplendent glory of his virtues, that they were to him now, since his death, perfectly invisible. He did not agree with the Right Honourable gentleman[5] that politicians were unfit for the government of the city: the city politicians had before now saved the city; and it was to the firmness of their politics that the house owed their existence; that a Sheriff, a privilege singular in its kind, could appear at their Bar; or indeed that there had been any parliamentary

---

[1] Langford, *Rockingham Administration*, pp. 230–3 ff.

[2] *Corr.* i. 250.

[3] Walter Spencer Stanhope (1749–1821) relates that Burke carried off part of the House to Westminster Abbey and there quoted Thomas Tickell's (1686–1740) 'Elegy on the Death of Addison' (A. M. W. Stirling, *Annals of a Yorkshire House*, 2 vols., London, 1911, ii. 31–3).

[4] *Morning Chronicle*: 'characters'.

[5] Richard Rigby. He had opposed a funeral procession through London involving the Common Council. He supported instead a monument to Chatham at Westminster Abbey and the burial there. He said that his 'respect for the corporation of London had ceased when it ceased to be governed by the most opulent and respectable characters'. His speeches are in *Parl. Hist.* xix. 1230, 1231–2.

bar for them to appear at. The petition, he declared, was worded in a manner which did the composers of it no less honour for the patriotic and respectful sentiment it breathed, than for the elegance and beauty of the stile in which it was written.[1]

As to the place of the Earl's interment he hoped the House would not interfere, and rob his family of a right of which it were a species of sacrilege to deprive them—that of depositing where they should think fit, the remains of this great ancestor, the pride and boast of their family, and the source of future emulation to glorious deeds, such as his example might prompt them to.

Chatham was buried on 9 June in Westminster Abbey, Burke being one of the pallbearers. The City erected a monument to him in Guildhall.

Speech on Hartley's Motion
28 May 1778

Source: *General Advertiser*, 2 June 1778

This report is repeated in *Parl. Reg.* ix. 266–7 and *Parl. Hist.* xix. 1223–4. Other reports are in the *Morning Post*, 30 May; *London Chronicle*, 30 May; *Westminster Journal*, 6 June; *Gazetteer*, 1 June; and *Whitehall Evening Post*, 4 June.

On 28 May David Hartley moved for an address to entreat the King not to prorogue Parliament in order that it might assist in measures already 'taken for the restoration of peace in America'. Burke spoke after Lord North who had praised the majorities in both Houses: 'They were respectable, unbiassed, and confident in their conduct: he paid the utmost deference to them, but, in the present case, he truly thought that Parliament might trust as safely in the ministry.'

Mr. Burke could not, he said, have the most distant comparison made between the majorities of Parliament, and the minority, without feeling resentment at the pretended equality. Depraved and corrupted, blind, biassed, and enchained, as the majorities have of late been, still the dignity of the House, and the recollection of what majorities have been, induced him to reprehend so unequal a comparison. Majorities have been composed, even in this session, of the independent part of

---

[1] Morning Chronicle: 'writen'.

the House. The opinion of the minority, by continuing the same for years together, brought them, by the transition of the contrary opinion, into the largest majority that ever the present administration were blest with. Minorities have become majorities, by the absurdity, in the first instance, and inflexibility in the second, of the Ministry. He could not avoid reverting to the dream of the learned gentleman,[1] nor enough wonder, reflecting on his amazing sagacity, that he should have been reduced to the incapacity of quoting examples from the records of barbarity.[2] The conduct of war, in the days of Rome, is, indeed, a very proper line for ours. It would have been the misfortune of that learned gentleman, if he had been made a prisoner in those days, to have been set up to public sale, with his *doubts*, and his ribbons about his neck, and been sold for a slave. He was happy that his dream was so soon, and so easily read, and that, like all dreams, it had been born in the weakness of the brain, and had ended in nothing. He begged leave to say, to an expression that had fallen from an honourable gentleman,[3] and answered to by the noble Lord,[4] something in favour of opposition. It was not his wish that any gentleman should join with opposition, before he had well considered the principles he entertained, and the conduct of the party he was about to join. To young members he invariably said, that he would rather wish them to join administration, than to adhere to opposition, before their minds are made up. It was so much more shameful to change from opposition to administration, than from the latter to the former, that he begged them to be cautious and considerate in their choice. If the honourable gentleman did mean to join with the part of the House to which he adhered, he would only say, that he would join with a set of men, as wise, as disinterested, and as worthy as ever existed, engaged in the greatest, and the best of causes. He begged to say to the noble Lord, who denied himself to be

---

[1] Wedderburn. Not all of Burke's allusion to his speech can be explained from the report of it in *Parl. Reg.* ix. 260.

[2] Wedderburn had used Roman history to argue that Burgoyne, as a prisoner of war on parole, was not entitled to vote in Parliament. Burgoyne claimed that under the terms of the Convention of Saratoga he was free to do so. The dispute turned on the difficult question of whether the Convention was still in force; there were those on both the British and American sides who argued that it had been abrogated. The difference was resolved when Burgoyne asserted that he had specifically clarified his status in this respect with agents of the Congress. The speaker therefore ruled in his favour.

[3] Burgoyne's speech as reported contained no expression in favour of opposition. But in his campaign to regain his credit after Saratoga he was plainly preparing to side with the Opposition.

[4] North.

the cause of American defalcation, that if he would not confess that he had, through wilful blindness, lost that continent, he must be forced to acknowledge that he had been the *dupe* of interested individuals. He had been misinformed, misadvised, and had misconducted the whole affair. He had not intended, perhaps, to lose, but he *had* lost America.

The motion was lost by 105 votes to 53.

Preamble for Catholic Relief Bill
[May 1778]

Source: MS. at Sheffield, R94.4

In Zouch's hand, corrected by Burke.

Burke is known to have drawn up a preamble for the Catholic Relief Bill which was presented to the House of Commons on 15 May: 'his draft did not give satisfaction.'[1]

Whereas it hath been the practice of all wise States by Acts of Indemnity and general pardon to put an End to the heats and animositys, which commonly attend and might otherwise survive, the most happy alterations in Government, and also in due time and on just occasion to relax those penalties on particular descriptions of Men which the exigency of critical circumstances and the publick safety on the formation of a new establishment had made adviseable. And Whereas the general peaceable demeanor of all his Majesties Roman Catholick Subjects for many years past hath shewn that they merit indulgence, and ought not to be molested in the enjoyment of their property or punished for a modest exercise of their religious persuasion upon the mere suggestion of malicious and interested persons. Therefore, in order to engage all his Majesty's Subjects in an affectionate and grateful Obedience to his Majestys Government, and in attachment to our excellent Constitution, as well as for the honour of the Protestant Religion, whose principles engage its true professors

---

[1] E. H. Burton, *The Life and Times of Bishop Challoner*, ii. 201.

to its support, without injury to any other persons. We therefore etc pray etc.

Brief for Lord Rockingham
[May 1778]

Source: MS. at Sheffield, R94.6

Burke evidently prepared this statement on the Catholic Relief Bill for Lord Rockingham to use in the House of Lords, where it was brought up on 22 May.

The Bill is for a repeal of certain parts of an act of the eleventh and twelfth of King William, which inflicts penalties and incapacities, of a very distressing kind, on the Roman Catholicks, both Clergy and Laity—

1. It destroys their property—
2. It subverts their families—
3. It prevents their Education at home or abroad—
4. It forbids the exercise of their religion—
5. The penalties are excessive and disproportiond—
6. Informers are invited by great rewards; and profligate relations encouraged by grants of the Estate of their popish Kindred.

The *Execution* of this act has been rare.

When *Laws* are worse than the *morals* of the people it is commonly the Case.

But *some* attempts have been made lately and successfully[1]—and there is reason to believe, that many attacks have been made on Estates, and compounded, and the proprietors kept under contribution.

That Severities may be necessary in times of publick confusion, and in great civil dissentions, which it would be wrong to continue afterwards.

Perhaps too there was something of Anger and resentment as well as policy, originally in the making this Statute. The attempts of a *popish Prince* had irritated the Legislature against *all* those of his Communion, however, innocent they might have been.

---

[1] Burke has written in the margin: 'One priest condemnd to be imprisond for Life—after some imprisonment, pardond on condition of perpetual transportation'.

385

This Law has continued *fourscore years*; without any *new* provocation or *cause* given for retaining it.

That we ought to lament the *Necessity* which had given rise to Laws so repugnant to the principles of *humanity*, of *Legislation* in general, of the *British Constitution in particular*, and indeed so contrary to the Genius of the *Protestant religion* itself; We ought not to continue them a Moment longer than the necessity which gave rise to them is evident.

That the principle of this Bill is to discriminate the *obnoxious politicks* from the simply *religious opinions* of the Roman Catholicks. Common justice requires, that when *one* of these is persecuted, upon account of its *supposed connexion with the other*, that the people may have an opportunity of seperating them, and shewing what they do and what they do not hold.

There was no pretence for persecuting papists, but *two*,—The first that they were supposed to acknowlege that kind of *Temporal power* in the Pope which gave him a *dominion over princes*, inconsistent with the Allegiance of Subjects.—The other that they were attached to the Interests of that family, whose Title is adverse to our happy establishment.

When they give satisfaction on these two points we ought to be as desirous to give, as they are to receive all reasonable indulgence, at least so far as to allow them the common rights of Mankind; 1. The power of acquiring and keeping property. 2. The modest exercise of their religion 3 and the power of giving Education to their Children.

That many harsh Laws remain, even harsher than this which is repeald[1]—The repeal of them too may become a matter of future consideration. But this act is the *latest*, and that on which most of the *prosecutions* have been grounded.

That the Bill has passed through the Commons, with unprecedented unanimity.[2] An unanimity which will do more service to the Cause of true religion, than all the persecuting Laws that ever were devised. Hope that it will meet the same reception from their Lordships.

---

[1] There is a summary by Burke of the remaining penalties on Catholics (MS. at Sheffield, Bk 27.205).
[2] There were no divisions on the Bill.

Speech on Commissioners' Manifesto
4 December 1778

Sources: *Parl. Reg.* xi. 116–17; *London Evening Post*, 5 December 1778

The beginning of the report reproduced here is only in *Parl. Reg.*, but the bulk of it is also in the *London Evening Post*, 5 December: for the material that is common to both the newspaper is followed. The same report is in the *General Advertiser*, 5 December, and *Westminster Journal*, 19 December. The *Parl. Hist.* xix. 1399–1400 repeats *Parl. Reg.* The report is abbreviated in *London Chronicle*, 5 December, and *Morning Chronicle*, 7 December. Other reports are in *Morning Post*, 5 December, and *Gazetteer*, 7 December. There are also no less than five rough drafts for this speech amongst Burke's papers at Northampton (A.xxxvii.61a, 62, 4, 5, 12).

On 3 October the Carlisle Commission[1] issued a Manifesto threatening 'the extremes of war' against the Americans. The Rockingham leaders in general viewed the measure with strong displeasure. The Marquess of Rockingham himself raised the matter in the Lords on 4 December promising a motion of censure 'when newspaper reports of the Commission's "Manifesto and Proclamation" could be authenticated'.[2] He produced such a motion three days later expatiating 'on the horrors which must ensue from pursuing the cruel system of desolation and savage cruelty'.[3] In the House of Commons a Foxite, Thomas William Coke,[4] moved on the fourth that an Address be presented to the King condemning the Manifesto. When Sir Grey Cooper[5] alleged that 'burning of towns that were nurseries of soldiers, or arsenals, or magazines of military stores, was perfectly consistent with the principles of civilized war', Burke felt obliged to reply.

Mr. *Burke* instanced the letter of the Marshall de Belleisle to Monsieur de Contades, in the last war, which was intercepted by the English. It was held in so disgracing a light, that it was published in the London Gazette, to prove to all the world, that the French, driven to extremities, were forced to renew the barbarities of war, and to desolate the country they could not subdue; and so strongly did this publication work on the French court, that in a proclamation they disavowed all knowledge of it: in so infamous a light did the barbarities of war appear to all Europe.[6] He thought the most exceptionable words

[1] See the headnote to Burke's speech of 23 February 1778 on North's Conciliation Bills, printed above.
[2] *London Chronicle*, 5 December 1778.
[3] Ibid. 8 December 1778.
[4] (1754–1842), 'Coke of Norfolk', later (1837) 1st Earl of Leicester, M.P. 1776–84, 1790–1832.
[5] (*c.*1726–1801), M.P. 1765–84, 1786–90.
[6] The letter (dated 23 July 1759) had been written by Charles-Louis-Auguste Fouquet, Duc de Belle-Isle (1684–1761) to Louis-Georges Érasme, Marquis de Contade (1704–95). In 1759

were, "that they had hitherto refrained from the extremes of war and the desolation of the country."[1] It is necessary, in order to decide on this point, to look back to the conduct of the war, had not almost every advantage been taken that the *rights of war* among civilized nations could authorize. Thus, if the war was to be changed—if the mode we had already practised—if the lenity, the humanity, the toleration which had been hitherto observed, was to be foregone, and we had forebore nothing that the rights of war could authorize, then the plan now to be prosecuted was different from lenity and toleration, and was different from the laws of war. The laws of war were the laws of limitation, for war was constantly to be limited by necessity, and its calamities and ravages bound in by that plea alone. But the *extremes of war*, and the *desolation of a country*, went beyond all limitations; and as no necessity could warrant them, no argument could excuse them. To prove by an example, the difference between the *limitations* of war, and the *extremes* of war, he stated that it would be right and pardonable, because it would be necessary to burn any fort, garrison, or town, that would give strength to the enemy, and enable them to annoy you; it would be proper to burn any house from which the enemy fired upon you; but it would not be lawful, right, nor pardonable, to burn any town, or house, that might, in process of time, give strength to the enemy, but which could not now shelter them. The *extremes of war* and the desolation of a country, were sweet sounding mutes and liquids, but their meaning was terrible; they meant the killing man, woman, and child, burning their houses, and ravaging their lands, annihilating humanity from the face of the earth, or rendering it so wretched that death would be preferable; and against whom was this dreadful menace pronounced, not against the virulent and the guilty, but against those who, conscious of rectitude, acted to the best of their ability in a good cause, and stood up to fight for freedom and their country. His arguments were too many for our small compass, but not too few, either for the importance

---

it had been 'found among Contades' papers after the battle of Minden', and had seemed to demonstrate 'the habitual villainy' of the French in plundering conquered territories. For the letter and the aftermath, see the *Annual Register* for 1759, pp. 234–8, and *London Gazette*, 18 August 1759.

[1] From this point the text of the speech in the *London Evening Post* is followed. The newspaper's report had begun: '*Mr. Burke*, in one of the most argumentative, most closely reasoned, and most conclusive speeches we ever heard, proved the contrary. The words in the passage were, "that they had hitherto refrained from the *extremes of war* and the *desolation* of the country".'

of the subject, or for their weight; one in particular we must advert to, which will come home to every breast: Lewis XIV. of France, ravaged and laid waste the Palatinate; and the great Duke of Marlborough, in retaliation ravaged Bavaria:[1] It was held pardonable and fair to revenge the barbarity on the *Ally*, rather than on the criminal herself, because there she was most vulnerable. Will not our enemies do the same? And will not every power be intimidated from allying with a nation who hath thrown away every shadow of principle, and renewed the savage horrors of ignorant and uncivilised war?

The motion was defeated by 209 votes to 122.

Speech on Luttrell's Motion on Palliser
11 December 1778

Source: *Gazetteer*, 15 December 1778

Burke spoke three times in this debate. The first and second speeches are in *Parl. Reg.* xi. 139, 143–4 and *Parl. Hist.* xx. 60, 64. The third is in *Gazetteer*, 15 December, reproduced in *Parl. Reg.* xi. 147–8 and *Parl. Hist.* xx. 67–9. This is the speech printed here. Reports of one or more of these speeches are in *Gazetteer*, 14 December; *General Evening Post* and *Whitehall Evening Post*, 12 December; *Morning Chronicle*, 11 December; *Morning Post*, 12 December (and other papers); *Public Ledger*, 12 December; *London Evening Post*, 12 December; *General Advertiser*, 12 December; and *Westminster Journal*, 19 December. There is also a MS. report of the debate at Sheffield (R90.4).

Admiral Augustus Keppel,[2] a longstanding member of the Rockingham party, had accepted the command of the Channel Fleet and on 27 July 1778 fought an indecisive battle off Ushant with the French. The conduct of Vice-Admiral Palliser,[3] a member of the Board of Admiralty, at this battle had been criticized in the press, the issue being his failure—for whatever reasons—to obey Keppel's signal to bring his squadron into line.[4] Palliser had asked Keppel to sign a statement to exculpate him, but Keppel had refused. Palliser had thereupon published his own version of what had happened and decided

---

[1] In 1704.
[2] See above, p. 325.
[3] Sir Hugh Palliser, 1st Baronet (1723–96), M.P. 1774–9, 1780–4.
[4] The affair is covered with noticeable sympathy for Keppel in *Rockingham Memoirs*, ii. 360–79.

to take action against Keppel.[1] The matter was first raised in the House of Commons on 2 December. On 9 December Palliser laid serious charges and the Admiralty ordered a Court Martial. If Keppel were to be found guilty, the death sentence was obligatory, and the subsequent trial, which began on 9 January 1779, received a great deal of public attention. Long excerpts from each hearing were transcribed by the press.[2] Burke played a very active part, both in speech and in print, in raising support for Keppel. Thus, for instance, the *Public Advertiser* would later announce that he had

declared in the House of Commons, that if Sir Hugh Palliser was to be tried, he would take Care it should not be a *sham* Trial ... It was, perhaps, not a little presumptuous in Mr. Edmund Burke to give himself such lofty Airs. He imagined, no Doubt, that his late influence on a *like* Occasion, might still continue.[3]

Burke's first opportunity to take a major part came on 11 December 1778 when Temple Simon Luttrell moved for an Address to the King for a Court Martial on Palliser.[4]

Mr. Burke now rose, and after declaring his intention of giving his dissent to the amended motion,[5] but not by way of a direct negative, entered into a minute and accurate investigation of the propriety of the conduct of the Admiralty Board, which, he affirmed, was the true substantial question before the House. Previous to his argument, however, he launched forth into the highest strains of panegyric on the conduct of the Honourable Admiral, absent from his place;[6] and, among a variety of other strong expressions, emphatically asked, was *this* the *return* he met with, after *forty years* painful and laborious service, and after being in *ten* capital engagements, or important conflicts, in every one of which he had, either as possessed of the sole command, or acting in a subordinate character, acquitted himself with the highest honour and reputation? Was it an adequate return for a person of his rank, consequence, and independent situation, stand-

---

[1] *Corr.* iv. 30; *Parl. Hist.* xix. 1382.
[2] See, for instance, *Public Advertiser* and *Gentleman's Magazine*, January and early February 1779.
[3] 28 April 1779.
[4] Palliser's trial began on 12 April.
[5] A proposed amendment deleted the end of Luttrell's motion: 'It appearing to this House, that the said Vice Admiral did not obey the signals of his superior commander, when preparing to re-engage the ships of the enemy.' Burke proposed to support this amendment (*St James's Chronicle*, 12 December), which was carried, and presumably supported the successful motion for the order of the day which effectually defeated Luttrell's motion.
[6] Keppel was not present at this debate; Palliser was and spoke on it.

ing forth as the favoured, selected Champion of his country, in the moment of danger and difficulty? He desired no return, but that which he had already *earned*, and was sure of receiving without diminution; a return which it was not in the power of the Admiralty to bestow, or with-hold—an inward consciousness of having performed his duty; of having stepped forward to shield his country from the ruin meditated by an insolent and ambitious foe; and the united thanks of his fellow-subjects, the gratitude and esteem of every good man of every party. These were the motives which called Mr. Keppel out into actual service; these were the rewards (and *nobler* and *greater* could not be) which he might count upon receiving.

He then entered into a short view of the action of the 27th of July, and endeavoured to shew, that though it did not carry the appearance of a victory, in point of consequence and effect, it was completely so. The enemy were driven into their lurking hole, where they remained in privacy and dishonour, while the British flag was borne triumphant on their coasts. He confirmed his assertions, by commenting on the account of the engagements that appeared in the French Gazette,[1] which he proved to consist of an heap of contradictions, absurdities, &c. and the whole taken together, as public information by authority, composing the *veriest gasconade* that ever disgraced the annals of any country;—such as running away under covert of the night, and pretending, that in the morning they found themselves *accidentally* at the mouth of Brest harbour; and their abandoning the whole of their commerce, in the most critical season of the year, to fall a prey to our privateers and letters of marque.

He then proceeded to consider the powers of the Admiralty Board, under the act of 22d of George the Second,[2] but before he proceeded any further, he begged leave to remind the House, that the noble Lord (Mulgrave)[3] who maintained, that the Board could only act ministerially, had indeed, in fact, (though, he presumed, not intentionally) given up the argument,—The noble Lord's principal defence consisted in asserting, that when charges were technically and

---

[1] See *Corr.* iv. 13.
[2] 22 Geo. II, c. 33. Much of the debate centred on the question of whether the Admiralty under this statute was obliged, after Palliser had brought his charges, to order the Court Martial on Keppel.
[3] Constantine John Phipps (1744–92), later (1790) 1st Baron Mulgrave, M.P. 1768–74, 1776–90, and Lord of the Admiralty 1777–82.

specifically made, and were of sufficient importance; the Board was compelled to act upon them, and give an order for immediate trial; but, adds the noble Lord, if they seem frivolous, or the accusation is such as will not admit of a negative; or, if proved, is not of sufficient importance; under such circumstances, the Board may, and will reject,[1] is not this at once substituting discretion, for acting merely as an instrument created by law? If the Board *can* deliberate, examine, and decide upon the nature of a complaint, by what is this discretionary power limited? The noble Lord has repeated frequently, that no such power is permitted, or created by the statute. If not, then it must have resided in the Board all along, and was not divested out of it by the statute. Should the noble Lord deny the latter, then his exception comes at once to nothing. The Board is not competent, in any instance, to judge; or, if competent, the Board, in every such act, exercises a discretionary power; the conclusion is clear and unavoidable either way. Every absurdity, villainy, and evil, which malice, rage, or folly, can suggest, is a proper subject to be sent to be enquired into by a Court-martial; or the Admiralty Board have the right contended for, that of judging of the magnitude, extent, and probability of the charge; the circumstances which brought it into existence, and every other matter connected with it; which may enable them to be the means of promoting general and particular justice.

He finally proceeded to consider the nature of the incompetency contended for by the noble Lord.

This, he observed, must be either *natural* or *artificial*; that is, it meant that the Admiralty Board *never* had the discretional power insisted upon; or, having it, that power was taken away by the statute.

That it had no *natural* incompetency would, he presumed, be hardly asserted seriously in debate. The clause read by the Clerk at the table proved it; and the very evils stated so ably by the noble Lord, which the statute, he said, was purposely framed to prevent, was the fullest evidence that this discretion existed previous to the act.

If then the Admiralty Board was not *naturally* incompetent, it followed of course, that its present supposed incompetency must have been caused by some subsequent act; which could be no other than that of 22d of George II, so[2] often alluded to.

---

[1] See Mulgrave's speeches in *Parl. Reg.* xi. 138–9, 139–40.
[2] *Gazetteer*: 'so so'.

Here then the issue lay between him and the noble Lord. It was brought upon its true ground, and was narrowed to the single question; Has the statute *taken away* the previous discretionary power existing in the Admiralty Board? He contended it did not, nor restrict it in a single instance but the one mentioned. The powers of the Board remained the same after as before the passing of that act; if they did not, in his opinion such was the rashness and hastiness, of those who now preside at that Board, respecting their conduct to the Honourable Admiral, that it was highly incumbent to give Parliament, and the nation, the most full and satisfactory proofs, that they could not have acted otherwise than they did without a breach of duty; for if this was *not* complied with, every evil and misfortune such as a *precipitate* conduct (he would call it *no worse*) might be productive of, would be laid at their door.

The order of the day was successfully moved in order to defeat Luttrell's motion.

Speech on Army Estimates
14 December 1778

Source: *Morning Chronicle*, 15 December 1778

This report is reproduced in *Parl. Reg.* xi. 161–4 and *Parl. Hist.* xx. 81–5. Other reports are in *London Chronicle*, 15 December (and other papers); *London Evening Post*, 15 December; and *Public Ledger*, 15 December.

On 14 December 1778 Charles Jenkinson introduced the army estimates. In response, Burke attempted to exploit growing public disillusionment with the American war. He also took the opportunity to explain his acceptance of American independence.

Mr. *Burke* declared that the Honourable Gentleman who spoke last but one,[1] had addressed himself chiefly to the passions of the House; this he thought a very improper moment for such[2] an address; he wished to speak to the good sense and reason of those who heard him. It was an easy thing, and to the ears of most Englishmen, a very

---

[1] Welbore Ellis.
[2] *Morning Chronicle*: 'such such'.

satisfactory one to boast of the magnanimity and the spirit of this country. Such arguments caught the passions, and while they proved nothing, tended to lead astray the judgment and bewilder the senses. Untill it was made evident to his understanding, that with thirty millions of debt, which had accumulated in consequence of the American war, we were richer than before we had incurred a shilling of that expence, and until he was convinced that we could do more with a small force than we had been able to effect with a Large army, the best appointed that the world had ever seen, he would not agree that this was a moment for us to adopt a pursuit of the same system which had put us in so much peril, or to continue a war in America, where all our schemes of conquest had been defeated, and where so much of our treasure, and so much of our national force had been sacrificed and thrown away. He contended that great as our resources might be, it was the certain way to exhaust them altogether, to apply them to the furtherance of a design, which experience ought long since to have taught us, it was impossible for us to accomplish.

With regard to avowing the Independency of America, Gentlemen looked at the position in a wrong point of view, and talked of it merely as a matter of choice, when in fact it was now become a matter of necessity. It was in this latter light only that he regarded it, in this latter light only that he maintained that it was incumbent on Great Britain to acknowledge it directly. On the day that he first heard of the American states having claimed Independency, it made him sick at heart; it struck him to the soul, because he saw it was a claim essentially injurious to this country, and a claim which Great Britain could never get rid of. Never! Never! Never! It was not therefore to be thought that he wished for the Independency of America.—Far from it.—He felt it as a circumstance exceedingly detrimental to the fame, and exceedingly detrimental to the interest of his country. But when by a wrong management of the cards a gamester had lost much, it was right for him to make the most of the game as it then stood, and to take care that he did not lose more. This was our case at present, the stake already gone was material, but the very existence of our empire was more, and we were now madly putting that to the risque. The argument of the Honourable Gentleman was in other words this: "I have lost my Lincolnshire estate—I have lost my coal-mines in Northumberland, and my tin-mines in Cornwall, but I have still left Goose Common and a Duck Decoy, and I have great magnanimity." It was exactly the language held by those who had gained the estates of minors, by Dice and Hazard. "You lost your estate at the gaming table—Go there again; there it is that you must look for another estate!"

He adverted a good deal to what had fallen from another Speaker [Governor Johnstone][1] relative to the folly of giving up the Independency of America, and the still remaining power of this country to conquer *and recover her*. The Honourable Gentleman had declared, that the majority of the people of America were still at heart the friends of this country; that they longed most ardently to avow their sentiments of loyalty, and to return to their allegiance. The Honourable Gentleman had said further, that the Congress were not chosen by the united voices of the people of America; that they held their situation by force, and that their tyranny was intolerable; and the Honourable Gentleman had mentioned, that the vote of Independency was carried by a majority of two only;[2] and that in the province of Pennsylvania where he was, there he was sure we had 30,000 friends. If these things were so, how happened it that when we had at Philadelphia an army, the finest ever seen, of 18,000 men, to support the thirty thousand provincials, who wished so well to Great Britain, that the 30,000 did not avow their loyalty to Great Britain, and did not deny the authority of the 600 tyrants who formed the monster called Congress, which held them in such oppressive subjection. If the 30,000 dare not oppose the usurped power of Congress, with such a powerful support at their back, was it likely, that they should hereafter do it, when we were not in the heart of them? The Honourable Gentleman had also said, that in New England and Massachusett's Bay, which was originally the centre of opposition to Great Britain; as it were the Head Quarters of rebellion, the people were divided into powerful factions, equally conducive and promising to the interests of this country; one party opposing Congress generally, and the other opposing Congress particularly, on account of the alliance she had made with France. Surely if this had been as the Honourable gentleman stated, his Majesty's commissioners would have

---

[1] The square brackets are in the newspaper.

[2] This was not true. Nine colonies voted for independence on 1 July 1776; they were joined the following day by South Carolina and Delaware. Pennsylvania joined them the day after that. New York did not vote because independence was not within the instructions of its delegates.

been more successful. The proposals they had made were sufficiently humiliating on the part of Great Britain, sufficiently advantageous, on the part of America!

After dwelling for some time on the argument of the Honourable Speaker, just returned from America; he reverted to a consideration of the present state of Great Britain in point of resource. Enterprize and spirit, he observed were good qualities in the field, but bad ones in the cabinet. Prudence, and a calm review of the financial powers of a country, were the first objects of a Statesman. It was a mad appeal to the passions of a people, whose resources were visibly decaying, that could carry them through where almost every thing depended upon the real sinews of war,—men, and money. He argued that we had exhausted thirty millions in the progress of the war hitherto; that we should have occasion for nine millions for the service of the ensuing year, and that we had already voted a land-tax of 4s in the pound; he compared this with the financial situation of France; introducing the conduct of Monsieur Neckar,[1] and the words of the edict lately published and registered by the Parliament of Paris, [mentioned by the Duke of Richmond in the other House, on Monday Dec. 7][2] from which it was evident, that France to put her navy on a respectable footing, only wanted eighteen hundred thousand pounds, and that she could raise that sum with the greatest ease, and without imposing any new tax on her subjects.[3] He compared the different necessities of the two kingdoms, and the different objects of attention, in the eyes of each, giving France the credit and advantage greatly, both in point of power of finance, and wisdom of application of her resources, deducing from his arguments on this point, a whimsical inference, that by going on with the American war, we were actually endeavouring to invert the order of nature, to change France into an island, and to render Great Britain continental, by suffering the former to acquire a great naval strength, while we were establishing a large military force.

In the course of his speech, he entered into an ample investigation of the propriety of America's joining with France, and contended, that in all ages, and in all countries, it was perfectly natural for revolted

[1] Jacques Necker (1732–1804), Directeur Général des Finances. For Burke's views of Necker in later years, see vol. viii, p. 278.

[2] The square brackets are in the newspaper. For Richmond's speech, see *Parl. Reg.* xiv. 70–5.

[3] The loan of November 1778, constituting life *rentes* of 4.5 million livres, brought in a capital of 48.36 million livres (R. D. Harris, *Necker: Reform Statesman of the Ancien Régime*, Berkeley, 1979, p. 30).

subjects to form an alliance with that power, known to be most inimical to the State from whose supremacy they had withdrawn, and to whom the destruction of the interest of the former parent state was obviously a matter of desirable advantage; proving his arguments on this head, by adducing instances from history. He particularly mentioned the interference of Great Britain to preserve the Low Countries from falling into the hands of France, and to secure them to the House of Austria,[1] and justified both France and America for their conduct in this respect on the broad ground of policy, expressing his astonishment, that any set of men should be so weak as to talk either of the treachery of France or the ingratitude of America, when they considered that America took the step after she had been forced into Independency, and that France acceded to it, when she saw Great Britain had failed in her efforts to conquer the United States, and when she had such extensive and lucrative offers made her by the Americans, provided she would assist them in their endeavours to establish their Independency.

Having spoken for near an hour with that enthusiasm of argument, that variety of metaphor, and volubility of oratory for which he is remarkable, Mr. Burke concluded his speech with urging Ministers to attack France formidably; to vote, if they could get the men, a still larger number than those moved for by the Honourable Member, but to employ them in any other service than against America.

Defence of Keppel
30 January 1779

Source: *Minutes of the Proceedings at a Court Martial*, London, 1779, pp. 102–9, 115–16

Burke was largely responsible for the narrative portion of Keppel's speech of defence in his Court Martial at Portsmouth. Keppel's specific answers (here omitted) to the charges brought against him were probably entirely the work of his lawyers: John Dunning, John Lee (1733–93), M.P. 1782–93, and Thomas Erskine (1750–1823), later (1806) 1st Baron Erskine, M.P. 1783–4, 1790–1806. The conclusion of the defence is largely by John Lee. The defence is here printed from the official *Minutes of the Proceedings* (Todd, 30h). The material available on its composition, however, is extensive. There are fragments of three early drafts in Burke's hand (MSS. at Sheffield, Bk 13.9; Bk 13.11, 13.10; Bk 13.15, 13.12, 13.14, 13.13). There is an incomplete 'fair

---

[1] By the Treaty of Utrecht in 1713 the Spanish Netherlands had passed to the Austrian Habsburgs.

draft' in Burke's hand (MSS. at Sheffield, R90.7, 1–4; Bk 13.23, 24) with some changes by Burke and some brief additions by Dunning. There is an incomplete 'final copy' (Bk 13.2–8) with heavy deletions, alterations by Burke himself, minor corrections in an unknown hand, and one passage changed by the Duke of Richmond. Finally there is John Lee's draft of the conclusion of the defence, with amendments by Burke, one paragraph being added by him as well as the last sentence of all (Bk 13.16, 25–7). It would be excessive to produce a text which contained all variants.

The procedure followed has been to ignore the early drafts, to reproduce in annotation major passages from the fair draft which were eliminated before the final copy was prepared, and to reproduce passages deleted in the final copy, but to ignore the handful of small changes which were made after the final copy was prepared and which appear in the printed version.

Keppel's Court Martial began at Portsmouth on 7 January. It assembled for the first day on board the *Britannia* and then, because of the Admiral's poor health, continued on shore at the Governor's House for the remaining five weeks. The court was presided over by Sir Thomas Pye,[1] Admiral of the Blue, and consisted as well of four admirals and eight captains. Keppel was charged with not marshaling his fleet, going into the fight in an unprofessional manner, scandalous haste in quitting the fight, running away, and not pursuing the enemy—all capital offences. Palliser himself was the prosecutor. A great number of officers ranging in rank from admiral to captain to lieutenant, were called as witnesses. The overwhelming majority testified that Keppel had conducted himself in a courageous and intelligent manner given the circumstances of the engagement. As a result, on 11 February, the court unanimously and honourably acquitted him.

There was some doubt expressed about the objectivity of the court. Rockingham kept the courtroom packed throughout with party supporters and Horace Walpole believed that some of the judges were so biased in favour of Keppel that Palliser should have refused to proceed.[2] However, Burke had reason to feel well pleased that his efforts helped to bring a favourable verdict for his friend. He might on the other hand have been less than delighted with the repercussions of the affair on the British navy. The armed forces generally had suffered from an appalling lack of unity since 1775, in part because officers like General Amherst[3] would not wage war on the colonists. Keppel himself had refused initially to serve and had agreed to command the Channel fleet only for the European theatre of operations. In the Court Martial the majority of the officers supported him,[4] but Palliser also had some influential friends in the naval establishment including the First Lord of the Admiralty, Lord Sandwich.[5] As the following speech helps to demonstrate, the trial drove a deep wedge between the two sides which could only have magnified existing tensions in the navy and done further damage to morale.[6]

[1] (*c.*1713–85).

[2] *Last Journals*, ii. 343.

[3] Jeffrey, 1st Baron Amherst (1717–97) Commander-in-Chief. For his refusal to serve in the war, see P. Mackesy, *The War for America, 1775–1783*, London, 1964, pp. 40, 214.

[4] See the Address of Admirals and Captains of February 1779, printed below.

[5] John Montagu, 4th Earl of Sandwich (1718–92).

[6] Mackesy, *The War for America*, pp. 239–44.

TWENTY-FIRST DAY
SATURDAY, the 30th of JANUARY, 1779

Court met according to Adjournment.

The Prisoner called in, and Audience admitted.

The Prisoner began his Defence, which he read, and is as follows:

Mr. President, and Gentlemen of the Court,

I AM brought before you, after Forty Years Service, on the Charge of an Officer under my Command, for a Variety of Offences; which, if true or probable, would be greatly aggravated by the Means I have had, from a long Experience, of knowing my Duty, and by the strong Motives of Honour, which ought to have incited me to perform it to the very utmost Extent of my Ability.[1]

Sir *Hugh Palliser*, an Officer under my Orders, conceives that I have acted very irregularly and very culpably in the Engagement with the *French* Fleet on the 27th of *July* last; so very irregularly, and so very faultily, that I have tarnished the Lustre of the Navy of *England*.

Possessed with this Opinion, on our Return to Port after the Action, he has a Letter from the Lords of the Admiralty[2] put into his Hands, giving me, in the most explicit Terms, his Majesty's Approbation, for a Conduct which he now affects to think deserves the utmost Disapprobation and the severest Censure; and he, with the other Admirals and Captains of the Fleet, to whom it was likewise communicated, perfectly acquiesces in it.

With the same ill Opinion of my Conduct in his Bosom, he goes to Sea again under my Command; he goes to Sea under me, without having given the least Vent to his Thoughts, either by Way of Advice to myself, or of Complaint to our common Superiors.

He afterwards corresponds with me in Terms of Friendship;[3] and in that Correspondence he uses Expressions which convey a very high Opinion of my Disinterestedness, and of my Zeal for the Service.

After all this I come home; I am received by his Majesty with the most gracious Expressions of Favour and Esteem; and I am received in the most flattering Manner by the First Lord of the Admiralty.[4]

---

[1] This first paragraph was rewritten by Burke on the final copy (Bk 13.2). The opening had previously read: 'I am brought to my Trial before you after forty years Service on the Charge of an Officer, under my Command for Negligence and ignorance of my Duty.'

[2] The letter of 2 August 1778 is printed in *Minutes of the Proceedings*, p. 166.

[3] Deleted here on the final copy (Bk 13.2): 'and particularly speaks of the event of that Engagement (which he now says has tarnished the Lustre of the Navy of Great Britain) as of a *Victory*'.   [4] Lord Sandwich.

Several Weeks pass—when at length, without giving me any previous Notice, the Board of Admiralty send me Five Articles of Charge, on which they declare their Intention of bringing me to my Trial. These Charges are brought by Sir *Hugh Palliser*; who nearly at the same Time publicly declared,[1] that he had taken this Step from an Opinion, that he himself lay under an Imputation of Disobedience to my Orders, and that this Imputation was countenanced by me.[2]

I may say without the least Hesitation, that if I should be censured on such a Charge (which in this Court and with my Cause I think impossible), there is an End of all Command in the Navy. If every subordinate Officer can set up his Judgment against[3] that of his Commander in Chief, and, after several Months of insidious Silence, can call him to Trial, whenever he thinks it useful for the Purpose of clearing away Imputations on himself, or in order to get the Start of a regular Charge, which he apprehends may possibly be brought on his own Conduct—there can be no Service.

If the Charges of my Accuser could be justified by his Apprehensions for himself, he has taken Care to prove to the Court, that he had very good Reason for his Fears; but if these Charges are to be considered as supported upon any rational Ground, with regard to the Nature of the Offence, or any satisfactory Evidence with regard to the Facts, as against me—he makes that Figure, which, I trust in God, all those who attack Innocence will ever make.[4]

---

[1] The fair copy adds: 'as he had done long before fortunately'.

[2] Palliser had made this charge in a speech in the Commons on 11 December 1778 (*Parl. Hist.* xx. 54–5).

[3] *Minutes of the Proceedings*: 'agianst'; 'in such attempts' deleted.

[4] R.90.7-2: 'Before I close my Evidence, I think I shall let you see to the very bottom of the malice, the falshood, the futility, and the folly of this accusation. I have not the smallest doubt that the same principles of honour and justice which have conducted you from the beginning of this Trial will lead you to a proper determination at the End of it; and that by your manly and upright Judgment you will confirm, what in my conscience I am persuaded, is already the formed opinion of the whole Navy of England.

I hope I shall prove to the Confusion of the Advocates of France that neither did I lead, nor did the British Fleet follow in that disgraceful flight which is so injuriously in the paper of accusation attributed to us both. I shall prove that with the Flag of England in my hands. I knew the full value of the pledge that was in them. I owe the clearest explanation of every thing to you and to the Service, and to the Glory of my Country. I want to prove to my profession that they have not been mistaken in me, to my King that he did not disgrace his Judgment when by his free choice he appointed me to that high Command. I owe even to an honourable enemy the satisfaction of knowing that he was not worsted by a blockhead and Poltroon'

R.90.7-1: 'As I am called to Trial under these unusual Circumstances, I must conform myself to them. The plan of my Defence must be that of a Commander in chief justifying his own

In your Examination into that Judgment, which my Officer, in order to depreciate my Skill and to criminate my Conduct, has thought proper to set up against mine, you have very wisely, and according to the evident Necessity of the Case, called for the Observations and Sentiments of all the Officers who have served in the late Engagement, so far as they have been brought before you by the Prosecutor. I take it for granted you will follow the same Course with those that I shall produce. If this should not be done, an Accuser (according to the Practice of mine), by the Use of leading Questions—by putting Things out of their natural Order—by confounding Times, and by a perplexed Interrogatory concerning an infinite Number of Manœuvres and Situations, might appear to produce a State of Things directly contrary to the Ideas of those who saw them with their own Eyes. I am astonished, that, when one Officer is accused by another of Crimes, which, if true, must be apparent to a very ordinary Observation and Understanding, that any Witness should, on being asked, refuse to declare his free Sentiments of the Manner in which the Matters to which he deposes have appeared to him. I never wished that any Gentleman should withhold that Part of his Evidence from Tenderness to me: what Motives the Accuser had for objecting to it, he knows.[1] The plainest and fullest speaking is best for a good Cause. The manifest View and Intention that Things are done with, constitutes their Crime or Merit. The Intentions are inseparably connected with the Acts; and a Detail of Military or Naval Operations, wholly separated from their Design, will be Nonsense. The Charge is read to a Witness, as I apprehend, that he may discern how the Facts he has seen agree with the Crimes he hears charged, otherwise I cannot conceive why a Witness is troubled with that reading. The Court

---

Judgment against that of his Subordinate officer. In that Trial of Judgments you have very wisely, and according to the evident Necessity of the Case, called for the Observations and Sentiments of all the Officers who have served in the late engagement so far as they have been brought before you by the prosecuter. There are some indeed more capable of giving the Court information; for I believe the Country was never served by Officers of more Gallantry honour, ability and skill in their profession.

When Sir H. P.'s accusations are stripped of the reproachful Terms, and the Criminal inferences, they amount to little else than this—"that if he had commanded on the 27th of July, he would not have acted as I have done".—In this opposition of Judgments you are put to decide between us;—and I have no doubt, that you will determine, (as far as such a Cause can be determined) with knowledge and integrity.'

[1] e.g. Captain Sir William Chaloner Barnaby, 2nd Baronet (1746–94), refused to give his opinion on Keppel's conduct and was supported by Palliser.

can hardly enter fully into the Matter without such Information; and the World out of our Profession, cannot enter into it at all. These Questions, I am informed, are properly Questions of Fact; and I believe it. They are perfectly conformable to the Practice of Courts-Martial. But if they were Questions to mere Opinion, yet the Court, not the Witness, is answerable for the Propriety of them. Masters have been called here by the Prosecutor (and the Propriety not disputed) for mere Opinions concerning the Effect of chacing on a Lee Shore. In higher Matters, higher Opinions ought to have Weight; if they ought, there are none more capable of giving the Court Information than those who are summoned here; for I believe no Country ever was served by Officers of more Gallantry, Honour, Ability, and Skill in their Profession. You are a Court of Honour as well as of strict Martial Law. I stand here for my Fame, as well as for my Life, and for my Station in the Navy. I hope therefore, that in a Trial, which is not without Importance to the whole Service, you will be so indulgent as to hear me with Patience, whilst I explain to you every Thing that tends to clear my Reputation as a Man, as a Seaman, and as a Commander. I will open it to you without any Arts; and with the plain Freedom of a Man bred and formed as we all are. As I am to be tried for my Conduct in Command, it is proper I should lay before you my Situation in that Command, and what were my Motives for the several Acts and Orders on account of which I stand charged. I must beg leave to make some Explanation of these, before I enter upon the Accusations, Article by Article. To the Five special Articles of the Charge, you may depend upon it, I shall give full, minute, and satisfactory Answers—even on the narrow and mistaken Principles on which some of them are made. But I beg Leave to point out to you, that there is a general false Supposition that runs through the Whole. In censuring me for Misconduct and Neglect of Duty, my Accuser has conceived very mistaken Notions of what my Duty was; and on that bad Foundation he has laid the whole Matter of his Charge.

I think myself particularly fortunate, in being able to make out by Evidence at this Distance of Time, with so much Exactness as I shall do, the various Movements which were made or ordered in the Action of the 27th of *July*. It is a Piece of good Fortune which cannot often happen to a Commander in Chief in the same Circumstances. In an extensive naval Engagement, and in the Movements preparatory to it, subordinate Officers, if they are attentive to their Duty, are fully employed in the Care of their own particular Charge; and they have but little Leisure for exact Observation on the Conduct of their Commander in Chief. It is their Business to watch his Signals, and to put themselves in a Condition to obey them with Alacrity and Effect. As they are looking towards one Thing, and he is looking towards another, it is always a great Chance whether they agree, when they come to form an Opinion of the whole.

You are sensible, Gentlemen, that one of the Things which distinguish a Commander is to know how to catch the proper Moment for each Order he gives. He is to have his Eye upon the Enemy. The rest ought to have their Eyes on him. If those subordinate Officers who are inclined to find Fault with him, do not mark the Instant of Time with the same Precision which he does, their Judgment will often be erroneous; and they will blame where perhaps there is the greatest Reason for Commendation.

Besides, it must be obvious, when we consider the Nature of general Engagements, that in the Multitude of Movements that are made, and the Variety of Positions in which Ships are successively found, with regard to one another, when in Motion over a large Space (to say nothing of the Smoke), Things scarcely ever appear exactly in the same Manner to any Two Ships. This occasions the greatest Perplexity and Confusion in the Accounts that go abroad, and sometimes produces absolute Contradictions between different Relators, and that too without any intentional Fault in those who tell the Story. But wherever the Commander in Chief is placed, *that* is the Center of all the Operations: *that* is the true Point of View from which they must be seen by those who examine his Conduct; because his Opinion must be formed, and his Conduct regulated by the Judgment of his Eye upon the Posture in which *he* sees his Objects, and not from the View which another in a different and perhaps distant Position[1] has of them; and in Proportion as he has judged well or ill upon that particular View, taken from that particular Position (which is the only Point of Direction he can have), he deserves either Praise or Censure.

On these Principles I wish my Manœuvres to be tried, when the proper Consideration is, whether they have been unskilfully conceived, or as the Charge expresses it, in an unofficer-like Manner.

But my Reasons for preferring any one Step to another stand upon

[1] The phrase 'in a different and perhaps distant position' was supplied by John Dunning (R 90.7-3).

different Grounds. All that he charges as Negligence was the Effect of Deliberation and Choice; and this makes it necessary for me to explain as fully, as I think it right to do, the Ideas I acted upon.

I am not to be considered in the Light in which Sir *Hugh Palliser* seems to consider me, merely as an Officer with a limited Commission, confined to a special Military Operation, to be considered upon certain Military Rules, with an Eye towards a Court Martial, for my Acquittal or Condemnation, as I adhered to those Rules, or departed from them. My Commission was of a very different Sort: I was intrusted with ample discretionary Powers for the immediate Defence of the Kingdom. I was placed, in some Sort, in a Political as well as a Military Situation; and though, at my own Desire, for the Purposes of Uniformity and Secrecy, my Instructions came to me through the Admiralty alone, yet Part of them originated from the Secretary of State as well as from the Board. Every Thing which I did as an Officer, was solely subservient and subordinate to the great End of the national Defence. I manœuvred; I fought; I returned to Port; I put to Sea; just as it seemed best to me for the Purpose of my Destination. I acted on these Principles of large Discretion; and on those Principles I must be tried. If I am not, it is another Sort of Officer, and not one with my Trust and my Powers that is on Trial.

It is undoubtedly the Duty of every Sea Officer to do his utmost to take, sink, burn, and destroy the Enemy's Ships wherever he meets them. Sir *Hugh Palliser* makes some Charge on this Head, with as little Truth, Reason, or Justice, as on any of the others. He shall have a proper Answer in its proper Place; that is, when I come to the Articles. But in Justice to the Principles which directed me in my Command, I must beg leave to tell you, that I should think myself perfectly in the Right, if I postponed, or totally omitted that Destruction of Ships in One, in Two, or in Twenty instances, if the Pursuit of that Object seemed to me detrimental to Matters of more Importance. Otherwise it would be a Crime for a Commander, entrusted with the Defence of the Kingdom, to have any Plan, Choice, or Foresight in his Operations. I ought to conduct myself, and I hope I did, in each Particular, by my Judgment of its probable Effect on the Issue of the whole Naval Campaign, to which all my Actions ought to have a Relation. Without attending to that Relation, some Particulars of my Conduct on the 27th and 28th of *July* cannot appear in the Light which I imagine they are fairly intitled to; and some Circumstances of my Lenity towards Sir *Hugh Palliser*, will incur a Censure they do not deserve.

I have reflected again and again on that Business; and if I were to be once more in that Situation, I am persuaded, that I should act in all Respects very much in the same Manner. I have done my best and utmost, not merely to comply with an Article of War (I should be ashamed that such a Thing at such a Time could have engaged my Thoughts), but to defend the Kingdom, and I have Reason to thank God, that whatever Obstructions I met with in Service, or whatever Slanders and Accusations have followed me afterwards, the Kingdom has been defended.

My Capacity may be unequal to the Trust which was placed in me. It is certainly very unequal to the warm Wishes I have ever felt for the Service of my Country. Therefore, if I had intrigued, or solicited the Command, or if I had bargained for any Advantage on accepting it, I might be blamed for my Presumption. But it came to me entirely unsought; and on accepting it, I neither complained of any former Neglect, nor stipulated for any future Gratification.[1]

It is upwards of Two Years ago, that is, in *November* 1776, that I received a Message from Lord *Sandwich*, brought to me by Sir *Hugh Palliser*; that the Appearance of Foreign Powers, in our Disputes, might require a Fleet at home, and that he had his Majesty's Orders to know, whether I would undertake the Command. I said, that I was ready to attend, and give my Answer in Person to the King. Being admitted into the Closet, I gave such an one as seemed satisfactory to his Majesty; and having delivered my Opinions with Openness, I ended with a Declaration of my Willingness to serve him, in the Defence of this Country and its Commerce, whenever I should be honoured with his Commands,[2] and as long as my Health permitted.

The Appearance on the Part of Foreign Powers not continuing (I suppose) to give so much Alarm, I heard no more of the Command from *November* 1776 to *February* or *March* 1778; at that Time I had Hints conveyed to me, that I might soon be wanted. I was as ready to obey the King as I had been Sixteen Months before; and when required to serve, I had Two or Three Audiences of his Majesty before I left *London* finally to hoist my Flag. I must remark, that I took

[1] Keppel himself supplied the account of events which follows this paragraph. One of Burke's early drafts (Bk 13.10) has a note: 'See Keppels Paper'. A copy of the paper, 'Narrative of Ad. Keppel', in Richard Burke sen.'s hand, is at Sheffield (Bk 13.19).
[2] The fair draft reads: 'with the openness which belongs to my character'.

the Freedom to express to his Majesty, that I served in Obedience to *his* Commands; that I was unacquainted with his Ministers, as Ministers; and that I took the Command as it was, without making any Difficulty, and without asking a single Favour; trusting to his Majesty's good Intentions, and his gracious Support and Protection.

Circumstanced as I was, I could have no sinister and no ambitious Views in my Obedience. I risqued a great deal, and I expected nothing.[1] Many Things disposed me rather to seek my Ease than any new Employment, and gave me a very natural Reluctance to put a Situation, so difficult to mend, to any new Hazard.

That Hazard, Gentlemen, is very great to a Chief commander, who is not well supported at Home. The greater the Command, and the larger the Discretion, the more liable the Commander is, in the Course of Service, to hasty, ignorant, envious, or mutinous Objections to his Conduct; and if he has not a candid and equitable Acceptance of his Endeavours at Home, his Reputation may be ruined. His Successes will be depreciated, and his Misfortunes, if such should befal him, will be turned into Crimes. But the Nation was represented to me, by those who ought best to know its Condition, as not in a very secure State. Although my Forty Years Endeavours were not marked by the Possession of any one Favour from the Crown (except that of its Confidence in Time of Danger),[2] I could not think it right to decline the Service of my Country.[3]

---

[1] After this sentence a long passage is deleted in the final copy (Bk 13.4): 'I must be allowed to say when I am treated thus unworthily, that the Day I went down to Portsmouth to hoist my Flag, there was not a fairer name in the Country than my own. From my Brethren the Admirals and Captains in the Navy down to the common Mariners I was regarded with affection and thought a Seaman and a friend to Seamen. I stood fair with the Mercantile Interest, who seemed to imagine that in my various Stations, I had been zealous to protect and serve them, and fortunate enough on many occasions to have effected it, As to my private Connexions they were among the best and most honourable Men in the Kingdom; and though it may be pride in me, I will not suppress it—I have reason to think I was exceedingly beloved by them. Even those with whom I differed in Politicks could take me by the hand; and I verily believe attributed my difference with them to conscience and honour, and not to picque or prejudice or any crooked motive whatever, there was nothing in my private Circumstances to make me eager for Service. My Constitution too was much shaken; and though at times I had health and spirits enough for any thing, and still have (or I could not support myself under the present tiresome attempt to persecute me) I had frequent returns of a violently painful Complaint, which I attribute to service in unwholesome Climates.' [Two phrases ('a seaman and' 'and fortunate enough on many occasions to have effected it') are by John Dunning (R90.7–4).]

[2] Deleted in the final copy: 'though I had received no Order, no Title, no high Civil employment, nor any one of those situations to which even Seniority might have entitled me.' After 'civil employment' the fair draft has deleted 'no command of Marines'.

[3] In the final copy this reads: 'I thought it did not become me to have any discussions with my country in the time of her real exigencies.'

I thought it expedient to lay before you a true State of the Circumstances under which I took the Command, that you may see that, if I am that incapable and negligent Officer which this Charge represents me, I did not intrude myself into Command; that I was called to it by the express Orders of my Sovereign; that these Orders were conveyed to me by his Chief Minister of the Marine, with great seeming Concurrence and Approbation; that the Messenger (who also appeared to be perfectly pleased with his Errand), was no other than Sir *Hugh Palliser*, my Accuser, who ought to have been a Judge of my Ability from a very long Acquaintance; and that, lastly, this was no Matter of Surprise and Hurry, since they had Sixteen Months Time to consider and canvass my Fitness for a great discretionary Trust, before they placed it in my Hands.

If I gave no just Cause of Doubt about my real Character before my Appointment, I gave as little Cause of Uneasiness afterwards.

From the Moment of my taking the Command, I laid down to myself one Rule, which, in my Opinion, where there are honest Intentions on all Sides, does more to ensure Success to Service, than almost any other than can be conceived, which was, *"To make the best of every Thing."* The whole Fleet will bear me Witness, that it was not my Custom to complain, though it is generally thought good Policy to be very exact by Way of Precaution. If any Thing was defective, I stated it in Confidence, and with good Humour, to the First Lord of the Admiralty.

I received my Supplies with Acknowledgment; what could not be helped, I concealed. I made no Noise, nor encouraged, much less excited any Murmurings in or out of the Fleet. I corresponded with the Noble Earl at the Head of the Admiralty; and I did every Thing with Reference to him, exactly in the same Way as if my best and dearest Friends were in that Department.[1] Having none but the plainest Intentions, I was much more willing to take any Blame upon myself, than to lay it upon those who sent me out, or on those who served under me. I was open and unguarded. In general I studied my Language very little, because I little suspected that Traps would be laid for me in my Expressions, when my Actions were above Reproach.

I very soon found how necessary it was for one in my Situation to be

---

[1] In the fair draft (Bk 13.23) this sentence reads: 'Whether it will be thought any Credit to my Judgment or not I cannot tell, but I assure you, that I corresponded with the Noble Earl at the head of the Admiralty, and did every thing with reference to him exactly in the same way as if my best and dearest friends were in that department.'

well supported by Office. On my first going to *Portsmouth*, which was in *March* last, I was made to believe, that I should see a strong and well appointed Fleet ready for Sea. An Opinion of that Kind was circulated very generally. There were not more than Six Ships of the Line assembled, and in any condition to go upon Service. Of them, all I shall say is, that on reviewing them with a Seaman's Eye, they gave me no Pleasure. Whilst I continued at *Portsmouth*, I believe Four or Five more arrived. I returned to Town without making any Noise—I represented amicably this State of Things. I was told, that the Ships were collecting from other Ports, and from Sea; and I must say, that from that Time forward great Diligence was used—as much, I believe, as was possible. If there had not, we never could have sailed, even with the Force we went out with.

On the Thirteenth of *June* I set Sail from *St Helens* with Twenty Ships of the Line, well enough equipped, that is, neither of the best nor the worst I had seen.

I was hardly on my Station, when a new Occasion occurred, to shew me how much a Commander, entrusted as I was, must take upon himself, how much he must venture on his own Discretion, and how necessary it is for him to have a proper Support. The Circumstances of my falling in with the *French* Frigates *Pallas* and *Licorne*, and of the Chace and the Engagement with the *Belle Poule* (so honourable to Captain *Marshall*),[1] are fresh in your Memories. I undertook the Affair at my own Risque; War had not been declared, nor even Reprisals ordered. My Situation was singular. I might be disavowed, and a War with *France* laid to the Account of my Rashness.

There was not wanting some Discourse of that Tendency among People whose Opinions are of Moment. I represented what I had done; and to this Hour I have not received one Syllable of direct or official Approbation of my Conduct.

I found, however, that the taking of the Ships was important to the State. The Papers I found in them, and the intelligence I received by that Means, filled me with the most serious Apprehensions. I was on the Enemy's Coast with Twenty Sail of the Line. There were Thirty-

---

[1] Samuel Marshall. On 13 June Admiral Keppel, commanding the Channel Fleet, sailed for his station off Brest, to assist a convoy taking troops to Gibralter, and to prevent the French fleet from Toulon, from joining that in Brest harbour. He sighted the two French frigates very soon; see T. Keppel, *The Life of Admiral Viscount Keppel*, 2 vols., London, 1842, ii. 29–34, and *Corr.* iii. 461.

two in *Brest* Road and Brest Water, and Frigates more than triple my Number.[1]

My Orders to sail with Twenty Ships could not have been upon a Supposition of my having to deal with such a Force. I know what can be done by *English* Officers and *English* Seamen, and I trust to it as much as any Man. I should not be discouraged by some Superiority against me in Ships, Men, and Metal; but I have never had the Folly to despise my Enemy. I saw, that an Engagement under such Circumstances of decided Superiority on the Part of *France*, would hazard the very Being of this Kingdom.

If our Fleet should be destroyed, it was evident that the *French* must become Masters of the Sea, for that Campaign at least.

Whether we could ever repair the Loss, is not very clear to me, when I consider the State of our naval Stores at that Time, and the extreme Difficulty of a Supply, as long as the *French* should continue superior in the Channel.

It is impossible to say to what such a Calamity might not lead. I was filled with the deepest Melancholy I ever felt in my Life. I found myself obliged to turn my Back on *France*; but I took my Resolution—I again risqued myself on my own Opinion—I quitted my Station. My Courage was never put to such a Trial as in that Retreat; *but my firm Persuasion is, that the Country was saved by it.*[2]

Those in Power, who must have understood the State of the Fleet and of the Kingdom, were best able to discern the Propriety of my Conduct. But I was permitted to go out again in the same important Command—very unworthy of the Trust, if I had done amiss; very deserving of Commendation and Thanks, if at my own Risque I had preserved the Country from no slight Danger. One or other of these was certainly the Case. But the Fact is, that I was continued in the Command—but did not then receive, nor have[3] I yet received, any more than I had on the former Occasion of taking the *French* Ships, one Word of official Approbation.

[1] In the fair draft (Bk 13.24) the paragraph ends: 'Before I left London, upon my representing some intelligence I had received, which I now found to be true, I had been given to understand that the French were not able to fit out above 20 or 25 at the utmost.'

[2] In the fair draft (Bk 13.24) the next paragraph begins: '⟨Had it⟩ pleased any accuser, or should it even now please any such, The Admiralty declares, they must put me on my Trial for this act. I am yet to know, whether the plea of that political discretion by which I saved the Kingdom, could properly be judged by a Court Martial so as to acquit me for leaving my Station.'

[3] The fair draft ends here.

All these discouraging Circumstances did not abate the Zeal I felt for the Safety of my Country, or disgust me with its Service, or disturb my Temper. On my Return to *Portsmouth* I made no Complaint. I did every Thing to stifle Discontent, and to get forward for Sea again, without divulging the true Situation of Affairs, although I found myself in Publications which are considered as countenanced by Authority, most grossly abused, and threatened with the Fate of Admiral *Byng*.[1]

I had returned to *Portsmouth* on the 27th of *June*, and on the 9th of *July*, finding my Fleet made up to Twenty-four Ships of the Line of Battle, with Four Frigates and Two Fireships, I sailed again, in Obedience to my Instructions, trusting to such Reinforcement as I was given to expect would join me.

At *Plymouth*, off the *Lizard*, and at Sea, by several Reinforcements of Ships, manned as the Exigency would permit, the Fleet was made up to Thirty Sail of the Line. After this, although I was much short of a proportionable Number of Frigates, and must naturally be subject to many Inconveniences from that Want, I had, on the whole, no just Cause for Uneasiness. The greatest Part of the Ships were in good Condition, and well appointed, and where any Thing was wanting, the Zeal of the Commanders abundantly supplied it.

The Appearance of the *French* Fleet confirmed the Ideas upon which I had returned to *Portsmouth*; for on the 8th of *July*, the Day before I left *St Helens*, they sailed out of *Brest* Thirty-two Sail of the Line. On the 23rd the Fleets of the two Nations first came in Sight of each other. I believe the *French* Admiral[2] found me much stronger than he expected; and from thence he all along shewed, as I conceived, a manifest Disinclination to come to an Engagement. I do not say this, as meaning to call his Courage in question—Very far from it. I am certain that he is a Man of Great Bravery; but he might have many very reasonable Motives for avoiding a decisive Action. Many Objects of the *French*, and those very important, might be obtained without a Battle. On my Part, I had every Motive which could make me earnest to bring it on, and I was resolved to do so whenever and by whatever Means I could. I should be criminal indeed, if I had not, for I had every Motive for desiring to press on an Action. The greatest Body of the *British* Trade was then on its Return Home. Two *East-India* and Two *West-India* Fleets of immense Value were hourly expected. From the Course

---

[1] Admiral John Byng (1704–57), court-martialled and shot after the loss of Minorca.
[2] Louis Guidlouet, Comte d'Orvilliers (1708–92).

it was probable they would hold, and from the Situation of the *French* Fleet, they might be taken in my Sight, without a Possibility of my preventing it. Besides this, I know that Two Fleets, where one of them chooses to decline Battle, may be for a very long Time near one another, without any Means of bringing on an Engagement. I cannot be certain whether the Account I have read be quite exact; but it should appear by that Account, that in King *William*'s Reign Admiral *Russell* continued for Two Months almost in the daily View of the *French* Fleet, without having it in his Power to fight them.[1] I do not think the Thing at all impossible.

I had also other Reasons for the greatest Anxiety to bring on an Engagement, upon any Terms that I could obtain it. These Reasons are weighty, and they are founded in my Instructions. I gave Notice to the Admiralty, that I might find it useful to my Defence to produce those Instructions on my Trial. They communicated to me his Majesty's Pleasure thereupon, and informed me, that they could not consent that my Instructions should be laid before my Counsel, or be produced at the Court-Martial. I was much surprised at this Answer— as I conceived that those who were much better Judges than I could be of what was Matter of State, could never have thought of putting me in a Situation, which might compel me, in my Defence, to produce the Instructions under which I acted, when, at the same Time, they meant to refuse me the fair and natural Means of my Justification.[2] It is my undoubted Right, if I think proper, to avail myself of them. On former Trials, they have been generally sent down with the Accusation, that the Conduct of the Admiral might be compared with his Instructions. But leaving the Admiralty to reflect on the Propriety of their Conduct, it is my Part to take care of my own. I have always been willing to run any Hazard for the Benefit of the State. I shall not produce those Instructions—I have not even shewn them to my Counsel, nor communicated their Contents; but my declining to make use of my

---

[1] Edward Russell (1652–1727), afterwards (1697) 1st Earl of Orford, in 1691 was at sea for nearly three months without being able to fight the French fleet (J. Ehrman, *The Navy in the War of William III, 1689–1697*, Cambridge, 1953, p. 378).

[2] This passage was written by the Duke of Richmond—certainly from 'thereupon, and informed me'. Burke's rather similar version can still be read beneath Richmond's emendation: 'think it proper for me to disclose them. I was much surprised at this answer, as I conceived that those who were much better judges than I could be of what was matter of State, could never have thought of putting me in a Situation, which might compel me in my defence to produce things which might be productive of publick ill consequences.' The final copy is incomplete at this point, so it is impossible to say how much Richmond contributed.

own Rights cannot in a like Case hereafter affect the Right of any other Man. The World will judge of the Wisdom and Equity of ordering Trials under such Circumstances.

On the 27th of *July* I came to an Action with the *French*. They were beaten, and obliged to retire into their own Port. No one can doubt but a Commander in Chief, who is to reap the principal Share of the Glory, will be earnest to have his Victory as complete as possible. *Mine did not* answer to my Wishes, nor to my just Expectations. I was fully resolved to renew the Engagement.[1] Why it was not renewed, will appear when I come to the Particulars of the Charge.

As to my Conduct after the Engagement, I might have pursued a fruitless and a most hazardous Chace of some few Ships (I know not to this Hour with Certainty what they were, nor does my Accuser), if I had had my Mind filled with Notions unworthy of my Station. I might easily[2] have paraded with my shattered Fleet off the Harbour of *Brest*.[3] I chose rather to return to *Plymouth* with all Expedition, to put my-self once more in a Condition to meet the Enemy, and defend the Kingdom. But on my Return, I took care to leave Two Men of War of the Line on a Cruise to protect the Trade. By the Vigilance of the Commanders, and the happy Effect of the late Advantage, the expected Fleets all came in safe.

At *Plymouth*, I lost no Time, and omitted no Means of putting myself in a State fit for Action. I did every Thing to promote an unanimous Exertion; and I found my Endeavours well seconded by all the Admirals and Captains of the Fleet. This Benefit I acquired, by avoiding a Retrospect into the Conduct of the Vice-Admiral of the Blue; for if I had instituted an Enquiry or Trial, it would have suspended the Operations of the whole Fleet, and would have sus-pended them in the Midst of the Campaign, when every Moment was precious, and the Exertion of every Officer necessary. The Delay which the present Court Martial has occasioned to the Service, even at this Time, is evident to all the World. How much more mischievous would it have been at that Period?—I was sensible of it, or rather to speak more correctly, my Mind was so fully taken up with carrying on

---

[1] There is a deleted phrase here on the final copy which cannot be read.

[2] Deleted in the final copy: 'If I had thought it a desirable'.

[3] Deleted here in the final copy: 'But I am not disposed to such Parade and ostentation. But whilst I continued on that Coast, with many of my Ships extremely hurt in the Action—The French would be employed in repairing their Fleet, and when they were ready for Service, I should have paid dearly for that piece of Vanity, by being obliged to relinquish the Seas to them.'

the great Service which was intrusted to my Care, that I could not admit the Thought of mispending my own Time, and wasting the Flower of the *British* Navy in attending on a Court-Martial.

My Letter to the Admiralty[1] was written in the Spirit which directed my Conduct at *Plymouth*. All my Letters were written in the same Spirit. My Letter published in the *Gazette*, has been brought before this court, for the Purpose of convicting me of Crimes, by the Person whose Faults it was intended to cover. He has attempted, very irregularly in my Opinion, to call upon Witnesses for their Construction of my Writing. No one has a Right to explain my Meaning, where it may be doubtful, but myself; and it is you, Gentlemen, who are to judge whether my Explanation is fair.

That letter (as far as it goes) is an Account of the Action, strictly true. It is indeed very short, and very general. But it goes as far as I intended it should. It commends Sir *Hugh Palliser*. It does what I meant to do. I meant to commend his Bravery (or what appeared to me as such) in the Engagement. As he stood high in Command, to pass over one in his Station, would be to mark him. It would have conveyed the Censure I wished for such good Reasons to avoid; and I should have defeated the one great Object I had in View, the Defence of the Nation.

In that Letter, I expressed also my Hopes of bringing the *French* Fleet to Action in the Morning:—I had such Hopes; and my Accuser, even in the second Edition of his Log-book, shews, that I was not wholly ungrounded in my Expectations; since he has recorded himself as of the same Opinion. I said, that I did not interrupt the *French* Fleet that Evening in the Formation of their Line. I shall shew you by Evidence (if it should not have already fully appeared) that I was not able to do it; and that any random Firing from me, under my Circumstances, would have been vain against the Enemy, and a disgraceful Trifling with regard to myself.

You have seen my Expressions, and such is their Meaning with regard both to the *French* and to Sir *Hugh Palliser*, so far as they applied to the particular Times to which they severally belonged. But there was an *intermediate Time* with regard to both, of which, when I wrote my Letter, I gave no Account. I intended to conceal it. I do not conceive that a Commander in Chief is bound to disclose to all

---

[1] Of 30 July 1778 (*Minutes of the Proceedings*, p. 52).

Europe, in the Midst of a critical Service, the real State of his Fleet, or his Opinion of any of his Officers. He is not, under such Circumstances, bound to accuse a *British* Admiral. To me, such an Accusation, under almost any Circumstances, is a very serious matter. Whilst a Possibility of Excuse for an Officer remains in my Mind, I am in my Disposition ready to lay hold of it; and I confess to you, that until Sir *Hugh Palliser* himself had brought out to this Court all the Particulars, I attributed much more to his Misfortune or Mistake, than I now find myself authorised to do; nor did I think his Conduct Half so exceptionable as he himself has proved it. After the Engagement, *he* never thought fit to explain to me the Reasons of his not bearing down into my Wake, to enable me to renew the Action, and I did not think fit to enquire into them.

I apprehend, that a Power of passing over Faults or Mistakes in Service (into which the very best Officers may be surprised) to be sometimes as necessary, if not to Discipline, yet to the End of all Discipline, the Good of the Service, as any Punishment of them can possibly be: And one of the ill Effects of this Prosecution will be, I fear, to terrify a Commander in Chief out of one of the most valuable Parts of his Discretion. By using the Discretion which I thought was in me, I preserved Concord in the Fleet, Promptitude in the Service, and Dignity to the Country. In my Opinion, any Complaint of such a Magnitude would have produced infinite Mischiefs. Nobody can imagine that, in that Moment, an Accusation of a Vice-Admiral, who was besides a Lord of the Admiralty, could be undertaken without a capital Detriment to our naval Operations, and even to the Quiet of the Public.

My Letter was written solely upon the Principles which I have now honestly and faithfully laid before you, and which I submit to your Judgment. If I have been more indulgent than was wise, the Public has had the Benefit, and all the Trouble and Inconvenience of my Indiscretion has fallen upon myself. I never had a more troublesome Task of the Sort, than in penning that letter, and it has ill answered my Pains. If I have not shewn myself able at Concealment, it is a Fault for which I hope I shall not lose much Credit with this Court-Martial. I shall not be very uneasy, if I have been thought to have wrote a bad Letter, if I shall be found, as I trust I shall be found, to have done my Duty in fighting the Enemy.[1]

---

[1] This passage was amended by Burke in the final copy (Bk 13.7) in the light of a memorandum written by the Duke of Richmond (Bk 13.21, 22).

The Intrusion of my Letter into the Trial, has made it necessary for me to explain it. I now proceed with the Account of my Conduct.

I got ready for Sea again with my usual Temper and Disposition to accommodate.[1] After this, I kept the Sea as long as I could. The *French* Fleet[2] carefully avoided my Station. I could obtain no distinct Intelligence of them, though I omitted no Means to procure it. In consequence of this their Desertion of the Seas, their Trade fell into the Hands of our Privateers, to a Number and Value that I believe was never equalled in the same Space of Time. His Majesty was pleased to speak of it in his Speech from the Throne; and to attribute it to the good Conduct of some of his Officers.[3]

When I considered this, when I considered the direct Approbation of my Conduct, and the Circumstances which attended my Appointment, it was with Difficulty I persuaded myself that I was awake; when I found that I was treated as a Criminal, and ordered, without the least Ceremony or previous Enquiry, to be tried at a Court Martial; on the Accusation of my Officer; my old Friend; one, over whose Faults I had so lately cast a Veil; the very Person who was the Messenger and Congratulator of my original Appointment. I acknowledge, it was for some Time before I could sufficiently master my Indignation, and compose myself to that Equality of Temper with which I came hither; and with which I have heard such shocking and reproachful Matter and Words read to my Face, in the Place of Support I was made to look for. I feel very much inward Peace at present, and the Event I consider with much less Concern for myself than for the Service.[4] Your Judgment, I am fully persuaded, will be wise and well weighed;[5] and such as will be of Credit to yourselves, and of Advantage and

---

[1] Deleted in the final copy: 'As soon as I had sailed I took care to secure in future against any misunderstanding as might the consequence of Errors in command, as I conceived had prevented me from reaping all the advantages of the Blow which had been given to the French on the 27th—Without making any complaint as soon as the Fleet had sailed from Plymouth, I gave it out in orders, that for the Future the Ships in every division should in time of action look to the Signals of the Commander in chief only. This I thought an abundant security against suffering the consequences One mistakes of orders from going to any length that might be mischievous.'

[2] Deleted in the final copy: 'they come to Sea at all'.

[3] The King's Speech of 26 November 1778 referred to the fact that 'the extensive Commerce of my Subjects has been protected in most of its Branches and large Reprisals have been made upon the injurious Aggressors, by the Vigilance of my Fleets, and by the active and enterprising Spirit of My People' (*Commons Journals*, xxxvii. 3).

[4] Deleted in the final copy: 'I have passed the middle of Life. My health is not the best. Honour well founded may be censured; but cannot be shaken.'

[5] Deleted in the final copy: 'and honourable'.

Encouragement to that Part of the Military which is the most interesting to this Kingdom. On my Part, I trust I shall entitle myself not only to an Acquittal, but to an honourable Reparation at your Hands, for the malicious Calumnies contained in the Charge against me.

Thus much I have said as to the general Matter, which has arisen on the Trial, and the Circumstances by which that Trial has been brought on, as well as to the Motives and Principles which regulated the Discretion that I conceive was in me.

If these Motives were probable and likely to be real, I cannot be Guilty of the criminal Negligence and Want of Knowledge in my Profession with which I stand charged. As to the Charges themselves, let the first Article be read again, and I will answer to it.

. . .

Having now offered to the Court precise Answers to all the Charges exhibited against me, I shall proceed to call my Witnesses, to support those Answers, and of course to refute the Charges in the Order in which they have been made—I shall call them, not as a Prisoner commonly calls his Witnesses—to oppose them to those which appear for the Prosecution.—Quite the contrary.—I bring them to support, confirm, enlarge, and illustrate, almost the Body of the Evidence which has been given by my Accuser.

But before I sit down, I must discharge a Duty which I feel myself to owe to the Reputation of a Service highly and justly favoured in this Country, and which can never suffer in its Honour, but the Nation itself will suffer in Proportion.

I have heard it asserted, and contended for during this Trial, as an essential and indispensable Right of a Captain of a Man of War, to make Additions and Alterations in the Ship's Log-book, even after the original Entries had been seen, examined, and approved by himself.—I have seen this attempted to be excused, nay, even justified and boasted of in a Case where the Alterations and Additions introduced Matter of criminal and capital Offence; acknowledged by the Party to have been introduced Months after the original Entries were inserted; and with Knowledge, that a criminal Charge had then been exhibited against the Person in whose Trial they were first heard of.—I have heard this attempted to be defended where the most material of the Alterations and Additions were certainly not supported by Fact.

Upon this Occasion surely I am called upon to enter my Protest against a Claim which subjects the Log-books of the King's Ships, that ought to contain, if not always a perfect, yet always a genuine Narrative of their Transactions, when the Events are fresh and recent; when they cannot be mistaken, and can hardly be misrepresented, and which ought never to be altered after the Entries have been made and authorised.[1]

This is the Case of the first Alteration of the Log-book.—Another Alteration has since appeared in another Log-book!—that of the Prosecutor himself! little differing from the former, except that the Person that has actually made it, does not appear to justify it; that the Witness to it states it to have been made soon after the Engagement, and that the Destruction of some Leaves, and the Substitution of others, seems to be rather made for the Purpose of exculpating another Person, than of criminating me.[2]—But whatever the Intention was, the thing is equally unjustifiable in all Respects; it tends equally to destroy all Sort of Use in these kind of Records, and to render them highly fallacious, and possibly highly dangerous.—I do not dwell on all the Particulars of that unhappy Business!—it is painful to me, and the Nature of the Transaction is but *too* visible.—There has always been, and probably will always be, something slovenly in these Books; and the Masters have thought they have more Power over them than is proper.—There is however a great Difference between Inaccuracy and malicious Design—there is a Difference between the Correction or Supply of indifferent Matters, and the cancelling of Pages and putting in others—omitting, adding to, and varying the most important Things, for the most important Purposes.[3]

It is also proper for me to state two or three Facts to the Court, in order to place the Conduct of my Accuser in its proper Point of View.

I admit that the Charges he has exhibited against me are very heinous.—They express Misconduct and Negligence, they imply (and so the Court has understood them to imply) Cowardice also.—If I ever committed them at all, it was in his Presence, and in the Presence

---

[1] The log-book of the *Robust*, one of the ships under Keppel's command during the engagement with the French, had been altered after the original entry. The alterations had been carried out by order of the ship's captain, Captain Alexander Hood (1727–1814); see *Public Advertiser*, 16 January 1779 and other newspapers.

[2] During the trial it had been discovered that 'three Leaves of the Narrative of the Proceedings of the Fleet on the 24th, 25th, 26th, 27th and 28th Days of July have been torn out of the Log Book of the *Formidable* and others placed in their Stead.' The description here of the circumstances surrounding the incident appears to be appropriate (ibid. 25 and 26 January 1779).

[3] This paragraph is by Burke (Bk 13.16).

of a numerous Corps of Officers, who being called upon by the Court, have all unanimously refused, or I trust will refuse to fix any one Charge upon me.—I have mentioned before, the Circumstance of my Accuser's Silence for Months, during which he was called upon by the Duty he owed his Country, to have stated my Misconduct, if any such had existed; and his Refusal to do so, is strong Evidence of itself, that even in his Opinion, my Conduct was liable to no Reproach.

But this is not all; even so late as the 5th of *October* last, I received a Letter from him,[1] dated at Sea, conceived in Terms of great Good-will and Respect for me—in which, having Occasion to mention some Prizes which had been taken by the Fleet; he considers *that* as a Subject of little Moment to me, assigning *this* as a Reason—"For I know you had rather meet the *French* Fleet."—*That Fleet* which he says I fled from!

Is this consistent with the Tenor of those Charges?—Could the Man who wrote the one believe the other?—it is absolutely impossible.— I cannot produce this Letter in Evidence, but when I go out of the Court, I will shew it to any Gentleman who is desirous to see it.

Another Thing more and I have done.—

Sir *Hugh Palliser* thought proper to address the Public, by a printed Newspaper, dated the 4th of *November*;[2]—principally, as it seems, for the Sake of asserting, that he was not, and insinuating that I *was*, the Cause of the *French* not being re-attacked in the Afternoon, the 27th of *July*.

In that Paper he positively denies that he received any Message by Captain Windsor[3] saying a Word about renewing the Attack; and he calls the contrary Assertion a false one. Captain *Windsor* has been called, and he has proved, that at Five o'Clock he received from me, and at about Half past Five he delivered to Sir *Hugh Palliser* himself the *Message* to come with the Ships of his Division into my Wake, and that I only waited for him to renew the Attack.

This Account of Captain *Windsor* has been attempted to be discredited by the Prosecutor, who has asked Captain *Bazeley*,[4] and I

---

[1] An extract printed, but dated 9 October 1778, in *The Proceedings at Large of the Court-Martial on the Trial of the Honourable Augustus Keppel*, ed. J. Almon, London, 1779, Appendix, p. 7.

[2] The *General Advertiser and Morning Intelligencer* of 15 October had an attack on Palliser, who replied in the newspaper of 4 November.

[3] Thomas Windsor (1752–1832).

[4] John Bazeley.

believe One or Two more, whether it was not a later Hour than Captain *Windsor* named,—I shall for that Reason call Witnesses to confirm Captain *Windsor* in all the Circumstances of his Testimony.

I owe it to him as an Honourable Man, to shew that his Evidence is correctly true.

I will prove that the Message sent by me was precisely the Message delivered by him at the Time he speaks to—and that it was exactly repeated by him to the Vice-Admiral.—Yet after his own Ears had heard at Half past Five in the Afternoon of a Summer's Day, that I waited only for him and his Division to renew the Attack,—this Gentleman applies to me, ignorant, negligent, cowardly, as he now represents me, to certify his good Behaviour, and to support his Character against the Malice of his Enemies.—He applies to me to sign a Paper, containing many Particulars directly contrary to the Evidence you have heard upon Oath, and which I will also shew to any one.[1]

At present, I have only to do with one of those Particulars.— That Paper (concurring with his Attempts in this Trial) contains this Assertion, that the calling his and Vice-Admiral sir *Robert Harland*'s[2] Divisions into my Wake in the Evening, was not for the Purpose of renewing the Battle at that Time;—but to be in readiness for it in the Morning.—This my Accuser had the Confidence to tender to me to sign.

To sign an Assertion of a Fact—absolutely unfounded,—the contrary of which, I knew to be true, and the contrary of which Captain *Windsor* has proved, my Accuser knew to be true.—How that Gentleman felt when this came out, I know not.—But if I could conceive myself in the same Situation, I know that it would be difficult to express what I should *feel.—I cannot wish so heavy a Punishment to my worst Enemy.*[3]

---

[1] Printed in Almon's *Proceedings at Large*, Appendix, p. 7.

[2] 1st Baronet (1715–84).

[3] The final paragraph is by Burke (Bk 13.27).

Address of Admirals and Captains
[February 1779]

Sources: MSS. at Sheffield, Bk 13.32, R154.40

A portion of Burke's draft of this Address survives (Bk 13.32) and there is a copy of the whole (R154.40). The first part of the text which follows reproduces the draft; the second part is taken from the copy. Considerable changes were made in Burke's draft and, where it can be compared with the copy, these changes are noted, except for differences in punctuation etc. In its final form the Address records the acquittal of Keppel on 11 February, but was being circulated in Portsmouth about 9 February when eighteen were said to have signed and six or eight more to have promised to do so (*Correspondence of King George the Third, 1760–83*, ed. Sir J. Fortescue, 6 vols., London, 1927–8, iv. 270–1).

The Court Martial of Admiral Keppel excited considerable public sympathy. On 12 February the *Public Advertiser* reported that on

Wednesday night Sir Hugh Palliser arrived at his House in Pall-Mall from Portsmouth having been ... greatly insulted almost all the way to Town, and Yesterday, about Six in the Evening, Admiral Keppel arrived at his House ... In consequence of the Admirals arrival ... being publicly known it was generally conceived that he had been honourably acquitted; This occasioned his Friends and wellwishers to testify to their Joy on the Occasion by lighting up their Houses, which was universally followed by the Inhabitants of London, Westminster and Southwark.

Indignation among those who had served under Keppel was particularly pronounced. Of the thirty-two Admirals and Captains who were at the Battle of Ushant twenty-three signed the following address. It appears never to have been presented.

We your Majesties most dutiful Subjects and servants several of the Officers who served your Majesty in the action with the French Fleet on the 27th of July last, beg leave to approach your Royal presence, and with the most perfect respect to lay ourselves at your Majesties feet,[1] in order to give your Majesty the most effectual proof which in this moment can be given, of our affection to your person and Government, by expressing the just indignation we feel against those who endeavour to injure the honour and safety of the Service to which we have the happiness to belong, and which is the distinguishing glory of the nation over which you reign.

The design long insidiously conceald, then audaciously avowed, and obstinately pursued through every species of evil practice,[2] against

---

[1] The copy continues: 'most dutifully to assure your Majesty of our perfect attachment and affection to your Person and Government, and to give a proof of it by expressing the just indignation we feel against the late endeavours to injure.'
[2] Copy: 'through much evil practice'.

the Life and reputation of Admiral Keppel is not the less resented by us all, because by the[1] marked interposition of providence in favour of oppressed Virtue it has been thoroughly defeated. The Malice of the prosecution is not lessend by the impartiality of the Trial and the Integrity of the final Sentence. The Martial Justice of the Nation has indeed shewn itself emulous of the purity and independence of the civil; and we trust in your Majesties goodness, that the Lustre of Office also should be placed[2] in the same clear light by your marking with your Royal displeasure those who have presumed to abuse,[3] one of the most sacred parts of your Royal prerogative the publick prosecution of Crimes, the Gratification of their own passions and designs.

Your Majesties Officers of your Navy are very plain men, occupied mostly on the Seas, and little versed in the common arts of the World, and little fitted to contend with them.[4] We neither wish nor desire[5] but rather think it our duty to expect, a full enquiry into all exceptionable conduct, either in or under command. But wanton and vexatious accusation tends to take off the weight and effect of what is rational and necessary and to make that which should be discipline appear as persecution. The honour of Officers cannot easily endure to be suspended; nor will any accusation be considerd as trivial, which is adopted by the State, as long as the State itself retains the respect which it ought to have.[6] We are fully sensible that in the infinite contingencies of service,[7] merit even as real as that of Mr Keppel, (though such merit is rare indeed) may not be so circumstanced as to be made equally clear with his. The anxiety trouble, fatigue, vexation, and expense attending such Trials are no trivial[8] things.[9] It behoves therefore the Office under whose immediate direction and control we

---

[1] Copy: 'a'.

[2] Copy: 'will also be placed'.

[3] The copy continues: 'to the Gratification of their own Passions and Designs one of the most sacred parts of your Prerogative, the public Prosecution of Crimes'.

[4] In the copy this sentence is omitted.

[5] Copy: 'desire to evade'.

[6] In the copy this sentence is omitted.

[7] In the copy: 'We know that in the infinite Contingencies of Service'.

[8] Copy: 'slight'.

[9] In the copy the next portion of the Address reads: 'The Office therefore, under which we immediately serve, and what ought to be cautious in receiving accusation, ought not, we presume, without conferring with any one Officer who could give them cool and impartial information, to commit the duty and Dignity of their Station on the passionate and recriminatory Charges of a Person, avowing an accusation of another as a means of exculpating himself and of revenging his own supposed Injuries. On this Subject we beg leave to express to your Majesty our hearty concurrence'.

serve to be extremely cautious and circumspect in receiving such accusations. They ought not we presume without conferring with any one who could give important and enlightend information commit the dignity of their Office on the passionate and recriminatory charges of a person avowing an accusation of another as a means of exculpating himself and revenging his own supposed Injuries. It is only from a consideration that we must be personally called on the Business of the 27th of July last which has prevented us hitherto from expressing most fully to your Majesty our hearty concurrence with the opinion of those respectable Admirals who have made an early and dutiful representation of this[1] matter to your Majesty.[2] We believe that theirs and ours, is the general opinion of the Navy of England.

It is a matter of respect which we owe to our Commander in Chief to leave the Conduct of a Subordinate Officer, which passes under his own Eye to his own discretion. But if the conduct of the Commander in Chief himself, entrusted with the most important of all Objects, had furnished occasion for a Charge so heinous as that exhibited by Sir Hugh Palliser, against Admiral Keppel, his guilt must have been visible to us all, and our Silence would have been participation. We humbly pray your Majesty, whose good opinion is amongst our first and dearest Objects to be assured, that we are not so wanting in Zeal and Loyalty to your Majesty as to have made so dangerous a Concealment, neither are we, we trust, so ignorant and supine in our Profession, as not to have seen gross Misconduct, where gross Misconduct was.

We also assure your Majesty that on the Day, which has been the Subject of the late Scandalous Accusation, we every one of us endeavoured to do his Duty with the utmost Zeal and Alacrity, and to the full extent of our Abilities, and that our exertions were animated by the consciousness that we acted under a Commander of long and most meritorious Service, of the most approved Courage and Conduct, of the clearest Honour and of the most obliging and endearing Attention to his Officers, of the greatest temper and Humanity in his Command, and who omitted nothing that could be done, to encourage the Efforts, and to promote the Union of all those who had the honour of serving under him.

We reject with the utmost disdain that false and malicious Aspersion,

---

[1] The draft breaks off at this point. The word 'Injuries' in the previous sentence is also supplied from the copy.
[2] The Address of the Admirals was probably drafted by Burke (*Corr.* iv. 32).

that the Lustre of the British flag suffered any diminution under that distinguished Commander who appeared to us by his Conduct on that day, fully to justify the high Opinion which the Navy entertained and still do entertain of him. The foreign Enemies to the Honour of the British Flag had no Ground for Triumph, the domestick for Accusation on that day, although Circumstances no way imputable to us, or to our Commander in Chief, prevented the destruction and capture of the Enemy's Ships, and favoured their flight into their own Harbour. Your Majesty and your people have had many of the solid and substantial effects of Victory: Your Fleet returned to the undisputed Dominion of the Sea: your Kingdom was freed from the terror of an Invasion: The Trade of this Nation was protected, and that of your Enemies distressed beyond example, whilst private Armaments amassed immense Riches under the cover and protection of a Royal Fleet, who in all their Operations disdained Interest, and made the Glory of their Sovereign and the Advantage of their Country their Sole Objects.

We hope we shall not appear presumptuous most gracious Sovereign, in saying, that having received your Majesty's Approbation we looked for other distinctions from the Admiralty than a Court Martial upon our Commander in Chief for tarnishing the Honour of the Flag of England. We must despair of an acceptance of our Endeavours if the Services of Admiral Keppel are held criminal.

We therefore implore your Majesty's most gracious protection to your Navy, which we trust we have hitherto deserved, and shall continue to deserve; most humbly requesting that we shall no longer be suffered to serve with, much less under a Person capable of such attrocious and ungrounded Accusation, and therefore so dangerous as an Associate, as a Commander, or as a Person under Command as Sir Hugh Palliser. Nor can we think ourselves perfectly Safe in our honest endeavours to serve your Majesty and the Country, whilst a Person holds any Direction or Superintendance over us, who may think himself injured by, and therefore may be disposed to resent the Truths, which (to the disgrace of his Accusation) our regard to our Consciences has obliged us publickly to declare upon Oath.

Robert Harland	John Leveson Gower	John Hamilton
John Campbell	J. Jervis	Evelyn Sutton
Richard Edwards	Charles Douglas	S Marshall

John Lockhart Ross	Phill. Cosby	I: Prescott
Robert Boyle Walsingham	Jnᵒ: N: P: Nott	Thomas Lloyd
Michael Clements	Robert Kingsmill	James Bradby[1]
John Carter Allen	John Macbride	
John Laforey		
Frederick Maitland		
Jonathan Faulknor		

Speech on Scottish Riots
15 March 1779

Source: *Gazetteer*, 17 March 1779

The Government had intended to follow the Catholic Relief Acts of 1778 for England and Ireland with the necessary separate Act for Scotland. However, riots had broken out against the legislation in Edinburgh and Glasgow. In May 1779 the celebrated anti-Papist, Lord George Gordon,[2] had stood up in the House of Commons and

entered at large into the Disturbances last Summer occasioned by the apprehension that the Act for the Relief of Roman Catholic Subjects in England would be extended to Scotland. He represented the Disposition of *One Million and a Half* of People to be so totally averse to any further Indulgence to the Papists that they were actually associating in different Parts to prevent it;[3] and if it was attempted to be carried into Execution, he foretold Rebellion.[4]

Thus the North ministry abandoned its purpose. The question of the Government's intentions was raised informally in the Commons by John Wilkes.[5]

---

[1] Vice-Admiral Sir Robert Harland and Rear-Admiral John Campbell (*c.*1720–90). Captains Richard Edwards (*c.*1771–88), John Lockhart Ross (1721–90), Robert Boyle Walsingham (1736–80), M.P. 1758–80, Michael Clements (d. *c.*1796), John Carter Allen (d. 1800), John Laforey (*c.*1729–96), later (1789) 1st Baronet, Frederick Lewis Maitland (1730–86), Jonathan Faulknor (d. 1794), John Leveson Gower (1740–92), John Jervis (1735–1823), later (1797) 1st Earl of St Vincent, Sir Charles Douglas, 1st Baronet (d. 1789), Phillips Cosby (*c.*1727–1808), John N. P. Nott (d. 1780), Robert Brice Kingsmill (1730–1805), later (1800) 1st Baronet, John MacBride (d. 1800), John Hamilton (d. 1787), Evelyn Sutton, Samuel Marshall, Isaac Prescott (1737–1830), Thomas Lloyd (d. 1780), James Bradby.

[2] (1751–93), M.P. 1774–80.

[3] Leadership in the campaign against Catholic relief was provided by the Friends of the Protestant Interest commonly called the Protestant Association (*Corr.* iv. 54).

[4] *Public Advertiser*, 6 May 1779.

[5] *Parl. Reg.* xii. 141–2.

Mr. Burke concluded by observing, that the city of Edinburgh had promised no satisfaction to the sufferers; that Glasgow had; but, nevertheless, nothing had been yet done for the Roman Catholics at either place in the way of either public or private satisfaction. The unfortunate objects of this paroxysm of religious phrenzy were ruined; and as they had not hitherto received any reparation on the spot, from those who were either wilfully culpable, or culpably negligent and remiss in their duty, he took the present opportunity of giving notice, that he would, on Thursday next, make a motion, both respecting the riots, the conduct of the Magistrates, and the compensation and the nature of the redress the sufferers were entitled to. It would, he observed, be highly cruel and impolitic to permit any description[1] of men to live in any part of this kingdom without affording them the protection which the laws and government held out to them.

Speech on Scottish Catholic Petition
18 March 1779

Sources: 1. *Public Advertiser*, 19 March 1779
2. MS. at Sheffield, Bk 8.49b
3. MS. at Sheffield, Bk 8.51

Other reports are in *Parl. Reg.* xii. 172, 176–7 and *Parl. Hist.* xx. 326–7; *General Advertiser*, 19, 22 March; *London Chronicle*, 20 March; *London Evening Post*, 20 March; *General Evening Post*, 20 March; *Morning Chronicle*, 19 March; *Morning Post*, 19 March; *St James's Chronicle*, 20 March; and *Lloyd's Evening Post*, 19 March.

On 18 March Burke presented a petition from the Roman Catholics of Scotland for compensation for their losses in the recent riots. He is said to have spoken for an hour and a half.[2]

(1) *PUBLIC ADVERTISER*, 19 MARCH 1779

Mr. Burke enlarged upon the Petition, and gave the House a more ample Detail of the Circumstances of the Riots at Glasgow and Edinburgh, which he justly observed were a Reproach to the Country;

---

[1] *Gazetteer*: 'desecration'.
[2] *Morning Chronicle*, 19 March 1779.

and he seemed to think the Magistrates had not been sufficiently vigilant and active in suppressing them, and punishing the Offenders. He then produced a most disgraceful Pamphlet artfully printed and circulated by an Association calling themselves "The Committee for the Protestant Interest".[1] These Men to give a Sanction to their Proceedings assembled in the principal Church (Calvinist)[2] at Edinburgh; and it is shocking to Humanity to reflect that such Bigotry, blind Zeal, and religious Barbarity should still subsist in any Part of the British Dominions, at a Time when Mens Minds in general are enlightened, and the most liberal Opinions in religious Matters universally prevail.

In this wretched Performance the Protestant Inhabitants are exhorted not to buy or sell to Roman Catholics, neither to borrow of them nor to lend to them; to hold no social Communication with them whatever; nor to harbour or conceal them, and to use their utmost Endeavours to banish them for ever from Scotland. Annexed to these pious Resolutions entered into by the Association, and recommended to all their Protestant Brethren, is a Catalogue of the Penal Laws of Scotland against Papists, not quite so bloody, but as severe as the Laws of Draco.

Mr. Burke followed the Line of the Petition; he did not wish to try a Repeal of these Laws in the present Disposition of the People of Scotland; but he insisted on an Indemnification for the Loss of Property, and Security for the Enjoyment of the Lives and Properties of the Roman Catholics, and the Enjoyment of the Exercise of their Religion in future, and that they might be reinstated in their Habitations and Callings by the Authority and under the Protection of Government.

In the Course of a very elaborate Comment on the Pamphlet, and reading Copious Extracts from it, Lord North had fallen into a sound Sleep, which the House did not perceive till these Words happened to drop from Mr. Burke in Support of an Argument; without adverting to the noble Lord's Situation—"Government is not dead, it only sleepeth." The Peals of Laughter upon this Occasion were universal, and the Minister Opening his Eyes was informed of the Occasion by his next Neighbour,[3] and then he joined in the Mirth. Mr. Burke pleasantly remarked, now the House was in good Humour, and

---

[1] The pamphlet Burke discusses, *A Letter to All Opposers of the Repeal of the Penal Laws against Papists in Scotland*, Edinburgh, 1779, was not in fact issued by the Committee (*Corr.* iv. 54).
[2] St Giles.   [3] Presumably Wedderburn, who woke him up.

Government awake, which he had long doubted of, he hoped it would be the proper Time to call them to the Exercise of Humanity. He then in a strain of manly and affecting Eloquence introduced his Motion, that the Petition be referred to a Committee of the whole House, to receive all Petitions, examine Witnesses, and report their Opinion thereon to the House.

(2) MS. AT SHEFFIELD, BK 8.49b

The question is now whether Magistracy has means to preserve peace; Government power to protect innocence; or the Legislature itself authority to make Laws upon the principles of Equity and justice.

The matter is great, and grave, and worthy of your most serious deliberation. The honour of the Nation, the age we live in, and the religion we profess.

The petition has stated to the house as much of the grievance of the sufferers as their prudence has permitted.

For it is a part of their misfortune, that any vehemence of complaint of the injuries they suffer, may[1] become a Cause of further injury; so much so that many people of a more timid discretion thought the very application for redress ought to be forborne.

For my part, I do not wish to open to you[2] the entire state of that part of the Kingdom under the present influence of its bigotted Phrensy. It will be enough to this House, that a man of the highest authority[3] in the Law in Scotland,[4] a man of great natural firmness and intrepidity, thinks that Phrensy to be such and to be so general, that it is advisable to suspend for a time the bringing in a Bill, which he thinks right on principles of Natural justice;[5] and which he thinks highly expedient in policy and necessary for producing union and harmony in the Laws of the Kingdom, and the State and Condition of the Subject.

Government has thought proper to go a Step further, it has thought proper formally [to] give up the design of bringing in such a Bill and to

---

[1] MS.: 'and may'.

[2] In the margin: 'Not disclose the State'.

[3] Henry Dundas, the Lord Advocate (*Parl. Reg.* xii. 141).

[4] In the margin: '1. Proof of it declining the Bill by the Ld. Ad. 2. government formally gives up the Bill and purges itself'.

[5] In the margin: 'Magistrates discharge the Rioters'.

confess before the[1] populace of Edinburg and to purge themselves and all their friends by a Letter from the Secretary of State from any designs in favour of toleration.[2]

All This indicates a great distemper in that Country, or what amounts nearly to the same thing a great weakness in the Organs of Government.

But when I find popular distempers raging, a Violent drastic medicine is not the first thing which occurs to me. The greater the distemper the greater the attention ought certainly to be given to it; but the greater at the same time the prudence, moderation and sobriety that is necessary. It requires a firm but a temperate and healing hand.

But in whatever state Government is found whether of *vigorous* exertion—or of *prudent relaxation—It owes as its first*, grand, indispensable duty—*protection to its Subjects.*

If it owes some attention and management even to those who *trample on Authority* and *defy the Laws*, how much does it owe regard to those who suffer by the *violence of these men*, and whose Cause of suffering is no other than their desire of *recommending themselves to Government by their Duty and submission?*

If we do not think it prudent to give them instant protection by our *power* we must *relieve* them with our *purse*. If we cannot *punish delinquency* let us not refuse *redress to suffering* and not to show ourselves at once impotent and uncharitable.

The *merits* of the suffering party is out of the question. They are *men and subjects* who have sufferd *illegal Violence.*[3]

If they were the *worst of men* and the worst of *Subjects* they are still intitled to that protection until *legal conviction.*

Nay after Legal Conviction. Robbery to rob an Outlaw—Murder to Kill a condemnd criminal is ⟨about⟩ a Robber must not be robbed—a murderer must not be murderd. But let it be rememberd that so far from being delinquents on account of their religion we thought them worthy of *relief* have actually relievd them *here* and only delayd their relief in Scotland on account of these very armies.

The persons most unexceptionable.[4]

---

[1] MS.: 'the the'.

[2] The letter was from Thomas Thynne, 3rd Viscount Weymouth (1734–96), later (1789) 1st Marquess of Bath, to Thomas Miller, styled Lord Glenlee (1717–89); see *Corr.* iv. 44.

[3] In the margin: 'This Hierarchy could not fall without a Struggle. All religious contests of any bitterness for power to give the reasons of the Struggle against future toleration—endless'.

[4] In the margin: 'cannot examine Tenets—our Business practical Government the obedient to us are Good in their principles the rebellious Evil'.

judge by their actions. These are of our competence.[1]
American sufferers to an immense amount[2] and that amount
Gentry of Scotland clear
Church of Scotland many men of the most *Liberal learning*—the most[3]
enlarged views, and the most *diffusive Benevolence*.

But in all churches there are a set of men of a very different
Character—who being neither able to give[4] the Church illumination
with their learning fervour with their piety, or consolation by their
Charity. Compensate all by their *Zeal*. A great auxiliary *Virtue* as giving
Effect and energy to other Virtues—but which independent of other
Virtues, or *supplemental* to them is the most mischievous thing in the
world.[5] This kind of Zeal requires no sort of Stock to set up; and
no wonder those choose to distinguish themselves by it who can
distinguish themselves by nothing else, especially when they engage in
combats with those who cannot resist, and in disputations with those
who dare not reply.

(3) MS. AT SHEFFIELD, BK 8.51

What must those suffer whose complaints are insults, and their very
desire of redress a provocation to punishment. Greatest sufferers—
greatest Objects of compassion. Writers hold the Magistrate has a right
to coerce. But never that individuals may fall upon and destroy them at
their pleasure vide our Oath.
Case of Calas[6] and the ground of it.
Walloon Synod. Bp. of Meaux[7]
Starchamber and Commission for the Church
Then Presbyterians

---

[1] In the margin: 'until this Country can be got into the Elements of Law and order and to the first principles of religion'.
[2] Financial provision for American refugees had been on a large scale since 1777 (M. B. Norton, *The British Americans: The Loyalist Exiles in England 1774–1789*, London, 1974, pp. 52–5).
[3] In the margin: 'respect it as I do every other great Christian and national Establishment'.
[4] MS.: 'give it the'.
[5] In rewriting this sentence Burke has failed to delete two words: 'the' and 'worst'.
[6] Jean Calas (1698–1762), a Protestant, executed for the alleged murder of his son to prevent him from changing his religion. He was later declared to have been innocent. Voltaire's interest in the case made it a matter of international importance.
[7] The reference to the Walloon Synod is not clear. Jacques-Bénigne Bossuet (1627–1704), Bishop of Meaux, strove to reconcile Protestants to the Catholic Church and praised the revocation of the Edict of Nantes.

1. Those who consider that this Storm fell upon them only for the supposed Good intentions of Parliament to them.

2. That it is struck directly at our authority.

3. That for the present at least they have lost the Benefit of those intentions and of that authority.

4. Those that think they can or ought to bear the loss of all they are worth will vote against us and I shall not envy them.

15 Mill of Subjects in the East Indies—enough that they are persecuted by Avarice and not to be exposed to Bigottry too—never enquire their principles.

Our Armies almost entirely composed of them.

Vote for the American sufferers on a blind Trust—knew neither numbers—merits or even Names.

I cannot say Bowie[1] and his Crew—and treat so great an Evil with contempt—Those who have shewn that they have *power* in a Country are not *contemptible*. Those whose *nonsense* persuades are *Eloquent*. Those who operate on a nation are *powerful*. Douglas—Hamilton—Scot—[2]

Lord North argued that compensation would be paid locally and the petition was ordered to lie on the table. Burke apparently spoke a second time in the debate.[3]

Speech on Scottish Catholics
31 March 1779

Source: *Morning Post*, 1 April 1779

Another report is in *London Chronicle*, 1 April; and *General Advertiser*, 1 April; and is abbreviated in *London Evening Post*, 1 April.

Burke took the opportunity of a debate on the Bill against Smuggling[4] to raise again the situation of the Catholics in Edinburgh and Glasgow.

---

[1] Patrick Bowie or Ralph Bowie, both members of the Protestant Association at Edinburgh (*Corr.* iv. 53–7).
[2] The allusion, presumably to the Douglas Cause, is not clear. The Douglas Cause was a celebrated Scottish case of 1769 between Archibald James Edward Douglas, later (1790) 1st Baron Douglas and James George Hamilton, 7th Duke of Hamilton (1755–69), disputing the succession to the Douglas estates (A. Francis, *The Douglas Cause*, Glasgow, 1909, p. 21).
[3] *Morning Chronicle*, 19 March 1779.   [4] 19 Geo. III, c. 19.

Mr. *Burke* could not approve of any law that condemned to the flames any thing that could be serviceable to mankind; he therefore must reprobate the idea of burning vessels taken from smugglers; they might be sold, or usefully employed in the service of the state. He then took occasion to mention the case of the Roman Catholics of Glasgow and Edinburgh, who were absolutely out of the protection of the laws; one of them indeed, a shoe-maker, had ventured to open his shop;[1] but none had been hardy enough as yet to follow his example. He had received a letter from the Secretary of the Protestant Association at Edinburgh,[2] declaring he had not been the author of the pamphlet which had been attributed to him: he therefore thought it proper to make a reparation to the Secretary, by contradicting, on the strength of the letter, the opinion he had formerly delivered in the House respecting the Secretary of the association as the supposed author of the pamphlet. But he observed, that this association for protecting the Protestant religion, as he said, from the claws of Parliament, still subsisted, and as the Roman Catholics were in no small danger from it, he gave notice, that after the holidays he would renew his motion on the petition he had already presented to the House, and which had been only put off for a time by the previous question.

No evidence has been found of Burke having done so.

Notes for Speech on Dissenters Bill
April 1779

Sources: MSS. at Sheffield, Bk 8.45, 36

The passage of the Catholic Relief Act of 1778 encouraged Sir Henry Hoghton[3] to move on 10 March 1779 for a Committee of the whole House to consider the granting of further relief to Protestant dissenting ministers and schoolmasters. Such relief had been considered in 1772 and 1773 but not implemented.[4] The motion was carried and a Bill prepared which relieved dissenting ministers and schoolmasters from the need to subscribe to the

---

[1] William Lockhart was the shoemaker at Edinburgh (MS. at Sheffield, Bk 8.53).
[2] From Patrick Bowie (Ralph Bowie was in fact secretary); see *Corr.* iv. 53–7.
[3] 6th Baronet (1728–95), M.P. 1768–95. Hoghton was a prominent member of a dissenting family in Lancashire.
[4] See vol. ii, pp. 368–70.

Thirty-nine Articles as laid down by the Toleration Act.[1] When this Bill was before a Committee of the whole House on 20 April, a petition from the University of Oxford was read which opposed the Bill unless a provision was inserted in it 'declaratory of the Christianity of those who were to be relieved by it'. Lord North, who was Chancellor of the University, proposed to include in the Bill the following declaration: 'I, A.B. do solemnly declare, that I am a Christian, and a Protestant Dissenter; and that I take the holy scriptures, both of the Old and New Testaments, as they are generally received in Protestant countries, for the rule of my faith and practice.'[2] The Committee accepted this declaration. Its report was debated on 28 April. John Dunning then

declared, that many of the protestant dissenting ministers had authorised him to give their reasons against signing the proposed declaration. He then read a paper, containing amongst other things, the distinguishing tenet by which Protestant dissenters are known throughout Europe, which is, that they deny the authority of the civil magistrate in matters of religion, and therefore they cannot consistently sign a test which admits of that authority.[3]

The Bill was passed with the declaration on 30 April. Burke is known to have spoken on 20 April (see Appendix A), but these notes were probably prepared for a speech which was never given. They appear to refer to Dunning's speech on the 30th.

(1) MS. AT SHEFFIELD, BK. 8.45

This is a *new* Ground of Objection. It is not on the difficulty of being called on to subscribe what they *do* not but what they *do believe*. It arises upon a question collateral to the matter of subscription—which is not a dispute concerning the articles of Religion but concerning the power of the Magistrate; concerning his power to annex any condition to the right of teaching religion publickly and under his protection. It is upon that abstract metaphysical proposition, that some refuse to subscribe to the holy Scriptures.

I am not ripe as *an abstract proposition* to give my opinion upon it in all its extent. These universal abstract propositions are not proper Legislative grounds—which are only the utility and convenience of the community as it happens[4] by accident to be constituted.

I think of Government as I do of every thing else made for the good of mankind—like their Cloaths made to fit them, not those who go by

---

[1] *Commons Sessional Papers*, xxix. 109–12.
[2] *Parl. Reg.* xii. 309; the wording was changed (19 Geo. III, c. 44).
[3] Ibid. 353.
[4] MS.: 'as it is happens'.

abstract rules to have their altitude taken by a quadrant and their solid content calculated by the cubick feet and inches.

This Bill has nothing to do with the individual private conscience—and therefore the rules of mere general Toleration do not apply to [it]—It regards the publick teaching by[1] a *certain description* of men whom we are to *know* by Law under the Name of Protestant Ministers dissenting. If by Law we are to know and to protect them, we have a full right to see whether they come under the description. In[2] my humble opinion it is their *duty when they claim immunity and protection* under this *description*, to shew that they belong to it.

To settle the grounds of distinction which makes a *protestant* as contradistinguishd from Catholicks is his rule of Faith—which in Catholicks is not the Scripture—but the Tradition of the Catholick Church and the scripture only as it is a part of that Tradition—a protestant is one, that holds the Scripture of the old and New Testament as his sole rule of faith. Now it is singular, that any man should desire protection[3] and immunity as *a protestant*, who refuses to qualifye himself by the sole characteristick distinction by which a *protestant can possibly be known*. It is a scruple perfectly extraordinary and a thing that I believe has no parralel since the beginning of the world. For a mere negation of any other religion a mere renunciation of Popery never made a man a protestant. Else a Jew would be a better Prot. than a Lutheran or a Calvinist, a Mahometan better than a Jew—and a Heathen much better than a Mahometan. So that merely proceeding in the infinity of Negation—the less a man was a Christian the better protestant he would be. It is as Christian and as protestant dissenter and says[4] their own paper.[5] And yet when I ask them what they mean by these words, they turn from me, and say do whip and persecute me as much as you please I had rather burn at the Stake than tell you. Sink or swim Mr. Faulkner[6] my secret shall go to the grave with me.

⟨The Casuists⟩ have disputed about the right of Christians to conceal their faith to avoid persecution. It is agreed on that as a piece of Charity any man ought to tell his faith and to give a reason for the faith which is in him. But this has been allowd like every principle of

---

[1] MS.: 'teaching of by'.
[2] MS.: 'and in'.
[3] MS.: 'protected'.
[4] MS.: 'and and says'.
[5] MS.: 'own own paper.' The paper is presumably that read to the House by Dunning.
[6] Probably George Faulkner (1699–75), editor of the *Dublin Journal*.

Charity to be governed by prudence; and the most rigid have gone no further that to say that when called on by a Magistrate they were obliged under ⟨every⟩ penalty to declare their religion—This has made the Confessors and Martyrs of older and of more recent times which are the Glory of the Church.

(2) MS. AT SHEFFIELD BK. 8.36

One ought to look on the whole Law together as it stands—and consider how the repeal of one part is likely to affect another[1] that is to stand and how far the present repeal of one part may not raise great Objections against the future correction of another.

If the Test now repeald might let dissenters whom we know to be Christians to be Magistrates. But then it would be argued as an Objection that we may put Magistracy in the hands of the very open and declared possibly zealous Enemies of the Christian Name.

relieve protestant dissenters—must intitle themselves to that Name. What Prot. what dissenter.

The Scource of Dissent is not a School question on *the rights of the Magistrate*. Those of the Ch. of England may hold that.

Scotch act of 1695. against irregular Baptism etc. perpetual imprisonment and Banishment of Episcopal Ministers. repeald 10. Ann. ch. 7.[2]

Many Casuists thought a Christian bound to make Profession of his Beliefs—what a Strange sort of Obstinacy to refuse to declare to a Christian Magistrate[3] wishing to protect and favour you[4] that you are a Christian.

What you were to an Heathen going to persecute you or an Inquisitor carrying you to the Stake. It looks ⟨underhand⟩ like a design to pick a Quarrel.

Is the question in which they dissent concerning the power of the Magistrate in point of religion. I dont see how this can divide us into separate congregations. A dissenter is a man who differs in doctrines

---

[1] The MS. has an undeleted 'other' as well.

[2] 10 Anne, c. 7, repealed an act passed by Parliament in Scotland 'in the year one thousand six hundred and ninety-five intitled *An Act against irregular Baptism and Marriage,* by which all Episcopal Ministers, who were turned out of their Churches, are prohibited to baptize any children, or to solemnize any Marriage, upon Pain of perpetual Imprisonment or Banishment'.

[3] Written above: 'dont believe it of dissenters'.

[4] MS.: 'you you'.

and ceremonies from an Establishment. Not he who has a controversy concerning the power of the Magistrate?

This is not a general declaratory Law made for the purpose of recognizing the rights of mankind and settling the bounds of the Magistrates jurisdiction. It is to the relief of Prot. dis. Min. They ought to qualifye themselves under that Name. Before a man can be a Prot. he must be a Christian—for it is a name of distinction among Christians. To say, that a man is not a Pap: is not to say that he is a Christian. If a mere negative not being a Pap. is enough to make a man a Prot. the Jews Mahometans Heathens are much better Prots than we.

Scotland—General Assembly they were bold in the Lord and in the name of the Church earnestly to ⟨obtain⟩ his Grace and the most honourable Estates that no such motion of any legal toleration to those of prelatical principles might be entertaind by the Parliament.[1]

Resolution on Ireland
11 May 1779

Source: MS. at Sheffield, R81.199

On 8 May 1779 Rockingham who was a very considerable landowner in Ireland[2] sent Burke a proposed resolution on Irish affairs which had been drafted by Lord Camden.[3] Burke sent back a heavily amended version on 9 May.[4] Two days later Rockingham introduced this revised motion in the House of Lords, where, after amendment, it was passed unanimously.[5]

(1) CAMDEN'S MOTION

That this House taking into Consideration the distressed and impoverished State of Ireland and observing[6] that the Measures that have been lately proposed in Parliament to relieve that Kingdom by extend-

---

[1] This last paragraph may have been intended as an insertion at a previous place.
[2] In *A List of the Absentees of Ireland, and an Estimate of the Yearly Value of their Estates and Incomes spent Abroad*, 3rd edn., Dublin, 1769, Rockingham's annual rents in Ireland are valued at more than £10,000.
[3] Charles Pratt, 1st Baron Camden (1714–94), later (1786) 1st Earl Camden.
[4] *Corr.* iv. 69–72.
[5] See vol. ix, p. 555.
[6] Burke has written in the margin: 'not necessary to accuse ourselves of our folly.'

ing the Trade thereof have been such as have[1] rather tended to disappoint than satisfy by the Smallness of the Benefit and finding ⟨now⟩ at last that the People there dispairing of any Relief from the Parliament of Great Britain by whose restrictive Laws they apprehend themselves reduced to their present State of Want and Misery, have begun to enter into dangerous[2] Associations not to import or use any British Commodities, and this House apprehending that this Spirit of discontent if it should be permitted to[3] encrease may take a deep Root and endanger the Safety of his Majesty's Kingdoms already too far engaged in a Civil as well as a foreign War.

And this House being of Opinion that it is more consonant to Justice and true Policy to remove the Causes of Discontent by a Redress of Grievances than to force a Submission by coercive Measures.

And to apprize his Majesty of these impending Evils as well as to demonstrate to that Loyal and well-deserving Nation that this House is not inattentive to such their Complaints; and to put this important Business forward in such manner as may best answer the Great End of Improving and augmenting the Wealth[4] Strength and Commerce of both Kingdoms. It is moved that an Humble Address be presented to his Majesty to take the Premises into his most serious Consideration and direct his Ministers[5] to prepare without delay some Plan for relieving his Good Subjects of Ireland whereby this House[6] may be enabled in concurrence with his Majesty to effectuate the same by good and wholesome Laws to the Common Benefit of all his Subjects in both Kingdoms.

(2) MS. AT SHEFFIELD, R. 81.199

I really think that all which is crossed, had better be fairly struck out of the motion.[7] It will stand then better, and with a more Parliamentary

---

[1] Rockingham has written in the margin: 'Quaere—May [so that the text would read 'such as may rather tend'].'

[2] Burke has written in the margin: 'danger not proper' Rockingham had asked: 'Quaere Propriety of the word dangerous'.

[3] Rockingham has underlined 'be permitted to' and asks in the margin: 'Quaere to omit the words underlined'.

[4] Under this Burke has written: 'N.B. this in effect is said in the last paragraph.'

[5] Burke has written in the margin: 'I would not go a begging to them for a plan.'

[6] Rockingham has written in the margin: 'Quaere Parliament'.

[7] Burke changed Camden's motion as he went along and then wrote out the motion again as he had changed it.

Appearance. Consult Lord John on it—who is a perfect judge of these matters—as is Montagu.[1]—It will stand thus as I correct it shorter as I imagine and less exceptionable.

"That this house, taking into Consideration the distressed and impoverishd State of the Kingdom of Ireland, and being of opinion, that it is consonant to Justice and true policy to remove the Causes of discontent by a redress of grievances, and in order to demonstrate the Sense, which this house entertains, of the merits of that Loyal and well deserving Nation this house doth conceive it highly expedient that this important Business should be enterd upon as soon as Circumstances will admit,[2] and that an humble address be presented to his Majesty, that his Majesty will be graciously pleased to take the matter into his most serious consideration, and to direct his Ministers to prepare and lay before Parliament, such particulars relative to the Trade and manufactures of Great Britain and Ireland as may enable the National Wisdom to pursue effectual methods for promoting the common strength, wealth and commerce of his Majesties Subjects in both Kingdoms."

Speech on Supply
31 May 1779

Source: *Gazetteer*, 2 June 1779

This report is followed by *Parl. Reg.* xiii. 181–7 and *Parl. Hist.* xx. 821–8 (both including an earlier intervention by Burke). It is also in *London Evening Post*, 3 June. Other reports are in *General Advertiser*, 1 June; *London Evening Post*, 1 June; *General Evening Post*, 1 June; *Lloyd's Evening Post*, 2 June; *London Chronicle*, 1 June; *Gazetteer*, 1 June; *St James's Chronicle*, 1 June; and *Morning Post*, 1 June.

On 31 May Lord North introduced the final financial measures for the year. This account of the Government's funding requirements was subjected to a searching scrutiny by David Hartley, who also pointed out that in the war

---

[1] Lord John Cavendish and Frederick Montagu. Montagu (1733–1800), M.P. 1759–90, sat for Rockingham's pocket borough of Higham Ferrers, yet enjoyed the friendship of Lord North to whom he was related through marriage. He was a respected figure in the House, and knowledgeable about its procedures. North even offered him the Speakership in 1780. Cavendish was not only a senior figure in the Rockingham party, but also one of its most experienced parliamentarians, having entered the House in 1754.

[2] Changed to 'should no longer be neglected' before submitted to the House of Lords.

at sea the forces of Britain and France were so nicely balanced that if Spain intervened, the naval consequences would be disastrous. Lord Nugent protested against some of the expressions which he used, and Burke called him to order, arguing that Hartley must be permitted to substantiate his claim. Hartley completed his speech and Burke rose again.

Burke's argument underlines the importance of the American war in the movement of the Rockingham party towards a moderate reform stance. Here Burke attacks above all the undue influence of the Crown in instigating and perpetuating a hopeless, expensive, and inhumane war. He was of course saying, as were so many others in Britain by the late 1770s, that only a corrupt and evil administration supported by a majority hungry for a plethora of Crown offices, pensions, and contracts could have brought the empire to such a state. It was substantially that belief which would soon encourage the Rockinghams to bring forth their celebrated economical reform programme.[1] It was also largely that which underlay the sudden dramatic increase in reform literature and ideas in Britain as a whole, by the late 1770s and early 1780s.[2]

He said, the public lay under great obligations to the Honourable Gentleman (Mr. Hartley) who had just sat down, as well on the present as on many former occasions. His details were always important and correct, and in particular well worthy of the attention of the noble Lord in the blue ribbon.

The Honourable Gentleman had stated, and truly stated, that the expence of the campaign 1779, would be little short of the enormous sum of *twenty millions*, including the navy debt, vote of credit, and services; which, from the manner they were necessarily incurred, could not be regularly passed in account within the year.—He had stated the unfunded debt only at *sixteen* millions, which he thought was considerably lower than it might be justly computed. He differed from the Honourable Gentleman with great reluctance and diffidence in matters of computation and finance; but he was convinced, that if the war was to cease the instant he was speaking, that a tail of *ten* additional millions of unfunded debt, which, with the eleven millions already

[1] See Burke's speech on public expenses of 15 December 1779 and his speech on economical reform of 11 February 1780, both printed below.

[2] See e.g. Willoughby Bertie, 4th Earl of Abingdon (1740–99), *Dedication to the Collective Body of the People of England, in which the Source of our Present Political Distractions are pointed out, and a Plan proposed for their Remedy and Redress*, Oxford, 1780; J. Cartwright, *A Letter to the Earl of Abingdon Discussing a Position Relative to a Fundamental Right of the Constitution*, London, 1778; *The People's Barrier against Undue Influence and Corruption* London, 1780; *An Essay on Constitutional Liberty: wherein the Necessity of Frequent Elections of Parliament is shewn to be superseded by the Unity of the Executive Power*, London, 1780; R. Price, *The General Introduction and Supplement to the Two Tracts on Civil Liberty, the War with America, and the Finances of the Kingdom*, London, 1778.

stated by his Honourable friend, would make in the whole twenty-one, or at least twenty millions of unfunded debt behind. The debt already funded bore an interest of nearly a *million* a year; this unfunded debt, when funded, would add to the interest paid to the public creditors about another million; so that the first face the American war at this stage of the business presented to the people of England, was, a mortgage on their lands, moveables, trade, and commerce, in perpetuity of two millions a year. America lost, and not a *shilling* to balance this unparalleled loss and insupportable burden in return.[1]

The noble Lord, if he could judge from his language, whatever his secret feelings might be, kept up his countenance tolerably well, and seemed to be already preparing for *another* American campaign.—Says the noble Lord, the sinking fund will be more productive this year than it was the last; the house and servants tax will come into its aid; and, instead of being a burden, as they were to the amount of seven hundred thousand pounds this year, they will considerably augment its receipt in the next.

Says the noble Lord, a sum of money is expected, the next year, from the East India Company; and in consideration of the territorial revenues, an *annual* supply will be expected by way of equivalent; and in a year or two, on the ceasing of some determinable annuities for years, the sinking fund will be further augmented, to the amount of 200,000l. per ann.[2]

For the present, I shall consider those *golden* premises in no other light than as they are held out, as stimulatives to induce this House, and the nation, to a further prosecution of the American War.

You hear no more of raising the supplies within the year, but you are told of the *increasing* state of the sinking fund, and of a standing fixed East India revenue, in which one supposition, perhaps impossible, is followed by another supposition, perhaps more impossible.—The first is, the supposed flourishing state of the sinking fund, and the certainty of obtaining a settled revenue from India; the second is, whether those resources, if real, can or will present such a security to the money-lenders, the next year, as they will be willing to advance their money upon; but of this, more hereafter.

---

[1] For the funded and unfunded debt, see B. R. Mitchell and P. Deane, *Abstract of British Historical Statistics*, Cambridge, 1962, p. 402.
[2] Burke is repeating information from North's speech (*Parl. Reg.* xiii. 178–80).

The noble Lord is preparing for another American campaign; that is the main object of my rising. He gave us to understand, early in the session, that it was his intention to do so; that the present was to be carried on upon a *moderate* scale; that it was to be *moderately fed*; but that the disposition of the people of America to return to their former state of obedience; and what from the inability of the Congress to support their usurped dominion, the loyalty of the majority or body of the people, and the *vigorous, unanimous* exertions of this country, the fate of America would be determined in the year 1780.—This was the substance of what fell in several conversations upon this subject.—If I have mis-stated the noble Lord's sentiments, his Lordship will rise and set me right: if not, I shall take it for granted; and his financial discourse this day confirms to me, that I neither misunderstood, nor have misrepresented him.—Here then is *another ten* millions to be added to our burdens, and an annual interest of half a million to be paid in perpetuity. If this however is certain loss, let us look forward to the probable gain.—Nothing! America is lost; and all we have to balance against this risque and loss is, a war with France, Spain, and America!—I shall beg leave to assign my reasons.

We have been sitting in this House, twice a week, till midnight, in examining officers upon the probability of success in the American war.[1] We have been informed, that the people in general are hostile to us; that the face of the country, at almost every mile's distance, presents a native fortress; that the rebels are well-disciplined; that they are the most dextrous in the world at raising field works and sudden defences; that, from the nature of the country, it is next to impossible to obtain intelligence; that the country in general is intersected by broad, deep, and rapid rivers; abounds in creeks, and is covered with woods and morasses. In short, that a successful war is totally impracticable, with any force or assistance we could be able to procure and send.

This is not the language of *declamation*, of *hearsay, or conjecture*; the two Generals[2] who commanded there, hold it; every officer of

[1] On 17 February Sir William Howe, in order to vindicate his own and his brother's reputation against the charges of incompetence laid against them on their return from their commands in America, moved successfully to have his correspondence with Lord George Germain placed before the House. In May a committee under the chairmanship of Frederick Montagu considered the papers and took expert testimony from a succession of officers concerning the conduct of the war in America.

[2] Howe and Burgoyne.

rank who served under them confirm[s] it.[1] What then is the next consideration?—Most assuredly, if we cannot recover America, or if even the probabilities were balanced, that it would be a most hazardous experiment, is to determine on the properest mode of relinquishing the attempt.

In the face of all these difficulties, however, the noble Lord appears determined to risque another campaign. The difficulties seem as nothing in his contemplation. The House and nation is *with* him, and all he looks for or attends to is the means. I recollect well when the noble Lord said on the first budget day, the American war must be "*moderately fed*," the House resounded with hear'ems! while twenty fat contractors at his Lordship's back, cried out with one voice, some in hoarser, some in more *sonorous* accents, *feed! feed! feed!* This deluded country was to be bled to death, to be plundered to the last shilling. What cared the contractors? like so many ravens and birds of prey they wished only to suck her inmost vitals, to feast on her entrails, and finally glut their all-devouring maws on her lifeless cadaver.

But to return to the means pointed out by the noble Lord for carrying on this ruinous war; an increase of the sinking fund! two hundred thousand pounds a year determinable annuities! and a permanent annual East-India revenue. The noble Lord knows that the sinking fund will not answer what it is already charged with; he knows that the surcharge of the Customs and Excises, the post-horse tax, nor that upon stamps, cannot, from the nature of collecting them, be brought into the receipt of the Exchequer by the end of the Christmas quarter. As he is sensible of all this, he must of course know, that instead of an increase of the sinking fund, there must be a decrease to the amount nearly of the interest of the whole loan of the present year, a sum of upwards of 400,000l. So much for his Lordship's expectations from that quarter.

As to the determinable annuities, which will fall in 1781 and 1782; surely the noble Lord does not mean to be serious when he states them as part of the ways and means for the year 1780.

The India Company, however, in his Lordship's opinion, holds out something more certain, and of greater magnitude; a fixed revenue to be obtained will be a good security. Here the same objection holds to

---

[1] This was the tendency of much of the evidence before the committee, not surprisingly, since the Howe brothers and Burgoyne were anxious to establish the difficulty and even impossibility of their task. None the less, Burke exaggerates.

this resource as to that of the sinking fund. Supposing the terms fixed, and the act passed, and the revenue certain, can the money be remitted, or investments made, time enough for the payment of the interest growing due in the year 1780? Impossible: but in my opinion the plan of a settled regular revenue is totally impracticable; and I dare say the noble Lord will be convinced of this melancholy truth, when he comes to negociate with the money-lenders; they will not trust to so precarious a security. The truth is, our territories in the East-Indies are able to render certain advantages, in commerce and military strength, to this country; and no more. We tried the experiment once before, and were at last obliged to forego an ideal revenue of 400,000l. per ann. but not until the Company became *bankrupt*, and were obliged to apply to this House for aid.[1] The great military establishment kept up in that country has swallowed up all the land-revenue; and all the real advantages we can ever expect to reap from it, is in the way of trade, and the increase of private property spent within the kingdom, and the power, and weight, and preference it has given to us in that quarter of the globe, over Holland, France, Spain, and all other European powers who possess any territories there. The Company will be able to defend their own possessions, and annoy our enemies there, and of course will add to the aggregate strength and dignity of the British empire; but, I fear, if our East-India possessions are to come under the patronage of the Crown, and are to be governed as a military province, that they will follow the fate of our dominions in the West, and will finally be wrested from this country. I do not mean however to disapprove of, or controvert the controuling power and guardianship of this House. Let this House and the Parliament be the medium of controul; but I hope I shall never behold it ingrafted or invested in the executive power of this country;[2] waving, however, every more remote consideration, so far as a fixed revenue may be applicable to the immediate relief of this country, to enable us to raise the supplies with greater facility, and upon better terms. I believe it is clearly demonstrable, that it can answer no such purpose for the ensuing year.

If then the American war is impracticable, I think I have proved that

---

[1] In the early 1770s; see L. Sutherland, *East Indies Company in Eighteenth-Century British Politics*, Oxford, 1952, pp. 182–268.

[2] This would of course be the rationalization behind Fox's East India Company legislation of 1783 in which Burke would play an instrumental part (ibid., p. 401; vol. v, pp. 378–451).

his Lordship's means are no less so, which clearly amounts to this; that the annuities payable on the loan of the next year must be paid by additional burdens, to be laid upon the people; and that the additional burdens thus to be laid, falling probably short of the sums they will be taken for, as in the three preceding years, must be drawn from the sinking fund, which will be an anticipation of the greatest part of its produce. Whether national aids procured in such a manner, and upon such terms, to carry on a war impracticable and destructive in its nature, would be a wise measure, I leave to this House and the noble Lord to determine: but I had an additional reason for rising on the present occasion, equally strong with any of the foregoing, to shew the folly and madness of prosecuting the American war; and it is connected with what fell from my honourable friend who spoke before me.

My honourable friend says, that he has strong reason to believe, that America would at present be willing to treat upon amicable terms with this country, if we desisted from further hostility, as they begin to see into the designs of France, and that Spain continues, and is determined, to preserve a neutrality.[1] My honourable friend, with his usual ability and zeal, has followed this information by earnestly pressing the noble Lord to make some proposition in Parliament, tending to a full reconciliation with the Colonies, because, said he, if from any accident Spain should depart from her neutrality, and be drawn in as a principal in the war, America will refuse to treat upon any terms. To strengthen this argument my honourable friend has stated the very formidable naval force of Spain, to shew that we should be overmatched by such an union of power as France, Spain, and America. I differ in part from my honourable friend, both in his facts and conclusions. I have strong doubts that America would not treat, because the condition precedent, that they would not, has already actually taken place, for Spain is no longer a neutral or mediating power; all neutrality and mediation is over, and that within a few days.[2] The treaty is determined very recently, within less than a week, perhaps five days. I agree with my honourable friend, that Spain, as she is now actually leagued with France, will turn the scale against us; but I do not despond, could we get rid of the American war. We often

---

[1] This is not recorded in Hartley's speech though it would correspond well with those remarks on an American negotiation which are (*Parl. Reg.* xiii. 181).

[2] Spain had signed the Convention of Aranjuez with France on 12 April.

contended with those powers, and vanquished them on our proper element, the ocean; and I trust still, if we were united, our councils wisely and vigorously conducted, and the spirit of the nation called forth, that we are able to resist their utmost efforts. If the confidence of the people was restored; if a dangerous Court system was broken; if the influence of the Crown was regulated and limited within its due and constitutional bounds, we should have no reason to despair; but the instant is critical; the moment must be seized; recall your troops from America; if she will not treat upon a political connexion, as soon as she perceives the House of Bourbon leagued for our total destruction, she will desist from all enmity, and forget all former injuries; she will feel all the emotions of a child for the miseries of an harsh or misled parent; but even were she to observe a neutrality, I would not despair but we should prevail in the contest. She must at once perceive, that it is no longer a struggle for her liberties, but a plan, concerted between our natural enemies, to erect schemes of ambition and endless destruction on the ruins of her once kind and indulgent parent.

I repeat once more, that all negociation is at an end, that Spain is openly leagued with France. The noble Lord knows it. I call upon him to contradict me; if he does not, I shall take it for granted.—If so, then I earnestly implore the noble Lord not to lose a moment's time, but instantly seize an occasion which the interval of a very few days may place for ever beyond his reach. The fate of the empire, the existence of this country depend upon celerity, vigour, and union in this very important concern.

I have but one word more to add; my Honourable friend has stated the naval force of Spain, I believe, very correctly; for I have a list myself in my hand which confirms it.[1] At present we are superior to France in the ocean, and the West-Indies, and I believe in the East. We are inferior only in the Mediterranean, where, most certainly, our two important fortresses[2] are at the mercy of the House of Bourbon; and for this single reason, if for no other, that we cannot at present send a single officer or man there, unless we shall be happy enough to smuggle him in a *rum* puncheon, or *brandy* cask. But Spain, says my Honourable friend, with forty or forty-eight ships of the line in

---

[1] Hartley had brandished two lists of his own before the House, one summarizing the strength of the Spanish fleet at Cadiz in September 1777 as forty ships of the line, the other naming eight ships built since that time.

[2] Minorca and Gibraltar.

Europe, will give to the House of Bourbon a decided majority—
Granted; and that, in its probable consequences, urges me to press the
matter more seriously on the noble Lord in the blue ribbon; because, if
the empire of the sea once leaves us, our distant dependencies must
follow of course. It is true, the East-Indies is able to defend itself, so is
the West; but no longer than we shall maintain the empire of the sea.
If the House of Bourbon have a superiority in the European seas, that
superiority will soon extend itself to the East and West Indies, because
having it in their power to cut off all supplies of men, ordnance, naval
stores, &c. those places must necessarily submit in time, be their local
strength ever so equal. Dispatch is therefore the only thing that can
save us from impending ruin, and the intention of pressing it forcibly
upon the noble Lord, was the true cause of giving the Committee so
much trouble.

He spoke to a great variety of matter of less consequence, particularly of the very critical and dangerous state of Ireland, which,
for want of room, the author of the above sketch has been obliged to
omit.

Burke spoke briefly again in the debate.[1]

Speech on Breach with Spain
16 June 1779

Source: *London Evening Post*, 17 June 1779

This report is followed by *Parl. Reg.* xiii. 419–20, 420–1 and *Parl. Hist.* xx. 895–7. Other reports
are in *Gazetteer*, 17 June; *General Advertiser*, 17 June; and *St James's Chronicle*, 17 June.

On 16 June North reported that the Government had received a manifesto
from the Spanish ambassador and that he would lay it before the House on
the following day. Unusually, Burke opened for the Opposition, speaking
immediately after North's statement. His emotional performance was almost
certainly in part at least the reflection of a feeling of self-righteous indignation
among the Rockingham leaders. Since the late 1760s they had been warning

---

[1] *General Evening Post*, 1 June 1779.

the ministry of the immense danger which the House of Bourbon posed to British security.[1] Now the apparent meddling of the Spanish along with the French in the American dispute seemed to them clearly to indicate that the ministry had criminally imperilled the nation by failing to heed their warnings. The *Public Advertiser* reported that in presenting the motion of impeachment which he finally dropped, Burke actually referred to North and his colleagues as 'wretched ministers'.[2] Considering the agitated state of his mind at the time this seems not improbable.

Mr. Burke immediately took fire, as it were, at the Minister's declaration, and reminded the noble Lord in particular, and the Ministerial side in general, how light they had made of the probability of such an event. Whenever we have talked of a Spanish war in addition to that of France and America, with what contempt have Ministry heard it? With what scorn have they scouted the very idea! Good God! with what joy have they triumphed as it were in our ignorance and folly! Spain we were told time after time could have no interest in joining our enemies. Spain had Colonies of her own, and would not set so bad an example, as to succour or aid those rebellious ones of America: besides, that Spain was naturally inclined to be at peace with Great Britain. In fine, the sincerity of that power was deemed of a fixed and lasting nature, and all suspicions to the contrary were treated as absurd and ridiculous. Such has been the constant and invariable language on the part of Government. Oh, Sir, how have we been deceived! How have we slept night after night, and dreamt of the *faith* of Spain! How long have Ministry retired to their beds, full of wholesome advice and admonition on that precarious point, and waked morning after morning trumpeting out their assurances of the pacific disposition of Spain! the Court of Spain they have had the effrontery to repeat again and again would be ruined by a war. We knew the interest of Spain better than it did herself, and Ministry must turn politicians for the House of Bourbon, and presume to point out, while they could not manage their own affairs, what would be to her advantage, and what would not. But now the unhappy, the dangerous crisis is arrived they were cautioned against. Oh, Sir, what a long, and dismal, what a dark and sad night has this Session been, to leave us at the end of it engaged in a war with the House of Bourbon and America joined to her against us! And how shall Ministry presume to exculpate

[1] See vol. ii, pp. 94–9. [2] 17 June 1779.

themselves? Was there nothing to incline them to expect this manifesto? Had they no opportunity of knowing the aid Spain has been giving to France, and the encouragement shewn to the ships and trade of America? Which ever way we consider this, they are equally culpable. If they really knew that we were exposed to the necessity of a Spanish war, they are not to be excused for their silence, and if they did not, they equally deserve punishment for their monstrous ignorance and want of information.

Burke was at this point called to order by the Speaker who enquired if he had a motion to make.

Mr. Burke was[1] all tumult upon this, and immediately exclaimed, "Oh, Sir, I *could* give the House a motion: THE IMPEACHMENT OF THE MINISTER (pointing to Lord North) MIGHT BE DEEMED A VERY PROPER ONE."

There was then some confusion in the House, at the end of which Burke spoke again.

Mr. Burke now informed the chair that he had a question to propose. It was, "That the House should immediately form itself into a committee to take into consideration the state of the nation." Before we talked of making war against the House of Bourbon, it was necessary for us to see what means we had left for that purpose, and a still more important thing to be thought of was, whether the present Ministers were persons fit to be entrusted with the conduct of this additional war. He reminded the House *what a shout of applause* had taken place, when the noble Lord some little [time] ago told the House of the *coolness* that subsisted between France and America, whereas the latter power was now joined by the other branch of the House of Bourbon.

Burke was persuaded by Lord John Cavendish to withdraw his motion.

[1] *London Evening Post*: 'was was'.

447

Thoughts
[July 1779]

Source: MS. at Sheffield, R155.1

This document, in Burke's hand, gives an outline of what Lord Rockingham should say to the King if the Marquess was asked for his views on the formation of a new administration. Its date is uncertain. It is docketed by Rockingham: 'Thoughts in July 1779 from E:B:'. The contents, however, make July 1780 at least as likely a date, especially as there was then a negotiation for a new ministry (I. R. Christie, 'The Marquis of Rockingham and Lord North's Offer of a Coalition, June–July 1780', in *Myth and Reality in Late Eighteenth-Century British Politics and Other Papers*, London, 1970, pp. 109–32).

Burke felt compelled to pen his thoughts about the conditions upon which the Rockingham party could take part in the formation of a new Government because he feared that overtures which had been made by the ministry were little more than trickery. He felt that the court was attempting merely to bolster its own strength and disunite the Opposition by buying off a few central figures. 'Fox thinks that you will have something like Carte blanche offered to you immediately,' he told the Duke of Portland,

I consider this as thrown out . . . to weaken your animosity towards the Court Faction, & to divide you among yourselves . . . I . . . told him of the strange Language of the Duke of Grafton,[1] relative to offers that might come from the Court; which was, that any two or three principal people, with the leader of any of the several branches that compose opposition, ought to come in with the present Ministry . . .[2]

This kind of arrangement was something which Burke was most anxious to avoid. Drawing on the experience of the Rockinghams' first short administration, he was still determined that their next Government should be broadly based, united with all those who would bow to the Marquess's leadership,[3] unthreatened by the meddling placemen and personal friends of the King whom the Rockinghams felt had constantly worked against their first regime,[4] and firmly under the control of the Marquess himself. These conditions had been set out by William Dowdeswell[5] some twelve years earlier and Burke himself had repeated them in his *Observations on a Late State of the Nation*[6] and in the *Thoughts on the Cause of the Present Discontents*.[7]

[1] Augustus Henry Fitzroy, 3rd Duke of Grafton (1735–1811).
[2] *Corr.* iv. 154.
[3] See W. M. Elofson, 'The Rockingham Whigs and the Country Tradition', *Parliamentary History*, viii (1989), 98–101.
[4] See Burke's *Short Account of a Late Short Administration* written just after the fall of the first Rockingham ministry (vol. ii, p. 56).
[5] In 1767 Dowdeswell, then the real brains behind Rockingham policies, had also written to the Marquess. He had entitled his work 'Thoughts on the Present State of Publick Affairs and the Propriety of Accepting or Declining Administration, written the 23 & 24 of July 1767' (MS. at Sheffield, R1.842).
[6] Vol. ii, pp. 209–15.
[7] Ibid. ii, pp. 320–3.

That I had significations made to me at various times within this twelvemonth that your Majesties affairs might require some change in your administration, and that it was wished that I should come again into your Service.[1]

That my Zeal, attachment, and devotion, to your Majesties person and Government, are points which can admit of no doubt. I have ever, and in all circumstances been uniform in my wishes for your honour, Ease, and happiness both publick and domestick; and your Majesty is, I believe, yourself perfectly convinced, that I have too much honour to attempt to deceive you in any representation that I shall make to you on the present or on any occasion.

That my inclinations and those of all my particular friends being as cordial to your Service as possible, I come to know from your Majesty yourself, and not from any one else, your own real Sentiments, and the real extent of your Intentions with regard to a change of your administration, because it frequently happens, that in conversations through the intervention of third persons, however honourable, very essential mistakes may be made; and in such circumstances your Majesties orders may be misconciev'd by me, or my humble opinions imperfectly conveyd to your Majesty.

That I fear pains have been taken to possess your Majesty with an opinion, that I meant to distress you, or to use compulsory, or other disagreeable ways of coming into your Service.

I beg leave with great Truth to assure you, that I am not, nor ever was at any time of my Life, an Ambitious man, nor of a violent Temper, nor of insolent and presumptuous manners, even to the meanest of your Subjects, much less to your Majesty, for whom I have always had all imaginable regard and reverence.

Your Honour is as dear to me as my own: and so far from wishing to force myself into power under your Majesty, that nothing, but the very unusual exigency of your affairs, could prevail upon me to accept of any Employment whatsoever; and certainly, there are no circumstances in which I shall accept of it, unless I have reason to understand, that on the part of your Majesty my appointment is one of the freest Acts of your whole Reign; and a thing which you not only consent to but actually command.

---

[1] The first proposals for a coalition seem to have been in May 1778 and they were revived in January 1779 (*Corr.* iv. 38–41).

That your Majesty may possibly recollect, that it was with the greatest reluctance I came into Office in the year 1765—and I had then reason to be persuaded, that my coming in was in conformity to your Majesty's most earnest desire—that afterwards I did not throw up in resentment; but went out of Office, as I had come into it, in consequence of your own pleasure.[1]

That without any intrigue, sollicitation or force, by your Majesties desire signified to me by the Duke of Grafton and General Conway I went again into your Closet in 1767; and did humbly present to your Majesty such a Plan of administration as I conceivd might most effectually serve you at that time.[2] It did not, (as I judged by not receiving your further orders on the Subject,) meet with your Majesties approbation.

Since that time, I have contented myself with doing my Duty as a Member of Parliament—Even any considerable exertion in that line I should probably in a great measure have discontinued; and should have been happy in becoming very much a private man, if I had not seen undertakings of great boldness taken in hand, and much above the powers of those who engaged in them; and that there seemd to me hardly one day in the course of several Years past in which the Kingdom was not in imminent danger. I was besides made to believe that my continuing in Business was in some degree conducive towards keeping together a set of valuable men, such as your Majesty might entirely rely upon in any trying Exigencies of your Government.

I hope therefore that the invidious language used by those, who I am bold to say have far less personal or publick attachment to your Majesties happiness and glory than I have, will have no weight with you. I am too well acquainted with the world to imagine, that I could have any hope of serving your Majesty reputably or effectually, or of doing any thing to draw this Country out of its present distressed Situation, unless I could make myself acceptable to you.

It is also said, that I desire to make a violent revolution in all the Establishments, and to drive from about your Majesty every person that is pleasing to you. Nothing has ever been further from my Intentions. Some about your Majesty are pleasing to myself. If others are pleasing to you Sir, it is reason enough for me to fall in with any[3]

---

[1] See Langford, *Rockingham Administration*, pp. 6–8, 16–18, 236–8.
[2] For these negotiations, see Brooke, *Chatham Administration*, pp. 162–217. Rockingham saw the King on 22 July 1767.   [3] MS.: 'with any with any'.

moderate wish of theirs. There are now in your Service men of very great natural Weight in the Country; and on that Ground I, who most earnestly desire that your Majesty should always be served in preference by that description of men, would rather incline to invite them into Office than forcibly to drive them from it. Altho', I confess, I have my affections and preferences very strong and unalterable, I have no persecuting party principle about me; and it is not in my Natural disposition to pursue Systems which must produce violent passions and convulsions in the Country.

That however if his Majesty wishes to new model his administration changes must be made; and those not[1] inconsiderable—else Government cannot possibly be strengthened as it ought to be, particularly at this time, for it is necessary to bring forward men of the greatest natural Weight and authority, of the best families, of the greatest Talents, and of the greatest Industry—for I humbly conceive, that all those descriptions of men, acting with united Efforts, will not be more than necessary at the present Crisis.

That they, who have enjoyd honours and advantages from the Crown in an encreasing measure for many years, can have little regard to your Majesties person and little gratitude for your favours, if at such a time as the present they should refuse to accomodate your affairs. When people talk to your Majesty of making a forcible Entry, they should recollect, that there is such a thing as holding a forcible possession.

That it is with the most perfect humility, I find myself obliged to represent to your Majesty, that if an administration were formed, in which any of the present Ministers should take the lead, the whole Benefit to be expected from a change would be lost. Nobody would consider me, or any of those who do me the honour to concur with me, in any other light, than that of venal men who wanted places—and this would, at the very first step, take away all heart and confidence from your people, at the time when they want most to be encouraged. They would be convinced that your Business would be conducted, or rather neglected in the manner, that has brought on the present difficulties and distresses of the Nation. The revolted Colonies would see no new inducements for reconciliation upon any plan which could be offerd; and the Courts of Europe would see no new Grounds of confidence

---

[1] MS.: 'those not not'.

and connexion laid for forming fresh engagements or for renewing the old. So that the present System, instead of being changed and amended, would seem only to be strengthend by the accession of Men, who, by a subordinate junction with those whom they opposed, had given both measures and means out of their own hands, and thereby renounced their principles, and justly forfeited every degree of publick confidence.

That if your Majesty should think it expedient to continue that eminent Trust in those who have sufferd Europe to unite against you, then my humble advice to your Majesty would be, to preserve the body of them as entire, and with as little foreign mixture as possible. For as probably none of them can justly accuse the other of past mismanagements, and that a sense of their very great common danger may promote their union, things might prosper better in their hands, than when they have a body of persons acting under their influence and direction, who cannot possibly have confidence in those whom they are to support. Indeed Sir dissensions must inevitably arise in such a System which would suffer nothing to prosper; and that unanimity in Measures, from whence we must derive all our hopes of salvation, instead of being promoted, would I greatly fear be effectually destroyed; and there is this further Evil in it, that if that Scheme should fail your Majesty would have no longer any Men of Character and reputation for Probity to whom you could apply yourself and this is a very serious consideration.

That on all these considerations, and many more which must occur to your Majesty['s] own penetration, it will be necessary, if your Majesty wishes any change, (and all I say is on a supposition that you do freely and entirely wish it) that your New Ministry may set out with every possible mark of your confidence and support, which they will want in the utmost extent in which it can be given in the arduous and dreadful undertaking they are to engage in.

If arrangements are made at setting out that decisively indicate this gracious resolution, I should not be the man to advise, that disagreeable things should be done to any Man whatsoever; but on the contrary, that nothing should be omitted to conciliate all those who shall be willing to lend their assistance towards carrying into execution your Majesties wise and benevolent purposes in favour of your people.

That your Majesties Servants have not been so attentive, as you had a right to expect, to the great Objects of their Trust, or not so judicious in the means they have chosen, or both, are matters which cannot admit of the smallest doubt. There are few Princes of more various and extensive knowlege than your Majesty; or of more application to your affairs or that God has blessed with a better understanding to determine on them. But in your high situation it is inevitable that you must depend very much on the information you receive, and it is very certain that some of your Ministers have communicated to your Majesty and your Parliament very imperfect and insufficient information upon Matters of the greatest moment as the Event has proved. I shall think myself bound not to fall into the same mistake; but to represent to you with the fidelity of a good Subject, and the Zeal of an humble friend to your person and your family, whatever regards the State of your affairs, and my own Views and intentions so far at least as any distinct intentions can be formed previously to the Events, which may arise, and which those Events must in a great measure determine.

That when the minds of men are disquieted and the State of publick affairs deranged some plan must be adopted, early declared, and steadily preserved in for giving some reasonable satisfaction to their feelings, and for bettering in some degree the Condition of the publick. To proceed in such an undertaking with caution and Temper, it will be necessary to lay a ⟨true⟩ and full State of the Nation before your Majesty and the Parliament.

It will be necessary to review and rectifye the whole of the affairs of Ireland, which have fallen, through some mismanagement or misfortune, into a State of astonishing disorder in every respect; and to settle something for the Benefit of that Country which will not be shocking to the prejudices of this.

To remove the fears of good men and to cut off the opportunities that factious men have of doing mischief, something ought to be done with regard to the freedom of Electing, and deciding on Elections,[1] as well as to the Seats of men interested in abuses with regard to publick money, and publick contracts. These I know by experience to be of no sort of use to the support of your Majesties government; on the contrary they bring a discredit upon it, of infinitely more prejudice than any advantages to be had from their Votes; and are felt to do so,

---

[1] A reference to Crewe's Bill; see below, p. 482.

by those who have long and regularly supported the measures of successive administrations.[1]

Above all, in the present deplorable State of the Finances, it will be necessary to adopt some vigorous and effectual plan of oeconomy, in almost every department.[2] This indeed is the first and the last; and it is not only wishd on account of the publick but on that of your Majesties growing family, which if something of that kind is not done, will be left either with a very incompetent provision, which none of your Subjects less desires than I do, or a disagreeable and invidious comparison made between their opulence and the publick poverty.

These are some of the outlines of what I wish with all Duty and reverence to lay at your Majesties feet; willing to open myself further and to bring more into Shape what is here but crudely conceivd. When I have the Sanction of your Majesties Orders and the assistance of your lights, and I leave this Substance of the conversation which your Majesty has so graciously indulged me in writing that your Majesty may reconsider at your Leisure, assuring you once more that none of your Subjects can have more real regard to the Strength, and lustre of your Government and its credit in every particular.

Articles of Impeachment
[Autumn 1779]

Sources: MSS. at Sheffield, Bk 6.184, 185, 186

In a moment of anger Burke had publicly spoken of impeaching North if not his colleagues.[3] There is no evidence in his correspondence that his party seriously considered formally doing so. But the existence of a draft among Burke's papers demonstrates that he gave the possibility some thorough

---

[1] Sir Philip Jennings Clerke had introduced a Bill in 1778 to exclude contractors from the House of Commons, unless their contract had been won at public auction. It was reintroduced in succeeding years and became law in 1782.

[2] A reference to Burke's own Civil Establishment Bills; his speech introducing them on 11 February 1780 is printed below.

[3] See Burke's speech of 16 June 1779 on the breach with Spain, above, pp. 445–7.

consideration. The Articles follow the same basic form as those used by the Whigs in the celebrated Sacheverell trial in 1710.[1]

Articles of impeachment for certain high Crimes and misdemeanors, agains[t], Frederick Lord North, George Sackville Germaine commonly called Lord George Germain,   Earl of Dartmouth—etc. etc. Earl of Sandwich Lord Viscount Weymouth, Earl Gower.[2]

Whereas the said etc. having been appointed and sworn of his Majestys most honourable Privy Council and still continuing Members of the Same, and holding certain offices of Profit and Trust under the Crown by which they were called as Privy Counsellors and Ministers of State to advise his Majesty in [the] conduct of the affairs of this Kingdom as well as to lay such full and true information before both houses of Parliament as might enable the house to pursue the proper measures on the important Business before them, according to the exigency thereof and being entrusted in the most ample manner by his Majesty, and by the said two houses of Parliament[3] with means of acting with Effect for the preservation and recovery of his Majesties Dominions in America, for ⟨preventing⟩ and frustrating the designs of foreign Enemies,[4] for preserving the Reputation and power of their Country, and in particular for the support of the Naval Strength of this Kingdom on which, under God, its force wealth, and importance, and even safety do principally depend, have, contrary to the duty of their Offices, and in violation of the high Trust reposed in them been, in the advice given to his Majesty and in the Conduct of his affairs guilty of sundry Criminal Neglects, omissions, and misdemeanours, as follow

1. That they the said[5] etc did advise his Majesty to send into North America for the purpose of subduing the rebellion then existing therein an Army not exceeding 7,000 men which with The Troops which could be collected and brought to act there did not exceed 10,000 Effective men by which Neglect of proportioning the force to the Necessity of the service, His Majesties Troops were blockaded within

---

[1] See G. Holmes, *The Trial of Doctor Sacheverell*, London, 1973, pp. 279–82.
[2] Granville Leveson Gower, 2nd Earl Gower (1721–1803), later (1786) 1st Marquess of Stafford.
[3] MS.: 'Parliament to'.
[4] In the MS. there is a semi-colon as well as a comma.
[5] There is an undeleted phrase in the MS.: 'That he the said'.

the Town of Boston and sufferd several heavy Losses and disgraces and were finally obliged to evacuate the said Town of Boston and to leave the same and thirteen Provinces of North America wholly in possession of Persons resisting his Majesties [Government] by which neglect they brought contempt on his Majesties Government and[1] on the forces and power of this Kingdom, and gave encouragement to Rebellion within the said provinces[2]

3dly[3] that when sundry military stores were sent for the supply of the said Troops and defence of the said Town they were embarked in ships of no Force nor properly armed nor provided with any sufficient convoy and that some of them fell into the hands of his Majesties Enemies, though attacked only by boats or other Vessels of very inconsiderable Strength, so that his Majesties Enemies were furnished at his Majesties expence; and from his Magazines with arms and ammunition of all kinds fit for carrying on a Siege for which they were before this supply very incompetently provided; and this criminal Neglect became one of the ⟨Causes⟩ of the loss to his Majesty of the said Town of Boston and several of the disasters that ensued therefrom.

4. That his Majesty having in the year 1775 taken a resolution by advice of his said Ministers to reduce the said Colonies then in great disorder to obedience to his Majesties Government did advise his Majesty instead of ⟨increasing⟩ to lessen the establishment which then subsisted for the Navy and to declare that it was intended to keep up a Naval force ⟨equal⟩ only to a provision [of] sixteen thousand seamen[4] and though in the Course of that session the said number was augmented and a Resolution moved in Parliament at the instigation of the said Ministers to eighteen thousand, yet the same was still less by two thousand than in the preceeding year of peace. Although it was evident from ⟨the⟩ great Extent of America along the sea coast that a naval force would [be] the most effectual means for suppressing the Rebellion [and] would be the most expedient for combining the

---

[1] MS.: 'and and'.

[2] An unattached phrase is in the margin: 'Officers Lawfully appointed and who had set up a Government in the same without his Majesties authority.'

[3] The second charge has been wholly deleted. It read: '2dly That for —— they did not dispatch any instructions for —— to the Officers commanding his Majesties Troops so blockaded as aforesaid.'

[4] In margin: 'and the chief strength of this Kingdom lying in its Navy.'

operations of his Majesties land forces; ⟨   ing⟩ and of preventing a military or other supply from abroad to the revolted provinces. By which insidious deceits and consequent Neglect the former insufficient provision of Land forces was coverd from the publick Eye; and the greatness and extent of the disorders in America suppressed; and the said Rebellion fomented and strengthend by the assistance of foreign powers; as well as an whole year allowd for the said powers to get the Start of this Kingdom in Naval preparation.

5. That his Majesty, in his gracious speech from the Throne[1] did lament the suffering of his Subjects in America under certain acts passed in the preceding Session of Parliament and which his Majesty was empowered to relax or amend by the means provided for in the said acts, which provisions of relaxation had been inserted in said acts on the advice and motion of his Majesties said Servants—and proposed to send Commissioners thither to relax the said acts etc—yet the said Ministers who had advised the reservation of the said powers did never send commissioners thither for the purpose of relaxing the said acts and relieving the distresses of the said Colonists which declaration with the subsequent Neglect had a tendency to lower in the minds of that people the opinion of his Majesties Clemency and the good faith of the Crown of Great Britain.

6. That the said ——— instead of sending the said Commissioners as aforesaid, did recommend to Parliament from the Knowlege of the state of the Country which the said Ministers pretended to have and which by the duty of their Offices were obliged to have as a fitting means to suppress the said Rebellion to pass an Act entitled an Act[2] ——— which act did pass accordingly on the ——— of February.—In the said act a power was reserved to his Majesty to send Commissioners to America to grant pardons etc. they the said ——— being then his Majesties Privy Councellours called to attend and counsel his Majesty, did advise and counsel his Majesty not to send the said Commissioners, neglected to advise to appoint and send them until the 6th day of May, near five months after the powers given by the said act and not until the News had arrived in G.B. of the evacuation of

---

[1] On 26 October 1775; the Speech did not connect suffering in America with the Acts of 1775. See above, p. 247.

[2] 'to Prohibit trade and intercourse with' the thirteen American colonies, commonly called the American Prohibitory Act, 16 Geo. III, c. 5. It actually passed the Commons and the Lords on 21 December 1775 and received the royal assent on 22 December (*Commons Journals*, xxxv. 492–4).

Boston by his Majesties Troops[1] the last Town in the 13 revolted Colonies which still remained under his Majesties authority to the great discredit of the Justice and Wisdom Magnanimity and Mercy of the British Government; And it ⟨further⟩ appears that the delay for some part of the time, arose from the difficulties which the said Ministers made in granting the powers which by the words of the said act they were enabled, and by the Spirit thereof were obliged, to grant. In consequence of the giving such ill or neglect of giving proper advice the Lord V. Howe one of the said Commissioners authorised and impowerd to grant said pardons etc. did not arrive in America, though with a passage as short as might be expected until—in the said interval the Colonies declared[2] themselves independent of his Majesties Government and of the Crown and Nation of Great Britain[3] assigning, in the instrument by which the said independence was declared, among other Causes of their seperation the Rigour of the said act of Parliament, which the Ministers were in duty bound, to send Commissioners to relax, as well as to treat of peace before the said desperate Step so difficult to be retracted was taken.

7. That when by the said Act in order to induce the people of the revolted Colonies to return to their allegiance a power was reserved to Commissioners to declare any Port place etc which should return to his Majesties obedience to be at the Kings peace and to have free Trade as before the Troubles—General Tryon Governor of New York did represent [the] Inhabitants [of the] Town of New York as obedient loyal and well disposed praying the restoration of the Trade[4] thereof which Letter and representation was printed in the London Gazette etc. yet the said Town of N. York notwithstanding the said powers and representation publishd by authority to acquaint the World with the Title it had to that Indulgence was not for two years after declared at the Kings peace; nor restored to free Traffick; to the great discouragement [of] the Inhabitants of any Port Town in the revolted Colonies which should be disposed to return to its allegiance.

---

[1] MS.: 'Majesties Troops of the'.
[2] MS.: 'declared themselves declared themselves'.
[3] Burke has failed to delete a full stop after Britain.
[4] Letters from William Tryon to Germain were printed in the *London Gazette* of 22 February and 20 March. In the first letter, written on 24 December 1776, Tryon had spoken of 'a general satisfaction expressed at my coming among ... [the inhabitants of Long Island] and to judge from the Temper and Disposition I perceived in them, there is not the least Apprehension of any farther commotion'.

8. That The American Congress did send over to G.B. in a certain Paper or Petition to his Majesty purporting to be a Petition etc. by the hands of Richard Penn Esquire[1] entreating etc. to which Petition The Earl of Dartmouth one of his Majesties principal Secretaries of State did advise his Majesty that no answer should be given, and the said Earl of Dartmouth did in his Majesties Name deliver a Message to that or the like Effect which contemptuous manner of treating the said petition had a tendency to produce, and was assigned as a Cause of declaring, the Independence of the said American Provinces.

9. That when by the said act, the Ships Merchandize etc. of the thirteen colonies thereby declared in Rebellion, were enacted to be Lawful prize[2] etc as if they were the ships of open Enemies etc. and that thereby it was to be apprehended, that the Enemy would without doubt endeavour to make reprisals no care was taken to provide any sort of Convoy for the[3] West India Trade by which Neglect a great Number of Vessels fell into their hands; and thereby not only strengthend the forces of the Rebellious Colonies by the wealth acquired by the said Capture; but supplied them with shipping and various stores of which they were in want. Several of these Ships were armed for War, and did much mischief to the Trade of this Kingdom.

10. That when it was notorious that France had protected an Agent from the Revolted American Provinces, had admitted Ships made prize from his Majesties Subjects to be sold in their Ports; and permitted the Cruizers of the said American Provinces to equip in their Ports; and had supplied them with arms and military stores and otherwise supported and encouraged them from the beginning of the Rebellion, and that it was equally notorious and announced from the Throne, that foreign Powers (meaning the Powers of France and Spain) were augmenting their Naval Forces and that his Majesty would etc. Yet they the said ———— did notwithstanding the Notoriety of the Facts aforesaid and notwithstanding the said declaration from the Throne abovementiond did not put the Nation in a respectable State of defence in any manner equal to the exigence nor did begin any effectual or Vigorous preparation, until France had publickly declared in favour of the American independency.

---

[1] See above, p. 183.   [2] Ibid.   [3] MS.: 'for the the'.

11. That upon the notoriety of these preparations, the said Ministers did not, as in Duty they were bound, levy and employ, that Naval force which the natural superiority of this Kingdom in Naval rescources and the vast sums granted by Parliament to the Navy, enabled them to[1] employ, in order to defeat the designs and frustrate the preparations of the Enemy by a timely and effectual Exertion, but permitted them to proceed without any disturbance until they had raised to a formidable height the Naval power of the House of Bourbon which had been nearly destroyd in the late War—and instead of taking the time most favourable to us, left those powers, to choose, each of them respectively, the time which they judged the most convenient for them to distress this Kingdom and to attack Great Britain when she had spent very great Sums and wasted great armies in the North American War.

12. That notwithstanding the aforesaid multiplied offensive acts, menacing preparations, and at last publick and avowed hostilities, of the Courts of France and Spain, the said Ministers neglected to station any effectual Naval Force at Gibraltar; though the use of that port and fortress is solely for the purpose of checking the Naval enterprises of France and Spain, and for that sole End it is kept at an immense expense to this Nation, through which Neglect or Treachery, not only the Meditterranean Sea was then and hath ever since [been] wholly abandond, but the Toulon Fleet under Count[2] of the Comte D'Estaign sailed without interruption into the Ocean, and this Neglect therefore became the original Cause of all the disasters, Calamities, and losses since then sustaind by this Nation in the West Indies and may be the Cause of many more.

13. That in consequence of the general Neglect of the Navy Admiral Byron[3] sailed later than he should do, and worse equipped than he ought to have been, to North America. And That Lord Viscount Howe commanding his Majesties Fleet in North America had but one Ship of the Line with him and that one was orderd to be sent home; though it was probable, by the connexions of France with the Revolted North American provinces, that in case of a rupture that part of the world would become the immediate Scene of their operations, by which Neglect of Stationing a proper Naval Force in North

---

[1] MS.: 'enabled them and to'.
[2] It seems likely from the MS that Burke intended to change this to 'Command'.
[3] Vice-Admiral John Byron (1723–86).

America, and by the delay of sending any reinforcement thither the whole British army and all the Fleet which was there collected was in the most imminent danger of being entirely destroyd, and was only saved by the French Fleets being detained on their Course from Toulon, by accidents upon which the Ministers aforesaid could not reckon, and ought not to have trusted to.

15.[1] That the said Ministers having orderd his Majesties Troops to evacuate Philadelphia and to retreat to New York, did through criminal negligence or Treachery, omit to give any Notice of the orders for evacuating the said Town to the Fleet of Victuallers then bound to Philadelphia insomuch that the victualing Ships did actually sail into the River Delawar, and would have, by proceeding to Philadelphia, inevitably fallen into the hands of the Enemy but were saved by information purely accidental; by which shameful and ⟨miserable⟩ Neglect the whole British Army might have sufferd the greatest distress and even been obliged through famine to have surrenderd to the Enemy.

16. That no timely or Effectual Provision of Sea or land forces was made for the defence of the West India Islands Admiral Barrington[2] having been left there with a force inadequate[3] to its purpose; and large quantities of Ordnance Stores being collected in Dominica with soldiers not above forty or fifty to defend or employ them; that in consequence of ⟨which⟩ Neglect [that] valuable Island and those Stores became an easy prey to the Enemy.

17. That no orders were given for stationing a Number of forces sufficient for the defence of the Islands of St Vincent and Grenada although a requisition was made to Lord George Germaine one of his Majesties principal Secretaries of State for a force to defend Grenada on a representation by the Governour of the danger to which that Island was exposed by which culpable Negligence or Treachery those important Islands also were lost to the dominion of Great Britain and added to the conquests of France.

18. That when Admiral Byrons Fleet was station'd in the West Indies no sufficient provision of Naval and military Stores was made for the supply of the same; by which Neglect the said Fleet was under much disadvantage in the engagement off Grenada; and was after-

---

[1] There is no Article 14.
[2] Samuel Barrington (1729–1800).
[3] MS.: 'inadquate'.

461

wards disabled from acting on the Offensive or preventing the further operations of the Comte d'Estaign.

19. That no measures have been taken for the protection of the Trade to the Coast of Africa or for the annoyance of the Enemy there; by which the said most valuable Branch of Commerce has been wholly lost.

20. That Admiral Keppel was sent from Portsmouth with orders to block up the Harbour of Brest with a Fleet not exceeding twenty Ships of the Line, although the Enemys Fleet in the said Port were 27 Ships of the Line or upwards.[1]

N.B. Further of Admiral Keppels agreeably to the resolutions moved last Session.

21. That when it was well known to his Majesties Ministers or might have been known to them that the Agents for the revolted Colonies at Paris, had made a considerable progress in a Treaty with the united Colonies, the said Ministers did not apply to Parliament for authority to name Commissioners for settling the matters in Dispute with the said Colonies in order to prevent the Treaty with France was actually signed;[2] by which [the] honour of the Crown and Kingdom were materially injured and the ample surrender advised by them, of the powers of Parliament and the repeal of Acts moved by themselves, which in a more seasonable time could hardly have failed of success, were renderd useless.

22. That they did authorise the said Commissioners to make several propositions to the American Congress, for which they had no authority from Parliament; and which were derogatory from the dignity of his Majesties Crown and the honour and advantage of the Nation.

23. That when Commissioners were appointed by his Majesty for treating with the revolted Colonies the said Ministers gave orders, without any apparent necessity, that the City of Philadelphia should be evacuated without communicating the said orders to the commissioners, who immediately after the declaration of their commission and full powers, were obliged precipitately and disgracefully to quit the principal City in America and to accompany a retreating Army; by

---

[1] On 13 June 1778 Keppel had set sail with 20 ships to see the Gibraltar reinforcements past Brest. While on the mission Keppel uncovered information that the Brest fleet numbered 27 sail of the line (Mackesy, *The War for America, 1775–83*, p. 207).

[2] Treaties were signed on 6 February. The Carlisle Commission did not embark until 16 April 1778.

which the congress again took possession of the said City, and the Commissioners lost Reputation and the opinion of power essential in a Transaction of that Nature.

24. That the said Ministers formed in 1777 the plan of an Expedition from Canada under Lieutenant General Burgoine an essential part in which was a cooperation from Sir Wm Howe and that no orders were given to secure such cooperation; by which criminal Neglect the Army under Lieutenant General Burgoine was obliged to surrender to the Enemy on Convention.

25. That when Spain had joined with France in Hostility against his Majesty and this Nation it was incumbent on the Ministers of this Kingdom to prevent a junction of the Fleets of the two hostile Crowns[1] and ought therefore to have sent a Fleet of sufficient force early in the summer to cruize off the Harbour of Brest. But the said Ministers did not send out such, or any Fleet to cruize before Brest nor did they make any other disposition of his Majesties Naval forces for that necessary purpose; by which Neglect or Treachery the Enemys Fleets effected a junction without any opposition whatsoever and became in consequence of that junction superior in the Channel during the whole Campaign.

25.[2] That his Majesties Ministers notwithstanding the large Grants made by Parliament, took no effectual means for the defence and security of several very important places in the Kingdom then threatned by the Superiour fleet of the Enemy.

26. That it does not appear that any orders were given or plans laid for an Offensive Campain by the main body of his Majesties army in America during the whole of the two last Summers; that the principal Part of the detached services under General Prevost[3] was not supported—although the nation has incurred during that time the charge of an Army of 62,000 men in that part of the world to no adequate purpose whatsoever.[4]

---

[1] Burke has failed to delete a full stop after 'Crowns'.

[2] This charge should have been numbered 26.

[3] General Augustine Prevost (1723–86), marched from Florida to beseige Charleston, whose surrender he demanded on 12 May 1779. He subsequently was forced to retreat without a battle in face of a colonial expeditionary force.

[4] Burke had some grounds for blaming the Government for inefficiency. In particular the failure of the First Lord of the Admiralty, Lord Sandwich, and Secretary of State, Lord George Germain, to agree on war policy appears to have made decisive action difficult. However, they operated under very difficult conditions, created by the entry of France into the conflict in 1778. See Mackesy. *The War for America*, pp. 162–234.

Petition
[*post* 13 December 1779]

Source: MS. at Sheffield, R155.3

The MS. is in Burke's hand. There is also a MS. copy (R155.5), in the hand of Rockingham's secretary, Jacob Brown, in which there are a few mistakes. This document can be dated by its reference to the Royal Proclamation of 13 December 1779.

It is not clear for whom Burke drafted this petition—possibly for a coastal county such as Sussex.[1] It evidently went no further. It displays in particular the sense of moral self-righteousness amongst the Rockinghams at the Government's failure to heed their warnings by preparing for the entry of Spain into the American war.[2]

The Humble Address and Petition of
   We your Majesties most faithful Subjects, the

being at this time called upon by your Majesties Royal proclamation[3] to attend more particularly to the difficulties and dangers into which we are brought, should think ourselves extremely defective in our Duty to your Majesty, as well as in regard to our own Welfare and that of our Posterity, if we neglected, in all humility, to represent to your Majesty, our real Sentiments on the present perilous State of our Affairs.

We assure your Majesty that we are not conscious to ourselves that the present calamitous State of the Nation is imputable to any fault in your loyal Subjects. The publick Service has been liberally provided for. The publick burthens have been patiently borne. Yet so far from having obtain by the encreasing profusion of our Grants for several years past an increase of reputation and power abroad, we are informed by your Majesties authority, that we are not in security in our own Houses.[4]

---

[1] The phrase 'and this ⟨County⟩ in particular' is deleted at the end. For Sussex (of which the Duke of Richmond was Lord Lieutenant), see A. T. Patterson, *The Other Armada: The Franco-Spanish Attempt to Invade Britain in 1779*, Manchester, 1960, pp. 125–7.

[2] See Burke's speech of 16 June 1779 on the breach with Spain, printed above.

[3] For a General Fast on 4 February 1780. The proclamation was dated 13 December 1779 and printed in the *London Gazette* of 14 December.

[4] A reference to the King's Speech of 25 November 1779. 'The designs and attempts of our enemies to invade this kingdom, have by the blessing of Providence, been hitherto frustrated and disappointed. They shall menace us with great armaments and preparations; but we are, I trust, on our part, well prepared to meet every attack, and repel every insult' (*Commons Journals*, xxxvii. 462).

We find with inexpressible sorrow that the Marine of our united Enemies has been sufferd to attain a marked superiority in Numbers over that of Great Britain. The progress of that marine, (nearly annihilated in the late glorious War) has been visible to the whole World; its destination was not doubtful; and its Effects are seriously to be apprehended. We are persuaded that means might have been found if proper care had been taken, to furnish a check to its alarming growth, and to provide a sufficient counterpoise against it, either by a timely increase of our own Naval Force; (the Natural Strength of this Kingdom) or by procuring such an Alliance among the Neighbouring Nations as our services to the Liberties of Europe on former occasions, had so abundantly merited. But we see with the deepest concern that Events, which have been in the hourly contemplation of almost all the world, appear to have come upon your Majesties Ministers by surprise. It was not until the actual declaration of Spain, which her armaments had long before indicated, that we began our preparation against the attempts of an additional Enemy. It was not until Hostilities were thus formally declared, that we began to think of raising those forces for our immediate defence, which ought now to be compleat in Numbers and discipline and in readiness for service, at a time when we are threatned with a War in the Heart of our Country.[1]

These things, we most humbly beg leave to represent to your Majesty, could not possibly have happend, without a Notorious want of Wisdom, or diligence, or fidelity in those who have been appointed to the highest Trusts in your affairs, and rewarded for their supposed assiduity and Vigilance with all the honours and emolluments which your Majesties Bounty and the ability of your subjects could furnish.

Having abundant reason to apprehend further mischiefs from the Neglects which have already produced such great Evils, in proportion as our Enemies encrease and our rescources diminish, we most humbly hope from your Majesties paternal regard to a people who deserve every thing at your hands, that you will provide for the security of your Subjects in the ability, Vigilance, industry and integrity of your Servants, without which we know experimentally that no supplies

---

[1] A Bill to double the Militia had been introduced on 21 June and a Bill to repeal exemptions from impressment into the Navy on 23 June. For a discussion of these Bills and their history, see Patterson, *The Other Armada*, pp. 113–17 and J. R. Western, *The English Militia in the Eighteenth Century*, London, 1965, pp. 210–15.

which can be granted will serve for any other purpose than further to exhaust instead of powerfully exerting the Strength of the Country.

We also lay before your Majesty our concern, that when an invasion was known to be meditated by such powerful Enemies; the maritime Counties were no otherwise enabled to exert themselves for the defence of their property, than by a general Warrant, requiring them to remove it to places unknown;[1] and No arms have been placed in the hands of the Inhabitants at large of these Counties, to enable them locally to co-operate with such Troops as your Majesty might send to their defence, or to supply the Want of them, when, in a Country, renderd destitute of subsistence by the said proclamation, they are left naked and exposed to the mercy of a resentful Enemy. We therefore most humbly Pray from your Majesties known goodness, the rational means of that general and local preservation for which [they] are so generally, as well as heavily burthend.

Speech on Public Expenses
15 December 1779

Source: *Substance of the Speeches made in the House of Commons, on Wednesday, the 15th of December, 1779, on Mr. Burke's giving Notice of his Intention to bring in a Bill after the Christmass Recess, for the Retrenchment of Public Expenses, and for the better securing the Independence of Parliament,* J. Almon, London, 1779, pp. 1–11.

The text is also in *Parl. Reg.* xvi. 188–94. There is a MS. copy at Sheffield (Bk 14.26–7), partly printed in *Corr.* (1844) ii. 332–4. It is in the hand of Jacob Brown and is endorsed by Rockingham. The MS. was almost certainly prepared under Burke's eye (*Corr.* iv. 175). It was carefully revised for publication, and the printed version has many small changes. A few of these changes—those not of a routine kind—are noted.

On 23 November 1779 the Reverend Christopher Wyvill took the first steps in the reform movement which is associated with his name.[2] This led to the Yorkshire County Meeting of 30 December. Wyvill's appeal amongst the country gentry in Rockingham's own home county caused real anxiety for

---

[1] Plans had been secretly made for 'driving' Suffolk, Essex, and the Channel coast counties. The policy of 'driving' had been made public by a Royal Proclamation of 9 July (Patterson, *The Other Armada*, pp. 124–5).

[2] See E. C. Black, *The Association: Extra-Parliamentary Political Organization, 1779–1783,* Cambridge, Mass., 1963.

the party leaders. The Marquess himself had always attempted to cultivate widespread support from that element, particularly through his friendship with the highly respected Sir George Savile who was himself attracted to Wyvill's movement.[1] The Rockinghams felt the need to compete with Wyvill and indeed with all the reform programmes which were currently being propagated in print and by radical elements particularly in the City of London.[2] 'I see no sort of Objection to any motion Which can be made for giving light, or strengthening the general principle upon which we proceed' Burke would argue in January. 'Little more time remains for us. It will not be borne by the people, who are hungering & thirsting after substantial reformation, that we should balk their appetite'.[3]

However, because of their defensive attitude towards the traditional constitution the Rockinghams could not propagate programmes which envisaged major changes to Parliament and the system of representation.[4] Therefore, they developed a proposal of their own which was more moderate than any adopted by other Opposition forces in or out of Parliament. It was based on two very broad and widely accepted objectives: greater economy in government—which had become a major concern to the landed classes as a result of very heavy taxation to support the American war; and a reduction of the undue influence of the Crown—which was the one principle shared by virtually all reform interests. Thus was born their celebrated economical reform programme first announced to the Commons by Burke on 15 December 1779.

Mr. *Burke*, after some observations upon the means which, he conceived, were used to prevent him from engaging the attention of the House to this interesting subject, said,[5]

"A general sense prevails of the profusion with which all our affairs are carried on, and with it a general wish for some sort of reformation.[6] That desire for reformation operates every where, except where it ought[7] to operate most strongly—in this House. The proposition which has been lately made by a truly noble Duke, and those propositions which are this very day making, in the other House, by a noble Lord of great talents, industry, and eloquence, are, in my opinion, a

[1] W. M. Elofson, 'The Rockingham Whigs and the Country Tradition', *Parliamentary History*, viii (1989), 104.
[2] Ibid. 102–11; above, p. 615.
[3] *Corr.* iv. 197: Burke to Portland, 16 January 1780.
[4] See Elofson, 'The Rockingham Whigs and the Country Tradition', pp. 102–11.
[5] The first paragraph is not in the MS.
[6] The MS. adds: 'grows every day more prevalent'.
[7] The MS. reads: 'naturally ought'.

reproach to us.[1] To us who claim the exclusive management of the public purse, all interference of the Lords, in our peculiar province, is a reproach. It may be something worse than a reproach:—For if the House of Lords should assume, or, if you please, should usurp, the performance of a duty of ours which we neglect, they will be supported in a usurpation that is necessary to the public. Privileges, (even such privileges as ours) are lost by neglect, as well as by abuse: and whenever it becomes evident, that they are kept up as gratifications of pride and self-importance, instead of being employed as instruments of public good, their stability will be only equal to their value. Old Parliamentary forms and privileges are no trifles. I very freely grant it. But the nation calls for something more substantial than the very best of them: and if form and duty are to be separated, they will prefer the duty without the form, to the form without the duty.[2] If both Lords and Commons should conspire in a neglect of duty, other ways, still more irregular than the interference of the Lords may now appear, will be resorted to: for I conceive the nation *will*, some way or other, have its business done, or it is a nation no longer.

It is not only the sense and feeling of our country that calls upon us; the call of our enemies is still louder. This is the second year in which France is waging upon us the most dreadful of all wars—*a war of œconomy.*[3] Monsieur Neckar has opened his second Budget. In the Edict of November last,[4] the King of France declares in the preamble, that he has brought his fixed and certain expences to an equilibrium with his receipt. In those fixed expences, he reckons *an annual sinking of debt.* For the additional services of the war, *he borrows only two millions.*[5] He borrows not for perpetuity but for *lives*; and *not a single tax*

---

[1] The Duke of Richmond had introduced a resolution on 7 December for the reduction of the Civil List. Lord Shelburne on 15 December moved two resolutions: the first attacked the alarming addition to the national debt under the heading of 'extraordinaries' and advocated governmental economy, while the second proposed a committee of both houses to examine public expenditure and to seek ways of saving money by reforming the structure of government.

[2] The MS. inserts here: 'If the House of Lords perform for the people a necessary service which we decline, the House of Lords will be supported in it.'

[3] Cf. with Burke's views of Necker and the French economy after the beginning of the French Revolution (vol. viii, p. 278).

[4] For this edict, see *Oeuvres complètes de M. Necker*, 15 vols., Paris, 1820, iii. 23–6. Extracts from the edict 'quoted by Mr. Burke in his Speech on the Necessity of Reformation in the Administration of the public Finance', were published in the *Annual Register* for 1780, p. 302.

[5] The loan constituting 6.75 million livres of rentes, brought a capital to the treasury of 67.12 million livres (Harris, *Necker*, p. 130).

is levied on the subject to fund this loan. The whole is funded on *œconomy*, and on improvement of the public revenue.[1]

This fair appearance, I allow, may have something at bottom, which is to be detracted from it. A large unfunded debt is probably left. Be it so. But what is *our* condition in respect of debts both funded and unfunded? What millions shall we not, must we not, borrow this year? What taxes are we to lay for funding these millions? Which of our taxes already granted, for these three years past, are not deficient? Not one, in my opinion. We must tax for what is to *come*; we must tax for what is *past*; or we shall be at dead stand in all the operations of the war.

Are we to conceal from ourselves, that the omnipotence of œconomy alone has, from the rubbish, and wrecks, and fragments of the late war, already created a marine for France?—Are we not informed, that in the disposition and array of the resources of that country, there is a reserve not yet brought forward, very little short of an annual two millions and an half, in the war taxes?[2] Against this masked battery, whenever it shall be opened in the conflict of finance between the two nations, we have not a single work thrown up to cover us. We have nothing at all of the kind to oppose to it. The keeping this supply in reserve by France, is the work of œconomy,—of œconomy, in the Court formerly the most prodigal, and in an administration of finance the most disorderly and corrupt. Absolute monarchies have been usually the seats of dissipation and profusion; republics of order and good management. France appears to be improved. On our part— indeed we are not—we are not indeed, what we *have* been.—And, in our present state, if we will not submit to be taught, by an enemy, we must submit to be ruined by him.

On this subject of œconomy on the other side of the House, they have not so much as dropped a single expression; they have not even thrown an oblique hint, which glances that way. A very in-genious gentleman of great consideration, connected with Ministry, has published,[3] a book, much of which is on the subject of finance;[4] the

---

[1] It was reported in the *London Evening Post*, on 7 January 1780, that 'Mons. Neckar ... has not only paid the interest of the two loans out of the savings in the household but so improved the revenues in the receipt, as to have certainly added by that means about a million sterling per annum.' Necker himself was grateful for Burke's praise and wrote to him directly (*Corr.* iv. 233).

[2] The MS. adds: 'which to a nation not loaded with new debts can not be intolerable'.

[3] The MS. adds: 'with his name'.

[4] Burke may be referring to Edward Gibbon (1737–94, M.P. 1774–84) who wrote *Mémoire Justificatif*, London, 1779, as a service to the ministry.

fruit of the throws and labour pangs of Ministry to bring forth taxes, in order to people the waste they have made in the public stock. This gentleman has ransacked every thing, every thing at home and abroad, antient and modern, to find taxes for that length of war, with the prospect of which he flatters his readers: But though he looks into every corner in the course of his inquisitive and learned research, and descends almost to thrust his nose into the urine tubs of Vespasian,[1]— yet in all this straining and stretching for revenue, he never has once so much as thought of œconomy. It seems to him a thing wholly out of the question; though the Dutch practice, and Roman principle, to which he looks on other occasions, might have taught him that old and true lesson, *Magnum vectigal parsimonia.*[2]

The noble Lord in the blue ribbon, has been so hard driven, that he has had recourse even to the impracticable in taxation. Last year he recommended the scheme of a worthy Member of this House, conceived[3] on the most laudable motives, though, in my opinion, not well considered. The scheme was for raising our supplies within the year. The noble Lord recommended that scheme—declaring at the same time that *he* did not know how to put it in practice.[4]—He, the Minister of Finance! It is however singular, that in all his begettings and adoptions, in all his schemes, practicable and impracticable, he has never once dreamt of œconomy.[5]

In the House of Lords, the first proposition towards œconomy, by a noble Duke,[6] was rejected by Ministers; and but for one reason;[7] and that just the most whimsical in the world—*That it would lower the spirits of the people.*[8] Very ingenious, indeed! that the œconomical conduct of

---

[1] See Suetonius, *De Vitae Caesarum*, VIII, Divus Vespanius, xxiii.

[2] 'Economy is a great revenue'; Cicero, *Paradoxa Stoicorum*, xlix.

[3] The MS. adds: 'as I am persuaded'.

[4] The scheme which would have imposed a tax of 15*s*. per cent on property in order to cover the cost of the supplies was suggested by William Pulteney (1729–1805), M.P. 1768–74, 1775–1805. Lord North had supported the idea of 'raising the supplies within the year' on 1 March 1779 (*Parl. Reg.* xiii. 16).

[5] This sentence reads in the MS.: 'Yet in all his own begettings and adoptions, in all his schemes, practicable and impracticable, no not so much in his visions and imaginations, ever once dreamt of œconomy'.

[6] Richmond on 7 December; see below, p. 482.

[7] The MS. adds: 'that ever I could learn'.

[8] The report of the debate on Richmond's motion in *Parl. Reg.* does not support Burke's account of it, though there was much reference to the importance of keeping up the 'splendour of the Crown'. Lord Onslow (George, 4th Baron Onslow, 1731–1814, and later, 1801, 1st Earl of Onslow, M.P. 1754–74) had said 'such a proceeding must sink us in the eyes of all Europe, and instead of assisting, must in fact injure us' (*Parl. Reg.* xvi. 106–7). The motion was defeated by 77 votes to 37.

their affairs would lower the spirits of the people. Not having any of their Lordships delicate feelings in my plebeian constitution, I know not what to make of this sort of irritability of their fibres. Such nervous sensations are always whimsical and distempered. I know that hypochondriacal people swoon at perfumes, and are recreated by a stench. But I trust there is still enough of health and sound stuff in the habits of Englishmen to relish things according to their genuine nature; that they will not take mortal offence at not being taxed to the quick; and that they will rather be animated with fresh spirit under their burthens, when they know that not a shilling is laid upon them beyond the absolute necessity of the case.

What the Ministers, whose duty it is, and whose place furnishes them with the best means of doing that duty, refuse to do, let us attempt to do for them. Let us supply our defects of power by our fidelity and our diligence. It is true, that we shall labour under great difficulties from the weight of office; and it is a weight that we must absolutely sink under, if we are not supported by the people at large. This House has so much sympathy with the feelings of its Constituents, that any endeavour after reformation which tends to weaken the influence of the Court, will be coldly received here, if it be not very generally and very warmly called for out of doors. But to offer is all that those out of power can do. If the people are not true to themselves, I am very sure it is not in us to save them.

I cannot help observing, that the whole of our grievances are owing to the fatal and overgrown influence of the Crown; and that influence itself to our enormous prodigality. They move in a circle; they become reciprocally cause and effect, and the aggregate product of both is swelled to such a degree, that not only our power as a State, but every vital energy, every active principle of our liberty will be overlaid by it. To this cause, I attribute that nearly general indifference to all public interests, which for some years has astonished every man of thought and reflection. Formerly the operation of the influence of the Crown only touched the higher orders of the State. It has now insinuated itself into every creek and cranny in the kingdom. There is scarce a family so hidden and lost in the obscurest recesses of the community, which does not feel that it has something to keep or to get, to hope or to fear, from the favour or displeasure of the Crown.

The worst of publick prodigality is, that what is squandered is not simply lost. It is the source of much positive evil. Those who are negligent Stewards of the public estate will neglect every thing else. It introduces a similar inaccuracy, a kindred slovenliness, a correspondent want of care, and a want of foresight into all the national management. What is worst of all, it soon surrounds a supine and inattentive Minister with the designing, confident, rapacious, and unprincipled men of all descriptions. They are a sort of animals sagacious of their proper prey;[1] and they soon drive away from their habitation all contrary natures. A prodigal Minister is not only not saving, but he cannot be either just or liberal. No revenue is large enough to provide both for the meritorious and undeserving; to provide for service which is, and for service which is not incurred.

I know that this influence is thought necessary for Government. Possibly, in some degree, it may. But I declare, it is for the sake of Government, for the sake of restoring to it that reverence, which is its foundation, that I wish to restrain the exorbitance of its influence. Is not every one sensible how much that influence is raised? Is not every one sensible how much authority is sunk? The reason is perfectly evident. Government ought to have force enough for its functions; but it ought to have no more. It ought not to have force enough to support itself in the neglect, or the abuse of them. If it has, they must be, as they are, abused and neglected. Men will throw themselves on their power for a justification of their want of order, vigilance, foresight, and all the virtues, and all the qualifications of a Statesman. The Minister may exist, but the Government is gone.

It is thus that you see the same men, in the same power, sitting undisturbed before you, though thirteen colonies have been lost. It is thus the marine of France and Spain has quietly grown and prospered under their eye, and been fostered by their neglect. It is thus that all hope of alliance in Europe is abandoned. It is thus that three of our West-India Islands have been torn from us in a Summer.[2] It is thus the most important of all, Jamaica, has been neglected, and all enquiry into that neglect, this day and in this House, stifled.[3] It is thus Ireland has been brought into such a state of distraction, that no one dares even to

---

[1] The MS. adds: 'they burrow in such a Minister'.

[2] St Vincent and Grenada had been captured by the French in the summer of 1779; Dominica had been taken earlier. Burke may be counting the Grenadines as his third island.

[3] A motion for all petitions, memorials, and addresses for protection from Jamaica had been defeated.

discuss it; that the bill relating to it, though making great and perplexing changes, is such, that no one knows what to say, or what not to say
upon it. Our Parliamentary capacity is extinguished by the difficulty of
our situation. The Bill has been mumbled over with rapidity; and
it passes in the silence of death.[1] Had Government any degree of
strength could this possibly have happened? Could the most ancient
prerogative of the Crown with relation to the most essential object,
the Militia, have been annihilated with so much scorn as it has been,
even at our doors?[2] Could his Majesty have been degraded from the
confidence of his people of Ireland in a manner so signal, and so
disgraceful, that they who have trusted his Predecessors in many
particulars for ever, and in all, for two years, should have contracted
their confidence in him to a poor stinted tenure of six months?[3] Could
the Government of this country have been thus cast to the ground, and
thus dashed to pieces in its fall, if the influence of a Court was its
natural and proper poise; if corruption was its soundness; and self-
interest had the virtue to keep it erect and firm upon its base?

I will not fatigue your patience, I will not oppress your humiliation with further instances of the debility and contempt of your
Government. The inference I draw from the whole is this, that the
present weakness of Government is a disease of repletion. The vigour
of the limbs is gone, because the stomach has been over-fed.

I have been clear on the nature of this disease, and on the specific
remedy for a long time. I however kept back my thoughts, partly
for reasons of personal want of importance, partly from my own
disposition. I am not naturally an œconomist. I am besides cautious of
experiment even to timidity—and I have been reproached for it.[4] But
times alter natures. Besides, I never, till lately, saw a temper in the
least favourable to reformation. There is now a dawning of hope. I
trusted that a Ministry might be formed, who would carry some such

---

[1] Lord North had given way to Irish pressure and had introduced propositions which allowed
Ireland direct trade to Africa and the Colonies (*Parl. Hist.* xx. 1272–85).
[2] A clause in the Militia Act of 1779 (19 Geo. III, c. 76) empowered the Crown to raise
volunteer regiments under the command of individuals. It was alleged that Lord Amherst, as
Commander-in-Chief, had used this clause to the detriment of the regular recruiting service and
at the expense of the King's own authority. Jenkinson had defended the procedure in less than
vigorous terms on 25 November (*Parl. Reg.* xvi. 44–6).
[3] The Irish Parliament had voted supplies for only nine months.
[4] The MS. adds: 'I thought too the public was not ripe' and omits 'But times alter natures'.

plan into effect with all the powers of Government; and much is lost in not possessing those powers for this purpose. But the present favourable moment is not to be neglected; even under this disadvantage, great as it is, and as I feel it to be.

I have a plan, that I think will serve for a basis (it is no more) for public œconomy and reduction of influence. I have communicated it to a very few friends, whose approbation I am strengthened by; and I will communicate it to more, who will make it worthy of being brought into Parliament. When it is thus matured, I mean to propose it to the consideration of the House, as soon after the Christmas recess as possible.

It will not be adviseable at this time to open all the particulars. Projectors see no difficulties; and criticks see nothing else. When any new propositions are made, unattended by their explanations, their qualifications, and a full stating of their grounds, they are very liable to be decried; especially where mens interests are concerned in decrying them.

But I will venture to state the *end and object* I aim at, though not the means, I will state too the *limits* I fix to myself in what I shall propose to the House.

I mean a regulation, substantial as far as it goes. It will give to the public service, two hundred thousand pounds a year. It will cut off a quantity of influence equal to the places of fifty members of parliament.

I rely more on a plan for removing the *means* of corruption, than upon any devices which may be used to prevent its *operation*, where these means are suffered to exist.[1] Take away the means of influence and you render disqualifications unnecessary. Leave them, and no disqualification can ever wholly prevent their operation on Parliament.

My plan stands in the way of no other reformation: but, on the contrary, it tends exceedingly to forward all rational attempts towards that great end. It certainly cannot make a careless Minister an œconomist. But the best Minister will find the use of it; and it will be no small check on the worst. For its main purpose is to correct the present prodigal *constitution* of the civil executive government of this kingdom;

---

[1] The MS. reads: 'I rely more on this than on regulations of disqualification, on which I intend to add very little to those for which I have voted on other Questions'.

and unless this be done, I am satisfied no Minister whatever can possibly introduce the best[1] œconomy into the *administration* of it.

As to my *limits*; the first is found in the rules of justice. And therefore, I do not propose to touch what any private man holds by a legal tenure.

The second is in the rules of equity and mercy. Where offices may be suppressed, which form the whole maintenance of innocent people, it is hard (and hardship is a kind of injustice) that they who were decoyed into particular situations of life, by our fault, should be made the sacrifice of our penitence. I do not mean to starve such people, because *we* have been prodigal in our establishments. The removals will fall almost wholly on those who hold offices by a tenure, in which they are liable to be, and frequently are, removed for accommodating the arrangements of Administration; and surely the accommodation of the public, in a great case like this, is full as material a cause for their removal, as the convenience of any Administration, or the displeasure of any Minister.

The third sort of limits are to be found in the service of the State. No one employment really and substantially useful to the public, and which may not very well be otherwise supplied, is to be retrenched; or to be diminished in its lawful and accustomed emoluments. To cut off such service, or such reward is what, I conceive, neither politic, nor rational in any sense.[2]

The fourth of my limits, is, that the *fund* for the reward of service, or merit, is to be left of sufficient solidity for its probable purposes.

The fifth, that the Crown shall be left an ample and liberal provision for personal satisfaction; and for as much of magnificence, as is suitable with the burthened state of this country; perhaps, some may think what I shall propose to leave, to be more than is decent.

I propose the idea with the properties, and with the qualifications I have now expressed. However presumptuous my attempt may appear, it is made with an humble and honest intention, and I will spare no pains to digest and ripen it. I trust it will give confidence to the people,

---

[1] The MS. has a pencilled amendment in the margin: 'least'. This reading was adopted in *Corr.* (1844), ii. 332–4.

[2] The MS. reads: 'It is what, I conceive, rather political or rational in any Sense to do; and this I shall fully explain hereafter'.

and strength to government; that it will make our state of war vigorous; and our state of peace and repose really refreshing and recruiting.

The House adjourned, no ministerial supporter having spoken.

Answers to Queries
[*post* 16 December 1779]

Source: MS. at Sheffield, R1.1875

When at the end of November Wyvill initiated the movement, which led to the Yorkshire County Meeting of 30 December, he got in touch with Stephen Croft,[1] an old friend of Lord Rockingham. Croft kept the Marquess in touch with events, and on 16 December sent him a set of queries to which Burke provided answers.[2] Evinced in Burke's replies is the desire to advance but at the same time to control and contain the Yorkshire movement. While the leading Rockinghams supported the latter for the potential collective challenge it was likely to be able to mount to the Government, they also had two major reasons for feeling threatened by it. The first was that it had a power of its own unlinked with the traditional aristocratic element which Rockingham himself represented and which for years he had headed in the county. Throughout his political life the Marquess had found it necessary to speak out against those who wished to block the 'operation of the landed *weight* in Peers Possession'[3] during elections. Now he feared plans promoted by some to 'bar all Members of Parliament'[4] from being on the proposed new Association Committees in Yorkshire because they were subject to aristocratic domination.

The second reason for the Rockinghams' trepidation was that some of the reform objectives called for by many of the Wyvill following were becoming too radical. Burke and the rest of the party could propagate economical reform because its aim was to fight increases in government expenditures and the Crown's influence which they felt certain were 'easily traced to ... new Circumstances and new modes of influence Subsequent to the Revolution'. To promote such a programme would not significantly alter the Revolution settlement—'the work and the Result of the Wisdom and Experience of

---

[1] 1712–98.
[2] MSS. at Sheffield, R134.4, R138.21.
[3] R1.996.
[4] R1.1881.

Ages'[1]—for which they credited their own Whig party.[2] 'I much wish—
Speculative propositions might be avoided,' Rockingham himself told Croft,
'*Short parliaments* or more *County Members*—or *diffusing the Right of Voting to
every Individual*—are at best but crude propositions—whereof perhaps no
man can well ascertain—what the Effects may be.'[3]

Quere. At the intended Meeting Decr 30th at York—who would *be* a proper Person as Chairman. Whether and what should be the Thing which should be adopted, as the essential one at the Meeting.

The Committee should appoint a Chairman[4]
Their Objects should not in general be more than two. 1. To enquire into the Conduct from whence the present State of the Nation is derived. 2. A plan of reform for the permanent establishment of publick œconomy and for lessening the influence of the Crown in and out of Parliament.

Whether

The Petition should be one to the King, one to the Lords and one to the Commons, or to who

To the two houses because the reform must be executed there according to the several powers of the two houses, keeping their Constitutional limits.

Whether

any thing should be hinted by any one about the approaching Election

Perhaps it might better be reserved for a seperate consideration.

Whether

The Petition should be signed by those present or by Numbers and whether it should go up with Parade to the House or in simple

By all present and then circulated about the County and signed by as many as possible, so as to let it come up in time. Freeholders as

---

[1] R1.1897: Rockingham to John Carr, 22 May 1780.
[2] See W. M. Elofson, 'The Rockingham Whigs and the Country Tradition', *Parliamentary History*, viii (1989), 102–11; and above, pp. 20–35.
[3] R1.1869: 12 December 1779.
[4] This first sentence is in Rockingham's hand.

dress and whether the Day of Meeting should get a Number of Freeholders or only simply Gentlemen

well as Gentlemen. It ought to be done with as much solemnity of every kind as the time and substance of the Business will allow.

Whether

It would not be possible to bring about an Association of the County with a large Comittee to meet at appointed times and to be acquainted of every Transaction by Letter but every thing to be transacted and determined by those who attend and if such a thing could be brought about, it would not have a good Effect upon Elections in every County.

Such a Committee would be proper. They ought to have powers to correspond with other petitioning Bodies; and directed to require an answer from the County Members, and Peers who deliver the Petitions to the two houses, and to report the same to a future meeting; the Committee to have power to call a meeting in order to receive such reports. The association would be a great means of strength and union, but the Objects of the association should be as distinct clear and few as possible the means to be pursued for obtaining those objects to be very well considerd.

Resolutions for Yorkshire Meeting
[December 1779]

Source: MS. at Sheffield, R136.20 (formerly R138.1)

Burke prepared resolutions for the Yorkshire Meeting, though they were not used.

Resolved,

1. That it is the opinion of this meeting that the present State of the Nation is in many respects and in an high degree distressful and perilous.

2. That such state of the Nation after the abundant supplies granted by Parliament, strongly indicates Neglect and mismanagement in the Conduct of the publick affairs.

3. That the continuance of such Neglect and mismanagement is owing to the excessive and dangerous influence of the Crown, which increases with the national Distress.

4. That the enormous publick Debt, and the many heavy burthens which have been, and are to be, imposed upon the people, do absolutely require a strict examination into the expenditure[1] of publick money, the speedy adoption of an effectual plan of œconomy and an essential reduction of expence in the administration of the Government, and the Revenues of this Kingdom.

5. That the County of York doth engage itself to the support of all constitutional Endeavours, which shall be used in Parliament for Enquiry into publick misconduct and for promoting a reformation of the abuses which prevail in the administration of affairs.

6. [2]that a Committee be appointed to draw up Petitions to be severally delivered to the houses of Lords and Commons, conveying to the said houses of Parliament the sense and the wishes of the County expressed in our resolutions of this day.

7. That a Committee be appointed to receive from time to time, from the Noblemen and Gentlemen who shall deliver the Petitions of this County accounts of the Steps taken by Parliament in consequence thereof, with powers to call another County Meeting, (if it should seem expedient to them) in order to receive their report; and that the said Committee be also empowerd to correspond with such other publick Bodies and persons who shall choose to petition Parliament in support of the Objects of this meeting.

Letter for Lord Rockingham
[January 1780]

Source: MS. at Sheffield, R1.1876b

In a letter of 13 January Rockingham asked Burke to draw up a general letter of thanks for the peers who had attended the Yorkshire meeting to send to its

---

[1] MS.: 'expediture'.
[2] MS. has 'Resolved' deleted.

chairman.[1] He enclosed the beginning of such a letter.[2] Burke appears merely to have drawn up the following letter for Rockingham to send as an individual. The stages of the composition of the letter actually sent can be followed in various drafts,[3] but Burke does not seem to have been concerned in it. The objective to involve the Marquess and the aristocratic element which he represented in the association movement, and to steer the cause of change along the paths of economical rather than more radical reform are evinced in this composition.

Sir,

I am extremely happy to find that my attendance at York on the late meeting was acceptable to the Gentlemen of the County.

On my part I assure you, with a sincerity, which I hope my Conduct through Life does not make doubtful, that the principles of that meeting, the Spirit and the Temper that were shewn there, and the resolutions with which you concluded,[4] gave me very real inward Satisfaction.

A Yorkshire man as I am, I must have particular pleasure to see the independent Spirit of English Country Gentlemen and English Freeholders, beginning to revive, and to shew itself first among you. If that Spirit should be kept up and spread, as I trust it will, the constitution which has always made this Country happy within itself, and made it often formidable to others, will recover its force and Virtue.

You have put your hands with sagacity and decision on the two main leading Causes of all our misfortunes—prodigality and corrupt influence. These are the things that weigh us down, that weaken our Strength as a Nation and deprive us as men not only of our Integrity but of our Understanding: for I am sure, no man can see distinctly what it is his private Interest not to see at all.

You have done well for your Country; and you never in any instance have given a greater proof of your fidelity and regard for your Sovereign than you have done at that meeting. For he never has been, nor will he ever be well advised, well served, or well supported, by those who shall

---

[1] *Corr.* iv. 192–3.
[2] MS. at Sheffield, R1.1876a.
[3] R140.60, 61, and R91.1, 5. The final version is printed *Wyvill Papers*, i. 44–6.
[4] Printed in *Wyvill Papers*, i. 4–6.

have no occasion to put him well with his Country, but trust wholly to influence to carry his affairs through Parliament.

You may be very sure of my most hearty concurrence in the general Objects of your Petition. I feel just as you do and I hope to shew that I shall not be the most backward in promoting our common End, the independence of Parliament, and the just and frugal application of that money which whoever has the voting of it or the expenditure of it is really yours.

Speech on Economical Reform
11 February 1780

Source: *Speech of Edmund Burke Esq., Member of Parliament for the City of Bristol, on Presenting to the House of Commons (on the 11th of February, 1780,) a Plan for the better Security of the Independence of Parliament and the Oeconomical Reformation of the Civil and Other Establishments*, 4th edn., J. Dodsley, London, 1780

At the end of this speech Burke departed from his notes (which have not survived) and had to rely on the memory of Arthur Young (1741–1820) and Hugh Macauley Boyd (1746–94) to recover some of the wording of his conclusion (*Corr.* iv. 212).

Having announced on 15 December his intention of presenting a plan 'for public economy and reduction of influence' 'as soon after the Christmas recess as possible',[1] Burke went ahead drawing up an outline of the plan and embodying it in a series of Bills.[2] He gave notice on 28 January that he would present the plan to the House on 11 February. The speech on economical reform ranks amongst Burke's very best and it received acclaim from his contemporaries at least equalling that drawn by his first speech on conciliation with America. Lord North himself 'paid Mr. Burke the compliment that he had never heard such a speech as his, and that he believed there was not a man in England who could have made such a one, or treated so very difficult a matter with so much perspicuity, clearness, and ability.'[3] The *London Evening Post* of 12 February reported that:

Mr. Burke rose to submit his promised important plan to the consideration of the House. He did it in a speech which we feel ourselves unable to do justice to... Memory alone is not equal to the task, memory may supply the outlines of his plan, but it would require talents equal to his own to reach the beauties of his detail.[4]

[1] See above, p. 474.
[2] The outline or sketch of the plan—which was circulated—survives (MSS. at Sheffield, Bk 14.30–4, printed *Corr.* (1844), ii. 321–32). For the Bills, see below, pp. 550–1.
[3] *Universal Magazine*, lxvi (1780), 97.
[4] On 12 February.

Burke's compelling performance may in part have been the result of his own sense of euphoria about the reform movement in general. At this point the Rockingham leaders had reason to believe that they and the forces of moderation would predominate. On 7 December the Duke of Richmond had presented a motion in the House of Lords which called for more economy in government and urged the Crown to set the example by diminishing the Civil List.[1] The Marquess of Rockingham spoke for the motion and 'enlarged upon the baneful Effects of . . . [the] Influence [of the Crown] and Corruption in the Minds of Men both *in* and out of *Parliament and . . . declared that a great Reduction of offices*' must be made. He was supported by two other important Opposition leaders in the House, Lords Shelburne and Grafton, and he later jubilantly spoke of the '*Union . . . declared* amongst us all on this Subject'.[2] Moreover, at the York county meeting on 30 December, Rockingham and his friends managed to gain the acceptance of moderate objectives. It was agreed that the county should simply present a petition to the commons requesting that

measures might be taken to enquire into, and correct the gross abuses in the expenditure of public money; to reduce all exorbitant salaries; to rescind and abolish all sinecure places and unmerited pensions; and to appropriate the produce to the necessities of the State.[3]

The Marquess intervened with friends in the county including Croft and Pemberton Milnes,[4] to resist the acceptance of more radical ideas such as annual Parliaments and changes in the system of representation which Wyvill and some of his colleagues were openly promoting by 21 January.[5]

As the weeks went on the Rockingham following would play an important role in the petitioning movement as it spread into other counties,[6] and Burke would receive official thanks from a number of counties for his plan.[7] It is distinctly possible that if his Bills had been successful the party just might have gained the advantage over more radical forces and managed to control and constrain the entire reform campaign. The Bills themselves were extensive enough to attract all the political forces which genuinely wanted to reduce government expenditure and place new limitations on the influence of the Crown. Burke claimed to be decreasing expenses by some £200,000 a year and promised to eliminate fifty placemen.[8] His measure, in combination with that of Sir Philip Jennings Clerke for the exclusion of government contractors from the House of Commons, and that of John Crewe[9] for the

[1] *Parl. Hist.* xx. 1255–8.
[2] MS. at Sheffield, R1.1869: Rockingham to Stephen Croft, 12 December 1779.
[3] *London Evening Post*, 4 January 1780.
[4] R1.1881: Rockingham to P. Milnes, 28 February 1780.
[5] *Wyvill Papers*, i. 67–8.
[6] F. O'Gorman, *The Rise of Party in England: The Rockingham Whigs, 1760–82*, London, 1975, p. 413.
[7] *Corr.* iv. 206–11.
[8] *Parl. Hist.* xx. 1293–1300; above, p. 424.
[9] (1742–1829), M.P. 1765–1802.

disfranchisement of revenue officers, went further than any similar legislation passed through Parliament in the eighteenth century. It also represented a more substantial step than the legislation which the Rockinghams would ultimately secure when they finally attained power in 1782.[1]

SPEECH

Mr. Speaker,

I Rise, in acquittal of my engagement to the house,[2] in obedience to the strong and just requisition of my constituents,[3] and, I am persuaded, in conformity to the unanimous wishes of the whole nation, to submit to the wisdom of parliament, "A plan of reform in the constitution of several parts of the public œconomy."

I have endeavoured, that this plan should include in its execution, a considerable reduction of improper expence; that, it should effect a conversion of unprofitable titles into a productive estate; that, it should lead to, and indeed almost compel, a provident administration of such sums of public money as must remain under discretionary trusts; that, it should render the incurring debts on the civil establishment (which must ultimately affect national strength and national credit) so very difficult, as to become next to impracticable.

But what, I confess, was uppermost with me, what I bent the whole force of my mind to, was the reduction of that corrupt influence, which is itself the perennial spring of all prodigality, and of all disorder; which loads us, more than millions of debt; which takes away vigour from our arms, wisdom from our councils, and every shadow of authority and credit from the most venerable parts of our constitution.

Sir, I assure you, very solemnly, and with a very clear conscience, that nothing in the world has led me to such an undertaking, but my zeal for the honour of this house, and the settled, habitual, systematic affection I bear to the cause, and to the principles of government.

I enter perfectly into the nature and consequences of my attempt; and I advance to it with a tremor that shakes me to the inmost fibre of my frame. I feel, that I engage in a business, in itself most ungracious; totally wide of the course of prudent conduct; and I really think, the most compleatly adverse that can be imagined, to the natural turn and

[1] O'Gorman, *The Rise of Party*, pp. 458–9.
[2] On 15 December 1779.
[3] In their petition presented to the Commons by Burke on 8 February.

temper of my own mind. I know, that all parsimony is of a quality approaching to unkindness; and that (on some person or other) every reform must operate as a sort of punishment. Indeed the whole class of the severe and restrictive virtues, are at a market almost too high for humanity. What is worse, there are very few of those virtues which are not capable of being imitated, and even outdone in many of their most striking effects, by the worst of vices. Malignity and envy will carve much more deeply, and finish much more sharply, in the work of retrenchment, than frugality and providence. I do not, therefore, wonder that gentlemen have kept away from such a task, as well from good nature as from prudence. Private feeling might, indeed, be over-borne by legislative reason; and a man of a long-sighted and strong-nerved humanity, might bring himself, not so much to consider from whom he takes a superfluous enjoyment, as for whom in the end he may preserve the absolute necessaries of life.

But it is much more easy to reconcile this measure to humanity, than to bring it to any agreement with prudence. I do not mean that little, selfish, pitiful, bastard thing, which sometimes goes by the name of a family in which it is not legitimate, and to which it is a disgrace;—I mean even that public and enlarged prudence, which, apprehensive of being disabled from rendering acceptable services to the world, with-holds itself from those that are invidious. Gentlemen who are, with me, verging towards the decline of life, and are apt to form their ideas of kings from kings of former times, might dread the anger of a reigning prince;—they who are more provident of the future, or by being young are more interested in it, might tremble at the resentment of the successor: they might see a long, dull, dreary, unvaried visto of despair and exclusion, for half a century, before them. This is no pleasant prospect at the outset of a political journey.

Besides Sir, the private enemies to be made in all attempts of this kind, are innumerable; and their enmity will be the more bitter, and the more dangerous too, because a sense of dignity will oblige them to conceal the cause of their resentment. Very few men of great families and extensive connections, but will feel the smart of a cutting reform, in some close relation, some bosom friend, some pleasant acquaintance, some dear protected dependant. Emolument is taken from some; patronage from others; objects of pursuit from all. Men, forced into an involuntary independence, will abhor the authors of a blessing which in their eyes has so very near a resemblance to a curse.

When officers are removed, and the offices remain, you may set the gratitude of some against the anger of others; you may oppose the friends you oblige against the enemies you provoke. But services of the present sort create no attachments. The individual good felt in a public benefit, is comparatively so small, and comes round through such an involved labyrinth of intricate and tedious revolutions; whilst a present personal detriment is so heavy where it falls, and so instant in its operation, that the cold commendation of a public advantage never was, and never will be, a match for the quick sensibility of a private loss: and you may depend upon it, Sir, that when many people have an interest in railing, sooner or later, they will bring a considerable degree of unpopularity upon any measure. So that, for the present at least, the reformation will operate against the reformers; and revenge (as against them) will produce all the effects of corruption.

This, Sir, is almost always the case, where the plan has compleat success. But how stands the matter in the mere attempt? Nothing, you know, is more common, than for men to wish, and call loudly too, for a reformation, who, when it arrives, do by no means like the severity of its aspect. Reformation is one of those pieces which must be put at some distance in order to please. Its greatest favourers love it better in the abstract than in the substance. When any old prejudice of their own, or any interest that they value, is touched, they become scrupulous, they become captious, and every man has his separate exception. Some pluck out the black hairs, some the grey; one point must be given up to one; another point must be yielded to another; nothing is suffered to prevail upon its own principle: the whole is so frittered down, and disjointed, that scarcely a trace of the original scheme remains! Thus, between the resistance of power, and the unsystematical process of popularity, the undertaker and the undertaking are both exposed, and the poor reformer is hissed off the stage, both by friends and foes.

Observe, Sir, that the apology for my undertaking (an apology which, though long, is no longer than necessary) is not grounded on my want of the fullest sense of the difficult and invidious nature of the task I undertake. I risque odium if I succeed, and contempt if I fail. My excuse must rest in mine and your conviction of the absolute, urgent *necessity* there is, that something of the kind should be done. If there is any sacrifice to be made, either of estimation or of fortune, the smallest is the best. Commanders in chief are not to be put upon the forlorn hope. But indeed it is necessary that the attempt should be made. It is necessary from our own political circumstances; it is necessary from the operations of the enemy; it is necessary from the demands of the people; whose desires, when they do not militate with the stable and eternal rules of justice and reason (rules which are above us, and above them) ought to be as a law to a House of Commons.

As to our circumstances; I do not mean to aggravate the difficulties of them, by the strength of any colouring whatsoever. On the contrary, I observe, and observe with pleasure, that our affairs rather wear a more promising aspect than they did on the opening of this session. We have had some leading successes.[1] But those who rate them at the highest (higher a great deal than I dare to do) are of opinion, that, upon the ground of such advantages, we cannot at this time hope to make any treaty of peace, which would not be ruinous and completely disgraceful. In such an anxious state of things, if dawnings of success serve to animate our diligence, they are good; if they tend to increase our presumption, they are worse than defeats. The state of our affairs shall then be as promising as any one may choose to conceive it: It is however but promising. We must recollect, that with but half of our natural strength, we are at war against confederated powers who have singly threatned us with ruin: We must recollect, that whilst we are left naked on one side, our other flank is uncovered by any alliance; That whilst we are weighing and balancing our successes against our losses, we are accumulating debt to the amount of at least fourteen millions in the year.[2] That loss is certain.

I have no wish to deny, that our successes are as brilliant as any one chooses to make them; our resources too may, for me, be as unfathomable as they are represented. Indeed they are just whatever the people possess, and will submit to pay. Taxing is an easy business. Any projector can contrive new impositions; any bungler can add to the old. But is it altogether wise to have no other bounds to your impositions, than the patience of those who are to bear them?

All I claim upon the subject of your resources is this, that they are not likely to be *increased* by wasting them.—I think I shall be permitted

---

[1] In 1779 the Government had decided to attack the southern colonies instead of New England. British troops took Charleston in 1780, but soon found themselves under constant siege by an American force under General Nathanael Greene (1742–86).
[2] The national debt increased from £153.4 million in 1779 to £167.2 million in 1780 (Mitchell and Deane, *Abstract of British Historical Statistics*, p. 402).

to assume, that a system of frugality will not *lessen* your riches, whatever they may be;—I believe it will not be hotly disputed, that those resources which lie heavy on the subject, ought not to be objects of *preference*; that they ought not to be the *very first choice*, to an honest representative of the people.

This is all, Sir, that I shall say upon our circumstances and our resources. I mean to say a little more on the operations of the enemy, because this matter seems to me very natural in our present deliberation. When I look to the other side of the water, I cannot help recollecting what Pyrrhus said on reconnoitering the Roman camp, "These Barbarians have nothing barbarous in their discipline."[1] When I look, as I have pretty carefully looked, into the proceedings of the French king, I am sorry to say it, I see nothing of the character and genius of arbitrary finance; none of the bold frauds of bankrupt power; none of the wild struggles, and plunges, of despotism in distress;—no lopping off from the capital of debt;—no suspension of interest;—no robbery under the name of loan;—no raising the value, no debasing the substance of the coin. I see neither Louis the fourteenth, nor Louis the fifteenth. On the contrary, I behold with astonishment, rising before me, by the very hands of arbitrary power, and in the very midst of war and confusion, a regular, methodical system of public credit; I behold a fabric laid on the natural and solid foundations of trust and confidence among men; and rising, by fair gradations, order over order, according to the just rules of symmetry and art. What a reverse of things! Principle, method, regularity, œconomy, frugality, justice to individuals, and care of the people, are the resources with which France makes war upon Great Britain. God avert the omen! But if we should see any genius in war and politics arise in France, to second what is done in the bureau!—I turn my eyes from the consequences.

The noble Lord in the blue ribbon, last year, treated all this with contempt.[2] He never could conceive it possible that the French minister of finance[3] could go through that year with a loan of but seventeen hundred thousand pounds; and that he should be able to fund that loan without any tax. The second year, however, opens the very same scene. A small loan, a loan of no more than two millions five hundred thousand pounds, is to carry our enemies through the service

---

[1] Plutarch, *Pyrrhus*, xvi.
[2] Probably a reference to Lord North's speech on 24 February 1779 (*Parl. Reg.* xii. 5–9).
[3] Jacques Necker; see above, p. 396.

of this year also. No tax is raised to fund that debt; no tax is raised for the current services. I am credibly informed that there is no anticipation whatsoever. Compensations* are correctly made. Old debts continue to be sunk as in the time of profound peace. Even payments which their treasury had been authorized to suspend during the time of war, are not suspended.

A general reform, executed through every *department of the revenue*, creates an annual income of more than half a million, whilst it facilitates and simplifies all the functions of administration. The king's *household*—at the remotest avenues to which, all reformation has been hitherto stopped—that household, which has been the strong hold of prodigality, the virgin fortress which was never before attacked—has been not only not defended, but it has, even in the forms, been surrendered by the king to the œconomy of his minister. No capitulation; no reserve. Œconomy has entered in triumph into the public splendour of the monarch, into his private amusements, into the appointments of his nearest and highest relations. Œconomy and public spirit have made a beneficent and an honest spoil; they have plundered, from extravagance and luxury, for the use of substantial service, a revenue of near four hundred thousand pounds. The reform of the finances, joined to this reform of the court, gives to the public nine hundred thousand pounds a year and upwards.[1]

The minister who does these things is a great man—But the king who desires that they should be done, is a far greater. We must do justice to our enemies—These are the acts of a patriot king. I am not in dread of the vast armies of France: I am not in dread of the gallant spirit of its brave and numerous nobility: I am not alarmed even at the great navy which has been so miraculously created. All these things Louis the fourteenth had before. With all these things, the French monarchy has more than once fallen prostrate at the feet of the public faith of Great Britain. It was the want of public credit which disabled France from recovering after her defeats, or recovering even from her victories and triumphs. It was a prodigal court, it was an ill-ordered

---

* This term comprehends various retributions made to persons whose offices are taken away, or who, in any other way, suffer by the new arrangements that are made.

[1] For Necker's reform of the financial system in France, see J. F. Bosher, *French Finances 1770–1795: From Business to Bureaucracy*, Cambridge, 1970, pp. 142–65. The edicts which Burke summarizes are quoted in the *Annual Register* for 1780 (Appendix to the Chronicles, pp. 302–4) and can be found in *Oeuvres complètes de M. Necker*, iii. 209–10, 211–18.

revenue, that sapped the foundations of all her greatness. Credit cannot exist under the arm of necessity. Necessity strikes at credit, I allow, with a heavier and quicker blow under an arbitrary monarchy, than under a limited and balanced government: but still necessity and credit are natural enemies, and cannot be long reconciled in any situation. From necessity and corruption, a free state may lose the spirit of that complex constitution which is the foundation of confidence. On the other hand, I am far from being sure, that a monarchy, when once it is properly regulated, may not for a long time, furnish a foundation for credit upon the solidity of its maxims, though it affords no ground of trust in its institutions. I am afraid I see in England, and in France, something like a beginning of both these things. I wish I may be found in a mistake.

This very short, and very imperfect state of what is now going on in France (the last circumstances of which I received in about eight days after the registry of the edict)* I do not, Sir, lay before you for any invidious purpose. It is in order to excite in us the spirit of a noble emulation.—Let the nations make war upon each other (since we must make war) not with a low and vulgar malignity, but by a competition of virtues. This is the only way by which both parties can gain by war. The French have imitated us; let us, through them, imitate ourselves; ourselves in our better and happier days. If public frugality, under whatever men, or in whatever mode of government, is national strength, it is a strength which our enemies are in possession of before us.

Sir, I am well aware, that the state and the result of the French œconomy which I have laid before you, are even now lightly treated by some, who ought never to speak but from information. Pains have not been spared, to represent them as impositions on the public. Let me tell you, Sir, that the creation of a navy, and a two years war without taxing, are a very singular species of imposture. But be it so. For what end does Neckar carry on this delusion? Is it to lower the estimation of the crown he serves, and to render his own administration contemptible? No! No! He is conscious, that the sense of mankind is so clear and decided in favour of œconomy, and of the weight and value of its resources, that he turns himself to every species of fraud and artifice, to obtain the meer reputation of it. Men do not affect a

---

* Edict, registered 29 Jan. 1780.[1]
[1] The material which Burke received from France is at Sheffield (Bk 25.50–2).

conduct that tends to their discredit. Let us, then, get the better of
Monsieur Neckar in his own way—Let us do in reality what he does
only in pretence—Let us turn his French tinsel into English gold. Is
then the meer opinion and appearance of frugality and good management of such use to France, and is the substance to be so mischievous
to England? Is the very constitution of nature so altered by a sea of
twenty miles, that œconomy should give power on the continent, and
that profusion should give it here? For God's sake let not this be the
only fashion of France which we refuse to copy.

To the last kind of necessity, the desires of the people, I have but a
very few words to say. The ministers seem to contest this point; and
affect to doubt, whether the people do really desire a plan of œconomy
in the civil government. Sir, this is too ridiculous. It is impossible that
they should not desire it. It is impossible that a prodigality which
draws its resources from their indigence, should be pleasing to them.
Little factions of pensioners, and their dependants, may talk another
language. But the voice of nature is against them; and it will be heard.
The people of England will not, they cannot take it kindly, that
representatives should refuse to their constituents, what an absolute
sovereign voluntarily offers to his subjects. The expression of the
petitions is, that "*before any new burthens are laid upon this country,
effectual measures be taken by this house, to enquire into, and correct, the
gross abuses in the expenditure of public money.*"[1]

This has been treated by the noble lord in the blue ribbon, as a wild
factious language. It happens, however, that the people in their address
to us, use almost word for word the same terms as the king of France
uses in addressing himself to his people; and it differs only, as it falls
short of the French king's idea of what is due to his subjects. "To
convince," says he, "our faithful subjects of *the desire we entertain not to
recur to new impositions,* until we have first exhausted all the resources
which order and œconomy can possibly supply"—&c. &c.

These desires of the people of England, which come far short of the
voluntary concessions of the king of France, are moderate indeed.
They only contend that we should interweave some œconomy with the
taxes with which we have chosen to begin the war. They request, not
that you should rely upon œconomy exclusively, but that you should

---

[1] This is from the Yorkshire petition which had been presented to the Commons on 8
February.

give it rank and precedence, in the order of the ways and means of this single session.

But if it were possible, that the desires of our constituents, desires which are at once so natural, and so very much tempered and subdued, should have no weight with an house of commons, which has its eye elsewhere; I would turn my eyes to the very quarter to which theirs are directed. I would reason this matter with the house, on the mere policy of the question; and I would undertake to prove, that an early dereliction of abuse, is the direct interest of government, of government taken abstractedly from its duties, and considered merely as a system intending its own conservation.

If there is any one eminent criterion, which, above all the rest, distinguishes a wise government from an administration weak and improvident, it is this;—"well to know the best time and manner of yielding, what it is impossible to keep."—[1] There have been Sir, and there are, many who chuse to chicane with their situation, rather than be instructed by it. Those gentlemen argue against every desire of reformation, upon the principles of a criminal prosecution. It is enough for them to justify their adherence to a pernicious system, that it is not of their contrivance; that it is an inheritance of absurdity, derived to them from their ancestors; that they can make out a long and unbroken pedigree of mismanagers that have gone before them. They are proud of the antiquity of their house; and they defend their errors, as if they were defending their inheritance: afraid of derogating from their nobility; and carefully avoiding a sort of blot in their scutcheon, which they think would degrade them for ever.

It was thus that the unfortunate Charles the First defended himself on the practice of the Stuart who went before him, and of all the Tudors; his partizans might have gone to the Plantagenets.—They might have found bad examples enough, both abroad and at home, that could have shewn an antient and illustrious descent. But there is a time, when men will not suffer bad things because their ancestors have suffered worse. There is a time, when the hoary head of inveterate abuse, will neither draw reverence nor obtain protection. If the noble Lord in the blue ribbon pleads, "*not guilty,*" to the charges brought against the present system of public œconomy, it is not possible to give a fair verdict by which he will not stand acquitted. But pleading is not

---

[1] The source of this quotation has not been found.

our present business. His plea or his traverse may be allowed as an answer to a charge, when a charge is made. But if he puts himself in the way to obstruct reformation, then the faults of his office instantly become his own. Instead of a public officer in an abusive department, whose province is an object to be regulated, he becomes a criminal who is to be punished. I do most seriously put it to administration, to consider the wisdom of a timely reform. Early reformations are amicable arrangements with a friend in power: Late reformations are terms imposed upon a conquered enemy; early reformations are made in cool blood; late reformations are made under a state of inflammation. In that state of things the people behold in government nothing that is respectable. They see the abuse, and they will see nothing else—They fall into the temper of a furious populace provoked at the disorder of a house of ill fame; they never attempt to correct or regulate; they go to work by the shortest way—They abate the nusance, they pull down the house.

This is my opinion with regard to the true interest of government. But as it is the interest of government that reformation should be early, it is the interest of the people that it should be temperate. It is their interest, because a temperate reform is permanent; and because it has a principle of growth. Whenever we improve, it is right to leave room for a further improvement. It is right to consider, to look about us, to examine the effect of what we have done.—Then we can proceed with confidence, because we can proceed with intelligence.—Whereas in hot reformations, in what men, more zealous than considerate, *call making clear work*, the whole is generally so crude, so harsh, so indigested; mixed with so much imprudence, and so much injustice; so contrary to the whole course of human nature and human institutions, that the very people who are most eager for it, are among the first to grow disgusted at what they have done. Then some part of the abdicated grievance is recalled from its exile in order to become a corrective of the correction. Then the abuse assumes all the credit and popularity of a reform. The very idea of purity and disinterestedness in politics falls into disrepute, and is considered as a vision of hot and inexperienced men; and thus disorders become incurable, not by the virulence of their own quality, but by the unapt and violent nature of the remedies. A great part therefore, of my idea of reform, is meant to operate gradually; some benefits will come at a nearer, some at a more remote period. We must no more make haste to be rich by parsimony, than by intemperate acquisition.

In my opinion, it is our duty when we have the desires of the people before us, to pursue them, not in the spirit of literal obedience, which may militate with their very principle, much less to treat them with a peevish and contentious litigation, as if we were adverse parties in a suit. It would, Sir, be most dishonourable for a faithful representative of the commons, to take advantage of any inartificial expression of the people's wishes, in order to frustrate their attainment of what they have an undoubted right to expect. We are under infinite obligations to our constituents, who have raised us to so distinguished a trust, and have imparted such a degree of sanctity to common characters. We ought to walk before them with purity, plainness, and integrity of heart; with filial love, and not with slavish fear, which is always a low and tricking thing. For my own part, in what I have meditated upon that subject, I cannot indeed take upon me to say I have the honour *to follow* the sense of the people. The truth is, *I met it on the way*, while I was pursuing their interest according to my own ideas. I am happy beyond expression, to find that my intentions have so far coincided with theirs, that I have not had cause to be in the least scrupulous to sign their Petition,[1] conceiving it to express my own opinions, as nearly as general terms can express the object of particular arrangements.

I am therefore satisfied to act as a fair mediator between government and the people, endeavouring to form a plan which should have both an early and a temperate operation. I mean, that it should be substantial; that it should be systematic; that it should rather strike at the first cause of prodigality and corrupt influence, than attempt to follow them in all their effects.

It was to fulfil the first of these objects (the proposal of something substantial) that I found myself obliged at the out-set, to reject a plan proposed by an honourable and attentive member of parliament,* with very good intentions on his part, about a year or two ago.[2] Sir, the plan I speak of, was the tax of *25 per cent.* moved upon places and pensions during the continuance of the American war.—Nothing, Sir,

---

* Thomas Gilbert, Esq; member for Litchfield.

[1] Presumably the Westminster petition, adopted on 2 February and presented to the Commons on 13 March.

[2] A proposal made on 9 March 1778; see Burke's speech of 10 March 1778 on the budget, printed above.

could have met my ideas more than such a tax, if it was considered as a practical satire on that war, and as a penalty upon those who led us into it; but in any other view it appeared to me very liable to objections. I considered the scheme as neither substantial, nor permanent, nor systematical, nor likely to be a corrective of evil influence. I have always thought employments a very proper subject of regulation, but a very ill-chosen subject for a tax. An equal tax upon property is reasonable; because the object is of the same quality throughout. The species is the same, it differs only in its quantity: but a tax upon salaries is totally of a different nature; there can be no equality, and consequently no justice, in taxing them by the hundred, in the gross.

We have, Sir, on our establishment, several offices which perform real service—We have also places that provide large rewards for no service at all. We have stations which are made for the public decorum; made for preserving the grace and majesty of a great people.—We have likewise expensive formalities, which tend rather to the disgrace than the ornament of the state and the court. This, Sir, is the real condition of our establishments. To fall with the same severity on objects so perfectly dissimilar, is the very reverse of a reformation. I mean a reformation framed, as all serious things ought to be, in number, weight, and measure.—Suppose, for instance, that two men receive a salary of £800 a year each.—In the office of one, there is nothing at all to be done; in the other, the occupier is oppressed by its duties.—Strike off twenty-five *per cent* from these two offices, you take from one man £200, which in justice he ought to have, and you give in effect to the other £600, which he ought not to receive. The public robs the former, and the latter robs the public; and this mode of mutual robbery is the only way in which the office and the public can make up their accounts.

But the balance in settling the account of this double injustice, is much against the state. The result is short. You purchase a saving of two hundred pounds, by a profusion of six. Besides, Sir, whilst you leave a supply of unsecured money behind, wholly at the discretion of ministers, they make up the tax to such places as they wish to favour, or in such new places as they may choose to create. Thus the civil list becomes oppressed with debt; and the public is obliged to repay, and to repay with an heavy interest, what it has taken by an injudicious tax. Such has been the effect of the taxes hitherto laid on pensions and employments, and it is no encouragement to recur again to the same expedient.

In effect, such a scheme is not calculated to produce, but to prevent reformation. It holds out a shadow of present gain to a greedy and necessitous public, to divert their attention from those abuses, which in reality are the great causes of their wants. It is a composition to stay enquiry; it is a fine paid by mismanagement, for the renewal of its lease. What is worse, it is a fine paid by industry and merit, for an indemnity to the idle and the worthless. But I shall say no more upon this topic, because (whatever may be given out to the contrary) I know that the noble lord in the blue ribbon perfectly agrees with me in these sentiments.

After all that I have said on this subject, I am so sensible, that it is our duty to try every thing which may contribute to the relief of the nation, that I do not attempt wholly to reprobate the idea even of a tax. Whenever, Sir, the incumbrance of useless office (which lies no less a dead weight upon the service of the state, than upon its revenues) shall be removed;—when the remaining offices shall be classed according to the just proportion of their rewards and services, so as to admit the application of an equal rule to their taxation, when the discretionary power over the civil list cash shall be so regulated, that a minister shall no longer have the means of repaying with a private, what is taken by a public hand—if after all these preliminary regulations, it should be thought that a tax on places is an object worthy of the public attention, I shall be very ready to lend my hand to a reduction of their emoluments.

Having thus, Sir, not so much absolutely rejected, as postponed, the plan of a taxation of office,—my next business was to find something which might be really substantial and effectual. I am quite clear, that if we do not go to the very origin and first ruling cause of grievances, we do nothing. What does it signify to turn abuses out of one door, if we are to let them in at another? What does it signify to promote œconomy upon a measure, and to suffer it to be subverted in the principle? Our ministers are far from being wholly to blame for the present ill order which prevails. Whilst institutions directly repugnant to good management, are suffered to remain, no effectual or lasting reform _can_ be introduced.

I therefore thought it necessary, as soon as I conceived thoughts of submitting to you some plan of reform, to take a comprehensive view of the state of this country; to make a sort of survey of its Jurisdictions, its Estates, and its Establishments. Something, in every one of them,

495

seemed to me to stand in the way of all œconomy in their administration, and prevented every possibility of methodizing the system. But being, as I ought to be, doubtful of myself, I was resolved not to proceed in an *arbitrary* manner, in any particular which tended to change the settled state of things, or in any degree to affect the fortune or situation, the interest or the importance, of any individual. By an arbitrary proceeding, I mean one conducted by the private opinions, tastes, or feelings, of the man who attempts to regulate. These private measures are not standards of the exchequer, nor balances of the sanctuary. General principles cannot be debauched or corrupted by interest or caprice; and by those principles I was resolved to work.

Sir, before I proceed further, I will lay these principles fairly before you, that afterwards you may be in a condition to judge whether every object of regulation, as I propose it, comes fairly under its rule. This will exceedingly shorten all discussion between us, if we are perfectly in earnest in establishing a system of good management. I therefore lay down to myself, seven fundamental rules; they might indeed be reduced to two or three simple maxims, but they would be too general, and their application to the several heads of the business, before us, would not be so distinct and visible. I conceive then,

First, That all jurisdictions which furnish more matter of expence, more temptation to oppression, or more means and instruments of corrupt influence, than advantage to justice or political administration, ought to be abolished.

Secondly, That all public estates which are more subservient to the purposes of vexing, overawing, and influencing those who hold under them, and to the expence of perception and management, than of benefit to the revenue, ought, upon every principle, both of revenue and of freedom, to be disposed of.

Thirdly, That all offices which bring more charge than proportional advantage to the state; that all offices which may be engrafted on others, uniting and simplifying their duties, ought, in the first case, to be taken away; and in the second, to be consolidated.

Fourthly, That all such offices ought to be abolished as obstruct the prospect of the general superintendant of finance; which destroy his superintendancy; which disable him from foreseeing and providing for charges as they may occur; from preventing expence in its origin, checking it in its progress, or securing its application to its proper purposes. A minister under whom expences can be made without his knowledge, can never say what it is that he can spend or what it is that he can save.

Fifthly, That it is proper to establish an invariable order in all payments; which will prevent partiality; which will give preference to services, not according to the importunity of the demandant, but the rank and order of their utility or their justice.

Sixthly, That it is right to reduce every establishment, and every part of an establishment (as nearly as possible) to certainty, the life of all order and good management.

Seventhly, That all subordinate treasuries, as the nurseries of mismanagement, and as naturally drawing to themselves as much money as they can, keeping it as long as they can, and accounting for it as late as they can, ought to be dissolved. They have a tendency to perplex and distract the public accounts, and to excite a suspicion of government, even beyond the extent of their abuse.

Under the authority and with the guidance of those principles, I proceed; wishing that nothing in any establishment may be changed, where I am not able to make a strong, direct, and solid application of those principles, or of some one of them. An œconomical constitution is a necessary basis for an œconomical administration.

First, with regard to the sovereign jurisdictions, I must observe, Sir, that whoever takes a view of this kingdom in a cursory manner, will imagine, that he beholds a solid, compacted, uniform system of monarchy; in which all inferior jurisdictions are but as rays diverging from one center. But on examining it more nearly, you find much excentricity and confusion. It is not a *Monarchy* in strictness. But, as in the Saxon times this country was an heptarchy, it is now a strange sort of *Pentarchy*. It is divided into five several distinct principalities, besides the supreme. There is indeed this difference from the Saxon times, that as in the itinerant exhibitions of the stage, for want of a complete company, they are obliged to cast a variety of parts on their chief performer; so our sovereign condescends himself to act, not only the principal, but all the subordinate parts in the play. He condescends to dissipate the royal character, and to trifle with those light, subordinate, lackered sceptres, in the hands that sustain the ball which represents the world, or which wield the trident that commands the ocean. Cross a brook, and you lose the king of England; but you have some comfort in coming again under his majesty, though "shorn of his beams,"[1] and

[1] *Paradise Lost*, i. 596.

497

no more than Prince of Wales. Go to the north, and you find him dwindled to a Duke of Lancaster; turn to the west of that north, and he pops upon you in the humble character of Earl of Chester. Travel a few miles on, the Earl of Chester disappears; and the king surprises you again as Count Palatine of Lancaster. If you travel beyond Mount Edgecombe, you find him once more in his incognito, and He is Duke of Cornwall. So that, quite fatigued and satiated with this dull variety, you are infinitely refreshed when you return to the sphere of his proper splendor, and behold your amiable sovereign in his true, simple, undisguised, native character of majesty.

In every one of these five Principalities, Dutchies, Palatinates, there is a regular establishment of considerable expence, and most domineering influence. As his majesty submits to appear in this state of subordination to himself, so his loyal peers and faithful commons attend his royal transformations; and are not so nice as to refuse to nibble at those crumbs of emolument, which console their petty metamorphoses. Thus every one of these principalities has the apparatus of a kingdom, for the jurisdiction over a few private estates; and the formality and charge of the exchequer of Great Britain, for collecting the rents of a country squire. Cornwall is the best of them; but when you compare the charge with the receipt, you will find that it furnishes no exception to the general rule.[1] The dutchy and county palatine of Lancaster do not yield, as I have reason to believe, on an average of twenty years, four thousand pounds a year, clear to the crown.[2] As to Wales, and the county palatine of Chester, I have my doubts, whether their productive exchequer yields any returns at all. Yet one may say, that this revenue is more faithfully applied to its purposes than any of the rest; as it exists for the sole purpose of multiplying offices, and extending influence.

An attempt was lately made to improve this branch of local influence, and to transfer it to the fund of general corruption. I have on the seat behind me, the constitution of Mr. John Probert; a knight-errant, dubbed by the noble lord in the blue ribbon, and sent to search for revenues and adventures upon the mountains of Wales.[3] The

---

[1] In the eight years from 1769 it produced £205,423.

[2] The Privy Purse received £64,800 from 1766 to 1783 (R. Somervile, *History of the Duchy of Lancaster*, 2 vols., London, 1953–72, ii. 169; there is a copy of the privately printed second volume of this work in the Institute of Historical Research).

[3] In November 1778 the Treasury had appointed John Probert at a salary of £300 a year to improve the diminished revenue derived from Wales. A movement of protest resulted with

commission is remarkable; and the event not less so. The commission sets forth, that "Upon a report of the *deputy auditor* (for there is a deputy auditor) of the principality of Wales, it appeared, that his majesty's land-revenues in the said principality, *are greatly diminished;*"— and "that upon a *report* of the *surveyor general* of his majesty's land revenues, upon a *memorial* of the auditor of his majesty's revenues *within the said principality*, that his mines and forests have produced very *little profit either to the public revenue or to individuals*,"—and therefore they appoint Mr. Probert, with a pension of three hundred pounds a year from the said principality, to try whether he can make any thing more of that very *little* which is stated to be so *greatly* diminished. *"A beggarly account of empty boxes."*[1] And yet, Sir, you will remark—that this diminution from littleness (which serves only to prove the infinite divisibility of matter) was not for want of the tender and officious care (as we see) of surveyors general, and surveyors particular; of auditors and deputy-auditors; not for want of memorials, and remonstrances, and reports, and commissions, and constitutions, and inquisitions, and pensions.

Probert, thus armed, and accoutred,—and paid, proceeded on his adventure;—but he was no sooner arrived on the confines of Wales, than all Wales was in arms to meet him. That nation is brave, and full of spirit. Since the invasion of king Edward, and the massacre of the bards, there never was such a tumult, and alarm, and uproar, through the region of *Prestatyn*. *Snowden* shook to its base; *Cader Edris* was loosened from its foundations. The fury of litigious war blew her horn on the mountains. The rocks poured down their goatherds, and the deep caverns vomited out their miners. Everything above ground, and every thing under ground, was in arms.

In short, Sir, to alight from my Welsh Pegasus, and to come to level ground; the *Preux Chevalier* Probert went to look for revenue, like his masters upon other occasions; and like his masters, he found rebellion. But we were grown cautious by experience. A civil war of paper might end in a more serious war; for now remonstrance met remonstrance, and memorial was opposed to memorial. The wise Britons thought it more reasonable, that the poor, wasted, decrepit revenue of the

---

meetings in London and in the Welsh counties. In face of the opposition Probert was told on 5 March to give up his efforts (P.R.O., T29/47, p. 393, T29/48, p. 139; *St James's Chronicle*, 23 January, 6 February, 25 February; *Corr.* iv. 239–40).

[1] *Romeo and Juliet*, v. i. 37.

principality, should die a natural than a violent death. They chose that their ancient moss-grown castles should moulder into decay, under the silent touches of time, and the slow formality of an oblivious and drowsy exchequer, than that they should be battered down all at once, by the lively efforts of a pensioned engineer. As it is the fortune of the noble lord to whom the auspices of this campaign belonged, frequently to provoke resistance, so it is his rule and his nature to yield to that resistance *in all cases whatsoever*.[1] He was true to himself on this occasion. He submitted with spirit to the spirited remonstrances of the Welch. Mr. Probert gave up his adventure, and keeps his pension— and so ends "the famous history of the revenue adventures of the bold Baron North, and the good Knight Probert, upon the mountains of Venodotia."[2]

In such a state is the exchequer of Wales at present, that, upon the report of the treasury itself, its *little* revenue is *greatly* diminished; and we see by the whole of this strange transaction, that an attempt to improve it, produces resistance; the resistance produces submission; and the whole ends in pension.*

It is nearly the same with the revenues of the dutchy of Lancaster. To do nothing with them is extinction; to improve them is oppression. Indeed, the whole of the estates which support these minor principalities, is made up, not of revenues, and rents, and profitable fines, but of claims, of pretensions, of vexations, of litigations. They are exchequers of unfrequent receipt, and constant charge; a system of finances not fit for an œconomist who would be rich; not fit for a prince who would govern his subjects with equity and justice.

It is not only between prince and subject, that these mock jurisdictions, and mimic revenues, produce great mischief. They excite among the people a spirit of informing, and delating; a spirit of supplanting and undermining one another. So that many in such circumstances, conceive it advantageous to them, rather to continue subject to vexation

---

* Here Lord North shook his head, and told those who sat near him, that Mr. Probert's pension was to depend on his success. It may be so. Mr. Probert's pension was, however, no essential part of the question; nor did Mr. B. care whether he still possessed it or not. His point was, to shew the ridicule of attempting an improvement of the Welsh revenue under its present establishment.

[1] A quotation from the Declaratory Act (6 Geo. III, c. 12).

[2] Venedotia, i.e. North Wales (Gwynedd).

themselves, than to give up the means and chance of vexing others. It is exceedingly common for men to contract their love to their country, into an attachment to its petty subdivisions; and they sometimes even cling to their provincial abuses, as if they were franchises, and local privileges. Accordingly, in places where there is much of this kind of estate, persons will be always found, who would rather trust to their talents in recommending themselves to power for the renewal of their interests, than to incumber their purses, though never so lightly, in order to transmit independence to their posterity. It is a great mistake, that the desire of securing property is universal among mankind. Gaming is a principle inherent in human nature. It belongs to us all. I would therefore break those tables; I would furnish no evil occupation for that spirit; I would make every man look every where, except to the intrigue of a court, for the improvement of his circumstances, or the security of his fortune. I have in my eye a very strong case in the dutchy of Lancaster (which lately occupied Westminster-hall, and the house of lords) as my voucher for many of these reflections.*

For what plausible reason are these principalities suffered to exist? When a government is rendered complex (which in itself is no desirable thing) it ought to be for some political end, which cannot be answered otherwise. Subdivisions in government, are only admissible in favour of the dignity of inferior princes, and high nobility; or for the support of an aristocratic confederacy under some head; or for the conservation of the franchises of the people in some privileged province. Such, for the two former of these ends, are the subdivisions in favour of the electoral, and other princes in the empire; for the latter of these purposes, are the jurisdictions of the imperial cities, and the Hanse towns. For the latter of these ends, are also the countries of the States [*Pais d'Etats*] and certain cities, and orders in France. These are all regulations with an object, and some of them with a very good object. But how are the prin-

* Case of Richard Lee, Esq; Appellant, against George Venables Lord Vernon, Respondent, in the year 1776.[1]

[2] George Venables Vernon, 1st Baron Vernon (1710–80) *v.* Richard Lee (b.c. 1743) of Clytha in Monmouth. Lee lost in the House of Lords (*Lords Journals*, xxxiv. 583–4; *The English Reports in Law and Equity*, 41 vols., Boston, 1851–8, ii. 500–6).

ciples of any of these subdivisions applicable in the case before us?[1]

Do they answer any purpose to the king? The principality of Wales was given by patent to Edward the Black Prince, on the ground on which it has stood ever since.—Lord Coke sagaciously observes upon it, "That in the charter of creating the Black Prince Edward prince of Wales, there is a *great mystery*—for *less* than an estate of inheritance, so *great* a prince *could* not have, and an *absolute estate of inheritance* in so *great* a principality as Wales (this principality being *so dear* to him) he *should* not have; and therefore it was made, *sibi et heredibus suis regibus Angliae*,[2] that by his decease, or attaining to the crown,[3] it might be extinguished in the crown."

For the sake of this foolish *mystery*, of what a great prince *could* not have *less*, and *should* not have *so much*, of a principality which was too *dear* to be given, and too *great* to be kept—and for no other cause, that ever I could find—this form and shadow of a principality without any substance, has been maintained. That you may judge in this instance (and it serves for the rest) of the difference between a great and a little œconomy, you will please to recollect, Sir, that Wales may be about the tenth part of England in size and population; and certainly not a hundredth part in opulence. Twelve judges perform the whole of the business, both of the stationary and the itinerant justice of this kingdom; but for Wales, there are eight judges. There is in Wales an exchequer, as well as in all the dutchies, according to the very best and most authentic absurdity of form. There are in all of them, a hundred more difficult trifles and laborious fooleries, which serve no other purpose than to keep alive corrupt hope and servile dependence.

These principalities are so far from contributing to the ease of the king, to his wealth, or his dignity, that they render both his supreme

[1] Later, in his *Reflections*, he was to tell the leaders of the Revolution that before they had destroyed their system of government they 'had all that combination, and all that opposition of interests ... that action and counteraction which, in the natural and in the political world, from the reciprocal struggle of discordant powers, draws out the harmony of the universe. These opposed and conflicting interests, which you considered as so great a blemish in your old and in our present constitution, interpose a salutary check to all precipitate resolutions; They render deliberation a matter not of choice, but of necessity; they make all change a subject of *compromise*, which naturally begets moderation; they produce *temperaments*, preventing the sore evil of harsh, crude, unqualified reformations; and rendering all the headlong exertions of arbitrary power, in the few or in the many, for ever impracticable. Through that diversity of members and interests, general liberty had as many securities as there were separate views in the several orders; whilst by pressing down the whole by the weight of a real monarchy, the separate parts would have been prevented from warping and starting from their allotted places.' See vol. viii, p. 86.
[2] To himself and to his heirs from the Kings of England.
[3] Sir Edward Coke, *The Fourth Part of the Institutes of the Laws of England*, 5th edn., London, 1671, p. 243.

and his subordinate authority, perfectly ridiculous. It was but the other day, that that pert, factious fellow, the duke of Lancaster, presumed to fly in the face of his liege lord, our gracious sovereign; and *associating with a parcel of lawyers as factious as himself, to the destruction of all law and order*, and *in committees leading directly to rebellion*—presumed to go to law with the king.[1] The object is neither your business, nor mine. Which of the parties got the better, I really forget. I think it was (as it ought to be) the king. The material point is, that the suit cost about fifteen thousand pounds. But as the duke of Lancaster is but a sort of *duke Humphrey*,[2] and not worth a groat, our sovereign was obliged to pay the costs of both. Indeed this art of converting a great monarch into a little prince, this royal masquerading, is a very dangerous and expensive amusement; and one of the king's *menus plaisirs*, which ought to be reformed. This dutchy, which is not worth four thousand pounds a year at best, to *revenue*, is worth forty or fifty thousand to *influence*.

The dutchy of *Lancaster*, and the county palatine of *Lancaster*, answered, I admit, some purpose in their original creation. They tended to make a subject imitate a prince. When *Henry the fourth* from that stair ascended the throne, high-minded as he was, he was not willing to kick away the ladder. To prevent that principality from being extinguished in the crown, he severed it by act of parliament.[3] He had a motive, such as it was. He thought his title to the crown unsound, and his possession insecure. He therefore managed a retreat in his dutchy; which *lord Coke* calls (I do not know why) *par multis regnis*.[4] He flattered himself that it was practicable to make a projecting point half way down, to break his fall from the precipice of royalty; as if it were possible for one who had lost a kingdom to keep any thing else. However, it is evident that he thought so. When *Henry the fifth* united, by act of parliament, the estates of his mother[5] to the dutchy, he had the same predilection with his father, to the root of his family honours,

---

[1] This case has not been found.

[2] 'To dine with Duke Humphrey' meant to go without a meal, from those who, unable to procure a dinner, loitered in Duke Humphrey's Walk in Old St Paul's. Humphrey, Duke of Gloucester (1390–1447) was brother of Henry V.

[3] See Somerville, *History of the Duchy of Lancaster*, i. 138 ff. In the passage which follows Burke is virtually quoting the views of Edmund Plowden (1518–85); see *The Commentaries, on Reports of Edward Plowden of Middle Temple, Esq. An Apprentice of the Common Law containing Diverse Cases upon Matters of Law, Argued and Adjudged in the Several Reigns of King Edward VI, Queen Mary, King and Queen Philip and Mary, and Queen Elizabeth*, London, 1779, p. 215.

[4] The equal of many kingdoms. Coke, *Fourth Part*, p. 205.

[5] Mary de Bohun (*c*.1369–94).

and the same policy in enlarging the sphere of a possible retreat from the slippery royalty of the two great crowns he held.[1] All this was changed by *Edward the fourth*. He had no such family partialities, and his policy was the reverse of that of Henry the fourth and Henry the fifth. He accordingly again united the dutchy of Lancaster to the crown.[2] But when *Henry the seventh*, who chose to consider himself as of the house of Lancaster, came to the throne, he brought with him the old pretensions, and the old politics of that house. A new act of parliament, a second time, dissevered the dutchy of Lancaster from the crown;[3] and in that line things continued until the subversion of the monarchy, when principalities and powers fell along with the throne. The dutchy of Lancaster must have been extinguished, if *Cromwell*,[4] who began to form ideas of aggrandizing his house, and raising the several branches of it, had not caused the dutchy to be again separated from the commonwealth, by an act of the parliament of those times.[5]

What partiality, what objects of the politics of the house of Lancaster, or of Cromwell, has his present majesty, or his majesty's family? What power have they within any of these principalities, which they have not within their kingdom? In what manner is the dignity of the nobility concerned in these principalities? What rights have the subject there, which they have not at least equally in every other part of the nation. These distinctions exist for no good end to the king, to the nobility, or to the people. They ought not to exist at all. If the crown (contrary to its nature, but most conformably to the whole tenor of the advice that has been lately given) should so far forget its dignity, as to contend, that these jurisdictions and revenues are estates of private property, I am rather for acting as if that groundless claim were of some weight, than for giving up that essential part of the reform. I would value the clear income, and give a clear annuity to the crown, taken on the medium produce for twenty years.

If the crown has any favourite name or title, if the subject has any matter of local accommodation within any of these jurisdictions, it is meant to preserve them; and to improve them, if any improvement can be suggested. As to the crown reversions or titles upon the property of the people there, it is proposed to convert them from a snare to their

---

[1] See Somerville, *History of the Duchy of Lancaster*, i. 177 ff.
[2] Ibid. i. 250.
[3] Private Act, 1 Hen. VII, c. 1.
[4] Thomas Cromwell (1485?–1540), 1st Earl of Essex, minister of Henry VIII.
[5] See Somerville, *History of the Duchy of Lancaster*, ii. 50 ff.

independance, into a relief from their burthens. I propose, therefore, to unite all the five principalities to the crown, and to its ordinary jurisdiction, to abolish all those offices that produce an useless and chargeable separation from the body of the people,—to compensate those who do not hold their offices (if any such there are) at the pleasure of the crown,—to extinguish vexatious titles by an act of short limitation,—to sell those unprofitable estates which support useless jurisdictions, and to turn the tenant-right into a fee, on such moderate terms as will be better for the state than its present right, and which it is impossible for any rational tenant to refuse.

As to the Dutchies, their judicial œconomy may be provided for without charge. They have only to fall of course into the common county administration. A commission more or less made or omitted, settles the matter fully. As to Wales, it has been proposed to add a judge to the several courts of Westminster-hall; and it has been considered as an improvement in itself. For my part, I cannot pretend to speak upon it with clearness or with decision; but certainly this arrangement would be more than sufficient for Wales. My original thought was to suppress five of the eight judges; and to leave the chief justice of Chester, with the two senior judges; and, to facilitate the business, to throw the twelve counties into six districts, holding the sessions alternately in the counties of which each district shall be composed. But on this I shall be more clear, when I come to the particular bill.[1]

Sir, the house will now see whether, in praying for judgment against the minor principalities, I do not act in conformity to the laws that I had laid down to myself, of getting rid of every jurisdiction more subservient to oppression and expence, than to any end of justice or honest policy; of abolishing offices more expensive than useful; of combining duties improperly separated; of changing revenues more vexatious than productive, into ready money; of suppressing offices which stand in the way of œconomy; and of cutting off lurking subordinate treasuries. Dispute the rules; controvert the application; or give your hands to this salutary measure.

Most of the same rules will be found applicable to my second object—*the landed estate of the crown.* A landed estate is certainly the

---

[1] The Bill retained the Chief Justice of Chester and one other justice for Chester and six Welsh counties, and two other justices for the other counties of Wales.

very worst which the crown can possess. All minute and dispersed possessions, possessions that are often of indeterminate value, and which require a continued personal attendance, are of a nature more proper for private management, than public administration.—They are fitter for the care of a frugal land steward, than of an office in the state. Whatever they may possibly have been in other times, or in other countries, they are not of magnitude enough with us, to occupy a public department, nor to provide for a public object. They are already given up to parliament, and the gift is not of great value. Common prudence dictates, even in the management of private affairs, that all dispersed and chargeable estates, should be sacrificed to the relief of estates more compact and better circumstanced.

If it be objected, that these lands at present would sell at a low market; this is answered, by shewing that money is at high price. The one balances the other. Lands sell at the current rate, and nothing can sell for more. But be the price what it may, a great object is always answered, whenever any property is transferr'd from hands that are not fit for that property, to those that are. The buyer and seller must mutually profit by such a bargain; and, what rarely happens in matters of revenue, the relief of the subject will go hand in hand with the profit of the exchequer.

As to the *forest lands*, in which the Crown has (where they are not granted or prescriptively held) the *dominion* of the *soil*, and the *vert* and *venison*; that is to say, the timber and the game, and in which the people have a variety of rights, in common of herbage, and other commons, according to the usage of the several forests;—I propose to have those rights of the crown valued as manerial rights are valued on an inclosure; and a defined portion of land to be given for them; which land is to be sold for the public benefit.

As to the timber, I propose a survey of the whole. What is useless for the naval purposes of the kingdom, I would condemn, and dispose of, for the security of what may be useful; and to inclose such other parts as may be most fit to furnish a perpetual supply; wholly extinguishing, for a very obvious reason, all right of *venison* in those parts.

The forest *rights* which extend over the lands and possessions of others, being of no profit to the crown, and a grievance, as far as it goes, to the subject; these I propose to extinguish without charge to the proprietors. The several commons are to be allotted and compensated for upon ideas which I shall hereafter explain. They are nearly the same with the principles upon which you have acted in private inclosures. I shall never quit precedents where I find them applicable. For those regulations and compensations, and for every other part of the detail, you will be so indulgent as to give me credit for the present.

The revenue to be obtained from the sale of the forest lands and rights, will not be so considerable, as many people have imagined; and it would be unwise to screw it up to the utmost; or even to suffer bidders to inhance, according to their eagerness, the purchase of those lands, when the expence of that purchase may weaken the capital to be employed in their cultivation. This, I am well aware, might give room for partiality in the disposal. In my opinion it would be the lesser evil of the two. But surely a rule of fair preference might be established, which would take away all sort of unjust and corrupt partiality. The principal revenue which I propose to draw from these uncultivated wastes, is to spring from the improvement and population of the kingdom; which never can happen, without producing an improvement more advantageous to the revenues of the crown, than the rents of the best landed estate which it can hold. It will hardly be necessary for me to add, that in this sale I naturally except all the houses, gardens, and parks belonging to the crown, and such one forest as shall be chosen by his majesty, as best accommodated to his pleasures.

By means of this part of the reform, will fall the expensive office of *surveyor general*, with all the influence that attends it. By this, will fall *two chief justices in Eyre*, with all their train of dependents. You need be under no apprehension, Sir, that your office is to be touched in its emoluments. They are yours by law; and they are but a moderate part of the compensation which is given to you for the ability with which you execute an office of quite another sort of importance: it is far from overpaying your diligence; or more than sufficient for sustaining the high rank you stand in, as the first gentleman of England. As to the duties of your chief justiceship, they are very different from those for which you have received the office. Your dignity is too high for a jurisdiction over wild beasts; and your learning and talents too valuable to be wasted as chief justice of a desert. I cannot reconcile it to myself, that you, Sir, should be stuck up as a useless piece of antiquity.[1]

I have now disposed of the unprofitable landed estates of the crown, and thrown them into the mass of private property; by which they will

---

[1] The Speaker, Sir Fletcher Norton (1716–89), later (1782) 1st Baron Grantley, M.P. 1756–82, was Chief Justice of Eyre South of the Trent.

come, through the course of circulation, and through the political secretions of the state, into our better understood and better ordered revenues.

I come next to the great supreme body of the civil government itself. I approach it with that awe and reverence with which a young physician approaches to the cure of the disorders of his parent. Disorders, Sir, and infirmities, there are—such disorders, that all attempts towards method, prudence, and frugality, will be perfectly vain, whilst a system of confusion remains, which is not only alien but adverse to all œconomy; a system, which is not only prodigal in its very essence, but causes every thing else which belongs to it to be prodigally conducted.

It is impossible, Sir, for any person to be an œconomist where no order in payments is established; it is impossible for a man to be an œconomist, who is not able to take a comparative view of his means, and of his expences, for the year which lies before him; it is impossible for a man to be an œconomist, under whom various officers in their several departments may spend,—even just what they please,—and often with an emulation of expence, as contributing to the importance, if not profit, of their several departments.—Thus much is certain; that neither the present, nor any other first lord of the treasury, has been ever able to take a survey, or to make even a tolerable guess, of the expences of government for any one year; so as to enable him with the least degree of certainty, or even probability, to bring his affairs within compass. Whatever scheme may be formed upon them, must be made on a calculation of chances. As things are circumstanced, the first lord of the treasury cannot make an estimate. I am sure I serve the king, and I am sure I assist administration, by putting œconomy, at least in their power. We must *class services*; we must (as far as their nature admits) *appropriate* funds; or every thing however reformed, will fall again into the old confusion.

Coming upon this ground of the civil list, the first thing in dignity and charge that attracts our notice, is the *royal household*. This establishment, in my opinion, is exceedingly abusive in its constitution. It is formed upon manners and customs, that have long since expired. In the first place, it is formed, in many respects, upon *feudal principles*. In the feudal times, it was not uncommon, even among subjects, for the lowest offices to be held by considerable persons; persons as unfit by their incapacity, as improper from their rank, to occupy such employments. They were held by patent, sometimes for life, and sometimes by inheritance. If my memory does not deceive me, a person of no slight consideration, held the office of patent hereditary cook to an earl of Warwick[1]—The earl of Warwick's soups, I fear, were not the better for the dignity of his kitchen. I think it was an earl of Gloucester, who officiated as steward of the household to the archbishops of Canterbury.[2] Instances of the same kind may in some degree be found in the Northumberland house-book,[3] and other family records. There was some reason in ancient necessities, for these ancient customs. Protection was wanted; and the domestic tie, though not the highest, was the closest.

The king's household has not only several strong traces of this *feudality*, but it is formed also upon the principles of a *Body-corporate*. It has its own magistrates, courts, and by-laws. This might be necessary in the antient times, in order to have a government within itself, capable of regulating the vast and often unruly multitude which composed and attended it. This was the origin of the antient court called the *Green Cloth*—composed of the marshal, treasurer, and other great officers of the household, with certain clerks. The rich subjects of the kingdom, who had formerly the same establishments (only on a reduced scale) have since altered their œconomy; and turned the course of their expence, from the maintenance of vast establishments within their walls, to the employment of a great variety of independent trades abroad. Their influence is lessened; but a mode of accommodation and a style of splendour, suited to the manners of the times, has been encreased. Royalty itself has insensibly followed; and the royal household has been carried away by the resistless tide of manners: but with this very material difference. Private men have got rid of the establishments along with the reasons of them; whereas the royal household has lost all that was stately and venerable in the antique manners, without retrenching any thing of the cumbrous charge of a Gothic establishment. It is shrunk into the polished littleness of modern elegance and personal accommodation. It has evaporated from

---

[1] Burke may be thinking of the famous banquet at the enthronment of George Neville (*c.*1433–76) as Archbishop of York, at which Richard Neville, 16th Earl of Warwick (1428–71), 'the King-maker', acted as Steward, and other nobles as Treasurer, Comptroller, and Carver (J. Leland, *Collections*, ed. T. Hearne, 6 vols., London, 1774, vi. 2–14).

[2] Richard de Clare, Earl of Gloucester (1222–62), was hereditary Steward of the Archbishop of Canterbury in right of his manor of Tonbridge.

[3] Of Henry Algernon Percy, 4th Earl of Northumberland (1478–1527). It had been published in 1770 by Thomas Percy (1729–81).

the gross concrete, into an essence and rectified spirit of expence, where you have tuns of antient pomp in a vial of modern luxury.

But when the reason of old establishments is gone, it is absurd to preserve nothing but the burthen of them. This is superstitiously to embalm a carcass not worth an ounce of the gums that are used to preserve it. It is to burn precious oils in the tomb; it is to offer meat and drink to the dead,—not so much an honour to the deceased, as a disgrace to the survivors. Our palaces are vast inhospitable halls. There the bleak winds, there, "Boreas, and Eurus, and Caurus, and Argestes loud,"[1] howling through the vacant lobbies, and clattering the doors of deserted guardrooms, appal the imagination, and conjure up the grim spectres of departed tyrants—the Saxon, the Norman, and the Dane; the stern Edwards and fierce Henrys—who stalk from desolation to desolation, through the dreary vacuity, and melancholy succession of chill and comfortless chambers. When this tumult subsides, a dead, and still more frightful silence would reign in this desert, if every now and then the tacking of hammers did not announce, that those constant attendants upon all courts, in all ages, Jobbs, were still alive; for whose sake alone it is, that any trace of ancient grandeur is suffered to remain. These palaces are a true emblem of some governments; the inhabitants are decayed, but the governors and magistrates still flourish. They put me in mind of *Old Sarum*, where the representatives, more in number than the constituents, only serve to inform us, that this was once a place of trade, and sounding with "the busy hum of men,"[2] though now you can only trace the streets by the colour of the corn; and its sole manufacture is in members of parliament.[3]

These old establishments were formed also on a third principle, still more adverse to the living œconomy of the age. They were formed, Sir, on the principle of *purveyance*, and *receipt in kind*. In former days, when the household was vast, and the supply scanty and precarious, the royal purveyors, sallying forth from under the Gothic portcullis, to purchase provision with power and prerogative, instead of money, brought home the plunder of an hundred markets, and all that could be seized from a flying and hiding country, and deposited their spoil in an hundred caverns, with each its keeper. There, every commodity,

[1] *Paradise Lost*, x. 699.

[2] Milton, *L'Allegro*, 118.

[3] Old Sarum was a burgage borough, all the burgages being owned by the Pitt family. The number of voters is given as seven in Namier and Brooke.

received in its rawest condition, went through all the process which fitted it for use. This inconvenient receipt produced an œconomy suited only to itself. It multiplied offices beyond all measure; buttery, pantry, and all that rabble of places, which, though profitable to the holders and expensive to the state, are almost too mean to mention.

All this might be, and I believe was necessary at first; for it is remarkable, that *purveyance*, after its regulation had been the subject of a long line of statutes, (not fewer, I think, than twenty-six) was wholly taken away by the twelfth of Charles the second; yet in the next year of the same reign, it was found necessary to revive it by a special act of parliament, for the sake of the king's journies.[1] This, Sir, is curious; and what would hardly be expected in so reduced a court as that of Charles the second, and in so improved a country as England might then be thought. But so it was. In our time, one well filled and well covered stage-coach, requires more accommodation than a royal progress; and every district at an hour's warning, can supply an army.

I do not say, Sir, that all these establishments whose principle is gone, have been systematically kept up for influence solely: neglect had its share. But this I am sure of, that a consideration of influence has hindered any one from attempting to pull them down. For the purposes of influence, and for those purposes only, are retained half at least of the household establishments. No revenue, no not a royal revenue, can exist under the accumulated charge of antient establishment; modern luxury; and parliamentary political corruption.

If therefore we aim at regulating this household, the question will be, whether we ought to œconomize by *detail*, or by *principle*? The example we have had of the success of an attempt to œconomize by detail, and under establishments adverse to the attempt, may tend to decide this question.

At the beginning of his majesty's reign, Lord Talbot[2] came to the administration of a great department in the household. I believe no man ever entered into his majesty's service, or into the service of any prince, with a more clear integrity, or with more zeal and affection for the interest of his master; and I must add, with abilities for a still higher service. Œconomy was then announced as a maxim of the reign.

---

[1] The index of Ruffhead's *Statutes at Large* suggests that Burke underestimates dealing with purveyance. The two statutes specifically referred to are 12 Car. II, c. 24, and 13 Car. II, stat. 1, c. 8.
[2] William Talbot, 1st Earl Talbot (1710–82), Lord Steward of the Household.

This noble lord, therefore, made several attempts towards a reform. In the year 1777, when the king's civil list debts came last to be paid, he explained very fully the success of his undertaking. He told the house of lords, that he had attempted to reduce the charges of the king's tables, and his kitchen.—The thing, Sir, was not below him. He knew, that there is nothing interesting in the concerns of men, whom we love and honour, that is beneath our attention.—"Love," says one of our old poets, "esteems no office mean;" and with still more spirit, "Entire affection scorneth nicer hands."[1] Frugality, Sir, is founded on the principle, that all riches have limits. A royal household, grown enormous, even in the meanest departments, may weaken and perhaps destroy all energy in the highest offices of the state. The gorging a royal kitchen may stint and famish the negotiations of a kingdom. Therefore, the object was worthy of his, was worthy of any man's attention.

In consequence of this noble lord's resolution, (as he told the other house) he reduced several tables, and put the persons entitled to them upon board wages, much to their own satisfaction. But unluckily, subsequent duties requiring constant attendance, it was not possible to prevent their being fed where they were employed—and thus this first step towards œconomy doubled the expence.

There was another disaster far more doleful than this. I shall state it, as the cause of that misfortune lies at the bottom of almost all our prodigality. Lord Talbot attempted to reform the kitchen; but such, as he well observed, is the consequence of having duty done by one person, whilst another enjoys the emoluments, that he found himself frustrated in all his designs. On that rock his whole adventure split— His whole scheme of œconomy was dashed to pieces; his department became more expensive than ever;—the civil list debt accumulated— Why? It was truly from a cause, which, though perfectly adequate to the effect, one would not have instantly guessed;—It was because the *turnspit in the king's kitchen was a member of parliament.** The king's domestic servants were all undone; his tradesmen remained unpaid, and became bankrupt—*because the turnspit of the kings kitchen was a member of parliament.* His majesty's slumbers were interrupted, his

---

* *Vide* Lord Talbot's speech, in Almon's Parliamentary Register, vol. vii. p. 79 of the Proceedings of the Lords.[2]

[1] The source of the first quotation has not been found; the second is from Spenser, *Faerie Queene*, I. vii. 40.

[2] Talbot may not have intended to be taken literally. If an M.P. was a turnspit he has not been identified.

pillow was stuffed with thorns, and his peace of mind entirely broken,—
because the king's turnspit was a member of parliament. The judges were
unpaid; the justice of the kingdom bent and gave way; the foreign
ministers remained inactive and unprovided; the system of Europe was
dissolved; the chain of our alliances was broken; all the wheels of
government at home and abroad were stopped;—*because the king's
turnspit was a member of parliament.*

Such, Sir, was the situation of affairs, and such the cause of that
situation, when his majesty came a second time to parliament, to desire
the payment of those debts which the employment of its members in
various offices, visible and invisible, had occasioned. I believe that a
like fate will attend every attempt at œconomy by detail, under similar
circumstances, and in every department. A complex operose office of
account and controul, is in itself, and even if members of parliament
had nothing to do with it, the most prodigal of all things. The most
audacious robberies, or the most subtle frauds, would never venture
upon such a waste, as an over careful, detailed guard against them will
infallibly produce. In our establishments, we frequently see an office of
account, of an hundred pounds a year expence, and another office, of
an equal expence, to controul that office, and the whole upon a matter
that is not worth twenty shillings.

To avoid, therefore, this minute care which produces the consequences of the most extensive neglect, and to oblige members of
parliament to attend to public cares, and not to the servile offices of
domestic management, I propose, Sir, to *œconomize by principle*, that is, I
propose, to put affairs into that train, which experience points out as
the most effectual, from the nature of things, and from the constitution
of the human mind. In all dealings, where it is possible, the principles
of radical œconomy prescribe three things; first, undertaking by the
great; secondly, engaging with persons of skill in the subject matter;
thirdly, engaging with those who shall have an immediate and direct
interest in the proper execution of the business.

To avoid frittering and crumbling down the attention, by a blind
unsystematic observance of every trifle, it has ever been found the best
way, to do all things, which are great in the total amount, and minute
in the component parts, by a *general contract*. The principles of trade
have so pervaded every species of dealing, from the highest to the
lowest objects; all transactions are got so much into system; that we
may, at a moment's warning, and to a farthing value, be informed at

what rate any service may be supplied. No dealing is exempt from the possibility of fraud. But by a contract on a matter certain, you have this advantage—you are sure to know the utmost *extent* of the fraud to which you are subject. By a contract with a person in *his own trade*, you are sure you shall not suffer by *want of skill*. By a *short* contract you are sure of making it the *interest* of the contractor to exert that skill for the satisfaction of his employers.

I mean to derogate nothing from the diligence or integrity of the present, or of any former board of green-cloth. But what skill can members of parliament obtain in that low kind of province? What pleasure can they have in the execution of that kind of duty? And if they should neglect it, how does it affect their interest, when we know, that it is their vote in parliament, and not their diligence in cookery or catering, that recommends them to their office, or keeps them in it?

I therefore propose, that the king's tables (to whatever number of tables, or covers to each, he shall think proper to command) should be classed by the steward of the household, and should be contracted for, according to their rank, by the head or cover;—that the estimate and circumstance of the contract should be carried to the treasury to be approved; and that its faithful and satisfactory performance should be reported there, previous to any payment; that there, and there only, should the payment be made. I propose, that men should be contracted with only in their proper trade; and that no member of parliament should be capable of such contract. By this plan, almost all the infinite offices under the lord steward may be spared; to the extreme simplification, and to the far better execution, of every one of his functions. The king of Prussia is so served. He is a great and eminent (though indeed a very rare) instance of the possibility of uniting in a mind of vigour and compass, an attention to minute objects, with the largest views, and the most complicated plans. His tables are served by contract, and by the head. Let me say, that no prince can be ashamed to imitate the king of Prussia;[1] and particularly to learn in his school, when the problem is—"The best manner of reconciling the state of a court with the support of war?"[2] Other courts, I understand, have followed him with effect, and to their satisfaction.

The same clue of principle leads us through the labyrinth of the

---

[1] Frederick II, the Great (1712–86).
[2] The source of this quotation has not been found.

other departments. What, Sir, is there in the office of *the great wardrobe* (which has the care of the king's furniture) that may not be executed by the *lord chamberlain* himself. He has an honourable appointment; he has time sufficient to attend to the duty; and he has the vice chamberlain to assist him. Why should not he deal also by contract, for all things belonging to this office, and carry his estimates first, and his report of the execution in its proper time, for payment, directly to the board of treasury itself? By a simple operation (containing in it a treble control) the expences of a department, which for naked walls, or walls hung with cobwebs, has in a few years cost the crown £150,000,[1] may at length hope for regulation. But, Sir, the office and its business are at variance. As it stands, it serves, not to furnish the palace with its hangings, but the parliament with its dependent members.

To what end, Sir, does the office of *removing wardrobe* serve at all? Why should a *jewel office* exist for the sole purpose of taxing the king's gifts of plate? Its object falls naturally within the *chamberlain's* province; and ought to be under his care and inspection, without any fee. Why should an office of the *robes* exist, when that of *groom of the stole* is a sinecure, and that this is a proper object of his department?

All these incumbrances, which are themselves nusances, produce other incumbrances, and other nusances. For the payment of these useless establishments, there are no less than *three useless treasurers*; two to hold a purse, and one to play with a stick. The treasurer of the household is a mere name. The cofferer, and the treasurer of the chamber, receive and pay great sums, which it is not at all necessary *they* should either receive or pay. All the proper officers, servants, and tradesmen, may be inrolled in their several departments, and paid in proper classes and times with great simplicity and order, at the exchequer, and by direction from the treasury.

The *board of works*, which in the seven years preceding 1777, has cost towards £400,000;* and (if I recollect rightly) has not cost less in proportion from the beginning of the reign, is under the very same description of all the other ill-contrived establishments, and calls for the very same reform. We are to seek for the visible signs of all this

* More exactly £378,616. 10s. 1d.¾.[2]

[1] Accounts at Sheffield (R.133.3), presumably used by Burke, demonstrate that payments to the Great Wardrobe from January 1769 to January 1777 totalled £141,314. 10s. 2d.

[2] For the expenditure of the Offices of Works (though not the precise account Burke cites), see H. M. Colvin et al., *The History of the King's Works*, 6 vols., London, 1963–82, v. 114–15.

expence.—For all this expence, we do not see a building of the size and importance of a pigeon-house. Buckingham-house was reprised by a bargain with the public, for one hundred thousand pounds;[1]—and the small house at Windsor has been, if I mistake not, undertaken since that account was brought before us.[2] The good works of that board of works, are as carefully concealed, as other good works ought to be. They are perfectly invisible. But though it is the perfection of charity to be concealed, it is, Sir, the property and glory of magnificence, to appear, and stand forward to the eye.

That board, which ought to be a concern of builders, and such like, and none else, is turned into a junto of members of parliament. That office too has a *treasury*, and a paymaster of its own; and lest the arduous affairs of that important exchequer should be too fatiguing, that paymaster has a deputy to partake his profits, and relieve his cares. I do not believe, that either now or in former times, the chief managers of that board have made any profit of its abuse. It is, however, no good reason that an abusive establishment should subsist, because it is of as little private as of public advantage. But this establishment has the grand radical fault, the original sin, that pervades and perverts all our establishments;—The apparatus is not fitted to the object, nor the workmen to the work. Expences are incurred on the private opinion of an inferior establishment, without consulting the principal; who can alone determine the proportion which it ought to bear to the other establishments of the state, in the order of their relative importance.

I propose, therefore, along with the rest, to pull down this whole ill-contrived scaffolding, which obstructs, rather than forwards our public works; to take away its treasury; to put the whole into the hands of a real builder, who shall not be a member of parliament; and to oblige him by a previous estimate and final payment, to appear twice at the treasury, before the public can be loaded. The king's gardens are to come under a similar regulation.

The *mint*, though not a department of the household, has the same vices. It is a great expence to the nation, chiefly for the sake of members of parliament.[3] It has its officers of parade and dignity. It

---

[1] See Burke's speech of 28 April 1775 on Somerset House, above, pp. 169–71.

[2] Alterations to the Queen's Lodge (previously the Garden House) had begun in 1776 (Colvin et al., *The History of the King's Works*, v. 338).

[3] For the mint as a source of patronage, see Sir John Craig, *The Mint*, Cambridge, 1953, pp. 223–38.

has its treasury too. It is a sort of corporate body; and formerly was a body of great importance; as much so, on the then scale of things, and the then order of business, as the bank is at this day. It was the great center of money transactions and remittances for our own, and for other nations; until king Charles the first, among other arbitrary projects, dictated by despotic necessity, made him withhold the money that lay there for remittance.[1] That blow, (and happily too) the mint never recover'd. Now it is no bank; no remittance-shop. The mint, Sir, is a *manufacture*, and it is nothing else; and it ought to be undertaken upon the principles of a manufacture; that is, for the best and cheapest execution, by a contract, upon proper securities, and under proper regulations.

The *artillery* is a far greater object; it is a military concern; but having an affinity and kindred in its defects with the establishments I am now speaking of, I think it best to speak of it along with them. It is, I conceive, an establishment not well suited to its martial, though exceedingly well calculated for its parliamentary purposes.—Here there is a *treasury*, as in all the other inferior departments of government. Here the military is subordinate to the civil, and the naval confounded with the land service. The object indeed is much the same in both. But when the detail is examined, it will be found that they had better be separated. For a reform of this office, I propose to restore things, to what (all considerations taken together) is their natural order; to restore them to their just proportion, and to their just distribution. I propose, in this military concern, to render the civil subordinate to the military; and this will annihilate the greatest part of the expence, and all the influence belonging to the office. I propose to send the military branch to the army, and the naval to the Admiralty: and I intend to perfect and accomplish the whole detail (where it becomes too minute and complicated for legislature, and requires exact, official, military, and mechanical knowledge) by a commission of competent officers in both departments. I propose to execute by contract, what by contract can be executed, and to bring, as much as possible, all estimates to be previously approved, and finally to be paid by the treasury.

Thus, by following the course of nature, and not the purposes of politics, or the accumulated patchwork of occasional accommodation,

---

[1] Charles I seized £100,000 at the mint in 1640 (J. S. Kepler, *The Exchange of Christendom: The International Entrepot at Dover*, Leicester, 1976, p. 69).

this vast expensive department may be methodized; its service proportioned to its necessities; and its payments subjected to the inspection of
the superior minister of finance; who is to judge of it on the result of
the total collective exigencies of the state. This last is a reigning
principle through my whole plan; and it is a principle which I hope
may hereafter be applied to other plans.

By these regulations taken together—besides the three subordinate
treasuries in the lesser principalities, five other subordinate treasuries
are suppressed. There is taken away the whole *establishment of detail*
in the household; the *treasurer*;—the *comptroller* (for a comptroller
is hardly necessary where there is no treasurer) the *cofferer of the
household*;—the *treasurer of the chamber*;—the *master of the household*;—
the whole *board of green cloth*;—and a vast number of subordinate
offices in the department of the *steward of the household*;—the whole
establishment of the *great wardrobe*;—the *removing wardrobe*;—the *jewel
office*;—the *robes*;—the *board of works*; almost the whole charge of the
civil branch of the *board of ordnance*, are taken away. All these arrangements together will be found to relieve the nation from a vast weight of
influence, without distressing, but rather by forwarding every public
service. When something of this kind is done, then the public may
begin to breathe. Under other governments, a question of expence
is only a question of œconomy, and it is nothing more; with us in
every question of expence, there is always a mixture of constitutional
considerations.

It is, Sir, because I wish to keep this business of subordinate
treasuries as much as I can together, that I brought the *ordnance-office*
before you, though it is properly a military department. For the same
reason I will now trouble you with my thoughts and propositions upon
two of the greatest *under treasuries*, I mean the office of *paymaster of the
land forces* or *treasurer of the army*; and that of the *treasurer of the navy*.
The former of these has long been a great object of public suspicion
and uneasiness. Envy too has had its share in the obloquy which is
cast upon this office. But I am sure that it has no share at all in
the reflections I shall make upon it, or in the reformations that I
shall propose. I do not grudge to the honourable gentleman who at
present holds the office,[1] any of the effects of his talents, his merit, or

---

[1] Richard Rigby.

his fortune. He is respectable in all these particulars. I follow the constitution of the office, without persecuting its holder. It is necessary, in
all matters of public complaint, where men frequently feel right and
argue wrong, to seperate prejudice from reason; and to be very sure,
in attempting the redress of a grievance, that we hit upon its real seat,
and its true nature. Where there is an abuse in office, the first thing
that occurs in heat is to censure the officer. Our natural disposition
leads all our enquiries rather to persons than to things. But this
prejudice is to be corrected by maturer thinking.

Sir, the profits of the *pay-office* (as an office) are not too great, in my
opinion, for its duties, and for the rank of the person who has generally
held it. He has been generally a person of the highest rank; that is to
say, a person of eminence and consideration in this house. The great
and the invidious profits of the pay-office, are from the *Bank* that is
held in it. According to the present course of the office, and according
to the present mode of accounting there, this bank must necessarily
exist somewhere. Money is a productive thing; and when the usual
time of its demand can be tolerably calculated, it may, with prudence,
be safely laid out to the profit of the holder. It is on this calculation,
that the business of banking proceeds. But no profit can be derived
from the use of money, which does not make it the interest of the
holder to delay his account. The process of the exchequer colludes
with this interest. Is this collusion from its want of rigour, and strictness, and great regularity of form? The reverse is true. They have in
the exchequer brought rigour and formalism to their ultimate perfection. The process against accountants is so rigorous, and in a manner
so unjust, that correctives must, from time to time, be applied to it.
These correctives being discretionary, upon the case, and generally
remitted by the barons to the lords of the treasury, as the best judges
of the reasons for respite, hearings are had; delays are produced; and
thus the extreme of rigour in office (as usual in all human affairs) leads
to the extreme of laxity. What with the interested slowness of the
officer; the ill-conceived exactness of the court; the applications for
dispensations from that exactness, the revival of rigorous process, after
the expiration of the time; and the new rigours producing new applications, and new enlargements of time, such delays happen in the public
accounts, that they can scarcely ever be closed.

Besides, Sir, they have a rule in the exchequer, which, I believe, they have founded upon a very ancient statute, that of the 51st of Henry III. by which it is provided, "That when a sheriff or bailiff hath began his account, none other shall be received to account, until he that was first appointed hath clearly accounted, and that the sum has been received."* Whether this clause of that statute be the ground of that absurd practice, I am not quite able to ascertain. But it has very generally prevailed, though I am told that of late they have began to relax from it. In consequence of forms adverse to substantial account, we have a long succession of pay-masters and their representatives, who have never been admitted to account, although perfectly ready to do so.

As the extent of our wars has scattered the accountants under the pay-master into every part of the globe, the grand and sure pay-master, Death, in all his shapes, calls these accountants to another reckoning. Death, indeed, domineers over every thing, but the forms of the exchequer. Over these he has no power. They are impassive and immortal. The audit of the exchequer, more severe than the audit to which the accountants are gone, demands proofs which in the nature of things are difficult, sometimes impossible to be had. In this respect, too, rigour, as usual, defeats itself. Then, the exchequer never gives a particular receipt, or clears a man of his account, as far as it goes. A final acquittance (or a *quietus*, as they term it) is scarcely ever to be obtained. Terrors and ghosts of unlaid accountants, haunt the houses of their children from generation to generation. Families, in the course of succession, fall into minorities; the inheritance comes into the hands of females; and very perplexed affairs are often delivered over into the hands of negligent guardians, and faithless stewards. So that the demand remains, when the advantage of the money is gone, if ever any advantage at all has been made of it. This is a cause of infinite distress to families; and becomes a source of influence to an extent, that can scarcely be imagined, but by those who have taken some pains to trace it. The mildness of government in the employment of useless and dangerous powers, furnishes no reason for their continuance.

As things stand, can you in justice (except perhaps in that over-perfect kind of justice which has obtained, by its merits, the title of

---

* Et quant viscount ou bailliff ait commence de accompter, nul autre ne seit resceu de acconter tanque le primer qe soit assis, eit peraccompte, et qe la somme soit resceu. Stat. 5.ann. dom. 1266.[1]

[1] Statutum de Scaccario (51 Hen. III, stat. 5, sect. vii).

the opposite vice*) insist that any man should, by the course of his
office, keep a *bank* from whence he is to derive no advantage? That a
man should be subject to demands below, and be in a manner refused
an acquittance above; that he should transmit an original sin, and
inheritance of vexation to his posterity, without a power of compensat-
ing himself in some way or other, for so perilous a situation? We know,
that if the pay-master should deny himself the advantages of his bank,
the public, as things stand, is not the richer for it by a single shilling.
This I thought it necessary to say, as to the offensive magnitude of the
profits of this office; that we may proceed in reformation on the
principles of reason, and not on the feelings of envy.

The treasurer of the navy[1] is, *mutatis mutandis*, in the same circumstances. Indeed all accountants are. Instead of the present mode, which
is troublesome to the officer, and unprofitable to the public, I propose
to substitute something more effectual than rigour, which is the worst
exactor in the world. I mean to remove the very temptations to delay;
to facilitate the account; and to transfer this bank, now of private
emolument, to the public. The crown will suffer no wrong at least from
the pay offices; and its terrors will no longer reign over the families of
those who hold or have held them. I propose, that these offices should
be no longer *banks* or *treasuries*, but mere *offices of administration.*—I
propose, first, that the present paymaster and the treasurer of the navy,
should carry into the exchequer the whole body of the vouchers for
what they have paid over to deputy paymasters, to regimental agents, or
to any of those to whom they have and ought to have paid money. I
propose that those vouchers shall be admitted as actual payments in
their accounts; and that the persons to whom the money has been paid,
shall then stand charged in the exchequer in their place. After this
process, they shall be debited or charged for nothing but the money-
balance that remains in their hands.

I am conscious, Sir, that if this balance (which they could not expect
to be so suddenly demanded by any usual process of the exchequer)
should now be exacted all at once, not only their ruin, but a ruin of
others to an extent which I do not like to think of, but which I can well
conceive, and which you may well conceive, might be the consequence.

* Summum jus summa injuria.[2]
[1] Richard Rigby and Welbore Ellis.
[2] The extremity of the law is the extremity of injustice; a maxim quoted by Cicero, *De Officiis*,
I. x. 33.

I told you, Sir, when I promised before the holydays to bring in this plan, that I never would suffer any man, or description of men, to suffer from errors that naturally have grown out of the abusive constitution of those offices which I propose to regulate. If I cannot reform with equity, I will not reform at all.[1]

For the regulation of past accounts, I shall therefore propose such a mode, as men, temperate and prudent, make use of in the management of their private affairs, when their accounts are various, perplexed, and of long standing. I would therefore, after their example, divide the public debts into three sorts; good; bad; and doubtful. In looking over the public accounts, I should never dream of the blind mode of the exchequer, which regards things in the abstract, and knows no difference in the quality of its debts, or the circumstances of its debtors. By this means, it fatigues itself; it vexes others; it often crushes the poor; it lets escape the rich; or in a fit of mercy or carelessness, declines all means of recovering its just demands. Content with the eternity of its claims, it enjoys its Epicurean divinity with Epicurean languor. But it is proper that all sorts of accounts should be closed some time or other—by payment; by composition; or by oblivion. *Expedit reipublicæ ut sit finis litium.*[2] Constantly taking along with me, that an extreme rigour is sure to arm every thing against it, and at length to relax into a supine neglect, I propose, Sir, that even the best, soundest, and the most recent debts, should be put into instalments, for the mutual benefit of the accountant and the public.

In proportion, however, as I am tender of the past, I would be provident of the future. All money that was formerly imprested to the two great *pay-offices*, I would have imprested in future to the *bank of England*. These offices should, in future, receive no more than cash sufficient for small payments. Their other payments ought to be made by drafts on the Bank, expressing the service. A cheque account from both offices, of drafts and receipts, should be annually made up in the exchequer, charging the bank, in account, with the cash-balance, but not demanding the payment until there is an order from the treasury, in consequence of a vote of parliament.

As I did not, Sir, deny to the paymaster the natural profits of the bank that was in his hands, so neither would I to the bank of England. A share of that profit might be derived to the public in various ways.

---

[1] In his speech of 15 December 1779, printed above.
[2] 'It is expedient for the state that there should be an end to litigation.'

My favourite mode is this; that, in compensation for the use of this money, the bank may take upon themselves, first, *the charge of the mint*; to which they are already, by their charter, obliged to bring in a great deal of bullion annually to be coined.

In the next place, I mean that they should take upon themselves the charge of *remittances to our troops abroad*. This is a species of dealing from which, by the same charter, they are not debarred. One and a quarter *per cent*. will be saved instantly thereby to the public, on very large sums of money. This will be at once a matter of œconomy, and a considerable reduction of influence, by taking away a private contract of an expensive nature. If the bank, which is a great corporation, and of course receives the least profits from the money in their custody, should of itself refuse, or be persuaded to refuse, this offer upon those terms, I can speak with some confidence, that one at least, if not both parts of the condition would be received, and gratefully received, by several bankers of eminence. There is no banker who will not be at least as good security as any paymaster of the forces, or any treasurer of the navy, that have ever been bankers to the public: as rich at least as my lord Chatham, or my lord Holland,[1] or either of the honourable gentlemen, who now hold the offices,[2] were, at the time that they entered into them; or as ever the whole establishment of the *mint* has been at any period.

These, Sir, are the outlines of the plan I mean to follow, in suppressing these two large subordinate treasuries. I now come to another subordinate treasury; I mean, that of the *paymaster of the pensions*; for which purpose I re-enter the limits of the civil establishment—I departed from those limits in pursuit of a principle; and following the same game in its doubles, I am brought into those limits again. That treasury, and that office, I mean to take away; and to transfer the payment of every name, mode, and denomination of pensions, to the *exchequer*. The present course of diversifying the same object, can answer no good purpose; whatever its use may be to purposes of another kind. There are also other lists of pensions; and I mean that they should all be hereafter paid at one and the same place. The whole of that new consolidated list, I mean to reduce to £60,000 a year, which sum I intend it shall never exceed. I think that sum will fully

---

[1] Henry Fox, 1st Baron Holland (1705–74).
[2] Richard Rigby and Welbore Ellis.

answer as a reward to all real merit, and a provision for all real public charity that is ever like to be placed upon the list. If any merit of an extraordinary nature should emerge, before that reduction is completed, I have left it open for an address of either house of parliament to provide for the case. To all other demands, it must be answered, with regret, but with firmness, "the public is poor."

I do not propose, as I told you before Christmas, to take away any pension. I know that the public seem to call for a reduction of such of them as shall appear unmerited. As a censorial act, and punishment of an abuse, it might answer some purpose. But this can make no part of *my* plan. I mean to proceed by bill; and I cannot stop for such an enquiry. I know some gentlemen may blame me. It is with great submission to better judgments, that I recommend it to consideration; that a critical retrospective examination of the pension list, upon the principle of merit, can never serve for my basis.—It cannot answer, according to my plan, any effectual purpose of œconomy, or of future permanent reformation. The process, in any way, will be entangled and difficult; and it will be infinitely slow: There is a danger that if we turn our line of march, now directed towards the grand object, into this more laborious than useful detail of operations, we shall never arrive at our end.

The king, Sir, has been, by the constitution, appointed sole judge of the merit for which a pension is to be given. We have a right, undoubtedly, to canvass this, as we have to canvass every act of government. But there is a material difference between an office to be reformed, and a pension taken away for demerit. In the former case, no charge is implied against the holder; in the latter, his character is slurred, as well as his lawful emolument affected. The former process is against the thing; the second against the person. The pensioner certainly, if he pleases, has a right to stand on his own defence; to plead his possession; and to bottom his title in the competency of the crown to give him what he holds. Possessed, and on the defensive as he is, he will not be obliged to prove his special merit, in order to justify the act of legal discretion, now turned into his property, according to his tenure. The very act, he will contend, is a legal presumption, and an implication of his merit. If this be so (from the natural force of all legal presumption) he would put us to the difficult proof, that he has no merit at all. But other questions would arise in the course of such an enquiry; that is, questions of the merit when weighed against the proportion of the reward; then the difficulty will be much greater.

The difficulty will not, Sir, I am afraid, be much less, if we pass to the person really guilty, in the question of an unmerited pension; the minister himself. I admit, that when called to account for the execution of a trust, he might fairly be obliged to prove the affirmative; and to state the merit for which the pension is given; though on the pensioner himself, such a process would be hard. If in this examination we proceed methodically, and so as to avoid all suspicion of partiality and prejudice, we must take the pensions in order of time, or merely alphabetically. The very first pension to which we come, in either of these ways, may appear the most grossly unmerited of any. But the minister may very possibly shew, that he knows nothing of the putting on this pension—that it was prior in time to his administration—that the minister, who laid it on, is dead; and then we are thrown back upon the pensioner himself, and plunged into all our former difficulties. Abuses, and gross ones, I doubt not, would appear; and to the correction of which I would readily give my hand; but, when I consider that pensions have not generally been affected by the revolutions of ministry; as I know not where such enquiries would stop; and as an absence of merit is a negative and loose thing, one might be led to derange the order of families, founded on the probable continuance of their kind of income. I might hurt children; I might injure creditors. I really think it the more prudent course, not to follow the letter of the petitions. If we fix this mode of enquiry as a basis, we shall, I fear, end, as parliament has often ended under similar circumstances. There will be great delay; much confusion; much inequality in our proceedings. But what presses me most of all is this; that though we should strike off all the unmerited pensions, while the power of the crown remains unlimited, the very same undeserving persons might afterwards return to the very same list: or if they did not, other persons, meriting as little as they do, might be put upon it to an undefinable amount. This I think is the pinch of the grievance.

For these reasons, Sir, I am obliged to wave this mode of proceeding as any part of my plan. In a plan of reformation, it would be one of my maxims, that when I know of an establishment which may be subservient to useful purposes, and which at the same time, from its discretionary nature, is liable to a very great perversion from those purposes, *I would limit the quantity of the power that might be so abused.*

For I am sure, that in all such cases, the rewards of merit will have very narrow bounds; and that partial or corrupt favour will be infinite. This principle is not arbitrary; but the limitation of the specific quantity must be so in some measure. I therefore state £60,000; leaving it open to the house to enlarge or contract the sum as they shall see, on examination, that the discretion I use is scanty or liberal. The whole amount of the pensions of all denominations, which have been laid before us, amount, for a period of seven years, to considerably more than £100,000 a year. To what the other lists amount, I know not. That will be seen hereafter. But from those that do appear, a saving will accrue to the public, at one time or other, of £40,000 a year, and we had better in my opinion to let it fall in naturally, than to tear it crude and unripe from the stalk.*

There is a great deal of uneasiness among the people, upon an article which I must class under the head of pensions. I mean the *great patent offices in the exchequer*. They are in reality and substance no other than pensions, and in no other light shall I consider them. They are sinecures. They are always executed by deputy. The duty of the principal is as nothing. They differ however from the pensions on the list, in some particulars. They are held for life. I think with the public, that the profits of those places are grown enormous; the magnitude of those profits, and the nature of them, both call for reformation. The nature of their profits which grow out of the public distress, is itself invidious and grievous. But I fear that reform cannot be immediate. I find myself under a restriction. These places, and others of the same kind, which are held for life, have been considered as property. They have been given as a provision for children; they have been the subject of family settlements; they have been the security of creditors. What the law respects shall be sacred to me. If the barriers of law should be broken down, upon ideas of convenience, even of public convenience, we shall have no longer any thing certain among us. If the discretion of power is once let loose upon property, we can be at no loss to determine whose power, and what discretion it is that will prevail at last. It would be wise to attend upon the order of things; and not to

* It was supposed by the Lord Advocate, in a subsequent debate, that Mr. Burke, because he objected to an enquiry into the pension list for the purpose of œconomy and relief of the public, would have it withheld from the judgment of parliament for all purposes whatsoever. This learned gentleman certainly misunderstood him. His plan shews, that he wished the whole list to be easily accessible; and he knows that the public eye is of itself a great guard against abuse.[1]
[1] Probably a reference to the speech of Henry Dundas on 21 February (*Parl. Reg.* xvii. 137–8).

attempt to outrun the slow, but smooth and even course of nature. There are occasions, I admit, of public necessity, so vast, so clear, so evident, that they supersede all laws. Law being only made for the benefit of the community cannot in any one of its parts, resist a demand which may comprehend the total of the public interest. To be sure, no law can set itself up against the cause and reason of all law. But such a case very rarely happens; and this most certainly is not such a case. The mere time of the reform is by no means worth the sacrifice of a principle of law. Individuals pass like shadows; but the common-wealth is fixed and stable. The difference therefore of to-day and to-morrow, which to private people is immense, to the state is nothing. At any rate it is better, if possible, to reconcile our œconomy with our laws, than to set them at variance; a quarrel which in the end must be destructive to both.

My idea, therefore, is to reduce those offices to fixed salaries, as the present lives and reversions shall successively fall. I mean, that the office of the great auditor (the auditor of the receipt) shall be reduced to £3,000 a year; and the auditors of the imprest and the rest of the principal officers, to fixed appointments of £1,500 a year each. It will not be difficult to calculate the value of this fall of lives to the public, when we shall have obtained a just account of the present income of those places; and we shall obtain that account with great facility, if the present possessors are not alarmed with any apprehension of danger to their freehold office.

I know too, that it will be demanded of me, how it comes, that since I admit these offices to be no better than pensions, I chose, after the principle of law had been satisfied, to retain them at all? To this, Sir, I answer, that conceiving it to be a fundamental part of the constitution of this country, and of the reason of state in every country, that there must be means of rewarding public service, those means will be incomplete, and indeed wholly insufficient for that purpose, if there should be no further reward for that service, than the daily wages it receives during the pleasure of the crown.

Whoever seriously considers the excellent argument of Lord Somers, in the banker's case,[1] will see he bottoms himself upon the very same maxim which I do; and one of his principal grounds of

---

[1] The judgment of Lord Chancellor Somers, in the Banker's Case of 1700 is in T. B. Howell, ed., *A Complete Collection of State Trials*, 33 vols., London, 1816–28, xiv. 2–114.

doctrine for the alienability of the domain in England* contrary to the maxim of the law in France, he lays in the constitutional policy, of furnishing a permanent reward to public service; of making that reward the origin of families; and the foundation of wealth as well as of honours. It is indeed the only genuine unadulterated origin of nobility. It is a great principle in government; a principle at the very foundation of the whole structure. The other judges who held the same doctrine, went beyond Lord Somers with regard to the remedy, which they thought was given by law against the crown, upon the grant of pensions. Indeed no man knows, when he cuts off the incitements to a virtuous ambition, and the just rewards of public service, what infinite mischief he may do his country, through all generations. Such saving to the public may prove the worst mode of robbing it. The crown, which has in its hands the trust of the daily pay for national service, ought to have in its hands also the means for the repose of public labour, and the fixed settlement of acknowledged merit. There is a time, when the weather-beaten vessels of the state, ought to come into harbour. They must at length have a retreat from the malice of rivals, from the perfidy of political friends, and the inconstancy of the people. Many of the persons, who in all times have filled the great offices of state, have been younger brothers, who had originally little, if any fortune. These offices do not furnish the means of amassing wealth. There ought to be some power in the crown of granting pensions out of the reach of its own caprices. An intail of dependence is a bad reward of merit.

I would therefore leave to the crown the possibility of conferring some favours, which, whilst they are received as a reward, do not operate as corruption. When men receive obligations from the crown through the pious hands of fathers, or of connections as venerable as the paternal, the dependences which arise from thence, are the obligations of gratitude, and not the fetters of servility. Such ties originate in virtue, and they promote it. They continue men in those habitudes of friendship, those political connections, and those political principles in which they began life. They are antidotes against a corrupt levity, instead of causes of it. What an unseemly spectacle would it afford, what a disgrace would it be to the commonwealth that suffered such things, to see the hopeful son of a meritorious minister begging his

---

* Before the statute of Queen Anne, which limited the alienation of land.[1]
[1] Presumably he is referring to 6 Anne, c. 34, which allowed a certain length of time for persons in Ireland to claim land wrongly sold by trustees as forfeited land.

bread at the door of that treasury, from whence his father dispensed the œconomy of an empire, and promoted the happiness and glory of his country? Why should he be obliged to prostrate his honour, and to submit his principles at the levee of some proud favourite, shouldered and thrust aside by every impudent pretender, on the very spot where a few days before he saw himself adored?—obliged to cringe to the author of the calamities of his house, and to kiss the hands that are red with his father's blood?—No, Sir,—These things are unfit—They are intolerable.

Sir, I shall be asked, why I do not chuse to destroy those offices which are pensions, and appoint pensions under the direct title in their stead? I allow, that in some cases it leads to abuse, to have things appointed for one purpose, and applied to another. I have no great objection to such a change: but I do not think it quite prudent for me to propose it. If I should take away the present establishment, the burthen of proof rests upon me, that so many pensions, and no more, and to such an amount each, and no more, are necessary for the public service. This is what I can never prove; for it is a thing incapable of definition. I do not like to take away an object that I think answers my purpose, in hopes of getting it back again in a better shape. People will bear an old establishment when its excess is corrected, who will revolt at a new one. I do not think these office-pensions to be more in number than sufficient: but on that point the House will exercise its discretion. As to abuse, I am convinced, that very few trusts in the ordinary course of administration, have admitted less abuse than this. Efficient ministers have been their own paymasters. It is true. But their very partiality has operated as a kind of justice; and still it was service that was paid. When we look over this exchequer list, we find it filled with the descendants of the Walpoles, of the Pelhams, of the Townshends;[1] names to whom this country owes its liberties, and to whom his majesty owes his crown. It was in one of these lines, that the immense and envied employment he now holds, came to a certain duke,* who is now probably sitting quietly at a very good dinner directly under us; and acting *high life below stairs*,[2] whilst we, his masters, are filling our mouths with unsubstantial sounds, and talking

---

* Duke of Newcastle, whose dining-room is under the House of Commons.[3]
[1] Charles Townshend, 2nd Vincount Townshend (1674–1738).
[2] A play by James Townley (1714–78) first performed in 1769.
[3] Henry Pelham Clinton, 2nd Duke of Newcastle (1720–94), Auditor of the Exchequer.

of hungry œconomy over his head. But he is the elder branch of an ancient and decayed house, joined to, and repaired by the reward of services done by another. I respect the original title, and the first purchase of merited wealth and honour through all its descents, through all its transfers, and all its assignments. May such fountains never be dried up. May they ever flow with their original purity, and refresh and fructify the commonwealth, for ages!

Sir, I think myself bound to give you my reasons as clearly, and as fully, for stopping in the course of reformation, as for proceeding in it. My limits are the rules of law; the rules of policy; and the service of the state. This is the reason why I am not able to intermeddle with another article, which seems to be a specific object in several of the petitions; I mean the reduction of exorbitant emoluments to efficient offices. If I knew of any real efficient office, which did possess exorbitant emoluments, I should be extremely desirous of reducing them. Others may know of them. I do not. I am not possessed of an exact common measure between real service and its reward. I am very sure, that states do sometimes receive services, which is hardly in their power to reward according to their worth. If I were to give my judgment, with regard to this country, I do not think the great efficient offices of the state to be overpaid. The service of the public is a thing which cannot be put to auction, and struck down to those who will agree to execute it the cheapest. When the proportion between reward and service, is our object, we must always consider of what nature the service is, and what sort of men they are that must perform it. What is just payment for one kind of labour, and full encouragement for one kind of talents, is fraud and discouragement to others. Many of the great offices have much duty to do, and much expence of representation to maintain. A secretary of state, for instance, must not appear sordid in the eyes of the ministers of other nations; neither ought our ministers abroad to appear contemptible in the courts where they reside. In all offices of duty, there is, almost necessarily, a great neglect of all domestic affairs. A person in high office can rarely take a view of his family-house. If he sees that the state takes no detriment, the state must see that his affairs should take as little.

I will even go so far as to affirm, that if men were willing to serve in such situations without salary, they ought not to be permitted to do it. Ordinary service must be secured by the motives to ordinary integrity. I do not hesitate to say, that, that state which lays its foundation in rare and heroic virtues, will be sure to have its superstructure in the basest profligacy and corruption. An honourable and fair profit is the best security against avarice and rapacity; as in all things else, a lawful and regulated enjoyment is the best security against debauchery and excess. For as wealth is power, so all power will infallibly draw wealth to itself by some means or other: and when men are left no way of ascertaining their profits but by their means of obtaining them, those means will be encreased to infinity. This is true in all the parts of administration, as well as in the whole. If any individual were to decline his appointments, it might give an unfair advantage to ostentatious ambition over unpretending service; it might breed invidious comparisons; it might tend to destroy whatever little unity and agreement may be found among ministers. And after all, when an ambitious man had run down his competitors by a fallacious shew of disinterestedness, and fixed himself in power by that means, what security is there that he would not change his course, and claim as an indemnity ten times more than he has given up?

This rule, like every other, may admit its exceptions. When a great man has some one great object in view to be atchieved in a given time, it may be absolutely necessary for him to walk out of all the common roads, and if his fortune permits it, to hold himself out as a splendid example. I am told, that something of this kind is now doing in a country near us.[1] But this is for a short race; the training for a heat or two, and not the proper preparation for the regular stages of a methodical journey. I am speaking of establishments, and not of men.

It may be expected, Sir, that when I am giving my reasons why I limit myself in the reduction of employments, or of their profits, I should say something of those which seem of eminent inutility in the state; I mean the number of officers who by their places are attendant on the person of the king. Considering the commonwealth merely as such, and considering those officers only as relative to the direct purposes of the state, I admit that they are of no use at all. But there are many things in the constitution of establishments, which appear of little value on the first view, which in a secondary and oblique manner, produce very material advantages. It was on full consideration that I determined not to lessen any of the offices of honour about the crown, in their number or their emoluments. These emoluments, except in

[1] Burke is probably referring to the methods employed by Necker in France (see above, pp. 396, 468).

531

one or two cases, do not much more than answer the charge of attendance. Men of condition naturally love to be about a court; and women of condition love it much more. But there is in all regular attendance, so much of constraint, that if it were a mere charge, without any compensation, you would soon have the court deserted by all the nobility of the kingdom.

Sir, the most serious mischiefs would follow from such a desertion. Kings are naturally lovers of low company. They are so elevated above all the rest of mankind, that they must look upon all their subjects as on a level. They are rather apt to hate than to love their nobility, on account of the occasional resistance to their will, which will be made by their virtue, their petulance, or their pride. It must indeed be admitted, that many of the nobility are as perfectly willing to act the part of flatterers, tale-bearers, parasites, pimps, and buffoons, as any of the lowest and vilest of mankind can possibly be. But they are not properly qualified for this object of their ambition. The want of a regular education, and early habits, and some lurking remains of their dignity, will never permit them to become a match for an Italian eunuch, a mountebank, a fidler, a player, or any regular practitioner of that tribe. The Roman emperors almost from the beginning, threw themselves into such hands; and the mischief increased every day till its decline, and its final ruin. It is therefore of very great importance (provided the thing is not overdone) to contrive such an establishment as must, almost whether a prince will or not, bring into daily and hourly offices about his person, a great number of his first nobility; and it is rather an useful prejudice that gives them a pride in such a servitude. Though they are not much the better for a court, a court will be much the better for them. I have therefore not attempted to reform any of the offices of honour about the king's person.

There are, indeed, two offices in his stables which are sinecures. By the change of manners, and indeed by the nature of the thing, they must be so; I mean the several keepers of buck-hounds, stag-hounds, fox-hounds, and harriers. They answer no purpose of utility or of splendor. These I propose to abolish. It is not proper that great noblemen should be keepers of dogs, though they were the king's dogs. In every part of my scheme, I have endeavoured that no primary, and that even no secondary service of the state, should suffer by its frugality. I mean to touch no offices but such as I am perfectly sure, are either of no use at all, or not of any use in the least assignable proportion to the burthen with which they load the revenues of the kingdom, and to the influence with which they oppress the freedom of parliamentary deliberation; for which reason there are but two offices which are properly state offices, that I have a desire to reform.

The first of them is the new office of *third secretary of state*, which is commonly called *secretary of state for the colonies*.

We know that all the correspondence of the colonies had been, until within a few years, carried on by the southern secretary of state; and that this department has not been shunned upon account of the weight of its duties; but on the contrary, much sought, on account of its patronage. Indeed he must be poorly acquainted with the history of office, who does not know how very lightly the American functions have always leaned on the shoulders of the ministerial *Atlas*, who has upheld that side of the sphere. Undoubtedly, great temper and judgment was requisite in the management of the colony politics; but the official detail was a trifle. Since the new appointment, a train of unfortunate accidents has brought before us almost the whole correspondence of this favourite secretary's office, since the first day of its establishment. I will say nothing of its auspicious foundation; of the quality of its correspondence; or of the effects that have ensued from it. I speak merely of its *quantity*; which we know would have been little or no addition to the trouble of whatever office had its hands the fullest. But what has been the real condition of the old office of secretary of state? Have their velvet bags, and their red boxes, been so full, that nothing more could possibly be crammed into them?

A correspondence of a curious nature has been lately published.* In that correspondence, Sir, we find, the opinion of a noble person, who is thought to be the grand manufacturer of administrations;[1] and therefore the best judge of the quality of his work. He was of opinion, that there was but one man of diligence and industry in the whole administration—it was the late earl of Suffolk.[2] The noble lord lamented very justly, that this statesman, of so much mental vigour, was almost wholly disabled from the exertion of it, by his bodily infirmities. Lord Suffolk, dead to the state, long before he was dead to

---

* Letters between Dr. Addington and Sir James Wright.[3]
[1] Lord Bute.
[2] Henry Howard, 12th Earl of Suffolk (1739–79), Secretary of State for the North.
[3] This correspondence between Dr. Anthony Addington (1713–90) and Sir James Wright, 1st Baronet (d. 1803) was reprinted in the *Annual Register* for 1778 'from papers now in possession, of the Earl of Chatham's family' (Appendix to the Chronicle, pp. 244–64).

nature, at last paid his tribute to the common treasury to which we must all be taxed. But so little want was found even of his intentional industry, that the office, vacant in reality to its duties long before, continued vacant even in nomination and appointment for a year after his death. The whole of the laborious and arduous correspondence of this empire, rested solely upon the activity and energy of Lord Weymouth.

It is therefore demonstrable, since one diligent man was fully equal to the duties of the two offices, that two diligent men will be equal to the duty of three. The business of the new office which I shall propose to you to suppress, is by no means too much to be returned to either of the secretaries which remain. If this dust in the balance should be thought too heavy, it may be divided between them both; North America (whether free or reduced) to the northern secretary, the West Indies to the southern. It is not necessary that I should say more upon the inutility of this office. It is burning day light. But before I have done, I shall just remark, that the history of this office is too recent to suffer us to forget, that it was made for the mere convenience of the arrangements of political intrigue, and not for the service of the state;[1] that it was made, in order to give a colour to an exorbitant increase of the civil list; and in the same act to bring a new accession to the loaded compost heap of corrupt influence.

There is, Sir, another office, which was not long since, closely connected with this of the American secretary; but has been lately separated from it for the very same purpose for which it had been conjoined; I mean the sole purpose of all the separations and all conjunctions that have been lately made—a job.—I speak, Sir, of the *board of trade and plantations*. This board is a sort of temperate bed of influence; a sort of gently ripening hot-house, where eight members of Parliament receive salaries of a thousand a year, for a certain given time, for doing little, in order to mature at a proper season, a claim to two thousand, to be granted for doing less, and on the credit of having toiled so long in that inferior laborious department.

I have known that board, off and on, for a great number of years. Both of its pretended objects have been much the objects of my study,

---

[1] For the creation of the office of the third Secretary of State—partly, as Burke says, for domestic political reasons, see M. A. Thomson, *The Secretaries of State 1681–1782*, Oxford, 1932, pp. 55–8.

if I have a right to call any pursuits of mine by so respectable a name. I can assure the house, and I hope they will not think that I risk my little credit lightly, that, without meaning to convey the least reflection upon any one of its members past or present,—it is a board which, if not mischievous, is of no use at all.

You will be convinced, Sir, that I am not mistaken, if you reflect how generally it is true, that commerce, the principal object of that office, flourishes most when it is left to itself. Interest, the great guide of commerce, is not a blind one. It is very well able to find its own way; and its necessities are its best laws. But if it were possible, in the nature of things, that the young should direct the old, and the in-experienced instruct the knowing; if a board in the state was the best tutor for the counting-house; if the desk ought to read lectures to the anvil, and the pen to usurp the place of the shuttle—yet in any matter of regulation, we know that board must act with as little authority as skill. The prerogative of the crown is utterly inadequate to its object; because all regulations are, in their nature, restrictive of some liberty. In the reign indeed, of *Charles the first*, the council, or committees of council, were never a moment unoccupied, with affairs of trade. But even where they had no ill intention (which was sometimes the case) trade and manufacture suffered infinitely from their injudicious tampering. But since that period, whenever regulation is wanting (for I do not deny, that sometimes it may be wanting) parliament constantly sits; and parliament alone is competent to such regulation. We want no instruction from boards of trade, or from any other board; and God forbid we should give the least attention to their reports. Parliamentary enquiry is the only mode of obtaining parliamentary information. There is more real knowledge to be obtained, by attending the detail of business in the committees above stairs, than ever did come, or ever will come from any board in this kingdom, or from all of them together. An assiduous member of parliament will not be the worse instructed there, for not being paid a thousand a year for learning his lesson. And now that I speak of the committees above stairs, I must say, that having till lately attended them a good deal, I have observed that no description of members give so little attendance, either to communicate, or to obtain instruction upon matters of commerce, as the honourable members of the grave board of trade. I really do not recollect, that I have ever seen one of them in that sort of business. Possibly, some members may have better memories; and may call to mind some job that may have accidentally brought one or other of them, at one time or other, to attend a matter of commerce.

This board, Sir, has had both its original formation, and its re-generation, in a job.[1] In a job it was conceived, and in a job its mother brought it forth. It made one among those shewy and specious imposi-tions, which one of the experiment making administrations of *Charles the second* held out to delude the people, and to be substituted in the place of the real service which they might expect from a parliament annually sitting. It was intended also to corrupt that body whenever it should be permitted to sit. It was projected in the year 1668, and it continued in a tottering and rickety childhood for about three or four years, for it died in the year 1673, a babe of as little hopes as ever swelled the bills of mortality in the article of convulsed or overlaid children, who have hardly stepped over the threshold of life.

It was buried with little ceremony; and never more thought of, until the reign of *King William*, when in the strange vicissitude of neglect and vigour, of good and ill success that attended his wars, in the year 1695, the trade was distressed beyond all example of former sufferings, by the piracies of the French cruisers. This suffering incensed, and, as it should seem, very justly incensed, the house of commons. In this ferment they struck, not only at the administration, but at the very constitution of the executive government. They attempted to form in parliament a board for the protection of trade; which, as they planned it, was to draw to itself a great part, if not the whole, of the functions and powers, both of the admiralty, and of the treasury; and thus, by a parliamentary delegation of office and officers, they threatened absolutely to separate these departments from the whole system of the executive government, and of course to vest the most leading and essential of its attributes in this board.[2] As the executive government

---

[1] The Council of Trade was first established in 1668 and consisted originally of 42 members. In 1670 its duties were taken over by the Council for Foreign Plantations and in 1621 the council was reconstituted as the Council of Trade and Foreign Plantations. It was purely an advisory council and it accomplished very little. After its president Anthony Ashley Cooper, 1st Earl of Shaftesbury (1621–83) went into opposition to the court in November 1673, it was disbanded, and in 1675 its work was transferred to a committee of the Privy Council (C. M. Andrews, *British Committees, Commissions, and Councils of Trade and Plantations, 1622–1675*, Johns Hopkins University Studies in History and Political Science, xxvi. 1–3, Baltimore, 1908, pp. 92, 106–7, 111, 127–32, 151).

[2] Clearly, Burke's view, supported by some historians, is that in the late seventeenth century the Tories had attempted through the formation of the Board of Trade to enable the House of Commons to encroach on the Crown's right to the patronage of all its offices and to the actual

was in a manner convicted of a dereliction of its functions, it was with infinite difficulty, that this blow was warded off in that session.[1] There was a threat to renew the same attempt in the next. To prevent the effect of this manœuvre, the court opposed another manœuvre to it; and in the year 1696, called into life this board of trade, which had slept since 1673.

This, in a few words, is the history of the regeneration of the board of trade. It has perfectly answered its purposes. It was intended to quiet the minds of the people, and to compose the ferment that then was strongly working in parliament. The courtiers were too happy to be able to substitute a board, which they knew would be useless, in the place of one that they feared would be dangerous. Thus the board of trade was reproduced in a job; and perhaps it is the only instance of a public body, which has never degenerated; but to this hour preserves all the health and vigour of its primitive institution.

This board of trade and plantations has not been of any use to the colonies, as colonies; so little of use, that the flourishing settlements of New England, of Virginia, and of Maryland, and all our wealthy colonies in the West Indies, were of a date prior to the first board of Charles the second. Pensylvania and Carolina were settled during its dark quarter, in the interval between the extinction of the first, and the formation of the second board. Two colonies alone owe their origin to that board. Georgia, which, till lately, has made a very slow progress; and never did make any progress at all, until it had wholly got rid of all the regulations which the board of trade had moulded into its original constitution.[2] That colony has cost the nation very great sums of

---

operation of the executive part of the government. See R. M. Lees, 'Parliament and the Proposal for a Council of Trade', *English Historical Review*, liv (1939), 38–66.

[1] Burke may be referring to the fact that in December 1695 the ministry, in an attempt to dampen enthusiasm for the board in the House of Commons, proposed among the resolutions for the Council of Trade, one in particular which stated that 'King William is lawful King of this realm' and that 'the late King James had no right or title there unto'. The purpose appears to have been to turn the Tories, many of whom apparently supported the board specifically as a means of reducing King William's power, against the plan. The resolution, however, was lost and the next year the court did indeed call the Council into life (H. Horwitz, *Parliament, Policy and Politics in the Reign of William III*, Manchester, 1977, p. 162).

[2] The charter was granted to the Trustees for the Establishment of the Colony of Georgia in 1732. However, the colony developed slowly until it reverted to the Crown in 1752. At that point it had a population of about 2,000 whites and 400 blacks. Between 1752 and 1773 its population grew to 33,000 (H. E. Davis, *The Fledgling Province: Social and Cultural Life in Colonial Georgia*, Williamsburg, 1976, pp. 3–32).

money;[1] whereas the colonies which have had the fortune of not being godfathered by the board of trade, never cost the nation a shilling, except what has been so properly spent in losing them. But the colony of Georgia, weak as it was, carried with it to the last hour, and carries, even in its present dead pallid visage, the perfect resemblance of its parents. It always had, and it now has, an *establishment* paid by the public of England, for the sake of the influence of the crown; that colony having never been able or willing to take upon itself the expence of its proper government, or its own appropriated jobs.

The province of Nova Scotia was the youngest and the favourite child of the board. Good God! What sums the nursing of that ill-thriven, hard-visaged, and ill-favoured brat, has cost to this wittol nation? Sir, this colony has stood us in a sum of not less than seven hundred thousand pounds. To this day it has made no repayment—It does not even support those offices of expence, which are miscalled its government; the whole of that job still lies upon the patient, callous shoulders of the people of England.

Sir, I am going to state a fact to you, that will serve to set in full sunshine the real value of formality and official superintendance. There was in the province of Nova Scotia, one little neglected corner; the country of the *neutral French*; which having the good fortune to escape the fostering care both of France and England, and to have been shut out from the protection and regulation of councils of commerce, and of boards of trade, did, in silence, without notice, and without assistance, increase to a considerable degree. But it seems our nation had more skill and ability in destroying, than in settling a colony. In the last war we did, in my opinion, most inhumanly, and upon pretences that in the eye of an honest man are not worth a farthing, root out this poor innocent deserving people, whom our utter inability to govern, or to reconcile, gave us no sort of right to extirpate.[2] Whatever the merits of that extirpation might have been, it was on the footsteps of a neglected people, it was on the fund of unconstrained poverty, it was on the acquisitions of unregulated industry, that any thing which deserves the name of a colony in that province, has been formed. It has been formed by overflowings from the exuberant

---

[1] The earliest industries including silk, wines, potash, pearl ash, and olives were heavily subsidized but they all failed. After 1752 the civil administration of the colony continued to be paid for by the mother country (ibid. pp. 33–100).
[2] The expulsion of the Acadians took place in 1755.

population of New England, and by emigration, from other parts of Nova Scotia of fugitives from the protection of the board of trade.

But if all of these things were not more than sufficient to prove to you the inutility of that expensive establishment, I would desire you to recollect, Sir, that those who may be very ready to defend it, are very cautious how they employ it; cautious how they employ it even in appearance and pretence. They are afraid they should lose the benefit of its influence in parliament, if they seemed to keep it up for any other purpose. If ever there were commercial points of great weight, and most closely connected with our dependences, they are those which have been agitated and decided in parliament since I came into it. Which of the innumerable regulations since made had their origin or their improvement in the board of trade? Did any of the several East India bills which have been successively produced since 1767, originate there?[1] Did any one dream of referring them, or any part of them thither? Was any body so ridiculous as even to think of it? If ever there was an occasion on which the board was fit to be consulted, it was with regard to the acts, that were preludes to the American war, or attendant on its commencement: those acts were full of commercial regulations, such as they were;—the intercourse bill; the prohibitory bill; the fishery bill? If the board was not concerned in such things, in what particular was it thought fit that it should be concerned? In the course of all these bills through the house, I observed the members of that board to be remarkably cautious of intermeddling. They understood decorum better; they know that matters of trade and plantations are no business of theirs.

There were two very recent occasions, on which, if the idea of any use for the board had not been extinguished by prescription, appeared loudly to call for their interference.

When commissioners were sent to pay his majesty's and our dutiful respects to the congress of the United States, a part of their powers under the commission were, it seems, of a commercial nature. They were authorized in the most ample and undefined manner, to form a commercial treaty with America on the spot.[2] This was no trivial object. As the formation of such a treaty would necessarily have been

---

[1] East India Dividend Act of 1767 (7 Geo. III, c. 47); East India Act (9 Geo. III, c. 24); East India Restraining Act (13 Geo. III, c. 9); The Tea Act (13 Geo. III, c. 44); East India Regulating Act (13 Geo. III, *c.* 63).

[2] The Carlisle Commission.

no less than the breaking up of our whole commercial system, and the giving it an entire new form; one would imagine, that the board of trade would have sat day and night, to model propositions, which, on our side, might serve as a basis to that treaty. No such thing. Their learned leisure was not in the least interrupted, though one of the members of the board was a commissioner,[1] and might, in mere compliment to his office, have been supposed to make a shew of deliberation on the subject. But he knew, that his colleagues would have thought he laughed in their faces, had he attempted to bring any thing the most distantly relating to commerce or colonies before *them*. A noble person, engaged in the same commission, and sent to learn his commercial rudiments in New York, (then under the operation of an act for the universal prohibition of trade) was soon after put at the head of that board.[2] This contempt from the present ministers of all the pretended functions of that board, and their manner of appointing to it the presiding commissioner, that is, the manner of breathing into that board its very soul, of inspiring it with its animating and presiding principle, puts an end to all dispute concerning their opinion of the clay it was made of. But I will give them heaped measure.

It was but the other day, that the noble lord in the blue ribbon carried up to the house of peers, two acts, altering, I think much for the better, but altering, in a great degree, our whole commercial system. These acts, I mean, for giving a free trade to Ireland in woollens and in all things else, with independent nations, and giving them an equal trade to our own colonies.[3] Here too the novelty of this great, but arduous and critical improvement of system, would make you conceive that the anxious solicitude of the noble lord in the blue ribbon, would have wholly destroyed the plan of summer recreation of that board, by references to examine, compare, and digest matters for parliament—You would imagine, that Irish commissioners of customs and English commissioners of customs, and commissioners of excise, that merchants and manufacturers of every denomination, had daily crowded their outer rooms. *Nil horum.*[4] The perpetual virtual adjournment, and the unbroken sitting vacation of that board, was no more disturbed by the Irish than by the plantation commerce,

---

[1] William Eden (1744–1814), later (1789) 1st Baron Auckland, M.P. 1774–89.
[2] Lord Carlisle was appointed President of the Board of Trade in 1779.
[3] See below, pp. 620–1.
[4] None of these.

or any other commerce. The same matter made a large part of the business which occupied the house for two sessions before; and as our ministers were not then mellowed by the mild, emollient, and engaging blandishments of our dear sister, into all the tenderness of unqualified surrender, the bounds and limits of a restrained benefit naturally required much detailed management and positive regulation. But neither the qualified propositions which were received, nor those other qualified propositions which were rejected by ministers, were the least concern of the board of trade, or were they ever thought of in the business.

It is therefore, Sir, on the opinion of parliament, on the opinion of the ministers, and even on their own opinion of their inutility, that I shall propose to you to suppress *the board of trade and plantations*; and to recommit all its business to the council from whence it was very improvidently taken; and which business (whatever it might be) was much better done and without any expence; and indeed where in effect it may all come at last. Almost all that deserves the name of business there, is the reference of the plantation acts, to the opinion of gentlemen of the law. But all this may be done, as the Irish business of the same nature has always been done, by the council, and with a reference to the attorney and solicitor general.

There are some regulations in the household, relative to the officers of the yeomen of the guards, and the officers and band of gentlemen pensioners, which I shall likewise submit to your consideration, for the purpose of regulating establishments, which at present are much abused.

I have now finished all, that for the present I shall trouble you with, on the *plan of reduction*. I mean next to propose to you the *plan of arrangement*, by which I mean to appropriate and fix the civil list money to its several services according to their nature; for I am sensible, that if a discretion, wholly arbitrary, can be exercised over the civil list revenue, although the most effectual methods may be taken to prevent the inferior departments from exceeding their bounds, the plan of reformation will still be left very imperfect. It will not, in my opinion, be safe to permit an entirely arbitrary discretion even in the first lord of the treasury himself: It will not be safe to leave with him a power of diverting the public money from its proper objects, of paying it in an irregular course, or of inverting (perhaps) the order of time dictated by the proportion of value, which ought to regulate his application of payment to service.

I am sensible too, that the very operation of a plan of œconomy which tends to exonerate the civil list of expensive establishments, may in some sort defeat the capital end we have in view, the independence of parliament; and that in removing the public and ostensible means of influence, we may increase the fund of private corruption. I have thought of some methods to prevent an abuse of surplus cash under discretionary application; I mean the heads of *secret service, special service, various payments*, and the like; which, I hope, will answer, and which in due time I shall lay before you. Where I am unable to limit the quantity of the sums to be applied, by reason of the uncertain quantity of the service, I endeavour to confine it to its *line*; to secure an indefinite application to the definite service to which it belongs; not, to stop the progress of expence in its line, but to confine it to that line in which it professes to move.

But that part of my plan, Sir, upon which I principally rest, that, on which I rely for the purpose of binding up, and securing the whole, is to establish a fixed and invariable order in all its payments, which it shall not be permitted to the first lord of the treasury, upon any pretence whatsoever, to depart from. I therefore divide the civil list payments into *nine* classes, putting each class forward according to the importance or justice of the demand, and to the inability of the persons entitled to enforce their pretensions; that is, to put those first who have the most efficient offices, or claim the justest debts; and, at the same time, from the character of that description of men, from the retiredness, or the remoteness of their situation, or from their want of weight and power to enforce their pretensions, or from their being entirely subject to the power of a minister, without any recip-rocal power of aweing him, ought to be the most considered, and are the most likely to be neglected; all these I place in the highest classes: I place in the lowest those whose functions are of the least importance, but whose persons or rank are often of the greatest power and influence.

In the first class I place the *judges*, as of the first importance. It is the public justice that holds the community together; the ease, therefore, and independence of the judges, ought to supersede all other con-siderations, and they ought to be the very last to feel the necessities of the state, or to be obliged either to court or bully a minister for their right: They ought to be as *weak solicitors on their own demands*, as strenuous assertors of the rights and liberties of others. The judges are, or ought to be, of a *reserved* and retired character, and wholly unconnected with the political world.

In the second class I place the foreign ministers. The judges are the links of our connections with one another; the foreign ministers are the links of our connection with other nations. They are not upon the spot to demand payment, and are therefore the most likely to be, as in fact they have sometimes been, entirely neglected, to the great disgrace, and perhaps the great detriment of the nation.

In the third class I would bring all the tradesmen who supply the crown by contract, or otherwise.

In the fourth class I place all the domestic servants of the king, and all persons in efficient offices, whose salaries do not exceed two hundred pounds a year.

In the fifth, upon account of honour, which ought to give place to nothing but charity and rigid justice, I would place the pensions and allowances of his majesty's royal family, comprehending of course the queen, together with the stated allowance of the privy purse.

In the sixth class, I place these efficient offices of duty, whose salaries may exceed the sum of two hundred pounds a year.

In the seventh class, that mixed mass, the whole pension list.

In the eight, the offices of honour about the king.

In the ninth and the last of all, the salaries and pensions of the first lord of the treasury himself, the chancellor of the exchequer, and the other commissioners of the treasury.

If by any possible mismanagement of that part of the revenue which is left at discretion, or by any other mode of prodigality, cash should be deficient for the payment of the lowest classes, I propose, that the amount of those salaries where the deficiency may happen to fall, shall not be carried as debt to the account of the succeeding year, but that it shall be entirely lapsed, sunk, and lost; so that government will be enabled to start in the race of every new year, wholly unloaded, fresh in wind and in vigour. Hereafter, no civil list debt can ever come upon the public. And those who do not consider this as saving, because it is not a certain sum, do not ground their calculations of the future on their experience of the past.

I know of no mode of preserving the effectual execution of any duty, but to make it the direct interest of the executive officer that it shall be faithfully performed. Assuming, then, that the present vast allowance to the civil list is perfectly adequate to all its purposes, if there should be any failure, it must be from the mismanagement or neglect of the first commissioner of the treasury; since, upon the proposed plan, there can be no expence of any consequence, which he is not himself previously to authorize and finally to control. It is therefore just, as well as politic, that the loss should attach upon the delinquency.

If the failure from the delinquency should be very considerable, it will fall on the class directly above the first lord of the treasury, as well as upon himself and his board. It will fall, as it ought to fall, upon offices of no primary importance in the state; but then it will fall upon persons, whom it will be a matter of no slight importance for a minister to provoke—it will fall upon persons of the first rank and consequence in the kingdom; upon those who are nearest to the king, and frequently have a more interior credit with him than the minister himself. It will fall upon masters of the horse, upon lord chamberlains, upon lord stewards, upon grooms of the stole, and lords of the bedchamber. The household troops form an army, who will be ready to mutiny for want of pay, and whose mutiny will be *really* dreadful to a commander in chief. A rebellion of the thirteen lords of the bedchamber would be far more terrible to a minister, and would probably affect his power more to the quick, than a revolt of thirteen colonies. What an uproar such an event would create at court! What *petitions*, and *committees*, and *associations* would it not produce! Bless me! what a clattering of white sticks and yellow sticks would be about his head—what a storm of gold keys would fly about the ears of the minister[1]—what a shower of Georges, and Thistles, and medals, and collars of S.S. would assail him at his first entrance into the antichamber, after an insolvent Christmas quarter. A tumult which could not be appeased by all the harmony of the new-year's ode.[2] Rebellion it is certain there would be; and rebellion may not now indeed be so critical an event to those who engage in it, since its price is so correctly ascertained;—ascertained at just a thousand pound.

Sir, this classing, in my opinion, is a serious and solid security for the performance of a minister's duty. Lord Coke says, that the staff was put into the treasurer's hand, to enable him to support himself when there was no money in the exchequer, and to beat away im-

---

[1] i.e. the symbols of office.

[2] i.e. by the goodwill associated with the honours (such as thistles and medals) traditionally bestowed on selected distinguished individuals on New Year's eve.

portunate solicitors.[1] The method, which I propose, would hinder him from the necessity of such a broken staff to lean on, or such a miserable weapon for repulsing the demands of worthless suitors, who, the noble lord in the blue ribbon knows, will bear many hard blows on the head, and many other indignities, before they are driven from the treasury. In this plan, he is furnished with an answer to all their importunity; an answer far more conclusive, than if he had knocked them down with his staff—"Sir, (or my Lord), you are calling for my own salary—Sir, you are calling for the appointments of my colleagues who sit about me in office—Sir, you are going to excite a mutiny at court against me—you are going to estrange his majesty's confidence from me, through the chamberlain, or the master of the horse, or the groom of the stole."

As things now stand, every man, in proportion to his consequence at court, tends to add to the expences of the civil list, by all manner of jobs, if not for himself, yet for his dependents. When the new plan is established, those who are now suitors for jobs, will become the most strenuous opposers of them. They will have a common interest with the minister in public œconomy. Every class, as it stands low, will become security for the payment of the preceding class; and thus the persons, whose insignificant services defraud those that are useful, would then become interested in their payment. Then the powerful, instead of oppressing, would be obliged to support the weak; and idleness would become concerned in the reward of industry. The whole fabric of the civil œconomy would become compact and connected in all its parts; it would be formed into a well organized body, where every member contributes to the support of the whole; and where even the lazy stomach secures the vigour of the active arm.

This plan, I really flatter myself, is laid, not in official formality, nor in airy speculation, but in real life, and in human nature, in what "comes home (as Bacon says) to the business and bosoms of men."[2] You have now, Sir, before you, the whole of my scheme, as far as I have digested it into a form, that might be in any respect worthy of your consideration.—I intend to lay it before you in five bills.* The

* Titles of the Bills read.

[1] 'when treasure failed, the white staff served him to rest him upon it, or to drive away importunate solicitors' (Sir Edward Coke, *Fourth Part of the Institutes of the Laws of England*, 5th edn., London, 1671, p. 104).

[2] Francis Bacon (1561–1626), 1st Baron Verulam and Viscount St Albans, in the dedication to the 1625 edition of his *Essays* wrote that they 'come home to men's business and bosoms'.

plan consists, indeed, of many parts; but they stand upon a few plain
principles. It is a plan which takes nothing from the civil list without
discharging it of a burthen equal to the sum carried to the public
service. It weakens no one function necessary to government; but on
the contrary, by appropriating supply to service, it gives it greater
vigour. It provides the means of order and foresight to a minister of
finance, which may always keep all the objects of his office, and their
state, condition, and relations, distinctly before him. It brings forward
accounts without hurrying and distressing the accountants: whilst
it provides for public convenience, it regards private rights. It extinguishes secret corruption almost to the possibility of its existence. It
destroys direct and visible influence equal to the offices of at least fifty
members of parliament. Lastly, it prevents the provision for his
Majesty's children, from being diverted to the political purposes of his
minister.

These are the points, on which I rely for the merit of the plan: I
pursue œconomy in a secondary view, and only as it is connected with
these great objects. I am persuaded, that even for supply, this scheme
will be far from unfruitful, if it be executed to the extent I propose it. I
think it will give to the public, at its periods, two or three hundred
thousand pounds a year; if not, it will give them a system of œconomy,
which is itself a great revenue. It gives me no little pride and satisfaction, to find that the principles of my proceedings are, in many
respects, the very same with those which are now pursued in the plans
of the French minister of finance. I am sure, that I lay before you a
scheme easy and practicable in all its parts. I know it is common at
once to applaud and to reject all attempts of this nature. I know it
is common for men to say, that such and such things are perfectly
right—very desirable; but that, unfortunately, they are not practicable.
Oh! no, Sir, no. Those things which are not practicable, are not
desirable. There is nothing in the world really beneficial, that does not
lie within the reach of an informed understanding, and a well directed
pursuit. There is nothing that God has judged good for us, that he has
not given us the means to accomplish, both in the natural and the
moral world. If we cry, like children for the moon, like children we
must cry on.

We must follow the nature of our affairs, and conform ourselves to
our situation. If we do, our objects are plain and compassable. Why
should we resolve to do nothing, because what I propose to you may

not be the exact demand of the petition; when we are far from resolved to comply even with what evidently is so? Does this sort of chicanery become us? The people are the masters. They have only to express their wants at large and in gross. We are the expert artists; we are the skilful workmen, to shape their desires into perfect form, and to fit the utensil to the use. They are the sufferers, they tell the symptoms of the complaint; but we know the exact seat of the disease, and how to apply the remedy, according to the rules of art. How shocking would it be to see us pervert our skill, into a sinister and servile dexterity, for the purpose of evading our duty, and defrauding our employers, who are our natural lords, of the object of their just expectations. I think the whole not only practicable, but practicable in a very short time. If we are in earnest about it, and if we exert that industry, and those talents in forwarding the work, which I am afraid may be exerted in impeding it—I engage, that the whole may be put in complete execution within a year. For my own part, I have very little to recommend me for this or for any task, but a kind of earnest and anxious perseverance of mind, which, with all its good and all its evil effects, is moulded into my constitution. I faithfully engage to the house, if they choose to appoint me to any part in the execution of this work, which (when they have made it theirs by the improvements of their wisdom, will be worthy of the able assistance they may give me) that by night and by day, in town, or in country, at the desk, or in the forest, I will, without regard to convenience, ease, or pleasure, devote myself to their service, not expecting or admitting any reward whatsoever. I owe to this country my labour, which is my all; and I owe to it ten times more industry, if ten times more I could exert. After all I shall be an unprofitable servant.

At the same time, if I am able, and if I shall be permitted, I will lend an humble helping hand to any other good work which is going on. I have not, Sir, the frantic presumption to suppose, that this plan contains in it the whole of what the public has a right to expect, in the great work of reformation they call for. Indeed, it falls infinitely short of it. It falls short, even of my own ideas. I have some thoughts not yet fully ripened, relative to a reform in the customs and excise, as well as in some other branches of financial administration. There are other things too, which form essential parts in a great plan for the purpose of restoring the independence of parliament. The contractors bill of last year it is fit to revive; and I rejoice that it is in better hands than mine.[1] The bill for suspending the votes of customhouse officers, brought into parliament several years ago, by one of our worthiest and wisest members,* (would to God we could along with the plan revive the person who proposed it.) But a man of very real integrity, honour, and ability will be found to take his place, and to carry his idea into full execution.[2] You all see how necessary it is to review our military expences for some years past, and, if possible, to bind up and close that bleeding artery of profusion: but that business also, I have reason to hope, will be undertaken by abilities that are fully adequate to it. Something must be devised (if possible) to check the ruinous expence of elections.

Sir, all or most of these things must be done. Every one must take his part.

If we should be able by dexterity or power, or intrigue, to disappoint the expectations of our constituents, what will it avail us? we shall never be strong or artful enough to parry, or to put by the irresistible demands of our situation. That situation calls upon us, and upon our constituents too, with a voice which *will* be heard. I am sure no man is more zealously attached than I am to the privileges of this house, particularly in regard to the exclusive management of money. The lords have no right to the disposition, in any sense, of the public purse; but they have gone further in self-denial than our utmost jealousy could have required.[†] A power of examining accounts, to censure, correct, and punish, we never, that I know of, have thought of denying to the House of Lords. It is something more than a century since we voted that body useless:[3] they have now voted themselves so. The whole hope of reformation is at length cast upon *us*; and let us not

---

* W. Dowdeswell, Esq; chancellor of the exchequer, 1765.

† In the Debate on the Rejection of Lord Shelburne's motion in the House of Lords.[4]

[1] Sir Philip Jennings Clerke.

[2] John Crewe (see above, p. 482).

[3] Presumably Burke refers in particular to the resolution of the House of Commons of 3 July 1678 that 'all Aids and Supplies, and Aids to his Majesty in Parliament are the sole Gift of the Commons: And all Bills for the Granting of any such Aids and Supplies ought to begin with the Commons: And that it is the undoubted and sole right of the Commons, to direct, limit and appoint, in such Bills, the Ends, Limitations, and Qualifications of such Grants, which ought not to be changed, or altered by the House of Lords.' See W. C. Costin and J. Steven Watson, *The Law and Working of the Constitution: Documents 1660–1914*, 2 vols., London, 1961, i. 154.

[4] The motion of 15 December 1779 on 'army extraordinairies'; see *Parl. Hist.* xx. 1285–93. Lord Shelburne on 15 December 1779 moved two resolutions: the first attacked the alarming addition to the national debt under the heading of 'extraordinaries' and advocated governmental economy, while the second proposed a committee of both Houses to examine public expenditures and to seek ways of saving money by reforming the structure of government.

deceive the nation, which does us the honour to hope every thing from our virtue. If *all* the nation are not equally forward to press this duty upon us, yet be assured, that they all equally expect we should perform it. The respectful silence of those who wait upon your pleasure, ought to be as powerful with you, as the call of those who require your service as their right. Some, without doors, affect to feel hurt for your dignity, because they suppose, that menaces are held out to you. Justify their good opinion, by shewing that no menaces are necessary to stimulate you to your duty.—But, Sir, whilst we may sympathize with them, in one point, who sympathize with us in another, we ought to attend no less to those who approach us like men, and who, in the guise of petitioners, speak to us in the tone of a concealed authority. It is not wise to force them to speak out more plainly, what they plainly mean.—But, the petitioners are violent. Be it so. Those who are least anxious about your conduct, are not those that love you most. Moderate affection and satiated enjoyment, are cold and respectful; but an ardent and injured passion, is tempered up with wrath, and grief, and shame, and conscious worth, and the maddening sense of violated right. A jealous love lights his torch from the firebrands of the furies.—They who call upon you to belong *wholly* to the people, are those who wish you to return to your *proper* home; to the sphere of your duty, to the post of your honour, to the mansion-house of all genuine, serene, and solid satisfaction. We have furnished to the people of England (indeed we have) some real cause of jealousy. Let us leave that sort of company which, if it does not destroy our innocence, pollutes our honour: let us free ourselves at once from every thing that can increase their suspicions, and inflame their just resentment: let us cast away from us, with a generous scorn, all the love-tokens and symbols that we have been vain and light enough to accept;—all the bracelets and snuff-boxes, and miniature pictures, and hair-devices, and all the other adulterous trinkets that are the pledges of our alienation, and the monuments of our shame. Let us return to our legitimate home, and all jars and all quarrels will be lost in embraces. Let the commons in parliament assembled, be one and the same thing with the commons at large. The distinctions that are made to separate us, are unnatural and wicked contrivances. Let us identify, let us incorporate ourselves with the people. Let us cut all the cables and snap the chains which tie us to an unfaithful shore, and enter the friendly harbour, that shoots far out into the main its moles and jettees

to receive us.—"War with the world, and peace with our constituents."
Be this our motto and our principle. Then indeed, we shall be truly
great. Respecting ourselves, we shall be respected by the world. At
present all is troubled and cloudy, and distracted, and full of anger and
turbulence, both abroad and at home: but the air may be cleared by
this storm, and light and fertility may follow it. Let us give a faithful
pledge to the people, that we honour, indeed, the crown; but that we
belong to them; that we are their auxiliaries, and not their task-masters;
the fellow-labourers in the same vineyard, not lording over their rights,
but helpers of their joy: that to tax them is a grievance to ourselves,
but to cut off from our enjoyments to forward theirs, is the highest
gratification we are capable of receiving. I feel with comfort, that we
are all warmed with these sentiments, and while we are thus warm, I
wish we may go directly and with a chearful heart to this salutary work.

Sir, I move for leave to bring in a bill, "For the better regulation of
his Majesty's civil establishments, and of certain public offices; for
the limitation of pensions, and the suppression of sundry useless,
expensive, and inconvenient places; and for applying the monies saved
thereby to the public service."[1]

Mr. Fox seconded the motion.

Lord North stated, that there was a difference between this bill for
regulating the establishments, and some of the others, as they affected
the antient patrimony of the crown; and therefore wished them to be
postponed, till the King's consent could be obtained. This distinction
was strongly controverted; but when it was insisted on as a point of
decorum *only*, it was agreed to postpone them to another day. Accordingly, on the Monday following, viz. Feb. 14, leave was given, on the
motion of Mr. Burke, without opposition, to bring in

1st, "A bill for the sale of the forest and other crown lands, rents,
and hereditaments, with certain exceptions; *and for applying the produce
thereof to the public service*; and for securing, ascertaining, and satisfying,
tenant-rights, and common and other rights."[2]

2d, "A bill for the more perfectly uniting to the crown the principality of Wales, and the county palatine of Chester, and for the more
commodious administration of justice within the same; as also, for

---

[1] For the Bill as printed, see *Commons Sessional Papers*, xxix. 361–88.
[2] A draft of this Bill is at Sheffield (Bk 14.20).

abolishing certain offices now appertaining thereto; *for quieting dormant claims, ascertaining and securing tenant-rights*; and for the sale of all forest lands, and other lands, tenements, and hereditaments, held by his Majesty in right of the said principality, or county palatine of Chester, *and for applying the produce thereof to the public service.*"[1]

3d, "A bill for uniting to the crown the duchy and county palatine of Lancaster; for the suppression of unnecessary offices now belonging thereto; for the *ascertainment and security of tenant and other rights*; and for the sale of all rents, lands, tenements, and hereditaments, and forests, within the said dutchy and county palatine, or either of them; *and for applying the produce thereof to the public service.*"[2]—*And it was ordered that* Mr. Burke, Mr. Fox, Lord John Cavendish, Sir George Savile, Colonel Barrè, Mr. Thomas Townshend, Mr. Byng,[3] Mr. Dunning, Sir Joseph Mawbey,[4] Mr. Recorder of London,[5] Sir Robert Clayton,[6] Mr. Frederick Montagu, the Earl of Upper Ossory,[7] Sir William Guise,[8] and Mr. Gilbert, *do prepare and bring in the same.*

At the same time, Mr. Burke moved for leave to bring in—4th, "A bill for uniting the dutchy of Cornwall to the crown; for the suppression of certain unnecessary offices now belonging thereto, for the *ascertainment and security of tenant and other rights*; and for the sale of certain rents, lands, and tenements, within or belonging to the said dutchy; *and for applying the produce thereof to the public service.*"[9]

But some objections being made by the surveyor general of the dutchy[10] concerning the rights of the Prince of Wales, now in his minority, and Lord North remaining perfectly silent, Mr. Burke, at length, though he strongly contended against the principle of the objection, consented to withdraw this last motion for the *present*, to be renewed upon an early occasion.

THE END

---

[1] See *Commons Sessional Papers*, xxix. 507–20. There is a draft at Sheffield (Bk 14.24).
[2] No copy appears to survive of this Bill.
[3] George Byng (*c.*1735–89), M.P. 1768–84.
[4] 1st Baronet (1730–98), M.P. 1761–74, 1765–90.
[5] James Adair
[6] (*c.*1740–99), M.P. 1768–99.
[7] John Fitzpatrick, 2nd Earl of Upper Ossory (1745–1818), M.P. 1767–94.
[8] 5th Baronet (1737–83), M.P. 1770–83.
[9] No copy appears to survive of this Bill.
[10] Sir Edward Bayntun Rolt, 1st Baronet (1710–1800), M.P. 1737–80.

Speech on Insolvent Debtors Bill
28 February 1780

Source: *Morning Chronicle*, 29 February 1780

This report is followed by *Parl. Reg.* xvii. 179 and *Parl. Hist.* xx. 1404, which mistakenly dates it 10 February 1780. Other reports are in *General Evening Post*, 29 February and *London Chronicle*, 29 February (and other papers).

On 9 February Lord Beauchamp introduced a Bill to prevent the perpetual imprisonment of insolvent debtors. The problem of imprisonment for debt was a substantial one in the eighteenth century. In 1776 'An Act for the Relief of Insolvent Debtors; and for the Relief of Bankrupts in Certain Cases',[1] the most recent of the amnesty acts for bankrupts, had been passed which allowed those in prison for debts which did not exceed £1,000 to any one person or institution, to apply to the courts for release after making all their assets available to their creditors. A perusal of the *London Gazette*, which published long lists on a regular basis of people taking advantage of the Act, demonstrates how badly such a measure was needed. Lord Beauchamp's Bill would have brought further relief. It required creditors to pay an allowance to debtors whom they insisted on keeping in jail and the courts were to be given the power to discharge any persons who were incapable of paying their debts. Burke spoke in support of the Bill on the second reading on 28 February.[2] His stand did more serious damage to his popularity amongst many of his constituents in Bristol who, as men of commerce, were constantly confronted with the problem of securing credit. In the city a public meeting was held and a petition against the Bill drawn up.[3] Both Burke and Henry Cruger were instructed to oppose it.[4]

Mr. *Burke* in a remarkably eloquent speech supported the Bill. He began with an ironical satire on Mr. Coventry,[5] for his having declared that men went to jail to enjoy the luxuries of a prison, and likewise for his having said four-pence a day was a luxury to a debtor, which he ought not to have.[6] Mr. Burke remarked, that the tables were now fairly turned on the noble Lord, and that so far from his Bill being

---

[1] 16 Geo. III, *c.* 38.
[2] For the Bill as introduced and as amended, see *Commons Sessional Papers of the Eighteenth Century*, xxix. 325–34, 335–60.
[3] See *Corr.* iv. 231.
[4] Ibid. 231–2.
[5] Thomas Coventry (*c.*1713–97), M.P. 1754–80. His speech is reported in *Parl. Reg.* xvii. 178.
[6] By the Bill it was intended that creditors should allow the debtors, confined for want of bail, 2*s.* 4*d.* a week.

founded, as every body had supposed, on benevolence and humanity, the Honourable Gentleman near him had proved that it was founded in inhumanity. For what was the avowed object of it?—To oblige men to come out of those prisons in which they lived so luxuriously! To force them to have that liberty which the Honourable Gentleman had proved to be so unpleasant to men who were debtors. Having carried this to a very laughable extent, Mr. Burke paid Lord Beauchamp a most handsome compliment, and went into a warm and persuasive description of the good effect the Bill would have, urging it so powerfully, that no man whose breast was not steeled against the impulse of humanity, could have heard him unmoved. He said, he wished the Bill to go still further than the noble Lord had intended; that the whitewashing clause ought to be inserted,[1] and that honest debtors should be cleared effectually upon a true *cessio bonorum*,[2] and not remain liable to the claim of their creditors ever afterwards.

The Bill met strenuous opposition, and having been through a select committee was recommitted to a Committee of the whole House, the meeting of which was continuously deferred until, on 23 May, it was put off for three months. For Burke's account of its history, see below, pp. 634–5.

Speech on Civil Establishment Bill
8 March 1780

Source: *Morning Chronicle*, 13 March 1780

Burke spoke three times in this debate on 8 March (*Parl. Reg.* xvii. 251–2, 255, 265–8; *Parl. Hist.* xxi. 190–1, 193–4, 203–6). The third speech is reproduced here. The first speech is reported in *Morning Chronicle*, 9 March; *Whitehall Evening Post*, 9 March; *London Courant*, 9 March; and *London Evening Post*, 9 March. The second, in which Burke accepted an amendment, is mentioned in a number of newspapers. Other reports of the third speech are in *General Advertiser*, 10 March; *London Chronicle*, 9 March (and other papers); *London Courant*, 10 March; and *Morning Post*, 10 March. The first part of the report of the third speech in *Parl. Reg.* follows that in *General Advertiser*.

[1] '*Mr. Burke*', the *London Chronicle* of 29 February reported, 'spoke very ably in support of the Bill, and wished to extend it further; notwithstanding the opprobrium fixed to what was called white-washing, he did not know if he should vote for the Bill, unless the white-washing clause, that is, the total discharge of the debtor, be inserted.'
[2] 'surrender of their property'.

On 8 March the House in committee on Burke's first Bill for Economical Reform debated the first clause—to abolish the office of Secretary of State for the Colonies. The Rockinghams found the third and most recently formed secretaryship a most inviting one to terminate. They felt obliged to defend any office or convention which had been established by Whig Governments between the Revolution and the fall of the 'Old Whigs' in the early 1760s. Thus, in his search for economies Burke marked for elimination only institutions which he could categorize as remnants of 'feudality'[1] on the one hand, or as the doings of those, other than the Rockinghams, who had taken over control of Government during the reign of George III. The third Secretary of State had been formed in 1768 and from the appointment of Hillsborough to the office in that year until 1779, the Secretary for the Colonies had also acted as the President of the Board of Trade which Burke had also marked for abolition.[2] Moreover, as a full-fledged ministerial department with its own bureaucratic network[3] and therefore numerous Crown appointees, the third secretaryship seemed in its own right to reflect a substantial expansion of the influence of the Crown in the present reign. 'We live at the period when for the first time since the Revolution, the power and influence of the Crown is held out, as the main and chief and only support to Government'[4], the Rockinghams had been claiming, and here was direct evidence that they were correct.

The Rockinghams' campaign against the influence of the Crown in the 1770s could have done little to bolster their standing in the eyes of George III. It seems reasonable to suppose that Burke's reminder here 'that his Majesty was the *creature of public institution*, and could not hold his throne a moment, if the other orders of the state chose to put a negative on his being any longer King', also did not help their cause. Such statements help to explain George III's well known antipathy in the early 1780s towards the second Rockingham Administration and perhaps even to the Fox–North coalition.

Mr. *Burke* spoke next, and after declaring that he could not possibly make a reply to what had been said, because nothing like a reason had been given to shew either the injustice, the impolicy, or the inexpediency of the Bill, very ably contended in favour of the principle of it, and in support of the clause then the subject of debate. He condemned the sentiments uttered by the noble Lord who began the debate,[5] and the

---

[1] See above, p. 509.
[2] See above, pp. 534–41.
[3] When the third Secretary of State was created, Opposition spokesmen attacked it as a direct attempt to expand the influence of the Crown. See, for instance, *The Political Register and Review of New Books*, ed. J. Almon, London, ii (1767), 29.
[4] *Corr.* ii. 194.
[5] Lord Beauchamp (*Parl. Reg.* xvii. 255–6).

Honourable Gentleman who spoke last,[1] as *Jacobitical*. He defined the distinction between Toryism and Jacobitism, shewing that the first was a leaning[2] towards the establishment of arbitrary monarchy and absolute power, accompanied with a declaration, that it nevertheless was subject to certain constitutional limitations and restrictions; whereas Jacobitism was a downright avowal of the unlimited power of sovereignty, a damnable doctrine that Kings derived not their power from the people, but governed *jure divino*,[3] were accountable to none but the Almighty, and had a right to expect passive obedience and non resistance at all times and on all occasions from their subjects. Jacobitism elevated Kings into the rank of Gods, and asserted, that the people were made for Kings, not Kings for the people. In the present case, the doctrines held out were but a bastard kind of Jacobitism, wanting the amiable prejudices of Jacobitism, and not having that strong plea of humanity in their favour, a desire to do justice to the descendants of a supposed injured family. There was something generous in a steady attachment to the persons of a royal family in distress, and the compassion of the heart made amends for the errors of the judgement. What was the doctrine avowed that day? That the King's Civil List, the liberal grant of Parliament, was his Majesty's freehold, in as full an extent as the freehold estate of any man in the kingdom was his sole right. Wherever Government wa[s] property, subjection must be slavery. The King was only a trustee for the public. Property and subjects existed before Kings were elected. Let Gentleman consider what a low, contemptible situation they sink Majesty to, when they attempt to make the King independent of Parliament. They render the Monarch the meanest and most wretched being in the whole realm. Let the Committee recollect, that the present Royal family were called to the Throne by the free voice of the people, that his Majesty was the *creature of public institution*, and could not hold his throne a moment, if the other orders of the state chose to put a negative on his being any longer King. The people collectively had made him what he was, by their universal consent; they had decorated his brow with the crown he wore, and they could snatch it from his temples, whenever they thought proper. His Majesty was the servant of his people, and let the King's friends remember, that to serve under a numerous and free people was the greatest glory humanity could be blessed with. To reign

---

[1] Charles Jenkinson (*Parl. Reg.* xvii. 262–5).
[2] *Morning Chronicle*: 'learning'   [3] By divine right.

absolute, over slaves, was a degradation of the most humiliating and contemptible kind. Let them tell his Majesty the real dignity of his station; let them convince him, that to be considered as the trustee of his subjects, was the highest post of honour; to self appropriate the trust, to claim an inherent, self-created, original and divine right in those grants, which his people freely voted him, was the essence, nay the quintessence of Jacobitism; it was high treason against the constitution!

After urging his idea in a repetition of glowing phrases, Mr. Burke replied to the other arguments which had been used against the principle of the Bill, especially those which pressed it upon the minds of the Committee, that proof of the right of Parliament to interfere was necessary. Parliament, he said, had a two-fold capacity, a judicial and legislative power; in all its judicial proceedings, like the inferior Courts, it was bound to proceed upon legal evidence; in its legislative, its dictatorial capacity, it was not obliged to act in the same manner; the wisdom of Parliament was then its guide, and that wisdom would ever direct it to take every step necessary to preserve the constitution; the present Bill was one of those steps, the influence of the Crown had shewn itself in a most alarming manner within those walls, that influence threatened danger to the constitution, and it was the duty of Parliament to lay the axe to the root, and cut down the noxious plant. With regard to the particular clause then agitating, were any proof necessary that three principal Secretaries of State was one too many, let Lord Suffolk, the late Lord Suffolk rise from the dead and give evidence at that Bar of the fact.[1] The late Lord Suffolk was a man of honour; was it likely that Lord Suffolk would have pocketed the income of the Secretary of Stateship, and sat for so long a time previous to his death, in his bed chamber with gouty legs, reposed on his crimson velvet bag, placed upon his red box, if he had not known that two Secretaries of State were equal to the publick duty? Let the Committee recollect how long Lord Suffolk had been unfit for business before he died! Let them remember that he had converted the office into an infirmary; that after his death it was changed into a grand cemetery, for the bones of a Secretary of State to repose in under a black velvet pall, and lay in state in, as in a kind of Jerusalem Chamber, for a whole year together! His wish was, that Lord Suffolk's

---

[1] He died on 7 March 1779; his successor was appointed on 27 October.

bones should be the last to lay in state there. His Bill professedly aimed at cutting off unnecessary pomp and splendour, the worst and most absurd of all pomp and pageantry, funereal pageantry!

It had been urged that the abolition of one secretary of stateship would save but little to the publick; true, it would not, but every plan must have a beginning, and every great plan must unavoidably exist of many small parts. The abolition of one office was the first part of his plan, and would lead to the abolition of many more; and with regard to the saving, the expense saved would pay a regiment of horse, or at the least, a regiment of infantry. But let Gentlemen consider what good the office of Secretary for the Colonies had done the publick? The first Secretary that had been appointed, was Lord Hillsborough, the only mark of whose conduct in the office, then in his recollection, was the famous circular letter that had set America in a flame, that had sown the seeds of discontent across the Atlantic, and had caused that damnable, that detestable war, which had cost Great Britain so much blood and treasure.[1] The noble Lord, who now held the office of Secretary for the Colonies,[2] he believed did his duty, and that the duty was laborious, but did not every man know that the servant last hired always did the most work? That the coachman rubbed down his horses, and kept his stable clean, till the groom was hired; that the business was then taken off the coachman's hands, and executed by the groom, till Tom the helper was hired, and that as soon as he was engaged, both groom and coachman were idle, and poor Tom did all the work. So with the objects of his Bill; useless supernumeraries were to be found in almost every one of the highest offices of the State. Additional Secretaries were from time to time created, and if an enquiry was made, why they were created, the only plea that could be adopted, would be that of the poor Irishman, who said "two people were doing nothing, and so he sent a third to help them." He instanced this by the late appointment of the Earl of Carlisle to be first Lord of Trade and Plantations, which he declared to be most clearly an office merely nominal.[3] He harangued, in very pointed terms, on the *laborious idleness* and the *idle labour* of office; said he was convinced, the public

[1] See vol. ii, p. 97.
[2] Lord George Germain.
[3] Carlisle was the first president of the Board of Trade since the appointment of Hillsborough in 1768 to hold the position without being Secretary of State for the Colonies. Burke is correct in calling the position 'nominal'. Its importance had been reduced significantly by Hillsborough in 1766; see Thomson, *The Secretaries of State*, p. 55.

business would be better done when it was in fewer hands, and therefore contested that the clause ought to stand, because it would lessen the number of Secretaries of State and save expence.

Mr. *Burke* supported his Bill with a great many more arguments forcibly put, and delivered in a most animated stile of oratory.

The clause was defeated by 208 votes to 201.

Speech on Commission of Accounts
13 March 1780

Source: *Morning Chronicle*, 15 March 1780

Burke spoke four times on 13 March when several subjects were before the House, the most important being Lord North's proposal for a commission to examine the public accounts and the clause of the Economical Reform Bill abolishing the Board of Trade. Burke's four speeches are reported in *Parl. Reg.* xvii. 284, 287–8, 296–300, 304–8, 414–18 and *Parl. Hist.* xxi. 280, 283–4, 235–9, 243–5. Other reports of the first speech—the one included here—are in *London Chronicle*, 14 March; *London Evening Post*, 14 March; and *London Courant*, 14 March. Reports of the other speeches are in *General Advertiser*, 15 March; *London Chronicle*, 14 March; *Morning Chronicle*, 15 March; *St James's Chronicle*, 14 March; *Whitehall Evening Post*, 16 March; and *Morning Post*, 14 March.

On 13 March Lord North moved for leave to bring in a Bill 'to appoint and enable Commissioners to take, state, and make up the public accounts, to ascertain what balances were in the hands of public officers; to discover what defects existed in the mode of making up accounts in the Exchequer, and to report to the House what they should deem the best method to remove them'.[1] He gave reasons why such commissioners should not be members of the House.

Mr. *Burke* said, the noble Lord[2] had given the House the very opinion of the matter which he entertained of it. He would however say a word or two in addition. The Petitions of the people ought to be listened to, and indeed he was happy to find, that they had already produced so good an effect within those walls; he believed the noble Lord in consequence had suggested a commission of accounts; but good God, what sort of a commission did the noble Lord now wish to have! not an

---

[1] *Parl. Reg.* xvii. 281.
[2] Simon Luttrell, 1st Baron Irnham (1713–87), M.P. 1755–80, later (1781) Viscount and (1785) Earl of Cathampton all in the Irish peerage.

able efficient commission composed of Members of Parliament, men of high character, whose names were known to the public and whose reputations were a bond of security and a seal of certainty, that they would honestly and faithfully discharge their duty as commissioners, but a weak and incapable commission composed of whom?—not of Members of Parliament! not of responsible men! but composed of obscure individuals, men, picked out of corners, and huddled together no man knew how! The petitions prayed redress of grievances, and the loud voice of the people called for reformation and œconomy. Was this commission a commencement of a plan of œconomy? Would it put an end to the abuses of the influence of the Crown? to the impositions of Contractors, to the profusion of the public expenditure? No such thing. It tended to increase the influence of the Crown, to create a new board, to create new dependents on the Minister, to create an un-necessary encrease of expence! He therefore for one would oppose the Bill. Every honest Member of Parliament ought to oppose it. Who were so competent to inspect the public accounts as Members of Parliament? What was their daily duty, but to call for accounts? He might have occasion to call for many in the progress of his Bill through the House, and if the noble Lord's Bill passed, it clogged and effectually damn'd up all enquiry, that he or any other member might think proper to institute, because when any papers was called for, how easy would it be for the Treasury Board to answer, "The subject the papers went to was before the Commissioners;" so that Commissioners, not authorized by the Constitution would possess a superseding power over members of Parliament. Mr. Burke concluded with objecting strongly to the Bill, and declaring, that though he was conscious there were many members more competent to the office of Commissioner of accounts than he was, yet he was ready and willing to be one, and to pay the business all possible attention without either fee or reward.

North's Commission was approved and passed into law (20 Geo. III, c. 54).

Form of Association
[April 1780]

Source: MS. at Sheffield, R91.12

In the hand of Zouch with corrections by Burke. There is also a copy at Sheffield (R165.1).

The leaders of the parliamentary Opposition agreed sometime in early 1780 to secede from Parliament, issue an Address, and establish an association based on support for economical reform. For various reasons, this policy had not been carried out.[1] Evidently attempts to draw up a form of association had been started, for the following appears to be Burke's text for it. There is also a longer text which survives in the hand of the Marchioness of Rockingham, with corrections by John Lee.[2]

The Rockinghams appear by this time to have viewed the association movement largely as a last ditch effort to establish their own leadership of the Opposition campaign and to unite it in support of temperate measures. When Burke drew up the following agreement the chances for a united front had dimmed after the loss of his measure in the House of Commons. In Parliament, most of the Rockinghams were becoming isolated not only from Lord Shelburne and his following but also from close friends including the Duke of Richmond and Sir George Savile over the question of parliamentary reform. Outside they were at odds with Wyvill and a total of twelve county and four town committees which had taken up the cause of annual Parliaments and a reform of the system of representation.[3] Rockingham had been able to convince himself to make a concession to more radical forces by accepting triennial Parliaments since this 'was the Term of duration fixed at the Revolution',[4] but he could go no further and this did little to ameliorate differences. He and Burke may well have anticipated vigorously promoting association, based strictly on economy in government and resistance to the undue influence of the Crown, as a means to overcome all the diversity of opinion. The fact that they did little or nothing after the following terms were drawn up suggests that they soon gave up that objective perhaps out of frustration.[5]

Whereas this Nation hath by the prevalence of Evil Councils, and by various neglects and Mismanagements been reduced in a few years from a most prosperous and flourishing State into a Condition of

---

[1] *Corr.* iv. 216–17.
[2] MS. at Sheffield R81.54; copy, R165(2).
[3] *Corr.* iv. 216, 217.
[4] R1.1883: to Henry Zouch, 23 March 1780.
[5] See Burke's speech of 8 May 1780 on the duration of Parliaments, below, pp. 588–602.

much distress and danger, and thereby discontents divisions and heartburnings have arisen, and are likely to encrease, we hold it therefore highly expedient at this time to make an open declaration of our Sentiments and our designs, in order to avoid as much as may be all Misunderstandings and to unite in one firm accord such of our good fellow Subjects as may be disposed to join with us in our endeavours for the redress of the Grievances which we suffer and for removing the Causes thereof so far as we have discovered or shall discover them.

First then, we profess and declare that, we are firmly attached to the present Constitution of our Country as it now stands and as it hath long stood, in King, Lords, and Commons. And neither propose or wish any alteration further than shall appear necessary for securing that great and evident principle, fundamental in our Constitution, namely the independency of Parliament.

We declare, that all the measures of reformation which we have pursued have been in affirmance and support of the said principle; and that we have not been nor are desirous of postponing, or setting aside any proposal of Amendment in the Constitution, further as it hath appeared to us of a doubtful Tendency with regard to that Object.

For the Sake of that principle we have supported in this Session three Bills; one for the suspending the Votes of Officers concerned in the collection of the Revenues; one for excluding Contractors from Seats in Parliament; and one for lessening publick expence, and the influence of the Crown in the Civil and other Establishments.

These three Bills had they been carried would have gone a great way towards the reduction of undue influence; would have obstructed no real Service and weakened no useful power of Government, and would have been attended with many collateral advantages.

If any thing more shall appear to be equally advisable for the same great purpose, and equally clear of reasonable objections, shall be proposed, we are open and desirous to consider and embrace it; but informed as we now are, we do not think it safe to engage for attempting any further alteration in the frame of our Government.

But with regard to the executive Administration of that Government in which the greatest abuses reside, and which being entrusted with the Conduct of all the affairs of the Kingdom abroad and at home hath by Misconduct brought his Majesty and this Nation into their present Condition, we mean strictly and diligently to enquire into the same without[1] passion or partiality; and to animadvert upon those who are by Law responsible for the Management thereof in such a manner as may be agreeable to Justice and a provident regard to the publick good— endeavouring to introduce a better order in the Administration of Affairs, and to employ the publick Money with that frugality which may give efficiency to the publick efforts and to secure the integrity of those who are entrusted with it.

For these purposes we do hereby associate ourselves faithfully and firmly promising to adhere and stand by one another in every Lawful and prudent means of promoting and forwarding the same, and we do invite the Gentlemen Clergy Freeholders Citizens and Burgesses of the Kingdom (without whose hearty and steady Aid this our strength against the above abuses will be as it has been vain and frivolous) to unite with us in this our Engagements.

Sketch of a Negro Code
[*post* 9 April 1780]

Source: Add. MS. 37,890, fos. 3–12

The MS., endorsed 'Sketch of the Negro Code', is in a clerk's hand with corrections and additions by Burke. All the square brackets are in the MS. The text printed in *Works* was from a rough draft, now missing, and the 'marginal references' 'marginal heads' were supplied by the editor (*Works*, 1792–1827, v. xiv; *Corr.* vii. 122) and are not reproduced here. In a letter to Henry Dundas of 9 April 1792, Burke described the Code as 'being done near twelve years ago' (*Corr.* vii. 122).

Burke had enunciated his disapproval of the Slave trade in the House of Commons on at least one occasion since his speeches of 5 June 1777.[2] In 1778 he praised the African Company but added:

He did not look upon the interference of Government as any benefit to commerce. If a branch of traffic will produce an adequate return, he was convinced the spirit of the merchants would prosecute. If it was not adequate, Government might squander the public money to little account. He did not therefore attribute the decay of the African trade to the non-interference of Administration, but to its own inadequate nature; and

[1] In deleting a word here, Burke has omitted to delete a comma.
[2] Printed above.

he confessed, that he was no advocate for a trade which consisted, in the greatest measure, of men's bodies, and not of manufactures.[1]

The following Negro Code evinces his genuine distaste for the trade and his desire to ameliorate some of its most inhuman practices. That Burke continued to recognize that his views were out of step with those of many of his friends and constituents at Bristol appears to be demonstrated by the fact that the code was not circulated publicly until just after the election in September 1780.[2]

Whereas it is expedient and conformable to the principles of true religion and morality, and to the Rules of sound policy, to put an end to all traffic in the persons of Men, and to the detention of their said persons in a State of Slavery, as soon as the same may be effected without producing great inconveniences in the sudden Change of practices of such long standing, and during the continuance of the said practices it is desirable and expedient, by proper regulations, to lessen the inconveniences and evils attendant on the said Traffic, and state of Servitude, until both shall be gradually done away.

And whereas the Objects of the said Trade and consequential servitude, and the Grievances resulting therefrom, come under the principal heads following, the Regulations ought thereto be severally applied—that is to say that Provisions should be made by the said Regulations,

1st for duly qualifying Ships for the said Traffic.

2ndly—For the mode and the Conditions of permi⟨tt⟩ing the said Trade to be carried on upon the Coast of Africa.

3rdly—For the Treatment of the Negroes in their Passage to the West India Islands.

4thly—For the Government of the Negroes which are or shall be employed in his Majesty's Colonies and plantations in the West Indies.

Be it therefore enacted etc.

1. That the Owner or Owners of every ship or trading Vessel which is intended for the Negro trade shall be enter'd and register'd as Ships

---

[1] *General Advertiser*, 14 May 1778. The *General Evening Post*, 14 May, and *Public Advertiser*, 14 May, reported this speech as follows: '*Mr. Burke* supported his Lordship's argument, and argued that the interference of Government in affairs of traffic was seldom of any good. The commerce that does not support itself can never be held up by the artificial supply of any Government; and for the trade of Africa in particular, he rather rejoiced at its downfall; for it was a trade of the most inhuman nature, a traffic for human bodies.'

[2] See P. T. Underdown, 'Edmund Burke, the Commissary of his Bristol Constituents', *English Historical Review*, lxxiii (1958), 252–69.

trading to the West Indies are by Law to be register'd with the further provisions following.

The said Entry and Register shall contain an Account of the greatest number of Negroes of all descriptions which are proposed to be taken into the said Ship or trading Vessel; and the said Ship, before she is permitted to be entered outwards shall be surveyed by a Ship Carpenter, to be appointed by the Collector of the Port from which the said Vessel is to depart, and by a Surgeon also appointed by the Collector who hath been conversant in the service of the said Trade, but not at the time actually engaged or convenanted therein, and the said Carpenter and Surgeon shall report to the Collector, or in his absence to the next principal Officer of the Port, upon oath, which Oath, the said Collector or principal Officer is hereby empower'd to administer, her measurement and what she contains in Builders' Tonnage and that she has [   ]¹ of grated Portholes between the Decks, and that she is otherwise fitly found, as a good Transport Vessel.

2. And be it enacted that no Ship employed in the said Trade, shall upon any pretence, take in more Negroes than one grown Man or Woman for—[one ton and half] of Builder's tonnage, nor more than one Boy or Girl for [one ton].

3. That the said Ship or other Vessel shall lay in, in proportion to the Ship's Company of the said Vessel, and the number of Negroes register'd a full and sufficient store of sound provision, so as to secure against all delays and accidents, namely, salted beef, Pork, saltfish, Butter, Cheese Biscuit, flour, Rice, Oatmeal and white Peas; but no Horse-beans or other inferior provisions—and the said Ship shall be properly provided with water-Casks, or Jars, in proportion to the intended number of the said Negroes; and the said Ship shall be also provided with a proper and sufficient stock of Coals or firewood.

4. And every Ship enter'd as aforesaid shall take out a coarse Shirt, and a pair of Trousers or Petticoat for each Negro, intended to be taken abroad, as also a Mat or coarse Mattrass or hammock for the use of the said Negroes.—The proportions of provision, fuel and Cloathing to be regulated by the Table annexed to this Act.

5. And be it enacted that no Ship shall be permitted to proceed on the said Voyage or Adventure until the Searcher of the Port from

---

¹ The square brackets here and throughout the text are in the MS.

whence the said Vessel shall sail or such Person as he shall appoint to act for him, shall report to the Collector that he hath inspected the said Stores, and that the Ship is accomodated and provided in the manner hereby directed.

6. And be it enacted that no Guns be exported to the Coast of Africa in the said or any other Trade unless the same be duly marked with the Maker's name on the barrels before they are put into the Stocks, and vouched by an Inspector in the place where the same are made, to be without fraud, sound, sufficient and merchantable Arms.

7. And be it enacted that before any Ship as aforesaid shall proceed on her Voyage, the Owner or Owners, or an Attorney by them named if the Owners are more than two, and the Master, shall severally give Bond, the Owners for themselves, and the Master for himself, that the said Master shall duly conform himself in all things to the Regulations in this Act contained, so far as the same regards his part in executing and conforming.

And whereas, in providing for the second Object of this Act, that is to say, for the Trade on the Coast of Africa, it is just and prudent, not only to provide against the manifold Abuses to which a Trade of that nature is liable, but that the same may be accompanied, as far as is possible, with such advantages to the Natives, as may tend to the civilizing them, and enabling them to enrich themselves by means more desirable, and to carry on hereafter a Trade, more advantageous and honorable to all parties.

And whereas Religion, Order, Morality and Virtue are the elemental principles, and the knowlege of Letters, Arts, and handicraft Trades, the chief means of such civilization and improvement. For the better attainment of the said good purposes, be it hereby enacted,

1. That the Coast of Africa on which the said Trade for Negroes may be carried on, shall be and is, hereby divided into [   ] Marts or Staples as follows [   ] And be it enacted that it shall not be lawful for the Master of any ship to purchase conclusively any Negro or Negroes, but at one of the said Marts or Staples and no Master of a Ship shall depart from any of the Marts aforesaid until his whole Cargo of slaves shall be examined attested, and duly cleared out from the Mart or Staple in which his ship shall have traded.

2. That the Directors of the African company shall appoint, where not already appointed, a Governor with three Counsellors at each of

the said Marts with a Salary of [   ] to the Governor, and of
[   ] to each of the said Counsellors. The said Governor, or in
his absence or illness, the senior Counsellors, shall and are hereby
empowered to act as a Justice of peace and they or either of them
are authorised, order'd and directed to provide for the peace of
the Settlement, and the good regulations of their Stations severally
according to the rules of Justice, and to the directions of this Act, and
to the instructions they shall receive from time to time from the said
African Company; and the said African Company is hereby authorised
to prepare instructions with the assent of the Lords of his Majesty's
privy Council, which shall be binding in all things not contrary to this
Act or to the Laws of England, or the said Governors and Counsellors,
every of them, and of all persons acting in commission with them
under this Act, and on all persons residing or trading within the
jurisdiction of the Magistrates of the said Mart.

3. And be it enacted that the Lord High Admiral or Commissioners
shall appoint one or more, as they shall see convenient of his Majesty's
Ships or Sloops of War, under the command severally of a post
Captain or Master and Commander, to each Mart, as a Naval Station.

4. And be it enacted that the Lord High Treasurer or the Commissioners for executing the Office of Vice Treasurer, shall name for
each Mart two Inspectors of the said Trade who shall provide for the
execution of this Act, according to the directions thereof, so far as shall
relate to them and shall examine the State and Condition of each
Slave before he be shipped from the Mart aforesaid; and it is hereby
provided and enacted that as Cases of sudden emergency may arise,
the said Governor or first Counsellor, and the first Commander of his
Majesty's Ship or Ships, on the said Station, and the said Inspectors or
the majority of them, the Governor having a double, or casting Voice,
shall have power and authority to make such occasional Rules and
Orders relative to the said Trade, as shall not be contrary to the
instructions of the African Company and which shall be valid until the
same are revoked by the said African Company.

5. That the said African Company is hereby authorized to purchase,
if the same may conveniently be done, with the consent of the Privy
Council, any Lands adjoining to the Fort or principal Mart aforesaid
not exceeding [   ] Acres, and to make allotments of the same. No
allotment to one person, to exceed (on pain of forfeiture) [   ]
Acres.

6. That the African Company shall at each Fort or Mart, cause to be erected in a convenient time and at a moderate Cost, the estimate of which shall be approved of by [the Treasury] one Church, one School house, and one Hospital and shall appoint one principal Chaplain, with a Curate and Assistant in holy orders, both of whom shall be recommended by the Lord Bishop of London with a Salary [   ] And the said Chaplain or his Assistant shall perform divine Service and administer the Sacraments according to the usage of the Church of England, or to such mode, not contrary thereto as to the said Bishop shall seem more suitable to the circumstances of the people; and the said principal Chaplain shall be the third Member in the Council, and shall be entitled to receive from the Directors of the said African Company, a Salary of [   ] and his Assistant a Salary of [   ]. And he shall have power to appoint one sober and discreet person, to be his Clerk and Catechist, at a Salary of [   ].

7. And be it enacted that the African Directors or Committee shall appoint one sufficient Schoolmaster who shall be approved by the Bishop of London, and who shall be capable of teaching Writing, Arithmetic, surveying and Mensuration, at a Salary of [   ] And the said African Committee is hereby authorised to provide for each settlement a Carpenter and Blacksmith with such encouragement as to them shall seem expedient, who shall take each, two Apprentices from amongst the Natives, to instruct them in their several Trades, the African Company allowing them as a fee for each Apprentice [   ]. And the said African Company shall appoint one Surgeon, and one Surgeon's Mate, who are to be approv'd on examination at Surgeon's Hall, to each Fort or Mart, with a Salary of [   ] for the Surgeon and for his mate [   ] and the said Surgeon shall take one native Apprentice, at a fee to be settled by the African Committee.

8. And be it enacted that the said Catechist, Schoolmaster, Surgeon, and Surgeon's Mate, as well as the Tradesmen in the Company's service, shall be obedient to the orders they shall from time to time receive from the Governor and Council of each Fort—and if they or any of them, or any person in whatever station, shall appear on Complaint and proof, to the majority of the Commissioners to lead a disorderly and debauched life, or use any profane or impious discourses to the danger of defeating the purposes of this Institution, and to the scandal of the Natives, who are to be led by all due means into a respect for our holy Religion, and a desire of partaking of the

benefits thereof, they are authorised and directed to suspend the said
Person from his Office or the exercise of his Trade, and to send him
to England (but without any hard confinement except in case of
resistance) with the Complaint, on which he hath been removed and
with the Enquiry and proofs adjoined, to the African Company.

9. And be it enacted that the Bishop of London for the time being,
shall have full authority to remove the said Chaplain on such causes as
to him shall seem reasonable.

10. And be it enacted that no Governor, Counsellor, Inspector,
Chaplain, Surgeon or Schoolmaster, shall be concerned or have any
share directly or indirectly, in the Negro Trade, on pain of [   ]

11. And be it enacted that the said Governor and Council shall keep
a Journal of all their proceedings and a Book in which Copies of all
their Correspondences shall be enter'd, and they shall transmit Copies
of the said Journals and Letter Book, and their Books of Accounts
to the African Company, who within [   ] of their Receipt
thereof shall communicate the same to one of his Majesty's principal
Secretarys of State.

12. And be it enacted that the said Chaplain or principal Minister
shall correspond with the Bishop of London, and faithfully and diligently transmit to him an account of whatever hath been done for the
advancement of Religion, morality and learning amongst the Natives.

13. And be it enacted that no Negro shall be conclusively sold, until
he shall be attested by the two Inspectors and Chaplain, or in case of
the illness of one Inspector, by one Inspector, and the Governor or one
of the Council—who are hereby authorised and directed, by the
best means in their power, to examine into the Circumstances and
Condition of the Persons exposed to sale.

14. And for the better direction of the said Inspectors, no persons
are to be sold, who to the best judgment of the said Inspectors, shall be
above thirty five years of Age, or who shall appear on examination to be
stolen, or carried away by the Dealers by surprize, nor any person who
is able to read in the Arabian or any other Book, nor any Woman who
shall appear to be advanced three Months in pregnancy, nor any
person distorted or feeble, unless the said Persons are consenting
to such sale—or any person afflicted with a grievous or contagious
distemper—But if any person so offer'd is only lightly disorder'd, the
said person may be sold; but must be kept in the Hospital of the
Mart—and shall not be shipped, until completely cured.

15. And be it enacted that no black or European Trader or Factor shall be permitted to Trade into the interior Country, or the Coast (the Masters of English Ships only excepted, for whose good Conduct provision is otherwise herein made) to buy or sell in any of the said Marts, unless he be approved by the Governor of the Mart in which he is to deal, or in his absence or disability, by the senior Counsellor for the time being—and obtaining a Licence from such Governor—and the said Traders and Factors shall severally or jointly, as they shall be concerned, before they shall obtain the said Licence be bound in a recognizance with one Security, for his or their good behaviour, as to the said Governor shall seem the best that can be obtained.

16. Be it enacted that the said Governor or other Authority afore-said shall examine as by his duty of Office into the conduct of all such Traders and Factors, as well as receive and publicly hear, with the Assistance of the Council and Inspectors aforesaid and of the Commodore, Captain or other principal Commander of one of his Majesty's Ships on the said Station, or as many of the same as can be assembled, two whereof, with the Governor, are hereby enabled to act, all complaints against them or any of them; and that if any black or white Trader or Factor (other than is in this Act excepted) and if either on inquisition of Office, or on Complaint, the said Traders or Factors, shall be convicted by a majority of the said Commissioners present, of stealing or taking by surprize, any person or persons whatsoever, whether free or the Slaves of others, without the consent of their Masters—or of wilfully and maliciously killing or maiming any person; or of any cruelty—necessary restraint only excepted, or of firing Houses, or destroying Goods, the said Trader or Factor shall be deemed to have forfeited his Recognizance, and his Security to have forfeited his, and the said Trader or Factor so convicted shall in case of murder or stealing, be deliver'd over to the Prince to whom he belongs to execute further justice on him, and shall be for ever dis-abled from dealing in any of the said Marts—unless the Offence shall be short of Murder, maiming, arson, stealing or surprizing the Person, and shall appear to the Commissioners aforesaid, to merit only, besides the penalty of his Bond, a suspension for one year. But it is hereby provided and enacted that if any European shall be con-victed of any of the said Offences, he shall be sent to Europe, together with the evidence against him, and on the warrant of the said Com-missioners, the Keeper of any of his Majesty's Jails in London,

Bristol, Liverpool, or Glasgow, shall receive him until he be deliver'd according to due course of Law, as if the said Offences had been committed within the Cities and Towns aforesaid.

17. Be it further enacted that if the said Governor, etc., shall be satisfied that any person or persons are exposed to sale who have been stolen or forced as aforesaid, or are not within the qualifications of Sale in this Act described, they are hereby authorised, if it can be done, to send the persons so described to their original habitation or settlement, in the manner they shall deem best for their security, allowing the said Governor, by the African Company, the reasonable Charges, unless they choose to sell themselves; and then, in that case, their Value in Money or Goods at their pleasure shall be secured to them, applicable to their use, without any dominion over the same of any Master to whom they may be sold, in the Colony or plantation in which they are to be disposed of, which shall always be in some of his Majesty's Colonies and plantations only—and the Master of the Ship in which such person shall embark, shall give bond for the faithful execution of his part of the trust at the Island on which he shall break bulk.

18. Be it further enacted, that besides the Hospital on Shore, one or more Hospital Ships shall be employed at each of the said chief Marts, wherein Slaves taken ill in the trading Ships shall be accomodated, until they shall be cured, and then that the owner may reclaim them, and shall again receive them on paying the Charges which shall be settled by regulation to be made by the Authority in this Act, enabled to provide such regulations.

And whereas it is necessary that Regulations be made to prevent abuses in the passage from Africa to the West Indies, be it further enacted—

1. That the Commander or Lieutenant of the King's Ship on each Station shall have authority, as often as he shall see occasion, attended with one of his Officers, and his Surgeon or Mate, to enter into and inspect every trading Ship, in order to provide for the due execution of this Act, and of any ordinances made in virtue thereof, and conformable thereto by the authorities herein constituted and appointed. And the said Officer or Officers are hereby required to examine every trading Ship, before she sails, and to stop the sailing of the said Ship or Ships, for the breach of the said Rules and Regulations,

until the Governor and Council shall order and direct otherwise; And the Master of the said Ship shall not presume, under the penalty of [   ] to be recover'd in the Courts of the West Indies, to sail without a Certificate from the Commander aforesaid, and one of the Inspectors in this Act appointed, that the said Vessel is provided with Stores, and other accomodations, sufficient for her Voyage, and has not a greater number of Slaves on board, than by the provisions of this Act is allowed.

2. And be it enacted that the Governor and Council, with the assistance of the said Naval Commander shall have power to give such special written Instructions for the health, discipline and care of the said Slaves, during their passage, as to them shall seem good.

3. And be it further enacted that each Slave at entering the said Ship is to receive some small present not exceeding in value [   ] to be provided according to the directions aforesaid; and musical Instruments according to the fashion of the Country are to be provided.

4. And be it further enacted that the Negroes on board the Transport, and the Seamen who navigate the same, are to receive their daily allowance according to the Table together with a certain quantity of Spirits to be mixed with their water. And it is enacted that the Table is to be fixed, and to continue for one week after sailing in some conspicuous part of the said Ship for the Seamen's inspection of the same.

5. And be it enacted that the Captain of each trading Vessell shall be enabled to appoint one Negro Man of every [ten or twenty] in his Ship, to have such authority over the other [   ] as according to his judgment, and the Master's and Surgeon's, he and they shall seem good to commit to them, and to allow to each of them some compensation in extraordinary diet and presents not exceeding [ten Shillings'].

6. And be it enacted that any European Officer or Seaman having unlawful communication with any Woman Slave, shall, if an Officer, pay five pounds to the use of the said Woman, on landing her from the said Ship, to be stopped out of his wages, or if a Seaman, forty Shillings; the said penalties to be recovered on the Testimony of the Woman so abused and one other.

7. And be it enacted that all, and every Commander of a Vessel or Vessels employed in that Trade having received Certificates from the

571

Port, of the outfit and from the proper Officers in Africa and the West Indies of their having conformed to the regulations of this Act, and not having lost more than one in thirty of their Slaves by death, shall be entitled to a bounty or premium of [ten pound].

WEST INDIES.

Whereas the condition of Persons in a state of servitude is such, that they are utterly unable to take advantage of any remedy which the Laws may provide for their protection and the amendment of their condition, and have not the proper means of pursuing any process for the same, but are, and must be, under Guardianship, and that it is not fitting that they should be under the sole Guardianship of their Masters, or their Attorneys and Overseers, from whom their grievances whenever they suffer any must ordinarily be oweing—

1. Be it therefore enacted that his Majestys Attorney General for the time being and successively, shall by his Office, exercise the Trust and Employment of Protector of Negroes within the Island in which he is or shall be Attorney General to his Majesty, his Heirs and Successors, and that the said Attorney General, Protector of Negroes, is hereby authorised to hear any Complaint on the part of any Negro or Negroes, and enquire into the same or may institute[1] an enquiry ex officio, and may call before him and examine Witnesses relative to the subject Matter of the said official enquiry or complaint. And it is hereby enacted and declared that the said Attorney General, protector of Negroes, is hereby authorised and empower'd at his discretion, to file an information ex officio, for any offences against the provisions of this Act, or for any misdemeanours or wrongs against the said Negroes, or any of them.

2. And it is further enacted that in all Trials of such information, the said Protector of Negroes, may and is hereby authorised to challenge peremptorily a number not exceeding [six] of the Jury who shall be impannelled to try the Charge in the said information contained.

3. And be it enacted that the said Attorney General, protector of Negroes shall appoint Inspectors, not exceeding the number of

[1] MS.: 'instute.'

[   ] at his discretion; and the said Inspectors shall be placed in convenient Districts in each Island severally, or shall, twice in the year, make a Circuit in the same according to the direction which they shall receive from the protector of Negroes aforesaid. And the said Inspectors shall, and they are hereby required twice in the year to report in writing to the Protector aforesaid, the state and condition of the Negroes in their Districts, or on their Circuit, severally—the number, Sex, age, and occupation of the said Negroes on each plantation; and the Overseer or chief Manager on each plantation, is hereby required to furnish an Account thereof within [ten days] after the demand of the said Inspectors, and to permit the Inspector or Inspectors aforesaid, to examine into the same; and the said Inspectors shall set forth in the said Report, the Distempers to which the Negroes are most liable in the several parts of the Island.

4. And be it enacted that the said Protector of Negroes, by and with the consent of the Governor and chief Judge of each Island, shall form instructions, by which the said Inspectors shall discharge their trust, in the manner the least capable of exciting any unreasonable hopes in the said Negroes, or of weakening the proper authority of the Overseer, and shall transmit them to one of his Majesty's principal Secretaries of State—and when sent back to him, with his approbation, the same shall become the Rule for the Conduct of the said Inspectors.

5. And be it enacted that the said Attorney General, protector of Negroes, shall appoint an office for registering all proceedings had relative to the duty of his place, as Protector of Negroes, and shall appoint his chief Clerk to such Register with a Salary not exceeding [   ].

6. And be it enacted, that no Negroes shall be landed for sale in any but the Ports following, that is to say [   ] and that the Collector of each of the said Ports, severally, shall in [   ] after the arrival of any Ship transporting Negroes, report the same to the Protector of Negroes, or to one of his Inspectors; and the said Protector is hereby authorised and required by one of his Deputies with the assistance of the said Collector or his Deputy, and a Surgeon to be called in on the occasion, diligently to examine, or cause to be examined the state of the said Ship and transport Negroes, and upon what shall appear to them the said Protector of Negroes, and the said Collector to be a sufficient proof, either as arising from their own inspection or sufficient information on a summary process, and if any contravention of

573

this Act, or cruelty to the Negroes or other malversation of the said
Captain or any of his Officers, to impose a fine on him or them, not
exceeding [   ] which shall not however weaken or invalidate any
penalty growing from the bond of the said Master, or his Owners. And
it is hereby provided that if the said Master etc, shall find himself
aggrieved by the said fine, he may within [   ] days appeal to the
Chief Judge, if the Court shall be sitting, or to the Governor who
shall and are required to hear the said parties, and on hearing, are
authorised to annul or confirm the same.

7. And be it enacted that no sale of Negroes shall be made but in
the presence of an Inspector and the said Negroes shall be sold
severally, or in known and ascertain'd lots, containing the description
of each lot, and not otherwise—and a paper containing the State and
description of each Negro severally sold, and of each lot, shall be
taken and register'd in the office aforesaid—and if on inspection or
information it shall be found that any Negro shall have in the same
ship, or any other at the same time examined, a wife, an Husband, a
Brother, Sister, or Child, the person or persons so related shall not be
sold separately at that or any future sale.

8. And be it enacted that each and every of his Majesty's Islands
and plantations, in which Negroes are used in cultivation, shall be by
the Governor and the Protector of Negroes for the time being, divided
into Districts, attending as much as convenience will admit, to the
present division into parishes, and subdividing them where necessary
into Districts according to the number of Negroes—and the said
Governor and protector of Negroes shall cause in each District, a
Church to be built in a convenient place with a Cemetery annexed, and
an house for the residence of a Clergyman with [   ] Acres of
Land, annexed—and they are hereby authorised to treat for the
necessary ground with the Proprietor, who is hereby obliged to sell and
dispose of the same to the said use; and in case of dispute concerning
the value, the same to be settled if required by the parties, by a Jury as
in like Cases is accustomed.

9. And be it enacted that in each of the said Districts shall be
established a presbyter of the Church of England as by law established,
who shall appoint under him one Clerk, who shall be a free Negro,
when such properly qualified can be found (otherwise a white Man)
with a Salary in each case of [   ], and the said Minister and Clerk,
both or one shall instruct the said Negroes in the Church Catechism

or such other as shall be provided by the authority in this Act named.

10. And the principal Overseer of each plantation is hereby required to deliver annually unto the Minister a list of all the Negroes upon his plantation, distinguishing their Sex, and age, and shall under a penalty of [   ] cause all the Negroes under his care, above the age of [   ] years, to attend divine Services once on every sunday, except in case of sickness, infirmity, or other necessary Cause to be given at the time, and shall, by himself or one of those who act under him, provide for the orderly behaviour of the Negroes under him, and cause them to return to his plantation, when divine Service, or administration of Sacraments, or Catechism is ended.

11. And be it enacted that the Minister shall have power to punish, by a punishment, not exceeding ten blows, to be given in one day and for one offence, which the Overseer or his under Agent or Agents, is hereby directed, according to the orders of the said Minister, effectually to inflict.

12. And be it enacted that no spirituous Liquors of any kind shall be sold, except in Towns, within [   ] distance of any Church, nor within any district, during divine Service, and an hour preceding and an hour following the same—and the Minister of each Parish shall, and is hereby authorised to act as a Justice of peace in enforcing the said Regulation.

13. And be it enacted that every Minister, as above described shall keep a Register of Births, Burials, and Marriages, of all Negroes and Mulattoes in his District.

14. And be it enacted that the Ministers of the several Districts shall meet annually on the [   ] of [   ] in a Synod of the Island, to which they belong; and the said Synod shall have for its[1] President, such person as the Bishop of London shall appoint for his Commissary; and the said synod[2] or general assembly is hereby authorised, by a majority[3] of voices, to make Regulations; which Regulations shall be transmitted by the said President or Commissary, to the Bishop of London, and when returned by the Bishop of London approved of, then and not before the said Regulations shall be in force to bind the said Clergy, their Assistants, Clerks and Schoolmasters only, and no other persons.

[1] The MS. is torn: 'for its' supplied from *Works*.
[2] 'synod' is supplied from *Works*.
[3] 'majority' is supplied from *Works*.

15. And be it enacted, that the said president shall collect matter in the said Assembly, and shall make a Report of the State of Religion, and Morals in the several parishes, from whence the Synod is deputed, and shall transmit the same, once in the Year, in duplicate thro' the Governor and the protector of Negroes to the Bishop of London.

16. And be it enacted and declared that the Bishop of London for the time being, shall be patron to all and every the said Cures in this Act directed, and the said Bishop is hereby required to provide for the due filling thereof, and is to receive from the Fund in this Act provided, for the due execution of this Act, a sum not exceeding [   ] for each of the said Ministers for his outfit and passage.

17. And be it enacted that on Misbehaviour, and on complaint from the said Synod, and on hearing the Party accused in a plain and summary manner, it shall and may be lawful for the Bishop of London to suspend or remove any Minister from his Cure, as his said offences shall appear to merit.

18. And be it enacted that for every two Districts a School shall be established for young Negroes, to be taught three days in the week, and to be detain'd from their Owner four hours in each day—The said number not to be more or fewer than twenty Males, who shall be chosen, and vacancies filled, by the Minister of the District; and the said Minister shall pay to the owners of the said Boys, and shall be allowed the same in his Accounts at the Synod, to the age of twelve years old, three pence by the day; and from every Boy from twelve years old to fifteen, five pence by the day.

19. And it is enacted, that if the President of the Synod aforesaid shall certify to the Protector of Negroes, that any Boys in the said school [provided that the number in no year shall exceed one in one year in the Island of Jamaica, and one in two years in the Island of Barbadoes, Antigua and Grenada and one in four years from any of the other,] do shew a remarkable aptitude for Learning, the said Protector is hereby authorised and directed, to purchase the said Boy at the best rate, at which Boys of that age and strength have been sold within the year; and the said Negro so purchased shall be under the entire Guardianship of the said Protector of Negroes, who shall send him[1] to the Bishop of London for his further education[2] in England, and

---

[1] 'send him' is supplied from *Works*.
[2] 'education' is supplied from *Works*.

may charge in his Accounts [   ] for the expence of transporting him to England—and the Bishop of London shall provide for the education of such of the said Negroes as he shall think proper Subjects until the age of twenty four years—and shall order those who shall fall short of expectation, after one year, to be bound Apprentice to some handicraft trade; and when his Apprenticeship is finished, the Lord Mayor of London is hereby authorised and directed to receive the said Negro from his Master, and to transmit him to the Island from which he came in the West Indies, to be there as a free Negro, subject however to the direction of the Protector of Negroes relatively to his behavior and employment.

20. And it is hereby enacted and provided that any Planter or Owner of Negroes not being of the Church of England, and not choosing to send his Negroes to attend divine Service in the manner by this Act directed, shall give jointly or severally, as the Case shall require, Security to the protector of Negroes, that a competent Minister of some Christian Church or Congregation shall be provided for the due instruction of the Negroes and for their performing divine Service, according to the description of the Religion of the Master or Masters in some Church or House thereto alloted in the manner and with the regulations in this Act prescribed, with regard to the exercise of Religion according to the Church of England.

Provided always that the Marriages of the said Negroes belonging to Dissenters, shall be celebrated only in the Church of the said District—and that a register of the Births shall be transmitted to the Minister of the said District. And the Minister aforesaid shall baptize and cause to be carefully instructed in the Christian Religion, all Negroes not baptized, or not belonging to Dissenters from the Church of England as aforesaid.

And whereas a state of Matrimony and the Government of a family is a principal means of forming men to a fitness for freedom, and to become good Citizens, be it enacted—

21. That all Negro Men and Women above eighteen years of age for the Men, and sixteen for the Women, who have cohabited together for twelve Months or upwards or who shall cohabit for the same time, and have a Child or Children, shall be deemed to all intents and purposes to be married; and either of the Parties is authorised to require of the Minister of the District, to be married in the face of the Church.

577

22. And be it enacted that from and after the [   ] of [   ] all Negro Men, in an healthy condition, and so reported to be in case the same is denied, by a Surgeon by the Inspector of Negroes to be appointed, and being twenty one years old or upwards, until fifty, and not being before married, shall, on requisition of the Inspector, be provided by their Masters or Overseers, with a Woman, not having Children living, and not exceeding the Age of the Man, and for any Man not exceeding the age of twenty five years, and such persons shall be married publicly in the face of the Church.

23. And be it enacted that the Minister in each District shall have, with the Assent of the Inspector, full power and authority to punish all Acts of Adultery, unlawful concubinage, and fornication, on hearing and a summary process, amongst Negroes, by ordering a number of blows not exceeding [thirty nine] for each offence. And if any white Person shall be proved on information in the Supreme Court, to be exhibited by the Protector of Negroes, to have committed Adultery with any Negro woman or to have corrupted any Negroe Woman under sixteen years of age, he shall be fined in the sum of [   ] and shall be for ever disabled from serving the Office of Overseer of Negroes, or being attorney to any Plantation.

24. And be it enacted that no Woman shall be obliged to field work, or any other laborious work for one month before her delivery or for six weeks afterwards.

25. And be it enacted that no Husband and Wife shall be sold separately, if originally belonging to the same Master nor shall any Children under sixteen be sold separately from their Parents, or one Parent, if one be living.

26. And be it enacted that if an Husband and Wife, which before their intermarriage belonged to different Owners, shall be sold, that they shall not be sold at such a distance as to prevent mutual help and cohabitation; and of this distance the Minister shall judge, and his Certificate of the inconvenient distance shall be valid, so as to make such sale unlawful, and to render the same null and void.

27. And be it enacted that no Negro shall be compelled to work for his Owner, at field work, or any service relative to a plantation, or to work at any handicraft trade from eleven OClock on Saturday forenoon, until the usual working hour on Monday Morning.

28. And whereas the habits of industry and sobriety and the means of acquiring and preserving property, are proper and reasonable

preparatives to freedom, and will secure against an abuse of the same, be it enacted that every Negroe Man who shall have served ten years, and is thirty years of age, and is married and has had two Children born of any Marriage, shall obtain the whole of Saturday for himself and his wife, for his own benefit, and after thirty seven years of age, the whole of friday for him and his wife, provided that in both Cases, the Minister of the District and the Inspector of Negroes shall certify that they know nothing against his peaceable, orderly, and industrious behavior.

29. And be it enacted that the Master of every plantation shall provide the materials of a good and substantial Hut for each married field Negro, and if his plantation shall exceed [   ] acres, shall allot a portion of Land not less than [   ] and the said Hut and Land annexed, shall remain to the said Negro for his natural life, or during his bondage, but the same shall not be alienated without the consent of the Owner.

30. And be it enacted that it shall not be lawful for the Owner of any Negro, by himself or any other, to take from him any land, house, Cattle, Goods, or Money acquired by the said Negro, whether by purchase, donation, or testament, whether the same has been derived from the Owner of the said Negro, or any other.

31. And be it enacted that if the said Negro should die possessed of any Lands, Goods, or Chattels, and dies without leaving a wife or issue, it shall be lawful for the said Negro to devise or bequeath the same by his last will—but in case the said Negro should leave a Wife and Children, the same shall be distributed amongst them according to the usage under the Statute commonly called the Statute of distributions.[1] But if the said Negro should die without Wife or Children, then and in that case, his Estate shall go to the Fund provided for the better execution of this Act.

32. And be it enacted that no Negro who is married and hath resided upon any plantation for twelve months, shall be sold either privately or by the decree of any Court, but along with the plantation on which he hath resided, unless he should himself request to be separated therefrom.

---

[1] The Statute of Distributions was 'An Act for the Better Settling of Intestates Estates' (22 and 23 Car. II, c. 10). It required ordinaries and judges to 'make just and equall distributions of what remaineth clear' of intestates' estates 'amongst the wife and children or next of kindred to the dead person' after debts, funeral costs, and so on had been paid.

33. And be it enacted that no blows or Stripes exceeding thirteen, shall be inflicted for one offence upon any Negro without the order of one of his Majesty's Justices of peace.

34. And it is enacted that it shall be lawful for the Protector of Negroes, as often as on complaint and hearing, he shall be of opinion that any Negro hath been cruelly and inhumanly treated, or when it shall be made to appear to him that an Overseer hath any particular malice, shall at the desire of the suffering Party, order the said Negro to be sold to another Master.

35. And be it enacted that in all Cases of injury to Member or life, the offences against a Negro shall be deemed and taken to all intents and purposes as if the same were perpetrated against any of his Majesty's Subjects; and the Protector of Negroes on complaint thereof, or if he shall receive credible information of any murder of a Negro, he shall cause the Coroner, or Officer acting as such to hold an Inquest into the same, or if this be not practicable, that he do cause, after examining a Witness or Witnesses, an Indictment to be presented for the same.

36. And in order to a gradual manumission of Slaves, as they shall seem fitted to fill the Offices of Freemen, be it enacted that every Negro Slave being thirty years of age and upwards, and who has had three Children born to him in lawful Matrimony and who hath received a Certificate from the Minister of his District, or any other Christian Teacher of his regularity in the duties of Religion, and of his orderly and good behaviour, may purchase at rates to be fixed by two Justices of peace the freedom of himself or his Wife, or Children, or of any of them separately, valuing the Wife and Children if purchased into liberty by the Father of the Family, at half only of their marketable value. Provided that the said Father shall bind himself in a penalty of [   ] for the good behaviour of his Children.

37. And be it enacted that it shall be lawful for the Protector of Negroes to purchase the freedom of any Negro who shall appear to him to excel in any mechanical Art or other knowledge or practice deem'd liberal and the value shall be settled by a Jury.

38. And be it enacted that the Protector of Negroes shall be and is authorised and required to act as a Magistrate for the coercion of all idle, dissolute, or disorderly free Negroes, and he shall by office prosecute them for the offences of idleness, drunkenness, quarreling, gaming or vagrancy, in the supreme Court, or cause them to

be prosecuted before one Justice of peace, as the Case may require.

39. And be it enacted that if any free Negro hath been twice convicted for any of the said Misdemeanors and is judged by the said Protector of Negroes, calling to his assistance, two Justices of the peace, that the said twice convicted free Negro is incorrigibly idle, dissolute, and vicious, it shall be lawful by the order of the said Protector and two Justices of peace, to sell the said free Negro into Slavery—the purchase money to be paid to the person so remanded into servitude, or kept in trust by the Protector and Governor, for the benefit of his Family.

40. And be it enacted that the Governor in each Colony shall be Assistant to the execution of this Act, and shall receive the Reports of the Protector, and such other Accounts as he shall judge material relative thereto, and shall transmit the same annually to one of his Majesty's principal Secretaries of State.[1]

Speech on Dunning's Motion
10 April 1780

Source: *Morning Chronicle*, 11 April 1780

This report is repeated in *Parl. Hist.* xxi. 384–5. Another report is in *Lloyd's Evening Post*, 12 April (and other newspapers). The report in *Parl. Reg.* xvii. 489 follows that in *London Courant*, 11 April.

On 10 April John Dunning moved to disqualify the holders of certain offices, the abolition of which formed a part of Burke's Bill that had already been rejected, from holding a seat in the House of Commons. During the debate Henry Dundas, the Lord Advocate, read a portion of Burke's *Thoughts on the Cause of Present Discontents*, which in 1770 had argued against a general place Bill because of the danger 'of disconnecting with Parliament, the greatest part of those who hold civil employments'. Burke had gone so far in the *Thoughts* as to state that it 'were better, perhaps, that ... [the latter] should have a

---

[1] The rough draft printed in *Works* has forty-two clauses in this section. The two omitted in the revised version are: '23. And be it enacted, that, if any negro shall refuse a competent marriage tendered to him, and shall not demand another specifically, such as it may be in his master's power to provide, the master or overseer shall be authorised to constrain him by an increase of work or a lessening of allowance.

25. And be it enacted, that no slaves shall be compelled to do any work for their masters for [three] days after their marriage.'

corrupt interest in the forms of the constitution than that they should have none at all'.[1] Essentially the following defence of his position was justified, since in 1770 he had been careful to distinguish between 'such mighty and important bodies as the military and naval establishments', which he had argued must be represented in Parliament, and 'Revenue Officers' and 'lower sorts' within the civil establishment, some of whom he had been prepared to disqualify even from voting in elections. Clearly, ten years later he still maintained that distinction.

Mr. Burke made a most able reply. He began with saying, that the learned Gentleman's feelings of surprize were of the most extraordinary kind.[2] Surprize to the learned Gentleman was preparation. The learned Gentleman's speech was the plainest and most direct answer to his argument against being taken by surprize, for though he had known nothing of the motion then under consideration, an invisible agent had conveyed into his pocket a long written extract, which the Honourable and learned Gentleman had thought convenient and applicable. The learned gentleman had descended to steal that from another which was little worth. He had confessed himself a plagiary of the most pitiful kind! He had robbed the poor, and taken what could avail him nothing. With regard to the author quoted by the Honourable Gentleman, would any man say that a writer was bound to follow in all cases, and under all circumstances, those arguments which he had thought wise and proper ten years ago, when times and circumstances were excessively different. At that time Influence was not carried to the extent to which it had been carried since. The American war had not been commenced. America was not lost to this country by influence. As far, however, as he was acquainted with that author, he would take upon him to assert, that what were his opinions, when he wrote the passages the learned Gentleman had cited, were his opinions now exactly and entirely. The Extract had no reference whatever to the point then under discussion; but he would appeal to the Committee if his conduct had differed from the doctrines contained in that Extract. What was the principal argument of them but this! That a general Place Bill, tending to disjoint the military and great professional departments from the Legislative, and give them separate feelings

---

[1] See vol. ii, p. 310.
[2] Dundas thought a Bill would have given the members of the House time for consideration; a resolution was a 'mode of taking the house by surprize' and 'was of itself sufficient to excite his objection to the motion'.

and separate interests, would not only be a violent, but a dangerous innovation on the Constitution? Who would now say otherwise? The Place Bill at present proposed, was not the sort of measure the Extract alluded to. After arguing this for some time, Mr. Burke went into a defence of the motion as perfectly consonant to his own Bill, though it fell somewhat short of it. The clause, however, having been lost, was it to be then wondered at, or charged against him as an inconstancy that he should take up his friend's proposition which came so near to his own meaning? This led him into a defence of his own clause which the Committee, who sat upon it before the holidays, had rejected. He declared it appeared to him that the offices aimed at in his plan of reform, such as the King's cooks, the King's dogkeepers, &c. &c. were, in his opinion, much too menial to be held by Members of Parliament, and therefore he had wished to abolish them. To do those Members who held these sort of places justice, it was but fair to say, they had a most *gentleman like ignorance* of the duties of the respective offices they filled. From this he returned to a defence of the present motion, and trusted that he and his friends should prove to be linked by a more tough and durable chain, than a rope of sand, by the decision of the question, which he justified from the Lord Advocate's attack on the ground, "that it would, if carried, do injury to many an honest man, but not prevent men willing to be corrupted, from being corrupted," by desiring the Committee, to remember that part of the Lord's Prayer, which says, "lead us not into temptation," and telling them it was their duty to lessen the inducements to Members to be corrupted by taking away the means of corruption.

Speech on Pillory
11 April 1780

Source: *Morning Chronicle*, 12 April 1780

The same report is in *General Evening Post*, 13 April, and is followed by *Parl. Reg.* xvii. 492–4 and *Parl. Hist.* xxi. 388–90. Other reports are in *Gazetteer*, 12 April; *London Evening Post*, 13 April (and other papers); *Public Advertiser*, 12 April; and *St James's Chronicle*, 13 April (and other papers).

On 10 April Theodosius Read and William Smith stood in the pillory as part
of their punishment for attempting to commit sodomy. Smith died as a result
of the mob's treatment.[1] Burke raised the matter in the House.

Mr. *Burke* called the attention of the House to a very particular matter.
He said, they sat there to make laws for the subject; that the laws
which chiefly came under their consideration were laws of Civil Polity,
but those which most claimed their attention and care were the
criminal laws. The first only regarded men's property, criminal laws
affected men's lives, a consideration infinitely superior to the former!

In making criminal laws, it behoved them materially to consider
how they proceeded, to take care wisely and nicely to proportion the
punishment so that it should not exceed the extent of the crime, and to
provide that it should be of that kind, which was more calculated to
operate as an example and prevent crimes, than to oppress and torment
the convicted criminal. If this was not properly attended to in the
criminal laws which passed the House, they forced his Majesty to
violate his Coronation Oath and commit perjury, because his Majesty,
when he was crowned, and was invested with the executive government, had solemnly sworn to temper mercy with justice, which it was
almost impossible for him to do if the House suffered any penal laws to
pass on principles repugnant to this idea, and in which justice, rigid
justice was solely attended to, and all sight of mercy lost, and foregone.
He said the matter which had induced him to make these reflections,
was the perusal of a melancholy circumstance stated in the newspapers
of that morning. He hoped to God the fact was mitigated, and that the
whole relation had no foundation in truth. It had, however, made a
very strong impression on his mind, and he conceived it of a nature
sufficiently interesting to merit the notice and attention of that House,
because if it should turn out to be true, he thought it would be
incumbent on that House, to take some measure in consequence of it.
The relation he alluded to, was that of the unhappy and horrid murder
of a poor wretch, condemned to stand in the pillory the preceding day.
The account stated that two men had been doomed to this punishment; that one of them being short of stature, and remarkably short-
necked, he could not reach the hole made for the admission of the head,
in the awkward and ugly instrument used in this mode of punishment;
that the officers of justice nevertheless forced his head through the

[1] *Corr.* iv. 230.

hole, and the poor wretch hung rather than walked as the pillory turned round; that previous to his being put in, he had deprecated the vengeance of the mob, and begged that mercy, which from their exasperation at his crime, and their want of considering the consequences of their cruelty, they seemed very little inclined to bestow. That he soon grew black in the face, and the blood forced itself out of his nostrils, his eyes, and his ears. That the mob nevertheless attacked him and his fellow criminal with great fury. That the officers seeing his situation, opened the pillory, and the poor wretch fell down dead on the stand of the instrument. The other man, he understood, was likewise so maimed and hurt by what had been thrown at him, that he lay now without hope of recovery.

Having stated this to the House, Mr. Burke proceeded to remark, that the punishment of the pillory had always struck him as a punishment of shame rather than of personal severity. In the present instance it had been rendered an instrument of death, and that of the worst kind, a death of torment. The crime for which the poor wretches had been condemned, was such as could scarcely be mentioned, much less defended or extenuated. The commission of sodomitical practices! A crime of all others the most detestable, because it tended to vitiate the morals of the whole community, and to defeat the first and chief end of society. Sodomitical practices was however of all other crimes a crime of the most equivocal nature, and the most difficult to prove. When criminals convicted of sodomitical practices were sentenced to the pillory, they were adjudged that punishment with a view to expose them to public reproach and contempt, not to popular fury, assault and cruelty. To condemn to the pillory with any such idea, would be to make it a capital punishment, and as much more severe than execution at Tyburn, as to die in torment, was more dreadful than momentary death, almost without sensation of pain. He submitted it, therefore to the consideration of the House, whether, if the facts turned out as they were stated in the newspapers, and as he had reported them to the House, on newspaper authority, it would not be right to abolish the punishment of the pillory since it was liable to such violent perversion, as to be rendered not the instrument of reproach and shame, but of death and murder. If no man would take the matter in hand, he would bring in a bill for this purpose; he saw, however, a learned and respectable gentleman in the House,[1] from whose high character and

[1] Alexander Wedderburn.

distinguished place, it was fair to infer that the matter would be much
better lodged in his hands, and would be more properly conducted
than it could be by him. He hoped that learned and respectable gentleman would take it up, and he hoped likewise that the House, if the
facts should turn out to be true, and the poor wretch to have been
murdered, as he had mentioned, would direct the learned gentleman to
proceed against those to whose neglect, or to whose cruelty, the
murder was ascribeable.[1]

Speech on Mutiny
1 May 1780

Source: *Morning Post*, 2 May 1780

A very similar report is in *St James's Chronicle*, 2 May. Other reports are in *London Chronicle*, 2
May; *Whitehall Evening Post*, 2 May; *London Courant*, 2 May; *London Evening Post*, 2 May; *Morning
Chronicle*, 2 May (which is repeated in *Parl. Reg.* xvii. 605); *Public Advertiser*, 2 May; *General
Evening Post*, 2 May; and *Lloyd's Evening Post*, 3 May.

On 1 May Temple Simon Luttrell raised the question of a mutiny on
the *Invincible*, caused by a delay in the payment of wages. Burke took this
opportunity to bring up another mutiny which had occurred on the *Eagle* when
under the authority of Captain Thomas Short. The two men convicted of
that crime were John Williams and James Stoneham.[2] In his speech Burke
demonstrated once again that he was prepared to speak out for the most
loathsome criminals when he felt they were being subjected to unfair or
unduly harsh treatment.

Mr. *Burke* coming in just when Mr. Luttrell was speaking of a mutiny,
took up the consideration of the two men who were condemned at the
Old Bailey, by the Court of Admiralty, to be hanged for a mutiny on
board a private ship of war. This ship had been fitted out at Bristol,
and instead of waging war against the enemies of this country, the
captain had carried on hostilities against neutral powers, and thereby
had turned pirate. Under American colours, he had plundered a
Dutchman, a Dane, and lastly a Portuguese, with many instances of
barbarity. After these acts of piracy, he was afraid to return to Bristol,

[1] The Under-Sheriff of Surrey was prosecuted, but was acquitted (*Corr.* iv. 230).
[2] For this affair, see P.R.O., HCA 24/74, 76, 80, 93, 94.

to his owners, and had resolved to put into Falmouth. The crew through fear of being pressed, refused to go into that port; and disobeyed the orders of their commander. The two unhappy convicts were of the number. He would not undertake to say, that according to the strict letter of the law, they were not guilty of an act of mutiny; but this much he would say, that equity might plead in favour of men, whose commander had, by his piracies, extinguished all discipline in his ship; and had consequently so far encouraged his men by his bad examples, that they acted in a manner in which they could not have dared to act, if they had not known, that their Captain had actually abdicated all authority among his men, when he turned pirate. This he[1] had been so conscious of himself, that though he was the principal prosecutor, he thought proper to forfeit his recognizance rather than appear in court against them. Another thing he had to urge against the execution of those unhappy men was, that the sentence pronounced upon them was informal, and incompatible, Sir James Marriot[2] appearing for the first time in his life, to pronounce sentence of death, was so affected at the time, that he condemned those men, that he only said; "You shall be carried to the place from whence you came and from thence to the place of execution—and the Lord have mercy on your souls." Mr. Burke trusted that mercy would likewise be extended to their bodies; for exclusive of what might be urged from equity in their favour, they perhaps might derive some advantage from law: for Sir Joseph Marriot had forgot to say, after mentioning the place of execution, "*and there you shall hang till you are dead;*" and from that omission it might, perhaps with some colour of law, be urged, that the sentence did not justify *hanging*. Many witnesses could be produced to prove this omission; and though the record was perfect, and contained the complete sentence, yet it contained more than had been pronounced by the Judge: there was certainly just ground to delay the sentence, at least till proper enquiry should be made into the transaction. The King, by his oath, was bound to execute justice in mercy: mercy was not dependent, at least it ought not to be dependent on the mere caprice of any man; it was absolutely part of the law of the land, and was as much to be attended to as justice: nay, justice itself called as loudly as human compassion could for mercy. He would

---

[1] i.e. Captain Thomas Short.
[2] Sir James Marriott (*c.*1730–1803), M.P. 1781–4, 1796–1802, judge of the Admiralty.

therefore move that the execution of these men be suspended till proper enquiry should be made into the affair.

The Speaker then interrupted Burke so that business on hand might be completed. When the matter was resumed, Burke made two further short speeches, but made no motion since Lord North promised to intervene. A stay of execution was granted on 3 May, and the two seamen were pardoned on 10 June on condition of serving in the Royal Navy.[1]

Speech on Duration of Parliaments
8 May 1780

Sources: MSS. at Northampton, A.xxxi.18, 19, 22, 23.

The date of the speech for which these drafts were prepared is established by the reports of the speech which Burke gave on Sawbridge's motion of 8 May in the *Morning Chronicle* of 9 May, and the *General Evening Post*, 9 May (*Parl. Hist.* xxi. 603–15). There are less substantial reports in other newspapers. The editors of *Works* (1792–1827), v. 373–86 altered Burke's text in order to make it read better. As with most of Burke drafts, the order of paragraphs and the place for intended insertions is often open to question, and the editors of *Works* rather disguised the uncertainties by running separated material together or failing to reproduce it at all. Although their order has been followed as far as possible the divisions of the MSS. are observed and all material printed. Two additional drafts, A. xxxi. 20, 21, which repeat portions of the argument, were left unpublished in the *Works* and are also excluded here.

On 8 May John Sawbridge made his annual motion for leave to introduce a Bill to shorten the duration of Parliaments. Burke spoke in opposition and 'was up near an hour and a half'.[2] This speech did a good deal to sound the death knell for whatever slim hopes remained of a united Opposition campaign based on economical reform. In early April some hope for unity had been revived by the success of John Dunning's famous motion in the House of Commons stating 'that the influence of the crown has increased, is increasing and ought to be diminished'.[3] However, the forces of discord had been at work since that time. The association movement had continued to embrace radical objectives which the Rockinghams could not support. John Crewe's Bill to exclude revenue officers from voting in elections had been lost in the House of Commons and Philip Jennings Clerke's Bill to prevent government contractors from becoming M.P.s had been lost in the House of Lords.[4] Thus Burke was in something other than a compromising frame of

---

[1] P.R.O., HCA 24/99, 100.
[2] *London Evening Post*, 9 May; *Gazetteer*, 9 May, says he spoke a full two hours.
[3] On 6 April 1780. See O'Gorman, *The Rise of Party in England*, p. 418.
[4] On 13 April and 14 April respectively.

mind. He separated over this particular motion from some close friends including Lord John Cavendish, who, for the sake of unity in opposition, voted with Sawbridge.[1] By calling for a strict adherence to the Septennial Act, he openly repudiated triennial Parliaments though the Marquess himself had agreed to support them,[2] and he took the opportunity to make it clear that he could not go along with other reform measures which aimed at meddling with the system of representation.

Later, Richard Champion would describe the damage done to the Opposition cause in Bristol when informing the Duke of Portland that the

Insinuations which have been used by many of our false friends, on account of Mr. B[urke]s having voted against shortening the duration of Parliaments, has disturbed so much our real ones, that they are out of Conceit with Committees of association, and dread the very Idea of them.[3]

After Burke's speech those who had aligned themselves against North would find it increasingly necessary to choose between conservative and radical ideals. The final blow to unity was to come on 3 June from a long-time staunch Rockingham friend, the Duke of Richmond, who would formally announce his conversion to the radical approach by moving a Bill in the House of Lords calling for annual Parliaments and universal suffrage.

It is always to be lamented when men are driven to search into the foundations of the Commonwealth; it is certainly necessary to resort to the Theory of your Government, whenever you propose any alteration in the frame of it, whether that alteration means the revival of some former antiquated and foresaken constitution, or the Introduction of some new improvement in the Commonwealth. The End of any institution is to promote its good purposes; and to prevent its inconveniences.

If we thought elections attended with no inconvenience or with but a triffling inconvenience the strong overruling principle of the Constitution would sweep [and] carry us like a torrent towards it.

Your Remedy is to be suited to your disease; and to your whole disease; to your present disease.

That man thinks much too highly, and therefore he thinks weakly and delusively of any contrivance of human Wisdom, who believes that it can make any sort of approach to perfection. There is not there never was a principle of Government under heaven, that does not in the very pursuit of the good it proposes, naturally and inevitably lead into some inconveniences, which makes it absolutely necessary to

---

[1] *Corr.* iv. 237 n.
[2] R1.1883: to Henry Zouch, 23 March 1780.
[3] Portland MSS., PwF 2,751: 29 May 1780.

counterwork and weaken the application of that first principle itself; and to abandon something of the extent of the advantage you had in View by it, in order to prevent also the inconveniences which have arisen from the Instrument of all the good you had in View.

To govern according to the Sense and agreeably to the interests of the People is a great and glorious Object of Government. This Object[1] cannot be obtaind but through the Medium of popular Election; and Popular Election is a mighty Evil. It is such, and so great an Evil; that there are few Nations whose Monarch was not originally elective; and very few who have not[2]

They are the distempers of elections that have destroyd all free States. To cure these distempers difficult if not impossible; The only thing therefore left to save the commonwealth is to prevent their return too frequently.

The Objects in view are to have Parliaments as frequent as they can be without distracting them in the prosecution of publick Business. On one hand to secure their dependence upon the people; on the other to give them that quiet in their minds and that Ease in their fortunes as to enable them to perform the most arduous and most painful Duty in[3] the world with Spirit, with Efficiency, with independency and with experience as real publick Counsellours not as the canvassers at a perpetual Election.

[It is] wise to Compass as many good Ends as possibly you can, and seeing there are inconveniences upon both sides with Benefits on both, to give up a part of the Benefit to soften the inconvenience.

The perfect cure [is] impracticable; because the disorder is dear to those from whom alone the cure can possibly be derived. The utmost to be done [is] to palliate—to mitigate, and to respite to put off the Evil day of the constitution to its latest possible hour and may it be a very late one. This I fear, would precipitate.[4]

One of two consequences, I know not which most likely, or which most dangerous; either that the Crown[5] by its constant, stated power,

---

[1] In margin: 'Another distemper besides the corruption of the Representative, the corruption of the constituent.'

[2] In margin: '⟨are⟩ few Elections.'

[3] In margin: 'I must see to satisfye me'.

[4] Below this section is written: 'To think a Government the same in Spirit and essence under different manners Customs and conditions opinion a vain thought'.

[5] In margin: 'Re-election how far answerd its purpose;'.

influence, and revenue, should wear out all opposition in Elections or that the violent and furious popular Spirit should arise.

Remedies—I must see their operation in the cure of the old Evil, and the cure of those new Evils which are inseperable from all remedies and how they balance each other—what is the total result— The excellence of Mathematics and Metaphysics is to have but one thing before you or a series but of one sort of thing, but he forms the best judgment in all moral disquisitions who has the greatest Number and variety of considerations in one View before him, and can take them in with the best possible consideration of the middle results of all.[1]

They who are not friends to the Bill. This pledge at least of their integrity and sincerity, they give to the people, that in this situation of Systematick opposition, in which all their hope of rendering it effectual depends upon popular interest and favour, they will not flatter them by a surrender of their uninfluenced Judgment and opinion; they give a Security, that if ever they should be in another situation no flattery to any other sort of power and influence, would induce them to act against that true interest of the people.

All are agreed that Parliament should not be perpetual, the only question is what is the most convenient time for their duration—on which there are three opinions.[2]

We are agreed too that the Term ought not to be chose most likely in its operation to spread corruption and to augment the already overgrown influence of the Crown. On these principles I mean to debate the Question.

Easy to pretend a Zeal for Liberty. Those who think themselves not likely to be encumberd with the performance of their promises either from their known inability or total indifference about the performance, never fail to entertain the most lofty Ideas. They are certainly the most specious and they cost them neither reflection to frame nor pains to modifye—nor management to support. The Task is of another nature to those who mean to promise nothing that it is not in their intention or may possibly be in their power to perform. To those who are bound and principled no more to delude the understandings than to violate the Liberty of their fellow Subjects. Faithful watchmen we ought to be

---

[1] Below this is written: 'I do not know that when the ground is prepared what I would ⟨do⟩—how much I would take'.
[2] In favour of annual, triennial, or septennial Parliaments.

over the[1] Rights and privileges of the people. But our Duty if we are qualified for it as we ought is to give them information and not to receive it from them[2] and are not to go to School to them to learn the principles of Law and Government.[3] In doing so, we should not dutifully serve, but we should basely and scandalously betray the people; who are not capable of this service by Nature; nor in any ⟨more⟩ instances called to it by the constitution. I reverentially look up to the opinion of the people and with an awe that is almost superstitious. I should be ashamed to shew my face before them. If I changed my Ground, cryd up or cryd down men, or things, or opinions if I wagged and shifted about with every change and joind in it or opposed as best answerd any low Interest or passion if I held them up hopes, which I knew I never intended or promised what I well knew I could not perform. Of all these things they are perfect sovereign Judges without appeal. But as to the detail of particular measures and or to any general Schemes of Policy. They have neither enough of Speculation in the Closet, nor of experience in business to decide upon it. They can well see whether we are tools of a Court or their honest Servants. Of that they can well judge, and I wish always exercised their Judgment but of the particular merits of a measure I have other standards.

That the frequency of Elections proposed by this Bill has a Tendency to increase the *power* and consideration of the Electors not lessen corruptibility; I do most readily admit. So far it is desirable;[4] it has no sort of tendency to increase their integrity and publick spirit, unless an encrease of[5] power has an operation upon Voters in Elections [that] it has in no other situation in the world and upon no other part of mankind.

2. This Bill[6] has no Tendency to limit the *quantity* of *influence in the Crown*;[7] to render its *operation* more difficult; or to *counteract* that operation which it cannot prevent in any way[8] whatsoever. It has its full

---

[1] MS.: 'their'.

[2] In margin: 'not lost my rights as a Citizen by becoming a Member of Parliament'.

[3] In margin: 'people to be gratified in any Object of Government they have at heart—I say as an Object of *Interest*. But if they go upon Theory, all disputants equal.'

[4] *Works* (1792–1827), v. 376, prints here a sentence from the margin which Burke appears to have deleted: 'This is what it has; I will tell you now what it has not—1st'.

[5] MS.: 'in' not deleted as presumably intended.

[6] In margin: 'I observe further'.

[7] In margin: 'not lessen means of corruption'.

[8] In margin: 'Travelled long through that ⟨Blind⟩ and obscure antiquity. Not an Idea of Election in the old times'.

weight, its full range, and its uncontrolled operation on the Electors exactly as it had before.

3. Nor thirdly, has it abated the interest and inclination of ministers to *apply*[1] that Influence to the Electors. Further to the Contrary, it has renderd it much[2] more necessary to them, if they seek to have a Majority in Parliament to increase the means of that Influence and redouble their diligence, and to sharpen dexterity in the application.

The whole Effect of the Bill is therefore the removing the application of some part of the influence from the Elected to the Electors; and further to strengthen and extend a court interest already great and powerful in Boroughs; here to fix their magazines and places of arms, and this to make the principal not the secondary Theatre of their manouvres for securing a determined Majority in Parliament.

I believe nobody will deny, that the Electors are corruptible. They are men; it is saying nothing worse of them; many of them are but ill informed in their minds, many feeble in their Circumstances; and easily overreachd; and easily seduced. If they are many; the wages of corruption are the lower; and would to God it were not rather a contemptible and hypocritical adulation than a Charitable Sentiment, to say that there is already no debauchery, no corruption, no Bribery, no perjury, no blind fury and interested faction among the Electors in many parts of this Kingdom. Nor is it surprising or at all blamable in that Class.

But admit it were true that the great Mass of the Electors were too vast an Object for Court influence to grasp [or] extend to[3] and that in despair they must abandon it. He must be very ignorant of the State of every popular interest, not to know that in all the Corporations open Boroughs indeed in every district of the Kingdom there is some leading man, some agitator, some wealthy merchant or considerable manufacturer, some active attorney, some popular preacher, some Money-Lender, &c., &c., who is followed by the whole Flock. This is the Style of all free countries. Multum in Fabia valet ille ille Velina;

---

[1] In margin: 'Freemen they were not lessen disposition to corrupt'.

[2] In margin: 'Ignorant whether Saxons formed ['assemblies' written above] a body sitting by their own right or in a representative capacity—whether several Orders ballancing one another or one assembly—whether they had any deliberative capacity—the Crown proposing and they rejecting or the contrary.'

[3] In margin: 'private men when they see their Neighbours aggrandized and themselves poor and virtuous without Eclat or dignity which attends men in higher situations.'

cuilibet hic fasces dabit eripietque curule;[1] these spirits, each of which informs and governs his own little Orb, are neither so many, nor so little powerful, or so incorruptible, but that a Minister may, as he does frequently find means of gaining them, and through them all their followers.

To establish, therefore a very general Influence among Electors will no more be found an impracticable project than to gain, an undue influence over Members of Parliament. Therefore I am apprehensive that this Bill though it shifts the place of the disorder does by no means relieve the Constitution. I went through almost every contested Election in the beginning of this Parliament; and acted as a manager in very many of them; by which (though as at a school of pretty severe and rugged Discipline) I came to have some degree of instruction, concerning the means by which Parliamentary interests are in general procured and supported. *Theory*, I know would suppose, that every general Election is to the Representative a day of Judgment, in which he appears before his constituents to account for the use of the Talent with which they intrusted him, and of the improvement he has made of it for the publick advantage; it would be so, if every corruptible representative[2] were to find an enlightend, and uncorruptible constituent. But the practice and knowlege of the world will not suffer us to be ignorant, that the constitution on Paper is one thing and in fact and experience is another. We must know that the Candidate instead of trusting at his Election the Testimony of his Behaviour in Parliament, he must bring the Testimony of a large sum of Money; the Capacity of Liberal expence in entertainments; the power of serving and obliging the Rulers of Corporations; of winning over the[3] popular Leaders of Political Clubs, associations, and neighbourhoods. It is ten thousand times more necessary to shew himself a man of power, than a man of integrity in almost all the Elections with which I have been acquainted. Elections therefore become a matter of heavy expence; and if contests are frequent, to many they will become a matter of an expence totally ruinous; which no fortunes can bear; but least of all the Landed fortunes; encumberd as they often, indeed as they mostly are, with

[1] In full, the passage from Horace translates: 'This man has much influence in the Fabian tribe; that in the Veline. This man will give the fasces to whom he will. Or if churlish will snatch the curule ivory from whom he pleases' (*Epistles*, I. vi. 52–3).
[2] MS.: 'corruptible were representative,'.
[3] MS.: 'to the'.

debts, with portions, with jointures and tied up in the hands of the possessor by the Limitations of settlement. It is a material, it is in my opinion a casting consideration in all the Questions concerning Election. Let no one think the charges of Elections a trivial matter.

The charge therefore of Elections, ought never to be lost sight of in a Question concerning their frequency; because the grand Object you seek is independence. Independence of mind will ever be more or less influenced by independence of Fortune and if every three years the exhausting Sluices of entertainments, drinkings open houses, to say nothing of Bribery are to be periodically drawn up and renewed. If Government favours for which now in some shape or other the whole race of men are candidates, are to be called for, upon every occasion I see that private fortunes will be washed away and every even to the least Trace of independence born down by the Torrent. I do not seriously think this constitution even to the wrecks of it could survive five Triennial Elections. If you are to fight the Battle you must put on the armour of the Ministry; you must call in [the] publick[1] to the aid of private money or you must give over the contest. The expence of [the] last Election has been computed (and I am persuaded that it has not been overrated) at 1,500,000L. 3 Shilling more in the Land Tax.[2] About the close of the last Parliament and the beginning of this several Agents for borroughs went about. I remember well that it was in every one of their mouths; "Sir your Election will cost you three thousand pound—if you are independent; but if the ministry supports you, it may be done for two; and perhaps for less."[3] And indeed the thing spoke itself. Where a Living was to be got for one; a Commission in the army for another; a Leftenancy in the Navy for a third, and Customhouse offices scatterd about without measure or Number who doubts that money may be saved? The Treasury may even add money;[4] but indeed it is superfluous. A Gentleman of two thousand a year who meets another of the same fortune fights with equal arms; but if to one of the Candidates you add a thousand a year in Places for himself, and a power of giving away as much among others one must, or there is[5] no

---

[1] MS.: 'call in of publick'.
[2] The land tax at 3*s.* in the pound yielded about £1,500,000.
[3] 'The average price demanded by a patron for a safe seat, in 1754 was £1,500; in 1774 it had risen to about £3,000' (Namier and Brooke, i. 77).
[4] The Government spent about £50,000 on the General Election of 1774 (ibid.).
[5] MS.: 'if there there is'.

truth in Arithmetical demonstration ruin his adversary if he is to meet him and fight with him every third year.

It will be said I do not allow for the operation of Character; but I do; and I know it will have its weight in most Elections; perhaps it may be decisive in some. But there are few in which it will prevent great expences.

The destruction[1] of independent fortunes will be the consequence on the part of the Candidate.

What will be the consequence of Triennial Corruption, Triennial Drunkenness, triennial Idleness,[2] triennial fury;[3] society dissolved, industry interrupted ruind. Those personal hatreds that will never [be] sufferd to soften; those animosities and feuds which will be renderd immortal; those Quarrels which are never to be appeased. Morals, vitiated and gangrened to the Vitals. I think no stable and useful advantages were ever made by the money got at Elections by the Voter but all he gets is doubly lost to the publick. It is money given to diminish the general Stock of the Community which is in the industry of the Subject. I am sure that it is a good while before he or his family settle again to their business. Their heads will never Cool. The temptations of Elections will be for ever glittering[4] before their Eyes. They will all grow Politicians. Every one quitting his Business will choose to enrich himself by his Vote. They will all take the gaging Rod. They will run to the Customhouse Key New places will be made for them their Looms and ploughs will be deserted.

So was Rome destroyd by the disorders of continual Elections; though those of Rome were sober disorders; they had nothing but faction, bribery, bread and stage Plays to debauch them. We have the inflammation of *Liquor* superadded; a fury hotter than any of them. There the contest was only between Citizen and Citizen; here you have the contests of ambitious Citizens of one side supported by the Crown, to oppose to the Efforts (let it be so) of private and unsupported ambition on the other. Yet Rome was destroyd by the frequency and charge of Elections, and the monstrous Expence of an unremitted courtship to the people.

I think therefore, the Independent Candidate and Elector may each

---

[1] In margin: 'India; and the West Indies furnish every year at least 3 Candidates.'
[2] In margin: 'Lawsuits a great article'.
[3] There is an undeleted phrase, 'of that to,' above the line.
[4] MS.: 'forever before glittering'.

be destroyd by it, the whole body of the community to be an[1] infinite sufferer. A Vitious ministry the only gainer.

Gentlemen I know, feel the weight of this argument, they agree that this would be the consequence of more frequent Elections if things were to continue as they are but they think the greatness and frequency of the Evil, would itself be a remedy for it; that sitting but for a short time the member would not find it worth while to make such Vast expences, while the fear of their constituents will hold them the more effectually to their Duty.

To this I answer, that experience is full against them. This is no new thing. We have had Triennial Parliaments;[2] At no period of time were seats more eagerly contested? The Expences of Elections ran higher, taking the State of all charges than they do now.[3] The expence of Entertainments was such, that an act, equaly Severe and ineffectual as most of the acts against corruption in Elections then made was made against it.[4] Every monument of the time bears witness of the Expence. All the writers talked of it and lamented it. Will any one think, that a Corporation will be contented with a Bowll of Punch or a piece of Beef the less because elections are every three, intead of every 7 Years? Will they change their Wine for ale; because they are to get more ale three years hence. Dont think it. Will they make fewer Demands for the advantages of Patronage in Favours and offices because their member is brought more under their power? We have not only our own historical experience upon this Subject in[5] England, but we have the experience coexisting with us in Ireland; where since their Parliament has been shortend; the expence of Elections has been so far from lowerd, that it has been very near doubled.[6] Formerly they sat for the King's Life;[7] the ordinary charge of a seat in Parliament was then

---

[1] MS.: 'to be be an'.

[2] Under the Triennial Act (6 and 7 Will. and Mary, c. 7).

[3] For the modern debate over election contests and expenses in the eighteenth century, see W. A. Speck, *Tory and Whig*, London, 1970, pp. 46, 59–60, 124–31; G. Holmes, *The Electorate and the National Will in the First Age of Party*, Kendal, 1976; J. A. Phillips, *Electoral Behavior in Unreformed England, Plumpers, Splitters, and Straights*, Princeton, 1982, esp. pp. 306–11; F. O'Gorman, *Voters, Patrons and Parties: The Unreformed Electoral System of Hanoverian England, 1734–1783*, Oxford, 1989, esp. pp. 141–70.

[4] The principal statute against corruption was 7 and 8 Will. III, c. 4.

[5] MS.: 'in in'.

[6] Burke appears to be exaggerating. The cost of the purchase of a seat in the Irish Parliament does not appear to have increased markedly (E. M. Johnston, *Great Britain and Ireland*, Edinburgh, 1963, pp. 199–200).

[7] i.e. until the passage of the Octennial Act (7 Geo. III, c. 3) in 1768.

1,500. They now sit 8 years 4 Sessions[1] it is now 2,500, and upwards. The Spirit of[2] emulation has also been extremely encreased and all who are acquainted with the true State of that Country have no doubt, that the Spirit[3] is still growing; that new Candidates will take the field; that the contests will be more Violent, and the Expence of Elections larger than ever.

It never can be otherwise. A Seat in this house, for good purposes, for bad purposes, for no purposes at all, (except the mere consideration derived from being concerned in the publick Counsels) will ever be a first rate Object of Ambition in England. Ambition is no exact calculator. Avarice itself does not calculate strictly when it games. One thing is certain that in this political Game The great Lottery of power is that, into which men will purchase with Millions of Chances against them; In Turkey where the place, where the fortune, where the head itself are so insecure, that scarcely any have died in their beds for ages; so that the bowstring is the natural Death of Bashaws; yet in no Country is power and Distinction (precarious enough God knows in all) sought for with such boundless avidity, as if the value of place was enhanced by the danger and insecurity of its Tenure. Nothing will ever make a seat in this house not an Object of desire to Numbers by any means or at any charge, but the depriving it of all power and all dignity, this would do it. This is the true and only Nostrum for that purpose. But an house of Commons without power and without dignity either in itself or its Members is no house of commons for the purposes of this constitution.

But they will be afraid to act ill if they know that the day of their account is always near. I wish it were true. But it is not; here again we have experience and Experience is against us. The distempers of this age are a poverty of Spirit and of Genius; it is triffling, it is futile; *worse* than ignorant, *superficially taught*; with politicks and morals of Girls[4] at a boarding school; rather than of men and statesmen. But it is not yet desperately wicked or so scandously venal as in former times. Did not a triennial Parliament give up the national Dignity approve the Peace of Utrecht and almost give up every thing else in taking every Step to defeat the Protestant Succession? Was not the constitution saved

---

[1] The Irish Parliament normally sat every two years.
[2] MS.: 'of of'.
[3] In margin: 'Emulation'.
[4] MS.: 'Morals of and Girls'.

by those who had no Election at all to go to the Lords because the Court applied to the *Electors* and by various means carried them from their true Interest; so that the Tory Ministry had a Majority without an application to a single Member?[1] Now as to the conduct of the Members; it was then far from pure and independent. Bribery was infinitely more flagrant. Your predecessor put the Question of his own expulsion for Bribery.[2] Sir C. Musgrave[3] was a wise Man; a grave Man; an independent man, a man of good fortune and good family; however he carried on while in opposition, a traffick with shameful traffick with the Ministry. Bishop Burnet knew of 6,000 pounds which he had received at one payment.[4] I believe, the payment of sums in hard money; plain naked bribery is rare amongst us. It was then far from uncommon. The shortness of the time in which they are to reap the profits of iniquity is far from checking the avidity of corrupt men. It renders them infinitely more ravenous. They rush violently and precipitately on their Object. They lose all regard to decorum. The moments of profits are precious. Never are men so wicked[5] as during a general Mortality. It was so in the great plague at Athens; every Symptom of which (and this its worst Symptom amongst the Rest) is so finely related by a great Historian of antiquity.[6] It was so in the plague of London in 1663.[7] [It] appears in soldiers, sailors, &c. Whoever would contrive to render the Life of man much shorter than it is would I am satisfied find the surest receipt for encreasing the wickedness of our Nature.

A triennial was near ruining; a Septennial Parliament saved your constitution; nor perhaps have you ever known a more flourishing period for the union of National Prosperity dignity and Liberty than the 60 of the years you have passed under that constitution of Parliament.

---

[1] Presumably Burke is referring to the transfer of the Crown to the Hanoverians on the death of Quan Anne in 1714 by a Council of Regency, which was dominated by Whig peers.

[2] Sir John Trevor (1637–1717), the Speaker, was rated guilty of a high crime and misdemeanour on 12 March 1695 for accepting £1,100 from the Common Council of London for promoting the Orphans Bill. He himself put the resolution from the chair.

[3] Sir Christopher Musgrave (*c.*1632–1704), M.P. 1661–1704. In the MS. the initial 'W' is used instead of 'C'.

[4] Gilbert Burnet (1643–1715), Bishop of Salisbury, records that Musgrave accepted £12,000 at various times for yielding points of importance (*History of his Own Times*, 6 vols., Oxford, 1833, v. 199).

[5] MS.: 'wicked wicked'.

[6] Thucydides, *The Peloponnesian War*, book II, chap. v.

[7] An error for 1665. Burke may have had Defoe's fictional account, *A Journal of the Plague Year*, in mind.

Thus in my opinion the shortness of a Triennial sitting, would have the following ill Effects; it [would] make the Member more shamelessly and shockingly corrupt; it would encrease his Dependence on those who could best support him at his Election. It would wrack and tear to pieces the fortunes of those who stood upon their own Fortunes and their private interest. It would make the Electors infinitely more venal; and it would make the whole body of the people who are whether they have votes or not concerned in Elections more Lawless; more idle, more debauchd; It would utterly destroy the Sobriety, the Industry, the integrity, the simplicity of all the people; and undermine I am much afraid, the deepest and best laid foundations of the commonwealth.[1]

Those who have spoken and written ⟨of⟩ this Subject without doors do not so much deny the probable existence of these inconveniences in their measure, as they trust for their prevention to remedies of various sorts which they propose. First a Place Bill; but if this wont do, as they fear it wont—Then, they say, we will have a Rotation, and a certain Number of you shall be render[ed] incapable of being elected for ten years. Then for the Electors they shall Ballot;[2] the members of parliament also shall[3] decide by Ballot. A fifth project [is] the Change of the present Legal representation of the Kingdom.[4]

On all this, I shall observe, that it will be very unsuitable to your Wisdom to adopt the project of a Bill to which there are objections, insuperable *by any thing in the Bill itself,* upon the hope, that those Objections may be removed, by *subsequent projects,* every one of which is full of difficulties, of its own and which are all of them very essential alterations in the constitution. This seems very irregular and unusual. If any thing should make this a very doubtful measure than that in the opinion of its advocates, it would so aggravate all our old inconveniences in such a manner as to require a total alteration in the constitution of the Kingdom.

If the remedies are proper in a Triennial, they will not be less so in Septennial Elections; let us try them first. See how the house relishes them, See how they will operate in the Nation, and then having felt your way and prepared against these inconveniences.

[1] In margin against this paragraph: '1.2.3.4.'

[2] By 1780 the secret ballot was being propagated by the Westminster Committee of the association movement, by the Society for Constitutional Information, and by noted radicals like James Burgh (1714–75); see H. T. Dickinson, *Liberty and Property: Political Ideology in Eighteenth-Century Britain,* London, 1977, pp. 225–8.

[3] MS.: 'shall shall'.

[4] A variety of proposed changes, including the abolition of 'rotten boroughs' and additional county represention, were under discussion.

The Honorable Gentleman sees, that I respect, the principle upon which he goes, as well as his intentions and his abilities.[1] He will believe that I do not differ from him wantonly and on trivial grounds. He is very sure, that it was not his engaging one way which determined me to take the other. I have not in Newspapers, to derogate from his fair fame with the Nation, printed the first Rude Sketch of his Bill with ungenerous and invidious comments;[2] I have not, in conversations industriously circulated about the Town and talked on the Benches of this house, attributed his conduct to motives low and unworthy, and as groundless as they are injurious; I do not affect to be frighted with his proposition as if some hideous Spectre had started from hell which was to be sent back again by every form of Exorcism and every kind of incantation. I invoke no Acheron[3] to overwhelm him in the whirlpools of its[4] muddy Gulf. I do not tell the respectable mover and seconder,[5] by a perversion of their Sense and expressions that their proposition halts between the ridiculous and the dangerous.[6] I am not one of those who start up, three at a time and fall upon and strike at him as at a Tyrant in the Senate house, with so much eagerness that *our daggers hack one another* in his sides.

My Honorable friend has not brought down a spirited and promising Imp of Chivalry to win the first atchievement and Blazon of Arms on his milkwhite shield, in [a] field listed against him—nor brought out the generous offspring of Lions, and said to them—not against that sign of the ⟨Power⟩. Beware of ⟨that⟩ of you here is the Prey where you are to fasten your Paws and seasoning his ⟨unpractised⟩ Jaws with blood, tell him; this is the Milk for which you are to thirst hereafter.

[1] In margin: 'Not contending that his ideas maybe more right than mine; that they are the Ideas of wise, informed, and virtuous men, that I do not go'.

[2] Burke's Civil Establishment Bill had been attacked by the London radicals before it was presented. However, the *London Evening Post* on 1 February defended the Bill as follows: 'We hear that it is the design of Mr. Burke's plan for a general œconomy in the State, which he has given notice to make a motion for on 11 February, not to strike at any of those offices where the labour is adequate to the reward, let the salary be never so large. Such an œconomy, that true friend to his country knows but too well, would be ill timed, narrow, and preventative of emulation—it is sinecures and inefficient places, together with those kind of offices whose growing perquisites, from the increase of business, have become enormous, that are properly the objects of reformation.'

[3] A fabulous river of the infernal regions. 'Under the sooty flag of Acheron' (Milton, *Comus*, 604); 'Acheron of sorrow, black and deep' (*Paradise Lost*, xi. 578); 'The poisonous exhalation of Acheron is not forgot' (see Burke's *Sublime and Beautiful* in *Works* (Bohn), i. 151).

[4] MS.: 'of of its'.

[5] The seconder was Frederick Bull.

[6] Burke intended apparently to delete the following sentence at this point: 'I am not in the Ranks of a formal Battle array, that is drawn up against him.'

We furnish at his expense no Holiday, nor suspend hell, that a crafty Sysiphus[1] has rest from his wheel,[2] and 〈   〉: nor give the common adversary if he be a common adversary, no reason to say I would have put in my word to oppose, but the eagerness of your allies in your social war was such that I could not break in upon you. I hope he sees and feels and that every Member sees and feels along with him the difference between amicable dissent and civil discord.

Speech on Gordon Riots
6 June 1780

Source: *Gazetteer*, 7 June 1780

This report is also in the *Whitehall Evening Post*, 8 June. Other reports are in *London Chronicle*, 8 June (and other papers), repeated in *Parl. Hist.* xxi. 662; *London Evening Post*, 8 June; and *London Courant*, 7 June, which is followed by *Parl. Reg.* xvii. 722.

On 2 June Lord George Gordon brought the petition of the Protestant Association for the repeal of the Catholic Relief Act of 1778[3] to the House. He was accompanied by a mob of some 60,000. The House decided, amid disorder, to take the petition into consideration on 6 June. By that time the Gordon riots had shocked the nation. Some 450 people had been killed in five days of utter chaos. In London, one

of the most dreadful spectacles this country ever beheld was exhibited.... [The] flames ascending and rolling in clouds from the King's Bench and Fleet Prisons, from New Bridewell, from the tollgates on Blackfriars Bridge, from houses in every quarter of the town, and particularly from the bottom and middle of Holborn, where the conflagration was horrible beyond description.... Six and thirty fires, and blazing at one time, and in different quarters of the city, were to be seen from one spot.[4]

Burke, himself, was at times threatened and in real physical danger from the mob[5] because of his well-known sympathy for the Catholic minority. His friend Sir George Savile, who had originally presented the Catholic Relief Act, was subjected to attacks on his home at Leicester Fields and the burning of much of his furniture.[6] Order was restored only after the militia was called out and a proclamation issued by George III announcing 'the most direct and effectual orders to all our officers, by an immediate exertion of their utmost force', to quash the disturbances.[7]

[1] The editors of *Works* (1792–1827) correctly changed this to Ixion, the legendary King of Thessaly whom Zeus punished by fastening him to an efernally revolving fiery wheel.
[2] MS.: 'whell'.
[3] See Burke's speeches of 15, 18, and 31 March 1779, printed above.
[4] *Annual Register*, for 1780, p. 261.
[5] *Corr.* iv. 246: Burke to Richard Shackleton, 13 June 1780.
[6] *Corr.* iv. 241 n.   [7] *Annual Register*, for 1780, pp. 261–2.

Mr. Burke condemned the riots in very strong terms; but said Ministers were much to blame for neglecting to take the proper precautions in time to prevent it, and doubly so now, by drawing out the army, and thereby establishing a military on the ruins of the civil government. The avenues near the House, and the streets leading to it, bore the appearance more of Paris, Berlin, or Petersburgh, than of the capital of a government limited by law. The streets were all lined as he came along with the horse and foot guards, and the Park looked more like a camp or a garrison than the Park belonging to the palace of a free monarch. He was of opinion that such an appearance of military preparation served only to create, not to suppress it. Government had lost all dignity and respect, and it was a mistaken idea to imagine the people of this country would be bullied by legions of armed men, or janissaries clothed in scarlet.

He said, in truth, that the Government had been abdicated, when it could be maintained with effect; but he feared the necessity of employing the military had been created on purpose to furnish a pretext for employing them; and that scenes would ensue, at which he was chilled with horror only to think of. The law officers of the Crown were much to blame, and they were responsible to that House and the nation for the consequences. They were responsible for resorting to the military, and not to constitutional means; and if any serious mischief should ensue, they would, he trusted, be called to an account; he was not now debating the bill, the repeal of which was prayed for by the petitions on the table; but this he might venture to say, that now was not the proper time to repeal it.

Resolutions after Gordon Riots
[*ante* 18 June 1780]

Source: MS. at Sheffield, Bk 8.21

These resolutions, surviving in a fair copy with one correction in Burke's hand, and endorsed 'Resolutions on the Riots', were written before 18 June 1780 when Lord North wrote to Burke about them (*Corr.* iv. 250–1).

Burke sent the resolutions to Lord North. They influenced the resolutions sponsored by the administration which Burke supported in the Commons and which the House adopted on 20 June 1780. North also sent Burke a copy of the latter. They were toned down somewhat from Burke's because North feared 'that many people would be alarm'd if the House of Commons were to adopt so large and extensive a plan of toleration as they seem to hold out'. He explained to Burke that while he did

not think that the bulk of my countrymen wish to see the Penal Laws strictly executed, I can not help being of opinion that any suspicion of an intention to repeal them would be of the worse consequence if it were to spread among the people at large, and countenanced by any vote of the House of Commons.

Resolved

That this House hath no cause to apprehend, that any detriment whatsoever hath arisen, or is likely to arise to our happy Constitution in Church and State, or to the national Prosperity and safety in any particular, from the Laws granting Indulgence to a conscientious dissent from the established Church, or particularly from the Operation of an Act passed two years since, allowing a certain very limited and conditional Relaxation to his Majesty's Roman Catholic Subjects of some Clauses of one only Law, among many penal Statutes, formerly made and still in force[1] against them.

Resolved

That the Truth and Evidence of the Christian Protestant Religion, the eminent Piety and Learning of sundry of its Professors, the Protection of the State, the Succession establish'd in his Majesty's Royal Family, the liberal Endowment of Churches, Universities, Schools, and Colleges, and the entire and exclusive possession of all offices and emoluments in Church, State, Law, Revenue, Army, and Navy, do, under the divine Providence, furnish a perfect Security to the said Protestant Religion, without any persecution of other his Majesty's Subjects.

Resolved

That all endeavours to disquiet the minds of the People, upon the said prudent and equitable Relaxation, as if any degree of Toleration were inconsistent with the safety, or irreconcileable to the Principles of the Protestant Religion, have a manifest tendency to disturb the public peace, to break the Union necessary at this time, to bring Dishonour on the national Character, to discredit the Protestant Religion, and to furnish occasion for the Renewal of the Persecution of our Protestant Brethren in other Countries.

[1] Only the words 'and still in force' are in Burke's hand.

Speech on Riots
20 June 1780

Source: *London Courant*, 22 June 1780

This report is repeated in *Parl. Reg.* xvii. 732 (erroneously dated 19 June) and *Parl. Hist.* xxi.
709–10. Other reports are in *General Advertiser*, 21 June; *London Evening Post*, 22 June; *London
Courant*, 21 June; *Morning Chronicle*, 21 June; *General Evening Post*, 22 June; and *Whitehall Evening
Post*, 22 June.

On 20 June the House went into committee to consider the petitions against
the Catholic Relief Act. Five Government resolutions were considered. Burke
spoke immediately after Alderman Frederick Bull[1] had declared his 'most
hearty concurrence with the petitions from the different Protestant Associations' and had claimed that he had 'a sanction for this opinion from that
corporation of which I have the honour to be a member'. The alderman had
also expressed his 'pleasure to see, at length, a spirit of opposition to that
encouragement which popery has been long receiving from the servants of the
Crown'.

Mr. *Burke* rose immediately, and with much passion, reprobated the
doctrines of Mr. Alderman Bull, and reflected upon him for his
ignorance and want of erudition; he stated, that the ablest arguments
that ever were used, had that day fallen from the ablest men, and that
they were opposed by ignorance, falsehood,[2] and fanaticism. He was
going on into a large and diffusive field of argument when he was
stopped and called to order by Sir James Lowther, who said he had
reflected in an unbecoming manner on the worthy Alderman, and was
deviating in an improper manner from the question. After some time,
  Mr. Burke proceeded, and said, the petitions had arisen from
bigotry and fanaticism; that the Church of England was struck at, and
the Crown itself, and he would defend both from the attempts and
malevolence of such men. He went into a full account of the late riots;
expatiated on the inhumanity of the mob; that Mr. Langdale, with
twelve children, had suffered to the amount of 50,000l.[3] he had lain in
a great stock against the commencement of new duties—he had since
been advised to go to Bath to relieve his mind—at his first arrival

---

[1] His speech is reported in *Parl. Reg.* xvii. 730–1, where the proceedings of 19 and 20 June are
not separated.
[2] *London Courant*: 'falshood'.
[3] Thomas Langdale, whose distillery at Holborn had been destroyed, alleged losses of
£52,674. 14s. 7d. (MS. at Sheffield, Bk 8.31). He received in 1782 compensation of £18,974.

there, he was treated with the sight of the chapel at that place in flames—he was obliged to return to the Devizes—the inhumanity of fanatics was such, that after the destruction of a school near the city, a petition had been presented, desiring the poor man, who owned it, might not have a lease of the land again to build another. He attacked the petitioners, and he read the names of several taken from thence with a mark—he threw others into ridicule, and he quoted, in a facetious manner, the names of several women—not being able to read and write themselves, these monsters were desirous of preventing others from receiving education. He had been educated as a Protestant of the church of England by a Dissenter;[1] he read the Bible there morning, noon, and night, and was the happier and better man for such reading: he had afterwards turned his attention to the reading of all the theological publications, on all sides, that were written with such wonderful ability in the last and present century; and at last thought such studies tended to confound and bewilder, and he dropped them, embracing and holding fast—[to] the church of England. He went into a large field of reasoning on toleration; vindicated the Papists from the charges brought against them, and decried the baseness of Payne, the constable, who, he said, had gone about, trying to find out matter to incarcerate for life, men against whom no complaint was made for any offence, other than saying their prayers in a language, which he did not understand, but they did. He had imprisoned Mr. Malony, an honest and inoffensive man, but the humanity of the Crown had released him—he had attempted to imprison Mr. Talbot, brother to the Earl of Shrewsbury, but had failed, very happily in proof.[2] He stated, in a very long speech, the means taken to bring about all the mischief that had happened, and he said it had happened by the zeal of wicked and abandoned men, who had gone about industriously misleading poor,

[1] Abraham Shackleton (1696–1771), Master of Ballitore School and a Quaker.

[2] William Payne made a profession of hunting Catholics (City of London Record Office, Indictments; *The Whole Proceedings on the King's Commission of the Peace, Oyer and Terminer and Gaol-Delivery for the City of London* [for 1771], pp. 149–51).

James Robert Talbot (1726–90), Bishop of Birtha, brother of George Talbot, 14th Earl of Shrewsbury (1719–87) was (apparently) six times brought into court between 1768 and 1777. His first name was twice wrongly given. But the basic reason why he was never convicted, apart from the probable hostility of judge and jury to the charge, was simple lack of evidence.

John Baptist Malony was arrested in February 1767 and sentenced to 'perpetual imprisonment' in August. His petition to be transferred from the Common Goal of the County of Surrey to the King's Bench Prison was granted by the Privy Council. He was released in June 1771 on condition that he would 'quit the Kingdom, and not return without leave' (P.R.O. Assizes, 31/8, pp. 114, 148, P.C. 2/112, pp. 481, 484, 491; E. H. Burton, *The Life and Times of Bishop Challoner*, ii. 88–9; *Annual Register* for 1771, p. 115.

ignorant, and deluded people; and he concluded, by moving a preface to the first motion, "that much industry had been used to misrepresent the intentions of Parliament, etc."[1]

Speeches on Bill to Secure Protestantism
26 June 1780

Source: *London Courant*, 28, 29 June 1780

These reports are repeated in *Parl. Reg.* xvii. 743–5, 750, 751 and *Parl. Hist.* xxi. 718–21, 725, 726.

On 23 June Sir George Savile who had originally presented the Catholic Relief Bill in 1778, demonstrated that he had lost some of his zeal for toleration when he presented a Bill to restrain Roman Catholics from educating the children of Protestants. It was debated on 26 June when Savile also produced an amendment preventing Papists from taking Protestant children as apprentices. The Bill was an expression of much current opinion which believed wholeheartedly in toleration but at the same time suspected that insidious forces were at work 'to seduce the youth of this kingdom from the established church to Popery'. These forces were considered 'highly criminal according to the laws' and were seen as a serious enough threat to society to be 'a proper subject of . . . regulation'.[2] Burke's views, as expressed in the following speech against Savile's Bill, thus appear distinctly liberal for the time.

Mr. *Burke* was sorry for the credulity of the age and country in which he lived: he himself had been obliged to ensure, though the *onus* properly lay on such as brought the charge; evidence of the facts complained of there was none; no accusers stand forth; they had been obliged to enquire and examine minutely where every school lay, boys and girls; none of them received the children of the Protestant parents; and this had been done to quiet the minds of a set of men, who have no possibility of being satisfied; but as these reports had operated on better minds than their own, he thought it right to give information.

He had observed the words seminary and seminaries had been used

---

[1] The *London Courant*, 21 June, adds: 'This proposition, after some debate was agreed to. He then moved, "that the act of the 18th was misrepresented and understood".'

[2] These words were used in North's resolutions of 20 June (*Commons Journals*, xxxvii. 911–12).

by these people indiscriminately; in the proper signification of them
(foundations for the instruction of youth, or colleges, or institutions
for orders) there were none such in England; he was sorry for it,
because he was sure men had better be so bred in England, than in
France, Flanders or Spain: there were no schools teaching liberal
science, or classics, not one that had any foundation. There was
one in Hertfordshire, which was supplied with boys chiefly from
Westminster.[1] There was a boarding-school at Sedgeley Park, in
Warwickshire,[2] which had 25 or 30 boarders before the act, and had
been of 16 years standing, tho' it had wickedly been said, in a paper he
had seen, to have arisen since it. It was supplied by two priests and
two lay-assistants, and four-fifths of the boys were educated for business. There were many foreigners, and many from the West Indies,
some Latin taught and languages, but it had no foundation. A certain
lady of fashion, Lady Stourton,[3] had maintained usually 12 boys at
school. He had list of them; none were the children of Protestants.
There are now but 9, though sometimes 12; and the suggestion of
their taking Protestant children was not founded in truth; one school
was gone at Hammersmith; one in another place; and one or two
more had dropped: in London he was not able to find any boarding-
school at all, nor in the northern parts of England, in Cumberland,
Northumberland, and those parts, except one that had been set up by a
house-painter, the better to procure a living.[4] As to day-schools, they
were never the objects of jealousy; there had indeed been brought to
town several little schools which had been consolidated into larger; one
of this sort was in the neighbourhood of Bloomsbury, another in the
Minories; and they may be traced by the fires: the master of one of
them had once 81 boys and 25 girls, though the latter were now
reduced to 15, and he had refused to teach the children of near
Protestant neighbours; they teach, what all men of liberal education
may know, the Doway catechism.[5] There was, indeed, another school

---

[1] Old Hall at Ware.
[2] In fact in Staffordshire. It is now Cotton College. Some of Burke's relations lived there
(*Corr.* iv. 93).
[3] Catherine, née Walmsley (1697–1785), widow of Robert Petre, 7th Baron (1690–1713) and
of Charles Stourton, 15th Baron (1702–53).
[4] It is not clear which school or 'house painter' Burke is referring to.
[5] Under the Patronage of Philip II of Spain, a Roman Catholic College was established in the
town of Douai in Northern France. The college was for English priests. The Old Testament of
the Douay Bible was prepared there in 1609.

in the Minories, the master of which was terrified and had run mad, of which he had no accounts, and there was not a single boarding-school existing in London.

There were several day schools, one of good character and estimation; a Protestant had been employed at one time to teach there, and all teach the catechism of the Church of England, and there was not a priest among them; they teach only the little rudiments of grammar.

Lord *Arundel of Wardour*[1] had, indeed, a little school in his own neighbourhood, where were only day scholars, about forty in all, and the noble Lord in his letter (which he read) had assured, that no boarders are or ever were admitted; there were only two instances of Protestant children taught, they were his own tenants, and were taught the catechism of the Church of England; children educated in schools were decreased from 355 to 350, and in the same proportion the Roman Catholic religion was diminishing; in many places a priest cannot be got for thirty or thirty-five pound per annum salary, such a salary, which was the most they in general received, gave poor encouragement.

There were great numbers of *Irish Roman Catholics*, who do almost all the labour of the metropolis; and he thought they should have some place where they may educate their children. The story of buying children, he was persuaded, originated from similar practices in Ireland. He did not wish to have opened his sentiments on this subject, but he could not now avoid it. There are Protestant charter schools in Ireland established, and money is voted and granted every year by the parliament there to maintain them: the Bishops and the Crown recommend, and they buy none but the children of Papists:—it may be right so far; but when children are taken or bought, they are sent from North to South, from East to West, their names changed, and the ties of affinity are snapped and broke asunder; we secrete ourselves, and yet complain of others doing that which cannot be proved. This blot and blemish should never have been mentioned, if he had not been forced to it; he quoted the opinion of Thomas Aquinas, in the 12th century, against breaking the law of nature,[2] and he contended, that the parent had full right to dispose of the education of the child,

---

[1] Henry Arundell, 8th Baron (1740–1808).

[2] 'Every human law has just so much of the nature of law as it is derived from the law of nature. But if at any point it deflects from the law of nature, it is no longer a law but a perversion of law' (*Summa Theologica*, i. 2. Q. xcv, Art. 5).

and said the darkness of the 12th century rises against the light of the 18th.

There were, he said, 50,000 Protestant children maintained at school in this town, and yet we were afraid of a miserable charity school of Papists. The reports originated from the loose suggestions of mean and base men, and many of them were false. He was now given to understand they would not be satisfied: why then, in God's name, go on with the bill? The petitioners had formidable names, and formidable hands; they did not petition till the 2d of June, and this was the 26th, and yet no evidence was offered till this day: he wished them to come, he wanted to see those men who were calumniators, and he wanted to know their names.

He saw no objection to shutting up boarding schools from educating Protestants, but objected to including apprentices.

During the debate Lord Beauchamp moved an amendment 'that would confine the offence to the keepers of boarding-schools only, by substituting the word *and*—instead of *or*; and then the clause would run, "*if* any Papist, or person professing the Popish religion, shall knowingly take upon him or herself the education, teaching, instruction, *and* boarding the child or children of any of his Majesty's protestant subjects"'.[1]

Mr. *Burke* The Papists are few in number, and extremely scattered, and children of such can have no education; at least such as their parents would wish, if the amendment be rejected. There are no persons keeping day schools to take the children of Papists, and the schools cannot be kept unless the owners of Popish schools be permitted to receive Protestant children; they will not afford a livelihood. No Popish child can be taught if the disjunctive *or* be admitted to stand in the bill, and no Protestant can teach a Popish child. He knows that some people get bread now, and this clause will certainly deprive them of it. Little day schools were not objects of jealousy; no harm could possibly arise from them, and therefore he must resist their abolition and ruin.

Lord Beauchamp withdrew his amendment.

---

[1] *Parl. Reg.* xvii. 749.

Mr. *Burke* said, gentlemen should consider how they would like to force Protestants into Popish schools; he was sure they would not like it, and yet this principle was what had been contended for against the Papists; for four-fifths of the children of poor Popish parents in this country must go without education: this was an improper thing to be done, and therefore, after the adoption of such a principle, he could not attend the bill any longer.

In the Bill, as passed by the Commons, this clause was amended, but not in a way to satisfy Burke. The Bill, as a whole, however, was defeated in the Lords probably in part at least because of Lord North's fear that anti-Catholic legislation would be seen as a concession to the rioters.[1]

Some Thoughts on the Approaching Executions
10 July 1780

Source: MS. at Sheffield, Bk 8.23, 24

The MS., endorsed 'Thoughts on the approaching Executions', is in Zouch's hand, with corrections and additions by Burke. It is probably the MS. used by the editors of *Works* (1792–1827), but variations between the MS. and the *Works* text are noted, if they are differences of substance. Burke sent 'Some Thoughts' to Lord Thurlow on 10 July 1780 (*Corr.* iv. 254).

When the issues raised by the Gordon riots in the House of Commons had been settled, and the House had adjourned, Burke turned his attention to the punishment of the rioters. He sent his views to Lord Thurlow, the Lord Chancellor. His main concern was to develop rational guidelines for determining civilized punishments. 'I am fully persuaded that a proper use of mercy would . . . recommend the wisdom and steadiness of government,' he told the Lord President of the Council, Lord Bathurst. He had cause to be concerned. In July sixty-two rioters were charged, brought to trial, and condemned to death. Twenty-five were actually executed.[2] Burke undoubtedly knew that some of them were so young that they could not be expected even to understand the seriousness of their crimes.[3] Just three days after he wrote

[1] See above, pp. 603–4.
[2] See G. Rudé, 'The Gordon Riots: A Study of the Rioters and their Victims', *Transactions of the Royal Historical Society*, 5th series, vi (1956), 99. The newspapers carried reports of the trials and executions. See, for instance, *London Evening Post*, 4, 6, 9, 12, 15 July 1780.
[3] Among them was 'a handsome young woman about 18' and 'a boy about 13' (*Annual Register* for 1780, pp. 275, 276).

the following piece London was witness to the execution of one Richard Roberts, 'a child of 14 years and seven months', who advised others 'particularly youth, to take warning by his unhappy fate'. He expressed remorse for his actions but claimed that he did not know 'the danger his life was in when he committed that for which he suffered'.[1]

Some Thoughts on the approaching Executions[2]

As the Number of persons convicted in the late[3] unhappy tumults will probably exceed what any ones Idea of vengeance or example would deliver to capital punishment, it is to be wished, that the whole Business, as well with regard to the Number and description of those who are [to] suffer Death, as with regard to those who shall be delivered over to lighter punishment, or wholly pardoned, should be entirely a work of reason.

It has happened frequently in cases of this Nature, that the fate of the Convicts has depended more upon the accidental circumstance of their being brought earlier or later to Trial, than to any steady principle of Equity applied to their several Cases. Without great care and sobriety, Criminal Justice generally begins with anger and ends in negligence. The first that are brought forward suffer the Extremity of the Law, with circumstances of Mitigation in their Case, and after a time, the most atrocious delinquents escape merely by the Satiety of punishment.

In the Business now before his Majesty, the following thoughts are humbly submitted.

If I understand the Temper of the publick at this moment, a very great part of the lower, and some of the middling people of this City, are in a very critical disposition, and such as ought to be managed with firmness and delicacy. In general, they rather approve than blame the principles of the Rioters; though the better sort of them are afraid of the consequences of those very principles, which they approve. This keeps their Minds in a suspended and anxious State, which may very easily be exasperated by an injudicious severity into desperate resolutions; or by weak measures on the part of Government may[4] be

---

[1] *London Evening Post*, 13 July 1780.
[2] *Works* adds: 'Humbly Offered To Consideration' [in small caps].
[3] *Works*: 'convicted on account of the late'.
[4] *Works*: 'Government it may'.

encouraged to the pursuit of Courses, which may be of the most dangerous consequence[1] to the publick.

There is no doubt that the approaching executions will very much determine the future conduct of those people. They ought to be such as will humble; not irritate. Nothing will make Government more awful to them than to see, that it does not proceed by chance or under the influence of passion.

It is therefore proposed, that no execution should be made, until the number of persons which Government thinks fit to try is compleated. When the whole is at once under the Eye—an examination ought to be made into the circumstances of every particular convict; and Six, at the very utmost, of the fittest examples may then be selected for execution, who ought to be brought out and put to death, on one and the same day, in Six different places, and in the most solemn manner that can be devised. Afterwards great care should be taken, that their Bodies may not be delivered to their friends, or to others, who may make them objects of compassion or even veneration; Some instances of the kind have happened with regard to the Bodies to those killed in the Riots.[2]

The rest of the Malefactors ought to be either condemned for larger or shorter terms to the Lighters,[3] houses of correction; service in the Navy;—and the like, according to the Case.

This small Number of executions and all at one time, though in different places, is seriously recommended; because it is certain, that a great havock among Criminals hardens rather than subdues the Minds of people inclined to the same Crimes; and therefore fails of answering its purpose as an example. Men who see their Lives respected and thought of value by others, come to respect that Gift of God themselves. To have compassion for oneself, or care, more or less, for ones own Life, is a Lesson to be learned just as every other; and I believe it will be found, that conspiracies have been most common and most desperate where their punishment has been most extensive and most severe.

Besides the least excess in this way excites a tenderness in the milder sort of people which makes them consider Government in an

---

[1] *Works*: 'consequences'.

[2] No information relative to the incident Burke mentions here has been found.

[3] Convicts had been employed in hulks on the Thames since 1776 by 16 Geo. III, c. 38 and 18 Geo. III, c. 52.

harsh and odious light. The sense of Justice in Men is overloaded and fatigued with a long series of executions, or with such a carnage at once as rather resembles a Massacre than a sober execution of the Laws. The Laws thus lose their Terror in the minds of the wicked, and their reverence in the minds of the Virtuous.

I have ever observed, that the execution of one Man fixes the attention and excites awe; The execution of Multitudes dissipates and weakens the Effect. But Men reason themselves into disapprobation and disgust; They compute more as they feel less; and every severe Act which does not appear to be necessary is sure to be offensive.

In selecting the Criminals a very different line ought to be followed from that recommended by the Champions of the Protestant Association. They recommend that the Offenders for plunder ought to be punished, and the Offenders from principle spared. But the contrary Rule ought to be followed. The ordinary executions, of which there are enough in conscience, are for the former species of delinquents—but such common plunderers would furnish no example in the present Case, where the false or pretended principle of religion which leads to crimes, is the very thing to be discouraged.

But the reason which ought to make these people objects of selection for punishment, confines the selection to very few. For we must consider, that the whole Nation has been for a long time guilty of their Crime. Toleration is a new virtue in any Country. It is a late ripe fruit in the best Climates. We ought to recollect the poison, which under the Name of antidotes against Popery, and such like Mountebank Titles, has been circulated from our Pulpits, and from our presses, from the heads of the Church of England, and the heads of the Dissenters. By degrees these publications have driven all religion[1] from our own Minds, and filled them[2] with nothing but a violent hatred of the religion of other people, and of course with a hatred of their persons, and so, by a very natural progression, has led them[3] to the destruction of their Goods and houses and to attempts upon their Lives.

This delusion furnishes no reason for suffering that abominable Spirit to be kept alive, by inflammatory Libels or seditious assemblies,

---

[1] *Works*: 'These publications, by degrees, have tended to drive all religion'.
[2] *Works*: 'and to fill them'.
[3] *Works*: 'progression, they have led men'.

or for Governments yielding to it, in the smallest degree any point of Justice, Equity, and sound[1] Policy. The King certainly ought not to give up any part of his Subjects to the prejudices of another. So far from it, I am clearly of opinion that on the late occasion, the Catholicks ought to have been taken more avowedly than they were, under the protection of Government, as the Dissenters had been on a similar occasion.[2]

But though we ought to correct the Bigottry of people, and to correct[3] our own too, if we have any left, we ought to reflect that an Offence, which in its Cause is National, ought not in its Effects to be vindicated on individuals but with a very well tempered severity.

For my own part I think the fire is not extinguished, on the contrary it seems to require the attention of Government more than Ever; But as a part of any methodical plan for extinguishing this flame it really seems necessary that the execution of Justice should be as steady and as cool as possible.

Additional Reflexions on the Executions
18 July 1780

Source: MS. at Sheffield, Bk 8.25, 26

The MS. is a draft in Burke's hand, endorsed: 'Draft Additional reflexions on the Executions'. Variations of substance between the MS. and the text in *Works* are noted.

Having in the first instance communicated his views to Lord Thurlow, Burke next approached Lord Bathurst, Lord President of the Council. These additional reflections were sent to Lord Bathurst on 18 July.[4]

Some additional reflexions on the Executions
humbly submitted to consideration[5]

---

[1] *Works*: 'or sound'.
[2] This may refer to the vigorous response of the Whig Government of the day to the riots directed against Dissenting meeting-houses at the beginning of George I's reign. Troops had then been extensively used in support of Dissenters and the Riot Act of 1714 passed to provide for effective prosecution of rioters.
[3] *Works*: 'But, though we ought to protect against violence the bigotry of other, and to correct'.
[4] *Corr.* iv. 256.
[5] *Works*: 'Some Additional Reflections on the Executions' [in small caps].

The great Number of the sufferers[1] seems to arise from the misfortune incident to the variety of judicatures which have tried the Crimes. It were well if the whole had been the business of one Commission[2]— For now every Trial seems as if it were a *seperate* Business, and in that light, each offence is not punished with greater severity than single offences of the Kind are commonly marked. But, in reality and fact, this unfortunate affair, though diversified in the Multitude of overt acts, has been one and the same riot, and therefore the executions, so far as regards the general effect on the Minds of men, will have a reference to the unity of the offence, and will appear to be much more severe than such a riot, atrocious as it was, can well justifye in Government. I pray that it may be recollected, that[3] the chief delinquents have hitherto escaped. Very many[4] of those who are fallen into the hands of justice are a poor thoughtless set of creatures, very little aware of the Nature of their offence. None of The List makers, the assemblers of the Mob, the directors and arrangers have been convicted. The preachers of mischief remain safe and are wicked enough not to feel for their deluded disciples;—no not [at] all.[5]

I would not plead the ignorance of the Law, in any even the most ignorant, as a justification; but I am sure, that when the question is of Mercy it is a very great and powerful argument. I have all the reason in the world to believe that they did not know that their[6] offence was capital.

There is one argument which I beg may not be considered as brought for any invidious purpose, or meant to impute[7] blame any where, but which, I think, with candid and considerate men, will have much weight. The unfortunate delinquents were perhaps much encouraged by some remissness on the part of Government itself. The absolute and entire impunity attending the same offence in Edinburgh,[8] which was over and over again urged as an example and encouragement to those unfortunate people, might be a means of

---

[1] *Works*: 'of sufferers'.
[2] A special Commission had been appointed to try rioters in Southwark. Rioters were tried also at the Old Bailey and at the Surrey Assizes.
[3] The preceding eight words are in the margin and have been accidentally deleted.
[4] *Works*: 'and very many'.
[5] The two preceding sentences are in the margin and have been deleted.
[6] *Works*: 'know their'.
[7] *Works*: 'as imputing'.
[8] See above, p. 424.

deluding them. Perhaps too a languor in the beginning of the Riots here (which sufferd the leaders to proceed, until very many, as it were by the contagion of a Sort of Fashion, carried to these excesses) might make the people think that there was something in the Cause[1] which induced Government to wink at the irregularity of the proceedings.

The conduct and condition of the Lord Mayor[2] ought in my opinion to be considerd. His answers to Lord Beauchamp,[3] to Mr. Malo,[4] and to Mr. Langdale[5] make him appear rather as an[6] accomplice in the Crimes than guilty of negligence as a Magistrate. Such an Example set to the Mob by the first Magistrate of the City, tends greatly to palliate their[7] offence.

The License and complete impunity too of the publications, which from the beginning instigated the people to such actions and in the midst of Trials and executions still continues does in a great degree render these Creatures an object of compassion. In the Publick advertiser of this morning there are two or three paragraphs strongly recommending such outrages; and stimulating the people to violence against the houses and persons of Roman Catholicks, and even against the Chappels of the foreign Ministers.[8]

I would not go so far as to adopt the Maxim, *Quicquid multis peccatur inultum*[9]—but certainly offences committed by vast *multitudes* are somewhat palliated in the *individuals*—who, when so many escape, are always looked upon rather as unlucky than criminal. All our loose

---

[1] *Works*: 'case'.

[2] Brackley Kennett (d. 1782).

[3] In an information to the Privy Council, Lord Beauchamp declared that when the mob was attacking houses in Moorfields and he begged the Lord Mayor to intervene: 'That the Lord Mayor answered they are the houses of People they do not like, and retired' (P.R.O., P.C.2/125, pp. 138–9).

[4] Malo—probably James Malo, merchant and weaver of 6 Moorfields, saw Kennett on the night of 3 June: '"You do not know," said his Lordship to Mr. Malo, "anything of the business. I have orders to employ the military if necessary, but I must be cautious what I do lest I bring the mob to my house. I can assure you there are very great people at the bottom of the riot."' On 5 June when Malo appealed to him again, Kennett merely enquired if he was a papist. On 6 June his house was destroyed (J. P. De Castro, *The Gordon Riots*, London, 1926, pp. 50, 66–7, 77).

[5] Thomas Langdale finding it was necessary to get the Lord Mayor's consent for troops to be brought into the City, was told by Kennett: 'if the Mob begin to pull your House down, come to me and I will order a Guard.' He was not quite so uncooperative afterwards. (See the statement of Langdale; MS. at Sheffield, Bk 8.31.)

[6] *Works*: 'rather an'.

[7] MS.: 'there'.

[8] Burke is probably referring to a paragraph in the *Public Advertiser* of 18 July 1780, arguing that no man can be lawfully punished for damaging what is unlawful (such as a Catholic Chapel).

[9] 'The sin of thousands always goes unpunished' (Lucan, *Pharsalia*, v. 260).

Ideas of Justice have something of comparison in them to[1] the situation of others; and no systematick reasoning can wholly free us from such impressions.

Phil. de Comines says our English Civil wars were less destructive than others; because the Cry of the conqueror always was "Spare the common people."[2] This principle of war should be at least as prevalent in the execution of Justice. The appetite of Justice is easily satisfied; and it best is nourished[3] with the least possible blood.

We may recollect, that[4] between capital punishment and total impunity there are many stages. On the whole, every Circumstance of Mercy and of comparative justice does,[5] in my opinion plead in favour of such low, untaught, or ill taught wretches. But above all the policy of Government is deeply interested, that the punishment[6] should appear *one* solemn deliberate act, aimed not at random; and at particular offences, but done with a relation to *the general Spirit of the tumults* and they ought to be nothing more than what is sufficient to mark and discountenance that Spirit.

Circumstances for Mercy

Not being principal.

Probable want of early and deliberate purpose.[7]

Youth.)
Sex.   ) where the highest malice does not appear.

Intoxication and Levity or mere wantonness of any kind.

---

[1] *Works*: 'justice, as it affects any individual, have in them something of comparison to'.

[2] Burke seems to be referring to two passages in the *Memoirs* of Philippe de Commynes (1447–1511): 'Now in my opinion, out of all the countries which I have personally known, England is the one where public affairs are best conducted and regulated with least violence to the people. There no buildings are knocked down or demolished through war, and disaster and misfortune befall those who make war'; 'But, as I said elsewhere, the realm of England enjoys one favour above all other realms, that neither the countryside nor the people are destroyed nor are buildings burnt or demolished' (Philippe de Commynes, *Memoirs*, trans. M. Jones, London, 1972, pp. 345, 353).

[3] *Works*: 'it is best nourished'.

[4] *Works*: 'may too recollect'.

[5] MS.: 'do'.

[6] *Works*: 'punishments'.

[7] *Works*: 'purposes'.

Election Advertisement
1 September 1780

Source: Bristol Public Library Handbill

Following are five pieces relative to Burke's ultimate decision in September 1780 not to contest the election in Bristol a second time. This decision led to his subsequent contesting and winning a seat in Rockingham's pocket borough of Malton.

Apparently there were rumours in August that Burke might withdraw from the race. His friends in the city found it necessary to publish an advertisement to the electors 'to contradict a Report *so very industriously circulated*, that he does not intend to offer you his Services at the next General Election'. This advertisement assured the electors that had Burke 'entertained such an Idea, he would have made it public before this Time'. It also expressed the 'hope, [that] the scandalous Whispers of designing Men will not prevail on any to engage themselves hastily, as they may depend Mr. Burke, is now preparing to pay a Visit to his constituents, to assure them of his Readiness to serve them'.[1] When Burke did appear in the city he had the following advertisement printed and circulated as a handbill.

To the Gentlemen, Clergy, Freeholders and Freemen of the City of BRISTOL

GENTLEMEN,

It is at the earnest Request of several of the most respectable Persons in this City, that I take the Liberty of soliciting your Votes at the approaching general Election. My friends are so indulgent, as to think, that I have not wholly fallen short of the Expectations upon which they brought me here some Years ago; a Stranger, and recommended only by my public Conduct.

I have served you, during one Parliament, with Fidelity and Diligence, both in your public and private Affairs. If it should be your Pleasure to continue me for another Parliament on the same Trust, I shall endeavour to execute it in the same Manner. I shall certainly receive that renewed Mark of your Confidence, as a Favour of very high Value, and with very sincere Gratitude,

> *I have the Honour to be with the greatest Respect and Esteem,*
> *Gentlemen, Your most obedient, and Most Humble Servant,*

Edmund Burke

Bristol, Sept. 1, 1780.

[1] Bristol Public Library.

Speech at Bristol Previous to the Election
6 September 1780

Source: *A Speech of Edmund Burke, Esq. at the Guildhall, in Bristol, Previous to the late Election in that City, upon Certain Points relative to his Parliamentary Conduct*, 3rd edn., J. Dodsley, London, 1780

Despite his public assertions to the contrary Burke had doubts about the propriety of contesting the election for Bristol well before the campaign began. The day after the following speech to his supporters at the guild-hall announcing his candidacy, he told Lord Rockingham that:

I had determined to resign my pretensions to the representation of Bristol; and nothing was left but for me to make that resignation in the most reputable manner. I was resolved to take my leave without meanness and without passion; and I had drawn up an advertisement for that purpose.[1]

Burke's ultimate decision to give up the election race seems to have centred on a realization that only one Whig could win and that between the two—Burke and Henry Cruger—the latter had the greater support. It is important to recognize, however, that that situation was at least in part related directly to Burke's conduct over the years that he had been a representative for the city.

Recent research has demonstrated that on the whole Burke did an excellent job of working to represent the interests of his constituents to authorities within the various departments of government.[2] But it is also clear that his conduct was not always based strictly on the best means of achieving the loyalty of the city of Bristol. In this final major appeal to his constituents, it is evident that Burke recognized that over the years he had failed sufficiently to cultivate his influence in the city. It is also clear that he understood that on a number of important issues he had taken positions which were not popular. As he well knew he had antagonized many of his constituents in recent years by working for a reduction of restrictions over the trade of Ireland.[3] In 1778 he had introduced a Bill for the free importation of Irish sail-cloth and when it was lost[4] he had actively supported three others.[5] The two which succeeded removed restrictions on Irish goods except woollens, cottons, hats, glass, hops, gunpowder, and coals; and British goods except woollens and glass when

---

[1] *Corr.* iv. 275.

[2] For this aspect of Burke's work as M.P., see P. T. Underdown, 'Edmund Burke, the Commissary of his Bristol Constituents, 1774–1780', *English Historical Review*, lxxiii (1958), 252–69.

[3] See vol. ix, pp. 504–63.

[4] It would appear that Burke actually gave it up. On 4 May he 'observed that it was he who through mistake had moved for leave to bring in the bill though upon enquiry he since discovered that such a law is already in being' (*Parl. Reg.* ix. 162–3).

[5] See *Parl. Hist.* xix. 1100–26.

imported into the colonies from Ireland, and of Irish cotton yarn when imported into Great Britain.[1] Burke's intentions had been thoroughly honourable. He had hoped to help bring relief to a country which was suffering a devastated economy in part as a result of the American dispute. However, the legislation had brought a storm of protest from commercial interests in various parts of England, including Burke's own constituency of Bristol, which had enjoyed protection from Irish competition.[2] Because of Burke's recognized stature as a parliamentarian his views on controversial issues always received wide circulation. It could have done his cause amongst his electors no good that in March 1779, it was reported that he had gone so far as to declare 'it for the interest of G[reat] Britain to lay the trade of Ireland open as well as that of Scotland; and if it were not done now voluntarily, it would soon be extorted by compulsion'.[3] Burke was also aware that his position with respect to insolvent debtors hurt his cause and that many of his electors did not support his fight for Catholic relief. The latter issue appears to have caused damage not just amongst those who objected on religious grounds or because of the chaos created by the Gordon riots. Based in part as it was on a concern to allow Catholics the privilege of prosperity through business and the ownership of property, it must have caused some ill-humour in a commercial city anxious to protect itself from increasing competition.

It is evident as well that Burke's reputation had suffered with respect to some issues other than those he spoke of publicly. He appears, for instance, to have been well out of step with many in Bristol on the question of the slave trade. His sketch of a Negro Code apparently was not circulated until after the 1780 election[4] but on at least three occasions he let his antipathy for the trade be known during speeches in the House of Commons[5] and this could well have hurt him in a metropolis so dependent on trade and commerce. Moreover, his public denunciation of radical measures during debates over subjects such as the duration of Parliaments appears to have splintered his own support amongst Opposition forces in Bristol more than that of Cruger who largely abstained from the fight. Burke felt no remorse, however, for having taken positions which were at variance with the views of his constituents. Indeed, in the following speech he pointed out that in the immense tragedy of the American war, he had originally taken the proper moderate path when many of his electors supported the misguided measures of administration. Rather than apologizing for his actions, Burke affirmed his belief in the principle which he had enunciated when seeking the support of the city some six years earlier. M.P.s must act according to their own judgement and principles rather than blindly following the will of their electorate. The people cannot be properly and strongly represented by men who are too

---

[1] 18 Geo. III, c. 55, and 18 Geo. III, c. 56.
[2] See *Corr.* iii. 426, 429, 440–4. There are copies of five Bristol petitions in *Parl. Reg.* (ix. 183–4, 193–4).
[3] *Gentleman's Magazine*, xlix (1779), 622.
[4] Underdown, 'Edmund Burke, the Commissary of his Bristol Constituents', pp. 252–69.
[5] See in particular his speeches of 5 June 1777 on the African slave trade, above, pp. 340–1.

weak to stand up for their beliefs. 'At present, it is the plan of the court to make its servants insignificant,' he argued.

If the people should fall into the same humour, and should choose their servants on the same principles of mere obsequiousness, and flexibility, and total vacancy or indifference of opinion in all public matters, then no part of the state will be sound; and it will be in vain to think of saving of it.[1]

Burke not only disagreed with his constituents, he rarely saw them. One of his most glaring mistakes was probably his failure to establish regular public contacts with the city. During his term in office he visited Bristol only twice prior to 1780.[2] One can appreciate that he had a difficult task getting to the city regularly, since he lived so far from it. However, before making his decision to run, he had been aware of this circumstance, and he also unquestionably had known that substantial effort would be required to nurse and sustain his interest with the third largest borough electorate in the kingdom.[3] Since their election he and Cruger had never been on good terms and the latter's friends had made strenous efforts to strengthen his interest. It would not have hurt Burke's cause to do something similar. From time to time he had lamented 'the indolence and the timidity which had destroyd ... [the] natural consequence' of his own friends in Bristol.[4] Surely much greater enthusiasm might have been expected had he been more visible more often amongst them to encourage *esprit de corps*. In truth Burke's basic view of the relationship between M.P.s and their electors was as much a handicap for him in courting his constituents as it was in representing their views. He was convinced that he was one of the élite who had been born to lead and therefore he considered himself a far better judge of what was right for the nation, the empire, and the people than the people themselves. As 'to leaving to the Crowd, to choose for me, what principles I ought to hold, or what Course I ought to pursue for their benefit', he told Portland, 'I had much rather, innocently and obscurely, mix with them, with the utter ruin of all my hopes, (which hopes are my all) than to betray them by learning lessons from them. They are naturally proud, tyrannical, and ignorant; bad scholars and worse Masters.'[5] After the 1780 election was over he observed that the campaign in Bristol had shown 'the madness of the common peoples dream, that they could be anything without the Aid of better fortunes and better heads than their own'.[6] From the beginning to the end of Burke's years as M.P. for Bristol he knew what he was risking by refusing to be the servant of

---

[1] See below, p. 626.

[2] Burke had come to Bristol for the election of 1774, had visited it in August–September 1775 and August 1776 (*Corr.* iii. 198, 206–7, 290). He arrived in Bristol just before the dissolution of Parliament in August 1780.

[3] Those of Westminster and London were larger.

[4] *Corr.* iv. 276.

[5] *Corr.* iv. 274.

[6] *Corr.* iv. 295.

his electors and it seems clear that he was prepared to pay the price which ultimately it cost him.

SPEECH, &c.

Mr. Mayor,[1] and Gentlemen,

I am extremely pleased at the appearance of this large and respectable meeting. The steps I may be obliged to take will want the sanction of a considerable authority; and in explaining any thing which may appear doubtful in my public conduct, I must naturally desire a very full audience.

I have been backward to begin my canvass. The dissolution of the Parliament was uncertain; and it did not become me, by an unseasonable importunity, to appear diffident of the effect of my six years endeavours to please you. I had served the city of Bristol honourably; and the city of Bristol had no reason to think, that the means of honourable service to the public, were become indifferent to me.

I found on my arrival here, that three gentlemen had been long in eager pursuit of an object which but two of us can obtain. I found, that they had all met with encouragement. A contested election in such a city as this, is no light thing. I paused on the brink of the precipice. These three gentlemen,[2] by various merits, and on various titles, I made no doubt, were worthy of your favour. I shall never attempt to raise myself by depreciating the merits of my competitors. In the complexity and confusion of these cross pursuits, I wished to take the authentic public sense of my friends upon a business of so much delicacy. I wished to take your opinion along with me; that if I should give up the contest at the very beginning, my surrender of my post may not seem the effect of inconstancy, or timidity, or anger, or disgust, or indolence, or any other temper unbecoming a man who has engaged in the public service. If, on the contrary, I should undertake the election, and fail of success, I was full as anxious, that it should be manifest to the whole world, that the peace of the city had not been broken by my rashness, presumption, or fond conceit of my own merit.

I am not come, by a false and counterfeit shew of deference to your

---

[1] John Bull (d. 1783).
[2] Cruger, Matthew Brickdale, and Richard Combe (?1728–80), M.P. 1772, 1774–80.

judgment, to seduce it in my favour. I ask it seriously and unaffectedly. If you wish that I should retire, I shall not consider that advice as a censure upon my conduct, or an alteration in your sentiments; but as a rational submission to the circumstances of affairs. If, on the contrary, you should think it proper for me to proceed on my canvass, if you will risque the trouble on your part, I will risque it on mine. My pretensions are such as you cannot be ashamed of, whether they succeed or fail.

If you call upon me, I shall solicit the favour of the city upon manly ground. I come before you with the plain confidence of an honest servant in the equity of a candid and discerning master. I come to claim your approbation not to amuse you with vain apologies, or with professions still more vain and senseless. I have lived too long to be served by apologies, or to stand in need of them. The part I have acted has been in open day; and to hold out to a conduct, which stands in that clear and steady light for all its good and all its evil, to hold out to that conduct the paltry winking tapers of excuses and promises—I never will do it.—They may obscure it with their smoke; but they never can illumine sunshine by such a flame as theirs.

I am sensible that no endeavours have been left untried to injure me in your opinion. But the use of character is to be a shield against calumny. I could wish, undoubtedly (if idle wishes were not the most idle of all things) to make every part of my conduct agreeable to every one of my constituents. But in so great a city, and so greatly divided as this, it is weak to expect it.

In such a discordancy of sentiments, it is better to look to the nature of things than to the humours of men. The very attempt towards pleasing every body, discovers a temper always flashy, and often false and insincere. Therefore, as I have proceeded strait onward in my conduct, so I will proceed in my account of those parts of it which have been most excepted to. But I must first beg leave just to hint to you, that we may suffer very great detriment by being open to every talker. It is not to be imagined, how much of service is lost from spirits full of activity and full of energy, who are pressing, who are rushing forward, to great and capital objects, when you oblige them to be continually looking back. Whilst they are defending one service, they defraud you of an hundred. Applaud us when we run; console us when we fall; cheer us when we recover; but let us pass on—for God's sake, let us pass on.

Do you think, Gentlemen, that every public act in the six years since I stood in this place before you—that all the arduous things which have been done in this eventful period, which has crowded into a few years space the revolutions of an age, can be opened to you on their fair grounds in half an hour's conversation?

But it is no reason, because there is a bad mode of enquiry, that there should be no examination at all. Most certainly it is our duty to examine; it is our interest too.—But it must be with discretion; with an attention to all the circumstances, and to all the motives; like sound judges, and not like cavilling pettyfoggers and quibbling pleaders, prying into flaws and hunting for exceptions. Look, Gentlemen, to the *whole tenour* of your member's conduct. Try whether his ambition or his avarice have justled him out of the strait line of duty; or whether that grand foe of the offices of active life, that master-vice in men of business, a degenerate and inglorious sloth, has made him flag and languish in his course? This is the object of our enquiry. If our member's conduct can bear this touch, mark it for sterling. He may have fallen into errors; he must have faults; but our error is greater, and our fault is radically ruinous to ourselves, if we do not bear, if we do not even applaud, the whole compound and mixed mass of such a character. Not to act thus is folly; I had almost said it is impiety. He censures God, who quarrels with the imperfections of man.

Gentlemen, we must not be peevish with those who serve the people. For none will serve us whilst there is a court to serve, but those who are of a nice and jealous honour. They who think every thing, in comparison of that honour, to be dust and ashes, will not bear to have it soiled and impaired by those, for whose sake they make a thousand sacrifices, to preserve it immaculate and whole. We shall either drive such men from the public stage, or we shall send them to the court for protection; where, if they must sacrifice their reputation, they will at least secure their interest. Depend upon it, that the lovers of freedom will be free. None will violate their conscience to please us, in order afterwards to discharge that conscience, which they have violated, by doing us faithful and affectionate service. If we degrade and deprave their minds by servility, it will be absurd to expect, that they who are creeping and abject toward us, will ever be bold and uncorruptible assertors of our freedom, against the most seducing and the most formidable of all powers. No! human nature is not so formed; nor shall we improve the faculties, or better the morals of public men, by our possession of the most infallible receipt in the world for making cheats and hypocrites.

Let me say with plainness, I who am no longer in a public character, that if by a fair, by an indulgent, by a gentlemanly behaviour to our representatives, we do not give confidence to their minds, and a liberal scope to their understandings; if we do not permit our members to act upon a *very* enlarged view of things; we shall at length infallibly degrade our national representation into a confused and scuffling bustle of local agency. When the popular member is narrowed in his ideas, and rendered timid in his proceedings, the service of the crown will be the sole nursery of statesmen. Among the frolics of the court, it may at length take that of attending to its business. Then the monopoly of mental power will be added to the power of all other kinds it possesses. On the side of the people there will be nothing but impotence: for ignorance is impotence; narrowness of mind is impotence; timidity is itself impotence, and makes all other qualities that go along with it, impotent and useless.

At present, it is the plan of the court to make its servants insignificant. If the people should fall into the same humour, and should choose their servants on the same principles of mere obsequiousness, and flexibility, and total vacancy or indifference of opinion in all public matters, then no part of the state will be sound; and it will be in vain to think of saving of it.

I thought it very expedient at this time to give you this candid counsel; and with this counsel I would willingly close, if the matters which at various times have been objected to me in this city concerned only myself, and my own election. These charges, I think, are four in number;—my neglect of a due attention to my constituents; the not paying more frequent visits here;—my conduct on the affairs of the first Irish trade acts;—my opinion and mode of proceeding on Lord Beauchamp's Debtors Bills;—and my votes on the late affairs of the Roman Catholics. All of these (except perhaps the first) relate to matters of very considerable public concern; and it is not lest you should censure me improperly, but lest you should form improper opinions on matters of some moment to you, that I trouble you at all upon the subject. My conduct is of small importance.

With regard to the first charge, my friends have spoken to me of it in the style of amicable expostulation; not so much blaming the thing, as lamenting the effects.—Others, less partial to me, were less kind in assigning the motives. I admit, there is a decorum and propriety in a member of parliament's paying a respectful court to his constituents. If I were conscious to myself that pleasure or dissipation, or low unworthy occupations, had detained me from personal attendance on you, I would readily admit my fault, and quietly submit to the penalty. But, Gentlemen, I live at an hundred miles distance from Bristol; and at the end of a session I come to my own house, fatigued in body and in mind, to a little repose, and to a very little attention to my family and my private concerns. A visit to Bristol is always a sort of canvass; else it will do more harm than good. To pass from the toils of a session to the toils of a canvass, is the furthest thing in the world from repose. I could hardly serve you *as I have done*, and court you too. Most of you have heard, that I do not very remarkably spare myself in *public* business; and in the *private* business of my constituents I have done very near as much as those who have nothing else to do. My canvass of you was not on the Change, nor in the county meetings, nor in the clubs of this city. It was in the House of Commons; it was at the Customhouse, it was at the Council; it was at the Treasury; it was at the Admiralty. I canvassed you through your affairs, and not your persons.[1] I was not only your representative as a body; I was the agent, the solicitor of individuals; I ran about wherever your affairs could call me; and in acting for you I often appeared rather as a ship-broker, than as a member of parliament. There was nothing too laborious, or too low for me to undertake. The meanness of the business was raised by the dignity of the object. If some lesser matters have slipped through my fingers, it was because I filled my hands too full; and in my eagerness to serve you, took in more than any hands could grasp.[2] Several gentlemen stand round me who are my willing witnesses; and there are others who, if they were here, would be still better; because they would be unwilling witnesses to the same truth. It was in the middle of a summer residence in London, and in the middle of a negociation at the Admiralty for your trade,[3] that I was called to Bristol; and this late visit, at this late day, has been possibly in prejudice to your affairs.

Since I have touched upon this matter, let me say, Gentlemen, that

[1] For this aspect of Burke's work as an M.P., see Underdown, 'Edmund Burke, the Commissary of his Bristol Constituents', pp. 252–69.
[2] Burke was indeed an exceptionally conscientious member; he did, however, in both 1775 and 1777 neglect the interests of the Bristol soap-makers (*Corr.* iii. 145, 357, 363).
[3] See *Corr.* iv. 263.

if I had a disposition, or a right to complain, I have some cause of complaint on my side. With a petition of this city in my hand,[1] passed through the corporation without a dissenting voice, a petition in unison with almost the whole voice of the kingdom, (with whose formal thanks I was covered over) whilst I laboured on no less than five bills for a public reform, and fought, against the opposition of great abilities, and of the greatest power, every clause, and every word of the largest of those bills, almost to the very last day of a very long session; all this time a canvass in Bristol was as calmly carried on as if I were dead. I was considered as a man wholly out of the question. Whilst I watched, and fasted, and sweated in the House of Commons—by the most easy and ordinary arts of election, by dinners and visits, by "How do you do's," and, "My worthy friends," I was to be quietly moved out of my seat—and promises were made, and engagements entered into, without any exception or reserve, as if my laborious zeal in my duty had been a regular abdication of my trust.

To open my whole heart to you on this subject, I do confess, however, that there were other times besides the two years in which I did visit you, when I was not wholly without leisure for repeating that mark of my respect. But I could not bring my mind to see you. You remember, that in the beginning of this American war (that æra of calamity, disgrace and downfall, an æra which no feeling mind will ever mention without a tear for England) you were greatly divided; and a very strong body, if not the strongest, opposed itself to the madness which every art and every power were employed to render popular, in order that the errors of the rulers might be lost in the general blindness of the nation. This opposition continued until after our great, but most unfortunate victory at Long Island.[2] Then all the mounds and banks of our constancy were borne down at once; and the phrensy of the American war broke in upon us like a deluge. This victory, which seemed to put an immediate end to all difficulties, perfected us in that spirit of domination, which our unparalleled prosperity had but too long nurtured. We had been so very powerful, and so very prosperous, that even the humblest of us were degraded into the vices and follies of kings. We lost all measure between means and ends; and

---

[1] See *Corr.* iv. 202–3, 206–11.

[2] In the battle of Long Island in August 1776. The news of it was known in London by 10 October.

our headlong desires became our politics and our morals. All men who wished for peace, or retained any sentiments of moderation, were overborne or silenced; and this city was led by every artifice (and probably with the more management, because I was one of your members) to distinguish itself by its zeal for that fatal cause. In this temper of yours and of my mind, I should sooner have fled to the extremities of the earth, than have shewn myself here. I, who saw in every American victory (for you have had a long series of these misfortunes) the germ and seed of the naval power of France and Spain, which all our heat and warmth against America was only hatching into life,—I should not have been a welcome visitant with the brow and the language of such feelings. When afterwards, the other face of your calamity was turned upon you, and shewed itself in defeat and distress, I shunned you full as much. I felt sorely this variety in our wretchedness; and I did not wish to have the least appearance of insulting you with that shew of superiority, which, though it may not be assumed, is generally suspected in a time of calamity, from those whose previous warnings have been despised. I could not bear to shew you a representative whose face did not reflect that of his constituents; a face that could not joy in your joys, and sorrow in your sorrows. But time at length has made us all of one opinion; and we have all opened our eyes on the true nature of the American war, to the true nature of all its successes and all its failures.

In that public storm too I had my private feelings. I had seen blown down and prostrate on the ground several of those houses to whom I was chiefly indebted for the honour this city has done me. I confess, that whilst the wounds of those I loved were yet green, I could not bear to shew myself in pride and triumph in that place into which their partiality had brought me, and to appear at feasts and rejoicings, in the midst of the grief and calamity of my warm friends, my zealous supporters, my generous benefactors.[1] This is a true, unvarnished, undisguised state of the affair. You will judge of it.

This is the only one of the charges in which I am personally concerned. As to the other matters objected against me, which in their turn I shall mention to you, remember once more I do not mean to extenuate or excuse. Why should I, when the things charged are

---

[1] Particularly Richard Champion and Paul Farr (d. 1794) and his father Richard (d. 1792) and brother Thomas (d. 1791).

among those upon which I found all my reputation? What would be left to me, if I myself was the man, who softened, and blended, and diluted, and weakened, all the distinguishing colours of my life, so as to leave nothing distinct and determinate in my whole conduct?

It has been said, and it is the second charge, that in the questions of the Irish trade, I did not consult the interest of my constituents, or, to speak out strongly, that I rather acted as a native of Ireland, than as an English member of parliament.

I certainly have very warm good wishes for the place of my birth. But the sphere of my duties is my true country. It was, as a man attached to your interests, and zealous for the conservation of your power and dignity, that I acted on that occasion, and on all occasions. You were involved in the American war. A new world of policy was opened, to which it was necessary we should conform whether we would or not; and my only thought was how to conform to our situation in such a manner as to unite to this kingdom, in prosperity and in affection, whatever remained of the empire. I was true to my old, standing, invariable principle, that all things, which came from Great Britain, should issue as a gift of her bounty and beneficence, rather than as claims recovered against a struggling litigant; or at least, that if your beneficence obtained no credit in your concessions, yet that they should appear the salutary provisions of your wisdom and foresight; not as things wrung from you with your blood, by the cruel gripe of a rigid necessity. The first concessions, by being (much against my will) mangled and stripped of the parts which were necessary to make out their just correspondence and connection in trade, were of no use.[1] The next year a feeble attempt was made to bring the thing into better shape. This attempt (countenanced by the minister) on the very first appearance of some popular uneasiness, was, after a considerable progress through the house, thrown out by *him*.[2]

What was the consequence? The whole kingdom of Ireland was instantly in a flame. Threatened by foreigners, and, as they thought, insulted by England, they resolved at once to resist the power of France, and to cast off yours. As for us, we were able neither to protect nor to restrain them. Forty thousand men were raised and disciplined without commission from the crown.[3] Two illegal armies were seen

---

[1] The proposals of April–May 1778.
[2] The proposals of January–March 1779.
[3] The Irish Volunteers.

with banners displayed at the same time, and in the same country. No executive magistrate, no judicature, in Ireland, would acknowledge the legality of the army which bore the king's commission; and no law, or appearance of law, authorised the army commissioned by itself. In this unexampled state of things, which the least error, the least trespass on the right or left, would have hurried down the precipice into an abyss of blood and confusion, the people of Ireland demand a freedom of trade with arms in their hands. They interdict all commerce between the two nations. They deny all new supply in the House of Commons, although in time of war. They stint the trust of the old revenue, given for two years to all the king's predecessors, to six months.[1] The British Parliament, in a former session frightened into a limited concession by the menaces of Ireland, frightened out of it by the menaces of England, was now frightened back again, and made an universal surrender of all that had been thought the peculiar, reserved, un-communicable rights of England;—The exclusive commerce of America, of Africa, of the West-Indies—all the enumerations of the acts of navigation—all the manufactures,—iron, glass, even the last pledge of jealousy and pride, the interest hid in the secret of our hearts, the inveterate prejudice moulded into the constitution of our frame, even the sacred fleece itself, all went together.[2] No reserve; no exception; no debate; no discussion. A sudden light broke in upon us all. It broke in, not through well-contrived and well-disposed windows, but through flaws and breaches; through the yawning chasms of our ruin. We were taught wisdom by humiliation. No town in England presumed to have a prejudice; or dared to mutter a petition. What was worse, the whole Parliament of England, which retained authority for nothing but surrenders, was despoiled of every shadow of its super-intendance. It was, without any qualification, denied in theory, as it had been trampled upon in practice. This scene of shame and dis-grace, has, in a manner whilst I am speaking, ended by the perpetual establishment of a military power, in the dominions of this crown, without consent of the British legislature,* contrary to the policy of the constitution, contrary to the declaration of right: and by this your liberties are swept away along with your supreme authority—and both,

---

* Irish Perpetual Muting Act.[3]
[1] The Irish Parliament adopted the Short Money Bill at the end of 1779.
[2] 'Free trade' was conceded to Ireland when Parliament met in November 1779.
[3] See vol. ix, pp. 563–4.

linked together from the beginning, have, I am afraid, both together perished for ever.[1]

What! Gentlemen, was I not to foresee, or foreseeing, was I not to endeavour to save you from all these multiplied mischiefs and disgraces? Would the little, silly, canvass prattle of obeying instructions, and having no opinions but yours, and such idle senseless tales, which amuse the vacant ears of unthinking men, have saved you from "the pelting of that pitiless storm,"[2] to which the loose improvidence, the cowardly rashness of those who dare not look danger in the face, so as to provide against it in time, and therefore throw themselves headlong into the midst of it, have exposed this degraded nation, beat down and prostrate on the earth, unsheltered, unarmed, unresisting? Was I an Irishman on that day, that I boldly withstood our pride? or on the day that I hung down my head, and wept in shame and silence over the humiliation of Great Britain? I became unpopular in England for the one, and in Ireland for the other.[3] What then! What obligation lay on me to be popular? I was bound to serve both kingdoms. To be pleased with my service, was their affair, not mine.

I was an Irishman in the Irish business, just as much as I was an American, when on the same principles, I wished you to concede to America, at a time when she prayed concession at our feet. Just as much was I an American when I wished Parliament to offer terms in victory, and not to wait the well-chosen hour of defeat, for making good by weakness, and by supplication, a claim of prerogative, pre-eminence, and authority.

Instead of requiring it from me, as a point of duty, to kindle with your passions, had you all been as cool as I was, you would have been saved disgraces and distresses that are unutterable. Do you remember our commission? We sent out a solemn embassy across the Atlantic ocean, to lay the Crown, the Peerage, the Commons of Great Britain, at the feet of the American Congress.[4] That our disgrace might want no sort of brightening and burnishing, observe who they were that composed this famous embassy. My Lord Carlisle is among the first ranks of our nobility. He is the identical man who but two years before,

---

[1] The Perpetual Mutiny Act was a defeat for the Irish Patriots and an alteration in London of the Mutiny Bill they supported.

[2] *King Lear*, III. iv. 29.

[3] See *Corr.* iv. 181–2.

[4] The Carlisle Commission.

had been put forward, at the opening of a session in the House of Lords, as the mover of an haughty and rigorous address against America.[1] He was put in the front of the embassy of submission. Mr. Eden[2] was taken from the office of Lord Suffolk, to whom he was then under secretary of state; from the office of that Lord Suffolk, who but a few weeks before, in his place in parliament, did not deign to enquire where a Congress of vagrants was to be found.[3] This Lord Suffolk sent Mr. Eden to find these vagrants, without knowing where his King's Generals were to be found, who were joined in the same commission of supplicating those whom they were sent to subdue.[4] They enter the capital of America only to abandon it; and these assertors and representatives of the dignity of England, at the tail of a flying army, let fly their Parthian shafts of memorials and remonstrances at random behind them.[5] Their promises and their offers, their flatteries and their menaces, were all despised; and we were saved the disgrace of their formal reception, only because the Congress scorned to receive them; whilst the State-house of independent Philadelphia opened her doors to the public entry of the ambassador of France.[6] From war and blood, we went to submission; and from submission plunged back again to war and blood; to desolate and be desolated, without measure, hope, or end. I am a Royalist, I blushed for this degradation of the Crown. I am a Whig, I blushed for the dishonour of Parliament. I am a true Englishman, I felt to the quick for the disgrace of England. I am a Man, I felt for the melancholy reverse of human affairs, in the fall of the first power in the world.

To read what was approaching in Ireland, in the black and bloody characters of the American war, was a painful, but it was a necessary part of my public duty. For, Gentlemen, it is not your fond desires or

---

[1] On 31 October 1776.

[2] See above, p. 540.

[3] He concluded his speech of 11 December 1777 'with declaring, that the conduct of a *vagrant* Congress, a Congress which no person at home knew where it had run to, was not to be held up as an object of example to their Lordships' (*Parl. Reg.* x. 119).

[4] The Commissioners sailed from England intending to go to Philadelphia but because of Howe's evacuation to New York went there. The Howe brothers were members of the Commission (P. Mackesy, *The War for America, 1775–83*, p. 189).

[5] The Manifesto and Proclamation of Carlisle and Eden were issued in October 1778 (see Burke's speech of 4 December 1778, printed above).

[6] On 6 February 1778 treaties of commerce and alliance were signed between America and France. The first French Ambassador to America, Conrad-Alexandre Gérard, was received by the Congress at Philadelphia on 12 July 1778 (M. Smelser, *The Winning of Independence*, Chicago, 1972, p. 264).

mine that can alter the nature of things; by contending against which what have we got, or shall ever get, but defeat and shame? I did not obey your instructions: No. I conformed to the instructions of truth and nature, and maintained your interest, against your opinions, with a constancy that became me. A representative worthy of you, ought to be a person of stability. I am to look, indeed, to your opinions; but to such opinions as you and I *must* have five years hence. I was not to look to the flash of the day. I knew that you chose me, in my place, along with others, to be a pillar of the state, and not a weathercock on the top of the edifice, exalted for my levity and versatility, and of no use but to indicate the shiftings of every fashionable gale. Would to God, the value of my sentiments on Ireland and on America had been at this day a subject of doubt and discussion! No matter what my sufferings had been, so that this kingdom had kept the authority I wished it to maintain, by a grave foresight, and by an equitable temperance in the use of its power.

The next article of charge on my public conduct, and that which I find rather the most prevalent of all, is Lord Beauchamp's bill. I mean his bill of last session for reforming the law-process concerning imprisonment. It is said, to aggravate the offence, that I treated the petition of this city with contempt even in presenting it to the House, and expressed myself in terms of marked disrespect.[1] Had this latter part of the charge been true, no merits on the side of the question which I took, could possibly excuse me. But I am incapable of treating this city with disrespect. Very fortunately, at this minute (if my bad eyesight does not deceive me)* the worthy gentleman deputed on this business stands directly before me. To him I appeal, whether I did not, though it militated with my oldest and my most recent public opinions, deliver the petition with a strong, and more than usual recommendation to the consideration of the House, on account of the character and consequence of those who signed it. I believe the worthy gentleman will tell you, that the very day I received it, I applied to the Solicitor, now the Attorney General,[2] to give it an immediate consideration; and he most obligingly and instantly consented to employ a great deal of his very valuable time, to write an explanation of

* Mr. Williams.
[1] The petition was presented on 10 April 1780. No record of Burke's speaking about it has been found.
[2] Alexander Wedderburn.

the bill. I attended the Committee with all possible care and diligence, in order that every objection of yours might meet with a solution; or produce an alteration. I entreated your learned Recorder[1] (always ready in business in which you take a concern) to attend. But what will you say to those who blame me for supporting Lord Beauchamp's bill, as a disrespectful treatment of your petition, when you hear, that out of respect to you, I myself was the cause of the loss of that very bill? for the noble Lord who brought it in, and who, I must say, has much merit for this and some other measures, at my request consented to put it off for a week, which the Speaker's illness lengthened to a fortnight; and then the frantic tumult about Popery, drove that and every rational business from the House.[2] So that if I chose to make a defence of myself, on the little principles of a culprit pleading in his exculpation, I might not only secure my acquittal, but make merit with the opposers of the bill. But I shall do no such thing. The truth is, that I did occasion the loss of the bill, and by a delay caused by my respect to you. But such an event was never in my contemplation. And I am so far from taking credit for the defeat of that measure, that I cannot sufficiently lament my misfortune, if but one man, who ought to be at large, has passed a year in prison by my means. I am a debtor to the debtors. I confess judgment. I owe, what, if ever it be in my power, I shall most certainly pay,—ample atonement, and usurious amends to liberty and humanity for my unhappy lapse. For, Gentlemen, Lord Beauchamp's bill was a law of justice and policy, as far as it went; I say as far as it went, for its fault was its being, in the remedial part, miserably defective.

There are two capital faults in our law with relation to civil debts. One is, that every men is presumed solvent. A presumption, in innumerable cases, directly against truth. Therefore the debtor is ordered, on a supposition of ability and fraud, to be coerced his liberty until he makes payment. By this means, in all cases of civil insolvency, without a pardon from his creditor, he is to be imprisoned for life:— and thus a miserable mistaken invention of artificial science, operates to change a civil into a criminal judgment, and to scourge misfortune

---

[1] John Dunning.
[2] The illness of the Speaker (Sir Fletcher Norton) led to an adjournment of the House from 14 to 24 April, which restricted the business the House could consider. The Gordon riots did not begin until 2 June.

or indiscretion with a punishment which the law does not inflict on the greatest crimes.

The next fault is, that the inflicting of that punishment is not on the opinion of an equal and public judge; but is referred to the arbitrary discretion of a private, nay interested, and irritated, individual. He, who formally is, and substantially ought to be, the judge, is in reality no more than ministerial, a mere executive instrument of a private man, who is at once judge and party. Every idea of judicial order is subverted by this procedure. If the insolvency be no crime, why is it punished with arbitrary imprisonment? If it be a crime, why is it delivered into private hands to pardon without discretion, or to punish without mercy and without measure?

To these faults, gross and cruel faults in our law, the excellent principle of Lord Beauchamp's bill applied some sort of remedy. I know that credit must be preserved; but equity must be preserved too; and it is impossible, that any thing should be necessary to commerce, which is inconsistent with justice. The principle of credit was not weakened by that bill. God forbid! The enforcement of that credit was only put into the same public judicial hands on which we depend for our lives, and all that makes life dear to us. But, indeed, this business was taken up too warmly both here and elsewhere. The bill was extremely mistaken. It was supposed to enact what it never enacted; and complaints were made of clauses in it as novelties, which existed before the noble Lord that brought in the bill was born. There was a fallacy that run through the whole of the objections. The gentlemen who opposed the bill, always argued, as if the option lay between that bill and the antient law.—But this is a grand mistake. For practically, the option is between, not that bill and the old law, but between that bill and those occasional laws called acts of grace. For the operation of the old law is so savage, and so inconvenient to society, that for a long time past, once in every parliament, and lately twice, the legislature has been obliged to make a general arbitrary jail-delivery, and at once to set open, by its sovereign authority, all the prisons in England.[3]

Gentlemen, I never relished acts of grace; nor ever submitted to them but from despair of better. They are a dishonourable invention, by which, not from humanity, not from policy, but merely because we

---

[1] Most recently by 16 Geo. III, c. 38, and 18 Geo. III, c. 52.

have not room enough to hold these victims of the absurdity of our laws, we turn loose upon the public three or four thousand naked wretches, corrupted by the habits, debased by the ignominy of a prison. If the creditor had a right to those carcases as a natural security for his property, I am sure we have no right to deprive him of that security. But if the few pounds of flesh were not necessary to his security, we had not a right to detain the unfortunate debtor, without any benefit at all to the person who confined him.—Take it as you will, we commit injustice. Now Lord Beauchamp's bill intended to do deliberately, and with great caution and circumspection, upon each several case, and with all attention to the just claimant, what acts of grace do in a much greater measure, and with very little care, caution, or deliberation.

I suspect that here too, if we contrive to oppose this bill, we shall be found in a struggle against the nature of things. For as we grow enlightened, the public will not bear, for any length of time, to pay for the maintenance of whole armies of prisoners; nor, at their own expence, submit to keep jails as a sort of garrisons, merely to fortify the absurd principle of making men judges in their own cause. For credit has little or no concern in this cruelty. I speak in a commercial assembly. You know, that credit is given, because capital *must* be employed; that men calculate the chances of insolvency; and they either withhold the credit, or make the debtor pay the risque in the price. The counting-house has no alliance with the jail. Holland understands trade as well as we, and she has done much more than this obnoxious bill intended to do. There was not, when Mr. Howard[1] visited Holland, more than one prisoner for debt in the great city of Rotterdam.[2] Although Lord Beauchamp's act[3] (which was previous to this bill, and intended to feel the way for it) has already preserved liberty to thousands; and though it is not three years since the last act of grace passed, yet by Mr. Howard's last account, there were near three thousand again in jail.[4] I cannot name this gentleman

---

[1] John Howard (*c.*1726–90).

[2] Howard found no debtors in Rotterdam 'at any of my former visits, but in 1781 there was one debtor' (Howard, *The State of the Prisons*, London, 1929, p. 49).

[3] An Act for Extending the Provisions of an Act . . . Intituled, An Act to Prevent Frivolous and Vexatious Arrests (19 Geo. III, c. 70).

[4] In 1779 there were 2,078 (Howard, *State of the Prisons*, p. 281).

without remarking, that his labours and writings have done much to open the eyes and hearts of mankind. He has visited all Europe,—not to survey the sumptuousness of palaces, or the stateliness of temples; not to make accurate measurements of the remains of ancient grandeur, nor to form a scale of the curiosity of modern art; not to collect medals, or collate manuscripts:—but to dive into the depths of dungeons; to plunge into the infection of hospitals; to survey the mansions of sorrow and pain; to take the gage and dimensions of misery, depression, and contempt; to remember the forgotten, to attend to the neglected, to visit the forsaken, and to compare and collate the distresses of all men in all countries. His plan is original; and it is as full of genius as it is of humanity. It was a voyage of discovery; a circumnavigation of charity. Already the benefit of his labour is felt more or less in every country: I hope he will anticipate his final reward, by seeing all its effects fully realized in his own. He will receive, not by retail but in gross, the reward of those who visit the prisoner; and he has so forestalled and monopolized this branch of charity, that there will be, I trust, little room to merit by such acts of benevolence hereafter.

Nothing remains now to trouble you with, but the fourth charge against me—the business of the Roman Catholics. It is a business closely connected with the rest. They are all on one and the same principle. My little scheme of conduct, such as it is, is all arranged. I could do nothing but what I have done on this subject, without confounding the whole train of my ideas, and disturbing the whole order of my life. Gentlemen, I ought to apologize to you, for seeming to think any thing at all necessary to be said upon this matter. The calumny is fitter to be scrawled with the midnight chalk of incendiaries, with "No Popery," on walls and doors of devoted houses, than to be mentioned in any civilised company. I had heard, that the spirit of discontent on that subject was very prevalent here. With pleasure I find that I have been grossly misinformed. If it exists at all in this city, the laws have crushed its exertions, and our morals have shamed its appearance in day-light. I have pursued this spirit where-ever I could trace it; but it still fled from me. It was a ghost, which all had heard of, but none had seen. None would acknowledge that he thought the public proceeding with regard to our Catholic dissenters to be blameable; but several were sorry it had made an ill impression upon others, and that my interest was hurt by my share in the business. I find with satisfaction and pride, that not above four or five in this city (and I dare say these misled by some gross misrepresentation) have signed that symbol of delusion and bond of sedition, that libel on the national religion and English character, the Protestant Association. It is therefore, Gentlemen, not by way of cure but of prevention, and lest the arts of wicked men may prevail over the integrity of any one amongst us, that I think it necessary to open to you the merits of this transaction pretty much at large; and I beg your patience upon it: for, although the reasonings that have been used to depreciate the act are of little force, and though the authority of the men concerned in this ill design is not very imposing; yet the audaciousness of these con-spirators against the national honour, and the extensive wickedness of their attempts, have raised persons of little importance to a degree of evil eminence, and imparted a sort of sinister dignity to proceedings that had their origin in only the meanest and blindest malice.

In explaining to you the proceedings of Parliament which have been complained of, I will state to you,—first, the thing that was done;—next, the persons who did it;—and lastly, the grounds and reasons upon which the legislature proceeded in this deliberate act of public justice and public prudence.

Gentlemen, The condition of our nature is such, that we buy our blessings at a price. The Reformation, one of the greatest periods of human improvement, was a time of trouble and confusion. The vast structure of superstition and tyranny, which had been for ages in rearing, and which was combined with the interest of the great and of the many; which was moulded into the laws, the manners, and civil institutions of nations, and blended with the frame and policy of states; could not be brought to the ground without a fearful struggle; nor could it fall without a violent concussion of itself and all about it. When this great revolution was attempted in a more regular mode by government, it was opposed by plots and seditions of the people; when by popular efforts, it was repressed as rebellion by the hand of power; and bloody executions (often bloodily returned) marked the whole of its progress through all its stages. The affairs of religion, which are no longer heard of in the tumult of our present contentions, made a principal ingredient in the wars and politics of that time; the enthusiasm of religion threw a gloom over the politics; and political interests poisoned and perverted the spirit of religion upon all sides. The Protestant religion in that violent struggle, infected, as the Popish had been before, by worldly interests and worldly passions, became a persecutor in its turn, sometimes of the new sects, which carried their own principles further than it was convenient to the original reformers; and always of the body from whom they parted; and this persecuting spirit arose, not only, from the bitterness of retaliation, but from the merciless policy of fear.

It was long before the spirit of true piety and true wisdom, involved in the principles of the Reformation, could be depurated from the dregs and feculence of the contention with which it was carried through. However, until this be done, the Reformation is not complete; and those who think themselves good Protestants, from their animosity to others, are in that respect no Protestants at all. It was at first thought necessary, perhaps, to oppose to Popery another Popery, to get the better of it. Whatever was the cause, laws were made in many countries, and in this kingdom in particular, against Papists, which are as bloody as any of those which had been enacted by the Popish princes and states; and where those laws were not bloody, in my opinion, they were worse; as they were slow, cruel outrages on our nature, and kept men alive only to insult in their persons, every one of the rights and feelings of humanity. I pass those statutes, because I would spare your pious ears the repetition of such shocking things; and I come to that particular law, the repeal of which has produced so many unnatural and unexpected consequences.

A statute was fabricated in the year 1699,[1] by which the saying mass (a church-service in the Latin tongue, not exactly the same as our Liturgy, but very near it, and containing no offence whatsoever against the laws, or against good morals) was forged into a crime punishable with perpetual imprisonment. The teaching school, an useful and virtuous occupation, even the teaching in a private family, was in every Catholic subjected to the same unproportioned punishment. Your industry, and the bread of your children, was taxed for a pecuniary reward to stimulate avarice to do what nature refused, to inform and prosecute on this law. Every Roman Catholic was, under the same act, to forfeit his estate to his nearest Protestant relation, until, through a profession of what he did not believe, he redeemed by his hypocrisy, what the law had transferred to the kinsman as the recompence of his profligacy. When thus turned out of doors from his paternal estate, he

---

[1] An Act for the Further Preventing the Growth of Popery (11 and 12 Will. III, c. 4).

was disabled from acquiring any other by any industry, donation, or charity; but was rendered a foreigner in his native land, only because he retained the religion, along with the property, handed down to him from those who had been the old inhabitants of that land before him.

Does any one who hears me approve this scheme of things, or think there is common justice, common sense, or common honesty in any part of it? If any does, let him say it, and I am ready to discuss the point with temper and candour. But instead of approving, I perceive a virtuous indignation beginning to rise in your minds on the mere cold stating of the statute.

But what will you feel, when you know from history how this statute passed, and what were the motives, and what the mode of making it? A party in this nation, enemies to the system of the Revolution, were in opposition to the government of King William. They knew, that our glorious deliverer was an enemy to all persecution. They knew that he came to free us from slavery and Popery, out of a country, where a third of the people are contented Catholics under a Protestant government. He came with a part of his army composed of those very Catholics, to overset the power of a Popish prince. Such is the effect of a tolerating spirit; and so much is liberty served in every way, and by all persons, by a manly adherence to its own principles. Whilst freedom is true to itself, every thing becomes subject to it; and its very adversaries are an instrument in its hands.

The party I speak of (like some amongst us who would disparage the best friends of their country) resolved to make the King either violate his principles of toleration, or incur the odium of protecting Papists. They therefore brought in this bill, and made it purposely wicked and absurd that it might be rejected. The then court-party, discovering their game, turned the tables on them, and returned their bill to them stuffed with still greater absurdities, that its loss might lie upon its original authors. They, finding their own ball thrown back to them, kicked it back again to their adversaries. And thus this act, loaded with the double injustice of two parties, neither of whom intended to pass, what they hoped the other would be persuaded to reject, went through the legislature, contrary to the real wish of all parts of it, and of all the parties that composed it. In this manner these insolent and profligate factions, as if they were playing with balls and counters, made a sport of the fortunes and the liberties of their fellow-creatures. Other acts of persecution have been acts of malice. This was a subversion of justice from wantonness and petulance. Look into the history of Bishop Burnet. He is a witness without exception.[1]

The effects of the act have been as mischievous, as its origin was ludicrous and shameful. From that time every person of that communion, lay and ecclesiastic, has been obliged to fly from the face of day. The clergy, concealed in garrets of private houses, or obliged to take a shelter (hardly safe to themselves, but infinitely dangerous to their country) under the privileges of foreign ministers, officiated as their servants, and under their protection. The whole body of the Catholics, condemned to beggary and to ignorance in their native land, have been obliged to learn the principles of letters, at the hazard of all their other principles, from the charity of your enemies. They have been taxed to their ruin at the pleasure of necessitous and profligate relations, and according to the measure of their necessity and profligacy. Examples of this are many and affecting.[2] Some of them are known by a friend who stands near me in this hall. It is but six or seven years since a clergyman of the name of Malony, a man of morals, neither guilty nor accused of any thing noxious to the state, was condemned to perpetual imprisonment for exercising the functions of his religion; and after lying in jail two or three years, was relieved by the mercy of government from perpetual imprisonment, on condition of perpetual banishment. A brother of the Earl of Shrewsbury, a Talbot, a name respectable in this county, whilst its glory is any part of its concern, was hauled to the bar of the Old Bailey among common felons, and only escaped the same doom, either by some error in the process, or that the wretch who brought him there could not correctly describe his person; I now forget which.—In short, the persecution would never have relented for a moment, if the judges, superseding (though with an ambiguous example) the strict rule of their artificial duty by the higher obligation of their conscience, did not constantly throw every difficulty in the way of such informers. But so ineffectual is the power of legal evasion against legal iniquity, that it was but the other day, that a lady of condition, beyond the middle of life, was on the point of being stripped of her whole fortune by a near relation, to whom she had been a friend and benefactor: and she must have been

---

[1] See Gilbert Burnet, *History of his Own Times*, iv. 420–1.
[2] See above, p. 377.

totally ruined, without a power of redress or mitigation from the courts of law, had not the legislature itself rushed in, and by a special act of Parliament rescued her from the injustice of its own statutes.[1] One of the acts authorising such things was that which we in part repealed, knowing what our duty was; and doing that duty as men of honour and virtue, as good Protestants, and as good citizens. Let him stand forth that disapproves what we have done!

Gentlemen, Bad laws are the worst sort of tyranny. In such a country as this, they are of all bad things the worst, worse by far than any where else; and they derive a particular malignity even from the wisdom and soundness of the rest of our institutions. For very obvious reasons you cannot trust the Crown with a dispensing power over any of your laws. However, a government, be it as bad as it may, will, in the exercise of a discretionary power, discriminate times and persons; and will not ordinarily pursue any man, when its own safety is not concerned. A mercenary informer knows no distinction. Under such a system, the obnoxious people are slaves, not only to the government, but they live at the mercy of every individual; they are at once the slaves of the whole community, and of every part of it; and the worst and most unmerciful men are those on whose goodness they most depend.

In this situation men not only shrink from the frowns of a stern magistrate; but they are obliged to fly from their very species. The seeds of destruction are sown in civil intercourse, in social habitudes. The blood of wholesome kindred is infected. Their tables and beds are surrounded with snares. All the means given by Providence to make life safe and comfortable, are perverted into instruments of terror and torment. This species of universal subserviency, that makes the very servant who waits behind your chair, the arbiter of your life and fortune, has such a tendency to degrade and debase mankind, and to deprive them of that assured and liberal state of mind, which alone can make us what we ought to be, that I vow to God I would sooner bring myself to put a man to immediate death for opinions I disliked, and

---

[1] This was the notorious Fenwick case in which the M.P. Thomas Fenwick (?1729–94, M.P. 1768–74) resorted to the anti-popery laws in order to deprive his brother's widow of her estate. A statute of 1774 (17 Geo. III, c. 37) provided her with protection; the unpopularity Fenwick had incurred in the process contributed to his failure to secure re-election for his Westmorland seat in 1774.

so to get rid of the man and his opinions at once, than to fret him with a feverish being, tainted with the jail-distemper of a contagious servitude, to keep him above ground, an animated mass of putrefaction, corrupted himself, and corrupting all about him.

The act repealed was of this direct tendency; and it was made in the manner which I have related to you. I will now tell you by whom the bill of repeal was brought into Parliament. I find it has been industriously given out in this city (from kindness to me unquestionably) that I was the mover or the seconder. The fact is, I did not once open my lips on the subject during the whole progress of the bill. I do not say this as disclaiming my share in that measure. Very far from it. I inform you of this fact, lest I should seem to arrogate to myself the merits which belong to others. To have been the man chosen out to redeem our fellow-citizens from slavery; to purify our laws from absurdity and injustice; and to cleanse our religion from the blot and stain of persecution, would be an honour and happiness to which my wishes would undoubtedly aspire; but to which nothing but my wishes could possibly have entitled me. That great work was in hands in every respect far better qualified than mine. The mover of the bill was Sir George Savile.[1]

When an act of great and signal humanity was to be done, and done with all the weight and authority that belonged to it, the world could cast its eyes upon none but him. I hope that few things, which have a tendency to bless or to adorn life, have wholly escaped my observation in my passage through it. I have sought the acquaintance of that gentleman, and have seen him in all situations. He is a true genius; with an understanding vigorous, and acute, and refined, and distinguishing even to excess; and illuminated with a most unbounded, peculiar, and original cast of imagination. With these he possesses many external and instrumental advantages; and he makes use of them all. His fortune is among the largest; a fortune which, wholly unincumbred, as it is, with one single charge from luxury, vanity, or excess, sinks under the benevolence of its dispenser. This private benevolence, expanding itself into patriotism, renders his whole being the estate of the public, in which he has not reserved a *peculium*[2] for

---

[1] The Catholic Relief Act.
[2] i.e. property of his own.

himself of profit, diversion, or relaxation. During the session, the first in, and the last out of the House of Commons; he passes from the senate to the camp; and, seldom seeing the seat of his ancestors, he is always in Parliament to serve his country, or in the field to defend it.[1] But in all well-wrought compositions, some particulars stand out more eminently than the rest; and the things which will carry his name to posterity, are his two bills; I mean that for a limitation of the claims of the crown upon landed estates;[2] and this for the relief of the Roman Catholics. By the former, he has emancipated property; by the latter, he has quieted conscience; and by both, he has taught that grand lesson to government and subject,—no longer to regard each other as adverse parties.

Such was the mover of the act that is complained of by men, who are not quite so good as he is; an act, most assuredly not brought in by him from any partiality to that sect which is the object of it. For, among his faults, I really cannot help reckoning a greater degree of prejudice against that people, than becomes so wise a man. I know that he inclines to a sort of disgust, mixed with a considerable degree of asperity, to the system; and he has few, or rather no habits with any of its professors. What he has done was on quite other motives. The motives were these, which he declared in his excellent speech on his motion for the bill; namely, his extreme zeal to the Protestant religion, which he thought utterly disgraced by the act of 1699; and his rooted hatred to all kind of oppression, under any colour or upon any pretence whatsoever.[3]

The seconder was worthy of the mover, and the motion. I was not the seconder; it was Mr. Dunning, Recorder of this city. I shall say the less of him, because his near relation to you makes you more particularly acquainted with his merits. But I should appear little acquainted with them, or little sensible of them, if I could utter his name on this occasion without expressing my esteem for his character. I am not afraid of offending a most learned body, and most jealous of its reputation for that learning, when I say he is the first of his

---

[1] Savile wrote to Rockingham on 22 November 1778 that he had not been at Rufford Abbey since the previous Christmas, except for about twenty-four hours in April (MS. at Sheffield, R.11821). He was Colonel of the West Riding Militia.

[2] The Nullum Tempus Act (9 Geo. III, c. 16); see vol. ii, pp. 75–83, 86.

[3] His speech is reported in *Parl. Reg.* viii. 287.

profession. It is a point settled by those who settle every thing else; and I must add (what I am enabled to say from my own long and close observation) that there is not a man, of any profession, or in any situation, of a more erect and independent spirit; of a more proud honour; a more manly mind; a more firm and determined integrity. Assure yourselves, that the names of two such men will bear a great load of prejudice in the other scale, before they can be entirely outweighed.

With this mover, and this seconder, agreed the *whole* House of Commons; the *whole* House of Lords; the *whole* Bench of Bishops; the King; the Ministry; the Opposition; all the distinguished Clergy of the Establishment; all the eminent lights (for they were consulted) of the Dissenting churches. This according voice of national wisdom ought to be listened to with reverence. To say that all these descriptions of Englishmen unanimously concurred in a scheme for introducing the Catholic religion, or that none of them understood the nature and effects of what they were doing, so well as a few obscure clubs of people, whose names you never heard of, is shamelessly absurd. Surely it is paying a miserable compliment to the religion we profess, to suggest, that every thing eminent in the kingdom is indifferent, or even adverse to that religion, and that its security is wholly abandoned to the zeal of those, who have nothing but their zeal to distinguish them. In weighing this unanimous concurrence of whatever the nation has to boast of, I hope you will recollect, that all these concurring parties do by no means love one another enough to agree in any point, which was not both evidently, and importantly, right.

To prove this; to prove, that the measure was both clearly and materially proper, I will next lay before you (as I promised) the political grounds and reasons for the repeal of that penal statute; and the motives to its repeal at that particular time.

Gentlemen, America—When the English nation seemed to be dangerously, if not irrecoverably divided; when one, and that the most growing branch, was torn from the parent stock, and engrafted on the power of France, a great terror fell upon this kingdom. On a sudden we awakened from our dreams of conquest, and saw ourselves threatened with an immediate invasion; which we were, at that time, very ill prepared to resist. You remember the cloud that gloomed over us all. In that hour of our dismay, from the bottom of the hiding-places, into which the indiscriminate rigour of our statutes had driven

646

them, came out the body of the Roman Catholics. They appeared before the steps of a tottering throne, with one of the most sober, measured, steady, and dutiful addresses, that was ever presented to the crown.[1] It was no holiday ceremony; no anniversary compliment of parade and show. It was signed by almost every gentleman of that persuasion, of note or property, in England. At such a crisis, nothing but a decided resolution to stand or fall with their country could have dictated such an address; the direct tendency of which was to cut off all retreat; and to render them peculiarly obnoxious to an invader of their own communion. The address shewed, what I long languished to see, that all the subjects of England had cast off all foreign views and connexions, and that every man looked for his relief from every grievance, at the hands only of his own natural government.

It was necessary, on our part, that the natural government should shew itself worthy of that name. It was necessary, at the crisis I speak of, that the supreme power of the state should meet the conciliatory dispositions of the subject. To delay protection would be to reject allegiance. And why should it be rejected, or even coldly and suspiciously received? If any independent Catholic state should choose to take part with this kingdom in a war with France and Spain, that bigot (if such a bigot could be found) would be heard with little respect, who could dream of objecting his religion to an ally, whom the nation would not only receive with its freest thanks, but purchase, with the last remains of its exhausted treasure. To such an ally we should not dare to whisper a single syllable of those base and invidious topics, upon which, some unhappy men would persuade the state, to reject the duty and allegiance of its own members. Is it then, because foreigners are in a condition to set our malice at defiance, that with *them*, we are willing to contract engagements of friendship, and to keep them with fidelity and honour; but that, because we conceive, some descriptions of our countrymen are not powerful enough to punish our malignity, we will not permit them to support our common interest? Is it on that ground, that our anger is to be kindled by their offered kindness? Is it on that ground, that they are to be subjected to penalties, because they are willing, by actual merit, to purge themselves from imputed crimes? Lest by an adherence to the cause of their country they should acquire a title to fair and equitable treatment, are we resolved to furnish them

---

[1] Drafted by Burke himself; see above, pp. 376–9.

with causes of eternal enmity; and rather supply them with just and founded motives to disaffection, than not to have that disaffection in existence to justify an oppression, which, not from policy but disposition, we have pre-determined to exercise?

What shadow of reason could be assigned, why, at a time, when the most Protestant part of this Protestant empire found it for its advantage to unite with the two principal Popish states, to unite itself in the closest bonds with France and Spain, for our destruction, that we should refuse to unite with our own Catholic countrymen for our own preservation? Ought we, like madmen, to tear off the plaisters, that the lenient hand of prudence had spread over the wounds and gashes, which in our delirium of ambition we had given to our own body? No person ever reprobated the American war more than I did, and do, and ever shall. But I never will consent that we should lay additional voluntary penalties on ourselves, for a fault which carries but too much of its own punishment in its own nature. For one, I was delighted with the proposal of internal peace. I accepted the blessing with thankfulness and transport; I was truly happy, to find *one* good effect of our civil distractions, that they had put an end to all religious strife and heart-burning in our own bowels. What must be the sentiments of a man, who could wish to perpetuate domestic hostility, when the causes of dispute are at an end; and who, crying out for peace with one part of the nation on the most humiliating terms, should deny it to those, who offer friendship without any terms at all?

But if I was unable to reconcile such a denial to the contracted principles of local duty, what answer could I give to the broad claims of general humanity? I confess to you freely, that the sufferings and distresses of the people of America in this cruel war, have at times affected me more deeply than I can express. I felt every Gazette of triumph as a blow upon my heart, which has an hundred times sunk and fainted within me at all the mischiefs brought upon those who bear the whole brunt of war in the heart of their country. Yet the Americans are utter strangers to me; a nation, among whom I am not sure, that I have a single acquaintance. Was I to suffer my mind to be so unaccountably warped; was I to keep such iniquitous weights and measures of temper and of reason, as to sympathise with those who are in open rebellion against an authority which I respect, at war with a country which by every title ought to be, and is most dear to me; and yet to have no feeling at all for the hardships and indignities suffered by men, who, by their very vicinity, are bound up in a nearer relation to us; who contribute their share, and more than their share, to the common prosperity; who perform the common offices of social life, and who obey the laws to the full as well as I do? Gentlemen, the danger to the state being out of the question (of which, let me tell you, statesmen themselves are apt to have but too exquisite a sense) I could assign no one reason of justice, policy, or feeling, for not concurring most cordially, as most cordially I did concur, in softening some part of that shameful servitude, under which several of my worthy fellow-citizens were groaning.

Important effects followed this act of wisdom. They appeared at home and abroad, to the great benefit of this kingdom; and, let me hope, to the advantage of mankind at large. It betokened union among ourselves. It shewed soundness, even on the part of the persecuted, which generally is the weak side of every community. But its most essential operation was not in England. The act was immediately, though very imperfectly, copied in Ireland; and this imperfect transcript of an imperfect act, this first faint sketch of toleration, which did little more than disclose a principle, and mark out a disposition, completed in a most wonderful manner the re-union to the state, of all the Catholics of that country.[1] It made us, what we ought always to have been, one family, one body, one heart and soul, against the family-combination, and all other combinations of our enemies. We have indeed obligations to that people, who received such small benefits with so much gratitude; and for which gratitude and attachment to us, I am afraid they have suffered not a little in other places.

I dare say, you have all heard of the privileges indulged to the Irish Catholics residing in Spain. You have likewise heard with what circumstances of severity they have been lately expelled from the sea-ports of that kingdom; driven into the inland cities; and there detained as a sort of prisoners of state.[2] I have good reason to believe, that it was the zeal to our government and our cause, (somewhat indiscreetly expressed in one of the addresses of the Catholics of Ireland)[3] which

---

[1] See *Corr.* iii. 448–50, 452–64; iv. 3–5, 5–10.
[2] The Spanish decree of 1779 requiring all natives of Ireland to retire twenty leagues inland from the coast had been reported in the English press (*St James's Chronicle*, 18 November 1779).
[3] Approved by the Catholic Committee on 15 July 1779 (*Archivium Hibernicum*, ix. 40–1).

has thus drawn down on their heads the indignation of the Court of Madrid; to the inexpressible loss of several individuals, and in future, perhaps, to the great detriment of the whole of their body. Now that our people should be persecuted in Spain for their attachment to this country, and persecuted in this country for their supposed enmity to us, is such a jarring reconciliation of contradictory distresses, is a thing at once so dreadful and ridiculous, that no malice short of diabolical, would wish to continue any human creatures in such a situation. But honest men will not forget either their merit or their sufferings. There are men, (and many, I trust, there are) who, out of love to their country and their kind, would torture their invention to find excuses for the mistakes of their brethren; and who, to stifle dissension, would construe, even doubtful appearances, with the utmost favour: such men will never persuade themselves to be ingenious and refined in discovering disaffection and treason in the manifest palpable signs of suffering loyalty. Persecution is so unnatural to them, that they gladly snatch the very first opportunity of laying aside all the tricks and devices of penal politics; and of returning home, after all their irksome and vexations wanderings, to our natural family mansion, to the grand social principle, that unites all men, in all descriptions, under the shadow of an equal and impartial justice.

Men of another sort, I mean the bigotted enemies to liberty, may, perhaps, in their politics, make no account of the good or ill affection of the Catholics of England, who are but an handful of people (enough to torment, but not enough to fear) perhaps not so many, of both sexes and of all ages, as fifty thousand.[1] But, Gentlemen, it is possible you may not know, that the people of that persuasion in Ireland, amount at least to sixteen or seventeen hundred thousand souls. I do not at all exaggerate the number.[2] A *nation* to be persecuted! Whilst we were masters of the sea, embodied with America, and in alliance with half the powers of the continent, we might perhaps, in that remote corner of Europe, afford to tyrannise with impunity. But there is a revolution in our affairs, which makes it prudent to be just. In our late awkward

[1] Probably sixty thousand (T. G. Holt, 'A Note on Some Eighteenth Century Statistics', *Recusant History*, x (1969–70), 3–11).
[2] The total population of Ireland was estimated in 1781 to be between 2,500,000 and 2,700,000. A modern estimate has put it as high as 4,048,000 (K. H. Connell, *The Population of Ireland*, Oxford, 1950, pp. 4–5, 25). More than two-thirds would be Catholics.

contest with Ireland about trade, had religion been thrown in, to ferment and embitter the mass of discontents, the consequences might have been truly dreadful. But very happily, that cause of quarrel was previously quieted by the wisdom of the acts I am commending.

Even in England, where I admit the danger from the discontent of that persuasion to be less than in Ireland; yet even here, had we listened to the counsels of Fanaticism and Folly, we might have wounded ourselves very deeply; and wounded ourselves in a very tender part. You are apprised, that the Catholics of England consist mostly of your best manufacturers.[1] Had the legislature chosen, instead of returning their declarations of duty with correspondent good-will, to drive them to despair, there is a country at their very door, to which they would be invited; a country in all respects as good as ours, and with the finest cities in the world ready built to receive them. And thus the bigotry of a free country, and in an enlightened age, would have repeopled the cities of Flanders, which, in the darkness of two hundred years ago, had been desolated by the superstition of a cruel tyrant. Our manufactures were the growth of the persecutions in the Low Countries. What a spectacle would it be to Europe, to see us at this time of day, balancing the account of tyranny with those very countries, and by our persecutions, driving back Trade and Manufacture, as a sort of vagabonds, to their original settlement! But I trust we shall be saved this last of disgraces.

So far as to the effect of the act on the interests of this nation. With regard to the interests of mankind at large, I am sure the benefit was very considerable. Long before this act, indeed, the spirit of toleration began to gain ground in Europe. In Holland, the third part of the people are Catholics; they live at ease; and are a sound part of the state. In many parts of Germany, Protestants and Papists partake the same cities, the same councils, and even the same churches. The unbounded liberality of the king of Prussia's conduct on this occasion is known to all the world; and it is of a piece with the other grand maxims of his reign.[2] The magnanimity of the Imperial

---

[1] i.e. artisans.

[2] 'All religions must be tolerated', wrote Frederick the Great in 1740, and held to this point of view throughout his life. He contributed to the building of the Catholic Cathedral in Berlin (W. Hubatsch, *Frederick the Great of Prussia: Absolutism and Administration*, London, 1975, pp. 41, 193–4).

Court, breaking through the narrow principles of its predecessors, has indulged its Protestant subjects, not only with property, with worship, with liberal education; but with honours and trusts, both civil and military.[1] A worthy Protestant gentleman of this country now fills, and fills with credit, an high office in the Austrian Netherlands.[2] Even the Lutheran obstinacy of Sweden has thawed at length, and opened a toleration to all religions.[3] I know myself, that in France the Protestants begin to be at rest. The army, which in that country is every thing, is open to them;[4] and some of the military rewards and decorations which the laws deny, are supplied by others, to make the service acceptable and honourable.[5] The first minister of finance in that country, is a Protestant.[6] Two years war without a tax, is among the first fruits of their liberality.[7] Tarnished as the glory of this nation is, and far as it has waded into the shades of an eclipse, some beams of its former illumination still play upon its surface; and what is done in England is still looked to, as argument, and as example. It is certainly true, that no law of this country ever met with such universal applause abroad, or was so likely to produce the perfection of that tolerating spirit, which, as I observed, has been long gaining ground in Europe; for abroad, it was universally thought that we had done, what, I am sorry to say, we had not; they thought we had granted a full toleration. That opinion was however so far from hurting the Protestant cause, that I declare, with the most serious solemnity, my firm belief, that no one thing done for these fifty years past, was so likely to prove deeply beneficial to our religion at large as Sir George Savile's act. In its effects it was, "an act for tolerating and protecting Protestantism throughout Europe:" and I hope, that those who were taking steps for the quiet and settlement of our Protestant brethren in other countries, will even yet, rather consider the steady equity of the greater and better part

[1] Tacitly rather than formally at this point. After the death of Maria Theresa in 1780, Joseph II (1741–90) was able to issue his Patent of Tolerance.

[2] Not identified. Protestants were excluded from civil office in the Austrian Netherlands, so presumably Burke is referring to a military personage.

[3] Gustavus III (1740–92), like Joseph II, brought his plans for toleration to fruition in 1781 (H. A. Barton, 'Gustavus III of Sweden and the Enlightenment', *Eighteenth Century Studies*, vi (1972–3), 1–34).

[4] It had never been officially closed to Protestants; Protestants from Lutheran Alsace indeed had a special position with regard to the army (A. Corvisier, *L'Armée française de la fin do xviii⁰ siècle au ministère de Choiseul, le soldat*, 2 vols., Paris, 1964, i. 288–94).

[5] The highest military order, the order of St Louis, was reserved to Catholics (A. T. Van Deursen, *Professions et métiers interdicts*, Gronique, 1960, p. 312).

[6] Necker.   [7] See above, pp. 487–9.

of the people of Great Britain, than the vanity and violence of a few.

I perceive, Gentlemen, by the manner of all about me, that you look with horror on the wicked clamour which has been raised on this subject; and that instead of an apology for what was done, you rather demand from me an account, why the execution of the scheme of toleration, was not made more answerable to the large and liberal grounds on which it was taken up. The question is natural and proper; and I remember that a great and learned magistrate,* distinguished for his strong and systematic understanding, and who at that time was a member of the House of Commons, made the same objection to the proceeding.[1] The statutes, as they now stand, are, without doubt, perfectly absurd. But I beg leave to explain the cause of this gross imperfection, in the tolerating plan, as well and as shortly as I am able. It was universally thought, that the session ought not to pass over without doing *something* in this business. To revise the whole body of the penal statutes was conceived to be an object too big for the time. The penal statute therefore which was chosen for repeal (chosen to shew our disposition to conciliate, not to perfect a toleration) was this act of ludicrous cruelty, of which I have just given you the history. It is an act, which, though not by a great deal so fierce and bloody as some of the rest, was infinitely more ready in the execution. It was the act which gave the greatest encouragement to those pests of society, mercenary informers, and interested disturbers of houshold peace; and it was observed with truth, that the prosecutions, either carried to conviction or compounded, for many years, had been all commenced upon that act. It was said, that whilst we were deliberating on a more perfect scheme, the spirit of the age would never come up to the execution of the statutes which remained; especially as more steps, and a co-operation of more minds and powers, were required towards a mischievous use of them, than for the execution of the act to be repealed: that it was better to unravel this texture from below than from above, beginning with the latest, which, in general practice, is the severest evil. It was alledged, that this slow proceeding would be attended with the advantage of a progressive experience; and that the

---

* The Chancellour.

[1] Thurlow is reported as saying: 'The House was first to determine how far they thought it safe to allow the free preaching and teaching of their religion. When this point had been settled, acts could be framed accordingly: Then the business could be effected on fixed principles, and not by piece-meal' (*Parl. Reg.* ix. 199).

people would grow reconciled to toleration, when they should find by the effects, that justice was not so irreconcileable an enemy to convenience as they had imagined.

These, Gentlemen, were the reasons why we left this good work in the rude unfinished state, in which good works are commonly left, through the tame circumspection with which a timid prudence so frequently enervates beneficence. In doing good, we are generally cold, and languid, and sluggish; and of all things afraid of being too much in the right. But the works of malice and injustice are quite in another style. They are finished with a bold masterly hand; touched as they are with the spirit of those vehement passions that call forth all our energies whenever we oppress and persecute.

Thus this matter was left for the time, with a full determination in Parliament, not to suffer other and worse statutes to remain for the purpose of counteracting the benefits proposed by the repeal of one penal law; for nobody then dreamed of defending what was done as a benefit, on the ground of its being no benefit at all. We were not then ripe for so mean a subterfuge.

I do not wish to go over the horrid scene that was afterwards acted. Would to God it could be expunged for ever from the annals of this country! But since it must subsist for our shame, let it subsist for our instruction. In the year 1780 there were found in this nation men deluded enough (for I give the whole to their delusion) on pretences of zeal and piety, without any sort of provocation whatsoever, real or pretended, to make a desperate attempt, which would have consumed all the glory and power of this country in the flames of London; and buried all law, order, and religion, under the ruins of the metropolis of the Protestant world. Whether all this mischief done, or in the direct train of doing, was in their original scheme, I cannot say; I hope it was not; but this would have been the unavoidable consequence of their proceedings, had not the flames they had lighted up in their fury been extinguished in their blood.

All the time that this horrid scene was acting, or avenging, as well as for some time before, and ever since, the wicked instigators of this unhappy multitude, quilty, with every aggravation, of all their crimes, and screened in a cowardly darkness from their punishment, continued, without interruption, pity, or remorse, to blow up the blind rage of the populace, with a continued blast of pestilential libels, which infected and poisoned the very air we breathed in.

The main drift of all the libels, and all the riots, was, to force Parliament (to persuade us was hopeless) into an act of national perfidy, which has no example. For, Gentlemen, it is proper you should all know what infamy we escaped by refusing that repeal, for a refusal of which, it seems, I, among others, stand somewhere or other accused. When we took away, on the motives which I had the honour of stating to you, a few of the innumerable penalties upon an oppressed and injured people, the relief was not absolute, but given on a stipulation and compact between them and us; for we bound down the Roman Catholics with the most solemn oaths, to bear true allegiance to this government; to abjure all sort of temporal power in any other; and to renounce, under the same solemn obligations, the doctrines of systematic perfidy, with which they stood (I conceive very unjustly) charged.[1] Now our modest petitioners came up to us, most humbly praying nothing more, than that we should break our faith without any one cause whatsoever of forfeiture assigned; and when the subjects of this kingdom had, on their part, fully performed their engagement, we should refuse, on our part, the benefit we had stipulated on the performance of those very conditions that were prescribed by our own authority, and taken on the sanction of our public faith—That is to say, when we had inveigled them with fair promises within our door, we were to shut it on them; and, adding mockery to outrage—to tell them, "Now we have got you fast—your consciences are bound to a power resolved on your destruction. We have made you swear, that your religion obliges you to keep your faith; fools as you are! we will now let you see, that our religion enjoins us to keep no faith with you." They who would advisedly call upon us to do such things, must certainly have thought us not only a convention of treacherous tyrants, but a gang of the lowest and dirtiest wretches that ever disgraced humanity. Had we done this, we should have indeed proved, that there were *some* in the world whom no faith could bind; and we should have *convicted* ourselves of that odious principle of which Papists stood *accused* by those very savages, who wished us, on that accusation, to deliver them over to their fury.

In this audacious tumult, when our very name and character, as gentlemen, was to be cancelled for ever along with the faith and honour of the nation, I, who had exerted myself very little on the quiet

---

[1] The Catholic Relief Act contained an oath that Catholics were required to take in order to benefit from it.

passing of the bill, thought it necessary then to come forward. I was not alone; but though some distinguished members on all sides, and particularly on ours, added much to their high reputation by the part they took on that day, (a part which will be remembered as long as honour, spirit, and eloquence have estimation in the world) I may and will value myself so far, that yielding in abilities to many, I yielded in zeal to none. With warmth, and with vigour, and animated with a just and natural indignation, I called forth every faculty that I possessed, and I directed it in every way which I could possibly employ it. I laboured night and day. I laboured in Parliament: I laboured out of Parliament. If therefore the resolution of the House of Commons, refusing to commit this act of unmatched turpitude, be a crime, I am guilty among the foremost. But indeed, whatever the faults of that House may have been, no one member was found hardy enough to propose so infamous a thing; and on full debate we passed the resolution against the petitions with as much unanimity, as we had formerly passed the law of which these petitions demanded the repeal.

There was a circumstance (justice will not suffer me to pass it over) which, if any thing could enforce the reasons I have given, would fully justify the act of relief, and render a repeal, or any thing like a repeal, unnatural, impossible. It was the behaviour of the persecuted Roman Catholics under the acts of violence and brutal insolence, which they suffered. I suppose there are not in London less than four or five thousand of that persuasion from my country,[1] who do a great deal of the most laborious works in the metropolis; and they chiefly inhabit those quarters, which were the principal theatre of the fury of the bigotted multitude. They are known to be men of strong arms, and quick feelings, and more remarkable for a determined resolution, than clear ideas, or much foresight. But though provoked by every thing that can stir the blood of men, their houses and chapels in flames, and with the most atrocious profanations of every thing which they hold sacred before their eyes, not a hand was moved to retaliate, or even to defend. Had a conflict once begun, the rage of their persecutors would have redoubled. Thus fury encreasing by the reverberation of outrages, house being fired for house, and church for chapel, I am convinced, that no power under heaven could have prevented a general conflagra-

---

[1] The total number of Catholics in London was about 14,000 (G. Rudé, 'The Gordon Riots', *Transactions of the Royal Historical Society*, 5th series, vi (1956), 108–9); probably half of them were Irish.

tion; and at this day London would have been a tale. But I am well informed, and the thing speaks it, that their clergy exerted their whole influence to keep their people in such a state of forbearance and quiet, as, when I look back, fills me with astonishment; but not with astonishment only. Their merits on that occasion ought not to be forgotten; nor will they, when Englishmen come to recollect themselves. I am sure it were far more proper to have called them forth, and given them the thanks of both Houses of Parliament, than to have suffered those worthy clergymen, and excellent citizens, to be hunted into holes and corners, whilst we are making low-minded inquisitions into the number of their people;[1] as if a tolerating principle was never to prevail, unless we were very sure that only a few could possibly take advantage of it. But indeed we are not yet well recovered of our fright. Our reason, I trust, will return with our security; and this unfortunate temper will pass over like a cloud.

Gentlemen, I have now laid before you a few of the reasons for taking away the penalties of the act of 1699, and for refusing to establish them on the riotous requisition of 1780. Because I would not suffer any thing which may be for your satisfaction to escape, permit me just to touch on the objections urged against our act and our resolves, and intended as a justification of the violence offered to both Houses. "Parliament," they assert, "was too hasty, and they ought, in so essential and alarming a change, to have proceeded with a far greater degree of deliberation." The direct contrary. Parliament was too slow. They took fourscore years to deliberate on the repeal of an act which ought not to have survived a second session. When at length, after a procrastination of near a century, the business was taken up, it proceeded in the most public manner, by the ordinary stages, and as

---

[1] 'Early in 1767, in consequence of criticism in the newspapers that the Anglican Bishops were being lax in restraining the spread of Catholicism in their dioceses, the House of Lords instituted an enquiry into the number of papists in each parish in England and Wales. On 22 May the House voted an Address to the King requesting that the bishops of England and Wales be directed to collect from their parish clergy and forward to the Clerks of the House "as correct and complete lists as can be obtained of the papists, or reported papists ... distinguishing their parishes, sexes, ages and occupations and how long they have been there resident." The information required was collected by the parish clergy and forwarded to the diocesan authorities, who, then passed it to the Clerk of the House as directed. The Dioceses of Chester and Durham sent in the original returns received from the parishes; the others sent in summaries giving the statistics called for omitting names' (*Returns of Papists 1767*, 2 vols., Catholic Record Soc., 1980, i, Diocese of Chester, p. x. See also *Lords Journals*, xxxvi. 169*b*, 174*a*). The returns made are in the House of Lords Record Office.

slowly as a law so evidently right as to be resisted by none, would naturally advance. Had it been read three times in one day, we should have shewn only a becoming readiness to recognise by protection the undoubted dutiful behaviour of those whom we had but too long punished for offences of presumption or conjecture. But for what end was that bill to linger beyond the usual period of an unopposed measure? Was it to be delayed until a rabble in Edinburgh should dictate to the Church of England what measure of persecution was fitting for her safety? Was it to be adjourned until a fanatical force could be collected in London, sufficient to frighten us out of all our ideas of policy and justice? Were we to wait for the profound lectures on the reason of state, ecclesiastical and political, which the Protestant Association have since condescended to read to us? Or were we, seven hundred Peers and Commoners, the only persons ignorant of the ribald invectives which occupy the place of argument in those remonstrances, which every man of common observation had heard a thousand times over, and a thousand times over had despised? All men had before heard what they have to say; and all men at this day know what they dare to do; and I trust, all honest men are equally influenced by the one, and by the other.

But they tell us, that those our fellow-citizens, whose chains we have a little relaxed, are enemies to liberty and our free constitution.—Not enemies, I presume, to their *own* liberty. And as to the constitution, until we give them some share in it, I do not know on what pretence we can examine into their opinions about a business in which they have no interest or concern. But after all, are we equally sure, that they are adverse to our constitution, as that our statutes are hostile and destructive to them? For my part, I have reason to believe, their opinions and inclinations in that respect are various, exactly like those of other men; and if they lean more to the Crown than I, and than many of you think *we* ought, we must remember, that he who aims at another's life, is not to be surprised if he flies into any sanctuary that will receive him. The tenderness of the executive power is the natural asylum of those upon whom the laws have declared war; and to complain that men are inclined to favour the means of their own safety, is so absurd, that one forgets the injustice in the ridicule.

I must fairly tell you, that so far as my principles are concerned, (principles, that I hope will only depart with my last breath) that I have no idea of a liberty unconnected with honesty and justice. Nor do I believe, that any good constitutions of government or of freedom, can find it necessary for their security to doom any part of the people to a permanent slavery. Such a constitution of freedom, if such can be, is in effect no more than another name for the tyranny of the strongest faction; and factions in republics have been, and are, full as capable as monarchs, of the most cruel oppression and injustice. It is but too true, that the love, and even the very idea, of genuine liberty, is extremely rare. It is but too true, that there are many, whose whole scheme of freedom, is made up of pride, perverseness, and insolence. They feel themselves in a state of thraldom, they imagine that their souls are cooped and cabbined in, unless they have some man, or some body of men, dependent on their mercy. This desire of having some one below them, descends to those who are the very lowest of all,—and a Protestant cobler, debased by his poverty, but exalted by his share of the ruling church, feels a pride in knowing, it is by his generosity alone, that the peer, whose footman's instep he measures, is able to keep his chaplain from a jail. This disposition is the true source of the passion, which many men in very humble life, have taken to the American war. *Our* subjects in America; *our* colonies; *our* dependants.[1] This lust of party-power, is the liberty they hunger and thirst for; and this Syren song of ambition, has charmed ears, that one would have thought were never organised to that sort of music.

This way, of *proscribing the citizens by denominations and general descriptions*, dignified by the name of reason of state, and security for constitutions and commonwealths, is nothing better at bottom, than the miserable invention of an ungenerous ambition, which would fain hold the sacred trust of power, without any of the virtues or any of the energies, that give a title to it; a receipt of policy, made up of a detestable compound of malice, cowardice, and sloth. They would govern men against their will; but in that government they would be discharged from the exercise of vigilance, providence, and fortitude; and therefore, that they may sleep on their watch, they consent to take some one division of the society into partnership of the tyranny over the rest. But let government, in what form it may be, comprehend the whole in its justice, and restrain the suspicious by its vigilance; let it

---

[1] Samuel Curwen (1714–82), the American Loyalist, living in Exeter, noted in his diary: 'It piques my pride (I confess it) to hear us called *our colonies* and *our plantations* as if our property and persons were absolutely theirs, like the Villeins and their cottages in the old feudal system' (*The Journals of Samuel Curwen Loyalist*, ed. A. Oliver, 2 vols., Cambridge, Mass., 1972, i. 284).

keep watch and ward; let it discover by its sagacity, and punish by its firmness, all delinquency against its power, whenever delinquency exists in the overt acts; and then it will be as safe as ever God and nature intended it should be. Crimes are the acts of individuals, and not of denominations; and therefore arbitrarily to class men under general descriptions, in order to proscribe and punish them in the lump for a presumed delinquency, of which perhaps but a part, perhaps none at all, are guilty, is indeed a compendious method, and saves a world of trouble about proof; but such a method, instead of being law, is an act of unnatural rebellion against the legal dominion of reason and justice; and this vice, in any constitution that entertains it, at one time or other will certainly bring on its ruin.

We are told, that this is not a religious persecution, and its abettors are loud in disclaiming all severities on account of conscience. Very fine indeed! then let it be so; they are not persecutors; they are only tyrants. With all my heart. I am perfectly indifferent concerning the pretexts upon which we torment one another; or whether it be for the constitution of the Church of England, or for the constitution of the State of England, that people choose to make their fellow-creatures wretched. When we were sent into a place of authority, you that sent us had yourselves but one commission to give. You could give us none to wrong or oppress, or even to suffer any kind of oppression or wrong, on any grounds whatsoever; not on political, as in the affairs of America; not on commercial, as in those of Ireland; not in civil, as in the laws for debt; not in religious, as in the statutes against Protestant or Catholic Dissenters. The diversified but connected fabric of universal justice, is well cramped and bolted together in all its parts; and depend upon it, I never have employed, and I never shall employ, any engine of power which may come into my hands, to wrench it asunder. All shall stand, if I can help it, and all shall stand connected. After all, to complete this work, much remains to be done; much in the East, much in the West. But great as the work is, if our will be ready, our powers are not deficient.

Since you have suffered me to trouble you so much on this subject, permit me, Gentlemen, to detain you a little longer. I am indeed most solicitous to give you perfect satisfaction. I find there are some of a better and softer nature than the persons with whom I have supposed myself in debate, who neither think ill of the act of relief, nor by any means desire the repeal, not accusing but lamenting what was done, on account of the consequences, have frequently expressed their wish, that the late act had never been made. Some of this description, and persons of worth, I have met with in this city. They conceive, that the prejudices, whatever they might be, of a large part of the people, ought not to have been shocked; that their opinions ought to have been previously taken, and much attended to; and that thereby the late horrid scenes might have been prevented.

I confess, my notions are widely different; and I never was less sorry for any action of my life. I like the bill the better, on account of the events of all kinds that followed it. It relieved the real sufferers; it strengthened the state; and, by the disorders that ensued, we had clear evidence, that there lurked a temper somewhere, which ought not to be fostered by the laws. No ill consequences whatever could be attributed to the act itself. We knew before-hand, or we were poorly instructed, that toleration is odious to the intolerant; freedom to oppressors; property to robbers; and all kinds and degrees of prosperity to the envious. We knew, that all these kinds of men would gladly gratify their evil dispositions under the sanction of law and religion, if they could: if they could not, yet, to make way to their objects, they would do their utmost to subvert all religion and all law. This we certainly knew. But knowing this, is there any reason, because thieves break in and steal, and thus bring detriment to you, and draw ruin on themselves, that I am to be sorry that you are in possession of shops, and of warehouses, and of wholesome laws to protect them? Are you to build no houses, because desperate men may pull them down upon their own heads? Or, if a malignant wretch will cut his own throat, because he sees you give alms to the necessitous and deserving; shall his destruction be attributed to your charity, and not to his own deplorable madness? If we repent of our good actions, what, I pray you, is left for our faults and follies? It is not the beneficence of the laws, it is the unnatural temper which beneficence can fret and sour, that is to be lamented. It is this temper which, by all rational means, ought to be sweetened and corrected. If froward men should refuse this cure, can they vitiate any thing but themselves? Does evil so react upon good, as not only to retard its motion, but to change its nature? If it can so operate, then good men will always be in the power of the bad; and virtue, by a dreadful reverse of order, must lie under perpetual subjection and bondage to vice.

As to the opinion of the people, which some think, in such cases, is to be implicitly obeyed; near two years tranquillity, which followed the act, and its instant imitation in Ireland, proved abundantly, that the late horrible spirit was, in a great measure, the effect of insidious art, and perverse industry, and gross misrepresentation. But suppose that the dislike had been much more deliberate, and much more general than I am persuaded it was—When we know, that the opinions of even the greatest multitudes, are the standard of rectitude, I shall think myself obliged to make those opinions the masters of my conscience. But if it may be doubted whether Omnipotence itself is competent to alter the essential constitution of right and wrong, sure I am, that such *things*, as they and I, are possessed of no such power. No man carries further than I do the policy of making government pleasing to the people. But the widest range of this politic complaisance is confined within the limits of justice. I would not only consult the interest of the people, but I would chearfully gratify their humours. We are all a sort of children, that must be soothed and managed. I think I am not austere or formal in my nature. I would bear, I would even myself play my part in, any innocent buffooneries, to divert them. But I never will act the tyrant for their amusement. If they will mix malice in their sports, I shall never consent to throw them any living, sentient, creature whatsoever, no not so much as a kitling, to torment.

"But if I profess all this impolitic stubbornness, I may chance never to be elected into Parliament." It is certainly not pleasing to be put out of the public service. But I wish to be a member of Parliament, to have my share of doing good, and resisting evil. It would therefore be absurd to renounce my objects, in order to obtain my seat. I deceive myself indeed most grossly, if I had not much rather pass the remainder of my life hidden in the recesses of the deepest obscurity, feeding my mind even with the visions and imaginations of such things, than to be placed on the most splendid throne of the universe, tantalized with a denial of the practice of all which can make the greatest situation any other than the greatest curse. Gentlemen, I have had my day. I can never sufficiently express my gratitude to you, for having set me in a place, wherein I could lend the slightest help to great and laudable designs. If I have had my share, in any measure giving quiet to private property, and private conscience; if by my vote I have aided in securing to families the best possession, peace; if I have joined in reconciling kings to their subjects, and subjects to their prince; if I have assisted to loosen the foreign holdings of the citizen, and taught him to look for his protection to the laws of his country, and for his comfort to the goodwill of his countrymen;—if I have thus taken my part with the best of men in the best of their actions, I can shut the book;—I might wish to read a page or two more—but this is enough for my measure.—I have not lived in vain.

And now, Gentlemen, on this serious day, when I come, as it were, to make up my account with you, let me take to myself some degree of honest pride on the nature of the charges that are against me. I do not here stand before you accused of venality, or of neglect of duty. It is not said, that, in the long period of my service, I have, in a single instance, sacrificed the slightest of your interests to my ambition, or to my fortune. It is not alledged, that to gratify any anger, or revenge of my own, or of my party, I have had a share in wronging or oppressing any description of men, or any one man in any description. No! the charges against me, are all of one kind, that I have pushed the principles of general justice and benevolence too far; further that a cautious policy would warrant; and further than the opinions of many would go along with me.—In every accident which may happen through life, in pain, in sorrow, in depression, and distress—I will call to mind this accusation; and be comforted.

Gentlemen, I submit the whole to your judgment. Mr. Mayor, I thank you for the trouble you have taken on this occasion. In your state of health, it is particularly obliging. If this company should think it adviseable for me to withdraw, I shall respectfully retire; if you think otherwise, I shall go directly to the Council-house and to the Change, and without a moment's delay, begin my canvass.

THE END

Bristol, Sept. 6, 1780.

At a great and respectable Meeting of the Friends of EDMUND BURKE, *Esq; held at the Guildhall this day;*

The Right Worshipful the Mayor in the Chair;

Resolved, That Mr. Burke, as a representative for this city, has done all possible honour to himself as a senator and a man, and that we do heartily and honestly approve of his conduct, as the result of an enlightened loyalty to his sovereign; a warm and zealous love to his country, through its widely-extended empire: a jealous and watchful care of the liberties of his fellow-subjects; an enlarged and liberal understanding of our commercial interest; a humane attention to the circumstances of even the lowest ranks of the community; and a truly wise, politic and tolerant spirit, in supporting the national church, with a reasonable indulgence to all who dissent from it; and we wish to express the most marked abhorrence of the base arts which have been employed, without regard to truth and reason, to misrepresent his eminent services to his country.

Resolved, That this resolution be copied out, and signed by the Chairman, and be by him presented to Mr. Burke, as the fullest expression of the respectful and grateful sense we entertain of his merits and services, public and private, to the Citizens of Bristol, as a man and a representative.

Resolved, That the thanks of this Meeting be given to the Right Worshipful the Mayor, who so ably and worthily presided in this Meeting.

Resolved, That it is the earnest request of this Meeting to Mr. Burke, that he should again offer himself a candidate to represent this city in Parliament; assuring him of that full and strenuous support which is due to the merits of so excellent a representative.

This business being over, Mr. Burke went to the Exchange, and offered himself as a candidate in the usual manner. He was accompanied to the Councilhouse, and from thence to the Exchange, by a large body of most respectable Gentlemen, amongst whom were the following Members of the Corporation, viz. Mr. Mayor, Mr. Alderman Smith, Mr. Alderman Deane, Mr. Alderman Gordon, William Weare, Samuel Munckley, John Merlott, John Crofts, Levy Ames, John Fisher Weare, Benjamin Loscombe, Philip Protheroe, Samuel Span, Joseph Smith, Richard Bright, and John Noble, Esquires.[1]

---

[1] John Bull, Morgan Smith (d. 1781), Thomas Deane (*c.*1717–98), Robert Gordon (d. 1784), William Weare (d. 1785), Samuel Munckley (*c.*1724–1801), not a member of the corporation, John Merlott (d. 1785), John Crofts (d. 1793), Levi Ames (d. 1820), John Fisher Weare (d. 1816), Benjamin Loscombe (d. 1796), Philip Protheroe (*c.*1747–1803), Samuel Span (d. 1795), Joseph Smith (1745–1815), Richard Bright (1754–1840), John Noble (1743–1826).

Election Advertisement
6 September 1780

Source: Bristol Public Library Handbill

To the Gentlemen, Clergy, Freeholders and Freeemen of the City of Bristol

Gentlemen,

My general Conduct in Parliament, and my humble Endeavours to serve the City, and the Citizens of Bristol in their particular Affairs, having been honored by the unanimous Approbation of a very large and very respectable Meeting at the Guildhall this day; in conformity with the Desire of that Meeting, and under the Sanction of their weighty Authority, I beg leave to renew to you my humble Solicitation for your Votes at this Election, and the Favour of your early Appearance at the Poll on Friday next; and if I have the Honour of being again chosen to represent you, I trust that I shall not shew myself less deserving of your Favour than formerly, or less sincerely grateful for it.

> *I have the Honour to be, With the most perfect Respect and Esteem,*
> *Gentlemen, Your most Obedient, and most obliged Servant,*
>
> Edmund Burke

Bristol, Sept. 6, 1780

Speech on the Hustings at Bristol
9 September 1780

Source: Bristol Public Library Broadsheet

This speech also appears in *Whitehall Evening Post, Morning Chronicle, Morning Post,* and *Public Advertiser,* 18 September (and other papers).

On 14 September the Duke of Portland informed Rockingham that:

A most respectable Body of ... [Burke's] friends met early on Saturday, and determined to decline. They then attended him to the Hustings, from whence he made a Speech, the effects of which were very visible in his Audience; from whom, not so much shouts of applause, as unaffected marks of affectionate Regard burst forth. Indeed, My Lord, it was a most moving Scene. There were few dry Eyes in Court. We returned with him in silent Procession to the Town House; not the smallest noise amongst the people, who of all ranks and descriptions crowded the Streets. There was a Solemnity attending the whole Scene, which struck every Spectator with Awe—The Solemnity of a suffering People, bewailing the Loss of their best friend.[1]

I decline the Election.—It has ever been my rule through life, to observe a proportion between my Efforts and my Objects. I have never been remarkable for a bold, active, and sanguine pursuit of advantages that are personal to myself.

I have not canvass'd the whole of this City in form. But I have taken such a view of it, as satisfies my own mind, that your choice will not ultimately fall upon me. Your City, Gentlemen, is in a state of miserable distraction: and I am resolved to withdraw whatever share my pretensions may have had in its unhappy divisions. I have not been in haste; I have tried all prudent means; I have waited for the effect of all contingencies. If I were fond of a contest, by the partiality of my numerous friends (whom you know to be among the most weighty and respectable people of the City) I have the means of a sharp one in my hands. But I thought it far better with my strength unspent, and my reputation unimpaired, to do, early and from foresight, that which I might be obliged to do from necessity at last.

I am not in the least surprised, nor in the least angry at this view of things. I have read the book of life for a long time, and I have read other books a little. Nothing has happen'd to me, but what has happen'd to men much better than me, and in times and in Nations full as good as the Age and Country that we live in. To say that I am no way concerned would be neither decent nor true. The Representation of *Bristol* was an Object on many accounts dear to me; and I certainly should very far prefer it to any other in the Kingdom. My habits are made to it; and it is in general more unpleasant to be rejected after long trial, than not to be chosen at all.

But, Gentlemen, I will see nothing except your former kindness, and I will give way to no other Sentiments than those of Gratitude. From the bottom of my heart I thank you for what you have done for me.

---

[1] Portland MSS., PwF 2,756.

You have given me a long term which is now expired. I have perform'd the conditions, and enjoy'd all the profits to the full; and I now surrender your Estate into your hands without being in a single tile, or a single stone impaired or wasted by my use. I have served the public for fifteen Years. I have served you in particular for six. What is passed is well stored. It is safe and out of the power of fortune. What is to come, is in wiser hands than ours; and he, in whose hands it is, best knows, whether it is best for you and me, that I should be in Parliament, or even in the World.

Gentlemen, the melancholly Event of yesterday reads to us an awfull lesson against being too much troubled about any of the objects of ordinary ambition. The worthy Gentleman,* who has been snatched from us at the moment of the Election, and in the middle of the contest, whilst his desires were as warm, and his hopes as eager as ours, has feelingly told us, what Shadows we are, and what Shadows we pursue.

It has been usual for a Candidate who declines, to take his leave by a letter to the Sheriffs, but I received your Trust in the face of day; and in the face of day, I accept your dismission. I am not,—I am not at all ashamed to look upon you; nor can my presence discompose the order of business here. I humbly and respectfully take my leave of the Sheriffs, the Candidates, and the Electors; wishing heartily that the Choice may be for the best, at a time which calls, if ever time did call, for service that is not nominal. It is no plaything you are about. I tremble when I consider the Trust I have presumed to ask. I confided perhaps too much in my intentions. They were really fair and upright; and I am bold to say, that I ask no ill thing for you, when on parting from this place I pray that whoever you chuse to succeed me, may resemble me exactly in all things,—except in my abilities to serve, and my fortune to please you.

* *Mr. Combe.*[1]
[1] R. Combe intended to offer himself a candidate for Bristol. He died on 8 September, apparently of a fever which came on suddenly during the campaign.

Letter to the Electors of Bristol
9 September 1780

Source: Bristol Public Library Handbill

To the Gentlemen Clergy, Freeholders, and Freemen of the City of Bristol

Gentlemen,

A very large and most respectable Meeting of the principal Citizens of Bristol did, by an unanimous Vote, authorise me to offer myself once more to your Service. My Deference to that Authority was my sole Motive for giving you one Moment's Trouble. On my Canvas, so far as it has proceeded, I found that my Pretensions were well received, and even with a Degree of Warmth in many of the Electors. But on a calm and very deliberate View of the State of the City, I am convinced that no other Consequence can be reasonably expected from my continuing a Candidate, than a long, vexatious and expensive Contest. Conscious that no Difference between my Service and that of any other Man, can be worth the Inconveniences of such a Struggle,—I decline the Election.

I return you my best Thanks, for having at any Time, or for any Period, condescended to think of me for your Representative. I have done my Duty towards you, and towards the Nation, as became me. You dispose of the future Trust, (as you have a Right to do) according to your Discretion. We have no Cause of Complaint on either Side. By being returned into the Mass of private Citizens, my Burthens are lessened; my Satisfactions are not destroyed. There are Duties to be performed, and there are Comforts to be enjoyed in Obscurity, for which I am not without a Disposition and Relish. I am sure that there is Nothing in the Retrospect of my public Conduct, which is likely to disturb the Tranquility of that Situation to which you restore me.

I have the Honour to be, with the utmost possible Respect,

gentlemen, *Your much Obliged,*
And most obedient, Humble Servant,

Edmund Burke

Bristol, Saturday, Morning, 9th *Sept.* 1780

APPENDIX A

List of Burke's Parliamentary Speeches 1774–1780

This list is designed to provide a summary of Burke's known speeches and interventions in debate, in the House of Commons in the period covered by this volume, and also to indicate the most useful, dependable, and accessible reports. (The only known speeches outside the Commons were those delivered at Bristol during the 1774 and 1780 election campaigns for which, see above, pp. 57, 63, 620, 666.) The sources for the debates are somewhat more complete for the 1774–80 Parliament than for the previous one. John Almon's *Parliamentary Register*, which started reporting the debates at the opening of the 1774–5 session (and thus began where the Cavendish Diary stopped), is most useful along with *Parl. Hist.* in helping to establish the subjects and occasions on which Burke spoke. Moreover, the great proliferation of reporting by the fiercely competitive British press, which had continued since 1770, provides access to relatively complete and reliable accounts of most parliamentary speeches. Variations from one parliamentary session to the other in the number of available accounts of Burke's performances would seem to reflect a change in the number of speeches actually given rather than inconsistency among reporters. The fact, therefore, that only eight speeches are transcribed in this volume from the 1776–7 session of Parliament (while an average of 11.4 are transcribed for the other sessions) does not suggest that for a short period the newspapers and other agencies were uncharacteristically erratic in providing accounts of Burke's speeches. It reflects instead the Rockingham Whigs' decision to secede from Parliament for a significant span of time starting in February 1777. The following points should be noted.

(i) The chronological sequence is broken thus ——— to indicate divisions into sessions, as defined by prorogation or dissolution of Parliament. Recesses of the Commons for such feasts as Christmas and Easter, as determined by the House itself, are not indicated.

(ii) The subject of the debate, and (if different) the particular subject to which Burke addressed himself, are described briefly, and with

669

a minimum of procedural detail. For example, the various stages which marked the passage of a Bill are not included.

(iii) A figure in parentheses, thus (2), indicates more than one intervention by Burke in a particular debate. Such interventions did not necessarily amount to what would conventionally be described as a 'speech', but were often a single remark or question.

(iv) Speeches represented by texts printed in this volume are shown with a cross-references thus: see above, p. 000. In these cases the sources and circumstances are discussed in the text.

(v) The sources listed have been selected with the intention of directing the reader to the most accessible and, in the editor's judgement, most reliable reports. Wherever possible a printed authority is listed, and reference is normally made to *Parl. Hist.* unless there are good reasons for disregarding it. The recently published Simmons and Thomas is referred to for the years in this volume (1774–6) which it includes. MS. reports are cited where the published version is either wanting or clearly inferior. Burke's own MSS. are also included where the editor feels able to relate notes, fragments, or other papers in Burke's hand to a specific debate or series of debates. In all cases the best source is placed first. It should be borne in mind that this and all other recommendations of sources depend heavily on the discretion and judgement of the editor. They are made to assist the reader who requires a ready guide to the principal authorities as a starting-point in the attempt to reconstruct Burke's speeches. They do not constitute a comprehensive list of parliamentary reports, nor do they presume to provide the authenticity of the modern Hansard. In a few cases, it has not proved possible to locate an adequate report. In these instances the authority from which it is known that Burke delivered a speech is cited, together with the phrase 'mention only'.

(vi) The abbreviations employed are the same as those listed above, pp. xviii–xx.

1774
  5 December   Address
                Parl. Hist. xviii. 44–5; Simmons and Thomas, v. 242; MSS. at Sheffield, Bk 27.231, 232; 6.34
                Motion to clear the public gallery
                Middlesex Journal, 6 December 1774
  6 December   Election petition
                Parl. Hist. xviii. 51 (mention only)

12 December   Exclusion of strangers
                     Parl. Hist. xviii. 53
                     Election petitions
                     Middlesex Journal, 13 December 1774
                     Indian Corn Bill
                     Morning Chronicle, 13 December 1774 (mention
                     only)
                     Dispute with House of Lords
                     Morning Chronicle, 13 December 1774 (mention
                     only)

13 December   Navy estimates
                     Parl. Hist. xviii. 57; Simmons and Thomas, v. 248

14 December   Indian Corn Bill
                     London Chronicle, 15 December 1774

16 December   Election petitioners in the gallery
                     St James's Chronicle, 17 December 1774

17 December   Indian Corn Bill
                     St James's Chronicle, 20 December 1774 (mention
                     only)

20 December   Land tax (2)
                     see above, p. 74

22 December   Exclusion of election petitioners
                     St James's Chronicle, 24 December 1774 (mention
                     only)

1775
19 January   American disturbances (2)
                     Parl. Reg. i. 33; Simmons and Thomas, v. 267

23 January   Petitions on America (3)
                     Parl. Hist. xviii. 172–3, 177, 177; Simmons and
                     Thomas, v. 292–3, 295–6, 297, 298, 299

25 January   Petitions on America (6)
                     St James's Chronicle, 26 January 1775; *Parl. Hist.*
                     xviii. 182, 183; Simmons and Thomas, v. 303–4,
                     305

26 January   Petitions on America
                     see above, p. 78

27 January   Birmingham American petitions
                     Morning Post, 28 January 1775

31 January	Birmingham American petitions (4) *Parl. Hist.* xviii. 195, 195–6, 196, 197; Simmons and Thomas, v. 326, 327–8
1 February	Birmingham American petitions *Morning Post*, 2 and 3 February 1775; MS. at Sheffield, Bk 6.59
2 February	American disturbances *Parl. Hist.* xviii. 233; Simmons and Thomas, v. 351, 353
6 February	American disturbances *see above*, p. 82
9 February	Restraining Bill *Universal Magazine*, lvi. 100 (mention only)
10 February	Restraining Bill *Parl. Hist.* xviii. 304–5; Simmons and Thomas, v. 411, 413, 416
17 February	Restraining Bill *London Chronicle*, 21 February 1775 (mention only); Simmons and Thomas, v. 430
20 February	North's Conciliatory Proposition *see above*, p. 86
22 February	Wilkes's motion *Lloyd's Evening Post*, 24 February 1775 (mention only) Nottingham American petition *Morning Post*, 24 February 1775; Simmons and Thomas, v. 454
6 March	Restraining Bill *see above*, p. 97
7 March	Restraining Bill *Universal Magazine*, lvi. 156–7 Irish Provisions Bill *Morning Chronicle*, 8 March 1775 (mention only); *Corr.* iii. 132 n.
8 March	Restraining Bill *see above*, p. 101
15 March	Bill to enable M.P.s to vacate seats *Parl. Hist.* xviii. 419–20
16 March	Burke's Conciliation Proposal *Morning Chronicle*, 17 March 1775 (mention only)

20 March	North American Merchants' petition (5)
	Parl. Reg. i. 361 (4), 362–3; Simmons and Thomas, v. 582, 583
22 March	Conciliation with America
	see above, p. 102
3 April	Petition on Small's lighthouse
	London Chronicle, 4 April 1775 (mention only)
6 April	Motion on wool manufacture
	Public Advertiser, 7 April 1775 (mention only)
7 April	Western Canal Bill
	Morning Post, 8 April 1775
10 April	Small's lighthouse
	Morning Post, 11 April 1775 (mention only)
11 April	Restraining Bill (2)
	see vol. ix, pp. 495–6
	East India Company (3)
	Parl. Hist. xviii. 617–19
28 April	Somerset House
	see above, p. 169
2 May	Small's lighthouse
	Parl. Reg. i. 446 (mention only)
2 May	Bill Incapacitating Hindon Electors
	Gazetteer, 3 May 1775
5 May	Champion's Porcelain Bill
	Gazetteer, 6 May 1775 (mention only)
8 May	Burke's Motion to Admit Merchants to Gallery
	Middlesex Journal, 14 May 1775
10 May	America
	Middlesex Journal, 18 May 1775
11 May	Bristol Porcelain Bill
	Morning Post, 12 May 1775
	New York petition
	General Evening Post, 13 May 1775 (mention only)
15 May	New York remonstrance
	see above, p. 171
	Bristol Porcelain Bill
	Middlesex Journal, 16 May 1775 (mention only)
17 May	Bristol Porcelain Bill
	St James's Chronicle, 18 May 1775 (mention only)

18 May	Bristol Porcelain Bill
	St James's Chronicle, 20 May 1775 (mention only)
	Savile's Bill to Repeal Quebec Act
	St James's Chronicle, 20 May 1775 (mention only)
22 May	Shipwreck Bill
	St James's Chronicle, 23 May 1775 (mention only)
	Doomsday Book
	Lloyd's Evening Post, 24 May 1775
24 May	Burke's Deer Stealing Bill
	St James's Chronicle, 25 May 1775
	Doomsday Book
	St James's Chronicle, 25 May 1775 (mention only)

---

26 October	Address
	Parl. Hist. xviii. 768–9; Simmons and Thomas, vi. 117, 119, 120; MS. at Sheffield, Bk 6.112
27 October	Address
	St James's Chronicle, 28 October (mention only)
1 November	Motion for accounts of British army in America
	Parl. Hist. xviii. 840; Simmons and Thomas, vi. 158, 161, 164
	Navy estimates
	Walpole, *Last Journals*, i. 490 (mention only)
2 November	Militia Bill
	see above, p. 181
	Notice of Bill for Conciliation with America
	Lloyd's Evening Post, 6 November 1775 (mention only)
	American petitions
	Parl. Reg. iii. 98–9; Simmons and Thomas, vi. 174–5
3 November	Employment of foreign troops in America
	Parl. Hist. xviii. 835–6; Simmons and Thomas, vi. 181; MS. at Sheffield, Bk 8.183
8 November	Army estimates (2)
	Parl. Hist. xviii. 894–5, 895; Simmons and Thomas, vi. 196, 198, 214–5, 215

10 November	Postponement of conciliation proposals
	Morning Chronicle, 11 November 1775 (mention only)
13 November	Postponement of conciliation proposals
	London Chronicle, 14 November 1775 (mention only)
16 November	Second Speech on Conciliation
	see above, p. 183
20 November	American Prohibitory Bill
	Parl. Hist. xviii. 999; Simmons and Thomas, vi. 279, 284; MSS. at Sheffield, Bks 6.119; 27.227, 228
22 November	Savile's motion to amend Militia Bill
	Parl. Hist. xviii. 863
	Fox's motion for army accounts
	Parl. Hist. xviii. 1001
	Burke's motion respecting duties in West Indies and quitrents in America
	Parl. Reg. iii. 206; Simmons and Thomas, vi. 287
	Militia Bill
	Parl. Reg. iii. 208
	Burke's motion respecting ordnance
	London Chronicle, 23 November 1775
	Nova Scotia Petition
	Middlesex Journal, 25 November 1775
23 November	Scottish Highlanders Recruitment Bill
	Parl. Reg. iii. 208–9
	Resolution of Committee of Supply
	St James's Chronicle, 25 November 1775
	Nova Scotia Bill
	Lloyd's Evening Post, 24 November 1775; Simmons and Thomas, vi. 289, 290
24 November	Indemnity Bill for Foreign Troops
	Parl. Hist. xviii. 1004–5; MS. at Northampton, A.xxxvii.9
29 November	Nova Scotia petition (3)
	Parl. Reg. iii. 231, 235, 236; for last two speeches only, *Parl. Hist.* xviii. 1026, 1026–7; Simmons and Thomas, vi. 305–6, 309
	Burke's motion on American taxation
	Morning Chronicle, 30 November 1775 (mention only)

1 December American Prohibitory Bill
            Parl. Hist. xviii. 1034; Simmons and Thomas, vi.
            313, 314, 381; MS. at Sheffield, Bk 6.61, 6.182

5 December American Prohibitory Bill
            Parl. Hist. xviii. 1041; Simmons and Thomas, vi.
            323, 325

6 December American Prohibitory Bill
            St James's Chronicle, 7 December 1775

7 December Hartley's proposals for conciliation
            Parl. Hist. xviii. 1054–5; Simmons and Thomas, vi.
            328, 339

8 December American Prohibitory Bill (2)
            Parl. Hist. xviii. 1060, 1060–1; Simmons and
            Thomas, vi. 345, 346

11 December American Prohibitory Bill
            Parl. Hist. xviii. 1063
            Burke's motion respecting georgia
            Craftsman, 16 December 1775 (mention only);
            Simmons and Thomas, vi. 349

1776
5 February Burke's motion respecting Irish cattle
            St James's Chronicle, 6 February 1776

8 February Stroudwater Navigation Bill
            St James's Chronicle, 10 February 1776 (mention
            only)
            Importation of Irish provisions
            Commons Journals, xxxv. 515–20; *Corr.* iii. 247

15 February Foreign troops in Ireland
            sse vol. ix, pp. 496–504

20 February Fox's motion respecting army in America
            Parl. Hist. xviii. 1154; Simmons and Thomas, vi.
            392, 395, 401; MSS. at Sheffield, Bk 6.179, 180

28 February Shaftesbury election petitions
            St James's Chronicle, 29 February 1776 (mention
            only)

29 February German treaties
            see above, p. 220

5 March   Scottish Militia Bill
            see above, p. 222

11 March	Army extraordinaries *Parl. Hist.* xviii. 1239; Simmons and Thomas, vi. 457, 458
12 March	Army extraordinaries *Parl. Hist.* xviii. 1246–7; Simmons and Thomas, vi. 465
20 March	Scottish Militia Bill *Lloyd's Evening Post*, 22 March 1776 (mention only)
22 March	Mariners Recruitment Bill *St James's Chronicle*, 23 March 1776 (mention only)
26 March	Butchers' Meat Bill *see above*, p. 224
27 March	Shipwreck Bill *see above*, p. 225
30 April	Shipwreck Bill *see above*, p. 227
1 May	Burke's motion on shipwrecks *see above*, p. 228
6 May	Loss of Boston *see above*, p. 229
8 May	Admiralty licenses (2) *Parl. Reg.* iv. 35, 37; Simmons and Thomas, vi. 523 Cross-Examination of Woolbridge (2) *London Chronicle*, 16 May, 18 May 1776; Simmons and Thomas, vi. 545–8; MS. at Sheffield, Bk 6.176
10 May	Sawbridge's motion Respecting America *Parl. Hist.* xviii. 1354–5; Simmons and Thomas, vi. 570
13 May	Grantham election warrant (2) *Parl. Reg.* iv. 116, 117 Convicts Bill *Parl. Reg.* iii. 117–18
22 May	Conway's motion *see above*, p. 232

6 November	Cavendish's motion on America *see above*, p. 251
22 November	Shaftesbury election petition *Parl. Reg.* vi. 77 (mention only)

1777

3 March	Gloucester election petition *Gazetteer*, 4 March 1777 (mention only)
7 March	Buckingham Church Bill Walpole, *Last Journals*, ii. 13
14 March	Burke's Dockyard Bill *St James's Chronicle*, 15 March 1777
17 March	Annuity Bill *General Evening Post*, 18 March 1777
21 March	Drainage Bill *Morning Post*, 22 March 1777
26 March	Birmingham Playhouse Bill *see above*, p. 286
16 April	Civil list debts *see above*, p. 330
18 April	Civil list debts (2) *see above*, p. 336
20 April	Lowther's motion respecting king's brothers *Public Advertiser*, 21 April 1777
28 April	British Museum *see above*, p. 336
29 April	Birmingham Playhouse Bill *see above*, p. 336
7 May	Landgrave of Hesse Cassel reimbursement *St James's Chronicle*, 8 May 1777
8 May	Landgrave of Hesse Cassel reimbursement (3) *Parl. Hist.* xix. 215–16, 216–17, 220–1; *Parl. Reg.* vii. 154–5, 156, 162–3 Reimbursement of American sufferers (2) *Parl. Reg.* vii. 157, 157–8
9 May	Income for Dukes of Cumberland and Gloucester *London Evening Post*, 13 May 1777
12 May	Burke's Osckyard Bill *St James's Chronicle*, 13 May 1777
13 May	Burke's Dockyard Bill *St James's Chronicle*, 13 May 1777 (mention only)
14 May	Budget *Parl. Hist.* xix. 251–2; MS. at Sheffield, Bk 6.105 Capital punishment *see above*, p. 338

15 May	Budget
	Gazetteer, 17 May 1777 (mention only)
22 May	East India Company
	see vol. v, pp. 35–40; MS. at Sheffield, Bk 9.5
23 May	African trade
	London Chronicle, 24 May 1777 (mention only)
26 May	Tax on servants
	Gazetteer, 28 May 1777
28 May	State of the African trade
	St James's Chronicle, 29 May 1777
	Tax on servants
	Gazetteer, 29 May 1777 (mention only)
2 June	African trade
	Parl. Hist. xix. 31
5 June	African slave trade (4)
	see above, p. 340

---

20 November	Address
	see above, p. 342
21 November	Address
	Parl. Hist. xix. 445
26 November	Navy estimates (2)
	Parl. Hist. xix. 447, 458–9; MS. at Sheffield, Bk 6.114
	Bill for Suspending Habeas Corpus (3)
	Parl. Hist. xix. 462–3, 465, 466
	American Treason Act
	Gazetteer, 28 November 1777
27 November	Bill for Suspending Habeas Corpus
	London Evening Post, 29 November 1777
	Navy estimates
	Public Advertiser, 28 November 1777 (mention only)
28 November	Augmentation of the navy
	St James's Chronicle, 29 November 1777 (mention only)
	Suspension of Habeas Corpus
	Gazetteer, 29 November 1777 (mention only)
2 December	Fox's motion
	see above, p. 344

3 December	Army estimates and Saratoga
	Parl. Hist. xix. 537–9
4 December	Ordnance estimates (3)
	Parl. Hist. xix. 547–8, 548, 549
5 December	War expenses (2)
	Parl. Hist. xix. 559, 560
10 December	Motion for adjournment
	Parl. Hist. xix. 590–1

1778

22 January	Subscriptions
	see above, p. 346
	Fox's motion for Burgoyne's instructions
	Parl. Reg. viii. 268; MS. at Northampton A.xxvii. 68
	Jennings Clerke's motion for address
	Walpole, *Last Journals*, ii. 94 (mention only)
29 January	Visitors' access to gallery
	Parl. Hist. xix. 649
2 February	Address from Council of Jamaica
	St James's Chronicle, 3 February 1778
	Call for American Papers
	Gazetteer, 4 February 1778
4 February	Burke's motion on raising troops without parliamentary consent
	St James's Chronicle, 5 February 1778 (mention only); MS. at Sheffield, Bk 8.181
6 February	Use of Indians
	see above, p. 354
11 February	Fox's motion on state of troops in America
	General Evening Post, 12 February 1778; *Parl. Hist.* xix. 730
13 February	Navy estimates
	Gazetteer, 16 February 1778
17 February	North's Conciliatory Bill
	General Evening Post, 19 February 1778
23 February	North's Conciliatory Bill
	see above, p. 367

24 February	North's Conciliatory Bill
	Parl. Hist. xix. 787; *London Chronicle*, 28 February 1778
25 February	Powys's Bill on American Taxation (4)
	Gazetteer, 28 February 1778
2 March	North's instructions to American Commission
	Parl. Reg. viii. 432; MSS. at Sheffield, Bk 27.13, 27.38, 6.121
6 March	Budget
	St James's Chronicle, 7 March 1778 (mention only); see Walpole, *Last Journals*, ii. 128 for comment
9 March	Budget
	Morning Post, 10 March 1778 (mention only); see Walpole, *Last Journals*, ii. 130 for comment
10 March	Budget
	see above, p. 372
11 March	State of the nation
	Morning Chronicle, 12 March 1778 (mention only)
12 March	Instructions of American Commission
	London Chronicle, 14 March 1778
16 March	Grenville's motion for communications with France and Spain
	London Evening Post, 17 March 1778
17 March	Motion of confidence
	Morning Post, 18 March 1778 (mention only); MS. at Sheffield, Bk 6.142
19 March	Fox's motion regarding the failed expedition from Canada
	Parl. Hist. xix. 958 (mention only)
23 March	Bill for Employing Convicts on Thames (2)
	Parl. Hist. xix. 970, 971; *General Evening Post*, 24 March 1778
	Burke's motion on army extraordinaries
	Parl. Hist. xix. 971–2
	Barré's motion for enquiry into public expenditures
	Parl. Hist. xix. 978
25 March	Army extraordinaries
	Gazetteer, 27 March 1778

26 March   House tax
     Parl. Reg. ix. 85
     Army extraordinaries
     Parl. Reg. ix. 87

30 March   Barré's motion for committee of public accounts
     Parl. Reg. ix. 93

2 April   Wilkes's motion respecting aids or loans to the
     Crown
     Parl. Hist. xix. 1009–10
     Irish trade
     see vol. ix, p. 504
     Grenville's motion for papers on French treaty with
     Americans
     St James's Chronicle, 4 April 1778

6 April   House Tax Bill
     London Chronicle, 7 April 1778
     Repeal of Declaratory Act
     see above, p. 373

7 April   Irish trade (2)
     see vol. ix, pp. 504–5

9 April   Irish trade
     see vol. ix, pp. 505–6

10 April   Powys's motion on American Commission
     see above, p. 374

13 April   Lord George Gordon
     Morning Post, 14 April 1778 (mention only)

15 April   American loyalists
     General Evening Post, 16 April 1778

4 May   Irish trade
     see vol. ix, p. 518

5 May   Irish trade
     see vol. ix, pp. 518–19

6 May   Irish trade
     see vol. ix, pp. 519–23
     Vote of credit
     see above, p. 379

7 May   Irish trade
     Universal Magazine, lxii. 266

12 May State of African trade
  General Evening Post, 14 May 1778
13 May African forts
  General Advertiser, 14 May 1778
19 May Irish trade
  see vol. ix, pp. 523–7
21 May Funeral of Lord Chatham
  see above, p. 380
26 May State of the army at Saratoga
  Morning Chronicle, 27 May 1778 (mention only)
27 May Admission of strangers to gallery
  Lloyd's Evening Post, 28 May 1778
28 May Hartley's motion
  see above, p. 382

—

26 November Address
  Public Ledger, 28 November 1778; MS. at Sheffield,
  Bk 6.138
4 December Commissioners' manifesto
  see above, p. 387
10 December Barré's motion on state of navy (2)
  Parl. Hist. xx. 49–50; *Parl. Reg.* x. 125–6, 131; MS.
  at Sheffield, Bk 6.123
11 December Luttrell's motion on Palliser
  see above, p. 389
  Fox's motion on taxation of Catholics
  Public Ledger, 12 December 1778
14 December Army estimates
  see above, p. 393
17 December Naval Court Martial Bill
  Morning Chronicle, 18 December 1778

1779
15 February Irish trade
  see vol. ix, pp. 527–9
17 February Howe's motion for American papers (2)
  Parl. Hist. xx. 139; *Gazetteer*, 18 February 1779

Riots against Palliser
Parl. Hist. xx. 144; *Parl. Reg.* xi. 246

19 February Fox's motion for address for dismissal of Palliser
Parl. Hist. xx. 147–8; *Morning Chronicle*, 22
February 1779

Burke presents petition concerning smuggling
London Chronicle, 20 February 1779 (mention only)

22 February Barré's motion respecting service in the army
Parl. Hist. xx. 150–1

24 February Budget (3)
Parl. Hist. xx. 155–6, 156, 161; *Morning Post*, 26
February 1779

25 February Naval Court Martial Bill
Public Advertiser, 26 February 1779

1 March Budget (2)
Parl. Hist. xx. 168–9, 172

3 March Keppel's orders
Morning Chronicle, 6 March 1779

8 March Fox's motion on state of the navy
Parl. Hist. xx. 235–7; MS. at Sheffield, Bk 13.37

9 March Trial of Palliser
St James's Chronicle, 11 March 1779

Bankrupt debtors
London Chronicle, 11 March 1779

12 March Irish trade
see vol. ix, pp. 529–31

13 March Irish trade
Whitehall Evening Post, 14 March 1779

15 March Scottish riots
see above, p. 424

Dunning's motion of censure of Admiralty Board
Parl. Hist. xx. 295–8

Trade of Ireland and Scotland
Gentleman's Magazine, xlviii. 622

16 March Luttrell's expression respecting Rigby
General Evening Post, 18 March 1779 (mention only)

17 March Relief of Protestant Dissenters
General Evening Post, 18 March 1779 (mention only)

18 March	Scottish Catholic petition
	see above, p. 425
19 March	Irish civil establishment
	see vol. ix, pp. 531–2
	Importation of sugar into Ireland
	Parl Reg. xii. 178 (erroneously dated 18 March
	1779)
22 March	Fox's motion of censure against Ministry
	Parl. Hist. xx. 337–8
24 March	Irish establishment
	Daily Advertiser, 26 March 1779
26 March	Army extraordinaries
	Parl. Reg. xii. 258
29 March	Army extraordinaries
	Gazetteer, 31 March 1779 (mention only)
	American Commission
	Gazetteer, 31 March 1779; *Parl. Hist.* xx. 361
	Howe's motion
	Gazetteer, 31 March 1779
31 March	Bill to Prevent Smuggling
	Lloyd's Evening Post, 1 April 1779
	Scottish Catholics
	see above, p. 430
	Augmentation of judges' salaries
	St James's Chronicle, 1 April 1779
16 April	East India Company
	Morning Chronicle, 17 April 1779 (mention only);
	MSS. at Sheffield, Bk 9.43, 45–7
28 April	American papers
	Public Advertiser, 29 April 1779; MS. at Sheffield,
	Bk 6.29
29 April	Enquiry into American war (2)
	Parl. Hist. xx. 724, 725; *Parl. Reg.* xii. 371, 372–3;
	MS. at Sheffield, Bk 6.98
[April]	Trial of Palliser
	Public Advertiser, 28 April 1779
3 May	Enquiry into American war
	Gazetteer, 5 May 1779

4 May	Bill for Preventing Adultery *Gazetteer*, 5 May 1779 (mention only)
11 May	Examination of Sir Andrew Hammond *St James's Chronicle*, 13 May 1779 (mention only) Resolution on Ireland *see above*, p. 435
13 May	American war (4) *Parl. Hist.* xx. 750, 750–1, 752, 758–9; *Parl. Reg.* xiii. 63, 64, 65–6, 71–3 Fox's motion on Palliser (3) *Parl. Hist.* xx. 626, 626, 628–30; *Gazetteer*, 17 May 1779 (1st speech)
17 May	Conduct of Navy *Parl. Reg.* xiii. 90–1
21 May	Surveys in America *St James's Chronicle*, 22 May 1779
27 May	American war *General Evening Post*, 29 May 1779
28 May	House tax *Parl. Reg.* xiii. 178 Burke Notice of Bill to Indemnify Scottish Catholics *St James's Chronicle*, 29 May 1779; *General Evening Post*, 29 May 1779
31 May	Speech on supply *see above*, p. 437
2 June	Vote of credit *General Advertiser*, 3 June 1779 Religion in Scotland *Parl. Hist.* xx. 831
7 June	Lord Hyde's seat in Commons *General Evening Post*, 8 June 1779
8 June	American war (3) *General Advertiser*, 10 June 1779; *Parl. Reg.* xiii. 273
9 June	Conduct of House of Lords *General Advertiser*, 10 June 1779 American war *Gazetteer*, 12 June 1779
11 June	Meredith's motion for peace with America *Parl. Hist.* xx. 853; *Gazetteer*, 15 June 1779

15 June   African Committee
General Advertiser, 16 June 1779
Thomas Townshend's American motion
Parl. Hist. xx. 872–3

16 June   Breach with Spain
see above, p. 445
Burke's motion respecting African Company
General Advertiser, 17 June 1779

17 June   Cavendish's motion on war with House of Bourbon
Parl. Hist. xx. 900; *Lloyd's Evening Post*, 21 June
1779

18 June   Enquiry into American war
Lloyd's Evening Post, 21 June 1779

21 June   North's motion on augmentation of Militia
Parl. Hist. xx. 922; *General Advertiser*, 22 June 1779

———

25 November   Address
see vol. ix, pp. 532–5

6 December   Upper Ossory's motion of censure
Parl. Hist. xx. 1200; *London Chronicle*, 7 December
1779; MSS. at Sheffield, Bk 6.61, 83, 90
Ireland
see vol. ix, pp. 535–42

9 December   Army extraordinaries
General Evening Post, 11 December 1779
Trade concessions to Ireland
London Courant, 19 December 1779

15 December   Public expenses
see above, p. 466
Pennant's motion respecting Jamaica
London Courant, 16 December 1779
Irish trade relief (3)
Public Ledger, 17 December 1779

23 December   Adjournment of the House (2)
General Advertiser, 24 December 1779

1780
28 January   Notice of Economical Reform Bills
London Chronicle, 29 January 1780

8 February	Yorkshire petition for economical reform
	Parl. Hist. xx. 1382–3
	Burke presents Bristol petition on public expenditure
	St James's Chronicle, 10 February 1780
10 February	Insolvent Debtors Bill
	Parl. Hist. xx. 1404
11 February	Economical reform
	see above, p. 481
14 February	Economical Reform Bills
	Parl. Hist. xxi. 73–4
16 February	Economical reform
	Craftsman, 4 March 1780 (mention only)
21 February	Nottingham petition for economical reform
	Parl. Reg. xvii. 130
	Savile's motion respecting pensions
	Parl. Hist. xxi. 92
	Nottingham protest
	Parl. Hist. xxi. 108–9
23 February	Economical reform (3)
	Parl. Hist. xxi. 111–35, 136, 137
28 February	Insolvent Debtors Bill
	see above, p. 552
29 February	Economical reform (2)
	Parl. Reg. xvii. 187, 188
	Thanks to Sir George Rodney
	Morning Post, 1 March 1780 (mention only)
2 March	Economical reform (2)
	Parl. Hist. xxi. 150, 154
6 March	Budget
	Morning Chronicle, 7 March 1780 (mention only)
8 March	Economical reform (2)
	see above, p. 553
13 March	Commission of Accounts
	see above, p. 558
	Economical Reform (2)
	Parl. Hist. xxi. 235–9, 243–8
20 March	Shelburne
	Parl. Reg. xvii. 374 (mention only)

	Establishment Bill (5)
	Parl. Hist. xxi. 300–1, 301–2, 303–7, 309 (2)
21 March	East India Company
	Parl. Hist. xxi. 313–14. Second intervention
	mentioned in *Morning Chronicle*, 22 March 1780
	Burke's motion for accounts
	Gazetteer, 22 March 1780
22 March	Economical reform
	Parl. Reg. xvii. 406–7
	Duel, Shelburne, and Fullarton (2)
	Parl. Hist. xxi. 323–4, 325–6
5 April	Army estimates
	Parl. Hist. xxi. 338–9
6 April	Dunning's motion (2)
	Parl. Hist. xxi. 367; *Gazetteer*, 11 April 1780; MS. at
	Sheffield, Bk 14.10
10 April	Dunning's motion
	see above, p. 581
11 April	Speech on pillory
	see above, p. 583
24 April	Burke's motion to defer Establishment Bills
	Parl. Hist. xxi. 522 (mention only)
27 April	Reply to Pownall
	Parl. Reg. xvii. 581, 586; *Morning Chronicle*, 28 April
	1780
	Stamp Tax Bill
	Parl. Hist. xxi. 535; *Morning Chronicle*, 28 April
	1780
28 April	Economical reform (5)
	Parl. Hist. xxi. 538–9, 541–4, 545 (2), 551–2; MS.
	at Sheffield, Bk 14.4
1 May	Mutiny
	see above, p. 586
	Public accounts
	Parl. Hist. xxi. 554
3 May	Army extraordinaries
	Parl. Reg. xvii. 626–7
8 May	Meredith's motion for call out of military (2)
	Parl. Hist. xxi. 592, 593

	Duration of Parliaments
	see above, p. 588
9 May	Importation of cotton wool
	Parl. Reg. xvii. 686 (mention only)
12 May	Malt Tax
	Gazetteer, 13 May 1780 (mention only)
18 May	Economical reform (2)
	Parl. Hist. xvii. 621 (2)
31 May	Thread Lace Bill
	London Courant, 1 June 1780
1 June	Commissioners for Public Accounts (2)
	London Courant, 2 June 1780; *General Evening Post*, 3 June 1780
6 June	Gordon riots
	see above, p. 602
19 June	Riots
	Parl. Hist. xxi. 700; MS. at Sheffield, Bk 8.32, 39, 40, 41, 43, 61
20 June	Riots
	see above, p. 607
21 June	Burke's motion for examination of Treasury officers
	General Advertiser, 22 June 1780 (mention only)
23 June	Economical reform
	General Advertiser, 24 June 1780
26 June	Bill to Secure Protestantism
	see above, p. 607
27 June	Hartley's motion for peace with America
	General Advertiser, 29 June 1780
28 June	Bill to Secure Protestantism
	General Advertiser, 29 June 1780
5 July	Economical reform
	Parl. Reg. xvii. 756

APPENDIX B

Collation of Texts

The following account, concerning the seven published writings represented in this volume, records for each, as applicable, several orders of information.

1. Printer's copy. The specific copy sent to press in xerographic form, identified by its bibliographical state, Todd item number, library, and, where necessary, shelf mark. 'Editorial copy' refers to an exemplar in the collection of the textual editor. All copies correspond to the detailed description given in the Todd bibliography and have been compared with certain of those there located.

2. Textual note. An account of any variant editions possibly affecting the text, though not represented in the bibliography, together with a summary notice of the present treatment of certain typographical peculiarities.

3. Collation. Since the editor has taken cognizance of surviving texts in manuscript or print anterior to the printer's copy, earlier superseded readings are noted here only when the purport of some revision remains in doubt. Accordingly this collation is confined, ordinarily, to those posterior substantive readings not in Burke's final revised issue of the separate publication, here submitted as printer's copy, but occurring later in the collected *Works*. These more significant readings are cited for several purposes:
(a) to disclose subsequent revisions in some manner conveyed by the author to his first editors: a circumstance which does not obtain in this volume.
(b) to disclose further any readings apparently unrevised by the author but regarded by his editors as a textual crux, which they then resolved in other language. Except as noted, such interference is now disallowed.
(c) to justify in the present edition the correction of misprints detected also by these editors.

(d) to record as unjustified numerous other and quite arbitrary amendments, all of which, along with countless alterations in pointing and orthography, have passed through these early *Works* to texts in current use.

For each work the textual collation is represented efficiently in a single schedule, the wording of the printer's copy always being given first, and the later alteration listed second. The latter variant is further identified by the numerals 1, 2, or 3, designating its first occurrence in the editions of the *Works* published in 1792, 1801, or 1803 (Todd 79*a*, 79*b*, 79*c*–*d*). Whenever this variant is adopted, according to the criteria cited above, its entry into the present edition is indicated by the plus sign, +. Otherwise, in this conservative text, the later reading is cited simply to illustrate an unacceptable deviant from what appears to be Burke's final intention.

Speeches at His Arrival at Bristol and at the Conclusion of the Poll
58–60, 64–70

Text from the authorised second edition 1775 (23*b*) editorial copy. This represents the two 1774 Bristol papers (18, 21) later collected in the *Works*. Three other papers (19, 20*a*, 22), all uncollected, are here printed directly from the broadsides.

58.12 expectation | expectations 3.   59.10 dwn | down 1+.   67.2 penetatring | penetrating 1+.

Speech on Conciliation
105–168

Text from third edition 1775 (25*c*), Univ. of Texas copy. Though this is evidently the last revised setting, the number of misprints cited below, as well as other aberrations noted in the bibliography,[1] would indicate that it was not carefully attended at press. Possibly for this reason, or perhaps simply through mischance, subsequent editions including the later *Works* derive ultimately from the second edition and therefore fail to incorporate the readings peculiar to this text.

Beginning on page 143 the variously styled petitions and resolutions

---

[1] To these may be added another typographical fault: on page 47 left margin the 't' in 'tasks' has slipped down to form, immediately below, the reading 'ttalk' (131.6 of the present edition).

are here uniformly represented in Roman type and enclosed in quotation marks.

109.n1 *engage* | engage 3.   109.n1 27 | 27th 2.   113.15 1722 | 1772 1+.   113.21 6,022,132 | 6,024,171 1.[1]   114.5 6,022,132 | 6,024,000 1.   114.6 487,868 | 485,000 1.   117.29 strike he | strike the 1+.   118.4 hardy | hard 3.   121.1 thier | their 1+.   126.7 been not | not been 1+.   126.29 exported | transmitted 1+.   127.5–6 plan (of punishing disorders by the denial of Government) | plan of punishing by the denial of the exercise of government 1.   127.14 uuheard | unheard 1+.   128.14 in | of 2.   130.26 their | the 3.   132.18 Rawleigh | Raleigh 1+.   133.10 tantamont | tantamount 1+.   133.29 in a | in 1.   133.30 as a | as 2.   137.3 well | so well 3.   140.2 antiquarians | antiquaries 3.   140.10 an | a 3.   140.15 liberties | liberty 2.   142.21 an | a 3.   151.30 millions | million 1.   153.24 province of the | province of 2.   155.23 come | came 3.   159.7 [*No* ¶] | ¶ It is 3.   162.1 for | as 1.   162.33 an | a 3.   163.5 government | governments 3.   165.11 waht | what 1+.   166.5 place | places 3.   166.35 Conrt | Court 1+.   168.18 province of the | province of 2.   168.20 in th | in the 1+.

Letter to the Sheriffs of Bristol   289–330

Text from third and last corrected edition 1777 (28*d*), editorial copy. Burke's editors, plausibly assuming the 'fourth edition' to represent the final state of text, did not realize that this is actually a London reissue with cancel title of the original Bristol publication, and therefore transmitted in *Works* 1 ninety-six early readings which the author later revised.

290.3 this | that 3.   291.2–3 (within the duration of the act) | [*om.*] 1.   291.35 it a | it would have been a 1.   292.5 those | these 1.   292.9 navy,—for the same legislature afterwards to treat | navy,—to consider 1.   292.11 piracy, seems harsh and incongruous. Such a procedure would | piracy, would 1.   292.13–14 do not | never 1.   292.19 as | as in 1.   293.1 by no means | never 1.   293.35 Americans | America 1.   294.10 made. For | made, to

---

[1] In this instance only *Works* 2–3 independently concur in the earlier third-edition reading.

be in any degree instructive: for 1.   294.10 instructing | teaching
1.   294.11 in their | their 1.   294.11–12 disobedient | undutiful 1.
294.39 we | you 1.   296.30–31 this great, steady, uniform
principle; | this; 1.   297.1 of mere | of 1.   297.7 *under* | in 1.
297.14 which | that 1.   297.18–19 a negro slave | negro slaves 1.
297.21–22 farther and farther | further and further 1.
297.26–27 this tends to dissolve it. It destroys *equality*, which is
the essence of community. As | this dissolves it. As 1.   298.14–15
struggle tended rather to inflame than to abate | struggle rather
inflamed than lessened 1.   298.17 could not | cannot 1.   298.20 ¶
Preserving | [*no* ¶] 1.   298.21 hope | hope that 1.   298.24 to a
station which | to what 1.   298.24 declining my | declining for
some time my 1.   299.12 I have said so much | I speak 1.   299.16
spirit are in danger of being | spirit appear to have been 1.   299.25
planted | exerted 1.   300.8 an | a 3.   300.10 bonds | bond 1.
300.17 in | of 3.   301.6 *Raille* | Rahl 3.   302.3 those powers |
them 1.   302.15 halloo | hollow 1.   302.35 in our | in a 2.
302.38 we shew | we should shew 1.   303.1 present zeal | zeal 1.
303.13 advantages | advantage 1.   303.26 awaken | awake 1.
303.29 affections | affection 1.   303.30 are | is 1.   304.7 any
ease | ease 1.   305.23 many a musket | many muskets 1.   305.34
began | begun 1.   306.3 facts | fact 1.   306.14 half | half the 1.
306.21 terrors? | terror? 1.   307.4 many in these places | many 1.
307.4 full even | very full 1.   308.13 and with | and as with 3.
309.19 tyrannic | tyrannical 1.   310.20 to make | to be 1.   310.29
who have | who 1.   311.12 their power is then | and then their
power is 1.   311.21 King Charles | Charles 2.   311.24 or to | or 1.
311.26 day: They were not | day; nor were they 1.   311.27 their |
the 2.   312.8 at that time | then 1.   313.28 or in | of 1.
313.29 or a | a 1.   314.10 affirm | say 1.   314.14 other | any 1.
314.37 ¶ I must | [*no* ¶] 1.   314.39 be safely | be 1.
315.2–3 the extent of legislative power | it 1.   315.5–6 yet
there are | yet 1.   315.7–8 which, being | yet, being 1.   315.9
such cases | that case 1.   315.11 that | which 1.   315.15 make
such attempts | attempt such things 1.   315.21 change | alter 1.
315.22 at | as 1+.   315.26–27 When it goes beyond this, its
authority will be precarious, let its rights be what they will. | [*om.*] 1.
316.3 ¶ As the | [*no* ¶] 1.   316.5 if ever | or ever 1.
316.34 I could never conceive | [*om.*] 1.   317.8 known character

of the people | [*om.*] 1.   317.20 must | should 1.   317.30 they
have questioned | [*om.*] 1.   318.4 freedom. | freedom; and every
government is called tyranny and usurpation which is not formed on
their fancies. 1.   318.10 depths | depth 1.   322.13 it gave | they
gave 1.   322.27 virtues | virtue 1.   322.30 an act of | a 1.   323.12
longer; | longer; because 1.   323.15–16 but as with | but as 1.
323.34 it. | it; something might possibly be gained by its
consequences. 1.   324.4 opinion | opinions 3.   324.5 these opinions
| they 1.   324.22 ¶ By the | [*no* ¶] 1.   324.31 have | had 3.
324.34 ¶ Not that [*no* ¶] 1.   324.36 [*no* ¶] | ¶ I hope 1.
325.21 a | any 1.   325.22 his | his own 1.   326.4 ¶ I hope |
[*no* ¶] 1.   326.5 greedily received | received 1.   326.8 lucre |
lure 1.   326.21 engaging in such a | taking this 1.   328.9–10 To
act on the principles of the constitution, with the best men the time
affords, | This, gentlemen, 1.   328.23 the | their 1.   328.24 union
of such men | union 1.   329.23 finding the| finding these 1.
329.26 some part | some 1.   329.28 mode. The | mode; and
those 1.

Speech on Economical Reform   483–551

Text from fourth edition 1780 (33*e*), Univ. of Texas copy. Again, as in
the *Letter to the Sheriffs*, the text given in *Works* 1 comes from the latest
authorized issue, in this instance a 'new' edition (*g*) reset directly from
an earlier 'new' edition (*c*), and thus fails to convey the revisions
successively introduced in the third and fourth impressions (*d–e*). Hence
the variants recurring in *Works* 1 constitute readings which Burke
had previously rejected, and those first appearing in 2–3 remain
unauthorized.

On pages 550–551 the bills are uniformly represented in roman
type, within quotation marks, and emphatic phrases therein given in
italics.

484.12 and | and a 3.   484.30 Besides | Besides this 1.   485.14
them | them at the least 1.   486.12 deal | deal indeed 1.   486.34
increased | increased 1.   487.1 *lessen* | lessen 1.   487.4 *preference* |
preference 1.   491.5 an | a 3.   497.26 *Monarchy* | monarchy 1.
497.31 cast | throw 1.   497.35 the hands | those hands 1.   497.35
which represents | representing 1.   498.14 so | [*om.*] 1.   498.16
emolument | emoluments 1.   498.17 these | those 1.   499.30

revenue | revenues 3.   500.1 death. | death. In truth, Sir, the
attempt was no less an affront upon the understanding of that
respectable people, than it was an attack on their property 1.   500.1
chose | chose rather 3.   500.7 his nature | nature 1.   501.24
Such, for | For 1.   501.24 ends, | ends, such 1.   501.26
jurisdictions | jurisdiction 3.   502.3 stood ever since | since stood 1.
502.20 the itinerant | itinerant 2.   503.16 *Lancaster* | Lancaster 1.
503.16 *Lancaster* | Lancaster 1.   503.18 *Henry the fourth* | Henry
the Fourth 1.   503.24 *lord Coke* | Lord Coke 1.   503.28 *Henry
the fifth* | Henry the Fifth 1.   504.3 *Edward the fourth* | Edward
the Fourth 1.   504.6 *Henry the seventh* | Henry the Seventh 1.
504.12 *Cromwell* | Cromwell 1.   505.27 down | [*om.*] 1.
506.14 at | at a 2.   507.6 considerable, | considerable, I
believe 1.   507.6 and | and I conceive 1.   507.8–9 those lands,
when | objects, wherein 1.   507.12 But surely | But I really conceive,
that 1.   507.18 It | I believe, Sir, it 2.   510.28 economy |
oeconomy 1+.   511.13 in | [*om.*] 2.   517.6 him | it 2.   519.32
slowness | delay 1.   521.24 to | to the 3.   522.32 in | in the 3.
523.35 that | the 3.   524.1 to | for 3.   524.10 might | it
might 2+.   527.13 offices | officers 1.   532.21–22 its decline, and
its final ruin | the decline and final ruin of the empire 3.   532.36 my
| the 2.   534.26 and all | and all the 2.   534.31 time, for doing
little | time 1.   534.32 to be | [*om.*] 1.   535.16 its | the 2.
535.22 tampering | tamperings 2.   535.25 instruction |
instructions 1.   537.3 attempt | [*om.*] 2.   537.9–10 then was | was
then 2.   539.4 would | will 3.   539.27 on | [*om.*] 2.   540.15–16
appointing . . . manner | [*om.*] 1.   540.16–17 that board | [*om.*] 1.
540.23 These | Those 1.   541.9 the board of trade | theirs 1.
541.12 suppress | *suppress* 1.   541.29 sensible | thoroughly sensible
1.   542.20 payments | payment 2.   542.28 him | [*om.*] 1.   544.30
ascertained;—ascertained | ascertained 1.   545.16 expences |
expence 3.   548.4 proposed | designed 1.   548.n.t In the Debate on
the | [*om.*] 1.   549.3 all | will 3.   550.20 Mr. . . . motion. |
[entered as note] 1.   551.2 forest | the forest 3.

Speech at Bristol Previous to the Election   623–664

Text from third, revised edition 1780 (39*c*), editorial copy. Two
apparantly unauthorized variants in the reset fourth edition (643.30,

646.33) and five others further accumulated in the fifth (623.9, 633.8, 642.23, 648.21, 652.14) are transmitted in collected *Works* 1 and subsequent editions.

623.9 effect | fact 1.   625.36 toward | towards 1.   625.36
uncorruptible | incorruptible 2.   626.23 saving of | saving 3.
629.6 sooner have | have sooner 1.   633.2 an | a 3.   633.8 his |
this 1.   639.24 structure | structures 3.   642.23 county |
country 1.   643.30 debase | abase 1.   644.18 possibly have | have
possibly 3.   645.4 Parliament | the senate 3.   645.15 to that | to
the 3.   646.33 engrafted | ingrafted 1.   648.21 could | would 1.
651.10 your | our 3.   652.5 an | a 3.   652.14 and | and as 1.
656.9 way | way in 3.   660.39 repeal, | repeal, yet who, 3.
663.28–664.29 [*text in italic*] | [*text in roman*] 1.

Speech on the Hustings at Bristol   666–667

Text from separate broadside 1780 (37*a*), Bristol Central Library, Accession B6979, page 225. Unlike two other handbills overlooked by Burke's editors (36, 38*a*), and therefore uncollected, this was belatedly discovered and reprinted, posthumously, in *Works* 2.

667.28 whoever | whomever 2.   667.28 may | he may 2.   667.n*
Combe | Coombe 2.

INDEX